THOU – YOU
THOU, THYSELF
YOURSELF

Shakespeare's Sonnets

SHAKESPEARE'S SONNETS

Edited with analytic commentary by

STEPHEN BOOTH

New Haven and London   Yale University Press

Designed by John O. C. McCrillis
and set in Times Roman type.
Printed in the United States of America by
The Murray Printing Co., Inc., Westford, Massachusetts.

Published in Great Britain, Europe, Africa, and Asia
(except Japan) by Yale University Press, Ltd.,
London. Distributed in Australia and New Zealand
by Book & Film Services, Artarmon, N.S.W., Australia;
and in Japan by Harper & Row, Publishers, Tokyo Office.

Library of Congress Cataloging in Publication Data

Shakespeare, William, 1564–1616.
  Shakespeare's Sonnets.

  Includes indexes.
  I.   Booth, Stephen.   II.   Title.
PR 2848.A2B6   821'.3   76–56161
ISBN 0–300–01959–9

79-2511

For
Philip J. Finkelpearl

Contents

Illustrations

Preface

The job of an editor is usually to establish as far as possible the author's text and to provide glosses for words, constructions, idioms, and allusions with which a modern reader may be unfamiliar. The job of an editor of Shakespeare's sonnets is somewhat different, and my own approach to it is somewhat different from that of previous editors of the sonnets. With two exceptions, sonnets 138 and 144, our only textual authority is the 1609 Quarto (see Appendix 1); therefore an editor has little comparing, choosing, and conflating to do. As to establishing Shakespeare's original text, that is either obviously unnecessary—or obvious (for instance, "beautits" in the Quarto text of 6.4 must be a misprint for *beauties*; Q's "Cha ter" in five of the surviving copies of 87.3 is obviously a misprint for *Charter* in the other eight; and Q's "fo" for "so" in 152.14 surely results from the tendency of *f* and the nearly identical long *s* to get confused in a printer's font)—or obviously beyond salvation except for a fanatically self-confident scholarly redeemer.

My primary purpose in the present edition is to provide a text that will give a modern reader as much as I can resurrect of a Renaissance reader's experience of the 1609 Quarto; it is, after all, the sonnets we have and not some hypothetical originals that we value. I have adopted no editorial principle beyond that of trying to adapt a modern reader—with his assumptions about idiom, spelling, and punctuation—and the 1609 text to one another. I do not modernize for the sake of modernizing or retain Quarto readings for the sake of retention, and I do nothing for the sake of methodical purity (to do that would be to let the means justify the end, and, since my modern text is physically coupled to the Quarto text reprinted in parallel with it, my lack of systematic rigor about particulars should not inconvenience anyone). Both my text and my commentary are determined by what I think a Renaissance reader would have thought as he moved from line to line and sonnet to sonnet in the Quarto. I make no major substantial emendations and few minor ones. It might therefore seem reasonable to reprint the Quarto text alone and simply comment on that, but the effects of almost four centuries are such that a modern reader faced with the Quarto text sees something that is effectively very different from what a seventeenth-century reader saw.

In modernizing spelling and punctuation I have taken each poem individually and tried to find a mid-point between following the punctuation and spelling of the Quarto text (which modern readers, accustomed to logically and semantically directive punctuation and spelling, are inclined to misinterpret) and modern directive spelling and punctuation (which often pays for its clarity by sacrificing a considerable amount of a poem's substance and energy). In each case I have tried to find the least distorting available compromise. Sometimes no compromise is satisfactory, and I describe the probable operation of a line or quatrain in a note.

ix

Some awkwardness occurs in the commentary because it is, in effect, interrupted several times by lengthy discussions of particular topics at the points which occasion them; little essays of that sort might have been relegated to a full-scale critical introduction or to an appendix, but to do so would be to mistake neatness for efficiency. Placed as they are, the long notes seem longer than they might otherwise seem, but in fact save the considerable repetition that isolating them from their subjects would entail. The long notes are these:

> On explications and emendations of unsatisfactory Shakespearian texts (in the notes on sonnet 112, pages 364–72).
> On the special grandeur of the best sonnets (in the notes on sonnet 116, pages 387–92).
> On spelling and punctuation (in the notes on sonnet 129, pages 447–52).
> On the functions of criticism (in the notes on sonnet 146, pages 507–17).

The longest of the long notes is the one on sonnet 146. A secondary purpose of this edition is to campaign for an analytic criticism that does not sacrifice—or at least tries not to sacrifice—any of a work of literature to logical convenience or even to common sense. The long note on sonnet 146 is an argument and plea for such a criticism. The fact that my commentary attempts also to exemplify such a criticism may be another source of discomfort to my reader. My notes can seem dedicated not to doing what the commentary should do—clarify the sonnets (which in fact rarely need much clarification)—but to transforming lines that are simple and clear into something complicated and obscure. If one accepts its terms, there is some validity to that charge, but I do not accept its terms. All of us were brought up on the idea that what poets say is sublime—takes us beyond reason; my commentary tries to describe the physics by which we get there. Notes designed to explain what the sonnets mean—what the poet is trying to get said—usually end up treating the actual words and their sequence as attendant inconveniences of verse. Such notes often begin with "i.e." and state the substance of a line in a syntax completely foreign to the one in the poem. Much of the time, to gloss a phrase or line in a way that indicates how the actual construction conveys its meaning is difficult, but I want notes that help a reader *with* the poems, not notes that substitute for them.

Scholarly glosses, particularly those for the sonnets, have commonly done a disservice both to readers and poems by ignoring the obvious fact that verse exists in time, that one reads one word and then another. A word or phrase can be incomprehensible at the moment it is read and then be effectively glossed by the lines that follow it; a word or phrase can (and in the sonnets regularly does) have one meaning as a reader comes on it, another as its sentence concludes, and a third when considered from the vantage point of a summary statement in the couplet. The notes to this edition attempt to indicate not only what words mean but when they mean it; the notes try actively to discourage analyses that treat syntax as if it existed in a static state.

Since these sonnets can easily become what their critical history has shown them to be, guide posts for a reader's journey to madness, I fear that much of what is sanest in what I say will look mad to a reader who forgets that when I say "suggestion" or "overtone," and when I talk about ideas and echoes that merely cross a reader's mind, I mean only what I say. In the course of the commentary I often caution readers against being misled by the generic implication that all notes to poems peddle their suggestions as substitute glosses on the words discussed (two particularly urgent instances are 78.3, 7, 11, note [on pens] and the long final note on sonnet 112). Some of the puns, allusions, suggestions, and implications I describe are farfetched; any that I fetch unbidden by the poems deserve to be sent back scornfully, but these poems go in generally for farfetched effects. As long as my reader remembers that I am describing *effects*, not trying to substitute ideational static for obvious surface meaning and intent, then the incidentals I describe and justify deserve, and can safely receive, a hearing.

(In talking about peripheral, rhyme-like repetitions of stock words [e.g. *in, but*, etc.] in different meanings or about possible puns on equally common words [e.g. *all* and *con-*] I have done what I could to acknowledge the commonness of such "effects" in everyday prose by duplicating them in the sentences in which I describe them. I want to forestall complaints that I am promoting accidents of the language to an exalted position they do not deserve. I can be said to exaggerate the value of such inevitabilities and accidents only if criticism is assumed to be a scorecard for rating the artist's ingenuity, and if poetic effects are taken to include only those that either import something [e.g. imitate, suggest, or complement the semantic substance of the passage where they appear] or call attention to their artificiality [e.g. end rhymes, heavy alliteration, or polyptoton in a significant word]. *In*significant and/or un*in*tentional verbal effects figure largely *in* casual conversation and *in* good and bad workaday prose; they trigger our *in*stinct for making and hearing puns, and they are often the unsought key by which we know when a paragraph addressed to the gas company is or is not as we want it. Such non-signifying patterns and tensions also occur in great poems—as little noticed and as undeniably there as the hundreds of slightly different leaf shapes and shades of green in a middle-sized maple tree in the back yard; they contribute to a great poem's identity just as—and just what—they contribute elsewhere. A literary effect need not be special to be.)

I think it will be profitable if I demonstrate the problems inherent in this sort of commentary by choosing one passage that both demands the analysis I provide and exemplifies the virtues and drawbacks of such analysis. I will discuss the third quatrain of sonnet 16 and couple further explanation of my methods and aims to that discussion. This is sonnet 16:

> But wherefore do not you a mightier way
> Make war upon this bloody tyrant time?
> And fortify yourself in your decay
> 4   With means more blessèd than my barren rhyme?
> Now stand you on the top of happy hours,
> And many maiden gardens yet unset,
> With virtuous wish would bear your living flowers,
> 8   Much liker than your painted counterfeit.
> So should the lines of life that life repair

> Which this time's pencil or my pupil pen
> Neither in inward worth nor outward fair
> 12   Can make you live yourself in eyes of men.
> To give away yourself keeps yourself still,
> And you must live, drawn by your own sweet skill.

One great problem for both editors and readers of the sonnets is that words, lines, and clauses often give a multitude of meanings—of which none fits a single "basic" statement to which the others can be called auxiliary. The problem is alleviated and at the same time complicated (particularly for an editor) because even where the lines are vaguest and most ambiguous they are usually *also* simple and obvious. The third quatrain of sonnet 16 provides a good example, one that offers a good occasion for explaining why my commentary is as it is. This quatrain is a devil's puzzle for an editor, but its first word makes it quite otherwise for a casual reader: *So. So* means "thus" here and signals a conclusion from the preceding facts. Moreover, the reader knows what to expect of that conclusion: quatrain 3 will say in terms appropriate to the particulars of lines 1–8 what the speaker has been saying in various ways during the preceding fifteen sonnets. The language that follows upon *So* pertains to and often echoes the language of lines 1–8, and a reader will see the speaker's point without understanding (or knowing that he has not understood and cannot in any usual sense understand) the sentence that makes that point. (Compare 8.5–8.) This quatrain obviously means "Thus children will give you the immortality that art cannot." No scholar or critic can deny this sense or say the quatrain means something else. Why then should an editor burden himself and his reader with what the words mean and how they fit together? Aside from the signal given by *So*, the editor will find no satisfactory logical explanation of how these four lines transmit their simple message. In demonstrating their complexity, will an editor not be guilty of making problems where he should be solving them? Where a Renaissance meaning for a word or a special, now-forgotten context exists or where modern usage will mislead a modern reader, editors' labors are justified, but no such considerations are more than incidentally relevant to this quatrain. Should editors not let well enough alone? An editor who takes it as his task to explain what the poet is driving at should indeed keep his unneeded hands off this quatrain. Once an editor has told him about the connotative and denotative significance of some of Shakespeare's words and phrases, a modern reader can read Shakespeare's sonnets and respond to them very much as a seventeenth-century reader would. He enjoys them and, I think, misses very little, if any, of their greatness and beauty.

This edition performs the usual tasks of glossing unfamiliar words and putting familiar ones into their Renaissance contexts; but since my commentary is explicitly designed to insure that a reader's experience of the sonnets will as far as possible approximate that of the first readers of the 1609 Quarto, I am also concerned with questions that are purely and unabashedly academic. My notes are as much occupied with investigating the sources of the greatness, the beauty, and, often, the obvious substantive meaning of Shakespeare's sentences as with reviving and revealing that meaning; the notes analyze the processes by which the relevant meanings of Shakespeare's words and phrases and the contexts they bring with them combine, intertwine, fuse, and conflict in the potentially dizzying complexity from which a reader's sense of straightforward simplicity emerges. It is the complexity, I think, that gives the sonnets what critics of eras less ambitious than this one for the clinical precision of natural science called the magic of the sonnets, the sense they give of effortless control of the uncontrollable. The notes to this edition investigate the particulars of the complexity. Any reader superstitiously fearful that the magic of a poem will vanish with knowledge of its sources need not worry any more than a student of zoology need worry that gazelles will slow down if he investigates the reasons why they can run so fast.

My commentary is designed not only to help a twentieth-century reader to a Renaissance reader's understanding of Shakespeare's idiom but also to answer academic questions about how the sonnets work—how they achieve the clarity and simplicity most of them have from the unstable and randomly dynamic locutions they employ. A reader who wants to know what it is that makes a sonnet he values so good will not achieve perfect understanding from this edition, but the commentary should help him to move in what common sense suggests is the most profitable direction—toward awareness of the multitudinous statements, ideas, ideals, standards, and references that almost every line of the 154 sonnets contains.

Let me turn again to quatrain 3 of sonnet 16. Although the general distinction that *So should the lines of life that life repair* makes between *lines of life* and lines of verse or lines in a drawing is immediately effective, editors worked and argued for many years over the precise meaning of *lines of life*. Finally, in 1930, William Empson in effect pointed out that *all* the suggested glosses for the phrase are right; this is from the second edition of *Seven Types of Ambiguity* (1947): "*Lines of life* refers to the form of a personal appearance, in the young man himself or repeated in his descendants (as one speaks of the lines of some one's figure); time's wrinkles on that face (suggested only to be feared); the young man's line or lineage—his descendants; lines drawn with a pencil—a portrait; lines drawn with a pen, in writing; the lines of a poem (the kind a Sonnet has fourteen of); and destiny, as in the life-line of palmistry—*Merchant of Venice*, II.ii.163" (pp. 54–55). The phrase also includes "lines of relationship (in a genealogical table)" and the obvious—but not quite demonstrable— meaning, "children." (*Line* may also play on "loin"; see the note on p. 579.)

Multitudinous meanings, overtones, and suggestions of reference that are relevant to their context but not necessarily compatible with each other or any single paraphrase are common in the sonnets. An editor of the sonnets who presents only the gloss demanded by the author's clear intent in the ongoing logic of a poem will not be incorrect but incomplete. There are some relatively rare instances where historical changes in idiom invalidate or distort a modern reader's probable response to a line (for instance, *astonishèd* in 86.8 *base* in 100.4, *brave* in 12.2 and 15.8, *closet* in 46.6, *eager* in 188.2, *fond* in 3.7, *go* in 130.11 *Intend* in 27.6, *interest* in 74.3, *level* in 117.11 and 121.9, *modern* in 83.7, *ow'st* in 18.10 and 70.14, *pencil* in 16.10, *policy* in 118.9 and 124.9, *prove* in 26.14, *reeks* in 130.8, *remember* in 120.9, *reviewest* in 74.5, *satire* in 100.11, *several* in 137.9, *store* in 11.9 and 14.12, *table* in 24.2 and 122.1,12; *translated* in 96.8,10; *will* in 134–136 and *wink* in 43.1 and 56.6). But most of the time when an editor offers the one obviously correct gloss on a word or phrase or line or quatrain, he is not so much explaining its meaning to his reader as lending scholarly sanction to the reader's own uneasy understanding of the text. The general effect of such a gloss is to tell the reader that he is foolish to have let his mind wander into any of the incidental byways toward which the accidents of particular words and idioms beckon him. The difficulty is that, since a modern reader is in obvious need of correction about those Renaissance words and phrases that he cannot understand or misunderstands because of changes the language has undergone in the time between Shakespeare and himself, a modern reader quickly develops the assumption that anything in a Renaissance text that does not accord with the general line of its argument is an illusion generated by his own ignorance and the assumption that "in those days" readers effortlessly understood a troublesome line as the unqualified and unclouded action that the logic of its context demands and an editor's gloss says it is. Some words, phrases, and lines only seem difficult to a reader unacquainted with the editor's special field of knowledge, but knowledge of Renaissance diction and idiom suggests that many of Shakespeare's locutions must have made his first readers as uneasy as they make modern readers. One can lose some of a poem if one forgets that a Shakespearian clause that makes straightforward logical sense after it has been sorted out and had its gaps filled in with probabilities must always have required some such exercise by its reader.

The notes in this edition are designed to admit that everything in a sonnet is there. Sometimes a line signals a syntactic action that later dissolves (see 33.2, 5, 7, note). Sometimes the syntax sends a reader on abortive side trips, often substantively gratuitous ones; for example, the word *that* in 16.9 can further crowd a complex line for a reader who understands *So should the lines of life that life repair* as "So should the lines of life *which* repair life"—a reading that cannot be denied even though it is cancelled, after the fact, by the actual appearance of *Which* to begin the next line.

In addition to containing the manifold significances of *lines of life* and the double action of *that*, line 9 also presents an example of another kind of fullness in the sonnets. As Empson goes on to say, *So should the lines of life that life repair* says both "that life thus should ['ought to' and 'would'] repair the lines of life" and "the lines of life thus should repair that life." The line is thus a syntactic mirror of a paradox, getting by giving, that is a recurrent theme in the preceding fifteen sonnets and is stated explicitly in the couplet of this one: *To give away yourself keeps yourself still.*

The second line of this quatrain is almost equally complex; moreover it demonstrates that discussion of Shakespeare's language is inseparable from discussion of punctuation and orthography. The spelling and punctuation of the 1609 Quarto are not necessarily or even probably Shakespeare's own, and, more importantly, even if they were it would not much matter. This is the Quarto text of 16.9–12:

> So should the lines of life that life repaire
> Which this (Times pensel or my pupill pen)
> Neither in inward worth nor outward faire
> Can make you live your selfe in eies of men,

No punctuation or orthography can satisfactorily retain all the superimposed meanings of line 10—meanings present in the Quarto but meanings that a modern reader can deny himself because of his habit of expecting punctuation and spelling to control logical relationships methodically.

The instinct of a modern reader will be to take the parenthetical material as an appositive identification: *this* equals *Times pensel or my pupill pen*. When one stops to think about it, that reading gives an understanding that comes close to sense but is not quite logical; before it is glossed by the parenthesis, *this* may, as Empson suggests, be taken as a contrast to *that* in the preceding line: "this life," the speaker's, spent on efforts to preserve the life of the young man in *barren rime* as opposed to *that life*, the young man's.

A more obvious and therefore more urgent understanding of *this* is as "this poem." Part of the apparent gloss in the parenthesis is thus easy to accept: the speaker's *pupill pen* may be read as a metonymy by which the product, the poem, is indicated by the tool with which it is made, the pen. However, *Times pensel*, which precedes *my pupill pen* in the apparent appositive, is another matter. In the sixteenth and seventeenth centuries "pencil" described a small brush, an instrument used in drawing not in writing. More important still, this pencil belongs to time; a pencil wielded by "time" would be used to mark the face of the young man, to age him, to do just the opposite of what the poem and the *pupill pen* attempt to do. Understanding the parenthetical words as appositional is additionally difficult because *Times pensel* relates to the idea of portraiture introduced at the end of the preceding quatrain; "time" as a personified malignancy cannot be thought of as an artist attempting to preserve the young man by an alternative method to the poet's.

Since the spelling and punctuation probably result from a printer's whims, errors, or idiosyncracies, most editors justly and sensibly abandon the quatrain's parenthesis and, since a modern reader is conditioned to take capitalizations like *Times* as a signal of personification, give *Times* as *time's* (the apostrophe added to genitives in *s* by modern editors can be a distorting limitation; but here, where *Times* is obviously genitive in any reading of line 10, the apostrophe simply makes the genitive construction as immediately obvious to a modern reader as context would have made it for a Renaissance reader). When an editor modernizes line 10, logic and the narrowed potential of modern language drive him to settle for *Which this time's pencil or my pupil pen*—perhaps followed by a comma. From the line thus printed a modern reader will understand "which the portraiture of this age or my poor writing." That orthography and punctuation effectively deny the personification of time and the relevant but syntactically unaccommodated suggestion of time drawing wrinkles on a face. They also cancel the possible reading of *this* as "this poem," the first element of a triple subject for *Can make*. The modern reading also tends to suppress some of the significance of *pupil*, which Empson glosses as "immature and unskilful: as pupil of that time whose sonnet tradition I am imitating; or of *Time* which matures me" (p. 55).

For Shakespeare's contemporaries all these meanings, contradictions, echoes, and suggestions would have been active in the line—all in some way appropriate but none appropriate to all of the others. A modern printing cannot retain all that is in this line and in others like it because a modern reader can probably never perfectly free himself from the assumption that punctuation and spelling follow rules and that a Renaissance writer would or could expect to succeed in exercising delicate control of his readers' responses by such means. The version of the Quarto's line 10 that I offer here is no less a compromise and no less unsatisfactory than those of other modernizers. In its favor one can, however, point out that it and my texts of other lines similarly resistant to translation into the twentieth century are accompanied by the Quarto text itself and by commentary that attempts to mark each unsatisfactory compromise for what it is.

In a case like line 10 some of the flexibility of Renaissance texts can be salvaged by resisting the temptation to put a comma after *pen*. Without a comma the relationship of *Which this time's pencil or my pupil pen* to line 11 does not solidify until one reaches *Can make* in line 12; the word *Neither* thus can momentarily act as a pronoun referring to *pencil* and *pen*, and the logical implications of the parallelism between *time's pencil or my pupil pen* in line 10 and *inward worth nor outward fair* in line 11 can have free play until line 12, which thus has the rhetorical effect of a certainty emerging from a maze of unsatisfactory alternative lines of thought.

I have tried also to offer notes that distinguish the now unfamiliar habits of Renaissance syntax and idiom from locutions that can never have been as straightforward as their practical efficiency suggests they are. For example, consider the three-line subordinate clause appended to *So should the lines of life that life repair*:

> Which this time's pencil or my pupil pen
> Neither in inward worth nor outward fair
> Can make you live yourself in eyes of men.

The clause conflates two incompatible constructions, one stating the positive case for *lines of life* (*Which . . . Can make you live*), the other stating the case against art (*this . . . Neither in . . . worth nor . . . fair Can make you live*). As the three lines are read, *Which* first seems to be the grammatical subject of its clause—its antecedent being *life* or *lines of life*. The next word, *this*, transforms a reader's understanding of *Which* from probable subject to probable direct object in a developing clause of which "this . . . " will be the grammatical subject; it also adds another possible antecedent for *Which*—"reparation," a noun extrapolation from the verb in the preceding line. Ultimately, however, the completed construction, *this . . . Can make you live*, ignores the word *Which* and cannot logically accommodate it at all: the word that links the clause to what precedes it vanishes in the course of our understanding. Moreover, a further complication of a reader's perception occurs because the clause is constructed positively; the action and power of the syntactical subject, *this time's pencil or my pupil pen*, is only qualified by a scarcely anchored syntactic appendage, *Neither in inward worth nor outward fair*. The logic of the situation urges a reader to understand the elements of the clause as if he heard "Neither in . . . worth nor . . . fair can this time's pencil or my . . . pen make you live . . . ," but the actual syntax cannot be discounted as a quaintness of archaic language: the thrust of the syntax and that of the substance and context pull against each other. A reader grasps the logically available statement he expects to hear, but it is wrapped in a syntax that suggests an opposite position. All this complexity and density is not only mastered by a reader but mastered without conscious effort or awareness. The word *So* led the reader into the quatrain confident of its direction; the couplet—a summary epigram that states a recurrent message in the preceding sonnets followed by a simple directive that echoes the language and topics of the quatrain—assures a reader that he has indeed read the simple statement he expected.

This third quatrain of sonnet 16 also offers occasion to comment on other editorial practices followed in my text. As I said, maintaining the Quarto capitalization of *Times* makes for a distortion in a modern reader's experience greater than the one that results from printing *time's*. What about *time* at the end of line 2? There, where *bloody tyrant* clearly personifies *time*, the Quarto text does not capitalize it. Many editors silently change *time* to *Time*, formalizing a personification surely evident to a Renaissance reader and, as the editorial silence testifies, evident to modern readers as well. In situations where indicating personification by capitalization does not result in a benevolent distortion, the indication is unnecessary. Much the same is true of words like *yourself*; in line 12 the Quarto gives *your selfe*, the usual Renaissance practice. The best way to duplicate the action of the Quarto line on its original readers is simply to print *yourself*—to do otherwise would be to preserve a distorting archaism for its own sake. Sometimes, however, retaining the Quarto spelling can take the place of an explanatory note; see, for example, line 13 of sonnet 62: *'Tis thee (my selfe) that for my selfe I praise*; there retention of the Quarto spelling would point up the wit of the line. I have chosen not to retain such accidentally informative spellings, not for the sake of consistency but because to create a physical distinction between standard reflexives and witty plays on them is to create an urgently etymological and ostentatiously artful effect from what would have seemed graceful wit to a Renaissance reader.

Dutiful retention of the Quarto's random use of italics (as in the Quarto text of sonnet 1, line 2) results in similar distortions by giving the sort of urgency orthographic emphases give to *Adolescent* prose. Renaissance texts do make purposeful use of such devices (e.g. *Will* in the Q text of 135.1, 2, 11, 12, and 14), but they do not do so consistently (e.g. *will* in the Q text of 135.4, 5, 6, 7, 8, and 12 and *Statues* in the Q text of 55.5). The literary experience of Shakespeare's contemporaries, not conditioned to look for meaning in orthographic variations, presumably let them recognize orthographic signals when their import assisted what was inherent in the rhythm and sense of a line but let them ignore orthographic peculiarities where they seem accidental; experience presumably also let them ignore the absence of such signals in situations where they are appropriate, and presumably preserved them from our modern temptation to study a printer's use or non-use of capitals and italics as a clue to what a Renaissance writer wished to convey. In modernizing the Q text I have used roman throughout and have not used informative capitals because where they are not unnecessary they are unwarranted. For a full discussion of the principles on which I modernize, see the long supplementary note on sonnet 129.

Except when there is practical value in doing otherwise, I have taken widely accepted glosses and suggestions by commentators whose work precedes and is covered by H. E. Rollins in his *New Variorum Edition* (1944) as in the public domain: I have not attempted to duplicate Rollins's effort in tracing back and acknowledging the first appearances of glosses and identifications that have become standard; nor have I troubled to consider suggestions that have been justly ignored by later commentators. Scholars of the caliber of Edmond Malone, Alexander Schmidt, and Hyder Rollins himself are in no danger of being forgotten; the bulk of the lesser scholars whose follies are displayed in the *Variorum* are in no danger *from* being forgotten. I have also chosen not to label each and every previously noted allusion and gloss with its donor's name because such scrupulosity seems less often prompted by generosity than by the hope that each *un*acknowledged perception will thereby be recognized and admired as the editor's own. I have drawn often on more recent commentaries, notably those in two editions that appeared in 1964, one by Gerald Willen and Victor Reed, the other by W. G. Ingram and Theodore Redpath; I acknowledge their contributions one by one because they are so many and because their authors are alive to hear my thanks. Bibliographical details on these and other works to which I refer regularly are given in the list of abbreviations (pp. 539–42).

Unless otherwise specified, all references to Shakespeare's plays and other poems are keyed to *The Tudor Shakespeare*, ed. Peter Alexander (London, 1951, and New York, 1952).

The spelling in my modernized text is British (because British readers seem to be more troubled by variations from the spellings normal to them than Americans are); however, where Q gives a spelling current in American usage but not in British, I have left it alone (e.g. *center* in 146.1). The spelling in the commentary is American because I am.

* * *

I am grateful to the Huntington Library for permission to reproduce the Bridgewater copy of the Apsley imprint of the 1609 Quarto and to The Elizabethan Club for permission to reproduce the title page from their copy of the Wright imprint. The two illustrations in the commentary are also by permission of the Huntington Library. I am indebted to Carey S. Bliss, Curator of Rare

Books at the Huntington, for his advice and counsel. I am equally grateful for the less specialized but equally practical bibliographical assistance of Julia Hess, Alyce Foley, Rochell Nemerov, Sylvia Bonnell, Sharon Osmond, Ilee Kaplan, Mary Booth, Peggy Chenier, and Kelly Cosandaey. This edition also owes an unreasonable amount to the wisdom and patience of Ellen Graham, Christine Froula, and Maureen Bushkovitch, my editors at the Yale University Press; to Thomas Tentler's generous, if grudging, technical assistance with the poems of John Donne; to Ruby Nemser, who let me see an advance copy of the critical commentary she provided for the new Oxford edition of the poems of Sir John Davies; and to unpublished essays by Barbara Walbolt, Marilyn Perry, William Buford, and Susan Nash.

I have worked six years on the commentary to this edition, and there now seem to be few living Americans who have not read, written, or corrected some of it. I was especially dependent on the assistance of three people who helped me on specialized topics: Florence Elon (on music), Ivan King (on astronomy), and A. J. Patek (on medicine); I thank them and apologize to them for phoning them at odd hours with odd questions; please keep in mind that I asked for their help only when I had the wit to know I needed it. I am also vastly indebted to Brent Cohen, Susan Harris, Richard Sylvester, William Buford, and—and most of all—Barbara Theiner; each of them read through the whole of the commentary, taking my foot out of my mouth more often than I care to recall and making more suggestions and additions than the economics of academic publishing allow me to acknowledge specifically. My own contribution to the commentary was *at least* as great as my wife's (for instance, I prepared the index all by myself); her name is Susan Patek Booth.

S. B.

Berkeley, California
May 3, 1976

Preface to the 1978 Printing

The present need to print more copies of this book gives me a chance to make up for some earlier lapses. I have silently corrected as many minor errors as I have so far found or been told about. I am indebted to various friends, relatives, and reviewers for catching escaped faults that would otherwise be still at large; I am most particularly indebted to W. L. Godshalk—who in the course of the last ten days' frantic correspondence has virtually become co-editor.

I am grateful also to the staff of the Huntington Library for permitting me—and helping me—to get six pages of the Huntington-Bridgewater copy of the 1609 Quarto re-photographed. The six pages—reproduced as pages 90, 93, 94, 97, 98, and 105 below—are signatures G2^v, G3^r, G3^v, G4^r, G4^v, and H2^r. For reasons beyond my severely limited technical scope, five of those six pages did not reproduce clearly in the first printing of this book. The sixth, H2^r, was reproduced without its catchword. (I wish I could say I wondered why. I know why. In a dim moment I blocked it out of the photograph. The catchword ["To"] on that page is severely damaged. In the Huntington-Bridgewater copy it looks like a smudge. I guess I must have taken it for an accident of the photograph—even though its position, its relative clarity in other copies of Q, and the absence of any other catchword for the page said otherwise and said it loudly. I feel appropriately foolish.)

This new printing also includes several pages of additional notes, notes largely derived from suggestions offered by reviewers. One of those notes (on 111.1) discusses the one substantial difference between the modernized text printed here and the one published in 1977. For obvious economic reasons the new notes are all together at the end of the book (pp. 579–83), but I have inserted a brief notice of the existence and location of each at the appropriate point in the body of the commentary to which it pertains.

S.B.

Berkeley, California
September 6, 1978

SHAKE-SPEARES

SONNETS.

Neuer before Imprinted.

_____

_____

AT LONDON
By *G. Eld* for *T. T.* and are
to be folde by *William Aspley.*
1609.

TO.THE.ONLIE.BEGETTER.OF.
THESE.INSVING.SONNETS.
Mr.W.H. ALL.HAPPINESSE.
AND.THAT.ETERNITIE.
PROMISED.

BY.

OVR.EVER-LIVING.POET.

WISHETH.

THE.WELL-WISHING.
ADVENTVRER.IN.
SETTING.
FORTH.

T. T.

1

From fairest creatures we desire increase,
That thereby beauty's rose might never die,
But as the riper should by time decease
His tender heir might bear his memory:
But thou, contracted to thine own bright eyes,
Feed'st thy light's flame with self-substantial fuel,
Making a famine where abundance lies—
Thyself thy foe, to thy sweet self too cruel.
Thou that art now the world's fresh ornament
And only herald to the gaudy spring
Within thine own bud buriest thy content,
And tender churl mak'st waste in niggarding.
  Pity the world, or else this glutton be—
  To eat the world's due, by the grave and thee.

2

When forty winters shall besiege thy brow
And dig deep trenches in thy beauty's field,
Thy youth's proud livery, so gazed on now,
Will be a tottered weed of small worth held.
Then being asked where all thy beauty lies—
Where all the treasure of thy lusty days—
To say within thine own deep-sunken eyes
Were an all-eating shame and thriftless praise.
How much more praise deserved thy beauty's use,
If thou couldst answer, "This fair child of mine
Shall sum my count and make my old excuse"—
Proving his beauty by succession thine.

SHAKE-SPEARES,
SONNETS.

FRom faireſt creatures we deſire increaſe,
　　That thereby beauties *Roſe* might neuer die,
But as the riper ſhould by time deceaſe,
His tender heire might beare his memory:
But thou contraĉted to thine owne bright eyes,
Feed'ſt thy lights flame with ſelfe ſubſtantiall fewell,
Making a famine where aboundance lies,
Thy ſelfe thy foe, to thy ſweet ſelfe too cruell:
Thou that art now the worlds freſh ornament,
And only herauld to the gaudy ſpring,
Within thine owne bud burieſt thy content,
And tender chorle makſt waſt in niggarding:
　　Pitty the world, or elſe this glutton be,
　　To eate the worlds due, by the graue and thee.

2

VVHen fortie Winters ſhall beſeige thy brow,
　　And digge deep trenches in thy beauties field,
Thy youthes proud liuery ſo gaz'd on now,
Wil be a totter'd weed of ſmal worth held:
Then being askt, where all thy beautie lies,
Where all the treaſure of thy luſty daies;
To ſay within thine owne deepe ſunken eyes,
Were an all-eating ſhame, and thriftleſſe praiſe.
How much more praiſe deſeru'd thy beauties vſe,
If thou couldſt anſwere this faire child of mine
Shall ſum my count, and make my old excuſe
Proouing his beautie by ſucceſſion thine.

B
　　　　　　　　　　　　　This

This were to be new made when thou art ould,
And see thy blood warme when thou feel'ſt it could,

3

Looke in thy glaſſe and tell the face thou veweſt,
Now is the time that face ſhould forme an other,
Whoſe freſh repaire if now thou not reneweſt,
Thou doo'ſt beguile the world, vnbleſſe ſome mother.
For where is ſhe ſo faire whoſe vn-eard wombe
Diſdaines the tillage of thy husbandry?
Or who is he ſo fond will be the tombe
Of his ſelfe loue to ſtop poſterity?
Thou art thy mothers glaſſe and ſhe in thee
Calls backe the louely Aprill of her prime,
So thou through windowes of thine age ſhalt ſee,
Diſpight of wrinkles this thy goulden time.
　　But if thou liue remembred not to be,
　　Die ſingle and thine Image dies with thee.

4

VNthrifty louelineſſe why doſt thou ſpend,
Vpon thy ſelfe thy beauties legacy?
Natures bequeſt giues nothing but doth lend,
And being franck ſhe lends to thoſe are free:
Then beautious nigard why dooſt thou abuſe,
The bountious largeſſe giuen thee to giue?
Profitles vſerer why dooſt thou vſe
So great a ſumme of ſummes yet can'ſt not liue?
For hauing traffike with thy ſelfe alone,
Thou of thy ſelfe thy ſweet ſelfe doſt deceaue,
Then how when nature calls thee to be gone,
What acceptable *Audit* can'ſt thou leaue?
　　Thy vnuſ'd beauty muſt be tomb'd with thee,
　　Which vſed liues th'executor to be.

5

THoſe howers that with gentle worke did frame,
The louely gaze where euery eye doth dwell
Will play the tirants to the very ſame,

And

This were to be new made when thou art old,
And see thy blood warm when thou feel'st it cold.

3

Look in thy glass and tell the face thou viewest,
Now is the time that face should form another,
Whose fresh repair if now thou not renewest,
4   Thou dost beguile the world, unbless some mother.
For where is she so fair whose uneared womb
Disdains the tillage of thy husbandry?
Or who is he so fond will be the tomb
8   Of his self-love to stop posterity?
Thou art thy mother's glass, and she in thee
Calls back the lovely April of her prime;
So thou through windows of thine age shalt see,
12   Despite of wrinkles, this thy golden time.
    But if thou live rememb'red not to be,
    Die single and thine image dies with thee.

4

Unthrifty loveliness, why dost thou spend
Upon thyself thy beauty's legacy?
Nature's bequest gives nothing but doth lend,
4   And being frank she lends to those are free.
Then beauteous niggard why dost thou abuse
The bounteous lárgess given thee to give?
Profitless usurer, why dost thou use
8   So great a sum of sums yet canst not live?
For having traffic with thyself alone,
Thou of thyself thy sweet self dost deceive.
Then how when nature calls thee to be gone,
12   What ácceptable audit canst thou leave?
    Thy unused beauty must be tombed with thee,
    Which uséd lives th' executor to be.

5

Those hours that with gentle work did frame
The lovely gaze where every eye doth dwell
Will play the tyrants to the very same

4   And that unfair which fairly doth excel:
For never-resting time leads summer on
To hideous winter and confounds him there,
Sap checked with frost and lusty leaves quite gone,
8   Beauty o'ersnowed and bareness everywhere.
Then were not summer's distillation left
A liquid pris'ner pent in walls of glass,
Beauty's effect with beauty were bereft,
12   Nor it nor no remembrance what it was.
       But flow'rs distilled, though they with winter meet,
       Leese but their show, their substance still lives sweet.

6

Then let not winter's ragged hand deface
In thee thy summer ere thou be distilled:
Make sweet some vial; treasure thou some place
4   With beauty's treasure ere it be self-killed.
That use is not forbidden usury
Which happies those that pay the willing loan;
That's for thyself to breed another thee,
8   Or ten times happier be it ten for one.
Ten times thyself were happier than thou art,
If ten of thine ten times refigured thee:
Then what could death do if thou shouldst depart,
12   Leaving thee living in posterity?
       Be not self-willed, for thou art much too fair,
       To be death's conquest and make worms thine heir.

7

Lo, in the orient when the gracious light
Lifts up his burning head, each under eye
Doth homage to his new-appearing sight,
4   Serving with looks his sacred majesty;
And having climbed the steep-up heav'nly hill,
Resembling strong youth in his middle age,
Yet mortal looks adore his beauty still,
8   Attending on his golden pilgrimage.
But when from highmost pitch, with weary car,

And that vnfaire which fairely doth excell:
For neuer resting time leads Summer on,
To hidious winter and confounds him there,
Sap checkt with frost and lustie leau's quite gon.
Beauty ore-snow'd and barenes euery where,
Then were not summers distillation left
A liquid prisoner pent in walls of glasse,
Beauties effect with beauty were bereft,
Nor it nor noe remembrance what it was.
　　But flowers distil'd though they with winter meete,
　　Leese but their show,their substance still liues sweet.

6

THen let not winters wragged hand deface,
　In thee thy summer ere thou be distil'd:
Make sweet some viall;treasure thou some place,
With beautits treasure ere it be selfe kil'd:
That vse is not forbidden vsery,
Which happies those that pay the willing lone;
That's for thy selfe to breed an other thee,
Or ten times happier be it ten for one,
Ten times thy selfe were happier then thou art,
If ten of thine ten times refigur'd thee,
Then what could death doe if thou should'st depart,
Leauing thee liuing in posterity?
　　Be not selfe-wild for thou art much too faire.
　　To be deaths conquest and make wormes thine heire.

7

LOe in the Orient when the gracious light,
　Lifts vp his burning head,each vnder eye
Doth homage to his new appearing sight,
Seruing with lookes his sacred maiesty,
And hauing climb'd the steepe vp heauenly hill,
Resembling strong youth in his middle age,
Yet mortall lookes adore his beauty still,
Attending on his goulden pilgrimage:
But when from high-most pich with wery car,

　　　　　　　　　　Like

Like feeble age he reeleth from the day,
The eyes(fore dutious)now conuerted are
From his low tract and looke an other way:
  So thou,thy selfe out-going in thy noon:
  Vnlok'd on dieſt vnleſſe thou get a ſonne.

8

MVſick to heare,why hear'ſt thou muſick ſadly,
  Sweets with ſweets warre not , ioy delights in ioy:
Why lou'ſt thou that which thou receauſt not gladly,
Or elſe receau'ſt with pleaſure thine annoy ?
If the true concord of well tuned ſounds,
By vnions married do offend thine eare,
They do but ſweetly chide thee, who confounds
In ſingleneſſe the parts that thou ſhould'ſt beare:
Marke how one ſtring ſweet husband to an other,
Strikes each in each by mutuall ordering;
Reſembling ſier,and child, and happy mother,
Who all in one,one pleaſing note do ſing:
  Whoſe ſpeechleſſe ſong being many,ſeeming one,
  Sings this to thee thou ſingle wilt proue none.

9.

IS it for feare to wet a widdowes eye,
  That thou conſum'ſt thy ſelfe in ſingle life?
Ah;if thou iſſuleſſe ſhalt hap to die,
The world will waile thee like a makeleſſe wife,
The world wilbe thy widdow and ſtill weepe,
That thou no forme of thee haſt left behind,
When euery priuat widdow well may keepe,
By childrens eyes,her husbands ſhape in minde:
Looke what an vnthrift in the world doth ſpend
Shifts but his place,for ſtill the world inioyes it
But beauties waſte hath in the world an end,
And kept vnvſde the vſer ſo deſtroyes it:
  No loue toward others in that boſome ſits
  That on himſelfe ſuch murdrous ſhame commits.

Like feeble age he reeleth from the day,
The eyes ('fore duteous) now converted are
12   From his low tract and look another way.
    So thou, thyself outgoing in thy noon,
    Unlooked on diest unless thou get a son.

8

Music to hear, why hear'st thou music sadly?
Sweets with sweets war not, joy delights in joy.
Why lov'st thou that which thou receiv'st not gladly,
4   Or else receiv'st with pleasure thine annoy?
If the true concord of well-tunèd sounds,
By unions married, do offend thine ear,
They do but sweetly chide thee, who confounds
8   In singleness the parts that thou shouldst bear.
Mark how one string, sweet husband to another,
Strikes each in each by mutual ordéring;
Resembling sire, and child, and happy mother,
12   Who all in one, one pleasing note do sing;
    Whose speechless song, being many, seeming one,
    Sings this to thee: "Thou single wilt prove none."

9

Is it for fear to wet a widow's eye
That thou consum'st thyself in single life?
Ah, if thou issueless shalt hap to die,
4   The world will wail thee like a makeless wife;
The world will be thy widow and still weep,
That thou no form of thee hast left behind,
When every private widow well may keep,
8   By children's eyes, her husband's shape in mind.
Look what an unthrift in the world doth spend
Shifts but his place, for still the world enjoys it;
But beauty's waste hath in the world an end,
12   And kept unused, the user so destroys it.
    No love toward others in that bosom sits
    That on himself such murd'rous shame commits.

For shame deny that thou bear'st love to any,
Who for thyself art so unprovident.
Grant if thou wilt, thou art belov'd of many,
4   But that thou none lov'st is most evident;
For thou art so possessed with murd'rous hate,
That 'gainst thyself thou stick'st not to conspire,
Seeking that beauteous roof to ruinate,
8   Which to repair should be thy chief desire.
O change thy thought, that I may change my mind.
Shall hate be fairer lodged than gentle love?
Be as thy presence is, gracious and kind,
12   Or to thyself at least kind-hearted prove.
    Make thee another self for love of me,
    That beauty still may live in thine or thee.

11

As fast as thou shalt wane so fast thou grow'st—
In one of thine, from that which thou departest,
And that fresh blood which youngly thou bestow'st
4   Thou mayst call thine, when thou from youth convertest.
Herein lives wisdom, beauty, and increase;
Without this, folly, age, and cold decay.
If all were minded so, the times should cease,
8   And threescore year would make the world away.
Let those whom nature hath not made for store,
Harsh, featureless, and rude, barrenly perish.
Look whom she best endowed, she gave the more;
12   Which bounteous gift thou shouldst in bounty cherish.
    She carved thee for her seal, and meant thereby
    Thou shouldst print more, not let that copy die.

12

When I do count the clock that tells the time,
And see the brave day sunk in hideous night,
When I behold the violet past prime,
4   And sable curls all silvered o'er with white,
When lofty trees I see barren of leaves,
Which erst from heat did canopy the herd,

10

FOr fhame dény that thou bear'ft loue to any
Who for thy felfe art fo vnprouident
Graunt if thou wilt, thou art belou'd of many,
But that thou none lou'ft is moft euident:
For thou art fo poffeft with murdrous hate,
That gainft thy felfe thou ftickft not to confpire,
Seeking that beautious roofe to ruinate
Which to repaire fhould be thy chiefe defire :
O change thy thought, that I may change my minde,
Shall hate be fairer log'd then gentle loue?
Be as thy prefence is gracious and kind,
Or to thy felfe at leaft kind harted proue,
    Make thee an other felfe for loue of me,
    That beauty ftill may liue in thine or thee.

11

AS faft as thou fhalt wane fo faft thou grow'ft,
In one of thine, from that which thou departeft,
And that frefh bloud which yongly thou beftow'ft,
Thou maift call thine, when thou from youth conuerteft,
Herein liues wifdome, beauty, and increafe,
Without this follie, age, and could decay,
If all were minded fo, the times fhould ceafe,
And threefcoore yeare would make the world away:
Let thofe whom nature hath not made for ftore,
Harfh, featurelefle, and rude , barrenly perrifh,
Looke whom fhe beft indow'd, fhe gaue the more;
Which bountious guift thou fhouldft in bounty cherrifh,
    She caru'd thee for her feale, and ment therby,
    Thou fhouldft print more, not let that coppy die.

12

VVHen I doe count the clock that tels the time,
    And fee the braue day funck in hidious night,
When I behold the violet paft prime,
And fable curls or filuer'd ore with white :
When lofty trees I fee barren of leaues,
Which erft from heat did canopie the herd
                B 3   And

And Sommers greene all girded vp in sheaues
Borne on the beare with white and bristly beard:
Then of thy beauty do I question make
That thou among the wastes of time must goe,
Since sweets and beauties do them-selues forsake,
  And die as fast as they see others grow,
    And nothing gainst Times sieth can make defence
    Saue breed to braue him, when he takes thee hence.

13

O That you were your selfe, but loue you are
  No longer yours, then you your selfe here liue,
Against this cumming end you should prepare,
And your sweet semblance to some other giue.
So should that beauty which you hold in lease
Find no determination, then you were
You selfe again after your selfes decease,
When your sweet issue your sweet forme should beare.
Who lets so faire a house fall to decay,
Which husbandry in honour might vphold,
Against the stormy gusts of winters day
And barren rage of deaths eternall cold?
    O none but vnthrifts, deare my loue you know,
    You had a Father, let your Son say so.

14

NOt from the stars do I my iudgement plucke,
  And yet me thinkes I haue Astronomy,
But not to tell of good, or euil lucke,
Of plagues, of dearths, or seasons quallity,
Nor can i fortune to breefe mynuits tell;
Pointing to each his thunder, raine and winde,
Or say with Princes if it shal go wel
By oft predict that I in heauen finde.
But from thine eies my knowledge I deriue,
And constant stars in them I read such art
As truth and beautie shal together thriue
If from thy selfe, to store thou wouldst conuert:

                                              Or

And summer's green all girded up in sheaves
8   Borne on the bier with white and bristly beard;
Then of thy beauty do I question make
That thou among the wastes of time must go,
Since sweets and beauties do themselves forsake,
12   And die as fast as they see others grow,
 And nothing 'gainst time's scythe can make defence
 Save breed to brave him when he takes thee hence.

13

O that you were yourself, but love you are
No longer yours than you yourself here live.
Against this coming end you should prepare,
4   And your sweet semblance to some other give.
So should that beauty which you hold in lease
Find no determination—then you were
Yourself again after your self's decease,
8   When your sweet issue your sweet form should bear.
Who lets so fair a house fall to decay,
Which husbandry in honour might uphold
Against the stormy gusts of winter's day
12   And barren rage of death's eternal cold?
 O none but unthrifts, dear my love you know,
 You had a father, let your son say so.

14

Not from the stars do I my judgement pluck,
And yet methinks I have astronomy;
But not to tell of good or evil luck,
4   Of plagues, of dearths, or seasons' quality;
Nor can I fortune to brief minutes tell,
Pointing to each his thunder, rain, and wind,
Or say with princes if it shall go well,
8   By oft predict that I in heaven find.
But from thine eyes my knowledge I derive,
And, constant stars, in them I read such art
As truth and beauty shall together thrive,
12   If from thyself to store thou wouldst convert;

Or else of thee this I prognosticate,
Thy end is truth's and beauty's doom and date.

15

When I consider everything that grows
Holds in perfection but a little moment,
That this huge stage presenteth nought but shows
4 Whereon the stars in secret influence commént;
When I perceive that men as plants increase,
Cheerèd and checked ev'n by the selfsame sky,
Vaunt in their youthful sap, at height decrease,
8 And wear their brave state out of memory;
Then the conceit of this inconstant stay
Sets you most rich in youth before my sight,
Where wasteful time debateth with decay
12 To change your day of youth to sullied night;
   And all in war with time for love of you,
   As he takes from you, I engraft you new.

16

But wherefore do not you a mightier way
Make war upon this bloody tyrant time?
And fortify yourself in your decay
4 With means more blessèd than my barren rhyme?
Now stand you on the top of happy hours,
And many maiden gardens yet unset,
With virtuous wish would bear your living flowers,
8 Much liker than your painted counterfeit.
So should the lines of life that life repair
Which this time's pencil or my pupil pen
Neither in inward worth nor outward fair
12 Can make you live yourself in eyes of men.
   To give away yourself keeps yourself still,
   And you must live, drawn by your own sweet skill.

17

Who will believe my verse in time to come
If it were filled with your most high deserts?

Or elſe of thee this I prognoſticate,
Thy end is Truthes and Beauties doome and date.

15

VV Hen I conſider euery thing that growes
    Holds in perfection but a little moment.
That this huge ſtage preſenteth nought but ſhowes
Whereon the Stars in ſecret influence comment.
When I perceiue that men as plants increaſe,
Cheared and checkt euen by the ſelfe-ſame skie:
Vaunt in their youthfull ſap, at height decreaſe,
And were their braue ſtate out of memory.
Then the conceit of this inconſtant ſtay,
Sets you moſt rich in youth before my ſight,
Where waſtfull time debateth with decay
To change your day of youth to ſullied night,
    And all in war with Time for loue of you
    As he takes from you, I ingraft you new.

16

BVt wherefore do not you a mightier waie
    Make warre vppon this bloudie tirant time?
And fortifie your ſelfe in your decay
With meanes more bleſſed then my barren rime?
Now ſtand you on the top of happie houres,
And many maiden gardens yet vnſet,
With vertuous wiſh would beare your liuing flowers,
Much liker then your painted counterfeit:
So ſhould the lines of life that life repaire
Which this (Times penſel or my pupill pen)
Neither in inward worth nor outward faire
Can make you liue your ſelfe in eies of men,
    To giue away your ſelfe, keeps your ſelfe ſtill,
    And you muſt liue drawne by your owne ſweet skill,

17

VV Ho will beleeue my verſe in time to come
    If it were fild with your moſt high deſerts?

Though

Though yet heauen knowes it is but as a tombe
Which hides your life , and fhewes not halfe your parts:
If I could write the beauty of your eyes,
And in frefh numbers number all your graces,
The age to come would fay this Poet lies,
Such heauenly touches nere toucht earthly faces.
So fhould my papers (yellowed with their age)
Be fcorn d,like old men of leffe truth then tongue,
And your true rights be termd a Poets rage,
And ftretched miter of an Antique fong.
    But were fome childe of yours aliue that time,
    You fhould liue twife in it,and in my rime.

18.

SHall I compare thee to a Summers day?
  Thou art more louely and more temperate:
Rough windes do fhake the darling buds of Maie,
And Sommers leafe hath all too fhort a date:
Sometime too hot the eye of heauen fhines,
And often is his gold complexion dimm'd,
And euery faire from faire fome-time declines,
By chance,or natures changing courfe vntrim'd:
But thy eternall Sommer fhall not fade,
Nor loofe poffeffion of that faire thou ow'ft,
Nor fhall death brag thou wandr'ft in his fhade,
When in eternall lines to time thou grow'ft,
    So long as men can breath or eyes can fee,
    So long liues this,and this giues life to thee,

19

DEuouring time blunt thou the Lyons pawes,
  And make the earth deuoure her owne fweet brood,
Plucke the keene teeth from the fierce Tygers yawes,
And burne the long liu'd Phænix in her blood,
Make glad and forry feafons as thou fleet'ft,
And do what ere thou wilt fwift-footed time
To the wide world and all her fading fweets:
But I forbid thee one moft hainous crime,

O

Though yet heav'n knows it is but as a tomb
4   Which hides your life, and shows not half your parts.
If I could write the beauty of your eyes,
And in fresh numbers number all your graces,
The age to come would say, "This poet lies—
8   Such heav'nly touches ne'er touched earthly faces."
So should my papers, yellowed with their age,
Be scorned, like old men of less truth than tongue,
And your true rights be termed a poet's rage
12   And stretchèd meter of an ántique song:
    But were some child of yours alive that time,
    You should live twice in it and in my rhyme.

18

Shall I compare thee to a summer's day?
Thou art more lovely and more temperate:
Rough winds do shake the darling buds of May,
4   And summer's lease hath all too short a date;
Sometime too hot the eye of heaven shines,
And often is his gold complexion dimmed;
And every fair from fair sometime declines,
8   By chance or nature's changing course untrimmed:
But thy eternal summer shall not fade,
Nor lose possession of that fair thou ow'st,
Nor shall death brag thou wand'rest in his shade,
12   When in eternal lines to time thou grow'st.
    So long as men can breathe or eyes can see,
    So long lives this, and this gives life to thee.

19

Devouring time, blunt thou the lion's paws,
And make the earth devour her own sweet brood;
Pluck the keen teeth from the fierce tiger's jaws,
4   And burn the long-lived phoenix in her blood;
Make glad and sorry seasons as thou fleet'st
And do whate'er thou wilt, swift-footed time,
To the wide world and all her fading sweets;
8   But I forbid thee one most heinous crime,

O carve not with thy hours my love's fair brow,
Nor draw no lines there with thine ántique pen.
Him in thy course untainted do allow,
12   For beauty's pattern to succeeding men.
    Yet do thy worst, old time; despite thy wrong,
    My love shall in my verse ever live young.

20

A woman's face, with nature's own hand painted,
Hast thou, the master mistress of my passion—
A woman's gentle heart, but not acquainted
4   With shifting change, as is false women's fashion;
An eye more bright than theirs, less false in rolling,
Gilding the object whereupon it gazeth;
A man in hue all hues in his controlling,
8   Which steals men's eyes and women's souls amazeth.
And for a woman wert thou first created,
Till nature as she wrought thee fell a-doting,
And by addition me of thee defeated,
12   By adding one thing to my purpose nothing.
    But since she pricked thee out for women's pleasure,
    Mine be thy love, and thy love's use their treasure.

21

So is it not with me as with that muse,
Stirred by a painted beauty to his verse,
Who heav'n itself for ornament doth use,
4   And every fair with his fair doth rehearse—
Making a couplement of proud compare
With sun and moon, with earth and sea's rich gems,
With April's first-born flow'rs, and all things rare
8   That heaven's air in this huge rondure hems.
O let me true in love but truly write,
And then believe me, my love is as fair
As any mother's child, though not so bright
12   As those gold candles fixed in heaven's air.
    Let them say more that like of hearsay well;
    I will not praise that purpose not to sell.

O carue not with thy howers my loues faire brow,
Nor draw noe lines there with thine antique pen,
Him in thy courfe vntainted doe allow,
For beauties patterne to fucceding men.
    Yet doe thy worft ould Time difpight thy wrong,
    My loue fhall in my verfe euer liue young.

20

A Womans face with natures owne hand painted,
Hafte thou the Mafter Miftris of my paffion,
A womans gentle hart but not acquainted
With fhifting change as is falfe womens fafhion,
An eye more bright then theirs, leffe falfe in rowling:
Gilding the obiect where-vpon it gazeth,
A man in hew all *Hews* in his controwling,
Which fteales mens eyes and womens foules amafeth,
And for a woman wert thou firft created,
Till nature as fhe wrought thee fell a dotinge,
And by addition me of thee defeated,
By adding one thing to my purpofe nothing.
    But fince fhe prickt thee out for womens pleafure,
    Mine be thy loue and thy loues vfe their treafure.

21

SO is it not with me as with that Mufe,
Stird by a painted beauty to his verfe,
Who heauen it felfe for ornament doth vfe,
And euery faire with his faire doth reherfe,
Making a coopelment of proud compare
With Sunne and Moone, with earth and feas rich gems:
With Aprills firft borne flowers and all things rare,
That heauens ayre in this huge rondure hems,
O let me true in loue but truly write,
And then beleeue me, my loue is as faire,
As any mothers childe, though not fo bright
As thofe gould candells fixt in heauens ayer:
    Let them fay more that like of heare-fay well,
    I will not prayfe that purpofe not to fell.

C   22

22

MY glaſſe ſhall not perſwade me I am ould,
So long as youth and thou are of one date,
But when in thee times forrwes I behould,
Then look I death my daies ſhould expiate.
For all that beauty that doth couer thee,
Is but the ſeemely rayment of my heart,
Which in thy breſt doth liue,as thine in me,
How can I then be elder then thou art?
O therefore loue be of thy ſelfe ſo wary,
As I not for my ſelfe,but for thee will,
Bearing thy heart which I will keepe ſo chary
As tender nurſe her babe from faring ill,
   Preſume not on thy heart when mine is ſlaine,
   Thou gau'ſt me thine not to giue backe againe.

23

AS an vnperfect actor on the ſtage,
Who with his feare is put beſides his part,
Or ſome fierce thing repleat with too much rage,
Whoſe ſtrengths abondance weakens his owne heart;
So I for feare of truſt,forget to ſay,
The perfect ceremony of loues right,
And in mine owne loues ſtrength ſeeme to decay,
Ore-charg'd with burthen of mine owne loues might:
O let my books be then the eloquence,
And do nb preſagers of my ſpeaking breſt,
Who pleade for loue,and look for recompence,
More then that tonge that more hath more expreſt.
   O learne to read what ſilent loue hath writ,
   To heare wit eies belongs to loues fine wiht.

24

MIne eye hath play'd the painter and hath ſteeld,
Thy beauties forme in table of my heart,
My body is the frame wherein ti's held,
And perſpectiue it is beſt Painters art.
For through the Painter muſt you ſee his skill,

To

22

My glass shall not persuade me I am old
So long as youth and thou are of one date,
But when in thee time's furrows I behold,
4 Then look I death my days should expiate.
For all that beauty that doth cover thee
Is but the seemly raiment of my heart,
Which in thy breast doth live, as thine in me.
8 How can I then be elder than thou art?
O therefore love, be of thyself so wary
As I not for myself, but for thee will,
Bearing thy heart, which I will keep so chary
12 As tender nurse her babe from faring ill.
  Presume not on thy heart when mine is slain,
  Thou gav'st me thine not to give back again.

23

As an unperfect actor on the stage,
Who with his fear is put besides his part,
Or some fierce thing replete with too much rage,
4 Whose strength's abundance weakens his own heart;
So I for fear of trust forget to say
The perfect ceremony of love's rite,
And in mine own love's strength seem to decay,
8 O'ercharged with burthen of mine own love's might.
O let my books be then the eloquence
And dumb presagers of my speaking breast,
Who plead for love and look for recompense
12 More than that tongue that more hath more expressed.
  O learn to read what silent love hath writ.
  To hear with eyes belongs to love's fine wit.

24

Mine eye hath played the painter and hath stelled
Thy beauty's form in table of my heart.
My body is the frame wherein 'tis held,
4 And pérspective it is best painter's art,
For through the painter must you see his skill

To find where your true image pictured lies,
Which in my bosom's shop is hanging still,
8   That hath his windows glazèd with thine eyes.
Now see what good turns eyes for eyes have done.
Mine eyes have drawn thy shape, and thine for me
Are windows to my breast, wherethrough the sun
12   Delights to peep, to gaze therein on thee.
    Yet eyes this cunning want to grace their art;
    They draw but what they see, know not the heart.

25

Let those who are in favor with their stars
Of public honour and proud titles boast,
Whilst I whom fortune of such triumph bars,
4   Unlooked for joy in that I honour most.
Great princes' favorites their fair leaves spread,
But as the marigold at the sun's eye,
And in themselves their pride lies burièd,
8   For at a frown they in their glory die.
The painful warrior famousèd for fight,
After a thousand victories once foiled,
Is from the book of honour razèd quite,
12   And all the rest forgot for which he toiled.
    Then happy I that love and am belovèd
    Where I may not remove, nor be removèd.

26

Lord of my love, to whom in vassalage
Thy merit hath my duty strongly knit,
To thee I send this written ambassage,
4   To witness duty, not to show my wit.
Duty so great, which wit so poor as mine
May make seem bare, in wanting words to show it,
But that I hope some good conceit of thine
8   In thy soul's thought, all naked, will bestow it;
Till whatsoever star that guides my moving
Points on me graciously with fair aspéct,
And puts apparel on my tottered loving,

To finde where your true Image pictur'd lies,
Which in my bosomes shop is hanging stil,
That hath his windowes glazed with thine eyes:
Now see what good-turnes eyes for eies haue done,
Mine eyes haue drawne thy shape,and thine for me
A re windowes to my brest, where-through the Sun
Delights to peepe,to gaze therein on thee
   Yet eyes this cunning want to grace their art
   They draw but what they see,know not the hart.

25

LEt those who are in fauor with their stars,
  Of publike honour and proud titles bost,
Whilst I whome fortune of such tryumph bars
Vnlookt for ioy in that I honour most;
Great Princes fauorites their faire leaues spread,
But as the Marygold at the suns eye,
And in them-selues their pride lies buried,
For at a frowne they in their glory die.
The painefull warrier famosed for worth,
After a thousand victories once foild,
Is from the booke of honour rased quite,
And all the rest forgot for which he toild:
   Then happy I that loue and am beloued
   Where I may not remoue,nor be remoued.

26

LOrd of my loue,to whome in vassalage
  Thy merrit hath my dutie strongly knit;
To thee I send this written ambassage
To witnesse duty, not to shew my wit.
Duty so great,which wit so poore as mine
May make seeme bare,in wanting words to shew it;
But that I hope some good conceipt of thine
In thy soules thought(all naked) will bestow it:
Til whatsoeuer star that guides my mouing,
Points on me gratiously with faire aspect,
And puts apparrell on my tottered louing,

To

To fhow me worthy of their fweet refpect,
  Then may I dare to boaft how I doe loue thee,
  Til then,not fhow my head where thou maift proue me.

27

WEary with toyle,I haft me to my bed,
  The deare repofe for lims with trauaill tired,
But then begins a iourny in my head
To worke my mind,when boddies work's expired.
For then my thoughts(from far where I abide)
Jntend a zelous pilgrimage to thee,
And keepe my drooping eye-lids open wide,
Looking on darknes which the blind doe fee.
Saue that my foules imaginary fight
Prefents their fhaddoe to my fightles view,
Which like a iewell(hunge in gaftly night)
Makes blacke night beautious,and her old face new.
  Loe thus by day my lims,by night my mind,
  For thee,and for my felfe,noe quiet finde.

28

HOw can I then returne in happy plight
  That am debard the benifit of reft?
When daies oppreffion is not eazd by night,
But day by night and night by day opreft.
And each(though enimes to ethers raigne)
Doe in confent fhake hands to torture me,
The one by toyle,the other to complaine
How far I toyle,ftill farther off from thee.
J tell the Day to pleafe him thou art bright,
And do'ft him grace when clouds doe blot the heauen:
So flatter I the fwart complexiond night,
When fparkling ftars twire not thou guil'ft th' eauen.
  But day doth daily draw my forrowes longer,(ftronger
  And night doth nightly make greefes length feeme

29

WHen in difgrace with Fortune and mens eyes,
  I all alone beweepe my out-caft ftate,

And

12   To show me worthy of thy sweet respect.
     Then may I dare to boast how I do love thee;
     Till then, not show my head where thou mayst prove me.

27

Weary with toil, I haste me to my bed,
The dear repose for limbs with travel tired,
But then begins a journey in my head
4   To work my mind, when body's work's expired.
'For then my thoughts, from far where I abide,
Intend a zealous pilgrimage to thee,
And keep my drooping eyelids open wide,
8   Looking on darkness which the blind do see.
Save that my soul's imaginary sight
Presents thy shadow to my sightless view,
Which like a jewel hung in ghastly night,
12   Makes black night beauteous, and her old face new.
     Lo thus by day my limbs, by night my mind,
     For thee, and for myself, no quiet find.

28

How can I then return in happy plight
That am debarred the benefit of rest—
When day's oppression is not eased by night,
4   But day by night and night by day oppressed?
And each, though enemies to either's reign,
Do in consent shake hands to torture me,
The one by toil, the other to complain
8   , How far I toil, still farther off from thee.
I tell the day to please him thou art bright,
And dost him grace when clouds do blot the heaven.
So flatter I the swart-complexioned night,
12   When sparkling stars twire not, thou gild'st the even.
     But day doth daily draw my sorrows longer,
     And night doth nightly make grief's length seem stronger.

29

When in disgrace with fortune and men's eyes,
I all alone beweep my outcast state,

And trouble deaf heav'n with my bootless cries,
4 And look upon myself and curse my fate,
Wishing me like to one more rich in hope,
Featured like him, like him with friends possessed,
Desiring this man's art, and that man's scope,
8 With what I most enjoy contented least;
Yet in these thoughts myself almost despising,
Haply I think on thee, and then my state,
Like to the lark at break of day arising
12 From sullen earth, sings hymns at heaven's gate;
  For thy sweet love rememb'red such wealth brings,
  That then I scorn to change my state with kings.

30

When to the sessions of sweet silent thought
I summon up remembrance of things past,
I sigh the lack of many a thing I sought,
4 And with old woes new wail my dear time's waste.
Then can I drown an eye, unused to flow,
For precious friends hid in death's dateless night,
And weep afresh love's long since cancelled woe,
8 And moan th' expense of many a vanished sight.
Then can I grieve at grievances foregone,
And heavily from woe to woe tell o'er
The sad account of fore-bemoanèd moan,
12 Which I new pay as if not paid before.
  But if the while I think on thee, dear friend,
  All losses are restored, and sorrows end.

31

Thy bosom is endearèd with all hearts,
Which I by lacking have supposèd dead;
And there reigns love and all love's loving parts,
4 And all those friends which I thought burièd.
How many a holy and obsequious tear
Hath dear religious love stol'n from mine eye,
As interest of the dead, which now appear
8 But things removed that hidden in thee lie.

And trouble deafe heauen with my bootlesse cries,
And looke vpon my selfe and curse my fate,
Wishing me like to one more rich in hope,
Featur'd like him,like him with friends possest,
Desiring this mans art,and that mans skope,
With what I most inioy contented least,
Yet in these thoughts my selfe almost despising,
Haplye I thinke on thee, and then my state,
(Like to the Larke at breake of daye arising)
From sullen earth sings himns at Heauens gate,
    For thy sweet loue remembred such welth brings,
    That then I skorne to change my state with Kings.

30

VVHen to the Sessions of sweet silent thought,
    I sommon vp remembrance of things past,
I sigh the lacke of many a thing I sought,
And with old woes new waile my deare times waste:
Then can I drowne an eye(vn-vs'd to flow)
For precious friends hid in deaths dateles night,
And weepe a fresh loues long since canceld woe,
And mone th'expence of many a vannisht sight.
Then can I greeue at greeuances fore-gon,
And heauily from woe to woe tell ore
The sad account of fore-bemoned mone,
Which I new pay as if not payd before.
    But if the while I thinke on thee (deare friend)
    All losses are restord,and sorrowes end.

31

Thy bosome is indeared with all hearts,
    Which I by lacking haue supposed dead,
And there raignes Loue and all Loues louing parts,
And all those friends which I thought buried.
How many a holy and obsequious teare
Hath deare religious loue stolne from mine eye,
As interest of the dead,which now appeare,
But things remou'd that hidden in there lie.

C 3   To

Thou art the graue where buried loue doth liue,
Hung with the tropheis of my louers gon,
Who all their parts of me to thee did giue,
That due of many, now is thine alone.
　　Their images I lou'd, I view in thee,
　　And thou(all they)haſt all the all of me.

32

IF thou ſuruiue my well contented daie,
When that churle death my bones with duſt ſhall couer
And ſhalt by fortune once more re-ſuruay:
Theſe poore rude lines of thy deceaſea Louer:
Compare them with the bett'ring of the time,
And though they be out-ſtript by euery pen,
Reſerue them for my loue, not for their rime,
Exceeded by the hight of happier men.
Oh then voutſafe me but this louing thought,
Had my friends Muſe growne with this growing age,
A dearer birth then this his loue had brought:
To march inranckes of better equipage:
　　But ſince he died and Poets better proue,
　　Theirs for their ſtile,ile read,his for his loue.

33

FVll many a glorious morning haue I ſeene,
Flatter the mountaine tops with ſoueraine eie,
Kiſſing with golden face the meddowes greene;
Guilding pale ſtreames with heauenly alcumy:
Anon permit the baſeſt cloud~s to ride,
With ougly rack on his celeſtiall face,
And from the for-lorne world his viſage hide
Stealing vn'eene to weſt with this diſgrace:
Euen ſo my Sunne one early morne did ſhine,
With all triumphant ſplendor on my brow,
But out alack, he was but one houre mine,
The region cloude hath mask'd him from me now.
　　Yet him for this,my loue no whit diſdaineth,
　　Suns of the world may ſtaine,whē heauens ſun ſtainteh.

Thou art the grave where buried love doth live,
Hung with the trophies of my lovers gone,
Who all their parts of me to thee did give;
12   That due of many now is thine alone.
    Their images I loved I view in thee,
    And thou, all they, hast all the all of me.

32

If thou survive my well-contented day,
When that churl death my bones with dust shall cover,
And shalt by fortune once more re-survey
4   These poor rude lines of thy deceasèd lover,
Compare them with the bett'ring of the time,
And though they be outstripped by every pen
Reserve them for my love, not for their rhyme,
8   Exceeded by the height of happier men.
O then vouchsafe me but this loving thought:
Had my friend's muse grown with this growing age,
A dearer birth than this his love had brought
12   To march in ranks of better equipage.
    But since he died, and poets better prove,
    Theirs for their style I'll read, his for his love.

33

Full many a glorious morning have I seen
Flatter the mountain tops with sovereign eye,
Kissing with golden face the meadows green,
4   Gilding pale streams with heav'nly alchemy,
Anon permit the basest clouds to ride
With ugly rack on his celestial face,
And from the fórlorn world his visage hide,
8   Stealing unseen to west with this disgrace.
Ev'n so my sun one early morn did shine
With all triumphant splendor on my brow;
But out alack, he was but one hour mine,
12   The region cloud hath masked him from me now.
    Yet him for this my love no whit disdaineth;
    Suns of the world may stain when heav'n's sun staineth.

34

Why didst thou promise such a beauteous day
And make me travel forth without my cloak,
To let base clouds o'ertake me in my way,
4   Hiding thy bravery in their rotten smoke?
'Tis not enough that through the cloud thou break,
To dry the rain on my storm-beaten face,
For no man well of such a salve can speak,
8   That heals the wound, and cures not the disgrace.
Nor can thy shame give physic to my grief;
Though thou repent, yet I have still the loss.
Th' offender's sorrow lends but weak relief
12   To him that bears the strong offence's cross.
    Ah, but those tears are pearl which thy love sheeds,
    And they are rich, and ransom all ill deeds.

35

No more be grieved at that which thou hast done:
Roses have thorns, and silver fountains mud,
Clouds and eclipses stain both moon and sun,
4   And loathsome canker lives in sweetest bud.
All men make faults, and even I in this,
Authórizing thy trespass with compare,
Myself corrupting salving thy amiss,
8   Excusing thy sins more than thy sins are;
For to thy sensual fault I bring in sense—
Thy adverse party is thy advocate—
And 'gainst myself a lawful plea commence.
12   Such civil war is in my love and hate,
    That I an áccessary needs must be
    To that sweet thief which sourly robs from me.

36

Let me confess that we two must be twain,
Although our undivided loves are one.
So shall those blots that do with me remain,
4   Without thy help by me be borne alone.
In our two loves there is but one respect,

34

VVHy didst thou promise such a beautious day,
 And make me trauaile forth without my cloake,
To let bace cloudes ore-take me in my way,
Hiding thy brau'ry in their rotten smoke.
Tis not enou h that through the cloude thou breake,
To dry the raine on my storme-beaten face,
For no man well of such a salue can speake,
That heales the wound, and cures not the disgrace:
Nor can thy shame giue phisicke to my griefe,
Though thou repent , yet I haue still the losse,
Th'offenders sorrow lends but weake reliefe
To him that beares the strong offenses losse.
    Ah but those teares are pearle which thy loue sheeds,
    And they are ritch,and ransome all ill deeds.

35

NO more bee greeu'd at that which thou hast don ,
 Roses haue thornes,and siluer fountaines mud,
Cloudes and eclipses staine both Moone and Sunne,
And loathsome canker liues in sweetest bud.
All men make faults,and euen I in this,
Authorizing thy trespas with compare,
My selfe corrupting saluing thy amisse,
Excusing their sins more then their sins are:
For to thy sensuall fault I bring in sence,
Thy aduerse party is thy Aduocate,
And gainst my selfe a lawfull plea commence,
Such ciuill war is in my loue and hate,
    That I an accessary needs must be,
    To that sweet theese which sourely robs from me,

36

LEt me confesse that we two must be twaine,
 Although our vndeuided loues are one:
So shall those blots that do with me remaine,
Without thy helpe , by me be borne alone.
In our two loues there is but one respect,

                                   Though

Though in our liues a seperable spight,
Which though it alter not loues sole effect,
Yet doth it steale sweet houres from loues delight,
I may not euer-more acknowledge thee,
Least my bewailed guilt should do thee shame,
Nor thou with publike kindnesse honour me,
Vnlesse thou take that honour from thy name:
   But doe not so,I loue thee in such sort,
   As thou being mine,mine is thy good report.

37

AS a decrepit father takes delight,
To see his actiue childe do deeds of youth,
So I , made lame by Fortunes dearest spight
Take all my comfort of thy worth and truth.
For whether beauty,birth,or wealth,or wit,
Or any of these all,or all,or more
Intitled in their parts,do crowned sit,
I make my loue ingrafted to this store:
So then I am not lame,poore, nor dispis'd,
Whilst that this shadow doth such substance giue,
That I in thy abundance am suffic'd,
And by a part of all thy glory liue:
   Looke what is best,that best I wish in thee,
   This wish I haue,then ten times happy me.

38

HOw can my Muse want subiect to inuent
While thou dost breath that poor'st into my verse,
Thine owne sweet argument,to excellent,
For euery vulgar paper to rehearse:
Oh giue thy selfe the thankes if ought in me,
Worthy perusal stand against thy sight,
For who's so dumbe that cannot write to thee,
When thou thy selfe dost giue inuention light?
Be thou the tenth Muse,ten times more in worth
Then those old nine which rimers inuocate,
And he that calls on thee,let him bring forth

Eternall

Though in our lives a separable spite,
Which though it alter not love's sole effect,
8   Yet doth it steal sweet hours from love's delight.
I may not evermore acknowledge thee,
Lest my bewailèd guilt should do thee shame;
Nor thou with public kindness honour me,
12   Unless thou take that honour from thy name.
    But do not so; I love thee in such sort,
    As, thou being mine, mine is thy good report.

37

As a decrepit father takes delight
To see his active child do deeds of youth,
So I, made lame by fortune's dearest spite,
4   Take all my comfort of thy worth and truth.
For whether beauty, birth, or wealth, or wit,
Or any of these all, or all, or more,
Entitled in thy parts do crownèd sit,
8   I make my love engrafted to this store.
So then I am not lame, poor, nor despised,
Whilst that this shadow doth such substance give,
That I in thy abundance am sufficed,
12   And by a part of all thy glory live.
    Look what is best, that best I wish in thee.
    This wish I have, then ten times happy me.

38

How can my muse want subject to invent,
While thou dost breathe, that pour'st into my verse
Thine own sweet argument, too excellent
4   For every vulgar paper to rehearse?
O give thyself the thanks, if aught in me
Worthy perusal stand against thy sight;
For who's so dumb that cannot write to thee,
8   When thou thyself dost give invention light?
Be thou the tenth muse, ten times more in worth
Than those old nine which rhymers invocate;
And he that calls on thee, let him bring forth

12   Eternal numbers to outlive long date.
              If my slight muse do please these curious days,
              The pain be mine, but thine shall be the praise.

39

O how thy worth with manners may I sing,
When thou art all the better part of me?
What can mine own praise to mine own self bring,
4   And what is't but mine own when I praise thee?
Even for this, let us divided live,
And our dear love lose name of single one,
That by this separation I may give
8   That due to thee which thou deserv'st alone.
O absence, what a torment wouldst thou prove,
Were it not thy sour leisure gave sweet leave
To entertain the time with thoughts of love,
12   Which time and thoughts so sweetly doth deceive,
              And that thou teachest how to make one twain,
              By praising him here who doth hence remain.

40

Take all my loves, my love, yea take them all:
What hast thou then more than thou hadst before?
No love, my love, that thou mayst true love call;
4   All mine was thine, before thou hadst this more.
Then if for my love thou my love receivest,
I cannot blame thee for my love thou usest;
But yet be blamed, if thou thyself deceivest
8   By wilful taste of what thyself refusest.
I do forgive thy robb'ry, gentle thief,
Although thou steal thee all my poverty;
And yet love knows it is a greater grief
12   To bear love's wrong than hate's known injury.
              Lascivious grace, in whom all ill well shows,
              Kill me with spites, yet we must not be foes.

41

Those pretty wrongs that liberty commits,
When I am sometime absent from thy heart,

Eternal numbers to out-liue long date.
  If my flight Muse doe pleafe thefe curious daies,
  The paine be mine, but thine fhal be the praife.

39

OH how thy worth with manners may I finge,
  When thou art all the better part of me?
What can mine owne praife to mine owne felfe bring;
And what is't but mine owne when I praife thee,
Euen for this, let vs deuided liue,
And our deare loue loofe name of fingle one,
That by this feperation I may giue:
That due to thee which thou deferu'ft alone:
Oh abfence what a torment wouldft thou proue,
Were it not thy foure leifure gaue fweet leaue,
To entertaine the time with thoughts of loue,
VVhich time and thoughts fo fweetly doft deceiue.
  And that thou teacheft how to make one twaine,
  By praifing him here who doth hence remaine.

40

TAke all my loues, my loue, yea take them all,
  What haft thou then more then thou hadft before?
No loue, my loue, that thou maift true loue call,
All mine was thine, before thou hadft this more:
Then if for my loue, thou my loue receiueft,
I cannot blame thee, for my loue thou vfeft,
But yet be blam'd, if thou this felfe deceaueft
By wilfull tafte of what thy felfe refufeft.
I doe forgiue thy robb'rie gentle theefe
Although thou fteale thee all my pouerty:
And yet loue knowes it is a greater griefe
To beare loues wrong, then hates knowne iniury.
  Lafciuious grace, in whom all il wel fhowes,
  Kill me with fpights yet we muft not be foes.

41

THofe pretty wrongs that liberty commits,
  When I am fome-time abfent from thy heart,

D
                      Thy

Thy beautie,and thy yeares full well befits,
For still temptacion followes where thou art.
Gentle thou art,and therefore to be wonne,
Beautious thou art,therefore to be assailed.
And when a woman woes,what womans sonne,
Will sourely leaue her till he haue preuailed.
Aye me,but yet thou mighst my seate forbeare,
And chide thy beauty,and thy straying youth,
Who lead thee in their ryot euen there
Where thou art forst to breake a two-fold truth:
  Hers by thy beauty tempting her to thee,
  Thine by thy beautie beeing false to me.

42

THat thou hast her it is not all my griefe,
  And yet it may be said I lou'd her deerely,
That she hath thee is of my wayling cheefe,
A losse in loue that touches me more neerely.
Louing offendors thus I will excuse yee,
Thou doost loue her,because thou knowst I loue her,
And for my sake euen so doth she abuse me,
Suffring my friend for my sake to approoue her,
If I loose thee,my losse is my loues gaine,
And loosing her,my friend hath found that losse,
Both finde each other,and I loose both twaine,
And both for my sake lay on me this crosse,
  But here's the ioy,my friend and I are one,
  Sweete flattery,then she loues but me alone.

43

WHen most I winke then doe mine eyes best see,
  For all the day they view things vnrespected,
But when I sleepe,in dreames they looke on thee,
And darkely bright,are bright in darke directed.
Then thou whose shaddow shaddowes doth make bright,
How would thy shadowes forme,forme happy show,
To the cleere day with thy much cleerer light,
When to vn-seeing eyes thy shade shines so?

How

Thy beauty and thy years full well befits,
4   For still temptation follows where thou art.
Gentle thou art, and therefore to be won,
Beauteous thou art, therefore to be assailed;
And when a woman woos, what woman's son
8   Will sourly leave her till he have prevailed?
Ay me, but yet thou might'st my seat forbear,
And chide thy beauty and thy straying youth,
Who lead thee in their riot even there
12   Where thou art forced to break a twofold truth:
    Hers, by thy beauty tempting her to thee,
    Thine, by thy beauty being false to me.

42

That thou hast her, it is not all my grief,
And yet it may be said I loved her dearly;
That she hath thee is of my wailing chief,
4   A loss in love that touches me more nearly.
Loving offenders, thus I will excuse ye:
Thou dost love her, because thou know'st I love her,
And for my sake ev'n so doth she abuse me,
8   Suff'ring my friend for my sake to approve her.
If I lose thee, my loss is my love's gain,
And losing her, my friend hath found that loss;
Both find each other, and I lose both twain,
12   And both for my sake lay on me this cross.
    But here's the joy, my friend and I are one;
    Sweet flatt'ry, then she loves but me alone.

43

When most I wink, then do my eyes best see,
For all the day they view things unrespected,
But when I sleep, in dreams they look on thee,
4   And darkly bright, are bright in dark directed.
Then thou, whose shadow shadows doth make bright—
How would thy shadow's form form happy show
To the clear day with thy much clearer light,
8   When to unseeing eyes thy shade shines so!

How would, I say, mine eyes be blessèd made,
By looking on thee in the living day,
When in dead night thy fair imperfect shade
12   Through heavy sleep on sightless eyes doth stay!
    All days are nights to see till I see thee,
    And nights bright days when dreams do show thee me.

44

If the dull substance of my flesh were thought,
Injurious distance should not stop my way;
For then, despite of space, I would be brought,
4   From limits far remote, where thou dost stay.
No matter then although my foot did stand
Upon the farthest earth removed from thee;
For nimble thought can jump both sea and land,
8   As soon as think the place where he would be.
But, ah, thought kills me that I am not thought
To leap large lengths of miles when thou art gone,
But that, so much of earth and water wrought,
12   I must attend time's leisure with my moan.
    Receiving naught by elements so slow
    But heavy tears, badges of either's woe.

45

The other two, slight air and purging fire,
Are both with thee, wherever I abide;
The first my thought, the other my desire,
4   These present-absent with swift motion slide.
For when these quicker elements are gone
In tender embassy of love to thee,
My life, being made of four, with two alone
8   Sinks down to death, oppressed with melancholy;
Until life's composition be recured
By those swift messengers returned from thee,
Who ev'n but now come back again, assured
12   Of thy fair health, recounting it to me.
    This told, I joy, but then no longer glad,
    I send them back again, and straight grow sad.

How would (I fay)mine eyes be bleffed made,
By looking on thee in the liuing day ?
When in dead night their faire imperfect fhade,
Through heauy fleepe on fightleffe eyes doth ftay?
   All dayes are nights to fee till I fee thee,
   And nights bright daies when dreams do fhew thee me,

44

IF the dull fubftance of my flefh were thought,
  Iniurious diftance fhould not ftop my way,
For then difpight of fpace I would be brought,
From limits farre remote,where thou dooft ftay,
No matter then although my foote did ftand
Vpon the fartheft earth remoou'd from thee,
For nimble thought can iumpe both fea and land,
As foone as thinke the place where he would be.
But ah,thought kills me that I am not thought
To leape large lengths of miles when thou art gone,
But that fo much of earth and water wrought,
I muft attend,times leafure with my mone.
   Receiuing naughts by elements fo floe,
   But heauie teares,badges of eithers woe.

45

THe other two,flight ayre,and purging fire,
  Are both with thee,where euer I abide,
The firft my thought,the other my defire,
Thefe prefent abfent with fwift motion flide.
For when thefe quicker Elements are gone
In tender Embaffie of loue to thee,
My life being made of foure,with two alone,
Sinkes downe to death,oppreft with melancholie.
Vntill liues compofition be recured,
By thofe fwift meffengers return'd from thee,
Who euen but now come back againe affured,
Of their faire health,recounting it to me.
   This told,I ioy,but then no longer glad,
   I fend them back againe and ftraight grow fad.

Mine

46

MIne eye and heart are at a mortall warre,
How to deuide the conquest of thy sight,
Mine eye,my heart their pictures sight would barre,
My heart,mine eye the freedome of that right,
My heart doth plead that thou in him doost lye,
(A closet neuer pearst with christall eyes)
But the defendant doth that plea deny,
And sayes in him their faire appearance lyes.
To side this title is impannelled
A quest of thoughts,all tennants to the heart,
And by their verdict is determined
The cleere eyes moyitie,and the deare hearts part.
    As thus,mine eyes due is their outward part,
    And my hearts right,their inward loue of heart.

47

BEtwixt mine eye and heart a league is tooke,
And each doth good turnes now vnto the other,
When that mine eye is famisht for a looke,
Or heart in loue with sighes himselfe doth smother;
With my loues picture then my eye doth feast,
And to the painted banquet bids my heart:
An other time mine eye is my hearts guest,
And in his thoughts of loue doth share a part.
So either by thy picture or my loue,
Thy seife away,are present still with me,
For thou nor farther then my thoughts canst moue,
And I am still with them and they with thee.
    Or if they sleepe, thy picture in my sight
    Awakes my heart,to hearts and eyes delight.

48

HOw carefull was I when I tooke my way,
Each trifle vnder truest barres to thrust,
That to my vse it might vn-vsed stay
From hands of falsehood,in sure wards of trust?
But thou,to whom my iewels trifles are,

Most

46

Mine eye and heart are at a mortal war,
How to divide the conquest of thy sight;
Mine eye my heart thy picture's sight would bar,
My heart mine eye the freedom of that right.
My heart doth plead that thou in him dost lie—
A closet never pierced with crystal eyes;
But the defendant doth that plea deny,
And says in him thy fair appearance lies.
To 'cide this title is impannellèd
A quest of thoughts, all tenants to the heart;
And by their verdict is determinèd
The clear eye's moiety, and the dear heart's part:
    As thus—mine eye's due is thy outward part,
    And my heart's right thy inward love of heart.

47

Betwixt mine eye and heart a league is took,
And each doth good turns now unto the other.
When that mine eye is famished for a look,
Or heart in love with sighs himself doth smother,
With my love's picture then my eye doth feast,
And to the painted banquet bids my heart.
Another time mine eye is my heart's guest,
And in his thoughts of love doth share a part.
So either by thy picture or my love,
Thyself away are present still with me;
For thou no farther than my thoughts canst move,
And I am still with them, and they with thee;
    Or, if they sleep, thy picture in my sight
    Awakes my heart to heart's and eye's delight.

48

How careful was I, when I took my way,
Each trifle under truest bars to thrust,
That to my use it might unusèd stay
From hands of falsehood, in sure wards of trust!
But thou, to whom my jewels trifles are,

Most worthy comfort, now my greatest grief,
Thou best of dearest, and mine only care,
8   Art left the prey of every vulgar thief.
Thee have I not locked up in any chest,
Save where thou art not, though I feel thou art,
Within the gentle closure of my breast,
12   From whence at pleasure thou mayst come and part;
      And even thence thou wilt be stol'n, I fear,
      For truth proves thievish for a prize so dear.

49

Against that time (if ever that time come)
When I shall see thee frown on my defects,
Whenas thy love hath cast his utmost sum,
4   Called to that audit by advised respects—
Against that time when thou shalt strangely pass,
And scarcely greet me with that sun thine eye,
When love converted from the thing it was
8   Shall reasons find of settled gravity—
Against that time do I ensconce me here
Within the knowledge of mine own desert,
And this my hand against myself uprear
12   To guard the lawful reasons on thy part—
      To leave poor me thou hast the strength of laws,
      Since why to love I can allege no cause.

50

How heavy do I journey on the way,
When what I seek (my weary travel's end)
Doth teach that ease and that repose to say,
4   Thus far the miles are measured from thy friend.
The beast that bears me, tired with my woe,
Plods dully on, to bear that weight in me,
As if by some instinct the wretch did know
8   His rider loved not speed, being made from thee.
The bloody spur cannot provoke him on,
That sometimes anger thrusts into his hide;
Which heavily he answers with a groan,

Moſt worthy comfort,now my greateſt griefe,
Thou beſt of deereſt,and mine onely care,
Art left the prey of euery vulgar theefe.
Thee haue I not lockt vp in any cheſt,
Saue where thou art not though I feele thou art,
Within the gentle cloſure of my breſt,
From whence at pleaſure thou maiſt come and part,
   And euen thence thou wilt be ſtolne I feare,
   For truth prooues theeuiſh for a prize ſo deare.

49

AGainſt that time (if euer that time come)
  When I ſhall ſee thee frowne on my defects,
When as thy loue hath caſt his vtmoſt ſumme,
Cauld to that audite by aduiſ'd reſpects,
Againſt that time when thou ſhalt ſtrangely paſſe,
And ſcarcely greete me with that ſunne thine eye,
When loue conuerted from the thing it was
Shall reaſons finde of ſetled grauitie.
Againſt that time do I inſconce me here
Within the knowledge of mine owne deſart,
And this my hand,againſt my ſelfe vpreare,
To guard the lawfull reaſons on thy part,
   To leaue poore me,thou haſt the ſtrength of lawes,
   Since why to loue,I can alledge no cauſe.

50

HOw heauie doe I iourney on the way,
  When what I ſeeke (my wearie trauels end)
Doth teach that eaſe and that repoſe to ſay
Thus farre the miles are meaſurde from thy friend.
The beaſt that beares me,tired with my woe,
Plods duly on,to beare that waight in me,
As if by ſome inſtinct the wretch did know
His rider lou'd not ſpeed being made from thee:
The bloody ſpurre cannot prouoke him on,
That ſome-times anger thruſts into his hide,
Which heauily he anſwers with a grone,

D 3

More

More sharpe to me then spurring to his side,
   For that same grone doth put this in my mind,
   My greefe lies onward and my ioy behind.

51

THus can my loue excuse the slow offence,
   Of my dull bearer, when from thee I speed,
From where thou art, why shoulld I hast me thence,
Till I returne of posting is noe need.
O what excuse will my poore beast then find,
When swift extremity can seeme but slow,
Then should I spurre though mounted on the wind,
In winged speed no motion shall I know,
Then can no horse with my desire keepe pace,
Therefore desire (of perfects loue being made)
Shall naigh noe dull flesh in his fiery race,
But loue, for loue, thus shall excuse my iade,
   Since from thee going he went wilfull slow,
   Towards thee ile run, and giue him leaue to goe.

52

SO am I as the rich whose blessed key,
   Can bring him to his sweet vp-locked treasure,
The which he will not eu'ry hower suruay,
For blunting the fine point of seldome pleasure.
Therefore are feasts so sollemne and so rare,
Since sildom comming in the long yeare set,
Like stones of worth they thinly placed are,
Or captaine Iewells in the carconet.
So is the time that keepes you as my chest,
Or as the ward-robe which the robe doth hide,
To make some speciall instant speciall blest,
By new vnfoulding his imprison'd pride.
   Blessed are you whose worthinesse giues skope,
   Being had to tryumph, being lackt to hope.

53

VVHat is your substance, whereof are you made,
   That millions of strange shaddowes on you tend?
                       Since

12   More sharp to me than spurring to his side;
      For that same groan doth put this in my mind—
      My grief lies onward and my joy behind.

51

Thus can my love excuse the slow offence
Of my dull bearer, when from thee I speed—
From where thou art, why should I haste me thence?
4   Till I return, of posting is no need.
O what excuse will my poor beast then find,
When swift extremity can seem but slow?
Then should I spur, though mounted on the wind—
8   In wingèd speed no motion shall I know.
Then can no horse with my desire keep pace;
Therefore desire, of perfect'st love being made,
Shall neigh no dull flesh in his fiery race,
12   But love, for love, thus shall excuse my jade—
      Since from thee going he went wilful slow,
      Towards thee I'll run, and give him leave to go.

52

So am I as the rich whose blessèd key
Can bring him to his sweet up-lockèd treasure,
The which he will not every hour survey,
4   For blunting the fine point of seldom pleasure.
Therefore are feasts so solemn and so rare,
Since seldom coming in the long year set,
Like stones of worth they thinly placèd are,
8   Or captain jewels in the carcanet.
So is the time that keeps you as my chest,
Or as the wardrobe which the robe doth hide
To make some special instant special blest,
12   By new unfolding his imprisoned pride.
      Blessèd are you whose worthiness gives scope,
      Being had to triumph, being lacked to hope.

53

What is your substance, whereof are you made,
That millions of strange shadows on you tend?

Since everyone hath, every one, one shade,
4   And you, but one, can every shadow lend.
Describe Adonis, and the counterfeit
Is poorly imitated after you;
On Helen's cheek all art of beauty set,
8   And you in Grecian tires are painted new.
Speak of the spring and foison of the year;
The one doth shadow of your beauty show,
The other as your bounty doth appear,
12   And you in every blessèd shape we know.
    In all external grace you have some part,
    But you like none, none you, for constant heart.

54

O how much more doth beauty beauteous seem,
By that sweet ornament which truth doth give.
The rose looks fair, but fairer we it deem
4   For that sweet odor which doth in it live.
The canker blooms have full as deep a dye
As the perfumèd tincture of the roses,
Hang on such thorns, and play as wantonly,
8   When summer's breath their maskèd buds discloses;
But for their virtue only is their show,
They live unwooed, and unrespected fade,
Die to themselves. Sweet roses do not so;
12   Of their sweet deaths are sweetest odors made.
    And so of you, beauteous and lovely youth,
    When that shall vade, by verse distils your truth.

55

Not marble nor the gilded monuments
Of princes shall outlive this pow'rful rhyme,
But you shall shine more bright in these conténts
4   Than unswept stone, besmeared with sluttish time.
When wasteful war shall statues overturn,
And broils root out the work of masonry,
Nor Mars his sword nor war's quick fire shall burn
8   The living record of your memory.

Since euery one,hath euery one,one shade,
And you but one,can euery shaddow lend:
Describe *Adonis* and the counterfet,
Is poorely immitated after you,
On *Hellens* cheeke all art of beautie set,
And you in *Grecian* tires are painted new:
Speake of the spring,and foyzon of the yeare,
The one doth shaddow of your beautie show,
The other as your bountie doth appeare,
And you in euery blessed shape we know.
   In all externall grace you haue some part,
   But you like none,none you for constant heart.

54

OH how much more doth beautie beautious seeme,
  By that sweet ornament which truth doth giue,
The Rose lookes faire, but fairer we it deeme
For that sweet odor,which doth in it liue:
The Canker bloomes haue full as deepe a die,
As the perfumed tincture of the Roses,
Hang on such thornes,and play as wantonly,
When sommers breath their masked buds disclofes:
But for their virtue only is their show,
They liue vnwoo'd, and vnrespected fade,
Die to themselues . Sweet Roses doe not so,
Of their sweet deathes, are sweetest odors made:
   And so of you,beautious and louely youth,
   When that shall vade,by verse distils your truth.

55

NOt marble, nor the guilded monument,
  Of Princes shall out-liue this powrefull rime,
But you shall shine more bright in these contents
Then vnswept stone, besmeer d with sluttish time.
When wastefull warre shall *Statues* ouer-turne,
And broiles roote out the worke of masonry,
Nor *Mars* his sword, nor warres quick fire shall burne:
The liuing record of your memory.

                         Gainst

Gainſt death,and all obliuious emnity
Shall you pace forth, your praiſe ſhall ſtil finde roome,
Euen in the eyes of all poſterity
That weare this world out to the ending doome.
    So til the iudgement that your ſelfe ariſe,
    You liue in this,and dwell in louers eies.

56

Sweet loue renew thy force , be it not ſaid
Thy edge ſhould blunter be then apetite,
Which,but too daie by feeding is alaied,
To morrow ſharpned in his former might.
So loue be thou,although too daie thou fill
Thy hungrie eies,euen till they winck with fulneſſe,
Too morrow ſee againe,and doe not kill
The ſpirit of Loue,with a perpetual dulneſſe:
Let this ſad *Intrim* like the Ocean be
Which parts the ſhore,where two contracted new,
Come daily to the banckes,that when they ſee.
Returne of loue,more bleſt may be the view.
    As cal it Winter,which being ful of care,
    Makes Somers welcome,thrice more wiſh’d,more rare:

57

BEing your ſlaue what ſhould I doe but tend,
Vpon the houres,and times of your deſire?
I haue no precious time at al to ſpend;
Nor ſeruices to doe til you require.
Nor dare I chide the world without end houre,
Whilſt I(my ſoueraine)watch the clock for you,
Nor thinke the bitterneſſe of abſence ſowre,
VVhen you haue bid your ſeruant once adieue.
Nor dare I queſtion with my iealious thought,
VVhere you may be,or your affaires ſuppoſe,
But like a ſad ſlaue ſtay and thinke of nought
Saue where you are , how happy you make thoſe.
    So true a foole is loue,that in your Will,
    (Though you doe any thing)he thinkes no ill.

58

58

THat God forbid,that made me firſt your ſlaue,
I ſhould in thought controule your times of pleaſure,
Or at your hand th' account of houres to craue,
Being your vaſſail bound to ſtaie your leiſure.
Oh let me ſuffer(being at your beck)
Th' impriſon'd abſence of your libertie,
And patience tame,to ſufferance bide each check,
Without accuſing you of iniury.
Be where you liſt,your charter is ſo ſtrong,
That you your ſelfe may priuiledge your time
To what you will,to you it doth belong,
Your ſelfe to pardon of ſelfe-doing crime.
  I am to waite,though waiting ſo be hell,
  Not blame your pleaſure be it ill or well.

59

IF their bee nothing new,but that which is,
Hath beene before , how are our braines beguild,
Which laboring for inuention beare amiſſe
The ſecond burthen of a former child ?
Oh that record could with a back-ward looke,
Euen of fiue hundreth courſes of the Sunne,
Show me your image in ſome antique booke,
Since minde at firſt in carrecter was done.
That I might ſee what the old world could ſay,
To this compoſed wonder of your frame,
Whether we are mended,or where better they,
Or whether reuolution be the ſame.
  Oh ſure I am the wits of former daies,
  To ſubiects worſe haue giuen admiring praiſe.

60

LIke as the waues make towards the pibled ſhore,
So do our minuites haſten to their end,
Each changing place with that which goes before,
In ſequent toile all forwards do contend.
Natiuity once in the maine of light.
                    E   Crawls

Crawles to maturity, wherewith being crown'd,
Crooked eclipses gainst his glory fight,
And time that gaue, doth now his gift confound.
Time doth transfixe the florish set on youth,
And delues the paralels in beauties brow,
Feedes on the rarities of natures truth,
And nothing stands but for his sieth to mow.
　　And yet to times in hope, my verse shall stand
　　Praising thy worth, dispight his cruell hand.

61

I S it thy wil, thy Image should keepe open
My heauy eie lids to the weary night?
Dost thou desire my slumbers should be broken,
While shadowes like to thee do mocke my sight?
Is it thy spirit that thou send'st from thee
So farre from home into my deeds to prye,
To find out shames and idle houres in me,
The skope and tenure of thy Ielousie?
O no, thy loue though much, is not so great,
It is my loue that keepes mine eie awake,
Mine owne true loue that doth my rest defeat,
To plaie the watch-man euer for thy sake.
　　For thee watch I, whilst thou dost wake elsewhere,
　　From me farre of, with others all to neere.

62

S Inne of selfe-loue possesseth al mine eie,
And all my soule, and al my euery part;
And for this sinne there is no remedie,
It is so grounded inward in my heart.
Me thinkes no face so gratious is as mine,
No shape so true, no truth of such account,
And for my selfe mine owne worth do define,
As I all other in all worths surmount.
But when my glasse shewes me my selfe indeed
Beated and chopt with tand antiquitie,
Mine owne selfe loue quite contrary I read

Selfe

Selfe,so selfe louing were iniquity,
  T'is thee(my selfe)that for my selfe I praise,
  Painting my age with beauty of thy daies,

63

AGainst my loue shall be as I am now
  With'times iniurious hand chrusht and ore-worne,
When houres haue dreind his blood and fild his brow
With lines and wrincles,when his youthfull morne
Hath trauaild on to Ages steepie night,
And all those beauties whereof now he's King
Are vanishing,or vanisht out of sight,
Stealing away the treasure of his Spring.
For such a time do I now fortifie
Against confounding Ages cruell knife,
That he shall neuer cut from memory
My sweet loues beauty,though my louers life.
  His beautie shall in these blacke lines be seene,
  And they shall liue, and he in them still greene.

64

VVHen I haue seene by times fell hand defaced
  The rich proud cost of outworne buried age,
When sometime loftie towers I see downe rased,
And brasse eternall slaue to mortall rage.
When I haue seene the hungry Ocean gaine
Aduantage on the Kingdome of the shoare,
And the firme soile win of the watry maine,
Increasing store with losse,and losse with store.
When I haue seene such interchange of state,
Or state it selfe confounded, to decay,
Ruine hath taught me thus to ruminate
That Time will come and take my loue away.
  This thought is as a death which cannot choose
  But weepe to haue,that which it feares to loose.

65

SInce brasse,nor stone,nor earth,nor boundlesse sea,
  But sad mortallity ore-swaies their power,

               How

How with this rage ſhall beautie hold a plea,
Whoſe action is no ſtronger then a flower?
O how ſhall ſummers hunny breath hold out,
Againſt the wrackfull ſiedge of battring dayes,
When rocks impregnable are not ſo ſtoute,
Nor gates of ſteele ſo ſtrong but time decayes?
O fearefull meditation, where alack,
Shall times beſt Iewell from times cheſt lie hid?
Or what ſtrong hand can hold his ſwift foote back,
Or who his ſpoile or beautie can forbid?
   O none, vnleſſe this miracle haue might,
   That in black inck my loue may ſtill ſhine bright.

66

TYr'd with all theſe for reſtfull death I cry,
  As to behold deſert a begger borne,
And needie Nothing trimd in iollitie,
And pureſt faith vnhappily forſworne,
And gilded honor ſhamefully miſplaſt,
And maiden vertue rudely ſtrumpeted,
And right perfection wrongfully diſgrac'd,
And ſtrength by limping ſway diſabled,
And arte made tung-tide by authoritie,
And Folly (Doctor-like) controuling skill,
And ſimple-Truth miſcalde Simplicitie,
And captiue-good attending Captaine ill.
   Tyr'd with all theſe, from theſe would I be gone,
   Saue that to dye, I leaue my loue alone.

67

AH wherefore with infection ſhould he liue,
  And with his preſence grace impietie,
That ſinne by him aduantage ſhould atchiue,
And lace it ſelfe with his ſocietie?
Why ſhould falſe painting immitate his cheeke,
And ſteale dead ſeeing of his liuing hew?
Why ſhould poore beautie indirectly ſeeke,
Roſes of ſhaddow, ſince his Roſe is true?

Why

Crawls to maturity, wherewith being crowned,
Crookèd eclipses 'gainst his glory fight,
8   And time that gave doth now his gift confound.
Time doth transfix the flourish set on youth,
And delves the parallels in beauty's brow,
Feeds on the rarities of nature's truth,
12   And nothing stands but for his scythe to mow.
    And yet to times in hope my verse shall stand,
    Praising thy worth, despite his cruel hand.

61

Is it thy will thy image should keep open
My heavy eyelids to the weary night?
Dost thou desire my slumbers should be broken,
4   While shadows like to thee do mock my sight?
Is it thy spirit that thou send'st from thee
So far from home into my deeds to pry,
To find out shames and idle hours in me,
8   The scope and tenor of thy jealousy?
O no, thy love, though much, is not so great.
It is my love that keeps mine eye awake,
Mine own true love that doth my rest defeat,
12   To play the watchman ever for thy sake.
    For thee watch I, whilst thou dost wake elsewhére,
    From me far off, with others all too near.

62

Sin of self-love possesseth all mine eye,
And all my soul, and all my every part;
And for this sin there is no remedy,
4   It is so grounded inward in my heart.
Methinks no face so gracious is as mine,
No shape so true, no truth of such account,
And for myself mine own worth do define,
8   As I all other in all worths surmount.
But when my glass shows me myself indeed
Beated and chopped with tanned antiquity,
Mine own self-love quite contrary I read;

12 Self so self-loving were iniquity.
   'Tis thee, myself, that for myself I praise,
   Painting my age with beauty of thy days.

63

  Against my love shall be as I am now,
  With time's injurious hand crushed and o'erworn,
  When hours have drained his blood and filled his brow
4 With lines and wrinkles, when his youthful morn
  Hath traveled on to age's steepy night,
  And all those beauties whereof now he's king
  Are vanishing, or vanished out of sight,
8 Stealing away the treasure of his spring—
  For such a time do I now fortify
  Against confounding age's cruel knife,
  That he shall never cut from memory
12 My sweet love's beauty, though my lover's life.
   His beauty shall in these black lines be seen,
   And they shall live, and he in them still green.

64

  When I have seen by time's fell hand defaced
  The rich proud cost of outworn buried age,
  When sometime lofty towers I see down razed,
4 And brass eternal slave to mortal rage,
  When I have seen the hungry ocean gain
  Advantage on the kingdom of the shore,
  And the firm soil win of the watery main,
8 Increasing store with loss, and loss with store,
  When I have seen such interchange of state,
  Or state itself confounded to decay,
  Ruin hath taught me thus to ruminate,
12 That time will come and take my love away.
   This thought is as a death, which cannot choose
   But weep to have that which it fears to lose.

65

  Since brass, nor stone, nor earth, nor boundless sea,
  But sad mortality o'ersways their power,

How with this rage shall beauty hold a plea,
4   Whose action is no stronger than a flower?
O how shall summer's honey breath hold out
Against the wrackful siege of batt'ring days,
When rocks impregnable are not so stout,
8   Nor gates of steel so strong but time decays?
O fearful meditation; where, alack,
Shall time's best jewel from time's chest lie hid?
Or what strong hand can hold his swift foot back?
12   Or who his spoil or beauty can forbid?
     O none, unless this miracle have might
     That in black ink my love may still shine bright.

66

Tir'd with all these, for restful death I cry,
As to behold desert a beggar born,
And needy nothing trimmed in jollity,
4   And purest faith unhappily forsworn,
And gilded honor shamefully misplaced,
And maiden virtue rudely strumpeted,
And right perfection wrongfully disgraced,
8   And strength by limping sway disablèd,
And art made tongue-tied by authority,
And folly, doctor-like, controlling skill,
And simple truth miscalled simplicity,
12   And captive good attending captain ill.
     Tir'd with all these, from these would I be gone,
     Save that to die, I leave my love alone.

67

Ah wherefore with infection should he live,
And with his presence grace impiety,
That sin by him advantage should achieve,
4   And lace itself with his society?
Why should false painting imitate his cheek,
And steal dead seeing of his living hue?
Why should poor beauty indirectly seek
8   Roses of shadow, since his rose is true?

Why should he live, now nature bankrout is,
Beggared of blood to blush through lively veins?
For she hath no exchequer now but his,
12   And, proud of many, lives upon his gains.
        O him she stores, to show what wealth she had,
        In days long since, before these last so bad.

68

Thus is his cheek the map of days outworn,
When beauty lived and died as flow'rs do now,
Before these bastard signs of fair were borne,
4   Or durst inhabit on a living brow—
Before the golden tresses of the dead,
The right of sepulchers, were shorn away,
To live a second life on second head—
8   Ere beauty's dead fleece made another gay.
In him those holy ántique hours are seen,
Without all ornament, itself and true,
Making no summer of another's green,
12   Robbing no old to dress his beauty new;
        And him as for a map doth nature store,
        To show false art what beauty was of yore.

69

Those parts of thee that the world's eye doth view
Want nothing that the thought of hearts can mend.
All tongues, the voice of souls, give thee that due,
4   Utt'ring bare truth, ev'n so as foes commend.
Thy outward thus with outward praise is crowned;
But those same tongues that give thee so thine own,
In other accents do this praise confound
8   By seeing farther than the eye hath shown.
They look into the beauty of thy mind,
And that in guess they measure by thy deeds;
Then, churls, their thoughts—although their eyes were kind—
12   To thy fair flow'r add the rank smell of weeds;
        But why thy odor matcheth not thy show,
        The soil is this, that thou dost common grow.

Why fhould he liue,now nature banckrout is,
Beggerd of blood to blufh through liuely vaines,
For fhe hath no exchecker now but his,
And proud of many,liues vpon his gaines?
  O him fhe ftores,to fhow what welth fhe had,
  In daies long fince,before thefe laft fo bad.

68

THus is his cheeke the map of daies out-worne,
  When beauty liu'd and dy'ed as flowers do now,
Before thefe baftard fignes of faire were borne,
Or durft inhabit on a liuing brow:
Before the goulden treffes of the dead,
The right of fepulchers,were fhorne away,
To liue a fcond life on fecond head,
Ere beauties dead fleece made another gay:
In him thofe holy antique howers are feene,
Without all ornament,it felfe and true,
Making no fummer of an others greene,
Robbing no ould to dreffe his beauty new,
  And him as for a map doth Nature ftore,
  To fhew faulfe Art what beauty was of yore.

69

THofe parts of thee that the worlds eye doth view,
  Want nothing that the thought of hearts can mend:
All toungs(the voice of foules)giue thee that end,
Vttring bare truth,euen fo as foes Commend.
Their outward thus with outward praife is crownd,
But thofe fame toungs that giue thee fo thine owne,
In other accents doe this praife confound
By feeing farther then the eye hath fhowne.
They looke into the beauty of thy mind,
And that in gueffe they meafure by thy deeds,
Then churls their thoughts(although their eies were kind)
To thy faire flower ad the rancke fmell of weeds,
  But why thy odor matcheth not thy fhow,
  The folye is this,that thou doeft common grow.

E 3   That

70

THat thou are blam'd shall not be thy defect,
For slanders marke was euer yet the faire,
The ornament of beauty is suspect,
A Crow that flies in heauens sweetest ayre.
So thou be good, slander doth but approue,
Their worth the greater beeing woo'd of time,
For Canker vice the sweetest buds doth loue,
And thou present'st a pure vnstayined prime.
Thou hast past by the ambush of young daies,
Either not assayld, or victor beeing charg'd,
Yet this thy praise cannot be soe thy praise,
To tye vp enuy, euermore inlarged,
    If some suspect of ill maskt not thy show,
    Then thou alone kingdomes of hearts shouldst owe.

71

NOe Longer mourne for me when I am dead,
Then you shall heare the surly sullen bell
Giue warning to the world that I am fled
From this vile world with vildest wormes to dwell:
Nay if you read this line, remember not,
The hand that writ it, for I loue you so,
That I in your sweet thoughts would be forgot,
If thinking on me then should make you woe.
O if(I say)you looke vpon this verse,
When I (perhaps) compounded am with clay,
Do not so much as my poore name reherse;
But let your loue euen with my life decay.
    Least the wise world should looke into your mone,
    And mocke you with me after I am gon.

72

O Least the world should taske you to recite,
What merit liu'd in me that you should loue
After my death(deare loue)for get me quite,
For you in me can nothing worthy proue.
Vnlesse you would deuise some vertuous lye,

To

70

That thou art blamed shall not be thy defect,
For slander's mark was ever yet the fair;
The ornament of beauty is suspéct,
4   A crow that flies in heaven's sweetest air.
So thou be good, slander doth but approve
Thy worth the greater, being wooed of time;
For canker vice the sweetest buds doth love,
8   And thou present'st a pure unstainèd prime.
Thou hast passed by the ambush of young days,
Either not assailed, or victor being charged;
Yet this thy praise cannot be so thy praise,
12   To tie up envy evermore enlarged.
    If some suspéct of ill masked not thy show,
    Then thou alone kingdoms of hearts shouldst owe.

71

No longer mourn for me when I am dead
Than you shall hear the surly sullen bell
Give warning to the world that I am fled
4   From this vile world with vildest worms to dwell.
Nay, if you read this line, remember not
The hand that writ it, for I love you so,
That I in your sweet thoughts would be forgot,
8   If thinking on me then should make you woe.
O if, I say, you look upon this verse,
When I, perhaps, compounded am with clay,
Do not so much as my poor name rehearse,
12   But let your love ev'n with my life decay,
    Lest the wise world should look into your moan,
    And mock you with me after I am gone.

72

O lest the world should task you to recite,
What merit lived in me that you should love
After my death, dear love, forget me quite,
4   For you in me can nothing worthy prove;
Unless you would devise some virtuous lie,

To do more for me than mine own desert,
And hang more praise upon deceasèd I,
8   Than niggard truth would willingly impart.
O lest your true love may seem false in this,
That you for love speak well of me untrue,
My name be buried where my body is,
12   And live no more to shame nor me nor you.
    For I am shamed by that which I bring forth,
    And so should you, to love things nothing worth.

73

That time of year thou mayst in me behold,
When yellow leaves, or none, or few, do hang
Upon those boughs which shake against the cold,
4   Bare ruined choirs, where late the sweet birds sang.
In me thou seest the twilight of such day,
As after sunset fadeth in the west,
Which by and by black night doth take away,
8   Death's second self, that seals up all in rest.
In me thou seest the glowing of such fire,
That on the ashes of his youth doth lie,
As the death-bed whereon it must expire,
12   Consumed with that which it was nourished by.
    This thou perceiv'st, which makes thy love more strong,
    To love that well which thou must leave ere long.

74

But be contented when that fell arrest
Without all bail shall carry me away,
My life hath in this line some interest,
4   Which for memorial still with thee shall stay.
When thou reviewest this, thou dost review
The very part was consecrate to thee.
The earth can have but earth, which is his due;
8   My spirit is thine, the better part of me.
So then thou hast but lost the dregs of life,
The prey of worms, my body being dead,
The coward conquest of a wretch's knife,

To doe more for me then mine owne defert,
And hang more praife vpon deceafed I,
Then nigard truth would willingly impart:
O leaft your true loue may feeme falce in this,
That you for loue fpeake well of me vntrue,
My name be buried where my body is,
And liue no more to fhame nor me, nor you.
　　For I am fhamd by that which I bring forth,
　　And fo fhould you, to loue things nothing worth.

73

THat time of yeeare thou maift in me behold,
　　When yellow leaues, or none, or few doe hange
Vpon thofe boughes which fhake againft the could,
Bare rn'wd quiers, where late the fweet birds fang.
In me thou feeft the twi-light of fuch day,
As after Sun-fet fadeth in the Weft,
Which by'and by blacke night doth take away,
Deaths fecond felfe that feals vp all in reft.
In me thou feeft the glowing of fuch fire,
That on the afhes of his youth doth lye,
As the death bed, whereon it muft expire,
Confum'd with that which it was nurrifht by.
　　This thou perceu'ft, which makes thy loue more ftrong,
　　To loue that well, which thou muft leaue ere long.

74

BVt be contented when that fell areft,
　　Without all bayle fhall carry me away,
My life hath in this line fome intereft,
Which for memoriall ftill with thee fhall ftay.
When thou reueweft this, thou doeft reuew,
The very part was confecrate to thee,
The earth can haue but earth, which is his due.
My fpirit is thine the better part of me,
So then hou haft but loft the dregs of life,
The pray of wormes, my body being dead,
The coward conqueft of a wretches knife,

To

To bafe of thee to be remembred,
 The worth of that, is that which jt containes,
 And that is this, and this with thee remaines.

75

SO are you to my thoughts as food to life,
 Or as fweet feafon'd fhewers are to the ground;
And for the peace of you I hold fuch ftrife,
As twixt a mifer and his wealth is found.
Now proud as an inioyer, and anon
Doubting the filching age will fteale his treafure,
Now counting beft to be with you alone,
Then betterd that the world may fee my pleafure,
Some-time all ful with feafting on your fight,
And by and by cleane ftarued for a looke,
Poffeffing or purfuing no delight
Saue what is had, or muft from you be tooke.
 Thus do I pine and furfet day by day,
 Or gluttoning on all, or all away,

76

VVHy is my verfe fo barren of new pride?
 So far from variation or quicke change?
Why with the time do I not glance afide
To new found methods, and to compounds ftrange?
Why write I ftill all one, euer the fame,
And keepe inuention in a noted weed,
That euery word doth almoft fel my name,
Shewing their birth, and where they did proceed?
O know fweet loue I alwaies write of you,
And you and loue are ftill my argument:
So all my beft is dreffing old words new,
Spending againe what is already fpent:
 For as the Sun is daily new and old,
 So is my loue ftill telling what is told,

77

THy glaffe will fhew thee how thy beauties were,
 Thy dyall how thy precious mynuits wafte,

The

12   Too base of thee to be rememb'red.
       The worth of that is that which it contains,
       And that is this, and this with thee remains.

75

So are you to my thoughts as food to life,
Or as sweet seasoned show'rs are to the ground;
And for the peace of you I hold such strife,
4   As 'twixt a miser and his wealth is found;
Now proud as an enjoyer, and anon
Doubting the filching age will steal his treasure;
Now counting best to be with you alone,
8   Then bettered that the world may see my pleasure;
Sometime all full with feasting on your sight,
And by and by clean starvèd for a look;
Possessing or pursuing no delight
12   Save what is had or must from you be took.
       Thus do I pine and surfeit day by day,
       Or gluttoning on all, or all away.

76

Why is my verse so barren of new pride,
So far from variation or quick change?
Why with the time do I not glance aside
4   To new-found methods, and to compounds strange?
Why write I still all one, ever the same,
And keep invention in a noted weed,
That every word doth almost tell my name,
8   Showing their birth, and where they did proceed?
O know, sweet love, I always write of you,
And you and love are still my argument.
So all my best is dressing old words new,
12   Spending again what is already spent:
       For as the sun is daily new and old,
       So is my love still telling what is told.

77

Thy glass will show thee how thy beauties wear,
Thy dial how thy precious minutes waste;

The vacant leaves thy mind's imprint will bear,
4   And of this book this learning mayst thou taste.
The wrinkles which thy glass will truly show,
Of mouthèd graves will give thee memory;
Thou by thy dial's shady stealth mayst know
8   Time's thievish progress to eternity.
Look what thy memory cannot contain,
Commit to these waste blanks, and thou shalt find
Those children nursed, delivered from thy brain,
12   To take a new acquaintance of thy mind.
    These offices, so oft as thou wilt look,
    Shall profit thee, and much enrich thy book.

78

So oft have I invoked thee for my muse,
And found such fair assistance in my verse,
As every alien pen hath got my use,
4   And under thee their poesy disperse.
Thine eyes, that taught the dumb on high to sing,
And heavy ignorance aloft to fly,
Have added feathers to the learnèd's wing,
8   And given grace a double majesty.
Yet be most proud of that which I compile,
Whose influence is thine, and born of thee.
In others' works thou dost but mend the style,
12   And arts with thy sweet graces gracèd be;
    But thou art all my art, and dost advance
    As high as learning my rude ignorance.

79

Whilst I alone did call upon thy aid,
My verse alone had all thy gentle grace,
But now my gracious numbers are decayed,
4   And my sick muse doth give another place.
I grant, sweet love, thy lovely argument
Deserves the travail of a worthier pen,
Yet what of thee thy poet doth invent
8   He robs thee of and pays it thee again.

The vacant leaues thy mindes imprint will beare,
And of this booke,this learning maift thou tafte.
The wrinckles which thy glaffe will truly fhow,
Of mouthed graues will giue thee memorie,
Thou by thy dyals fhady ftealth maift know,
Times theeuifh progreffe to eternitie.
Looke what thy memorie cannot containe,
Commit to thefe wafte blacks,and thou fhalt finde
Thofe children nurft,deliuerd from thy braine,
To take a new acquaintance of thy minde.
 Thefe offices,fo oft as thou wilt looke,
 Shall profit thee,and much inrich thy booke.

78

SO oft haue I inuok'd thee for my Mufe,
 And found fuch faire affiftance in my verfe,
As euery *Alien* pen hath got my vfe,
And vnder thee their poefie difperfe.
Thine eyes, that taught the dumbe on high to fing,
And heauie ignorance aloft to fl e,
Haue added fethers to the learneds wing,
And giuen grace a double Maieftie.
Yet be moft proud of that which I compile,
Whofe influence is thine,and borne of thee,
In others workes thou dooft but mend the ftile,
And Arts with thy fweete graces graced be.
 But thou art all my art,and dooft aduance
 As high as learning,my rude ignorance.

79

WHilft I alone did call vpon thy ayde,
 My verfe alone had all thy gentle grace,
But now my gracious numbers are decayde,
And my fick Mufe doth giue an other place.
I grant (fweet loue)thy louely argument
Deferues the trauaile of a worthier pen,
Yet what of thee thy Poet doth inuent,
He robs thee of,and payes it thee againe,

F   He

He lends thee vertue,and he ftole that word,
From thy behauiour,beautie doth he giue
And found it in thy cheeke: he can affoord
No praife to thee,but what in thee doth liue.
 Then thanke him not for that which he doth fay,
 Since what he owes thee,thou thy felfe dooft pay.

80

O How I faint when I of you do write,
 Knowing a better fpirit doth vfe your name,
And in the praife thereof fpends all his might,
To make me toung-tide fpeaking of your fame.
But fince your worth(wide as the Ocean is)
The humble as the proudeft faile doth beare,
My fawfie barke (inferior farre to his)
On your broad maine doth wilfully appeare.
Your fhalloweft helpe will hold me vp a floate,
Whilft he vpon your foundleffe deepe doth ride,
Or (being wrackt) I am a worthleffe bote,
He of tall building,and of goodly pride.
 Then If he thriue and I be caft away,
 The worft was this,my loue was my decay.

81

O R I fhall liue your Epitaph to make,
 Or you furuiue when I in earth am rotten,
From hence your memory death cannot take,
Although in me each part will be forgotten.
Your name from hence immortall life fhall haue,
Though I (once gone) to all the world muft dye,
The earth can yeeld me but a common graue,
When you intombed in mens eyes fhall lye,
Your monument fhall be my gentle verfe,
Which eyes not yet created fhall ore-read,
And toungs to be, your beeing fhall rehearfe,
When all the breathers of this world are dead,
 You ftill fhall liue (fuch vertue hath my Pen)
 Where breath moft breaths,euen in the mouths of men.

I grant

He lends thee virtue, and he stole that word
From thy behaviour; beauty doth he give
And found it in thy cheek; he can afford
12   No praise to thee but what in thee doth live.
    Then thank him not for that which he doth say,
    Since what he owes thee thou thyself dost pay.

80

O how I faint when I of you do write,
Knowing a better spirit doth use your name,
And in the praise thereof spends all his might,
4   To make me tongue-tied speaking of your fame.
But, since your worth, wide as the ocean is,
The humble as the proudest sail doth bear,
My saucy bark, inferior far to his,
8   On your broad main doth wilfully appear.
Your shallowest help will hold me up afloat,
Whilst he upon your soundless deep doth ride;
Or, being wracked, I am a worthless boat,
12   He of tall building and of goodly pride.
    Then, if he thrive and I be cast away,
    The worst was this: my love was my decay.

81

Or I shall live your epitaph to make,
Or you survive when I in earth am rotten,
From hence your memory death cannot take,
4   Although in me each part will be forgotten.
Your name from hence immortal life shall have,
Though I, once gone, to all the world must die.
The earth can yield me but a common grave,
8   When you entombèd in men's eyes shall lie.
Your monument shall be my gentle verse,
Which eyes not yet created shall o'er-read,
And tongues to be your being shall rehearse,
12   When all the breathers of this world are dead,
    You still shall live—such virtue hath my pen—
    Where breath most breathes, ev'n in the mouths of men.

82

I grant thou wert not married to my muse,
And therefore mayst without attaint o'erlook
The dedicated words which writers use
4   Of their fair subject, blessing every book.
Thou art as fair in knowledge as in hue,
Finding thy worth a limit past my praise,
And therefore art enforced to seek anew
8   Some fresher stamp of the time-bett'ring days.
And do so, love; yet when they have devised
What strainèd touches rhetoric can lend,
Thou truly fair wert truly sympathized
12   In true plain words by thy true-telling friend;
          And their gross painting might be better used,
          Where cheeks need blood; in thee it is abused.

83

I never saw that you did painting need,
And therefore to your fair no painting set;
I found, or thought I found, you did exceed
4   The barren tender of a poet's debt;
And therefore have I slept in your report,
That you yourself, being extant, well might show
How far a modern quill doth come too short,
8   Speaking of worth, what worth in you doth grow.
This silence for my sin you did impute,
Which shall be most my glory, being dumb;
For I impair not beauty, being mute,
12   When others would give life, and bring a tomb.
          There lives more life in one of your fair eyes
          Than both your poets can in praise devise.

84

Who is it that says most, which can say more
Than this rich praise, that you alone are you—
In whose confíne immurèd is the store
4   Which should example where your equal grew?
Lean penury within that pen doth dwell,

82

I Grant thou wert not married to my Muse,
  And therefore maiest without attaint ore-looke
The dedicated words which writers vse
Of their faire subiect, blessing euery booke.
Thou art as faire in knowledge as in hew,
Finding thy worth a limmit past my praise,
And therefore art inforc'd to seeke anew,
Some fresher stampe of the time bettering dayes.
And do so loue, yet when they haue deuisde,
What strained touches Rhethorick can lend,
Thou truly faire, wert truly simpathizde,
In true plaine words, by thy true telling friend.
　　And their grosse painting might be better vs'd,
　　Where cheekes need blood, in thee it is abus'd.

83

I Neuer saw that you did painting need,
  And therefore to your faire no painting set,
I found (or thought I found) you did exceed,
The barren tender of a Poets debt:
And therefore haue I slept in your report,
That you your selfe being extant well might show,
How farre a moderne quill doth come to short,
Speaking of worth, what worth in you doth grow,
This silence for my sinne you did impute,
Which shall be most my glory being dombe,'
For I impaire not beautie being mute,
When others would giue life, and bring a tombe.
　　There liues more life in one of your faire eyes,
　　Then both your Poets can in praise deuise.

84

WHo is it that sayes most, which can say more,
　　Then this rich praise, that you alone, are you,
In whose confine immured is the store,
Which should example where your equall grew,
Leane penurie within that Pen doth dwell,

F 2　　　　　　　　　　　That

That to his subiect lends not some small glory,
But he that writes of you,if he can tell,
That you are you,so dignifies his story.
Let him but coppy what in you is writ,
Not making worse what nature made so cleere,
And such a counter-part shall fame his wit,
Making his stile admired euery where.
    You to your beautious blessings adde a curse,
    Being fond on praise,which makes your praises worse.

85

MY toung-tide Muse in manners holds her still,
While comments of your praise richly compil'd,
Reserue their Character with goulden quill,
And precious phrase by all the Muses fil'd.
I thinke good thoughts,whilst other write good wordes,
And like vnlettered clarke still crie Amen,
To euery Himne that able spirit affords,
In polisht forme of well refined pen.
Hearing you praisd,I say 'tis so, 'tis true,
And to the most of praise adde some-thing more,
But that is in my thought,whose loue to you
(Though words come hind-most)holds his ranke before,
    Then others,for the breath of words respect,
    Me for my dombe thoughts,speaking in effect.

86

VVAs it the proud full saile of his great verse,
Bound for the prize of (all to precious) you,
That did my ripe thoughts in my braine inhearce,
Making their tombe the wombe wherein they grew?
Was it his spirit,by spirits taught to write,
Aboue a mortall pitch,that struck me dead ?
No,neither he,nor his compiers by night
Giuing him ayde,my verse astonished.
He nor that affable familiar ghost
Which nightly gulls him with intelligence,
As victors of my silence cannot boast,

                                        I was

That to his subject lends not some small glory,
But he that writes of you, if he can tell
8   That you are you, so dignifies his story.
Let him but copy what in you is writ,
Not making worse what nature made so clear,
And such a counterpart shall fame his wit,
12   Making his style admired everywhere.
      You to your beauteous blessings add a curse,
      Being fond on praise, which makes your praises worse.

85

My tongue-tied muse in manners holds her still,
While comments of your praise, richly compiled,
Reserve their character with golden quill
4   And precious phrase by all the muses filed.
I think good thoughts, whilst other write good words,
And like unlettered clerk still cry amen,
To every hymn that able spirit affords,
8   In polished form of well-refinèd pen.
Hearing you praised, I say, " 'tis so," " 'tis true,"
And to the most of praise add something more;
But that is in my thought, whose love to you,
12   Though words come hindmost, holds his rank before.
      Then others for the breath of words respect,
      Me for my dumb thoughts, speaking in effect.

86

Was it the proud full sail of his great verse,
Bound for the prize of all too precious you,
That did my ripe thoughts in my brain inhearse,
4   Making their tomb the womb wherein they grew?
Was it his spirit, by spirits taught to write
Above a mortal pitch, that struck me dead?
No, neither he, nor his compeers by night
8   Giving him aid, my verse astonishèd.
He, nor that affable familiar ghost
Which nightly gulls him with intelligence,
As victors, of my silence cannot boast;

12   I was not sick of any fear from thence.
       But when your countenance filled up his line,
       Then lacked I matter, that enfeebled mine.

87

       Farewell, thou art too dear for my possessing,
       And like enough thou know'st thy estimate.
       The charter of thy worth gives thee releasing;
4   My bonds in thee are all determinate.
       For how do I hold thee but by thy granting,
       And for that riches where is my deserving?
       The cause of this fair gift in me is wanting,
8   And so my patent back again is swerving.
       Thyself thou gav'st, thy own worth then not knowing,
       Or me, to whom thou gav'st it, else mistaking;
       So thy great gift, upon misprision growing,
12   Comes home again, on better judgement making.
         Thus have I had thee as a dream doth flatter:
         In sleep a king, but waking no such matter.

88

       When thou shalt be disposed to set me light,
       And place my merit in the eye of scorn,
       Upon thy side against myself I'll fight,
4   And prove thee virtuous, though thou art forsworn.
       With mine own weakness being best acquainted,
       Upon thy part I can set down a story
       Of faults concealed, wherein I am attainted,
8   That thou in losing me shall win much glory.
       And I by this will be a gainer too,
       For bending all my loving thoughts on thee,
       The injuries that to myself I do,
12   Doing thee vantage, double vantage me.
         Such is my love—to thee I so belong—
         That for thy right myself will bear all wrong.

89

       Say that thou didst forsake me for some fault,
       And I will comment upon that offence.

I was not sick of any feare from thence.
But when your countinance fild vp his line,
Then lackt I matter,that infeebled mine.

87

FArewell thou art too deare for my poſſeſſing,
And like enough thou knowſt thy eſtimate,
The Chaꝛter of thy worth giues thee releaſing:
My boꝰds in thee are all determinate.
For how do I hold thee but by thy granting,
And for that ritches where is my deſeruing?
The cauſe of this faire guiſt in me is wanting,
And ſo my pattent back againe is ſweruing.
Thy ſelfe thou gau'ſt,thy owne worth then not knowing,
Oꝛ mee to whom thou gau'ſt it,elſe miſtaking,
So thy great guiſt vpon miſpriſion growing,
Comes home againe,on better iudgement making.
Thus haue I had thee as a dreame doth flatter,
In ſleepe a King,but waking no ſuch matter.

88

VVHen thou ſhalt be diſpode to ſet me light,
And place my merrit in the eie of ſkorne,
Vpon thy ſide,againſt my ſelfe ile fight,
And proue thee virtuous,though thou art forſworne:
With mine owne weakeneſſe being beſt acquainted,
Vpon thy part I can ſet downe a ſtory
Of faults conceald,wherein I am attainted :
That thou in looſing me ſhall win much glory:
And I by this wil be a gainer too,
For bending all my louing thoughts on thee,
The iniuries that to my ſelfe I doe,
Doing thee vantage,duble vantage me.
Such is my loue,to thee I ſo belong,
That for thy right,my ſelfe will beare all wrong.

89

SAy that thou didſt forſake mee for ſome fait,
And I will comment vpon that offence,

F 3

The

Speake of my lamenesse, and I straight will halt:
Against thy reasons making no defence.
Thou canst not(loue)disgrace me halfe so ill,
To set a forme vpon desired change,
As ile my selfe disgrace,knowing thy wil,
I will acquaintance strangle and looke strange:
Be absent from thy walkes and in my tongue,
Thy sweet beloued name no more shall dwell,
Least I(too much prophane)should do it wronge:
And haplie of our old acquaintance tell.
   For thee,against my selfe ile vow debate,
   For I must nere loue him whom thou dost hate.

90

THen hate me when thou wilt, if euer,now,
  Now while the world is bent my deeds to crosse,
Ioyne with the spight of fortune,make me bow,
And doe not drop in for an after losse:
Ah doe not,when my heart hath scapte this sorrow,
Come in the rereward of a conquerd woe,
Giue not a windy night a rainie morrow,
To linger out a purposd ouer-throw.
If thou wilt leaue me, do not leaue me last,
When other pettie griefes haue done their spight,
But in the onset come,so stall I taste
At first the very worst of fortunes might.
   And other straines of woe, which now seeme woe,
   Compar'd with losse of thee,will not seeme so.

91

SOme glory in their birth,some in their skill,
  Some in their wealth, some in their bodies force,
Some in their garments though new-fangled ill:
Some in their Hawkes and Hounds,some in their Horse.
And euery humor hath his adiunct pleasure,
Wherein it findes a ioy aboue the rest,
But these perticulers are not my measure,
All these I better in one generall best.

                                 Thy

Speak of my lameness, and I straight will halt,
4   Against thy reasons making no defence.
Thou canst not, love, disgrace me half so ill,
To set a form upon desired change,
As I'll myself disgrace, knowing thy will,
8   I will acquaintance strangle and look strange,
Be absent from thy walks, and in my tongue
Thy sweet belovèd name no more shall dwell,
Lest I, too much profane, should do it wrong
12   And haply of our old acquaintance tell.
    For thee, against myself I'll vow debate,
    For I must ne'er love him whom thou dost hate.

90

Then hate me when thou wilt, if ever, now,
Now while the world is bent my deeds to cross,
Join with the spite of fortune, make me bow,
4   And do not drop in for an after-loss.
Ah do not, when my heart hath 'scaped this sorrow,
Come in the rearward of a conquered woe;
Give not a windy night a rainy morrow,
8   To linger out a purposed overthrow.
If thou wilt leave me, do not leave me last,
When other petty griefs have done their spite,
But in the onset come; so shall I taste
12   At first the very worst of fortune's might,
    And other strains of woe, which now seem woe,
    Compared with loss of thee will not seem so.

91

Some glory in their birth, some in their skill,
Some in their wealth, some in their body's force,
Some in their garments, though new-fangled ill,
4   Some in their hawks and hounds, some in their horse;
And every humor hath his adjunct pleasure,
Wherein it finds a joy above the rest.
But these particulars are not my measure;
8   All these I better in one general best.

Thy love is better than high birth to me,
Richer than wealth, prouder than garments' cost,
Of more delight than hawks or horses be;
12   And having thee, of all men's pride I boast;
     Wretched in this alone, that thou mayst take
     All this away, and me most wretched make.

92

But do thy worst to steal thyself away,
For term of life thou art assurèd mine,
And life no longer than thy love will stay,
4   For it depends upon that love of thine.
Then need I not to fear the worst of wrongs,
When in the least of them my life hath end.
I see a better state to me belongs
8   Than that which on thy humor doth depend.
Thou canst not vex me with inconstant mind,
Since that my life on thy revolt doth lie.
O what a happy title do I find,
12   Happy to have thy love, happy to die!
     But what's so blessèd-fair that fears no blot?
     Thou mayst be false, and yet I know it not.

93

So shall I live, supposing thou art true,
Like a deceivèd husband—so love's face
May still seem love to me, though altered new:
4   Thy looks with me, thy heart in other place.
For there can live no hatred in thine eye,
Therefore in that I cannot know thy change.
In many's looks, the false heart's history
8   Is writ in moods and frowns and wrinkles strange,
But heav'n in thy creation did decree,
That in thy face sweet love should ever dwell,
Whate'er thy thoughts or thy heart's workings be,
12   Thy looks should nothing thence but sweetness tell.
     How like Eve's apple doth thy beauty grow,
     If thy sweet virtue answer not thy show.

Thy loue is bitter then high birth to me,
Richer then wealth,prouder then garments coſt,
Of more delight then Hawkes or Horſes bee:
And hauing thee,of all mens pride I boaſt.
   Wretched in this alone,that thou maiſt take,
   All this away,and me moſt wretched make.

92

BVt doe thy worſt to ſteale-thy ſelfe away,
  For tearme of life thou art aſſured mine,
And life no longer then thy loue will ſtay,
For it depends vpon that loue of thine.
Then need I not to feare the worſt of wrongs,
When in the leaſt of them my life hath end,
I ſee,a better ſtate to me belongs
Then that,which on thy humor doth depend.
Thou canſt not vex me with inconſtant minde,
Since that my life on thy reuolt doth lie,
Oh what a happy title do I finde,
Happy to haue thy loue, happy to die!
   But whats ſo bleſſed faire that feares no blot,
   Thou maiſt be falce, and yet I know it not.

93

SO ſhall I liue,ſuppoſing thou art true,
  Like a deceiued husband ſo loues face,
May ſtill ſeeme loue to me,though alter'd new:
Thy lookes with me,thy heart in other place.
For their can liue no hatred in thine eye,
Therefore in that I cannot know thy change,
In manies lookes,the falce hearts hiſtory
Is writ in moods and frounes and wrinckles ſtrange,
But heauen in thy creation did decree,
That in thy face ſweet loue ſhould euer dwell,
What ere thy thoughts, or thy hearts workings be,
Thy lookes ſhould nothing thence, but ſweetneſſe tell.
   How like *Eaues* apple doth thy beauty grow,
   If thy ſweet vertue anſwere not thy ſhow.

94

THey that haue powre to hurt, and will doe none,
 That doe not do the thing, they moſt do ſhowe,
Who mouing others, are themſelues as ſtone,
Vnmooued, could, and to temptation ſlow:
They rightly do inherrit heauens graces,
And husband natures ritches from expence,
They are the Lords and owners of their faces,
Others, but ſtewards of their excellence:
The ſommers flowre is to the ſommer ſweet,
Though to it ſelfe, it onely liue and die,
But if that flowre with baſe infection meete,
The baſeſt weed out-braues his dignity:
    For ſweeteſt things turne ſowreſt by their deedes,
    Lillies that feſter, ſmell far worſe then weeds.

95

HOw ſweet and louely doſt thou make the ſhame,
 Which like a canker in the fragrant Roſe,
Doth ſpot the beautie of thy budding name?
Oh in what ſweets doeſt thou thy ſinnes incloſe!
That tongue that tells the ſtory of thy daies,
(Making laſciuious comments on thy ſport)
Cannot diſpraiſe, but in a kinde of praiſe,
Naming thy name, bleſſes an ill report.
Oh what a manſion haue thoſe vices got,
Which for their habitation choſe out thee,
Where beauties vaile doth couer euery blot,
And all things turnes to faire, that eies can ſee!
    Take heed(deare heart)of this large priuiledge,
    The hardeſt kniſe ill vſ'd doth looſe his edge.

96

SOme ſay thy fault is youth, ſome wantoneſſe,
 Some ſay thy grace is youth and gentle ſport,
Both grace and faults are lou'd of more and leſſe:
Thou makſt faults graces, that to thee reſort:
As on the finger of a throned Queene,

The

94

They that have pow'r to hurt, and will do none, *a*
That do not do the thing they most do show, *b*
Who moving others are themselves as stone, *a*
4   Unmovèd, cold, and to temptation slow *b*
They rightly do inherit heaven's graces, *c*
And husband nature's riches from expense; *d*
They are the lords and owners of their faces, *c*
8   Others but stewards of their excellence. *d*
The summer's flow'r is to the summer sweet, *e*
Though to itself it only live and die; *f*
But if that flow'r with base infection meet, *e*
12   The basest weed outbraves his dignity. *f*
    For sweetest things turn sourest by their deeds;
    Lilies that fester smell far worse than weeds.

95

How sweet and lovely dost thou make the shame
Which, like a canker in the fragrant rose,
Doth spot the beauty of thy budding name!
4   O in what sweets dost thou thy sins enclose!
That tongue that tells the story of thy days,
Making lascivious comments on thy sport,
Cannot dispraise but in a kind of praise;
8   Naming thy name blesses an ill report.
O what a mansion have those vices got
Which for their habitation chose out thee,
Where beauty's veil doth cover every blot,
12   And all things turns to fair that eyes can see!
    Take heed, dear heart, of this large privilege;
    The hardest knife ill used doth lose his edge.

96

Some say thy fault is youth, some wantonness,
Some say thy grace is youth and gentle sport;
Both grace and faults are loved of more and less;
4   Thou mak'st faults graces that to thee resort.
As on the finger of a thronèd queen

The basest jewel will be well esteemed,
So are those errors that in thee are seen,
8   To truths translated, and for true things deemed.
How many lambs might the stern wolf betray,
If like a lamb he could his looks translate;
How many gazers mightst thou lead away,
12   If thou wouldst use the strength of all thy state!
   But do not so; I love thee in such sort,
   As thou being mine, mine is thy good report.

97

How like a winter hath my absence been
From thee, the pleasure of the fleeting year!
What freezings have I felt, what dark days seen!
4   What old December's bareness everywhere!
And yet this time removed was summer's time,
The teeming autumn big with rich increase,
Bearing the wanton burthen of the prime,
8   Like widowed wombs after their lords' decease.
Yet this abundant issue seemed to me
But hope of orphans, and unfathered fruit;
For summer and his pleasures wait on thee,
12   And thou away, the very birds are mute;
   Or if they sing, 'tis with so dull a cheer,
   That leaves look pale, dreading the winter's near.

98

From you have I been absent in the spring,
When proud-pied April, dressed in all his trim,
Hath put a spirit of youth in everything,
4   That heavy Saturn laughed and leapt with him.
Yet nor the lays of birds, nor the sweet smell
Of different flow'rs in odor and in hue,
Could make me any summer's story tell,
8   Or from their proud lap pluck them where they grew.
Nor did I wonder at the lily's white,
Nor praise the deep vermilion in the rose;
They were but sweet, but figures of delight,

The baseft Iewell wil be well esteem'd:
So are thofe errors that in thee are feene,
To truths tranflated,and for true things deem'd.
How many Lambs might the fterne Wolfe betray,
If like a Lambe he could his lookes tranflate.
How many gazers mighft thou lead away,
If thou wouldft vfe the ftrength of all thy ftate?
   But doe not fo,I loue thee in fuch fort,
   As thou being mine,mine is thy good report.

97

How like a Winter hath my abfence beene
From thee,the pleafure of the fleeting yeare?
   What freezings haue I felt,what darke daies feene?
What old Decembers bareneffe euery where?
And yet this time remou'd was fommers time,
The teeming Autumne big with ritch increafe,
Bearing the wanton burthen of the prime,
Like widdowed wombes after their Lords deceafe:
Yet this aboundant iffue feem'd to me,
But hope of Orphans,and vn-fathered fruite,
For Sommer and his pleafures waite on thee,
And thou away,the very birds are mute.
   Or if they fing,tis with fo dull a cheere,
   That leaues looke pale,dreading the Winters neere.

98

From you haue I beene abfent in the fpring,
When proud pide Aprill (dreft in all his trim)
Hath put a fpirit of youth in euery thing:
That heauie *Saturne* laught and leapt with him.
Yet nor the laies of birds,nor the fweet fmell
Of different flowers in odor and in hew,
Could make me any fummers ftory tell:
Or from their proud lap pluck them where they grew:
Nor did I wonder at the Lillies white,
Nor praife the deepe vermillion in the Rofe,
They weare but fweet,but figures of delight:

G   Drawne

Drawne after you, you patterne of all those.
　Yet feem'd it Winter still, and you away,
　As with your shaddow I with these did play.

99

THe forward violet thus did I chide,
　Sweet theefe whence didst thou steale thy sweet that
If not from my loues breath, the purple pride, 　(smels
Which on thy soft cheeke for complexion dwells?
In my loues veines thou hast too grosely died,
The Lillie I condemned for thy hand,
And buds of marierom had stolne thy haire,
The Roses fearefully on thornes did stand,
Our blushing shame, an other white dispaire:
A third nor red, nor white, had stolne of both,
And to his robbry had annext thy breath,
But for his theft in pride of all his growth
A vengfull canker eate him vp to death.
　More flowers I noted, yet I none could see,
　But sweet, or culler it had stolne from thee.

100

VV Here art thou Muse that thou forgetst so long,
　To speake of that which giues thee all thy might?
Spendst thou thy furie on some worthlesse songe,
Darkning thy powre to lend base subiects light,
Returne forgetfull Muse, and straight redeeme,
In gentle numbers time so idely spent,
Sing to the eare that doth thy laies esteeme,
And giues thy pen both skill and argument.
Rise resty Muse, my loues sweet face suruay,
If time haue any wrincle grauen there,
If any, be a *Satire* to decay,
And make times spoiles dispised euery where.
　Giue my loue fame faster then time wasts life,
　So thou preuenst his sieth, and crooked knife.

101

OH truant Muse what shalbe thy amends,

　　　　　　　　　　　　　　　　　　　For

12   Drawn after you, you pattern of all those.
        Yet seemed it winter still, and, you away,
        As with your shadow I with these did play.

99

The forward violet thus did I chide:
Sweet thief, whence didst thou steal thy sweet that smells
If not from my love's breath? The purple pride
Which on thy soft cheek for complexion dwells,
5   In my love's veins thou hast too grossly dyed.
The lily I condemnèd for thy hand,
And buds of marjoram had stol'n thy hair;
The roses fearfully on thorns did stand,
9   One blushing shame, another white despair;
A third, nor red nor white, had stol'n of both,
And to his robb'ry had annexed thy breath;
But for his theft, in pride of all his growth
13   A vengeful canker ate him up to death.
        More flow'rs I noted, yet I none could see,
        But sweet or colour it had stol'n from thee.

100

Where art thou, muse, that thou forget'st so long
To speak of that which gives thee all thy might?
Spend'st thou thy fury on some worthless song,
4   Dark'ning thy pow'r to lend base subjects light?
Return, forgetful muse, and straight redeem
In gentle numbers time so idly spent;
Sing to the ear that doth thy lays esteem,
8   And gives thy pen both skill and argument.
Rise, resty muse; my love's sweet face survey
If time have any wrinkle graven there;
If any, be a satire to decay,
12   And make time's spoils despisèd everywhere.
        Give my love fame faster than time wastes life;
        So thou prevent'st his scythe and crookèd knife.

101

O truant muse, what shall be thy amends

For thy neglect of truth in beauty dyed?
Both truth and beauty on my love depends;
4 So dost thou too, and therein dignified.
Make answer, muse, wilt thou not haply say,
Truth needs no colour with his colour fixed,
Beauty no pencil, beauty's truth to lay;
8 But best is best, if never intermixed?
Because he needs no praise, wilt thou be dumb?
Excuse not silence so, for 't lies in thee,
To make him much outlive a gilded tomb,
12 And to be praised of ages yet to be.
　　Then do thy office, muse, I teach thee how
　　To make him seem long hence as he shows now.

102

My love is strengthened, though more weak in seeming;
I love not less, though less the show appear.
That love is merchandised, whose rich esteeming
4 The owner's tongue doth publish everywhere.
Our love was new, and then but in the spring,
When I was wont to greet it with my lays,
As Philomel in summer's front doth sing,
8 And stops his pipe in growth of riper days.
Not that the summer is less pleasant now
Than when her mournful hymns did hush the night,
But that wild music burthens every bough,
12 And sweets grown common lose their dear delight.
　　Therefore, like her, I sometime hold my tongue,
　　Because I would not dull you with my song.

103

Alack what poverty my muse brings forth,
That, having such a scope to show her pride,
The argument all bare is of more worth
4 Than when it hath my added praise beside.
O blame me not if I no more can write!
Look in your glass, and there appears a face
That overgoes my blunt invention quite,
8 Dulling my lines, and doing me disgrace.

For thy neglect of truth in beauty di'd?
Both truth and beauty on my loue depends:
So doft thou too, and therein dignifi'd:
Make anſwere Muſe, wilt thou not haply ſaie,
Truth needs no collour with his collour fixt,
Beautie no penſell, beauties truth to lay:
But beſt is beſt, if neuer intermixt.
Becauſe he needs no praiſe, wilt thou be dumb?
Excuſe not ſilence ſo, for't lies in thee,
To make him much out-liue a gilded tombe:
And to be praiſd of ages yet to be.
　　Then do thy office Muſe, I teach thee how,
　　To make him ſeeme long hence, as he ſhowes now.

102

MY loue is ſtrengthned though more weake in ſee-
I loue not leſſe, thogh leſſe the ſhow appeare, (ming
That loue is marchandiz'd, whoſe ritch eſteeming,
The owners tongue doth publiſh euery where.
Our loue was new, and then but in the ſpring,
When I was wont to greet it with my laies,
As *Philomell* in ſummers front doth ſinge,
And ſtops his pipe in growth of riper daies:
Not that the ſummer is leſſe pleaſant now
Then when her mournefull himns did huſh the night,
But that wild muſick burthens euery bow,
And ſweets growne common looſe their deare delight.
　　Therefore like her, I ſome-time hold my tongue:
　　Becauſe I would not dull you with my ſonge.

103

ALack what pouerty my Muſe brings forth,
That hauing ſuch a skope to ſhow her pride,
The argument all bare is of more worth
Then when it hath my added praiſe beſide.
Oh blame me not if I no more can write!
Looke in your glaſſe and there appeares a face,
That ouer-goes my blunt inuention quite,
Dulling my lines, and doing me diſgrace,

Were it not sinfull then striuing to mend,
To marre the subiect that before was well,
For to no other passe my verses tend,
Then of your graces and your gifts to tell.
   And more,much more then in my verse can sit,
   Your owne glasse showes you,when you looke in it.

104

TO me faire friend you neuer can be old,
  For as you were when first your eye I eyde,
Such seemes your beautie still:Three Winters colde,
Haue from the forrests shooke three summers pride,
Three beautious springs to yellow *Autumne* turn'd,
In processe of the seasons haue I seene,
Three Aprill perfumes in three hot Iunes burn'd,
Since first I saw you fresh which yet are greene.
Ah yet doth beauty like a Dyall hand,
Steale from his figure,and no pace perceiu'd,
So your sweete hew,which me thinkes still doth stand
Hath motion,and mine eye may be deceaued.
   For feare of which,heare this thou age vnbred,
   Ere you were borne was beauties summer dead.

105

LEt not my loue be cal'd Idolatrie,
  Nor my beloued as an Idoll show,
Since all alike my songs and praises be
To one,of one,still such,and euer so.
Kinde is my loue to day,to morrow kinde,
Still constant in a wondrous excellence,
Therefore my verse to constancie confin'de,
One thing expressing,leaues out difference.
Faire,kinde,and true,is all my argument,
Faire,kinde and true,varrying to other words,
And in this change is my inuention spent,
Three theams in one,which wondrous scope affords.
   Faire,kinde,and true,haue often liu'd alone.
   Which three till now,neuer kept seate in one.

When

Were it not sinful then, striving to mend,
To mar the subject that before was well?
For to no other pass my verses tend,
12   Than of your graces and your gifts to tell;
    And more, much more than in my verse can sit,
    Your own glass shows you, when you look in it.

104

To me, fair friend, you never can be old,
For as you were when first your eye I eyed,
Such seems your beauty still. Three winters cold
4   Have from the forests shook three summers' pride,
Three beauteous springs to yellow autumn turned
In process of the seasons have I seen,
Three April pérfumes in three hot Junes burned,
8   Since first I saw you fresh, which yet are green.
Ah yet doth beauty, like a dial hand,
Steal from his figure, and no pace perceived;
So your sweet hue, which methinks still doth stand,
12   Hath motion, and mine eye may be deceived:
    For fear of which, hear this, thou age unbred,
    Ere you were born was beauty's summer dead.

105

Let not my love be called idolatry,
Nor my belovèd as an idol show,
Since all alike my songs and praises be
4   To one, of one, still such, and ever so.
Kind is my love today, tomorrow kind,
Still constant in a wondrous excellence;
Therefore my verse to constancy confined,
8   One thing expressing, leaves out difference.
Fair, kind, and true, is all my argument,
Fair, kind, and true, varying to other words;
And in this change is my invention spent—
12   Three themes in one, which wondrous scope affords.
    Fair, kind, and true, have often lived alone,
    Which three, till now, never kept seat in one.

106

When in the chronicle of wasted time
I see descriptions of the fairest wights
And beauty making beautiful old rhyme
4   In praise of ladies dead and lovely knights,
Then in the blazon of sweet beauty's best,
Of hand, of foot, of lip, of eye, of brow,
I see their ántique pen would have expressed
8   Ev'n such a beauty as you master now.
So all their praises are but prophecies
Of this our time, all you prefiguring,
And for they looked but with divining eyes,
12   They had not skill enough your worth to sing;
      For we which now behold these present days,
      Have eyes to wonder, but lack tongues to praise.

107

Not mine own fears nor the prophetic soul
Of the wide world dreaming on things to come
Can yet the lease of my true love control,
4   Supposed as forfeit to a cónfined doom.
The mortal moon hath her eclipse endured,
And the sad augurs mock their own preság e,
Incertainties now crown themselves assured,
8   And peace proclaims olives of endless age.
Now with the drops of this most balmy time
My love looks fresh, and death to me subscribes,
Since spite of him I'll live in this poor rhyme,
12   While he insults o'er dull and speechless tribes.
      And thou in this shalt find thy monument,
      When tyrants' crests and tombs of brass are spent.

108

What's in the brain that ink may character,
Which hath not figured to thee my true spirit?
What's new to speak, what now to register,
4   That may express my love, or thy dear merit?
Nothing, sweet boy, but yet, like prayers divine,

106

WHen in the Chronicle of wasted time,
  I see discriptions of the fairest wights,
And beautie making beautifull old rime,
In praise of Ladies dead,and louely Knights,
Then in the blazon of sweet beauties best,
Of hand,of foote,of lip,of eye,of brow,
I see their antique Pen would haue exprest,
Euen such a beauty as you maister now.
So all their praises are but prophesies
Of this our time,all you prefiguring,
And for they look'd but with deuining eyes,
They had not still enough your worth to sing :
    For we which now behold these present dayes,
    Haue eyes to wonder,but lack toungs to praise.

107

NOt mine owne feares,nor the prophetick soule,
  Of the wide world,dreaming on things to come,
Can yet the lease of my true loue controule,
Supposde as forfeit to a confin'd doome.
The mortall Moone hath her eclipse indur'de,
And the sad Augurs mock their owne presage,
Incertenties now crowne them-selues assur'de,
And peace proclaimes Oliues of endlesse age.
Now with the drops of this most balmie time,
My loue lookes fresh,and death to me subscribes,
Since spight of him Ile liue in this poore rime,
While he insults ore dull and speachlesse tribes.
    And thou in this shalt finde thy monument,
    When tyrants crests and tombs of brasse are spent.

108

VVHat's in the braine that Inck may character,
   Which hath not figur'd to thee my true spirit,
What's new to speake,what now to register,
That may expresse my loue,or thy deare merit ?
Nothing sweet boy,but yet like prayers diuine,

G 3   I must

I muſt each day ſay ore the very ſame,
Counting no old thing old,thou mine,I thine,
Euen as when firſt I hallowed thy faire name,
So that eternall loue in loues freſh caſe,
Waighes not the duſt and iniury of age,
Nor giues to neceſſary wrinckles place,
But makes antiquitie for aye his page,
 Finding the firſt conceit of loue there bred,
 Where time and outward forme would ſhew it dead,

109

O Neuer ſay that I was falſe of heart,
 Though abſence ſeem'd my flame to quallifie,
As eaſie might I from my ſelfe depart,
As from my ſoule which in thy breſt doth lye:
That is my home of loue, if I haue rang'd,
Like him that trauels I returne againe,
Iuſt to the time,not with the time exchang'd,
So that my ſelfe bring water for my ſtaine,
Neuer beleeue though in my nature raign'd,
All frailties that beſiege all kindes of blood,
That it could ſo prepoſterouſlie be ſtain'd,
To leaue for nothing all thy ſumme of good :
 For nothing this wide Vniuerſe I call,
 Saue thou my Roſe,in it thou art my all.

110

A Las 'tis true,I haue gone here and there,
 And made my ſelfe a motley to the view,
Gor'd mine own thoughts, ſold cheap what is moſt deare,
Made old offences of affections new.
Moſt true it is,that I haue lookt on truth
Aſconce and ſtrangely: But by all aboue,
Theſe blenches gaue my heart an other youth,
And worſe eſſaies prou'd thee my beſt of loue,
Now all is done,haue what ſhall haue no end,
Mine appetite I neuer more will grin'de
On newer proofe,to trie an older friend,
A God in loue,to whom I am confin'd.

Then

I must each day say o'er the very same;
Counting no old thing old, thou mine, I thine,
8   Ev'n as when first I hallowed thy fair name.
So that eternal love in love's fresh case
Weighs not the dust and injury of age,
Nor gives to necessary wrinkles place,
12   But makes antiquity for aye his page,
  Finding the first conceit of love there bred,
  Where time and outward form would show it dead.

109

O never say that I was false of heart,
Though absence seemed my flame to qualify.
As easy might I from myself depart,
4   As from my soul, which in thy breast doth lie.
That is my home of love; if I have ranged
Like him that travels I return again,
Just to the time, not with the time exchanged,
8   So that myself bring water for my stain.
Never believe, though in my nature reigned
All frailties that besiege all kinds of blood,
That it could so preposterously be stained
12   To leave for nothing all thy sum of good—
  For nothing this wide universe I call,
  Save thou, my rose; in it thou art my all.

110

Alas 'tis true, I have gone here and there,
And made myself a motley to the view,
Gored mine own thoughts, sold cheap what is most dear,
4   Made old offences of affections new.
Most true it is, that I have looked on truth
Askance and strangely. But by all above,
These blenches gave my heart another youth,
8   And worse essays proved thee my best of love.
Now all is done, have what shall have no end—
Mine appetite I never more will grind
On newer proof, to try an older friend,
12   A god in love, to whom I am confined.

Then give me welcome, next my heav'n the best,
Ev'n to thy pure and most most loving breast.

111

O for my sake do you wish fortune chide,
The guilty goddess of my harmful deeds,
That did not better for my life provide
4   Than public means which public manners breeds.
Thence comes it that my name receives a brand,
And almost thence my nature is subdued
To what it works in, like the dyer's hand.
8   Pity me then, and wish I were renewed,
Whilst like a willing patient I will drink
Potions of eisel 'gainst my strong infection;
No bitterness that I will bitter think,
12   Nor double penance, to correct correction.
    Pity me then, dear friend, and I assure ye,
    Ev'n that your pity is enough to cure me.

112

Your love and pity doth th' impression fill,
Which vulgar scandal stamped upon my brow;
For what care I who calls me well or ill,
4   So you o'er-green my bad, my good allow?
You are my all the world, and I must strive
To know my shames and praises from your tongue;
None else to me, nor I to none alive,
8   That my steeled sense or changes right or wrong.
In so profound abysm I throw all care
Of others' voices, that my adder's sense
To critic and to flatt'rer stoppèd are.
12   Mark how with my neglect I do dispense:
    You are so strongly in my purpose bred,
    That all the world besides me thinks y' are dead.

113

Since I left you, mine eye is in my mind,
And that which governs me to go about
Doth part his function, and is partly blind,

Then giue me welcome,next my heauen the beſt,
Euen to thy pure and moſt moſt louing breſt,

III

O For my ſake doe you wiſh fortune chide,
   The guiltie goddeſſe of my harmfull deeds,
That did not better for my life prouide,
Then publick meanes which publick manners breeds,
Thence comes it that my name receiues a brand,
And almoſt thence my nature is ſubdu'd
To what it workes in,like the Dyers hand,
Pitty me then,and wiſh I were renu'de,
Whilſt like a willing pacient I will drinke,
Potions of Eyſell gainſt my ſtrong infection,
No bitterneſſe that I will bitter thinke,
Nor double pennance to correct correction.
   Pittie me then deare friend,and I aſſure yee,
   Euen that your pittie is enough to cure mee.

112

YOur loue and pittie doth th'impreſſion fill,
   Which vulgar ſcandall ſtampt vpon my brow,
For what care I who calles me well or ill,
So you ore-greene my bad,my good alow?
You are my All the world,and I muſt ſtriue,
To know my ſhames and praiſes from your tounge,
None elſe to me,nor I to none aliue,
That my ſteel'd ſence or changes right or wrong,
In ſo profound Abiſme I throw all care
Of others voyces,that my Adders ſence,
To cryttick and to flatterer ſtopped are:
Marke how with my neglect I doe diſpence.
   You are ſo ſtrongly in my purpoſe bred,
   That all the world beſides me thinkes y'are dead,

113

SInce I left you,mine eye is in my minde,
   And that which gouernes me to goe about,
Doth part his function,and is partly blind,

Seemes

Seemes seeing, but effectually is out:
For it no forme deliuers to the heart
Of bird, of flowre, or shape which it doth lack,
Of his quick obiects hath the minde no part,
Nor his owne vision houlds what it doth catch:
For if it see the rud'st or gentlest sight,
The most sweet-fauor or deformedst creature,
The mountaine, or the sea, the day, or night:
The Croe, or Doue, it shapes them to your feature.
  Incapable of more repleat, with you,
  My most true minde thus maketh mine vntrue.

114

OR whether doth my minde being crown'd with you
Drinke vp the monarks plague this flattery?
Or whether shall I say mine eie saith true,
And that your loue taught it this *Alcumie?*
To make of monsters, and things indigest,
Such cherubines as your sweet selfe resemble,
Creating euery bad a perfect best
As fast as obiects to his beames assemble:
Oh tis the first, tis flatry in my seeing,
And my great minde most kingly drinkes it vp,
Mine eie well knowes what with his gust is greeing,
And to his pallat doth prepare the cup.
  If it be poison'd, tis the lesser sinne,
  That mine eye loues it and doth first beginne.

115

THose lines that I before haue writ doe lie,
Euen those that said I could not loue you deerer,
Yet then my iudgement knew no reason why,
My most full flame should afterwards burne cleerer.
But reckening time, whose milliond accidents
Creepe in twixt vowes, and change decrees of Kings,
Tan sacred beautie, blunt the sharp'st intents,
Diuert strong mindes to th' course of altring things:
Alas why fearing of times tiranie,

Might

4 Seems seeing, but effectually is out;
   For it no form delivers to the heart
   Of bird, of flow'r, or shape, which it doth latch.
   Of his quick objects hath the mind no part,
8 Nor his own vision holds what it doth catch;
   For if it see the rud'st or gentlest sight,
   The most sweet favor or deformèd'st creature,
   The mountain, or the sea, the day, or night,
12 The crow, or dove, it shapes them to your feature.
     Incapable of more, replete with you,
     My most true mind thus maketh m'eyne untrue.

114

   Or whether doth my mind, being crowned with you,
   Drink up the monarch's plague, this flattery?
   Or whether shall I say mine eye saith true,
4 And that your love taught it this alchemy—
   To make of monsters and things indigest
   Such cherubins as your sweet self resemble,
   Creating every bad a perfect best
8 As fast as objects to his beams assemble?
   O 'tis the first, 'tis flatt'ry in my seeing,
   And my great mind most kingly drinks it up.
   Mine eye well knows what with his gust is greeing,
12 And to his palate doth prepare the cup.
     If it be poisoned, 'tis the lesser sin
     That mine eye loves it and doth first begin.

115

   Those lines that I before have writ do lie,
   Ev'n those that said I could not love you dearer.
   Yet then my judgement knew no reason why
4 My most full flame should afterwards burn clearer.
   But reck'ning time, whose millioned accidents
   Creep in 'twixt vows, and change decrees of kings,
   Tan sacred beauty, blunt the sharp'st intents,
8 Divert strong minds to th' course of alt'ring things—
   Alas, why, fearing of time's tyranny,

Might I not then say, now I love you best,
When I was certain o'er incertainty,
12   Crowning the present, doubting of the rest?
   Love is a babe; then might I not say so,
   To give full growth to that which still doth grow.

116

Let me not to the marriage of true minds
Admit impediments. Love is not love
Which alters when it alteration finds,
4   Or bends with the remover to remove.
O no, it is an ever-fixèd mark
That looks on tempests and is never shaken;
It is the star to every wand'ring bark,
8   Whose worth's unknown, although his height be taken.
Love's not time's fool, though rosy lips and cheeks
Within his bending sickle's compass come.
Love alters not with his brief hours and weeks,
12   But bears it out ev'n to the edge of doom.
   If this be error and upon me proved,
   I never writ, nor no man ever loved.

117

Accuse me thus: that I have scanted all
Wherein I should your great deserts repay,
Forgot upon your dearest love to call,
4   Whereto all bonds do tie me day by day;
That I have frequent been with unknown minds,
And giv'n to time your own dear purchased right;
That I have hoisted sail to all the winds
8   Which should transport me farthest from your sight.
Book both my wilfulness and errors down,
And on just proof surmise accumulate;
Bring me within the level of your frown,
12   But shoot not at me in your wakened hate,
   Since my appeal says I did strive to prove
   The constancy and virtue of your love.

Might I not then say now I loue you best,
When I was certaine ore in-certainty,
Crowning the present,doubting of the rest:
   Loue is a Babe , then might I not say so
   To giue full growth to that which still doth grow.

119

LEt me not to the marriage of true mindes
  Admit impediments,loue is not loue
Which alters when it alteration findes,
Or bends with the remouer to remoue.
O no,it is an euer fixed marke
That lookes on tempests and is neuer shaken;
It is the star to euery wandring barke,
Whose worths vnknowne,although his higth be taken.
Lou's not Times foole,though rosie lips and cheeks
Within his bending sickles compasse come,
Loue alters not with his breefe houres and weekes,
But beares it out euen to the edge of doome:
   If this be error and vpon me proued,
   I neuer writ,nor no man euer loued.

117

ACcuse me thus,that I haue scanted all,
  Wherein I should your great deserts repay,
Forgot vpon your dearest loue to call,
Whereto al bonds do tie me day by day,
That I haue frequent binne with vnknown mindes,
And giuen to time your owne deare purchas'd right,
That I haue hoysted saile to al the windes
Which should transport me farthest from your sight.
Booke both my wilfulnesse and errors downe,
And on iust proofe surmise,accumilate,
Bring me within the leuel of your frowne,
But shoote not at me in your wakened hate:
   Since my appeale saies I did striue to prooue
   The constancy and virtue of your loue

118

Like as to make our appetites more keene
With eager compounds we our pallat vrge,
As to preuent our malladies vnseene,
We sicken to shun sicknesse when we purge.
Euen so being full of your nere cloying sweetnesse,
To bitter sawces did I frame my feeding;
And sicke of wel-fare found a kind of meetnesse,
To be diseas'd ere that there was true needing.
Thus pollicie in loue t'anticipate
The ills that were, not grew to faults assured,
And brought to medicine a healthfull state
Which rancke of goodnesse would by ill be cured.
  But thence I learne and find the lesson true,
  Drugs poyson him that so fell sicke of you.

119

What potions haue I drunke of *Syren* teares
Distil'd from Lymbecks foule as hell within,
Applying feares to hopes, and hopes to feares,
Still loosing when I saw my selfe to win?
What wretched errors hath my heart committed,
Whilst it hath thought it selfe so blessed neuer?
How haue mine eies out of their Spheares bene fitted
In the distraction of this madding feuer?
O benefit of ill, now I find true
That better is, by euil still made better.
And ruin'd loue when it is built anew
Growes fairer then at first, more strong, far greater.
  So I returne rebukt to my content,
  And gaine by ills thrise more then I haue spent.

120

That you were once vnkind be-friends mee now,
And for that sorrow, which I then didde feele,
Needes must I vnder my transgression bow,
Vnlesse my Nerues were brasse or hammered steele.
For if you were by my vnkindnesse shaken

As

118

Like as to make our appetites more keen
With eager compounds we our palate urge—
As to prevent our maladies unseen,
4 We sicken to shun sickness when we purge—
Ev'n so, being full of your ne'er-cloying sweetness,
To bitter sauces did I frame my feeding;
And sick of welfare found a kind of meetness
8 To be diseased ere that there was true needing.
Thus policy in love t' anticipate
The ills that were not grew to faults assured,
And brought to medicine a healthful state,
12 Which rank of goodness would by ill be cured.
But thence I learn and find the lesson true,
Drugs poison him that so fell sick of you.

119

What potions have I drunk of siren tears,
Distilled from limbecks foul as hell within—
Applying fears to hopes, and hopes to fears,
4 Still losing when I saw myself to win!
What wretched errors hath my heart committed,
Whilst it hath thought itself so blessèd never!
How have mine eyes out of their spheres been fitted
8 In the distraction of this madding fever!
O benefit of ill, now I find true
That better is by evil still made better;
And ruined love when it is built anew
12 Grows fairer than at first, more strong, far greater.
So I return rebuked to my content,
And gain by ills thrice more than I have spent.

120

That you were once unkind befriends me now,
And for that sorrow which I then did feel
Needs must I under my transgression bow,
4 Unless my nerves were brass or hammered steel.
For if you were by my unkindness shaken,

As I by yours, y' have passed a hell of time,
And I, a tyrant, have no leisure taken
8   To weigh how once I suffered in your crime.
O that our night of woe might have rememb'red
My deepest sense, how hard true sorrow hits,
And soon to you as you to me then tend'red
12   The humble salve which wounded bosoms fits!
But that your trespass now becomes a fee;
Mine ransoms yours, and yours must ransom me.

121

'Tis better to be vile than vile esteemed,
When not to be receives reproach of being,
And the just pleasure lost, which is so deemed,
4   Not by our feeling but by others' seeing.
For why should others' false adulterate eyes
Give salutation to my sportive blood?
Or on my frailties why are frailer spies,
8   Which in their wills count bad what I think good?
No, I am that I am, and they that level
At my abuses reckon up their own;
I may be straight though they themselves be bevel.
12   By their rank thoughts my deeds must not be shown,
Unless this general evil they maintain—
All men are bad and in their badness reign.

122

Thy gift, thy tables, are within my brain
Full charactered with lasting memory,
Which shall above that idle rank remain
4   Beyond all date ev'n to eternity—
Or at the least, so long as brain and heart
Have faculty by nature to subsist—
Till each to razed oblivion yield his part
8   Of thee, thy record never can be missed.
That poor retention could not so much hold,
Nor need I tallies thy dear love to score.
Therefore to give them from me was I bold

As I by yours , y'haue paſt a hell of Time,
And I a tyrant haue no leaſure taken
To waigh how once I ſuffered in your crime.
O that our night of wo might haue remembred
My deepeſt ſence,how hard true ſorrow hits,
And ſoone to you,as you to me then tendred
The humble ſalue,which wounded boſomes fits!
   But that your treſpaſſe now becomes a fee,
   Mine ranſoms yours,and yours muſt ranſome mee,

121

TIS better to be vile then vile eſteemed,
  When not to be,receiues reproach of being,
And the iuſt pleaſure loſt,which is ſo deemed,
Not by our feeling,but by others ſeeing.
For why ſhould others falſe adulterat eyes
Giue ſalutation to my ſportiue blood?
Or on my frailties why are frailer ſpies;
Which in their wils count bad what I think good?
Noe,I am that I am,and they that leuell
At my abuſes,reckon vp their owne,
I may be ſtraight though they them-ſelues be beuel
By their rancke thoughtes,my deedes muſt not be ſhowa.
   Vnleſſe this generall euill they maintaine,
   All men are bad and in their badneſſe raigne.

122.

THy guift,,thy tables,are within my braine
  Full characterd with laſting memory,
Which ſhall aboue that idle rancke remaine
Beyond all date euen to eternity.
Or at the leaſt,ſo long as braine and heart
Haue facultie by nature to ſubſiſt,
Til each to raz'd obliuion yeeld his part
Of thee,thy record neuer can be miſt:
That poore retention could not ſo much hold,
Nor need I tallies thy deare loue to skore,
Therefore to giue them from me was I bold,

To truſt thoſe tables that receaue thee more,
  To keepe an adiunckt to remember thee,
  Were to import forgetfulneſſe in mee.

133

NO! Time, thou ſhalt not boſt that I doe change,
  Thy pyramyds buylt vp with newer might
To me are nothing nouell,nothing ſtrange,
They are but dreſſings of a former ſight:
Our dates are breefe,and therefor we admire,
What thou doſt foyſt vpon vs that is ould,
And rather make them borne to our deſire,
Then thinke that we before haue heard them tould:
Thy regiſters and thee I both defie,
Not wondring at the preſent,nor the paſt,
For thy records,and what we ſee doth lye,
Made more or les by thy continuall haſt:
    This I doe vow and this ſhall euer be,
    I will be true diſpight thy ſyeth and thee.

124

YF my deare loue were but the childe of ſtate,
  It might for fortunes baſterd be vnfathered,
As ſubiect to times loue,or to times hate,
Weeds among weeds,or flowers with flowers gatherd.
No it was buylded far from accident,
It ſuffers not in ſmilinge pomp,nor falls
Vnder the blow of thralled diſcontent,
Whereto th'inuiting time our faſhion calls:
It feares not policy that *Heriticke,*
Which workes on leaſes of ſhort numbred howers,
But all alone ſtands hugely pollitick,
That it nor growes with heat,nor drownes with ſhowres,
    To this I witnes call the foles of time,
    Which die for goodnes,who haue liu'd for crime.

125

VVEr't ought to me I bore the canopy,
  With my extern the outward honoring,

Or

12   To trust those tables that receive thee more.
      To keep an adjunct to remember thee
      Were to import forgetfulness in me.

123

No! Time, thou shalt not boast that I do change.
Thy pyramids built up with newer might
To me are nothing novel, nothing strange;
4   They are but dressings of a former sight.
Our dates are brief, and therefore we admire
What thou dost foist upon us that is old,
And rather make them born to our desire
8   Than think that we before have heard them told.
Thy registers and thee I both defy,
Not wond'ring at the present, nor the past;
For thy recórds, and what we see, doth lie,
12   Made more or less by thy continual haste.
      This I do vow, and this shall ever be,
      I will be true despite thy scythe and thee.

124

If my dear love were but the child of state,
It might for fortune's bastard be unfathered,
As subject to time's love, or to time's hate,
4   Weeds among weeds, or flow'rs with flowers gathered.
No, it was builded far from accident;
It suffers not in smiling pomp, nor falls
Under the blow of thrallèd discontent,
8   Whereto th' inviting time our fashion calls.
It fears not policy, that heretic
Which works on leases of short numb'red hours,
But all alone stands hugely politic,
12   That it nor grows with heat, nor drowns with show'rs.
      To this I witness call the fools of time,
      Which die for goodness, who have lived for crime.

125

Were't ought to me I bore the canopy,
With my extern the outward honoring,

Or laid great bases for eternity,
4   Which proves more short than waste or ruining?
Have I not seen dwellers on form and favor
Lose all and more by paying too much rent
For compound sweet forgoing simple savor,
8   Pitiful thrivers, in their gazing spent?
No, let me be obsequious in thy heart,
And take thou my oblation, poor but free,
Which is not mixed with seconds, knows no art,
12   But mutual render, only me for thee.
    Hence, thou suborned informer! A true soul
    When most impeached stands least in thy control.

126

O thou, my lovely boy, who in thy pow'r
Dost hold time's fickle glass, his sickle hour,
Who hast by waning grown, and therein show'st
4   Thy lovers withering, as thy sweet self grow'st—
If nature, sovereign mistress over wrack,
As thou goest onwards still will pluck thee back,
She keeps thee to this purpose, that her skill
8   May time disgrace, and wretched minute kill.
Yet fear her, O thou minion of her pleasure;
She may detain but not still keep her treasure.
Her audit, though delayed, answered must be,
12   And her quietus is to render thee.

127

In the old age black was not counted fair,
Or if it were it bore not beauty's name.
But now is black beauty's successive heir,
4   And beauty slandered with a bastard shame;
For since each hand hath put on nature's pow'r,
Fairing the foul with art's false borrowed face,
Sweet beauty hath no name, no holy bow'r,
8   But is profaned, if not lives in disgrace.

Or layd great bafes for eternity,
Which proues more fhort then waft or ruining?
Haue I not feene dwellers on forme and fauor
Lofe all, and more by paying too much rent
For compound fweet; Forgoing fimple fauor,
Pittifull thriuors in their gazing fpent.
Noe, let me be obfequious in thy heart,
And take thou my oblacion, poore but free,
Which is not mixt with feconds, knows no art,
But mutuall render onely me for thee.
        Hence, thou fubbornd *Informer*, a trew foule
        When moft impeacht, ftands leaft in thy controule.

126

O Thou my louely Boy who in thy power,
    Doeft hould times fickle glaffe.his fickle, hower:
Who haft by wayning growne, and therein fhou'ft,
Thy louers withering, as thy fweet felfe grow'ft.
If Nature(foueraine mifteres ouer wrack)
As thou goeft onwards ftill will plucke thee backe,
She keepes thee to this purpofe, that her skill.
May time difgrace, and wretched mynuit kill.
Yet feare her O thou minnion of her pleafure,
She may detaine, but not ftill keepe her trefurel
Her *Audite*(though delayd)anfwer'd muft be,
And her *Quietus* is to render thee.
        (   )
        (   )

127

IN the ould age blacke was not counted faire,
    Or if it weare it bore not beauties name:
But now is blacke beauties fucceffiue heire,
And Beautie flanderd with a baftard fhame,
For fince each hand hath put on Natures power,
Fairing the foule with Arts faulfe borrow'd face,
Sweet beauty hath no name no holy boure,
But is prophan'd, if not liues in difgrace,

Therefore

Therefore my Misterſſe eyes are Rauen blacke,
Her eyes ſo ſuted,and they mourners ſeeme,
At ſuch who not borne faire no beauty lack,
Slandring Creation with a falſe eſteeme,
　　Yet ſo they mourne becomming of their woe,
　　That euery toung ſaies beauty ſhould looke ſo.

128

HOw oft when thou my muſike muſike playſt,
Vpon that bleſſed wood whoſe motion ſounds
With thy ſweet fingers when thou gently ſwayſt,
The wiry concord that mine eare confounds,
Do I enuie thoſe Iackes that nimble leape,
To kiſſe the tender inward of thy hand,
Whilſt my poore lips which ſhould that harueſt reape,
At the woods bouldnes by thee bluſhing ſtand.
To be ſo tikled they would change their ſtate,
And ſituation with thoſe dancing chips,
Ore whome their fingers walke with gentle gate,
Making dead wood more bleſt then liuing lips,
　　Since ſaufie Iackes ſo happy are in this,
　　Giue them their fingers,me thy lips to kiſſe.

129

TH'expence of Spirit in a waſte of ſhame
Is luſt in action,and till action , luſt
Is periurd,murdrous,blouddy full of blame,
Sauage,extreame,rude,cruell,not to truſt,
Inioyd no ſooner but diſpiſed ſtraight,
Paſt reaſon hunted, and no ſooner had
Paſt reaſon hated as a ſwollowed bayt,
On purpoſe layd to make the taker mad.
Made In purſut and in poſſeſſion ſo,
Had,hauing,and in queſt,to haue extreame,
A bliſſe in proofe and proud and very wo,
Before a ioy propoſd behind a dreame,
　　All this the world well knowes yet none knowes well,
　　To ſhun the heauen that leads men to this hell.

My

Therefore my mistress' eyes are raven black,
Her eyes so suited, and they mourners seem
At such who, not born fair, no beauty lack,
12   Sland'ring creation with a false esteem.
    Yet so they mourn becoming of their woe,
    That every tongue says beauty should look so.

128

How oft, when thou my music music play'st
Upon that blessèd wood whose motion sounds
With thy sweet fingers when thou gently sway'st
4   The wiry concord that mine ear confounds,
Do I envý those jacks that nimble leap
To kiss the tender inward of thy hand,
Whilst my poor lips, which should that harvest reap,
8   At the wood's boldness by thee blushing stand.
To be so tickled they would change their state
And situation with those dancing chips,
O'er whom thy fingers walk with gentle gait,
12   Making dead wood more blest than living lips.
    Since saucy jacks so happy are in this,
    Give them thy fingers, me thy lips to kiss.

129

Th' expense of spirit in a waste of shame
Is lust in action, and till action lust
Is perjured, murd'rous, bloody, full of blame,
4   Savage, extreme, rude, cruel, not to trust,
Enjoyed no sooner but despisèd straight,
Past reason hunted, and no sooner had,
Past reason hated as a swallowed bait,
8   On purpose laid to make the taker mad;
Mad in pursuit, and in possession so,
Had, having, and in quest to have, extreme,
A bliss in proof, and proved, a very woe,
12   Before, a joy proposed, behind, a dream.
    All this the world well knows, yet none knows well
    To shun the heav'n that leads men to this hell.

130

My mistress' eyes are nothing like the sun—
Coral is far more red than her lips' red—
If snow be white, why then her breasts are dun—
4   If hairs be wires, black wires grow on her head:
I have seen roses damasked, red and white,
But no such roses see I in her cheeks,
And in some pérfumes is there more delight
8   Than in the breath that from my mistress reeks.
I love to hear her speak, yet well I know
That music hath a far more pleasing sound.
I grant I never saw a goddess go;
12   My mistress when she walks treads on the ground.
    And yet by heav'n I think my love as rare
    As any she belied with false compare.

131

Thou art as tyrannous, so as thou art,
As those whose beauties proudly make them cruel;
For well thou know'st to my dear doting heart
4   Thou art the fairest and most precious jewel.
Yet in good faith some say that thee behold
Thy face hath not the pow'r to make love groan;
To say they err I dare not be so bold,
8   Although I swear it to myself alone.
And to be sure that is not false I swear
A thousand groans but thinking on thy face
One on another's neck do witness bear
12   Thy black is fairest in my judgement's place.
    In nothing art thou black save in thy deeds,
    And thence this slander as I think proceeds.

132

Thine eyes I love, and they as pitying me,
Knowing thy heart torment me with disdain,
Have put on black, and loving mourners be,
4   Looking with pretty ruth upon my pain.

130

MY Miſtres eyes are nothing like the Sunne,
Currall is farre more red,then her lips red,
If ſnow be white,why then her breſts are dun:
If haires be wiers,black wiers grow on her head:
I haue ſcene Roſes damaskt,red and white,
But no ſuch Roſes ſee I in her cheekes,
And in ſome perfumes is there more delight,
Then in the breath that from my Miſtres reekes.
I loue to heare her ſpeake,yet well I know,
That Muſicke hath a farre more pleaſing ſound:
I graunt I neuer ſaw a goddeſſe goe,
My Miſtres when ſhee walkes treads on the ground.
　　And yet by heauen I thinke my loue as rare,
　　As any ſhe beli'd with falſe compare.

131

THou art as tiranous,ſo as thou art,
As thoſe whoſe beauties proudly make them cruell;
For well thou know'ſt to my deare doting hart
Thou art the faireſt and moſt precious Iewell.
Yet in good faith ſome ſay that thee behold,
Thy face hath not the power to make loue grone;
To ſay they erre,I dare not be ſo bold,
Although I ſweare it to my ſelfe alone.
And to be ſure that is not falſe I ſweare
A thouſand grones but thinking on thy face,
One on anothers necke do witneſſe beare
Thy blacke is faireſt in my iudgements place.
　　In nothing art thou blacke ſaue in thy deeds,
And thence this ſlaunder as I thinke proceeds.

132

THine eies I loue,and they as pittying me,
Knowing thy heart torment me with diſdaine,
Haue put on black,and louing mourners bee,
Looking with pretty ruth vpon my paine.

And

And truly not the morning Sun of Heauen
Better becomes the gray cheeks of th' Eaft,
Nor that full Starre that vfhers in the Eauen
Doth halfe that glory to the fober Weft
As thofe two morning eyes become thy face:
O let it then as well befeeme thy heart
To mourne for me fince mourning doth thee grace,
And fute thy pitty like in euery part.
   Then will I fweare beauty her felfe is blacke,
    And all they foule that thy complexion lacke.

133

BEfhrew that heart that makes my heart to groane
For that deepe wound it giues my friend and me;
I'ft not ynough to torture me alone,
But flaue to flauery my fweet'ft friend muft be.
Me from my felfe thy cruell eye hath taken,
And my next felfe thou harder haft ingroffed,
Of him,my felfe,and thee I am forfaken,
A torment thrice three-fold thus to be croffed:
Prifon my heart in thy fteele bofomes warde,
But then my friends heart let my poore heart bale,
Who ere keepes me,let my heart be his garde,
Thou canft not then vfe rigor in my Iaile.
   And yet thou wilt,for I being pent in thee,
    Perforce am thine and all that is in me.

134

SO now I haue confeft that he is thine,
And I my felfe am morgag'd to thy will,
My felfe Ile forfeit,fo that other mine,
Thou wilt reftore to be my comfort ftill:
But thou wilt not,nor he will not be free,
For thou art couetous,and he is kinde,
He learnd but furetie-like to write for me,
Vnder that bond that him as faft doth binde.
The ftatute of thy beauty thou wilt take,
Thou vfurer that put'ft forth all to vfe,

                        And

And truly not the morning sun of heav'n
Better becomes the gray cheeks of the east,
Nor that full star that ushers in the ev'n
8 Doth half that glory to the sober west
As those two mourning eyes become thy face.
O let it then as well beseem thy heart
To mourn for me, since mourning doth thee grace,
12 And suit thy pity like in every part.
Then will I swear beauty herself is black,
And all they foul that thy complexion lack.

befitting or suitable

133

Beshrew that heart that makes my heart to groan
For that deep wound it gives my friend and me.
Is't not enough to torture me alone,
4 But slave to slavery my sweet'st friend must be?
Me from myself thy cruel eye hath taken,
And my next self thou harder hast engrossed.
Of him, myself, and thee, I am forsaken—
8 A torment thrice threefold thus to be crossed.
Prison my heart in thy steel bosom's ward,
But then my friend's heart let my poor heart bail;
Whoe'er keeps me, let my heart be his guard,
12 Thou canst not then use rigor in my jail.
And yet thou wilt, for I being pent in thee
Perforce am thine, and all that is in me.

134

So now I have confessed that he is thine,
And I myself am mortgaged to thy will,
Myself I'll forfeit, so that other mine
4 Thou wilt restore to be my comfort still.
But thou wilt not, nor he will not be free,
For thou art covetous, and he is kind;
He learned but surety-like to write for me,
8 Under that bond that him as fast doth bind.
The statute of thy beauty thou wilt take,
Thou usurer that put'st forth all to use,

And sue a friend came debtor for my sake;
12 So him I lose through my unkind abuse.
    Him have I lost; thou hast both him and me;
    He pays the whole; and yet am I not free.

135

Whoever hath her wish, thou hast thy will,
And will to boot, and will in overplus;
More than enough am I that vex thee still,
4 To thy sweet will making addition thus.
Wilt thou, whose will is large and spacious,
Not once vouchsafe to hide my will in thine?
Shall will in others seem right gracious,
8 And in my will no fair acceptance shine?
The sea, all water, yet receives rain still,
And in abundance addeth to his store;
So thou being rich in will add to thy will
12 One will of mine, to make thy large will more.
    Let no unkind, no fair beseechers kill;
    Think all but one, and me in that one will.

136

If thy soul check thee that I come so near,
Swear to thy blind soul that I was thy will,
And will thy soul knows is admitted there;
4 Thus far for love my love-suit sweet fulfil.
Will will fulfill the treasure of thy love,
Ay fill it full with wills, and my will one.
In things of great receipt with ease we prove,
8 Among a number one is reckoned none.
Then in the number let me pass untold,
Though in thy store's account I one must be,
For nothing hold me, so it please thee hold
12 That nothing me, a something sweet to thee.
    Make but my name thy love, and love that still,
    And then thou lov'st me for my name is Will.

137

Thou blind fool love, what dost thou to mine eyes,

And fue a friend,came debter for my fake,
So him I loofe through my vnkinde abufe.
  Him haue I loft, thou haft both him and me,
  He paies the whole,and yet am I not free.

135

WHo euer hath her wifh,thou haft thy *Will*,
  And *Will* too boote,and *Will* in ouer-plus,
More then enough am I that vexe thee ftill,
To thy fweet will making addition thus.
Wilt thou whofe will is large and fpatious,
Not once vouchfafe to hide my will in thine,
Shall will in others feeme right gracious,
And in my will no faire acceptance fhine:
The fea all water,yet receiues raine ftill,
And in aboundance addeth to his ftore,
So thou beeing rich in *Will* adde to thy *Will*,
One will of mine to make thy large *Will* more.
  Let no vnkinde,no faire befeechers kill,
  Thinke all but one,and me in that one *Will*.

136

IF thy foule check thee that I come fo neere,
  Sweare to thy blind foule that I was thy *Will*,
And will thy foule knowes is admitted there,
Thus farre for loue, my loue-fute fweet fullfill.
Will, will fulfill the treafure of thy loue,
I fill it full with wils,and my will one,
In things of great receit with cafe we prooue,
Among a number one is reckon'd none.
Then in the number let me paffe vntold,
Though in thy ftores account I one muft be,
For nothing hold me,fo it pleafe thee hold,
That nothing me,a fome-thing fweet to thee.
  Make but my name thy loue,and loue that ftill,
  And then thou loueft me for my name is *Will*.

137

THou blinde foole loue,what dooft thou to mine eyes,
                      I   That

That they behold and fee not what they fee :
They know what beautie is,fee where it lyes,
Yet what the beft is,take the worft to be.
If eyes corrupt by ouer-partiall lookes,
Be anchord in the baye where all men ride,
Why of eyes falfchood haft thou forged hookes,
Whereto the iudgement of my heart is tide?
Why fhould my heart thinke that a feuerall plot,
Which my heart knowes the wide worlds common place?
Or mine eyes feeing this,fay this is not
To put faire truth vpon fo foule a face,
    In things right true my heart and eyes haue erred,
    And to this falfe plague are they now tranfferred.

138

WHen my loue fweares that fhe is made of truth,
    I do beleeue her though I know fhe lyes,
That fhe might thinke me fome vntuterd youth,
Vnlearned in the worlds falfe fubtilties.
Thus vainely thinking that fhe thinkes me young,
Although fhe knowes my dayes are paft the beft,
Simply I credit her falfe fpeaking tongue,
On both fides thus is fimple truth fupprest :
But wherefore fayes fhe not fhe is vniuft ?
And wherefore fay not I that I am old ?
O loues beft habit is in feeming truft,
And age in loue,loues not t'haue yeares told.
    Therefore I lye with her,and fhe with me,
    And in our faults by lyes we flattered be.

139

O Call not me to iuftifie the wrong,
    That thy vnkindneffe layes vpon my heart,
Wound me not with thine eye but with thy toung,
Vfe power with power,and flay me not by Art,
Tell me thou lou'ft elfe-where;but in my fight,
Deare heart forbeare to glance thine eye afide,
What needft thou wound with cunning when thy might

Is

That they behold and see not what they see?
They know what beauty is, see where it lies,
4   Yet what the best is take the worst to be.
If eyes corrupt by over-partial looks
Be anchored in the bay where all men ride,
Why of eyes' falsehood hast thou forgèd hooks,
8   Whereto the judgement of my heart is tied?
Why should my heart think that a several plot,
Which my heart knows the wide world's common place?
Or mine eyes, seeing this, say this is not
12   To put fair truth upon so foul a face?
    In things right true my heart and eyes have erred,
    And to this false plague are they now transferred.

138

When my love swears that she is made of truth, *good*
I do believe her though I know she lies,
That she might think me some untutored youth,
4   Unlearnèd in the world's false subtleties.
Thus vainly thinking that she thinks me young,
Although she knows my days are past the best,
Simply I credit her false-speaking tongue:
8   On both sides thus is simple truth suppressed.
But wherefore says she not she is unjust?
And wherefore say not I that I am old?
O love's best habit is in seeming trust,
12   And age in love loves not to have years told.
    Therefore I lie with her, and she with me,
    And in our faults by lies we flattered be.

139

O call not me to justify the wrong
That thy unkindness lays upon my heart;
Wound me not with thine eye but with thy tongue;
4   Use pow'r with pow'r, and slay me not by art.
Tell me thou lov'st elsewhére; but in my sight,
Dear heart, forbear to glance thine eye aside.
What need'st thou wound with cunning when thy might

8   Is more than my o'erpressed defence can bide?
Let me excuse thee; ah, my love well knows,
Her pretty looks have been mine enemies,
And therefore from my face she turns my foes,
12   That they elsewhére might dart their injuries.
      Yet do not so, but since I am near slain,
      Kill me outríght with looks, and rid my pain.

140

Be wise as thou art cruel, do not press
My tongue-tied patience with too much disdain:
Lest sorrow lend me words, and words express
4   The manner of my pity-wanting pain.
If I might teach thee wit, better it were,
Though not to love, yet, love, to tell me so;
As testy sick men, when their deaths be near,
8   No news but health from their physicians know.
For if I should despair I should grow mad,
And in my madness might speak ill of thee.
Now this ill-wresting world is grown so bad,
12   Mad sland'rers by mad ears believèd be.
      That I may not be so, nor thou belied,
      Bear thine eyes straight, though thy proud heart go wide.

141

In faith I do not love thee with mine eyes,
For they in thee a thousand errors note;
But 'tis my heart that loves what they despise,
4   Who in despite of view is pleased to dote.
Nor are mine ears with thy tongue's tune delighted;
Nor tender feeling to base touches prone,
Nor taste, nor smell, desire to be invited
8   To any sensual feast with thee alone.
But my five wits, nor my five senses can
Dissuade one foolish heart from serving thee,
Who leaves unswayed the likeness of a man,
12   Thy proud heart's slave and vassal wretch to be.
      Only my plague thus far I count my gain,
      That she that makes me sin awards me pain.

Is more then my ore-preſt deſence can bide?
Let me excuſe thee,ah my loue well knowes,
Her prettie lookes haue beene mine enemies,
And therefore from my face ſhe turnes my foes,
That they elſe-where might dart their iniuries :
　　Yet do not ſo,but ſince I am neere ſlaine,
　　Kill me out-right with lookes,and rid my paine.

140

BE wiſe as thou art cruell,do not preſſe
My toung tide patience with too much diſdaine :
Leaſt ſorrow lend me words and words expreſſe,
The manner of my pittie wanting paine.
If I might teach thee witte better it weare,
Though not to loue,yet loue to tell me ſo,
As teſtie ſick-men when their deaths be neere,
No newes but health from their Phiſitions know.
For if I ſhould diſpaire I ſhould grow madde,
And in my madneſſe might ſpeake ill of thee,
Now this ill wreſting world is growne ſo bad,
Madde ſlanderers by madde eares beleeued be.
　　That I may not be ſo, nor thou be lyde,　　　　(wide.
　　Beare thine eyes ſtraight , though thy proud heart goe

141

IN faith I doe not loue thee with mine eyes,
For they in thee a thouſand errors note,
But 'tis my heart that loues what they diſpiſe,
Who in diſpight of view is pleaſd to dote.
Nor are mine eares with thy toungs tune delighted,
Nor tender feeling to baſe touches prone,
Nor taſte, nor ſmell, deſire to be inuited
To any ſenſuall feaſt with thee alone :
But my fiue wits,nor my fiue ſences can
Diſwade one fooliſh heart from ſeruing thee,
Who leaues vnſwai'd the likeneſſe of a man,
Thy proud hearts ſlaue and vaſſall wretch to be :
　　Onely my plague thus farre I count my gaine,
　　That ſhe that makes me ſinne,awards me paine.

142

LOue is my sinne, and thy deare vertue hate,
Hate of my sinne, grounded on sinfull louing,
O but with mine, compare thou thine owne state,
And thou shalt finde it merrits not reproouing,
Or if it do, not from those lips of thine,
That haue prophan'd their scarlet ornaments,
And seald false bonds of loue as oft as mine,
Robd others beds reuenues of their rents.
Be it lawfull I loue thee as thou lou'st those,
Whome thine eyes wooe as mine importune thee,
Roote pittie in thy heart that when it growes,
Thy pitty may deserue to pittied bee.
    If thou doost seeke to haue what thou doost hide,
    By selfe example mai'st thou be denide.

143

LOe as a carefull huswife runnes to catch,
One of her fethered creatures broake away,
Sets downe her babe and makes all swift dispatch
In pursuit of the thing she would haue stay:
Whilst her neglected child holds her in chace,
Cries to catch her whose busie care is bent,
To follow that which flies before her face:
Not prizing her poore infants discontent;
So runst thou after that which flies from thee,
Whilst I thy babe chace thee a farre behind,
But if thou catch thy hope turne back to me:
And play the mothers part kisse me, be kind.
    So will I pray that thou maist haue thy *Will*,
    If thou turne back and my loude crying still.

144

TWo loues I haue of comfort and dispaire,
Which like two spirits do sugiest me still,
The better angell is a man right faire:
The worser spirit a woman collour'd il.
To win me soone to hell my femall euill,

Tempteth

142

Love is my sin, and thy dear virtue hate,
Hate of my sin, grounded on sinful loving.
O but with mine compare thou thine own state,
4   And thou shalt find it merits not reproving,
Or if it do, not from those lips of thine,
That have profaned their scarlet ornaments,
And sealed false bonds of love as oft as mine,
8   Robbed others' beds' revénues of their rents.
Be it lawful I love thee as thou lov'st those
Whom thine eyes woo as mine impórtune thee.
Root pity in thy heart, that when it grows,
12   Thy pity may deserve to pitied be.
    If thou dost seek to have what thou dost hide,
    By self-example mayst thou be denied.

143

Lo, as a careful housewife runs to catch
One of her feathered creatures broke away,
Sets down her babe, and makes all swift dispatch
4   In púrsuit of the thing she would have stay—
Whilst her neglected child holds her in chase,
Cries to catch her whose busy care is bent
To follow that which flies before her face,
8   Not prizing her poor infant's discontent:
So run'st thou after that which flies from thee,
Whilst I, thy babe, chase thee afar behind;
But if thou catch thy hope, turn back to me,
12   And play the mother's part, kiss me, be kind.
    So will I pray that thou mayst have thy will,
    If thou turn back and my loud crying still.

144

Two loves I have of comfort and despair,
Which like two spirits do suggest me still;
The better angel is a man right fair,
4   The worser spirit a woman coloured ill.
To win me soon to hell, my female evil

Tempteth my better angel from my side,
And would corrupt my saint to be a devil,
8   Wooing his purity with her foul pride.
And, whether that my angel be turn'd fiend,
Suspect I may, yet not directly tell,
But being both from me both to each friend,
12   I guess one angel in another's hell.
      Yet this shall I ne'er know, but live in doubt,
      Till my bad angel fire my good one out.

145

Those lips that love's own hand did make
Breathed forth the sound that said, I hate,
To me that languished for her sake.
4   But when she saw my woeful state
Straight in her heart did mercy come,
Chiding that tongue that ever sweet
Was used in giving gentle doom;
8   And taught it thus anew to greet:
I hate she altered with an end,
That followed it as gentle day
Doth follow night, who like a fiend
12   From heav'n to hell is flown away.
      I hate from hate away she threw,
      And saved my life saying, not you.

146

Poor soul, the center of my sinful earth,
. . . . these rebel pow'rs that thee array,
Why dost thou pine within and suffer dearth,
4   Painting thy outward walls so costly gay?
Why so large cost, having so short a lease,
Dost thou upon thy fading mansion spend?
Shall worms, inheritors of this excess,
8   Eat up thy charge? Is this thy body's end?
Then, soul, live thou upon thy servant's loss,
And let that pine to aggravate thy store:
Buy terms divine in selling hours of dross;

Tempteth my better angel from my fight,
And would corrupt my faint to be a diuel:
Wooing his purity with her fowle pride.
And whether that my angel be turn'd finde,
Suspect I may, yet not directly tell,
But being both from me both to each friend,
I geffe one angel in an others hel.
   Yet this fhal I nere know but liue in doubt,
   Till my bad angel fire my good one out.

145

THofe lips that Loues owne hand did make,
   Breath'd forth the found that faid I hate,
To me that languifht for her fake:
But when fhe faw my wofull ftate,
Straight in her heart did mercie come,
Chiding that tongue that euer fweet,
Was vfde in giuing gentle dome:
And tought it thus a new to greete:
I hate fhe alterd with an end,
That follow'd it as gentle day,
Doth follow night who like a fiend
From heauen to hell is flowne away.
   I hate, from hate away fhe threw,
   And fau'd my life faying not you.

146

POore foule the center of my finfull earth,
   My finfull earth thefe rebbell powres that thee array,
Why doft thou pine within and fuffer dearth?
Painting thy outward walls fo coftlie gay?
Why fo large coft hauing fo fhort a leafe,
Doft thou vpon thy fading manfion fpend?
Shall wormes inheritors of this exceffe,
Eate vp thy charge? is this thy bodies end?
Then foule liue thou vpon thy feruants loffe,
And let that pine to aggrauat thy ftore;
Buy tearmes diuine in felling houres of droffe:

Within

Within be fed, without be rich no more,
So shalt thou-feed on death,that feeds on men,
And death once dead,ther's no more dying then,

147

MY loue is as a feauer longing still,
For that which longer nurseth the disease,
Feeding on that which doth preserue the ill,
Th'vncertaine sicklie appetite to please:
My reason the Phisition to my loue,
Angry that his prescriptions are not kept
Hath left me,and I desperate now approoue,
Desire is death,which Phisick did except.
Past cure I am,now Reason is past care,
And frantick madde with euer-more vnrest,
My thoughts and my discourse as mad mens are,
At randon from the truth vainely exprest.
　　For I haue sworne thee faire,and thought thee bright,
　　Who art as black as hell,as darke as night.

148

O Me! what eyes hath loue put in my head,
Which haue no correspondence with true sight,
Or if they haue,where is my iudgment fled,
That censures falsely what they see aright?
If that be faire whereon my false eyes dote,
What meanes the world to say it is not so?
If it be not,then loue doth well denote,
Loues eye is not so true as all mens:no,
How can it? O how can loues eye be true,
That is so vext with watching and with teares?
No maruaile then though I mistake my view,
The sunne it selfe sees not, till heauen cleeres.
　　O cunning loue,with teares-thou keepst me blinde,
　　Least eyes well seeing thy foule faults should finde.

149

CAnst thou O cruell,say I loue thee not,
When I against my selfe with thee pertake:

Doe

12   Within be fed, without be rich no more.
    So shalt thou feed on death, that feeds on men,
    And death once dead, there's no more dying then.

147

    My love is as a fever, longing still
    For that which longer nurseth the disease,
    Feeding on that which doth preserve the ill,
4   Th' uncertain sickly appetite to please.
    My reason, the physician to my love,
    Angry that his prescriptions are not kept,
    Hath left me, and I desp'rate now approve
8   Desire is death, which physic did except.
    Past cure I am, now reason is past care,
    And frantic mad with evermore unrest,
    My thoughts and my discourse as madmen's are,
12   At random from the truth vainly expressed;
      For I have sworn thee fair, and thought thee bright,
      Who art as black as hell, as dark as night.

148

    O me! what eyes hath love put in my head,
    Which have no correspondence with true sight!
    Or if they have, where is my judgment fled,
4   That censures falsely what they see aright?
    If that be fair whereon my false eyes dote,
    What means the world to say it is not so?
    If it be not, then love doth well denote,
8   Love's eye is not so true as all men's: no.
    How can it? O how can love's eye be true,
    That is so vexed with watching and with tears?
    No marvel then though I mistake my view;
12   The sun itself sees not till heaven clears.
      O cunning love, with tears thou keep'st me blind,
      Lest eyes, well seeing, thy foul faults should find.

149

    Canst thou, O cruel, say I love thee not,
    When I against myself with thee partake?

Do I not think on thee when I forgot
4   Am of myself all tyrant for thy sake?
Who hateth thee that I do call my friend?
On whom frown'st thou that I do fawn upon?
Nay, if thou lour'st on me, do I not spend
8   Revenge upon myself with present moan?
What merit do I in myself respect,
That is so proud thy service to despise,
When all my best doth worship thy defect,
12   Commanded by the motion of thine eyes?
But, love, hate on, for now I know thy mind;
Those that can see thou lov'st, and I am blind.

150

O from what pow'r hast thou this pow'rful might,
With insufficiency my heart to sway?
To make me give the lie to my true sight,
4   And swear that brightness doth not grace the day?
Whence hast thou this becoming of things ill,
That in the very refuse of thy deeds
There is such strength and warrantise of skill,
8   That, in my mind, thy worst all best exceeds?
Who taught thee how to make me love thee more,
The more I hear and see just cause of hate?
O, though I love what others do abhor,
12   With others thou shouldst not abhor my state:
If thy unworthiness raised love in me,
More worthy I to be belov'd of thee.

151

Love is too young to know what conscience is,
Yet who knows not conscience is born of love?
Then, gentle cheater, urge not my amiss,
4   Lest guilty of my faults thy sweet self prove.
For thou betraying me, I do betray
My nobler part to my gross body's treason;
My soul doth tell my body that he may
8   Triumph in love; flesh stays no farther reason,

Doe I not thinke on thee when I forgot
Am of my selfe, all tirant for thy sake?
Who hateth thee that I doe call my friend,
On whom froun'st thou that I doe saune vpon,
Nay if thou lowrst on me doe I not spend.
Reuenge vpon my selfe with present mone?
What merrit do I in my selfe respect,
That is so proude thy seruice to dispise,
When all my best doth worship thy defect,
Commanded by the motion of thine eyes.
   But loue hate on for now I know thy minde,
   Those that can see thou lou'st,and I am blind.

150

OH from what powre hast thou this powrefull might,
  VVith insufficiency my heart to sway,
To make me giue the lie to my true sight,
And swere that brightnesse doth not grace the day?
Whence hast thou this becomming of things il,
That in the very refuse of thy deeds,
There is such strength and warranti'e of skill,
That in my minde thy worst all best exceeds?
Who taught thee how to make me loue thee more,
The more I heare and see iust cause of hate,
Oh though I loue what others doe abhor,
VVith others thou shouldst not abhor my state.
   If thy vnworthinesse raisd loue in me,
   More worthy I to be belou'd of thee.

151

LOue is too young to know what conscience is,
  Yet who knowes not conscience is borne of loue;
Then gentle cheater vrge not my amisse,
Least guilty of my faults thy sweet selfe proue.
For thou betraying me, I doe betray
My nobler part to my grose bodies treason,
My soule doth tell my body that he may,
Triumph in loue,flesh staies no farther reason,

                                                                But

But ryfing at thy name doth point out thee,
As his triumphant prize,proud of this pride,
He is contented thy poore drudge to be
To ftand in thy affaires,fall by thy fide.
   No want of confcience hold it that I call,
   Her loue,for whofe deare loue I rife and fall.

152

IN louing thee thou know'ft I am forfworne,
But thou art twice forfworne to me loue fwearing,
In act thy bed-vow broake and new faith torne,
In vowing new hate after new loue bearing:
But why of two othes breach doe I accufe thee,
When I breake twenty:I am periur'd moft,
For all my vowes are othes but to mifufe thee:
And all my honeft faith in thee is loft.
For I haue fworne deepe othes of thy deepe kindneffe:
Othes of thy loue,thy truth,thy conftancie,
And to inlighten thee gaue eyes to blindneffe,.
Or made them fwere againft the thing they fee.
   For I haue fworne thee faire:more periurde eye,
   To fwere againft the truth fo foule a lie.

153

CVpid laid by his brand and fell a fleepe,
A maide of *Dyans* this aduantage found,
And his loue-kindling fire did quickly fteepe
In a could vallie-fountaine of that ground:
Which borrowd from this holie fire of loue,
A dateleffe liuely heat ftill to indure,
And grew a feething bath which yet men proue,
Againft ftrang malladies a foueraigne cure:
But at my miftres eie loues brand new fired,
The boy for triall needes would touch my breft,
I fick withall the helpe of bath defired,
And thether hied a fad diftemperd gueft.
   But found no cure,the bath for my helpe lies,
   Where *Cupid* got new fire;my miftres eye.

But rising at thy name doth point out thee,
As his triumphant prize—proud of this pride,
He is contented thy poor drudge to be,
12   To stand in thy affairs, fall by thy side.
     No want of conscience hold it that I call
     Her love for whose dear love I rise and fall.

152

In loving thee thou know'st I am forsworn,
But thou art twice forsworn to me love swearing,
In act thy bed-vow broke and new faith torn
4   In vowing new hate after new love bearing.
But why of two oaths' breach do I accuse thee,
When I break twenty? I am perjured most,
For all my vows are oaths but to misuse thee,
8   And all my honest faith in thee is lost.
For I have sworn deep oaths of thy deep kindness,
Oaths of thy love, thy truth, thy constancy,
And to enlighten thee gave eyes to blindness,
12   Or made them swear against the thing they see,
     For I have sworn thee fair: more perjured eye,
     To swear against the truth so foul a lie.

153

Cupid laid by his brand and fell asleep.
A maid of Dian's this advantage found,
And his love-kindling fire did quickly steep
4   In a cold valley-fountain of that ground,
Which borrowed from this holy fire of love
A dateless lively heat, still to endure,
And grew a seething bath which yet men prove
8   Against strange maladies a sovereign cure.
But at my mistress' eye love's brand new-fired,
The boy for trial needs would touch my breast.
I sick withal the help of bath desired,
12   And thither hied, a sad distempered guest,
     But found no cure; the bath for my help lies
     Where Cupid got new fire—my mistress' eye.

154

The little love-god lying once asleep
Laid by his side his heart-inflaming brand,
Whilst many nymphs that vowed chaste life to keep
4   Came tripping by, but in her maiden hand
The fairest votary took up that fire,
Which many legions of true hearts had warmed;
And so the general of hot desire
8   Was sleeping by a virgin hand disarmed.
This brand she quenchèd in a cool well by,
Which from love's fire took heat perpetual,
Growing a bath and healthful remedy
12   For men diseased; but I, my mistress' thrall,
    Came there for cure, and this by that I prove:
    Love's fire heats water, water cools not love.

154

THe little Loue-God lying once a sleepe,
  Laid by his side his heart inflaming brand,
Whilst many Nymphes that vou'd chast life to keep,
Came tripping by,but in her maiden hand,
The fayrest votary tooke vp that fire,
Which many Legions of true hearts had warm'd,
And so the Generall of hot desire,
Was sleeping by a Virgin hand disarm'd.
This brand she quenched in a coole Well by,
Which from loues fire tooke heat perpetuall,
Growing a bath and healthfull remedy,
For men diseasd,but I my Mistrisse thrall,
    Came there for cure and this by that I proue,
    Loues fire heates water,water cooles not loue.

FINIS.

K   A

Commentary

SONNET 1

Katharine M. Wilson has recently explored the interrelation of sonnets 1–17 and "arguments from a very lengthy, learned, and earnest 'Epistle to persuade a young gentleman to marriage,' which was written by Erasmus and had appeared in Thomas Wilson's [widely influential] *The Arte of Rhetorique* in 1553" (*Shakespeare's Sugared Sonnets* [London and N.Y., 1974], pp. 146–67); for earlier comment on Erasmus as model, see *Variorum* I, 7 and II, 192.

2. *That* so that. *thereby* (1) by means of fairest creatures (echoing the use of "by" in the locution "have a child by"); (2) by means of increase. *beauty's rose* (1) the bloom of youth (beauty's prime); (2) the most perfect example of beauty (see 109.14, note); and, by virtue of the image evoked, perhaps (3) the beauty of the rose. (The vagueness and ambiguity of *beauty's rose* opens the way for a rhetorically useful blurring of distinction between a *rose*—one flower, which blooms and dies—and a rosebush, which goes on generating new flowers indefinitely.) *rose* Q has *rose* capitalized and in italics; numerous commentators have pounced on this to read special emblematic significance and biographical hints into what is probably a typesetter's whim; see *Variorum* II, 8 and the discussion of random capitalization and italics, Preface, pp. xvii–xviii.

2,3. *thereby*, *by* Note the balance of conflicting forces embodied in the two "by's."

3–4. As a reader comes upon *But*, it can momentarily seem to mean "except" and to introduce a modification of *rose might never die*: "might never die except in so far as the riper should . . . decease." That reading, which tests and discredits the possibility of immortality proffered by line 2, evaporates when line 4 reveals the larger construction of lines 2–4: ". . . never die, but instead its heir might bear its memory," which the logic of the speaker's argument invites us to clarify syntactically and flesh out so as to understand lines 3 and 4 as if they said "but instead, when the elder bloom (or parent bush) withers, buds (or seedlings or rooted slips) live on, and thus in a way perpetuate the life of the withered bloom (and/or of the parent bush)." Quatrain 1 deals with two different kinds of mortality and immortality, one simple (each individual mortal creature lives briefly and dies) and one complex (in recreating themselves individual mortal creatures can be said to live on in their seed). The persuasiveness and comfort of the logic through which immortality is possible is nothing as compared to the inevitable despair inherent in the fact of individual mortality. This quatrain, designed to recommend and advertise the potency of the idea that mortals are immortal in their generation, is strengthened by including and overwhelming the fact it attempts to combat (the beauty of each beautiful creature is mortal, each must *by time decease*); when the sentence emerges from the muddy syntax of line 3 into the relative clarity of line 4, the assertion that immortality is possible through progeny overwhelms the depressing acknowledgment of individual mortality, and the syntactic triumph acts rhetorically to suggest that the fact of mortality can be balanced out by a comforting idea.

3. *as* (1) in so far as (a sense rejected later; see the preceding note); (2) in as much as, because; (3) when; (4) even as. *should* (1) shall; (2) ought properly to. *decease* In this context *decease* delivers its own meaning, "die," and suggestions of "decrease" ("shrivel"), the precise opposite of the rhyme word, *increase*.

4. *His . . . his* its . . . its (but see 73.10, note). *tender* (1) young (the word suggests an immature plant, "a tender shoot," and thus contrasts well with *riper*, to which it is also related both phonetically and by the logic of the statement); (2) loving, gentle, kind (as in line 12 and 22.12). *bear his memory* be a living reminder of the father. The metaphor is heraldic: the resemblance of the child's face to the father's is likened to the bearing of heraldic arms (*bear* also carries logically inappropriate suggestions of "bearing fruit" and "bearing young," which are pertinent to the previous botanical metaphor and to the general topic of procreation; see 13.8, note). Also see 1.4, note on p. 579.

5. *contracted to* betrothed to (but with a suggestion of "drawn together into"—shrunken rather thain increased).

6,8. *fuel, cruel* = dissyllabic; see 129.4, note.

6. *with self-substantial fuel* with your own substance (like a candle); *self-substantial* also carries suggestion of "unique," "sui generis."

8. *Thyself* Q gives "Thy selfe"; for a defense of this and similar modernizations, see Preface, p. xvii.

10. *only* principal (with overtones of "single," "solitary," and also of *only* meaning "merely"—see 94.10, note). *gaudy* joyous, luxurious, showy (though not necessarily excessively so); the color called "gaudy-green"—the yellowish green of fabric dyed with weld—is the predominant color of spring.

11. See 99.12–13, note. *own* Note the phonetic and ideational play on *only* in line 10; *own* also pertains to the ongoing dissolution of the distinction between what is owned and what is owed. *buriest* = dissyllabic, by syncopation. *thy contént* what is contained in you—potential fatherhood—and what would make you contented—marriage (see 151.11, note) and fatherhood (see 119.13 and note).

12. *tender churl* gentle boor (an oxymoron). (*Tender* echoes and plays on *tender* meaning "young" in line 4; *churl* was commonly used in a special sense—as a synonym for "miser" [compare *R&J* V.iii.163, and see *AYLI* II.iv.75–77: "My master is of churlish disposition, / And little recks to find the way to heaven / By doing deeds of hospitality"]. Since *tender* carries a reminder of tendering, offering, giving *tender churl* embodies suggestion of another oxymoron: "generous miser.") *niggarding* hoarding.

13. *glutton* = a one-word emblem of one of the poem's paradoxes; gluttony suggests both selfish hoarding and extravagant waste.

14. *by* The relationship the preposition indicates is unfixed: *by* modifies *eat* and thus suggests that the person addressed anticipates, imitates, and doubles the efficacy of the grave by devouring (line 5–6) and burying (line 11) himself in

voluntary celibacy; *by* also modifies *due* and thus suggests that the addressee devours not only what he owes to the world but, confusingly, what the grave owes to the world. Line 14 sounds clear and—since it echoes all the poem's earlier assertions—summary as well; the line feels meaningful, but it neither invites nor can sustain a precise gloss.

1,12,14. *increase, churl, niggarding, due* These words cooperate to ellect a metaphoric undercurrent that anticipates the distinction in sonnets 2 and 4 between investment for profit and miserly self-defeating financial conservatism. The conjunction of *due* and *grave* also anticipates sonnet 4 by raising unharnessed suggestions of the idea of death as "paying one's debt to nature."

SONNET 2

See the final note to sonnet 1.

3. *Thy youth's proud livery* the marks and trappings of your youthful beauty (the metaphor of fine new clothing for youthful beauty is made pertinent to the military metaphors among which it appears by the word *livery*, which indicated soldiers' uniforms as well as servants'). *livery* = trisyllabic. *proud* splendid, gorgeous (with suggestions of "which makes you so confident and haughty").

3. *tottered weed* tattered garment (and—because of the context of beauty's field—with a play on the botanical sense of *weed*; compare 94.12).

5. *lies* is; *lies* carries appropriate overtones of "lies buried."

5–12. See Matt. 25:14–30, the parable of the talents.

6. *lusty* spirited and gallant (although in this context *lusty* has overtones of "lustful," "full of carnal desire").

8. *all-eating* describes both the extent of the disgrace (total) and the nature of the offense (miserly greed in hoarding and thus devouring the vigor and beauty of youth): see Ovid, *Met.* XV.234–36 (lines 258–60 in Arthur Golding's translation; see Appendix 2). *thriftless* describes both the value of the praise (profitless) and the nature of the quality offered as praiseworthy (wastefulness).

9. *deserved* would deserve. *use* use for procreative purposes, sexual use (compare 4.7, 6.5, 20.14, 40.6, 48.3, 78.3, 134.10, and *Tim* IV.iii.82: "Be a whore still; they love thee not that use thee")—but presented in a metaphor of usury—investment for profit, as opposed to the thriftlessness of miserly hoarding.

10. The comma after *answer*, the quotation marks, and the capital *T* of *This* are editorial additions and are justifiable on grounds that the Q text, grossly puzzling to a reader raised on logically directive typographical signals, is less likely to evoke an approximation of the response it presumably evoked in Shakespeare's reader than the modernization is. No modern orthography can satisfactorily retain the momentary misreadings invited by the potential "this" has in the Q text for being read as a pronoun ("answer this" = "answer as follows"), and, when "faire" makes an adjectival reading of "this" probable, invited by the fleeting potential "this faire child" has for indicating the person answered. See Preface, pp. xiv–xviii.

11. *sum my count* complete my account and present the balanced audit (the

child will in effect act both as evidence and lawyer). *make my old excuse* justify, when I am old, the consumption of the beauty expended during my life (taking *old* as an ellipsis for "when I am old"; the context demands that the phrase be understood by synesis, i.e. as meaning what it must mean rather than what its syntax would otherwise indicate ["make my usual excuse"]).

12. This line continues the legal language of the preceding lines and, because the logic of the emergent metaphorical situation requires not "proving his . . . to be thine" but "thine . . . to be his," intensifies the paradox of increasing wealth by expending it. This line exemplifies the constructive vagueness by which Shakespeare makes a word or phrase do double duty. He regularly places a word or phrase in a context to which it pertains but which it does not quite fit idiomatically; the context dictates the sense the word or phrase must have, and that sense is colored by the sense and context the word or phrase ordinarily has. Here *Proving* and *by succession* evoke a metaphoric situation in which a son demonstrates his right to his deceased father's possessions ("proving thine to be his"); *his beauty* and *thine* pertain to a different but related demonstration—the presentation of evidence of the source of what the son indisputably possesses ("proving his to be thine"). The line does not seem complicated until it is explained; the easy conflation of the two related situations actually makes a miraculous paradox occur in the fabric of lines 9–14, lines that have miraculous paradox as their topic. In fact, the metaphoric use of idiom and syntax is itself miraculously multiple in line 12; *thine* not only participates in the double situation described in the line but also suddenly reveals the line to be a resumption of the speaker's syntax—in which he addresses the young man (*If thou couldst . . .*)—and not a continuation of the hypothetical statement by the young man himself (*this fair child of mine . . .*). The miraculousness derives from the fact that the signal, *thine*, occurs after the reversion to the speaker's voice has been in effect for the whole length of the line. (Although modern punctuation explains and justifies the logic by which lines 10–12 are organized, the modernization does not, I think, diminish the syntactic surprise effected by *thine*.)

13. *were* would be.

SONNET 3

1,9–10. Compare 62.9, 13–14.

1,9–12. See Ovid, *Met.* XV.232–33 (lines 255–57 in Golding's translation; see Appendix 2).

1. *glass* mirror. (Note, however, that in the proper context [e.g. 126.2], *glass* means "hourglass," and that the substantively irrelevant conjunction of *tell* and *time* in this and the following line presents the raw materials for such a context; in quatrain 3 the action of *thy mother's glass* and the *windows* is comparable to reversing the action of an hourglass, making time run backwards. Compare 77.1.)

2. *another* Q gives "an other"; on the folly of retaining invitingly informative Q spellings, see Preface, pp. xiv–xviii.

3. *fresh repair* unfaded condition. *renewest* make again, duplicate. (The

juxtaposition of *fresh repair* and *renewest* colors the line with suggestions of "repair" meaning "restoration" and "to renew" meaning "to rejuvenate" and thus with suggestions of "repair a face that is in no apparent need of repair." Moreover, there may also be a macaronic pun on *repair*—taken as if it were compounded of the Latin prefix *re-* and the French noun *père* and meant "fathering again"; Shakespeare uses *repair* twice more in the sonnets [10.8, 16.9—both times as a verb], and in both cases the context suggests a similar punning meaning for *repair*. Compare *WT* V.i.31, *Lear* IV.vii.28, *Cymb* I.i.132, *Per* II.i.120, and *AW* I.ii.30–31: "It much repairs me / To talk of your good father.")

4. *beguile*   cheat or disappoint (but with flattering overtones of "charm"). *unbless some mother*   cheat some woman of maternity.

5. *uneared*   This word carries two related meanings at once. An uneared womb is one not yet fruitful (an eared stalk of wheat or corn is one matured to the point where fruiting spikes have formed). An uneared womb is also one that is untilled (literally "unploughed"—from Old English "erian," to plough; for a similarly bawdy use of this metaphor, see *A&C* II.ii.232, "He plough'd her and she cropp'd").

5–6. Contrast Donne's homosexual poem "Sapho to Philaenis":

> Thy body is a naturall *Paradise*,
>   In whose selfe, unmanur'd, all pleasure lies,
> Nor needs *perfection*; why shouldst thou than
>   Admit the tillage of a harsh rough man?
> Men leave behinde them that which their sin showes.
>
>   [35–39]

6. *husbandry*   agricultural management (with a pun on "husband," "a man who has a wife").

7. *fond*   foolish (with· a play on *fond* meaning "loving"; see 84.14).   *will be*   as to become, that is willing to be.

8. *to stop posterity*   with the result that your family will end with you (*to* gives the phrase overtones of deliberate intent).

9–10. "In the April of one's age" was proverbial (Tilley, A310).

10. *lovely*   See 5.2, note.   *prime*   height of perfection, time of being at one's best (with a play on "springtime" evoked by the context of *April*; see the similar play on *prime* meaning "the spring of the year" in 12.3).

11. *through windows of thine age*   through your age-dimmed eyes. The phrase loses its precision if a modern reader forgets that non-distorting, fully transparent window glass is an achievement of recent technology. (In this logically primary sense of the phrase, *through* denotes a medium passed, as in "gaze through" or "passed through" constructions; however, because of the reminder here of another kind of glass—the mirrors of lines 1 and 9—this phrase also suggests "by means of your progeny.")

13. *rememb'red not to be*   (1) in such a way that you will not be remembered; (2) with the intent of being forgotten.

14. *image*   (1) memory, fame in the world; (2) mirror image; (3) potential offspring.

SONNET 4

This sonnet plays on the proverbial idea of "paying one's debt to nature" (Tilley, D168); see the final note to sonnet 1.

1. *Unthrifty* profitless and wasteful. (See *thriftless*, 2.8. This sonnet echoes the diction of sonnet 2.)

1–4. The quatrain echoes the stock expression "fair and free" (which may also be glanced at in *LLL* IV.i.23: "A giving hand, though foul, shall have fair praise").

2. *beauty's legacy* the qualities you now possess, an inheritance *from* your parents and *for* your children; *beauty* is grammatically the possessor and logically also the thing possessed. (See 2.12, note—on constructive vagueness.)

3–14. See Matt. 25:14–30, the parable of the talents.

4. *frank* generous. *free* generous (with overtones of *free* meaning "noble" [see *Oth* II.iii.308, quoted in 134.5, note], and of *free* meaning "licentious" [compare the following lines from number 11 in a series of satires on the marriage of Edward Coke attributed to John Davies by Robert Krueger and Ruby Nemser in their forthcoming edition of Davies: "A covetous lawier a free Lady wonne; / Ere he began, yet had another donne . . . "]). Ingram and Redpath suggest that "the alliteration may reinforce a wordplay which is both English and bilingual (cf. It. *franco* = 'free')."

5. *niggard* miser. See *waste in niggarding*, 1.12.

5,6. *beauteous, bounteous* = dissyllabic, by syncopation.

7,8. The paradox of this sentence is augmented by conflict between the senses of *use* and *live* evoked by the metaphor and those demanded by the situation described in the preceding lines. In the context of *usurer*, *use* ought to mean "invest for profit"; the preceding lines cause the reader to understand the exactly opposite meaning—"expend," "use up." In the financial metaphor *live* means "support yourself," but, in the larger context of the topic of the poem, *live* must be understood as "have physical immortality in a child"; when read after 3.13–14, *live* also suggests "be remembered after death." For *use* meaning "use sexually," see 2.9, note.

8. *sum of sums* The phrase plays casually with "some"; compare *MofV* III.ii.157–58: "But the full sum of me / Is sum of something . . . . "

9. *traffic* commerce, dealings. Translated from the metaphor of finance to the topic of the poem, procreation, *having traffic with thyself alone* not only means "keeping yourself single" (i.e. avoiding sexual intercourse), but specifically suggests "masturbating." See lines 1–2, 5, 7 above; 6.4; and 9.14.

12. *ácceptable* On the accent, see 50.7, note. *audit* final, summary accounting—as by a steward. (Q capitalizes and italicizes *audit* here and in 126.11; see Preface, pp. xvii–xviii.)

SONNET 5

Sonnets 5 and 6 are logically linked.
1. *hours* = dissyllabic.

2. *lovely* (1) beautiful; (2) loveable (as in 126.1). *gaze* object eagerly looked on.

4. *unfair* deface (compare *Fairing* in 127.6). *fairly* in and by means of beauty. (The construction here gives the word flattering extra overtones of three commoner sixteenth-century meanings: "legitimately," "completely," and "beautifully." It also activates the suggestion that "to unfair" is "unfair," is illegitimate.)

5–8. Compare 97.1–4, and see Ovid, *Met.* XV. 212–13 (lines 233–35 in Golding's translation; see Appendix 2).

5. *leads . . . on* (1) directs the forward progress of, guides the advancing steps of; (2) lures, entices (as in *MWW* II.i.83: ". . . give him a show of comfort in his suit, and lead him on with a fine-baited delay")

6. *hideous* = dissyllabic, by syncopation. *confounds* destroys (although this use of "to confound" is perfectly standard, Shakespeare may have been drawn to it because he heard a punning relationship between it and 'to confine"; see *pent* and *pris'ner* in line 10).

7. The conjunction of *leaves* and *gone* generates a syntactically and logically unharnessed play on "to leave"; note *left* in line 9. See 6.12, 51.14, 73.14, 77.3, 97.14 and notes.

9–14. See 54.9–14.

9. *summer's distillation* the essence of summer (gradually specified in lines 10 and 13 as perfumes made from flowers).

10. *pris'ner* The dissyllabic pronunciation is common in Shakespeare (e.g. *Lucrece* 1608, 1652).

11. *were bereft* would be snatched away.

12. The verb here is missing but understood: "neither it nor any remembrance of what it was would exist" (for *nor . . .* nor meaning "neither . . . nor," see 55.7). *remembrance* memory and reminder (the word does double duty).

14. *Leese* lose. *substance* See 53, headnote. "More show than substance" was proverbial (Tilley, S408). *still* (1) even afterward, nevertheless; (2) always, forever (with a play on *distilled*—compare 119.2–4, 10).

SONNET 6

1. *ragged* rough (torn and capable of causing tearing).

2. *distilled* See sonnet 5, to which this sonnet is so tightly linked as practically to make it the second half of a 28-line unit.

3. *Make sweet some vial* The specific meaning "impregnate the womb of some woman" is suggested by the metaphor and the context of the preceding sonnets and is confirmed in line 7. (The logically incidental wit of a probably audible play on "make sweet some vile," i.e. "something vile," contributes a casual demonstration of the ease by which complete reversals can be effected. *Make sweet some vial* can also carry suggestions of "make some sweet vial," "create a child to contain and preserve your essence.") *vial* = dissyllabic. *treasure* (1) fill with treasure; (2) make precious. (Until a reader reaches *With* in line 4, *treasure* can seem to mean "value highly.")

5. *use* See 2.9 and note. *forbidden usury* Although "use," lending money at interest, was no longer illegal in England, it was still considered sinful. (Partridge suspects a reference to masturbation; see 4.9, note.)

6. *happies* makes happy. *pay* (1) repay with interest; (2) make. *willing* voluntarily given. Syntactically, *willing* describes the attitude of the lenders (fathers), but the substance of the line causes *willing* also to reflect on the borrowers (mothers), who, by giving birth, willingly repay the loan with interest. (In this context of procreation, *willing* carries pertinent overtones of the sexual senses of the noun "will"; see 135, headnote. Note also that this sonnet, like those that precede it, is informed by the then current pseudo-medical belief that each sexual emission diminished a man's lifespan; see 11.3 and 129.1.)

8,9. *happier* = dissyllabic, by syncopation.

8. *ten for one* The interest rate forcefully attests to the excellence of the investment—both because the figures mentioned suggest the highest rate then legally permitted (10 percent, one for ten), and because the rate here is actually 1000 percent.

9. *than* = a simple modernization of Q's "then" (see 16.4, 8, note; here syntactical necessity requires a reader to understand Q's "then" as *than*, but the logic and the rhetorical thrust of the statement include the ideas "then" expresses: "therefore" and "at that time" [as opposed to "now"]).

10. *refigured* duplicated (with a play on "figure" meaning a numerical symbol, like 1 or 10).

11. This line echoes the Elizabethan marriage service; see 11.2, note (here the echo is merely superficial because *depart* in this line has only its modern sense, "go away [die]").

12. *Leaving thee living* The phonetic play of *Leaving* and *living* calls attention to this phrase; it is a simple summary of the paradox that the poem explains. However, the wit of the phrase is also unobtrusively complex. *Leaving* indicates the condition in which its object, *thee*, will be at the time of departure (compare the "leave to" construction in *John* IV.iii.145–56: "England now is left / To tug and scramble"); but, since this sense of *Leaving* derives from "to leave" meaning "to depart," *Leaving* also puns on the sense *depart* has in line 11 (see 134.9, note—on ideational puns); moreover, *Leaving* pertains (non-logically) to the botanical metaphor of sonnet 5 and the opening lines of this poem (see *leaves quite gone* and *left* in 5.7, 9), and to the arithmetical language of lines 8–10 (for the use of "leaves" to indicate the result of subtracting one number from a larger one, see *OED*, 3c), and to the idea of leaving—of bequeathing—one's worldly goods to one's heirs. The logic of its context dictates that *thee* be understood as "thyself," but Shakespeare's non-idiomatic use of *thee* instead of a reflexive allows the line to be read both as modifying *depart* and as modifying *death*: "what could death do if he had to leave you behind, if he could not take you." *in posterity* (1) in the persons of your descendants; (2) in perpetuity, on into the times of all future generations.

13. *self-willed* obstinate (with a play on "bequeathed to yourself"). (Note the complex phonetic and ideational relationship between *self-killed* in line 4 and *willing* in line 6. *Self-willed* also has some bawdy potential as a reference to

masturbation; see 135, headnote, and the notes to 112.3 and 154.9; if Shakespeare's reader heard any such joking here, it would have been enhanced by the bawdy potential of *conquest* in line 14; see 151.1, 2, 13, note.)

14. *conquest*   The primary meaning must be the usual one: "spoils of war," but the context of inheritance invokes a play on a sense *conquest* has in Scottish law—the sense Ingram and Redpath argue is primary here: "real estate acquired otherwise than by inheritance." See 46.2, 8.6, notes.

SONNET 7

This sonnet echoes various elements in *Met.* XV.184–227 (lines 202–49 in Golding's translation; see Appendix 2).

1. *Lo*   behold (with a play on "low"; see line 12).   *orient*   (= dissyllabic, by syncopation) East.   *light*   sun.

2. *under eye*   (1) eye that is below; (2) subservient being. (For Shakespeare's license in using adverbs as adjectives, see Abbott, par. 22, and compare *seldom* in 52.4 and *evermore* in 147.10.)

1–2. The likeness between the sun and an eye is a commonplace (see 49.6, note); the justice of the analogy was increased by the belief that eyes emit light (see 20.6, note).

2,3,4, etc. *his, he*   its, it (but see 73.10, note).

4. *his sacred majesty*   (1) its sacred glory, the holy splendor of the sun; (2) his sacred majesty (= a title of honor on the model of "his sacred majesty, the king").

5. *steep-up*   precipitous.   *heav'nly*   (1) of the sky; (2) sacred. (The conjunction of the rising sun, religious language, and the climbing of a hill gives the whole poem vague, substantively unharnessed, but pervasive reference to the crucifixion and resurrection of Christ; the pun on "sun" and *son* in line 14 is obviously also pertinent to Christ, but the Christian references never solidify, never add up to the sacrilegiously complimentary analogy they point toward; they do, however, give an air of solemnity and miraculousness to the equation the poem implies between the sun's cyclical birth, death, and rebirth and human victory over mortality by procreation.)

6. (1) "At noon (*his middle age*), the sun retains its youthful vigor"; (2) "The sun resembles a strong youth as he comes to look in middle age" (the second reading takes *strong youth* as a metonymy for "a strong young man"). The two concurrent meanings that result from the syntactically ambiguous relationship between *in his middle age* and the rest of the line begin a gradually developing analogy between the diurnal lifespan of the sun and a human lifespan; the analogy is not made explicit until the couplet, where it is promptly capped by the pun on "sun" and *son*.

7. *Yet mortal looks adore*   (1) mortal looks continue to adore, mortals gaze no less and no less adoringly than before; (2) nevertheless mortal gazes adore; and, in context of religious language, perhaps (3) gazes that are yet mortal, not yet immortal, adore.   *still*   repeats the senses of *Yet*.

8. *Attending on*   watching, following the course of, paying attention to (with

metaphoric suggestions of "traveling along with him as his attendants, his servants, during").

9. *highmost pitch* apex. *car* = an allusion to Phoebus's chariot in classical mythology.

9–12. This quatrain echoes a proverb for which Tilley (S979) gives many Renaissance variants: "The rising, not the setting, sun is worshipped by most men." See *Tim* I.ii.138: "Men shut their doors against a setting sun."

11. *'fore* before. *duteous* = dissyllabic, by syncopation. *converted* turned away (see 49.7, note). (Many of the words in this sonnet are religious in derivation or common usage—*gracious, homage, sacred, heav'nly, adore, pilgrimage.* In such a context, the choice of the verb "convert" to describe the simple physical act of averting the eyes gives the action overtones of apostasy; however—and moreover—it simultaneously suggests a conversion from superstitious heathen fear to a higher religion.)

12. *tract* path.

13. A full reading of this line conflates four complementary and simultaneously active separable meanings: (1) "So you, outlasting your prime" (for this meaning of *outgoing*, see *A&C* III.ii.60–61; "the time shall not / Out-go my thinking on you"); (2) "So you, at the moment when you surpass yourself" (see *Tim* I.i.276–77: "He outgoes / The very heart of kindness"); (3) "So you, yourself already in the process of departing (i.e. dying) at the moment of your prime"; (4) "So you, yourself already in the process of going out (as a light goes out, is extinguished) at the moment of your prime."

14. *diest* = monosyllabic, by syncopation. *get* (1) obtain; (2) beget. *son* The pun on "sun" capsules the paradox by which the dying father lives again in—is—his child. (Note that "sun," the key word in this sonnet, never appears in it; see 141.13–14, note.)

SONNET 8

1. *Music to hear* You, whose voice is music. (The phrase is revealed as a vocative epithet by the syntax of the rest of the line; it can momentarily register as "in order to hear music.") *sadly* mournfully.

1–4. The wit of this quatrain is derived from a playful perversity in which a commonplace observation—that music often makes its listeners feel sad and that the listeners enjoy the feeling—is treated as if it revealed a serious logical inconsistency. The inconsistency is first exaggerated by means of the contrast between the chiasmically balanced epithet and question in line 1; the next three lines then analyze the inconsistency with inappropriately rigorous logic.

4. *thine annoy* what gives you pain.

3–4. *lov'st thou, thou receiv'st, receiv'st with pleasure* Why *lov'st thou* means simply "Why do you like," but *thou receiv'st*, a chiasmic echo of *lov'st thou*, can activate casual sexual overtones of "to love" meaning "to have sexual intercourse with"—overtones subsequently strengthened by *receiv'st with pleasure* in line 4. (For the sexual potential of *receiv'st*, see *things of great receipt* in 136.7 and—for the idea of one sexual partner physically receiving the other—122.12

and note. For the specifically sexual sense of *with* as "wit" and the sexual suggestiveness of "wit," see 23.14 and 26.1–14, notes.)

5. *true* (1) honorable; (2) genuine, abiding; (3) lawful, legitimate (note the
legal senses of *concord* and *unions*). (Like many of the words that follow in this
quatrain, *true* is a musical term; see *MND* III.i.116: "The throstle with his note
so true.") *concord* agreement, accord. (See the note on lines 5–8 below. Like
its synonym, "harmony," *concord* is a musical term; see the *OED* example in
the following note. In view of the substantively incidental legal undercurrent in
lines 5 and 6, note that in property law a *concord* is an agreement about fines for
trespass [*OED* gives examples from 1531 onward].)

6. *Unions* joinings, unifications, marriages. (Note that in Scots law [see
6.14, note] a "union" is a "uniting into one tenantry of lands or tenements not
lying contiguous" [*OED* gives examples from 1605 onward]; the traditional
means of unifying properties was by the intermarriage of interested parties or
their children. A "union" is also appropriately reminiscent of a "unison," a
musical term meaning "a sound or note of the same pitch as another" or "the
agreement of the sounds of two or more bodies vibrating at different rates"
[*OED* cites a music text of 1596: "A concord is divided into a Unison, Third,
Fifth, Sixt . . . ."].)

5–6. *the true concord of well-tunèd sounds, | By unions married* polyphonic
music.

5–8. Often Shakespeare's use of language is such that a reader can make no
paraphrase that both follows the syntax of the lines and says what he knows the
lines mean. One can almost always make a general paraphrase of a Shakespeare
sonnet and give a satisfactory gloss for any particular word in it, but if one puts
together a new sentence replacing Shakespeare's words with their glosses, one
will often get a sentence that makes no sense at all. Sometimes Shakespeare's
own sentences can be demonstrated to mean nothing at all—even where readers
actually understand them perfectly. This second quatrain of sonnet 8 is an
excellent example. Lines 5–6 introduce the running theme of the preceding seven
sonnets (all of which urge a young man to marry and beget children) by using
language that is both musical and marital (e.g. *unions, married,* and *concord*
[literally "hearts together"]) to say, "If polyphonic music is distasteful to you."
The language of lines 7–8 continues the double frame of reference, music and
marriage. Going along at a normal reading speed a reader will presumably
recognize an appropriate, if imprecise, metaphor of a musician "bearing a
part" (*one* of the parts) in a piece of polyphonic music and understand *who con-
founds | In singleness the parts that thou shouldst bear* as a repetition of what
several sonnets have just said: "who are doing wrong in remaining single."
Editors and students are pressed for something more specific; the best paraphrase I have seen is this one by Ingram and Redpath (who make a point of its
insufficiency): "who, by remaining single, suppress those roles (of husband and
father) which you should play." The clause effectively says much more than
that and literally says much less. The coherence of the paraphrase is achieved
by means of substitutions whose meanings are not quite those of the original
words: *confounds* is replaced by "suppress" and *bear* by "play." The plurality of

parts is explained by a reasonable extrapolation, "of husband and father." The paraphrase gives precise form to the obvious purport of the clause and does so in one of the sets of terms in which the poem operates. The paraphrase is absolutely just, but necessarily ignores several common meanings of "to confound" that also pertain in this context and impinge upon it: (a) "to ruin," "to destroy" (the sense it has in 5.6); (b) "to waste" (a theme of the sonnets since sonnet 1); and (c) "to throw into confusion," "to disorder," "to destroy the harmony of." Taking *parts* to mean "roles," no reader can be expected to understand *confounds . . . the parts* as "ruins the parts" or "wastes the parts" or "disorders the parts," but several other meanings of *parts* are invoked by this context, and they act to sustain the illusion that the clause actually says what it so obviously means: *parts* means "talents," "good qualities," "abilities" (as in 17.4), and "who waste your abilities" makes good sense until one comes to *bear*; moreover, *parts* appears here in context of *singleness* and gives the lines the pertinent—though logically and syntactically unmanageable—richness of a vaguely meaningful opposition between the unity suggested by *singleness* and the division suggested by *parts* as a word meaning "pieces"; moreover, the context of marriage invokes a logically casual play on *parts* meaning "sex organs" (see 151.6 and note). Similarly, *bear*, as a word meaning "give birth to," is substantively irrelevant to this clause but so urgently relevant to its occasion that it gives a feeling of rightness, a sound of sense, to the lines. A complementary and equally easy victory over reasonable probability occurs in the grammatically unusual *who confounds* (for "who confoundst"—see Abbott, par. 247) and in the oxymoron *sweetly chide*. The quatrain is an emblem of the paradoxical conditions it recommends, harmony and marriage—unities that supersede common sense in being more unified than singleness, unities made by literally "confounding," "pouring together," individual elements and potentially disabled by a confusion that results from failure to mix.

9–12. The metaphor here is of lute strings, which are tuned in pairs; when one is plucked, the other of the same pitch produces a sympathetic vibration.

10. *mutual* = dissyllabic by syncopation (as in 125.12).

11. *sire, and child, and happy mother* This trio suggests the paradox of the Holy Trinity and multiplies our sense of paradox by also and simultaneously suggesting the Holy Family—Jesus, his mother Mary, and his foster father Joseph.

2,3,12. *not, not, note* The two words were apparently never homonyms, but they may have been pronounced enough alike for a Renaissance reader to have heard a complex play on *not, note*, and "knot" in this context of negation, music, and union. Shakespeare rhymes *note* with "pot," *not* with "smote," *note* with "coat," "got" with "coat," and *not* with "got"; he puns on *not* and "knot" in *AW* III.ii.20–22: "she hath recovered the king and undone me. I have wedded her, not bedded her; and sworn to make the 'not' eternal"; Webster may intend a pun on *not, note*, and "knot" (meaning "ornamental garden" [*OED*, 7]) when in his Induction to Marston's *Malcontent* he has Burbadge say the additions introduced into the play are "only as your salad to your great feast, to entertain a little more time, and to abridge the not-received custom of music in our theatre" (*The Malcontent*, Induction, 88–91 in *The Works of*

John Marston, ed. A. H. Bullen, I.204). See *noted weed* in 76.6 and 76.9, note.

13. *speechless* wordless (but with a paradoxical play on "silent"). *being many, seeming one* This inversion of the paradox of the Holy Trinity continues from suggestion of the Trinity in quatrain 3.

14. *Sings . . . single* The overt play on *sings* and *single* is shadowed in lines 8 and 12. *Thou single wilt prove none* (1) unmarried—and thus without an heir—your line will become extinct with your death; (2) being single (one, 1), you will turn out to be nothing (zero, 0). (There is incidental allusion here to the ancient mathematical principle that "one is no number," which—as the embodiment of the quibble on the number "one" and "one" as opposed to a multitude—became proverbial [Tilley, O54; see 136.8]. Another proverb, "One is as good as none" [Tilley, O52], also pertains; Whitney gives it thus: "The proverbe saieth, one man is deemed none, / And life, is deathe, where men doo live alone" [p. 66].) *none* It is possible that Shakespeare had a pun on "nun" in mind. Barrenness suggests nuns to him, and nuns suggest barrenness; see *MND* I.i.69–78 and the "self-loving nuns" passage in *V&A* (752–68). For a similarly suggestive use of *none*, see *Measure* II.iv.134–38, Angelo's attempted seduction of Isabella, a novice from a nunnery: "Be that you are, / That is, a woman; if you be more, you're none; / If you be one, as you are well express'd / By all external warrants, show it now / By putting on the destin'd livery"; also see *Measure* III.i.62–63: *Claudio.* "Is there no remedy?" / *Isabella.* "None . . ." (since Isabella is herself the potential "remedy," her response has something like the effect that occurs in *AW* I.i.141–42, where Helena asks how a maiden can lose her virginity to her own liking, and Parolles introduces his answer with the expletive "marry"). For a simpler play on "nun" and "none", see *The Jew of Malta,* lines 491–92: "a Nunnery, where none but their owne sect / Must enter in . . . ." (The evidence for the pronunciations of *one* and *none* is inconclusive; Shakespeare rhymes *one* with "sun" and "sun" with "nun," but he also rhymes both *one* and *none* with "bone" and—like Whitney—with "alone"; see the *noon* / *son* rhyme in 7.13–14.)

SONNET 9

3. *issueless* childless. *hap* happen.

4. *makeless* mateless (with some suggestion of "non-creating," "who makes nothing"). *wife* (1) woman (as in *HV* V. Chorus. 9–10: "the English beach / Pales in the flood with men, with wives, and boys"); (2) married woman. *like a makeless wife* (1) in the manner of a widow; (2) as it would lament a single woman's unmarried state. (The following line is in effective apposition to this one and limits the meaning of *like a makeless wife* to sense (1).)

5. *still* (1) continually; (2) forever; (3) in any case, even so (i.e. even though you take pains to have no widow).

7. *private widow* ordinary individual woman—as opposed to the general widow, the whole world (this odd phrase may result from Shakespeare's wish to make a macaronic pun on the root meaning of the Latin word from which *private* is derived: *privare*, to bereave).

9. *Look what* whatever. (The use of *look*-plus-pronoun or adverb to make

an indefinite relative appears to have been reasonably common in the sixteenth and seventeenth centuries; see *OED*, 4b. However, this and Shakespeare's three other uses of the construction in the sonnets [11.11, 37.13, and 77.9] all occur in contexts of eyes, looking, and appearance and thus have logically incidental extra pertinence and resonance in the poems where they appear.) *unthrift* prodigal.

10. *his* its (but see 73.10, note). *still* (1) even after that has happened; (2) nevertheless; (3) forever. *enjoys* (1) has the use of; (2) takes pleasure from (with a play on *enjoy* meaning "use sexually"—as in 129.5).

11. *beauty's waste* (1) beauty wasted, the profitless use of beauty, waste of beauty; (2) the wasting away (deterioration) of beauty; (3) what is wasted by a beautiful person.

12. *unused . . . user* See 4.7–8; here Shakespeare plays on "use" meaning "utilize," meaning "expend," and meaning "invest for profit."

14. *himself* itself (but see 47.4, note; here the word's flexibility of reference allows it to refer directly both to the synecdoche, *bosom*, and to its tenor, the young man addressed). *murd'rous shame* shameful murder (the construction allows *murd'rous* both to specify the shame and to act as an intensifying adjective). See 4.9, note. *shame* Note the link between this sonnet and the next that *shame* in 10.1 provides.

SONNET 10

1. *For shame deny* (1) shame on you! you should deny; (2) to avoid shame you should deny; (3) from a sense of your shame you should deny. Many modern editors print "For shame! deny" or "For shame, deny"—thus making (1) explicit at the cost of (2) and (3); Q has no stop after *shame*, and none is needed because, since "For shame!" is and was such a common remonstrance, and since the unpunctuated construction is the inverse of usual word order for (2) and (3) (deny for shame), all three meanings occur one after another in the sequence of reading. *shame* See 9.14.

2. *thyself* See Preface, p. xvii.

3. *Grant if thou wilt* In context of lines 1 and 2, the phrase is an imperative: "agree please"; in context of the rest of line 3 and the argument that follows, the phrase has the meaning signaled by *if thou wilt* (which is usually found introducing concessions in an argument): "I grant (*or* granted), if you insist." *belov'd of* loved by. (The word "beloved" is dissyllabic here and in 150.14 and, perhaps, in 25.13; elsewhere it is trisyllabic in the sonnets.)

6. *thou stick'st not* you do not scruple.

7. *roof* The word acts as a synecdoche for "house," which means both "a place of habitation" (*that . . . roof* = "your body, the house of your spirit"), and "family," as in "the House of Tudor" (*that . . . roof* = "your family line").

8. *repair* keep in good condition (but with a suggestion inherent in the context of the commoner meaning "restore after decay"; for the possible play on "re-father" see 3.3, note).

9. *thought* attitude. *mind* opinion. The wit of line 9 derives from the distinction it puts between the potentially synonymous words *thought* and *mind*: "oh, change your mind (about marrying) so that I can change my mind (about you)."

11. *presence* appearance. *gracious* noble, beautiful, and benevolent. *kind* benevolent, affectionate (but other Renaissance meanings of *kind* [see 105.5, note] are also pertinent—e. g. "be kind" suggests "act according to your nature" and so partially recapitulates *Be as thy presence is* [see 134.6, note]).

12. *kind-hearted* benevolent, affectionate (with suggestions of "in accordance with your nature" and "with care for your species").

13. *Make thee another self* duplicate yourself in a child (but with a suggestion of "change your ways," which echoes the imperatives beginning lines 9 and 11). *for love of me* Martin (p. 27) notes that this is the first point in the 1609 sequence where the speaker implies close personal friendship between himself and the young man he is addressing; except in this line and 13.1, 13 the grounds for referring to the young man of sonnets 1–17 as "the beloved" are derived from previous readings of the rest of the collection. See 18.12, note.

14. *still may* (1) may continue to; (2) may always. *live in* (1) continue to exist in the form of; (2) dwell in (continuing the language of lines 7, 8, and 10).

SONNET 11

1–2. Q punctuates these lines thus: *As fast as thou shalt wane so fast thou grow'st,* | *In one of thine, from that which thou departest,* but most modern editors put a comma after *wane* and no punctuation after *grow'st*; the logical smoothness of such modern texts denies confirmation of the inevitable formal pause at the end of line 1, and thus can suggest to a modern reader that the exaggerated paradox that line 1 expresses in its temporary identity as a self-contained unit is only an accident of the verse form.

1. *As fast as . . . so fast* (1) as rapidly as . . . just that rapidly; (2) as rapidly as . . . just that steadily (for a similar use of *fast*, see *2HVI* V.ii.21: "thou art so fast mine enemy"); (3) as rapidly as . . . just that stable and secure (taking the second *fast* as an adjective). Shakespeare sometimes uses "as fast as" to mean "as soon as" (see *AYLI* IV.i.117–18: *Rosalind.* "Ay, but when?" | *Orlando.* "Why, now; as fast as she can marry us"). A Renaissance reader used to the idiom might well have understood "As soon as thou shalt wane" up to the point in the line where the completed "as . . . so" construction makes that reading impossible.

2. *In one of thine* (1) in the womb of your wife; (2) in the person of your child. *from that which thou departest* (1) out of that (i. e. sperm) which you bestow (this reading enhances a probable sexual meaning of *wane* in line 1 as male loss of tumescence after sexual emission; for other Renaissance examples of "depart" and "depart from" meaning "bestow," see *OED*, 2, 13); (2) as a result of that (your youth) which you now leave behind. No note can take in all the permutations that occur among the various meanings of the words and phrases in lines 1 and 2 in all their relationships to one another. The crush of

meanings in these lines is further swelled by overtones of three other common uses of "depart"—all pertinent to this context, all called up in a reader's mind, but, unlike the two meanings given above, not syntactically harnessed to the sentence in which they appear or capable of inclusion in its particular logic: (a) "depart" meant "put asunder" (OED, 3), and the use of the word here invokes an echo of the Elizabethan marriage service (in which its use—"to have and to hold . . . till death us depart"—would have been as familiar as the words that replaced it in 1622—"till death us do part"—are now), an echo that relates to two topics of the sonnet, marriage and death; (b) "depart" was used intransitively as a synonym for "die" (OED, 7); (c) the common construction "depart from," which ordinarily means "go away from," appears here in a context in which that meaning is substantially relevant but syntactically impossible.

3. *blood* life (the sum of four common Renaissance meanings of *blood*: "vital fluid," "vigor," "sensual appetite," and "offspring"; see 6.6, note). *youngly* (1) in youth; (2) youthfully (i.e. zestfully).

4. *convertest* (probably pronounced "convartest"; see 12.6,8 and 17.2, notes) (1) turn away; (2) change ("convert" was already much used as a financial term; its use here thus helps to link this sonnet with the metaphors of investment in preceding sonnets and confirms the suggestion by Ingram and Redpath of "a secondary train of associations in this sonnet, viz. investment, appearing in 'bestow'st' (line 3) and continuing in the ambiguity of 'increase,' which would thus make the transition back to the seminal associations of 'store' and 'barrenly' ").

5–6. *Herein lives . . . Without this* This construction suggests several different sentences, no one of which is fully realized: (1) in this course of action is . . . outside this course of action is; (2) in such a course of action is . . . not having this (a child) results in; (3) in this place (see the opening phrase of line 2) dwells (or is alive) . . . external to this place lives. The text given here follows the majority of modern editions by putting a comma after *Without this*; the comma gives emphasis to the linked and antithetical triplets in lines 5 and 6. The Q punctuation of line 6 (*Without this folly, age, . . .*) also makes good modern sense and gives another reading for lines 5 and 6, one that prepares a reader for *If all were minded so* in the next line: (4) wisdom, etc., live here without the company of the folly, etc., inherent in your present way of life.

5. *lives* Shakespeare often uses a singular verb for a plural subject, especially when the verb comes first. Here the singular verb tends to help persuade a reader that *wisdom*, *beauty*, and *increase* are synonyms for one another.

7. *times* the generations of men.

8. *year* years. (In Old English the nominative plural of this word was the same as the nominative singular—*year*; in the sixteenth century *year* was still often used for "years"; some very old farmers still say it today.)

9. *for store* as a source of supply, for breeding (livestock kept for breeding were called "store beasts"). ("Store" was also a common synonym for "hoarded wealth," and its use here therefore relates—non-logically—to the topic of hoarding in sonnets earlier in the collection; moreover, in *made for store* there

is a relevant echo of another idiom, "to make store of," meaning "to value highly.")

10. *featureless* shapeless (see 113.12, note). *barrenly* Compare the double senses of *barren* in 13.12 and 16.4.

11. "To those that she made most beautiful (not *harsh, featureless, and rude*) she gave extra powers of generation." (Renaissance printers often spelled "thee" with only one "e"; many editors have therefore read "she gave thee more," which makes this line say that nature gave the young man addressed more good qualities than she gave even the best endowed of other people.) *Look whom* whomever (see 9.9, note).

12. *in bounty cherish* foster (take care of, as a child is taken care of) by being bountiful (i.e. prolific). (*Cherish* also meant "guard carefully"; thus this phrase embodies the paradox of several previous sonnets, that of keeping by giving, increasing by diminishing.)

13. *seal* stamp from which impressions are made.

14. *copy* pattern (that from which a copy is made, here specifically the *seal* in line 13). There is also a play on the meaning of *copy* that has since become its only common one, "reproduction," and on *copy* in the equally common Renaissance sense of "abundance," the sense closest to the Latin root (*copia*: "abundance," "riches," "store," "ability," "power," "means"). (In context of *seal, print*, and *copy*, a modern reader may hear a logically casual pun on a "die," an engraved stamp for impressing a design upon metal; the pun is particularly inviting in this context of procreation since a die is often used in conjunction with a "matrix." However, *OED* gives no example of this sense of "die" before 1699 and none for the relevant sense of "matrix" before 1626.)

SONNET 12

See *Met.* XV. 199–213 (lines 221–35 in Golding, Appendix 2).

1. *count* count the strokes of. *tells* (1) utters; (2) counts out (as in Modern English "bank teller").

2. *brave* resplendent. *hideous* = dissyllabic, by syncopation.

3. *violet* = trisyllabic (as in 99.1). *past prime* which is past its prime, is declining from its point of perfection (= an adjectival phrase modifying *violet*, but with a play on its adverbial potential for indicating the time of seeing: "after the spring, after the season [*prime*] when violets are at their prime"; for *prime* meaning "the spring of the year," see 3.10 and 97.7).

4. *sable* black (a heraldic term). *all silvered o'er* Q has "or silver'd ore." (The emendation given here has been most popular among editors; among other and equally likely suggestions are "o'er silvered are," "o'er silvered all," and "are silvered o'er." A case can be made for retaining the Q reading on grounds that meanings of "or" and "ore" pertain to contexts suggested by other words in the line ["or" is the heraldic term for gold as *sable* is for black, and "ore" is material containing valuable metallic constituents such as silver and gold]; those ideas do relate to the line and can color a reader's perceptions in any case, but such readings give no coherent surface sense for line 4 as a whole; Q's version

looks, and presumably always looked, like a printer's error; Shakespeare's contemporaries probably emended the line as they read, just as modern readers do.)

6. *erst*   formerly.

6,8. *herd, beard*   *Beard* was probably pronounced something like Modern English "bird." Shakespeare rhymes "heard" and *beard* in *LLL* II.i.201–02. Renaissance pronunciations of vowel-plus-r are extremely problematic; see 17.2, note and Kökeritz, pp. 204–09.

7. *summer's green*   (1) the greenness (freshness, youth) of summertime; (2) the fresh green plants of summertime.   *girded up*   tied around.

8. *bier*   (1) a handbarrow, a frame for carrying such things as harvested grain; (2) a movable stand on which a corpse is carried to the grave.   *beard* awn (of such grains as wheat). This line conflates two very different and yet similar public processions: a funeral procession and an Elizabethan harvest-home, in which the last sheaf of grain was brought to the barn with great ceremony and celebration (see W. B. Rye, *England as Seen by Foreigners*, 1865, p. 111, and *Variorum* I, 33).

9. *of thy beauty do I question make*   I speculate about your beauty (with inherent suggestions of "I question the reality of your beauty [and/or of mortal beauty]").

10. *among the wastes of time must go*   must become one of the things destroyed by time (but complicated both by an echo of the stock phrase "waste of time," meaning "frivolous expense of time" [see 100.13, note], and by overtones inherent in the verb "go" of "must travel" either "in the wastelands made by time" or—taking *of* as it is used in "deserts of Arabia"—"in the deserts of Time").

11. *do themselves forsake*   (1) abandon their natures, depart from being what they were; (2) give themselves up (Ingram and Redpath point out that the phrase is a literal translation of the Latin idiom *sese deserere*).

12. *others*   other sweets and beauties.

13. *'gainst*   in opposition to (and, because of the context of time, with a play on "in anticipation of," "in preparation for"; this is the gentlest of Shakespeare's plays on "against" in the sonnets; see 13.3,11; 49.1,5,9,11; and 63.1,10). *time's scythe*   See 60.12, note.

12,13. *see, scythe*   See 123.14, note.

14. *breed*   offspring.   *brave*   defy (contrast *brave* in line 2).

SONNET 13

1. *love*   my love (a vocative; see 10.13, note).

1–2. These lines present four different sentences; each succeeding phrase changes the nature of what precedes it. *O that you were yourself* is a standard idiomatic expression meaning "I wish you were in good health" or "I wish you were as you usually are"; the completed line presents a simple contradiction, an apparent paradox: "I wish you were yourself (i.e. in good health), but you *are* yourself"; the next potential sentence demands that a reader take conscious note of the possessive element, "your," in *yourself* (which Q prints as two words—see Preface, p. xvii): *O that you were yourself, but love you are | No longer yours*, "O that you were your own (i.e. were free, were owner of yourself [with a play on the idea of being self-possessed—compare 94.7]), but, my love, you are not in possession anymore"; the final phrase of line 2 reveals the "no longer than" construction and again changes the meaning of the whole by making the reader's understanding of *No longer* obsolete: "you own yourself only as long as you remain alive." See 141.13–14, note; and compare 133.5.

2. *than*   See *then* in line 6 and 16.4,8, note.   *here live*   continue alive on this earth (with a play on "dwell at this place"). (Willen and Reed suggest that *here* may have been homonymous with "heir"; the probability of the pun in line 2 is vouched for by the same pun in *1HIV*, I.ii.55–56: "were it not here apparent that thou art heir apparent." The pun gives a fifth sentence, ending in "only as long as you continue to be your self-heir, that is, your own heir."

3. *Against*   in anticipation of. (The word is repeated in line 11, but there it means "in opposition to"; see 12.13, note.)

5. *in lease*   by lease (i.e. for a limited term).

6. *determination*   ending (= legal language: an estate held in lease determines at the end of a fixed term; one held for life determines at the death of the holder).   *then*   (1) at that time; (2) thus, as a result.

7. *Yourself*   Q gives "you selfe."   *your self's*   Here I retain Q's division into two words because the genitive construction would have made this use of "yourself" as self-assertively unusual for Shakespeare's contemporaries as for modern readers.

6–7. *you were | Yourself again*   (1) you would live again; (2) you would own yourself again. It is possible that Shakespeare also intended—and that some of his readers could perceive—a play on "you yourself would be a gain" (i.e. you yourself would get yourself back as interest on your investment of yourself). The suggestion is farfetched, but not quite so farfetched as it may seem at first glance. This poem appears among sonnets in which Shakespeare is pressing the idea of investment for every dram of wit it will yield (see 2.9, note). This sonnet is cast in terms of profitable property management. The word *again* appears here in company with the play on *against* in lines 3 and 11. Moreover, although there is no clear instance of a pun on *again* (which Shakespeare rhymes with *slain* [22.14], "brain," "pain," "gain," etc. and also with *pen* [79.6,8], "men," "then," etc.), seven out of the ten instances of *again* in the sonnets occur in conjunction with language of finance, profit, and monetary value (and in an eighth, 22.14, it figures in a refusal to return the beloved's heart—*Thou gav'st me thine not to give back again*): in 56.7 *again* is followed by non-financial uses of *contracted, banks*, and *return*; in 76.12 it appears in company with non-financial uses of *spending* and *spent*; *again* also appears in 79.8 in *pays it thee again*, twice in sonnet 87 (a sonnet entirely phrased in language of loans, gifts, and possession), and in 109.6, where it is followed by *exchanged* (line 7) and *leave for nothing all thy sum of good* (line 12). Since the meaning of *again* recommends it to most of these contexts, this shadow of a pun may be cast only by my ingenuity; but I would not want to bet on it.

6,8. *were, bear*   See 140.5,7, note (on similar rhymes).

8. (1) "When your children would bear your likeness (i.e. have your appear-ance, look like you)"; (2) "When your children would bear (give birth to) children who would resemble you." For the heraldic sense of *bear*, see 1.4, note.

9. *lets . . . a house*   permits . . . a house (with a play on "rents a house out," "leases a house out"). *a house*   (1) a dwelling place (the building); (2) a family.

10. *husbandry*   (1) careful management; (2) tillage (with a play on "mar-riage" from "husband," "married man"—see 3.5–6).

12. *barren rage*   barren-making passion; Abbott (par. 4) cites this phrase to demonstrate that "adjectives signifying effect were often used to signify the cause"; he also cites "weak evils" (*AYLI* II.vii.132) meaning evils that cause weakness and the Elizabethan use of "barren curses" to mean curses that wish barrenness upon the person cursed; compare *razed oblivion* in 122.7 and the somewhat similar inversions listed in 51.1, note. Shakespeare often uses *rage* where we would use "lust" or "desire" or "passion"; see *Lucrece* 463–69. (In this context a simpler meaning of *barren rage*, "ineffectual anger," allows the phrase to describe both a powerful threat—"barren-making passion"—and the threat foiled as it can be by *husbandry*.)

13. *dear my love*   See 10.13, note.

13–14. The punctuation here is that of Q, and allows *you know* to be read first with the preceding phrase ("my love, you know that only prodigals do that") and then with the phrase that follows ("my love, you know that you had a father").

SONNET 14

1. *pluck*   The use of the word *pluck* gives the line the contemptuous tone that "starcatcher" (the term Donne plays on in "Goe and catche a falling starre") had as an epithet for astrologers.

2. *I have astronomy*   I am skilled in astrology.   *methinks*   it seems to me.

5. *to brief minutes*   (1) for each individual minute; (2) to within minutes (i.e. very precisely).

6. *Pointing to each*   appointing (assigning) to each minute. (Before the com-pleted line makes the reading impossible, however, a reader presumably thinks of an astrologer pointing his finger imperiously at a succession of particular minutes.)   *his*   its (but see 73.10, note).

7. *Or say with princes*   The completed line reveals *with princes* as indirect object of *go well* ("or say whether things will go well for princes"), but, as the opening phrase is read, *with* can seem to express likeness or association and so continue previous overtones of mockery by giving a momentary impression of a self-aggrandizing astrologer delivering decrees as if he were a king or royal minister.   *shall . . . well*   For the phonetic likeness of *well* and "will," see 112.3, note. See 134.9, note (on ideational puns).

8. *By oft predict that*   by means of frequent predictions based on what. The perversity of the diction (*oft* is almost never used as an adjective, and this is the

only recorded use of *predict* as a noun) and the awkwardly elliptical syntax suggest the pompous obfuscations of a smug hack.

10. *read such art*   derive such specialized knowledge. (The sense of the phrase is determined by the information given in line 9.)

10,12. *art, convert*   See 11.4, note.

11. *As*   as that, as—for example—that. (The gloss reflects the logic revealed by *shall together thrive*. However, the standard idiom *such* . . . / *As* in lines 10 and 11 may lead a reader to expect something like "such art as no ordinary astrologer can have"; even after *truth and beauty* are added to *such* . . . / *As*, a reader may expect a construction like "such art as truth and beauty give.")

12. *store*   provision for future use (see 11.9, note—on "store beasts"). *convert*   turn—meaning both (1) "turn your attention" and (2) "change" (see 49.7, note).

14. *doom*   end, death (compare the proverb, "Death's day is doomsday" [Tilley, D161]). *date*   end, stipulated limit.

SONNET 15

1–2. Line 1 is an example of a potentially complete syntactical unit whose grammatical nature is redefined by what follows it (compare 33.1–2); under pressure of syntactical necessities introduced by *Holds*, a simple subject-verb-object construction comes to be understood as if it had been "When I consider *that* everything that grows."

2. *Holds in perfection*   (1) retains perfection within itself (*in* expressing location); (2) stays in a state of perfection (*in* expressing condition).

3. *That*   Note that this conjunction indicates a construction parallel to line 2—in which the same conjunction was only elliptically present, but which followed upon a pronominal use of *that* in *everything that grows*; compare 131.5–6.

4. *influence*   power exerted by celestial bodies on earthly affairs (an astrological term). *commént*   See 85.2, note. On the accent, see 50.7, note. This line is metrically unusual; it asks to be pronounced as a twelve-syllable, six-stress line, and sounds good when pronounced that way. Compare lines 6 and 8, which rhyme a stressed final syllable, *sky*, and the unstressed final syllable of *memory*.

1–4. The quatrain moves in an appropriately orbital path. It begins with *I consider* and concludes with *the stars* . . . *commént*; it travels far from its starting place and ends up far from its starting place, but, in a way, the quatrain returns to its starting point because line 4 can activate the atrophied literal meaning of "to consider": "to look at the stars" (from Latin *cum* and *sidus, sider-*). Lines 3 and 4 are a complicated inversion of *I consider*.

The whole of this sonnet is an exercise in relativity (see, for example, the ongoing demonstration of the semantic effects of context on *in* [the word and the sound] and the similar mutability of *with* in lines 11 and 13 and *that* in this quatrain). In these first four lines the speaker's estimate of his relation to the universe diminishes in passage—first in a developing syntax where each addition subtracts from the scope of the assertion and of the speaker's consideration ("I consider everything" is more than "I consider everything that grows," and that consideration is broader than "I consider that everything that grows contains perfection and remains perfect only briefly"), then in the overt assertions of line 3 (where *this huge stage* is only a stage) and line 4 (where the considerer of line 1 has become one of myriad mortals considered).

6. *Cheerèd* encouraged ("to cheer" did not yet have its modern and special theatrical meaning "to shout applause"). *checked* (1) repressed, stopped; (2) taunted, rebuked (as in 136.1). (The interrelation of *Cheerèd* and *checked* is emblematic of the relativity explored by the sonnet. They are antonyms, linked phonetically by alliteration and logically by *and*. Each is a participial adjective effected by adding a dental consonant sound [indicated by *ed* in modern spelling] to a root verb. But one is dissyllabic and the other monosyllabic—and they are so *only* because of their positions in the line; if they were reversed they would be pronounced "checkèd" and "cheered.") *ev'n* The second syllables of "even" and "heaven" are so light that they can both be pronounced dissyllabically throughout the sonnets without metrical inconvenience. However, dissyllabic spellings of "even" and "heaven" were probably read monosyllabically or dissyllabically as the rhythm dictated. Whether Shakespeare's reader pronounced monosyllabic "even" as "e'en," "en," "in," or "ev'n" is never clear (see Kökeritz, pp. 25, 203–04; F spells "even" as "in" in *A&C* IV.xv.73; the Q spelling of the rhyme "heaven"/"eaven" in 28.10,12 and 132.5,7 may indicate the sounds we now would understand from "heaven"/"even" or "hayvun"/ "ayvun" or "hev'n"/"ev'n" or "hen"/"en" or "hin"/"in"). Rhythm indicates that "even" is dissyllabic in 35.5, 39.5, 41.11, and 48.13; 28.10,12 and 132.5,7 are doubtful, since dissyllabic "heaven" and "even" would be ordinary feminine rhymes. I adopt *ev'n* (and *heav'n*) in the present text merely as a means to indicate instances of possible or probable monosyllabic pronunciation.

3–6. Ben Jonson seems to have had these lines in mind in line 78 of "To the Memory of . . . Shakespeare," the tribute prefaced to the 1623 Folio: "Or influence, chide or cheer the drooping stage." (That poem shares some commonplaces with the sonnets—the idea of verse as monument in lines 22–24 [see 55 and 18.13–14] and the idea of poet as parent in lines 65–68 [see 76.8, note]—but seems specifically to echo this context and these lines; moreover, lines 47–49 and 69 seem to refer to the clothing metaphor in 76.6,11 and to 76.7: *every word doth almost tell my name.*)

7. *Vaunt in their youthful sap* exult in the fact that they possess youthful sap (*in* expressing the relation of the verb to the indirect object as it does in 91.1: *Some glory in their birth, some in their skill*). (The topic—mutability—and the word *youthful* give the phrase overtones of another kind of *in* construction, one where *in* indicates duration: "exult during the time of their youthful vitality." Moreover, although nothing can be thought to wear sap, *wear their brave state* in the next line seems to recapitulate this phrase and thus retroactively colors it with suggestions of another shade of meaning for *vaunt* and still another *in* construction: "swagger in new clothes.") *at height decrease* having reached their prime, begin to decline (*height* describes the peak of an actor's career—or that of one of the heroes he plays, the full growth of a plant, and the highest point reached by a celestial body in its passage across the sky).

8. "And wear their splendid finery (*brave state*) beyond the time when anyone remembers them or the outdated fashions they wear." Ingram and Redpath
suspect that the line alludes specifically to the clothes of actors: "A decayed
player continued to wear the finery (often originally handed over from noblemen's wardrobes) long after it had lost both gloss and fashion." (This line contains—in a context of clothing—the constituents of the standard expression
"wear out," and thus carries a syntactically irrelevant but otherwise appropriate
auxiliary suggestion of decay.) *out of* beyond. (Note that *out*, a potential
antonym for *in*, occurs here in company with nine *in*'s [ten, if one counts *ev'n*],
but in a sense that does not relate precisely to any of them; see 134.9, note [on
ideational puns].) *memory* = trisyllabic.
    9. *conceit* thought, idea. *this inconstant stay* this mutability (the phrase
functions like an oxymoron: its terms—*inconstant* and *stay*, i.e. "continuance"
—are contradictory; other meanings of *stay* make its presence here particularly
apt: *stay* meaning "support" was regularly used to mean a support for a plant,
and "stay of the sun" was a synonym for "solstice," the time when the sun
reaches its highest point—see *height* in line 7—and seems to stand still in its
northward or southward passage). Note the interplay among *Then the conceit*
and *inconstant* in this line, *When I consider* in line 1, and *When I perceive* in line
5: phonetic and ideational interplay among *When, When,* and *Then,* among
consider, preceive, and *conceit,* and among *con-, con-,* and *incon-*.
    10. *Sets you* places you, i.e. evokes your image. *rich in youth* (1) opulent,
magnificent during the time of your youthfulness (*in* indicating duration); (2)
possessed of abundance of youthfulness (*in* indicating that to which the attribute
is limited); (3) richly clothed in youthfulness (*in* expressing relation to that which
covers). The line pertains to all three of the metaphorical contexts introduced in
quatrain 1: the situation described suggests a theatrical presentation, and *Sets*
(although not yet a theatrical term), is both a botanical term (see *maiden gardens
yet unset* in 16.6), and an astronomical one (the sun sets). Also note that *Sets*
(places, locates in a fixed position) presents an incidental contrast to *inconstant*
in line 9. *before* Although *before* can only indicate place here, note that its
temporal senses (e.g. "earlier in time than") and qualitative senses (e.g. "in a
higher position than") pertain generally to this context. See 134.9, note (on
ideational puns), and compare *HVIII* II.iv.227–30: "we are contented / To
wear our mortal state to come with her, / . . . before the primest creature /
That's paragon'd o'th' world."
    11. *Where* in my sight (with a suggestion of "during the time of your youth-
fulness" which arises from a combination of a meaning that *in youth* has in line
10 and the reflection back upon *in youth* of the logical necessities introduced by
Where and answered by the potential *in* has for expressing location). *wasteful*
devastating, destructive, decay-causing (see *HV* III.i.13: "the wild and wasteful
ocean"). (Here its conjunction with *time* gives *wasteful* suggestions of other
meanings relevant to *time*: (1) "unoccupied," "spare," "profitlessly used"
[*OED* cites a passage from 1593 in which Archbishop Parker talks about riding
his "hobby horse" and "so spending my wasteful time within mine own walls"");
(2) "extravagant," "prodigal," "thriftless" [see 100.13, note].) *time debateth*

with decay   (1) time strives together with decay (*with* expressing association); or (2) time strives by means of decay (*with* expressing instrumentality); at first reading, however—before one realizes that time and decay are obvious allies, and before *To change* in line 12 makes the reading still less acceptable—one is likely to understand (3) time fights against decay (*with* expressing opposition—as it does in line 13); the false start is made probable by the commonness of such constructions as "debate with" and "fight with" to indicate opposition. See *Met.* XV.234–35: *tempos edax rerum, tuque, invidiosa vestustas, | omnia destruitis* (Golding recasts the construction, lines 258–59).

13. *all in war*   entirely at war (*in* expressing relation between the subject and an occupation).   *for love of you*   on account of my love for you (and, because of the context of contention, with non-logical overtones of "in order to obtain your love").

14. "As time withers you, I give you new life (by writing about you)." Despite a probable pun on *engraft* (in which the prefix presents *in* for the ninth time in the poem—see 81.2, note) and its Greek root *graphein*, "to write," and despite some likeness between a stylus (*graphis*) and a scion, a reader presumably does not recognize this first of several traditional claims for the immortalizing power of verse (see sonnets 18 and 19) until the line is glossed by the first quatrain of sonnet 16, which is both logically and syntactically linked with this one. As a reader comes upon it in the 1609 sequence, this line gives no hint as to which of the speaker's activities is described by *engraft*; he can be said to have been doing two things—writing verse and urging the young man to marry. He has previously called no attention to the power of his verse or to himself as writer; he has offered no alternatives to procreation as a way to immortality. The gloss given here, the one made obvious in sonnet 16, demands that the reader understand *I engraft you* as a metaphor from the practice of replacing the wasted limbs of old trees with slips that grow to be new boughs. However, except for this line, I find no recorded Renaissance use of the verb "to engraft" where its direct object is the receiving stock and not the grafted scion; the usual way to understand the metaphor would be "I insert you, a scion of one tree, into another tree." The reader's lack of foreknowledge about sonnet 16, the speaker's previous single-mindedness about urging procreation, and the similarities between grafting and sexual intercourse make it probable that a first reading of this line would suggest "As time withers you, I renew you by joining you to a wife." (Compare the French *enter au coin*. Also see 26.1–14, note, and consider *all* in *all in war*.)   *engraft*   Q gives "ingraft"; for a justification of the modern form, see 37.7, note.

SONNET 16

1. *But*   This sonnet is a syntactic, logical, and metaphorical continuation from the last lines of sonnet 15.   *mightier*   = dissyllabic, by syncopation.

3. "And secure yourself during your decline (and for the time of your ruin)." (In this context of warfare, *fortify yourself in* must suggest "And fortify yourself within . . . ." Even though the grammatical object, *your decay*, turns out

to be not a place but a condition, the initial suggestion of siege colors the completed clause.)

4. See 15.14, 17.13–14 and notes. *barren* (1) valueless, worthless; (2) incapable of bearing children. *rhyme* verses, poetry (see 107.11, note).

4,8. *than* = a modernization of the usual Q spelling, "then." (In Renaissance spellings "then" and "than" are interchangeable and both spellings are used to indicate both words. In line 4, the time-related topic of the poem and *Now* in line 5 generate ideational static that borders on punning. Compare 6.9; 17.10; 22.8; 23.9; 32.11; 40.2; 71.2; 92.3,5,8; 102.5,10; and 103.4,9,12,13; see also 111.4, note and 21.10 (where *then*, meaning both "at that time" and "as a result," appears in context of the topic of comparison and amid comparative constructions that are not "then" constructions).

5. *stand . . . on* See 52.1–2, note. *hours* See 58.3, note.

5,7. *hours, flowers* = perhaps monosyllables and perhaps dissyllables.

6. *And* As the quatrain is read a reader will presumably take *And* as introducing a second object for *stand . . . on* in line 5. (At the end of a line of verse neither a comma—like the one at the end of line 5—nor the absence of a comma is as efficient in the experience of even a modern reader as grammar-school rules of logical punctuation suggest; see my comments on punctuation in the Preface [pp. xiv–xvi] and in the long final note on sonnet 129.) The probability that *And* will seem to introduce a second direct object is increased because standing on top of *gardens* is more easily imagined than standing on top of *hours*. Only when he comes to *would bear* in line 7 can a reader know that *And* introduces a new clause. *unset* unplanted.

7. *With virtuous wish* innocently (presumably because in wedlock) and eagerly. (This phrase turns out to modify *maiden gardens*, but can first seem to indicate that with which the gardens are *yet unset*—as a garden can be said to be still unplanted with marigolds or zinnias.) *virtuous* = dissyllabic, by syncopation.

8. *liker* more like. *counterfeit* portrait (see *MofV* III.ii.114–15: "What find I here? / Fair Portia's counterfeit!") Shakespeare elsewhere plays on this meaning and *counterfeit* meaning "fraudulent imitation"; see *Tim* V.i.78–80.

9–12. This complex quatrain is discussed in detail in the Preface, pp. xi–xvii.

9. *repair* For the possible play on "re-father," see 3.3, note.

10. *pencil* painter's brush (the word was not used to describe an instrument for writing until the eighteenth century).

11. *fair* beauty.

12. *in eyes of men* See 55.11, note.

13. *give away yourself* (1) give yourself in marriage; (2) transfer yourself into children (see 77.10–12, note). *still* (1) even after that has happened; (2) forever (see 81.13).

14. *drawn* Shakespeare may be playing on the likeness of shape between the phallus—the instrument by which the young man will draw living pictures (and draw out, continue, the length of his life)—and the artist's instruments mentioned in line 10.

SONNET 17

2. *were* should be. *deserts* pronounced to rhyme with *parts* (see 11.4, note; 14.12; 49.10, note; and 72.6).

3. *heav'n* See 15.6, note. *tomb* See 83.12, note.

4. *parts* good qualities (as in the expression "a man of parts"). (This line may be intended to contain a crude and gratuitous play on "bodily parts" and/ or an allusion to a funeral effigy—a representation in half or three-quarter relief of the deceased, recumbent on top of his tomb; see 81.8.)

6. See 106.5, note (on blazons). *fresh* (1) new; (2) lively. *numbers* verses (as in 38.12, 79.3, and 100.6).

8. *touches* strokes of artistry. *ne'er* never (but see 118.5, note).

10. *than* = a modernization of Q's "then"; but see 16.4, 8, note.

11. *your true rights* the estimation to which you are entitled; Ingram and Redpath suggest the possibility "that there is also a pun here (as perhaps again in 23.6) on 'right' and 'rite.'" *a poet's rage* the products of the poet's inspiration, "heavenly touches" not in the subject but imagined by the divinely inspired poet (see 100.3, note).

12. *stretchèd meter* (1) poetic exaggeration ("meter" was regularly used as a synonym for "verse," composition *in* meter, in systematic rhythm); (2) strained meter, forced meter; Ingram and Redpath suggest (3) "the elongated metres used by some contemporary poets but beginning to go out of fashion— e.g. Poulter's Measure (12, 14 alternate), 'fourteeners' and continuous Alexandrines." (Richard Sylvester suggests to me that "reference may be to the sequence as a whole, 'stretched out' for 154 poems; the 'antique song' then becomes the whole previous Petrarchan convention.") A modern reader may be tempted to point out this line as an example of the artificially *stretchèd meter* it talks about; remember that the dissyllabic pronunciation of *stretched* was the Renaissance norm and the monosyllabic pronunciation was the exception. Compare 82.10. *ántique* old (but with a play on "antic"—"bizarre," "fantastic"; in the Renaissance "antique" and "antic" were pronounced alike and shared a variety of spellings; a similar pun may be intended in *1HIV* I.ii.58, where Falstaff says "old father antic").

13–14. Both this sonnet and sonnet 16 make oblique reference to the traditional notion of poet and poem as parent and child (see 76.8, note).

14. (1) "You would live twice in it (i.e. have a second life, live again, in your child) and [have a third life] in my verse." (2) "You would have two chances at immortality, in your child and in my verse." Neither a modern logical reading of the Q punctuation nor a more obvious and more satisfying substitute punctuation ("you should live twice, in it and in my rhyme") can include all the substance of the line or retain the metaphor of procreation (a pair turns into a trio) or do justice to the dazzling emblem of infinity that the line is by virtue of its construction (the young man is only one mortal; the line specifies that he will live *twice*; the line refers to three different kinds of "lives" [of which two can expand infinitely]: (a) the young man's own lifespan, (b) the lives of his child and his child's children, and (c) his survival as the subject of potentially eternal

and infinitely reproducible poems).   *my rhyme*   (1) this poem of mine; (2) my verse, my poems (see 107.11, note).

SONNET 18

1. This poem plays on the proverbial comparative formula "as good as one shall see in a summer's day" (Tilley, S967), meaning "as good as the best there is."
2. *temperate*   (= trisyllabic) not susceptible to extremes. The poem develops into a comparison between things of lasting duration—things that are unchanging—and things of limited duration—things that change. In that connection it is worth noting that the Latin source of *temperate* (*temperatus*—"moderate," "calm," "steady") is derived from *tempus*—"a period of time" or "time" in general. The word *temperate* thus embodies both of the qualities contrasted in the poem, and anticipates the paradox of line 12, where the beloved, bound to time the destroyer, grows to—fuses with—time, as a grafted scion grows to—and thus along with—a tree.
4. *lease*   allotted time. *hath all to short a date*   has too brief a duration. The phrase also has overtones of *date* in a sense incompatible with *short* but inherent in the legal language (a *lease* has a *date*, a fixed point of expiration): "comes too soon to its end." See *RII* I.iii. 150–51 (quoted in 87.4, note).
5. *Sometime*   sometimes (a common Renaissance variant; see 41.2, 64.3, 75.9, and 102.13).
6. *his*   its (but see 73.10, note).   *leath bed.*
7. *fair from fair*   (1) beautiful thing from beauty; (2) beautiful face from being beautiful (for *fair* meaning "fair face," see *AYLI* III.ii.84–85: "Let no face be kept in mind / But the fair of Rosalinde"; compare 83.2).   *sometime*   at some time, eventually.   *declines*   Although this use is metaphoric and indicates diminishment, not the relevance of *declines* to the sun in the preceding lines. Compare *Met.* XV.225–27 (lines 247–49 in Golding's version; see Appendix 2).
8. *untrimmed*   stripped of ornament (see *trim* in 98.2).
9. *fade* See 146.6, note (on *fading*).
10. *lose*   Q reads "loose," the most usual Renaissance spelling; the only instance where Q gives the modern spelling is 125.6. The words we spell "lose" and "loose" were not orthographically distinguished; see 88.8, 134.12, notes. *fair thou ow'st*   beauty you own (with a play on "to own" meaning "to be under obligation to render up").
11. *his shade*   The reference here is probably to "the valley of the shadow of death" (Psalm 23), the *umbra mortis* of the Vulgate; at any rate, *his shade* is presented as a place; the word is suggestive both of "the shades" (meaning the classical underworld, Hades) and of its inhabitants (Latin: *umbra*, "a spirit"), who wander there. (*Shade—darkness*—concludes a sequence of words that suggest the inevitable transitoriness of *a summer's day* in terms of light: *the eye of heaven shines, dimmed, declines,* and *fade*.)
12. Lines 13 and 14 establish "in lines of immortal verse" as the primary, if not the exclusive, meaning of *in eternal lines*. As he comes upon line 12, however, a reader may well understand *lines* in its root meaning, "cords" or "ropes," and

take *in eternal lines* as "bound eternally." That reading is sustained—though finally made less ominous—by *to time thou grow'st*, which recurs to the grafting metaphor of 15.14 (see note to line 3, above); a graft is usually bound in place by cords until it has coalesced with the stock. *Lines* also suggests "lines of life," the threads spun by the Fates in classical mythology; the Fates decided the length of each human life and cut each man's thread accordingly. *Eternal lines* would be threads never cut; they call to mind the progeny alluded to by *lines of life* in 16.9, *So should the lines of life that life repair.* Since a reader cannot be expected to know either that sonnet 17 was the last of the poems in support of procreation or that Shakespeare is about to claim an immortality for his verse that the two preceding poems specifically question, line 12 will probably appear to lead into another exhortation to marry. The imperceptibility of the dividing line between the procreation sonnets and sonnets 18–126 is a primary reason for assuming that 1–126 all concern the same relationship.

SONNET 19

1–2. See *Met.* XV.234–35 (lines 258–59 in Golding's translation; see Appendix 2). "Time devours all things" was proverbial (Tilley, T326).

4. *the . . . phoenix*   = a legendary bird, said to live several centuries, then to consume itself in fire, and then to rise from its own ashes ready to repeat the cycle forever; the phoenix, which time cannot defeat, is a symbol of immortality; see *Met.* XV.391–407 (lines 432–48 in Golding's translation; see Appendix 2). *in her blood*   (1) while she is still young and vigorous ("in blood" is a hunting term meaning "in good condition," "vigorous"); (2) alive, while the blood still moves in her veins (the phoenix always burned itself alive, so Time's victory here is dubious even if the burning is premature); (3) brutally, violently.

5. *thou fleet'st*   = Q's reading; many editors emend to "thou fleets," a common Renaissance variant on the second-person singular of verbs ending in *t*. The emendation, designed to perfect the rhyme with *sweets* in line 7, is unnecessary to the overall harmony of the quatrain.

5–6. See *Met.* XV.176–227 (196–251 in Golding) and 60, headnote. Tilley (T327) suggests that these lines reflect proverbial expressions like "Time has wings," "Time flees away without delay," and "Time flies." In 97.2 Shakespeare uses "fleeting" in another time-context where this class of proverbs pertains.

10. *ántique*   (1) old (with a suggestion "old-making"); (2) antic, capricious (see 17.12, note).

11. *course*   progress, passage (but with overtones of two other pertinent meanings of *course*: "pursuit" [of game with hounds—a hunting term] and "the charge of opposing knights in a tournament"). *untainted*   (1) unsullied; (2) not hit (by his opponent's lance—from "taint"—a jousting term, which *OED* demonstrates with this example from 1525: "They ran togider, & tainted eche other on the helmes").

14. *My love*   my beloved (as in line 9, but "the affection I feel" is possible and can be invoked by *my verse*). Line 14 is metrically limp and thus—whether by design or not—ironically undercuts its substance.

13–14. The proverb, "A faithful friend is like a phoenix" (Tilley, F688), may pertain here.

SONNET 20

Only this sonnet and sonnet 87 use feminine rhymes throughout.

On grounds of its vocabulary—though not of its final statement—this sonnet has been carelessly cited as evidence of its author's homosexuality. See 126.4, note, and Appendix 1.

1. *with*   by (but, before he finishes reading the line, a reader may take *with* to mean "that has" and so expect a construction similar to "a little whey face, with a little yellow beard" (*MWW* I.iv.20–21).   *painted*   (1) made; (2) colored—as with cosmetics.

2. *master mistress*   Q has "Master Mistris." Most editors give "master-mistress"; regardless of punctuation, however, the expression plays on (1) "supreme mistress" and (2) "male beloved" (*mistress* here is an almost technical term of courtly love: a lady to whom the lover swears allegiance—on the pattern of a vassal who swore allegiance to a lord, his master—and to whom he addresses his love poems; *mistress* was not yet a euphemism for "concubine"). In "Shakespeare's 'Master Mistris': Image and Tone in Sonnet 20" (*SQ*, XXII.2 [Spring 1971], 189–91), M. B. Friedman points out that "the terms 'Master' and 'Mistress,' used interchangeably to refer—as here—to something which is an object of passionate interest or a center of attention, come from the game of bowls. They are names for the small bowl thrown out at the beginning of the game . . . called the 'jack' . . . ."   *passion*   (1) emotion; (2) love; (3) poem (poems and speeches that expressed strong feeling were often called passions: in 1582 Thomas Watson called the individual sonnets of his *Hecatompathia* "passions"; see *MND* V.i.307: "her passion ends the play").

3. *heart*   See 24.13–14, note.   *acquainted*   Shakespeare may intend, and in this context his reader might have heard, a casual pun on the noun "quaint," which was still current as a term for the female sex organ (*OED* gives an example from 1598).

4. *false*   (1) deceitful; (2) fickle; (3) artificial (i.e. artificially beautified).

5. *rolling*   wandering, changing the direction of their attention.

6. *Gilding*   (1) making bright (as the rising sun seems to turn objects golden as it strikes them; the most popular Renaissance theory of vision held that the eye, like the sun, is a source of light, which it emits in beams; see 114.8 and *V&A* 1051, where Shakespeare says that Venus's eyes, "being open'd, threw unwilling light"); (2) imparting an appearance of beauty to, covering the imperfections of (see *2HIV* I.ii.139–41: "Your day's service at Shrewsbury hath a little gilded over your night's exploit on Gadshill").

7. Several Renaissance meanings of *hue* are pertinent in this context: (1) form, shape, appearance; (2) complexion; (3) color; and perhaps (4) apparition, phantasm, specter (*OED* demonstrates "hue" meaning "apparition" with this from 1603: "I conjure thee . . . Be [by] Sanctis of Hevin and hewis of Hell"). Moreover, *in his controlling* is ambiguous in construction (*controlling* operates

both like a noun and like an adjective); the phrase presents several meanings of both *in* and *controlling*: (1) "[are] in his power;" (2) "[are] held, contained, in his [hue]"; (3) "dominating by means of his [hue]"; (4) " challenging by means of his [hue]" (*OED* illustrates *to control* meaning "to challenge," "deny the value of" with this from 1582: "Heretikes controule the old authentical translation"). Since the word *hue* is repeated, the permutations of overlapping meanings and suggestions in the line are too numerous to spell out; these are a few: (1) A man in form, all forms (i.e. people of both sexes), are subject to his power (see line 8); (2) A man in complexion, he has power over all other complexions (i.e. causes people to flush or grow pale); (3) Although he has a man's complexion, it challenges all others; (4) A man in appearance, he is capable of presenting any appearance he chooses; (5) He has a man's complexion, but can have any complexion he chooses (suggesting a capacity for the cosmetic deceit denied in line 1; the contradiction has invited arguments that the line is corrupt and needs emendation); and perhaps (5) A human being in form, he has [magical] power over phantasms (see 18.11, note, and 53.1–2).

This line may be further complicated by a possible pun that Kökeritz (p. 77) says is "now probably lost beyond recovery"; we do not, of course, know just how *hue*, *hues*, and *his* were pronounced; in particular we do not know whether the initial *h* was pronounced in any of them. Perhaps in *hues* Shakespeare's contemporaries heard a pun on "use" meaning "employment for sexual purposes" (see line 14); they may also have heard a pun on "you" in *hue* (see 104.11 and *Titus* IV.ii.89–127), and/or a logically wanton play on "cunt rolling" (see *nothing* in line 12 and 58.2 and 3, notes). See also sonnet 82, where *use* and *hues* both figure prominently, and 104.11. In this context there is a chance that *all* would have had a bawdy anatomical reference too (see 26.1–14, note).

Q capitalizes and italicizes *hues*, thus fathering "W. Hughes" (or "Hewes"), a candidate for Mr. W. H. (see Appendix 1, p. 547); for a discussion of randomly italicized and capitalized words in Q, see Preface, pp. xvii–xviii.

8. *Which* The antecedent is imprecise—either *his [hue]* or (taking the participle as a noun), *his controlling. amazeth* throws into confusion, stuns ("amaze" was sometimes used as a synonym for "infatuate").

9. *for a woman* to be a woman (but with a play on "to be used by a woman," which anticipates *for women's pleasure* in line 13).

10,12. *a-doting, nothing* "Noting" was the usual Renaissance pronunciation of *nothing*; see 108.5, note.

11. *defeated* deprived, cheated (the word also carries overtones of a Renaissance meaning of "defeat" that is pertinent to the sonnet at large but inadmissible in the syntax of this line: "destroy the beauty, form, or figure of"—see *Oth* I.iii.346, "defeat thy favour [i.e. appearance] with an usurp'd beard").

12. See 136.11, note. *thing* (1) object; (2) generative organ (used both for "penis" [as in *Lear* I.v.49; see Florio, s.v., *cotale*] and for "vulva" [see *2Gent* III.i.340–43; Florio glosses *cotalina* as "a little pretty thing or quaint"]. *nothing* (1) worthless; (2) no-thing, a non-thing. "Nothing" and "naught" were popular cant terms for "vulva" (perhaps because of the shape of a zero); compare the use of *nothing* in *Ham* III.ii.105–16 (the "country matters" passage), and see Thomas

Pyles, "Ophelia's Nothing," *MLN*, XLIV (May 1949), 322–23; and Paul
Jorgensen, "Much Ado About *Nothing*," *SQ*, V,3 (Summer 1954),287–95. Here
the word adds an extra fillip of wit: the assertion that nature's addition is useless
for the speaker's male purposes incidentally designates the *thing* which would
be to his purpose something.

13. *pricked thee out* (1) selected you (to "prick" someone is to mark his
name with a puncture or a dot); (2) furnished you with a penis (for "prick"
meaning "penis," see Partridge). *for women's pleasure* (1) to be a delight to
women, to give pleasure to women; (2) to give sexual satisfaction to women, to
accommodate the lust of women (the specifically sexual sense of *pleasure* survived into modern times in the expression "to have one's pleasure" of a woman;
see Genesis 18.12, which the Geneva text renders "Therefore Sarah laughed
within her selfe, saying, After I am waxed olde, & my lord also, shal I have lust?"
and which AV renders ". . . Shall I have pleasure . . . ?"; see 48.12, 58.2,
97.2, and 121.3.

14. *use* employment for sexual purposes (but with a suggestion of "interest paid on a loan"—i.e. children; see 2.9; 4.7; 6.5; and 40.6). *and thy love's
use their treasure* (1) and let the privilege of using your love be a much valued
possession of theirs (2) and let their treasury (that in which they store treasure,
their "nothings"—see 6.3–4, and 52.2, 136.5, notes) be what your love uses.
(Note that *thy love's* can mean not only "of your lovemaking and of the passion
you feel" but also "your beloved's"—i.e. "of him who has your love," "my.")

13–14. By tradition the lady for whom a courtly lover languished was
physically unattainable; usually she was married. Martin points out that in
substituting a male subject for the Petrarchan mistress Shakespeare only enlarged upon the tradition; the *master mistress* "is beautiful, he prompts the
lover's highest idealism, and [being male rather than female] he is [literally]
inaccessible" (p. 84).

9–14. Compare Martial, *Epigrams* XI.22.9–10: *divisit natura marem: pars
una puellis, / una viris genita est.* (Nature has divided the male: one part is made
for girls, one for men.)

See 21.1, note. That poem, which is also on improbable couplements, makes
an illustratively improbable pair with this one.

SONNET 21

See the final note on sonnet 20.

1. *So is it not with me as with* my condition—my state—is not the same as
that of, things with me are not the way [such as] they are with. (For the *with*
construction see *Ham* III.iv.116: "How is it with you, lady?") The foregoing
gloss reflects the speaker's intention to declare a contrast between himself and
the kind of poet who writes less *truly*—a contrast that only becomes clear when
the piling-up of examples of poetic irresponsibility in lines 3–8 makes poetic
tactics the sole object of our attention. As the line is first read, however, the
inversion of "It is not so" in *So is it not* can seem to introduce a question, a
rhetorical question like 133.3: *Is't not enough to torture me alone. So is it not*

asks to be read as "That being the case, do you not agree that" (taking *So* as introducing a conclusion based on previously established facts), or as "Is it not the same" (taking *So* to mean "that way," "thus"), or, most probably, as a conflation of the two in which both syntactically appropriate senses of *So* are activated (note, also, that a third sense of *So*, "true," pertains to and sustains the interrogative gesture—even though the word order of *So is it not* does not invite a reader to seek out "Is it not so" within it). The interrogative reading is momentarily probable even if the poem is read in isolation; if the poem is read in the Q order, lines 2 and 3 make a just comment on sonnet 20: a male beloved who has the beauty of a woman stirs the speaker to address him as one would expect a woman to be addressed; the condition of the speaker is thus comparable to that of a poet inspired by an illusion—by a picture or by a woman whose beauty is cosmetically achieved. (Note *painted* in 20.1.) Moreover, at the same time that the speaker's actual intent in *So is it not* is emerging in lines 3–8, the injustice of the contrast between *that muse* and the couplement-making, earnestly poetic speaker becomes evident too. Thus the rejected reading of line 1 comes ironically to be just: it is indeed with the speaker as with that other muse.

    muse   poet (a standard metonymy activated by the logic inherent in the comparison with *me*).

    2. *a painted beauty*   (1) a work of art (a painting or someone else's poetry); (2) a person whose beauty is cosmetically achieved.

    3. "Who [i.e. *that muse*] even uses heaven as an ornament for his poem and/ or for his beloved." See sonnets 105 and 130. *heav'n*   (1) the sky and the things in it—the sun, moon, and stars; (2) the highest things (an example of literal height used as an emblem for height of worth—compare 116.8); (3) deities or near-deities (a synecdoche for gods and goddesses and/or the Christian god, the angels, saints, etc.; see 105, 130, and notes). (Technically, the syntax limits the reference of *Who* to *that muse*, but Renaissance readers and writers were even less scrupulous than we are about distinguishing between "who," the nominative, and "whom," the accusative [see "Between who?" in *Ham* II.ii.193]. The inverted syntax of this line thus lets it include the shadow of an example of the sort of hyperbolic compliment *that muse* might crank out: "a . . . beauty . . . who [i.e. 'whom'] even heaven uses to ornament itself.") *heav'n it-*   = two syllables: "hev nit."

    4. *every fair with his fair*   every kind of beauty and/or beautiful thing with the beautiful subject of his poem, his fair one. *rehearse* name over, mention (as in 38.4—with substantively unharnessed but pertinent overtones of "say over mechanically," "practice repeating," as an actor does words written for him).

    5. *Making a couplement*   Note that this phrase actually makes a strained and unexpected couplement with the self-contained unit that appeared syntactically complete with the completion of quatrain 1. (A similar sense of unnecessary couplement is evoked when line 8 tacks an unexpected adjectival clause to the last of the three exemplary pairs in lines 6 and 7. Those three pairs also illustrate the unreasonable extension the speaker asserts. The first, *With sun and moon*, presents two huge and properly paired entities in the four syllables of a perfectly uncomplicated *with* construction. The second, *with earth and sea's rich gems*,

presents a disruptively expansive addition to the category inhabited by the first
syntactically defined pair [*sun and moon* and *earth* are comparable as bodies in
the cosmos], but, when *earth* is linked by *and* to *sea's*, the second pair emerges as
smaller in scope than the first [*sun* and *moon* are two comparable variously
contrasting entities; paired with "sea," *earth* comes to mean not "the earth" but
"the land," and *earth* and "sea" are two comparable contrasting parts of "the
earth," which, in the cosmological terms in which the previous pair operated, is
only one entity]. The lesser pair, which takes momentary shape in a phrase
syllabically equal and syntactically identical with the first, turns out to be lesser
still [not "earth and sea," but *earth and sea's . . . gems; gems* are smaller than
the places where they are found], longer syllabically, more complicated syntactically, less clearly a pair [gems of the earth and gems of the sea are two varieties
within one category], less clearly a proper pair [syntactically the phrase can be
read as a couplement of *earth* on the one hand and *sea's rich gems* on the other],
and less clear generally [what is paired here? *earth* and *gems* or two kinds of
gem? and, if it is two kinds of gem, are they the minerals of the earth and the
pearls of the sea or the minerals found underground and those rumored to lie on
and beneath the floor of the sea?]. Moreover, when *gems* establishes the final
form of the second pair, it again blurs the distinction between its elements and
those of the first [by reducing *sun* and *moon* to the size and function of sparkling
pendants for *ornament*]. The third pair takes up as many syllables as the first two
together; its genitive first element is syntactically comparable to the genitive
construction that emerged at the end of the second and transformed it; and so
April's . . . flow'rs in one respect continues—and thus threatens the closed
identity of—the second pair, while *first-born* reaches back to invade the first pair
by its relation to the sound of *sun*, "son"; within line 7 the contrast between the
paired elements is so great that they do not seem properly comparable at all [the
first element—in which the *flow'rs* are not only *April's* but *April's first-born*—is
highly specific, takes up five syllables, and presents a traditional emblem of
littleness, frailty, and inconsequentiality; the second element, *all things rare*—
which fulfills the ironic trend of the two lines toward increasing numerousness
and thus toward undercutting one of the ideas inherent in *rare*, and which
thereby points up the potential contradiction in terms inherent in a phrase that
couples *all things* with *rare*—is totally unspecific, takes up only three syllables,
and takes in *sun, moon, gems, flow'rs*, and anything else imaginable]; and yet the
third pairing is perversely and illogically apt [consider the phonetic likeness
between the genitive *April's* and the plural *all things*; and compare the way the
easy jingle of *and all things rare* and *That heaven's air* strengthens the link by
which the small second element in the *flow'rs–things* pair in line 7 is augmented
by the whole unexpected length of line 8].)

proud In effect the word operates twice: it registers the presumptuousness of
such a poet in making such extravagant comparisons, and it describes the stuff
of his similes as *proud*—"grand," "exalted," "splendid" (see 2.3, note). *of
proud compare* (1) consisting of proud comparisons (see *compare* in 35.6 and
130.14; *OED* gives this from 1589: "What need compare where sweet exceeds
compare?"); (2) with an exalted compeer, with a noble equal (as in the phrase

"without compare"; *OED* gives this from the 1580's: "The envious man / That dares avow there liveth her compare"); (3) which is comparable with the most splendid similes of better writers, which is of compare with what is proud (for *of*-plus-noun to denote a quality, see *of trust* in 48.4 and *Ham* II.i.64 and IV.vi. 18: "we of wisdom and of reach" and "They have dealt with me like thieves of mercy"). (This phrase is just sufficiently awkward, inefficient, and non-idiomatic to contribute to the poem's ongoing demonstration of the strained poetizing it deprecates. Moreover, the interplay among the senses of *compare* points toward the inherent paradox of the poetic practice of using comparisons to assert that a beloved is unique, is without compeer.)

   a couplement of proud compare   Shakespeare may intend a play on the phonetically, ideationally, and etymologically related words *compare* and "pair"; *couplement* and *compare* ("comparison," "pairing with") are not here used as synonyms but are potentially synonymous. (The poetic effect of using synonyms non-synonymously is comparable to that of meter, in which urgent continuity and equally urgent change coexist harmoniously in a meta-rational—a supernatural—unity of conflicting organizational systems which fuse perfectly and yet retain their independence and vigor undiminished and unmodified. The unforced, unostentatious coexistence of these two pairable words has the kind of effect unavailable in the mechanical verse the speaker mocks and parodies in the sonnet at large. Among the dizzying multitude of different kinds of couplement this poem exemplifies, it manages to include demonstrations of both true poetic wit and grotesque caricatures of the empty gestures it scorns; here Shakespeare makes one phrase simultaneously exemplify both. For a similar coexistence of successful and unsuccessful poetic effects, compare, on the one hand, the delicate variation between *heav'n* in line 3 and *heaven's* in lines 8 and 12 [see 86.5, note] and, on the other, the hollow thud in line 12 when *in heaven's air* ostentatiously echoes *heaven's air in* from line 8.)

   5–6. *compare / With*   "To compare [something] with [something else]" is a standard locution, a locution that might naturally occur in this poem about comparisons. The fact that the construction never quite occurs in the sonnet could be presented as an emblem of its appropriately perverse method of illustrating contorted comparison. The word *with* occurs six times in the first two quatrains; in line 1 it occurs twice (and in a comparative construction), but not in the sense it has in "to compare with"; here, where *compare* and *with* are in actual conjunction, the standard construction is replaced by *couplement . . . with*, and *compare* is only part of a modifying phrase.

   7. *rare*   splendid, precious, excellent (with ironic overtones of "unusual," "scarce"; see the note on line 5 above, 56.14, and 52.5, note). (In specifying *April's first-born flow'rs* [i.e. spring flowers, rather than flowers of summer], Shakespeare refers to the metaphoric popularity of violets, but in this context the epithet is comically suggestive of one more kind of unnatural and contrived couplement, one that is premature; see 60.9 and 94.9, notes—on *flos aetatis*.)

   8. *rondure*   sphere (an Anglicization of the French *rondeur*, glossed by Cotgrave [1611] as "Roundnesse," "globinesse"; by using so self-consciously abstruse a word, Shakespeare mocks poetic affectation by illustration; the joke is

ironically underscored by a standard figurative use—similar to those of "round," "roundly," "roundness" in Renaissance English—of *rondeur* in French: after the literal meanings Cotgrave adds "plainenesse," "bluntnesse," "free speech," "good earnest"). *hems* encircles, bounds. (Note that this line would have been aurally indistinguishable from "That heaven's heir [possessor] in this huge rondure hymns." For the likeness of *air* and "heir," see the note below on line 13; for the likeness of *hems* and "hymns" see Kökeritz, p. 187 and *AYLI* I.iii.19: "cry 'hem' and have him." *OED* credits Milton with initiating the use of "hymn" as a verb, but Shakespeare adapted parts of speech at will [see 101.7, note—on *beauty's truth to lay*] and was generally appreciative of the likeness of "hymn" and "him"; see 85.7, note, 102.8, note, and *Per* I.iv.74: "Thou speak'st like him's ['himnes' in Q1] untutor'd to repeat." Also see Donne's plays on "him" and "hymn" in "To the Lady Magdalen Herbert" ["Her of your name . . ."] and in lines 33–38 of "The Second Anniversary" [for the sexual senses of "wit," see 26.1–14, note]:

> Immortall Maid, who though thou would'st refuse
> The name of Mother, be unto my Muse
> A Father, since her chast Ambition is,
> Yearely to bring forth such a child as this.
> These Hymnes may worke on future wits, and so
> May great Grand children of thy prayses grow.)

5–8. Note that as this quatrain piles up its stylistic ironies it also develops a larger, gentler, and more paradoxical irony in being so good—so stirring, such a good example of the efficacy of hyperbolic comparisons and of the potential credibility of a comparer's voice. At the point where the speaker's demonstration of hyperbolic excess reaches its height, the *this* of *in this huge rondure* and the sweep that results from the final couplement of the whole length of line 8 to the last small unit of line 7 turn the quatrain into a convincing, immediate, personal testimony to an infatuation that transcends rational perspectives. The quatrain is not only an example of what it mocks but evidence that such mockery is not always justified.

9. "I pray that I, who am true in love (a faithful lover) and true in love (truly in love, genuinely feel the passion I report) may in love (for love's sake, in charity) but (only, do no more than) write truly (tell the truth) in love (about love, with regard to love)." *In love* operates four times (compare *in love* in 118.9, and see 118.9–10, note); *true* operates twice and also participates in the interplay between it and *truly*. Also note the potential but unexploited pun that relates *truly* and *write*: the variously relevant, absent words "rightly" and "right" are a synonym for *truly* and a homonym of *write* (see 141.13–14, note).

10. *then* (1) on that occasion; (2) therefore, in that case.

11. *any mother's child* Note the echo of *April's first-born flow'rs* in line 7. *not so bright* The idiom in which this phrase = "not very intelligent" is modern and American.

13. *like of* like. *hearsay* unverified reports (Q: "heare-say"). The word is curiously weak and flat here; its choice was probably dictated by Shakespeare's

desire to include the idea that other poets write (say) only what they have heard, i.e. stock phrases (like *gold candles* in line 12) and ideas they have mechanically acquired from their reading. (Richard Sylvester points out to me that the inclusion of that idea adds "I am not writing for profit.") Shakespeare may also have been attracted to the word *hearsay* by its potential for play on "heresy," "here-say," "air-say" (see *heaven's air* in line 12), and possibly "her-say" or "hare-say"; the evidence of Elizabethan puns and rhymes is not definitive, but the words we spell "her," "here," "hear," "hair," "hare," "heir," and—since initial *h* was ordinarily silent in common words—"ear" and "air," all apparently sounded enough alike to be confusable (see Kökeritz, pp. 90, 103, 111, 448, and 449). "Heresy" is trisyllabic in Shakespeare; "heretic" is dissyllabic in one instance, *Lear* III.ii.84, where it may be purposefully syncopated to accentuate a pun on "her" and/or "hare": "No heretics burn'd but wenches' suitors." For "hare" meaning "whore" see Partridge and *R&J* II.iv.125–35; in this context the bawdy connotations of the syllable might have colored not only *hearsay* but *air* in lines 8 and 12 and—just possibly—*compare* in line 5. Note, moreover, that *fixed in heaven's air* in line 12 would have been capable of an incidental but pertinent suggestion of "stuck in heaven's hair [as ornaments]."

14. The line alludes to a proverb: "he praises who wishes to sell" (Tilley, P546); see 102.3–4. *that purpose not* who do not intend.

SONNET 22

1. *glass* See 3.1, note.

2. *of one date* of an age, the same age.

4. *expiate* end, bring peace to (for another instance of this odd use of *expiate*, see Marlowe, *Dido* V.i. 1724–25: "dye to expiate / The griefe that tires upon thine inward soule"; the word carries overtones of its more usual meanings: "purify" and "extinguish the guilt of").

5–6. "The lover is not where he lives but where he loves" was proverbial (Tilley, L565).

5–14. The wit of these lines derives from seeming to take a metonymy literally. The particular metonymy (substitution of "heart" for "love," "affection," or "devotion") was so common that it has passed into the language as a special meaning for "heart"; see Spenser, *FQ* I.xii.40: "Thrise happy man . . . possessed of his Ladies hart and hand," and Sidney's "My true love hath my hart, and I have his" (Ringler, pp. 75–76). See also Ephesians 5:29, which is part of the marriage service and is quoted in 36, headnote.

6. *seemly* becoming and appropriate.

6–7. Compare 109.3–4 and 133.13–14.

8. *then . . . than* = a modernization of Q's "then . . . then"; see 16.4, 8, note.

9. *love* my love, my beloved (this sense—a noun, vocative—is revealed by the necessities of the completed line; as a reader comes upon *love*, however, he may take it as an imperative verb).

10. *for myself* (1) of me; (2) for my own benefit. *for thee will* (1) will [be

careful of myself] for your benefit; (2) will [be careful] of you. (Only sense (1)
fits the premise of lines 5–7 and 11–12, but the involved syntax of lines 9–10 and
the two ambiguous appearances of *for* make this line demonstrate a reality in the
fanciful fusion of identities that the poem discusses: within the line, to safeguard
either is actually to safeguard the other. This phrase may also play on the poet's
name: "I am Will for your benefit"; or—since the speaker is the beloved and the
beloved is the speaker—"you who are Will"; see 135, 136, and 143.)

  11. *bearing*   carrying (but in a context that invokes overtones of "baring"
[see lines 5 and 6] and "bearing a child" [see line 12]).   *chary*   carefully.

  13. *Presume not on*   do not expect to regain.

SONNET 23

  1. *As an unperfect actor*   (1) like an actor who has not properly learned his
part (Shakespeare sometimes uses "perfect" to mean "word-perfect"; see line 6
and *MND* I.ii.95–6: "There we may rehearse . . . . Take pains; be perfect");
(2) like an actor who has not properly learned his craft. Considering the fact that
Shakespeare was an actor by profession, there is also an initial suggestion of a
positive fault inherent in being an actor: (3) since I am a mere actor.

  2. *with*   by.   *put besides*   put out of, made to forget (*besides* was a standard
variant on "beside").

  3. *Or*   Before a reader comes to line 4 and sees that *Or* introduces a parallel
construction that presents an alternative for the whole of lines 1 and 2, *Or* can
seem to introduce an alternative only to *fear* in line 2, an alternative cause of the
actor's lapse of memory.   *some fierce thing replete with too much rage*   some
wild beast too full of anger (but *rage* also meant "lust," and gives the line and
those that follow it bizarre sexual undermeaning; for the sexual meanings of
thing, see 20.12, note).

  4. *heart*   capacity for action (but, in this context, with overtones of "affection," "love," "devotion"; see 22.5–14, note. Shakespeare may have picked
the word because its pronunciation invited confusion with "art"; see 24.13–14,
note).

  5. *for fear of trust*   (1) afraid to trust myself; (2) afraid of responsibility; (3)
afraid that I will not be trusted (Willen and Reed point out that "the curious
phrasing here is probably partly owing to Shakespeare's interest in the paradoxical conjunction of 'fear' and 'trust' ").

  6. *perfect*   (1) memorized; (2) exact, unalloyed, not marred by errors; (3)
holy.   *of love's rite*   (Q has "right"; the two words were not then differentiated
by spelling; see 17.11.) (1) that is love's ritual; (2) that is love's due (Shakespeare
elsewhere uses "rite of love" specifically to mean "sexual intercourse"; see *AW*
II.iv.39–40—where, incidentally, the "rite"–"right" pun is underscored by the
inclusion of the word "due": "The great prerogative and rite of love, / Which,
as your due, time claims, he does acknowledge").

  7–8. *mine own love's strength* and *mine own love's might*   (1) the strength/
might of my passion; (2) the strength/might of my beloved (see 34.13, note).

  7. *decay*   become weak.

8. *O'ercharged* overloaded. *burthen* burden.

9. *books* writings. ("Book" was not limited to its modern sense; Ingram and Redpath cite *Cymb* V.iv.133 as an instance where Shakespeare uses "book" to describe a single sheet of paper with writing on it; *books* could describe a sheaf of manuscript poems. Here Shakespeare may intend a play on "book" meaning the written text of a stage play. *OED* [Supplement I, 1972] cites Florio's 1598 *Worlde of Wordes*: "Buriasso . . . a prompter or one that keeps the book for plaiers." Although *books* is the Q reading and makes sense, most editors have emended it to "looks"; see note on *presagers*, below.)

9, 12. *then, than* Q spells both words "then"; see 16.4, 8, note.

10. *presagers* messengers? (This word has not been satisfactorily explained, and is the probable source of the wish to change *books* in line 9 to "looks." No other instance of "presager" or any form of "presage" is known where the reference is not to foreshowing the future. *OED*'s one supposed example of a use of "presage" in a sense similar to the one *presagers* seems to have here is based on a careless reading of *FQ* I.x.53–61. Supporters of the substitution of "looks" for *books* point to the stage simile in the first two lines and argue that *dumb presagers* alludes to the dumb shows that preceded and summarized the acts in some early Elizabethan plays.)

11. *Who* the antecedent is *books* (although a reader presumably extrapolates an additional antecedent from *my* in line 10 and understands *Who* as also indicating "I").

12. *more hath more expressed* has more often said more.

14. *with* The Q spelling, "wit," probably reflects only the printer's inclination or carelessness, but, whatever the spelling, Shakespeare and his readers probably heard some kind of likeness between contemporary pronunciations of *with* and *wit*, the last word of the poem. Shakespeare puns on "withe" (often spelled "with") and "wit" in *LLL* I.ii.90–94; see Kökeritz, p. 154. *fine wit* acute intelligence. *wit* See 26.1–14, note and the Donne passage in 21.8, note.

SONNET 24

The body of this poem is a playfully grotesque and literal-minded elaboration on a traditional topic of courtly love poetry: the reflection a lover sees of himself in the beloved's eye (see 55.14). The sonnet is carefully designed to boggle its reader's mind (make his eyes glaze), but some sanity may be retained if one holds on to the idea of two people looking into one another's eyes.

1, 2. *eye, heart* See the final note to sonnet 141.

1. *stelled* portrayed. This is the generally accepted emendation for Q's "steeld." Emendation may not be justified; the arguments for and against are given by Ingram and Redpath, who retain the Q reading as a typically Shakespearian innovation in language; "steeld," they say, "can bear an intelligible and vigorous meaning, 'engraved' or 'indelibly carved.'" They suggest that "steeld" may be a nonce use not of "to steel," here meaning "to engrave with a steel point," but of "to style," here meaning "to inscribe with a stylus": "'style' used

as a noun meaning 'stylus' could, in the sixteenth and seventeenth centuries, be spelled [and pronounced] 'steele.' " The arguments for "stelled," "steeled," and "styled" are lengthy, manifold, and valid; they cancel one another out. Fortunately, the intended sound and sense are generally obvious and are not much affected by an editor's choice. Note, however, that "steel" would participate in a constellation of words that pertain to reflection and vision (e.g. *pérspective* [line 4] occurs in a context of *windows* and *glazèd* [line 8], and "perspective" and "perspective glass" were terms for "telescope" [*OED*, 2]; *table* [line 2] was already used to mean the flat upper surface of a cut gem and to refer to a diamond cut with such an upper surface, a "table diamond" [*OED*, 18; this connotation of *table* also pertains to *stelled*, "cut"]): in this context any use of "steel" could suggeśt a "steel glass," a mirror. Note also that Q's "steel'd" in 112.8 is the occasion of one of the other major cruxes in the sonnets; see the final note to 112.

2. *table*   tablet, board on which a picture is drawn or words are written. See 122.1, 1–2, notes.   *heart*   The device here is a variation on that in 22.5–13; the context involves organs of the body (eye, heart) and also the emotions for which "heart" is synonymous. "To write something in the table of one's heart" was a stock metaphor (see Proverbs 3:3: "write them upon the table of thine heart," which the margin of the Geneva Bible glosses as "Have them ever in remembrance"). The wit here is in revivifying the metaphor to the point of literalness. (Also see the note on lines 13–14 below.)

3. *frame*   picture frame (but with a play on "skeletal structure" and "corporeal frame").

4. The conjunction of *pérspective* and *it* here is unusual; since a reader is called upon to decide whether *pérspective* is used adverbially—as Renaissance practice allowed any noun or adjective to be—or as a noun (of which the pronoun *it* is a redundant duplication), the reader is likely to understand the construction both ways. In addition, both the noun form of *pérspective* and *best painter's art* have several pertinent senses here: (1) "And, seen from the proper angle, the picture is an example of the best work of which a painter is capable (or is the finest work of *Mine eye*, the painter)"; (2) "And the skill to make 'perspectives' is the best skill a painter can have" (both (1) and (2) allude to a kind of picture that was particularly popular with the Elizabethans; a "perspective" is a picture drawn so as to appear distorted except from one particular point of view—see the quotation in the note to line 8 below; the allusion is particularly apt because one's reflection in another person's eye is, like any reflection on a convex surface, distorted); (3) "And the skill of drawing objects so that they look as they do in reality is the best skill a painter can have (or is the skill of the best painters)"; (4) "And the science of sight (optics, perspective), is the best skill a painter can have (see *Mine eye*, line 1). (See the note to line 1. Note also that line 5 presents a retroactive play on the Latin root of *pérspective*: *perspicere*, "to see through.")

5. *through the painter*   by means of the painter (but with a strong suggestion of "by looking through me," i.e. through flesh and rib cage to the heart).   *see his skill*   perceive his ability.

5–6. *must you see his skill | To find . . .*   (1) in order to discover . . . , you must see his skill; (2) you must see his skill in finding, his ability to find, . . . (Q's comma after *skill* does not effectively limit the relationship between lines 5 and 6).

7. *still*   (1) always, forever; (2) constantly; (3) now no less than before.

8. *his*   its (but see 73.10, note).   *glazèd*   furnished with glass (but with a suggestion of "covered with a film," the meaning "glazed" has in *RII* II.ii.16–20, a passage that shares much of the language of this sonnet: "For sorrow's eye, glazed with blinding tears, / Divides one thing entire to many objects, / Like perspectives which, rightly gaz'd upon, / Show nothing but confusion—ey'd awry, / Distinguish form").

9. *good turns*   Note the same expression in a related context in 47.2.

10. *drawn*   (1) delineated, pictured; (2) extracted, drawn out.

13. *this cunning want*   lack this skill.   *art*   skill. (There are overtones here of *cunning* meaning "craftiness" and of *art* meaning "trickery," "use of wiles.")

14. *draw*   delineate (but with plays on "attract" and on "extract"). This line simultaneously exploits and undercuts the concept of the heart as drawing board and the body as display case by leaping to another rhetorical stance and using the traditional metonymy of *heart* as "inmost thoughts and feelings," "essence," in the traditional assertion that everyone's true thoughts are invisible (compare *Oth* III.iii.138–45).

13–14. *art, heart*   These two words, pronounced enough alike for punning, capsule the wit of the poem. See 23.4, Kökeritz, pp. 92, 307–08, and the word-play of *Shrew* IV.ii.8–10:

> *Lucentio.*   I read that I profess, 'The Art to Love'.
> *Bianca.*   And may you prove, sir, master of your art!
> *Lucentio.*   While you, sweet dear, prove mistress of my heart.

On the other hand, Shakespeare's practice of saying "mine art," "an art," "my heart," and "a heart" testifies that the two words were not exactly the same in pronunciation; *heart* had not clearly lost its initial *h*, and *art* had not acquired one. Moreover, the play on *art/heart* in *Shrew* is sustained by the ideational rhyme, "master of" / "mistress of," and works in any pronunciation of *art* and *heart*.

SONNET 25

1. *who are in favor with their stars*   whose stars are propitious (the astrological statement is cast in a metaphor of court politics; see *RIII* I.i.79: "we will keep in favour with the King").

1,4,7,8. *in*   See 81.2, note.

3. *of*   from (see *Cymb* III.iii.102: "to bar thee of succession").

4. *Unlooked for*   (1) unregarded, ignored; (2) unexpectedly, beyond expectation (taking the expression adverbially).   *joy in that I honour most*   (1) take pleasure from, delight in, what I most honor; (2) exult because I am more devoted, give more honor, than anyone else. (*Joy* and *in* also have pertinent

overtones of their astrological uses. *OED* cites a fifteenth-century reference to
the "Joys of the Planets," and explains the term with these later examples:
"Joyes of the Planets are when they are in those houses where they are most
powerful and strong, as Saturn joyeth in [i.e. when its location is] Scorpio"—
1658; "Joyes of the Planets . . . are certain Dignities [i.e. augmentations of
their influence] that befall them, either by being in the place of a Planet of like
Quality or Condition, or when they are in a House of the Figure agreeable to
their own Nature"—1706; "Every planet, according to Ptolemy, is in his joy
when another is dignified in any of his dignities"—1819).

    5. *favorites* = trisyllabic.

    6. *But* only. *marigold* = "named ye husbandmans Dyall, for that the
same so aptlye declareth the houres of mornyng and evening, by the opening
and shutting of it" (T. Hill, *Profitable Art of Gardening*, 1597); the flower then
called marigold was probably an old strain of "pot marigold," *calendula of-
ficinalis*).

    7. *pride* (1) inordinate self-esteem; (2) splendid display; (3) prime (see
99.12). See also *Lucrece* 705–06: "While Lust is in his pride, no exclamation /
Can curb his heat" and the notes to 151.10; 52.12; 64.2; 75.5; 76.1; 98.8; 99.12–
13; 103.1,2; and 104.4.

    9. *painful* (1) pain-giving; (2) full of pain, often wounded; (3) painstaking,
diligent. *warrior* = dissyllabic, by syncopation. *fight* This is the more popular of two generally favored emendations of Q's "worth." The other, "might,"
is somewhat more likely to have been misread as "worth" when written in
sixteenth-century secretary script. However, this looks less like the result of a
printer's misreading than of a printer or copyist remembering the sense and
rhythm and neglecting to check his copy. All else being equal, *famousèd for
fight* may be preferred as more pompous and imitative of military glory. (A few
editors have retained "worth" and changed *quite* in line 11 to "forth.")

    10. *foiled* (1) defeated; (2) defiled; (3) thwarted, disappointed.

    11. *razèd quite* erased completely.

    13–14. *belovèd, removèd* Q has "beloved" and "removed." The printer's
usual (though not invariable) practice suggests that, if these words were intended
to be pronounced as we now pronounce them, they would have been spelled
"belov'd" and "remov'd" in Q.

    14. *remove* depart (with a suggestion of "change," "be fickle," as in 116.4).
be removèd be dismissed (from office or favor).

SONNET 26

    This sonnet uses language and conceits traditional in Elizabethan literary
dedications. Shakespeare used some of the same ones in dedicating *Lucrece* to
Southampton. Although the likeness between this poem and the *Lucrece* dedication is purely generic, the likeness has been frequently pressed into service to
support Southampton's candidacy as the addressee in the sonnets.

    2. *duty* respect, devotion.

3. *ambassage* message (like those, often oral, carried by official ambassa-
dors). The word was apparently stressed on the first syllable and, more lightly,
on the third.

4. *To witness* to bear witness to. *wit* literary cleverness.

5. *wit* (1) intelligence; (2) skill.

6. *bare* meager (with a suggestion of "naked"; see line 8). *wanting* lacking.

7. *But* except. *conceit* opinion, idea (with a play on *conceit* meaning "ingenious expression," "product of literary cleverness"; see *wit*, line 4).

8. *In thy soul's thought* The phrase operates as it would if it appeared twice;
first it locates *conceit of thine*; then it indicates the place of bestowal. *naked*
(1) unclothed; (2) deficient; (3) unprotected, defenseless. *all naked* = a modifier for *wit* (called *bare* in lines 5 and 6) and/or for *soul's thought* (because of
proximity and because it complements the intimacy *soul's thought* implies).
bestow (1) place; (2) give lodging to. (This line has some echoes of another
familiar conceit of Elizabethan dedications, one not found in the *Lucrece*
dedication: the author's modest comparison of his book or poem to a sickly
baby or deformed child thrown upon the charity of the patron, who is asked to
cherish it not for itself but for its father's sake; see 76.8, note.)

9. *moving* actions, course of life (there is some wit in the choice of this word:
in astrology and astronomy the "moving" of a heavenly body referred to the
course it followed).

10. See 25.1, note. *Points on* directs its rays at (see *RII* I.iii.146–47: "his
golden beams . . . / Shall point on me and gild my banishment"). *fair* auspicious, propitious, promising (as in 78.2; *OED* gives this from 1550: "Ther
is no better . . . nor no fayrer cure"). In this context of appearances, *fair* also
carries suggestions of its use as a synonym for "beautiful." *aspéct* astrological influence (but with overtones of three other meanings pertinent to the relationship either of lord and vassal or of lover and beloved: (a) "regard," "consideration"; (b) "appearance"; (c) "look," "glance").

11. *tottered* tattered (see 2.4).

12. *thy* an almost universally accepted emendation for Q's "their"; the
same easy printer's error occurs or is suspected thirteen more times in the collection: 27.10; 35.8; 37.7; 43.11; 45.12; 46.3, 8, 13, 14; 69.5; 70.6; and 128.11, 14.
worthy of thy sweet respect (1) worthy of your kind regard; (2) fit to be seen
(because now clothed). The phrase = "respectable"—in both senses. (Sisson
retains Q's "their" on the grounds that "their sweet respect" can mean "their
sweet object of regard"; even granting that argument, however, the emendation is probably called for if only because "their" pulls a reader up short; antecedents for "their" can be found, but only by a reader driven to the search.)
worthy For the possible pun on "worth thee," see 72.4, note.

14. *prove* test.

1–14. This poem is netted together by a series of variations on the idea of
showing; see *show my wit* in line 4, *show it* in line 6, *show me worthy* in line 12,
and *show my head* in line 14. The play on *witness* and *wit* in line 4, the curious
linkage among *wit so poor* in line 5, *bare* (meaning "poor"), *show it* in line 6, and

all naked in line 8, all combine to give the poem overtones of witty—though puerile—obscenity. *Wit*, as Ellis clearly demonstrates (pp. 103–10), was commonly used in punning contexts like this one to mean "penis" (and "vulva" as well—see 21.8, note); Ellis cites French *vit*, Italian *vitto*, and a great deal of evidence in English including *AYLI* IV.i.142–52. Note also *conceit* (line 7) and *head* (line 14). Like any word beginning *con*, *conceit* is always open to sexual joking in Shakespeare (see *HVIII* II.iii and 151.1, 2, 13, note). *Head* is used to mean "penis" and/or "foreskin" in *Measure* IV.ii.1–4 (where its first use is literal; its second plays on "male sexual organs" and "lord and master" [see Ephesians 5:23, quoted in the marriage service: "For the housband is the wives head"]; and the third means "maidenhead"): — ". . . Can you cut off a man's head?" —"If the man be a bachelor, sir, I can; but if he be a married man, he's his wife's head, and I can never cut off a woman's head." (There may also be an illogical extra fillip of wit in Hamlet's "I mean my head upon your lap" in the "country matters" passage [*Ham* III.ii.110].)

It is possible that *all* (the opposite of *nothing* [see 20.12, note]), also had a sexual sense (probably derived from "awl" and meaning "penis"—but, perhaps under the influence of a phonetic likeness to "hole," used for female genitalia also). If such a pun existed, it would have given *all naked* a logically casual suggestion of "with penis bared." Ellis says this:

> For the suggestiveness of *all*, compare Lyly's *Mother Bombie*, 4.2: *Accius. My father? What need you to care, I hope hee was none of yours! Halfepenie.* A hard question, for it is oddes that one begat them both, he that cut out the upper leather, cut out the inner, and so with one *awle* stitcht two soles together. See *The Dramatic Works of John Lilly*, ed. F. W. Fairholt (2 vols.; London: 1858), II, 123. [p. 47]

See the "all" / "awl" / "women's matters" passage, *JC* I.i.22–24: "Truly, sir, all that I live by is with the awl. I meddle with no tradesman's matters nor women's matters, but with awl. I am indeed [*or*: . . . but with all. I am indeed . . . *or* . . . but withal I am indeed . . .], sir, a surgeon to old shoes." An anatomical sense for *all* would give clarity to the last line of the following pseudo–Sidneian exercise and justify the triumphant flourish with which that line is delivered; the poem is number ten in *The Arbor of Amorous Devices* (1597):

> Leaue me O life, the prison of my minde,
> Since nought but death can take away my loue,
> For she which likes me wel is most unkinde,
> And that which I loue best my death doth prooue.
> Loue in her eyes my hopes againe reuiue,
> Hopes in my thoughts doe kindle my desires,
> Desire enflam'd through loue and beauty striue,
> Til she (displeased with loue) my death conspires:
>   That loue for me, and for Loue doe cal,
>   Yet she denies because she graunts not al.

Also see "my parts, or all" and "that part that all must bind" in the first quotation in 151.6, note. I know of no clearcut instance of a sexual sense for *all*; the word is so common and so necessary to simple communication that a pun on it would require an urgently specialized context. But *all* does repeatedly occur in such contexts throughout the sonnets. Consider *all the all of me* in 31.14; *all alone stands hugely politic* in 124.11; and *all* in 40.4,13; 61.14; 68.10; and 75.9,14. In the plays, consider *MND* I.ii.85 ("Some of your French crowns have no hair at all"); *2HIV* II.i.1–17 and V.iii.32–36 (Silence's song, "Be merry, be merry, my wife has all"); *HVIII* II.iii.67 ("More than my all is nothing"—in context of a scene full of labored double entendres); and *Cymb* I.vi.120–23 (". . . to be partner'd / With tomboys hir'd . . . with diseas'd ventures / That play with all infirmities for gold"). I would not want to argue for any of those as examples of a sexual sense of *all* or evidence that such senses existed. Since the word is so common and the topic so inviting to punsters, one would expect to find some crude example in which *all* is meaningless in its ordinary sense. I cannot make or recommend any decision on the matter.

SONNET 27

See the headnotes to 28 and 61.

1. *Weary with toil* = a translation of Ovid's *cum lassa quiete* (*Met.* XV.188, line 208 in Golding, Appendix 2).

2. *travel* (1) journeying; (2) toil, painful labor (Q has "travaill"; Elizabethans made no regular distinction in spelling between "travel" and "travail"; see 50.2 where Q's "travels" also carries both meanings).

3. *a journey* (1) a trip (of unspecified duration—our modern sense); (2) a day's travel; (3) a day's work (*OED* gives examples from the fourteenth through nineteenth centuries; this is from 1706: "*Journey* [:] Among Farmers a Days Work"). In this context the etymological roots of *journey* in *jour* make it epitomize the paradox by which the speaker's day continues into the night.)

4. *work* (1) set to laboring; (2) agitate (see *Macb* I.iii.150–51: "My dull brain was wrought / With things forgotten"). *expired* ended (but expressed in a word that suggests the death of the body and pertains to language and ideas later in the poem: "to expire" means "to breathe out," specifically "to breathe one's last," "breathe out the soul," "give up the ghost"—i.e. give up the soul).

1–4. The syntax of this quatrain is generally imitative of the situation it describes. Line 1 presents a condition, *Weary with toil*, which enters a reader's consciousness unlocated; the phrase takes literal precedence over—and rhetorically outweighs— *I*,the word it modifies. Then, after the syntax of line 3 has come to rest as a complete assertion ("then a mental journey begins"), line 4 continues it and recasts its elements to fit the new logic that emerges with the appended words, a logic by which *journey* becomes the grammatical subject of the transitive verb *work*, an agent acting upon the speaker ("then a mental journey begins to agitate my mind"). (The metamorphosis of the sentence is incidentally disturbed and cumbered by the momentary, tentative emergence of a "journey to" construction like *pilgrimage to thee* in line 6.)

5. *from far* from afar.

6. *Intend* (1) set out upon (as in the Latin phrase *iter intendere*; see *Per*

I.ii.115–16: "I now . . . to Tharsus / Intend my travel"); (2) have in mind as a
fixed purpose (see *T&C* II.ii.39: "an enemy intends you harm"). (Shakespeare
may allude to the same double meaning in *1HIV* IV.i.91–92: "The King himself in person is set forth, / Or hitherwards intended speedily." Since *thoughts*
is the subject of the sentence here, the choice of *Intend* may have been influenced
by a wish to play on the common Latin idiom *intendere animum*, "to direct one's
thoughts to"; moreover, in the context of *from far, Intend* may also have been
recommended by its basic Latin meaning: "to stretch out.")

   8. *Looking*   Since the antecedent, *eyelids*, is imprecise, it must be understood as "eyes" or "me" or a loose amalgam of the two.

   9. *Save that*   except that. The logical link between line 9 and quatrain 2
is imprecise: *Save that* seems logically to modify *Looking on darkness*: "[my
eyes] would be looking on darkness, seeing only what the blind see, except that
my imagination presents your image." The connection is, however, so vague
syntactically that quatrain 3 sounds like a qualification of lines 1–8 and seems
to be admitting a compensation inherent in the speaker's insomnia: the thoughts
that keep him awake are delightful to contemplate.   *imaginary*   (1) imaginative; (2) imagined, unreal.   *sight*   (1) power to see; (2) thing seén.

   10. *thy*   Q has "their"; see 26.12, note.   *shadow*   image. (The word is apt
because of its commonest meanings, which are associated with darkness and
night, and because of its use as a synonym for "ghost.")

   11–12.   = an allusion to the general belief in the existence of precious stones
that shone in the dark, had the power to emit light; see *Titus* II.iii.226–30.

   11. *ghastly*   terrifying, horrible (but with a suggestion of "ghost-like,"
"apparition-like").

   12. Shakespeare often treats *black* as if it were a simple antonym for *beauteous*; see 127.1, note.   *old*   In classical mythology, Nox, the night personified
as a goddess, was usually a withered old woman.

   14. *For*   on account of.   *for*   (1) on account of; (2) to the benefit of (the
use *for* has in such expressions as "a gift for you" and "no rest for the weary"):
"My limbs find no quiet by day for myself (= are active on account of my journey)
and find me no rest; my mind finds me no rest by night for thee (= because of
you) and for myself (= because of my love)." (Moreover, the double meaning
of the second *for* reflects on the first and—in conjunction with *myself*, which
was commonly used in hyperbolic testimony to the truth that lover and beloved
are one flesh [see 36, headnote]—leaves a shadowy suggestion that the beloved,
whose shadow is so active, gets no rest either.)

SONNET 28

This sonnet continues from the previous one.
1. *happy plight*   good condition.
3, 4. *by*   (1) at, during the; (2) through the agency of.
4. Note the echo of "day by day," a stock phrase for indicating regular,
monotonous, repetitive continuation (as in *Titus* V.ii.58).
5. *either's*   (Q has "ethers") each other's.
6. *shake hands*   unite, become friends.

9. *to please him*   The phrase first indicates the motive for telling; then the developing logic of lines 9 and 10 makes *to please him* part of what is told—the imputed motive for being *bright*.

10, 12. *heaven, even*   See 15.6, note.

12. *twire*   peek (not an especially rare word in the early seventeenth century). *gild'st*   Q has "guil'st," which (as a form of the verb "to beguile") might be correct. *even*   evening.

14. *length*   This, the Q reading, makes sense, although most editors have (not unreasonably) emended to "strength." (Note that this line is itself very long and seems particularly long physically in Q because the couplet indentation made it impossible for the printer to get it all in one line of type. Compare the content and Q printing of 140.14.)

SONNET 29

The Christian distinction between material and spiritual well-being functions as a hyperbolic metaphor throughout this sonnet; line 3, for example, suggests the sin of despair. In lines 9–12 the beloved's love functions as the love of the deity does in Christian theology. Note the ideational interplay among *fortune* (line 1), *rich in hope* (line 5), and *wealth* (line 13). Compare sonnet 105; both poems derive energy from activating the literal implication in the courtly love conceit of love as a religion in which the lover "worships" the beloved.

1. *in disgrace*   out of favor.

2, 10, 14. *state*   (1) condition (social, economic, mental, emotional, or spiritual); (2) status, rank.

3. This line is metrically puzzling; its rhythm invites a reader to swallow the second syllable of *trouble* and pronounce the second syllable of "heaven"—even though *And trouble deaf heav'n with* gives two iambs and a trochee (as in 2.14); see 15.6, 86.5, notes and Abbott, par. 465.   *deaf heav'n*   (1) the skies; (2) God, who does not answer my prayers (both senses are recalled in lines 11–12). *bootless*   unavailing, useless.

5. *more rich in hope*   (1) who has more hope, who is richer with respect to hope; (2) who is prospectively more wealthy, who has better expectations of wealth.

6. *Featured*   (1) handsome (*OED* cites George Turberville's 1567 version of Ovid's *Heroides*, in which a Latin phrase meaning "beauty" is translated "featured face"); (2) shaped, formed.   *like him, like him*   (1) like *one more rich* (in line 5); (2) like a second man, like a third.

7. *art*   (1) skill; (2) learning; and possibly (3) deviousness.   *scope*   (1) freedom, range of opportunity; (2) range of ability (but with suggestions of both "person who is an object of desire or pursuit," the sense it has in *FQ* III.iv.52, and "subject, argument, or theme for debate or literary treatment"; *OED* exemplifies this last meaning with a quotation from 1549, one that is interesting in light of *state* in line 2: "The scope or state of the boke, tendes to dysuade the kinge from his supremycye").

8. *enjoy*   (1) take pleasure in; (2) possess (but see 129.5–12, note; here *enjoy*

appears in the potentially suggestive context of *in/outcast, all, Desiring, contented, arising,* and *hymns;* see 26.1–14, note and the notes to 21.8; 4.9; and 151.11).

9. *thoughts* ideas, considerations, reflections ("thought" was also often used to mean "grief," "sorrow"). *despising* Although this word has its usual meaning here, the context of lines 1, 4, and 11–12 make its simple literal meaning, "look down" (*de*-plus-*specere*), relevant also.

10–12. *and . . . sings* Q's punctuation is this: "and then my state, (Like to the lark at break of day arising) From sullen earth sings". That punctuation can mislead a modern reader into assuming that he should understand *lark* as the only riser, *state* as the only singer, and *From sullen earth* as designating only the place from which *state sings.* Actually, the general context (downcast spirits and low status), on the one hand, and both common knowledge of birds and the inevitable unity of the standard phrase "arising from," on the other, make any punctuation powerless to deny that *state* and *lark* are both singers and risers. However, both the Q punctuation and the line-end pause between *arising* and *From* carry a syntactically blurred image of the speaker('s state) sending hymns aloft from the earth, sending up hymns to heaven: "then my state from sullen earth sings hymns . . . like to the lark arising at daybreak."

10. *Haply* perchance (but with a suggestion of "happily," "fortunately").

11. *arising* There is a quiet play here on the fact that this word is appropriate both to a human being getting up in the morning and to the behavior of larks, which are noted for flying straight up into the air at dawn while singing a "tireless torrent of runs and trills." In addition *arising* is also pertinent to dawn, sunrise. In the context of *state, arising* also suggests "advancement in rank" (*OED* cites this from 1534: "Some by handy crafte . . . arise & come forward"), as well as general revival of a person who is "down," "depressed."

12. *sullen* (1) dull colored (see *1HIV* I.ii.205–07: "like bright metal on a sullen ground, / My reformation . . . / Shall show more goodly"); (2) sluggish; (3) melancholy (in this context *sullen* also gives a free-floating suggestion of its commonest meaning: "ill-humored," which describes the speaker in the first eight lines; moreover, the context of the lark and its song suggests *sullen* meaning "of a deep dull or mournful tone" [see *R&J* IV.v.88: "Our solemn hymns to sullen dirges change"]).

SONNET 30

Both this sonnet and sonnet 31 are elaborately metaphysical *exempla* for the homely proverb, "In love is no lack"; they may have been intended as such (see *lack,* 30.3 and *lacking,* 31.2).

1. *sessions* the periodic sittings of judges, a court of law (Seymour-Smith notes that the legal metaphor "adds the notion of guilt and punishment to that of nostalgia." Ingram and Redpath point out that "the atmosphere suggested by the language of the sonnet is that of an enquiry in a manorial court, presided over by Thought, the Lord of the Manor, or his Steward, into the condition of the estate, its losses and resources. Relevant words are: 'waste,' 'dateless,' 'cancell'd,' 'expense,' 'vanish'd,' 'tell o'er,' 'account,' 'pay,' 'losses,' 'restor'd' ").

thought   (1) the action or process of thinking; (2) anxiety or mental distress; (3) melancholy (see *JC* II.i.186–87: "If he love Caesar, all that he can do / Is to himself take thought and die for Caesar").

2. *summon*   (1) cite by authority to appear at a specified place, require an appearance before a court either to answer a charge or to give evidence (= summon *to* the sessions); (2) call a faculty or other insubstantial quality into action (= summon *up* remembrance).

3. *sigh*   lament with sighing.   *many a* = two syllables ("men yuh," as in 31.5 and 33.1).

4. *with*   (1) by means of; (2) together with.   *new*   newly, anew. (However, the parallel meanings of *old* and *new* suggest at first glance that their grammatical functions are also parallel, that *new* acts adjectively: "with old woes [made] new, bewail"; compare 76.11. A pause after *woes* makes *new* an adverb; a pause after *new* makes it an adjective.)   *my*   can modify *time's* or *waste* or both (moreover, since these are love poems, and since *my dear* is such a common construction, *my dear* can be momentarily taken as "my beloved," "my love").   *dear*   (1) precious; (2) grievous, dire; (3) costly (*dear* acts on both *time's* and *waste*).   *time's* = the commonest modern emendation for Q's "times"; some editors read "times'." Several senses of "time" are relevant here: (1) "lifetime" (as in *AYLI* II.vii.142: "one man in his time plays many parts"); (2) "opportunity" (as in *MWW* V.iii.2: "when you see your time, take her by the hand"); and (3) designating the general idea of continuous duration—the sense in which "time" is often personified as a destroyer, a waster.   *waste*   (1) useless expenditure; (2) consumption, using up; (3) gradual loss or diminishment; (4) refuse, remnants; (5) destruction, devastation (the legal context also activates overtones of a technical legal sense of *waste*: "an unauthorized act of a tenant which tends to the destruction of the tenement").   *My dear time's waste*   (1) my costly, grievous, and useless expenditure of my precious time (or of valuable opportunities); (2) the grievous consumption of my span of life; (3) the precious remnants of my lifetime (= *things past*); (4) time's grievous destruction of things precious to me. (Most of the possible syntaxes presented by this line are indicated in the notes to its individual words. Whatever syntax a reader assumes or chooses, the context will cause the meanings given by the others to impinge on his consciousness. One syntax, however, is hidden by modern punctuation. In Q either "woes" or "times" could be a possessive; taking *woes* as "woe's," *wail* as a noun meaning "bewailing," *new* as an adjective, *time's* as "times," and *waste* as a verb, one gets this pertinent extra reading [see *Variorum* I, 87]: "and waste my precious opportunities in the new bewailing of old woes.")

6. *dateless*   endless, without limit or fixed term (for the legal sense of "date," see 18.4, note).

7. *afresh*   Q has "a fresh," which, considering the vagaries of Elizabethan spelling, is not a surprising form of *afresh*; it does, however, point up the potential (always present to the ear) for momentarily taking *afresh love's* as "a fresh (i.e. new) love's"; like *my dear* in line 4 the phrase thus anticipates the thought of the dear friend in line 13 and makes the shift less sudden.   *long since*   an adverbial phrase modifying *cancelled*; however, *love's long* can momentarily

signal an adjectival construction (*love's long* something) and thus color the line
with pertinent suggestions of the traditionally interminable anguish of lovers
(compare Wyatt's "The longe love, that in my thought doeth harbar"). *woe*
Willen and Reed note that *woe* and "woo" are often treated as homonyms by
Renaissance writers; Shakespeare's contemporaries may have heard a pun here
and in line 10.

8. *expense*   (1) loss; (2) expenditure.   *sight*   (1) thing seen; (2) sigh (*OED*
gives this from 1584: "Not waying of her many loving sightes, Her watrie eyes,
her secret moane by nights").

9. *foregone*   past, gone before (but with freefloating overtones of three other
Renaissance meanings of *foregone*: "lost," "wearied," and "given up").

10. *heavily*   (1) in a heavy manner, laboriously; (2) sorrowfully.   *tell*   (1)
say; (2) count (see 12.1, note).

11. *account*   (1) narrative report; (2) record of financial debts and credits.
fore-bemoanèd moan   already-lamented cause of grief (compare 149.8).

SONNET 31

1. *bosom*   (1) chest cavity (as in *V&A* 646–47: "Within my bosom . . . /
My boding heart pants, beats, and takes no rest"); (2) the same, but considered as the seat of thoughts and feelings, here nearly a synonym for "self."
(In company with *endearèd* two other meanings also pertain: *bosom* was used as
we use "pocket," to indicate the place where money is carried [*OED* gives
several Renaissance examples]; *bosom* also means "the enclosure formed by the
chest and arms in an embrace" ["in one's bosom" meant "clasped to one's
breast"].)   *endearèd with*   made precious by (*with* is used as it is in the construction "filled with"); (although *OED* gives no example earlier than 1622 of
"to endear" meaning "to love," it is probable that, until the meaning of the
phrase is limited by line 2, Shakespeare's reader would have taken the additional meaning "beloved by," "valued highly in the estimation of" from *endearèd with*. Q puts a comma at the end of line 1, but no punctuation can make
line 2 a nonrestrictive clause, even for a reader geared to systematic punctuation.
The formal pause at the end of line 1 does, however, give the line a momentary
identity as a complete statement, one sense of which is "you are beloved by
everyone").   *hearts*   Shakespeare is playing on two meanings of "heart": the
literal sense—a bodily organ lodged in the chest—and the standard figurative
use in which "heart" is a synecdoche for "loved one," "friend," or "companion."

2. *lacking*   not having (perhaps with an allusion to the stock phrase "to lack
heart," "to be wanting in zest, courage, hope"); see also 30, headnote.

3. *reigns*   holds sway (see 109.9, note).   *love, love's*   capitalized in Q.
parts   attributes (but with a suggestion, arising from the context, of "parts of
the body"; Willen and Reed suggest "acts" and cite Sir Walter Raleigh, *Dis-
coverie of Guiana*: "For your . . . friendly parts, I have hitherto only returned
promises"; for *parts* used to mean sex organs, see 151.6, note). (*All love's loving
parts* is one of several phrases, words, and statements that have unexploited

potential for sexual meaning—e.g. *holy* [see 127.7, note] and *the grave where buried love doth lie*—and that, being in one another's company, give the poem a persistent though muted and casual undercurrent of sexual innuendo. Compare sonnets 48, 98, and 99; and see line 14 below.)

5. *many a* = dissyllabic (see 30.3, note). *obsequious* (probably trisyllabic, by syncopation of "-quious") dutiful (commonly used with the special meaning "dutiful in performing funeral rites"; see 125.9, note).

6. *dear* (1) severe, keen (see 37.3); (2) heartfelt, earnest (see *LLL* II.i.1: "summon up your dearest spirits"); (3) loving, tender (see *Ham* I.ii.110–11: "love . . . which dearest father bears his son"); (4) honorable, worthy, precious. (The context established by *endearèd* gives the word overtones of two further meanings: "costly" and "beloved.") *religious* (1) scrupulous, exact, conscientious; (2) pious.

7. *interest* (dissyllabic, by syncopation) the rightful due, the legal right (with a play on *interest* meaning "interest-money," "return on an investment"). *the dead, which now appear* The occurrence of *appear* at the end of a line underscores and prolongs the temporary identity of *the dead, which now appear* as a self-contained noun unit (see the Q punctuation). The apparitions briefly visible in the mind's eye of the reader or listener vanish instantly as the apparently completed clause resumes in the next line, superseding the syntax in which *appear* meant "come into sight" and revealing *the dead, which now appear* to have been a mere syntactic apparition, a ghost sense: *the dead, which now appear / But things removed.* The momentarily apparent resurrection of the dead in line 7 is not finally included in the sense one understands from the quatrain, but the apparition *is* part of one's experience of the quatrain, and, in a poem where the speaker says he sees his dead friends live again in his friend, a pertinent one. Compare *my dear* in 30.4 and *no man well* in 34.7.

7–8. *appear / But* (1) are revealed to be merely; (2) seem to be merely.

8. *things* See 136.7,11, and 20.12, notes (on sexual senses of "thing"). *removed* (1) that are absent, that have gone elsewhere (in the Renaissance "remove" had a specific idiomatic meaning that "move" has now: *removed* suggests "that have changed their residence, moved to another house"; *OED* gives several examples of the idiom); (2) that have been taken away. *thee* = the generally accepted emendation for Q's "there"; taken as a reference to *Thy bosom* in line 1 and *there* in line 3, "there" makes sense here, but it also makes the line flat and awkward. *lie* are (but with pertinent suggestions from *lie* meaning lodge, dwell temporarily [as in *AW* III.v.28: "here comes a pilgrim . . . she will lie at my house"], and from "to lie" meaning "to be buried").

9. *doth live* (1) has life; (2) resides.

10. *trophies of my lovers* (1) memorials of victories by my lovers (who conquered the speaker); (2) memorials of victories over my lovers (who were conquered by the speaker). (In ancient Greece and Rome a trophy was a tree or pillar or scaffold hung with the arms and treasure of a conquered enemy as a memorial of the victory; "trophy" was also used to mean both a funeral monument or anything hung on such a monument to honor the dead person; see *Titus* I.i.388). *lovers* On the kind of relationship indicated, see 126.4, note.

11. *parts of* shares in, claims upon (note the play on this use of "parts" and its use in line 3; see 8.8, 17.4, 37.7, 12).

12. *That due of many* what was due to many (*due* and "dew" were not distinguished in sixteenth-century spelling; Shakespeare's contemporaries may have seen a pun here; see *tear*, line 5).

13. *images* mental pictures (Renaissance Englishmen wrote harshly and often against "images"—symptoms of the pagan idolatry deplored by Protestants; see sonnet 105; in context of the religious language in lines 5 and 6, the couplet suggests a conversion to monotheism; "image" meaning "ghost" also is pertinent here).

14. *all the all of me* me, everything I have, and everything I ever had (but see 26.1–14, note).

13–14. For the Platonic overtones of these lines, see 53, headnote.

SONNET 32

The sexual innuendo of sonnet 31 seems—almost mindlessly—to continue in 32. See 154.9, note (on *well*), 112.3, note (on the phonetic likeness of *well* and *will*), and 151.11 and 26.1–14, notes (on *content* and *con-*); note *pen* in line 6 (and see 78.3, 7, 11, note).

1. *my well-contented day* Willen and Reed point out that "to content" meant "to pay in full"; *OED* cites a legal document of 1531 which mentions sums "now to be paide or otherwise contented." Shakespeare's phrase contains all of the following: (1) the day when I am paid in full (have had my measure of life); (2) the day when I "pay my score," my debt to nature; (3) a day that I am willing to see come.

3. *by fortune* by chance. *re-survey* look at again. (Although the overall effect of the line is to suggest a casual glance, "survey" was ordinarily used to describe exacting examination; here it prepares for the following lines by suggesting "inspect carefully with a view to re-evaluation." The commonest use of "survey" was and is to describe an examination to establish boundaries, legal rights, and value for real estate; such a survey is customarily made of property before it is transferred to the survivors of a deceased owner).

4. *lover* On the kind of relationship indicated, see 126.4, note.

5. *bett'ring* progress, improvement. (If one follows the grammar strictly, line 5 cannot be paraphrased because lines of verse cannot be compared with progress. However, since comprehension is more flexible than grammar, the sum effect of the line is to say both "compare them with the improved writing done since they were written" and "make allowance for the advantage that progress in poetic technique will give the poets of that day.")

7. *Reserve* preserve, keep (see *TN* I.v.177: "what is yours to bestow is not yours to reserve"). *rhyme* poetry (see 107.11, note). *for my love* (1) for the sake of my love for you; (2) for the sake of me, for the sake of your love for me.

8. *happier* (= dissyllabic, by syncopation) (1) luckier; (2) more able.

9. *then* (1) on that occasion; (2) therefore. (See *than* in line 11 below and note.)

11. *than* = a simple modernization of Q's "then"; see 16.4, 8, note; here the word derives logically incidental energy from the context provided by *then* in line 9 and by the poem's topic generally. *brought* brought forth, given birth to (see 76.8, note).

12. *in ranks* In context of *march* and *equipage* the dominant idea is of rows of soldiers, but there is also a play on *ranks* meaning simply "lines," "orderly rows," and lines of verse; *ranks* also carries suggestions of rows of print on a page (see 122.3, note). The military language here suggests a mechanical precision analogous to the metric precision lacking in *poor rude lines.* *of better equipage* better, or more grandly, equipped ("to march in equipage with" was idiomatic and meant "to keep step with" and hence "to be equal with"; see *outstripped*, line 6). *in ranks of better equipage* (1) in company with better poems; (2) in better made verse. *equipage* = accented on the first and third syllables.

SONNET 33

That "the morning sun never lasts the day" was proverbial (Tilley, S978). See 109.8, note.

1. *Full many a glorious morning* The whole phrase turns out to be the object of *seen*, but it can initially be read adverbially: "on many mornings," "often." *many a* = dissyllabic (as in 30.3). *glorious* = dissyllabic, by syncopation (as in *Lucrece* 109, 1013).

2. *Flatter* (1) caress, stroke (*OED* cites this example from 1599: "Trout is a fish that loveth to be flattered and clawed in the water"); (2) gratify the self-esteem of (as the notice of a king would flatter a courtier); (3) encourage with hopeful signs; (4) delude (see 42.14, note). (The word *flatter* in this context may also have reminded Shakespeare's contemporaries of the expression "make fair weather with" meaning "curry favor with.")

2, 5, 7. *Flatter, permit, hide* Q closes line 1 with a comma (here deleted in deference to a modern reader's inclination to read punctuation as logically directive). Regardless of punctuation, however, the mere fact that the completion of a potentially complete assertion coincides with the physical and rhythmic completion of a line is enough to establish the self-sufficient unit "I have seen many mornings" temporarily in the reader's mind as a completed statement which then suddenly loses its syntactic stability when *Flatter* continues the clause and changes its syntactic nature. The same sort of sudden transformations occur when *Anon* in line 5 and *Stealing* in line 8 abruptly cancel a conceptual completeness temporarily achieved at the ends of lines 4 and 7. (Compare 15.1–2 and 30.7–8.) Here the mutability of syntactic identities acts as a stylistic metaphor for the unexpected inconstancy the poem talks about: the reader's syntactic experience is to his expectations about sentences as sudden changes in weather or in a beloved's mood are to the non-literary situations described.

4. *heav'nly* (1) of the sky; (2) splendid, superhuman.

4, 9, 14. *heav'nly, Ev'n, heav'ns* See 15.6, note.

5. *Anon* soon; almost immediately. *basest* (1) darkest, least bright (see

100.4, note); (2) lowest (in the sky); (3) most ignoble, lowest (in dignity, rank). Note that *basest* pertains to its metallurgic context: the alchemists' best-known aim was to turn "base" metals like lead and iron into gold; see line 4 and "base lead" in *MofV* II.ix.20.

6. *rack* mass of scraggly, smoke-like, wind-driven cloud. (However, *With ugly rack* carries appropriate overtones of "with ugly wrack" [see 126.5], and thus both suggests "ruinously" and echoes the sailing metaphor implied by *ride* in line 5.)

7. *fórlorn* is stressed on the first syllable.

8. *disgrace* (1) disfigurement, loss of ("dis-") beauty ("grace"), blemish (*OED* gives this from 1581: "wart, moale, spot, or such disgrace"); (2) dishonor, shame (*disgrace* also means "the disfavor of a powerful person"; *OED* cites a passage from 1600 that speaks of courtiers' fear of the king's disgrace; that sense of the word recalls the courtly metaphor of line 2 and underscores the transformation in the sovereign sun that formerly condescended to the courtier-like mountains; note also that in Shakespeare's time "to be under a cloud" already meant "to be in disgrace").

9. *shine* In this context the literal sense is augmented by .common metaphoric uses of *shine*; see 135.8, note.

11. *out alack* alas (but with a play on "gone out," "extinguished" [see 7.13, note]). *hour* = monosyllabic.

12. *region cloud* the clouds of that part of the sky where he now is (Shakespeare elsewhere uses *region* to mean "the heavens," "the upper air"; see *Ham* II.ii.480–81: "thunder / Doth rend the region"; in Renaissance meteorology the atmosphere was conceived of as divided into successive regions by height. Here there might be a play on "regent" meaning "kinglike," "sovereign"; see the usurping clouds of lines 5–8).

13. *no whit disdaineth* disdains not at all (but see 26.1–14, note [on *wit*], and 51.9–14, note [the commentary on *neigh no dull flesh* in 51.11]).

14. This line has the ring of a proverb and its substance is similar to the proverb Chaucer attributes to the Parson in the general prologue to *The Canterbury Tales*: "If gold rust what shall iron do?" In view of the metallurgic language of the first quatrain, it is possible that Shakespeare had Chaucer's proverb in mind. *Suns of the world* (1) great men (whose power and splendor is sun-like); (2) *sons* of the world, human beings, mere mortals. *stain* (1) lose color and luster (*OED* gives this from 1579: "purple dye will never staine"); (2) sustain a moral blot, suffer dishonor (used of the conscience). (A once common, now forgotten, transitive use of "stain" is also pertinent to this context: "to stain" meant "to outshine," "deprive lesser luminaries of their lustre" and was used literally of the sun and figuratively of people whose brilliance obscured that of their associates; see 35.3. Note that "to stain" did not yet have the meaning "to be readily stainable" [as in "white flannel looks good, but it stains"].) *when* Q's "whē" was a common abbreviation for *when*; the mark, placed above vowels, indicated an *m* or *n* omitted for the printer's convenience. Seymour-Smith inexplicably but deliberately "changed 'whē' to 'where' without note" (p. 39). *heav'n's sun* the actual sun, the sun in the sky (but with

an inevitable suggestion of "heaven's son," which in turn floods the poem with vague and unharnessed suggestions of the incarnation and crucifixion).

SONNET 34

This sonnet continues the topic of sonnet 33.

1. *beauteous*   = dissyllabic, by syncopation.

3. *base* See 33.5, note.

1-4. "Although the sun shines, leave not thy cloak at home" was proverbial (Tilley, S968).

4. *bravery* splendor, finery (see 15.8, note).   *rotten smoke* unwholesome mist.

5-14. Compare the similar themes and metaphors in sonnet 120.

5. *cloud* clouds (compare 33.12).   *thou break*   = a subjunctive (see Abbott, par. 368).

6. *my storm-beaten face* In the metaphor, this phrase refers to the appearance of a person caught in a storm. In terms of the speaker's relationship with the beloved it refers to the speaker's face when frowned upon and, in a separate but related logic, suggests that he has wept at being rebuffed.

7. *well of* anything good about (but note that *no man well* contains logically unexploited potential for meaning "no healthy man," "no one in good health," and thus anticipates and prepares the way for the metaphors of medicine and wounds that follow; compare *my dear* in 30.4 and *the dead, which now appear* in 31.7).

7-8. See 35.7 and note.

8. *disgrace* (1) shame, dishonor; (2) disfigurement, scar (see 33.8, note).

9-14. Much of the language of these lines contributes to a general tendency of the sonnet to fuse the speaker and the beloved by describing guilty action and reaction in terms that also fit innocent action and reaction or by describing the victim in words that also describe the offender.

9. *thy shame* your regret, your sense of having done wrong (but "your disgrace" and "your wrongdoing," although not pertinent to this sentence, are pertinent to the general situation).   *give physic to* (1) act as remedy, medicine, for; and, more specifically, (2) wash away, purge ("a physic" = "a cathartic").

10. *yet, still* See 7.7, note.   *the loss* the loss of beauty, the disfigurement of having a *storm-beaten face*. (*Loss* is an excellent example of a word given meaning by the lines that precede and follow it. The gloss above reflects only a literal reading of line 5. As the line is read, the logic of the situation, and the speaker's tone, combine to dictate that *I have still the loss* be understood as an amalgam of "I have nonetheless been injured," "I still bear the scars," "I have nonetheless suffered disgrace," and "you might just as well still be lost to me." *Loss*, which can carry its unaccustomed load of meaning because it so obviously does the same job in this line that *disgrace* did in line 8, is also bolstered by a punning equation [similar to those described in the notes to 50.6, 109.6–7, 142.13, 149.2, and 152.11]: since *disgrace* can mean loss of beauty [as in 33.8], it illogically follows that *loss* can be used as a general synonym for *disgrace*. [The

interplay of *disgrace* and *loss* here has some likeness to the interplay of the two senses of *shame* in line 9.] In this case Shakespeare was probably incidentally attracted by the paradox of possessing a loss—a paradox present but entirely dormant in the idiom "to have losses" [as in *Much Ado* IV.ii.81].)

12. *cross* = the almost universally accepted emendation for Q's "losse." ("Bear" suggests *cross; loss* is the last word of line 10, and its repetition is an easily imagined printer's error. However, since the speaker's point about *loss* in line 10 is that it persists, the repetition might possibly be purposeful and intended illustratively; "bears the . . . offense's loss" would mean "endures the loss incurred as a result of your offense.") *bears the . . . cross* endures the . . . affliction (with an implication of "in a Christ-like manner" or "for the sake of Christ"—see Matt. 10:38 and the common expression "that is the cross I bear").

13. *sheeds* = a variant spelling of "sheds"—possibly indicating that "sheds" —*deeds* was a true rhyme. Elsewhere Shakespeare rhymes "shed" (in various spellings) with "dead," "encounterèd," "head," and "bed"; he rhymes the plural with "bleeds" and "proceeds." Nowhere else does he rhyme *deeds* with a word that does not rhyme with it in Modern English pronunciations. Perhaps the vowel sound in the plural of "shed" was different from that in the singular. *thy love sheeds* which your affection [for me] causes you to shed (but the simple meaning of *thy love*, "your lover," "your friend," may cause "which I shed" to hover in a reader's understanding of the phrase; see line 6; for other double uses of *love*, see 23.7–8, 40, 49.3, 51.1, 107.3, and 124.1).

14. *ransom* (1) atone for (see 1Timothy 2:6: "[Jesus] gav him self a raunsome for all men"); (2) buy back (note *rich*).

13–14. The couplet recalls elements prominent in the first part of the poem: the shedding of tears mirrors both the storm metaphor used for the beloved's offense (lines 1–4) and the speaker's tears in line 6; *pearl*, noted among Renaissance physicians and apothecaries for its supposed medicinal properties, relates to the medical metaphor of lines 7–9; *ransom* recalls the ambush metaphor in lines 3–4, and—accepting the emendation *cross* for "loss" in line 12—also pertains to *bears the . . . cross* because "our ransom," like "the redeemer," is a byname for Christ. The paradox by which rain, the metaphor expressing the injury, could just as well express the reparation (tears) resembles both the Christian paradox by which the sin of Adam was paid for by the injured party and the miniature paradox inherent in the play on the speaker's *disgrace* and the beloved's *shame* in lines 8 and 9. Sonnet 35 makes still another experiment in confusing the identities of injurer and injured party.

SONNET 35

2. *Roses have thorns* "No rose without a thorn" and variants like "The sweetest rose hath his prickle" were common proverbs; see Tilley, R182. Shakespeare makes bawdy fun with the proverb in *AYLI* III.ii.101–02: "He that sweetest rose will find / Must find love's prick and Rosalinde." *silver* (1) silvery, shining, silvery in color (see *RII* II.i.46: "the silver sea"); (2) made of

silver. (Note the continued reference to precious metals and jewels; see 33 and
pearl in 34.13.) *fountains* (1) springs, sources of water issuing naturally from
the earth and collecting in pools; (2) structures built for jets or streams of water
to spout from and into (the use that has become the only modern sense of the
word). See 154.9, note.

3. *stain* (1) obscure the luster of, eclipse; (2) defile, corrupt (see the intransitive use in 33.14 and note).

4. *canker* cankerworm, a caterpillar that consumes the bud from within.
That "the canker soonest eats the fairest rose" was proverbial (Tilley, C56);
Shakespeare uses the proverb in *2Gent* I.i.45–50 and in 70.7; see also 95.2 and
99.13.

4,5,9,12. *in* See 81.2, note.

5. *All men make faults* (yet another common proverb; see Tilley, M116,
MWW I.iv.14–15, and *Tim* III.i.29) (1) everyone makes some mistakes; (2)
everyone commits some sins (the next three lines, however, suggest a sense of
make that it does not have as it is read, its basic meaning—"create": "all men
fabricate faults"—as, for example, by exaggerating the beloved's trifling error
into a sin). *make faults* Shakespeare's contemporaries may have heard a pun
here on "make farts" (a pun that would have given cogency to a complementary
pun on *in sense* in line 9). Ellis (pp. 128–30) gives plentiful evidence of the *fault/*
"fart" pun (e.g. *LLL* IV.iii.64–67 and Launce's plays on "fault," "fart," and
"for't" in *2Gent* IV.iv.1–36); a similar but farfetched play may have been
audible in 148.14. *even I* I myself. (The force of *even* emphasizes identity [as
in *Much Ado* V.i.250: "Yea, even I alone"]. The commonest modern use of
even—to emphasize the unexpected or an extreme case or the magnitude of a
statement [as in 48.13]—is here only a secondary meaning.) *in this* (1) by
doing the following things; (2) in this poem (sense (2) activates a pun on *Authóri-*
zing in the following line).

5–8. That "a fault once excused is twice committed" was proverbial (Tilley,
F104)—but so was "to excuse is to accuse" (Tilley, E215); see the final note on
this sonnet.

6. *Authórizing* and *trespass* are both legal terms. For the accentuation of
Authórizing, see 50.7, note. *compare* comparison (see 21.5, note).

7. Many editors separate *corrupting* and *salving* with a comma—thus accen-
tuating the identity of *Authórizing, corrupting, salving,* and *excusing* as logically
independent actions. The Q punctuation (given here) tends to accentuate the
implication that the salving corrupts the speaker (corrupting myself [by] salving
thy amiss). No interpretation of either punctuation can exclude either reading
from a reader's consciousness because a comma suggests apposition of the two
rhythmically and syntactically complementary half lines, while the formal
likeness of the two participles to each other and to the participles in lines 6 and
8 suggests an equality of function for all four whether these two are separated by
a comma or not. *salving* (1) explaining, making acceptable, palliating (*OED*,
v.² 2, 3—see 34.8: *and cures not the disgrace*); (2) soothing and healing as with
an ointment (*OED* v.¹ 1—see 34.8: *That heals the wound*). *thy amiss* your
misdeed, your offense (but with overtones of "your state of being in bad order,

in ill health"; in *Macb* II.iii.94–96 Shakespeare uses the adjective from which this substantive is derived in a quasi-medical sense: *Donalbain.* "What is amiss?" / *Macbeth.* "You are, and do not know't. / The spring, the head, the fountain of your blood / Is stopp'd . . . "; see also *Tim* III.i.208–09).

8. *thy . . . thy* Q reads "their . . . their"—on the frequency of this supposed printer's error, see 26.12, note; the emendation is standard, but cases have been made for the Q reading (Ingram and Redpath), for "thy . . . their" (Sisson), and for most conceivable other emendations (see *Variorum*). *more* modifies both *Excusing* and *sins*: "Excusing your sins to a greater extent than is warranted by the size of your sins."

9. *sensual* of the senses (merely physical, non-intellectual; but also often with pejorative overtones of "lewd," "lustful," and "voluptuous"); *sensual* is dissyllabic, by syncopation (as in 141.8). *sense* (1) reason, intellect as opposed to sensation; the wit of the line extends beyond the simple polyptoton (*sensual* and *sense* derive from the same root) and paranomasia (*sensual* and *sense* are alike in sound and contrast in meaning); in one of its common uses *sense* is simply the noun form of *sensual* and thus means both "reason" and its opposite; (2) sensation, faculties of corporeal sensation as opposed to intellect (*OED* gives this from 1586: "This bastard Love . . . subverts . . . nature, in making reason give place to sense"). A third meaning of *sense* is also pertinent here: "the capacity to feel." Compare sonnet 141. *in sense* Some commentators suspect a pun on "incense."

8–9. Kökeritz (p. 85) suggests that Shakespeare gave roughly the same pronunciation to *sins, sense,* and the first syllable of *sensual;* see *AYLI* II.vii.64–66 and 141.13–14, note.

10. *adverse party* adversary.

11. *lawful* (1) just; (2) legalistic ("law-full," "full of law").

1–14. This sonnet is a variation of Shakespeare's habits of damning with fulsome praise (as in 87.1) and of making flattering accusations (as in 33). It evokes responses contrary to those its rhetorical gestures seem designed to elicit. Quatrain 1 seems to be a loving effort to relieve the beloved's sense of guilt, but the easiness of its not-quite-appropriate platitudes gives it a lack of conviction that advertises the speaker's earnest benevolence rather than the justice of the defense he offers. The platitude that begins quatrain 2 is the first in the poem that has any rhetorical energy, but *and even I in this* suddenly turns the reference of *All men make faults* from the beloved to the speaker. The quatrain develops a competition in guilt between the speaker and the beloved: line 5 first says "no one is perfect" and, by implication, "you are no more guilty than other mortals"; the line then says "I am guilty too; I am in the act of sinning now," and opens the way for "I am more guilty than you" and "I have become so for your sake" in lines 6 and 7. From there the speaker goes on to belittle the beloved (lines 8 and 9), to call attention to his own superiority as both sinner and sacrificer (lines 9–11), and to reassert the beloved's wrongdoing (line 14). The poem leaves the beloved diminished and under a new guilt—the guilt of being beneficiary of the speaker's ostentatious sacrifice. All in all, the manner of this poem is that of a long-suffering and relentlessly selfless wife. The facts the poem reports should make the speaker seem admirable in a reader's eyes; the speaker's manner, however, gives conviction to the idea that he is worthy of the contempt he says he deserves. Everything about the poem—its substance, its structure, its syntax, its effect—suggests *civil war* (courteous, legalistic, *and* intestine).

SONNET 36

The theme of this sonnet (the paradox by which a pair of lovers are "one flesh," an indivisible unit, as well as distinct, separable individuals) appears and reappears in its incidentals—see, for example, the line ends of quatrain 1 (*twain, one, with me remain, alone*), and the paradox of grammatical number in *our undivided loves* in line 2. The idea and variations on it appear in 22, 34, 39, 42, 62, 109, 134, and 135. The most efficient source of the idea is Ephesians 5: 25–33, which, in the following form, was part of the marriage service:

> Ye husbands love your wives, even as Christ loved the church, and hath given himself for it, to sanctify it purging it in the fountain of water, through thy word, that he might make it unto himself a glorious congregation, not having spot or wrinkle, or any such thing, but that it should be holy and blameless. So men are bound to love their own wives as their own bodies. He that loveth his own wife, loveth himself: for never did any man hate his own flesh, but nourisheth and cherisheth it, even as the Lord doth the congregation: for we are members of his body, of his flesh and of his bones.
>
> For this cause shall a man leave father and mother, and shall be joined unto his wife, and they two shall be one flesh. This mystery is great: but I speak of Christ and of the congregation. Nevertheless, let every one of you so love his own wife, even as himself.   [*BCP*, p. 223]

(Ephesians 5 appears to have been deeply embedded in Shakespeare's consciousness; he drew on the chapter regularly: verses 14–16 are echoed in 116.9 and in *1HIV* V.iv.81; verse 16, which—in a context of light and darkness—speaks of "Redeming the tyme" is echoed—in contexts of light and darkness—in 100.5–6 [where "wrinkle" follows in line 10] and in Hal's soliloquy at the end of *1HIV* I.ii. See Noble, p. 297. The *blots* in line 3 of the present sonnet may be an echo of "spot" in Ephesians 5:27 [see the note on *wrinkles* in 93.8]; at any rate, the speaker's self-sacrifice in accepting divorce for his beloved's sake and Christ's marriage to the church are similarly motivated.)

1. *Let me confess* In context of the speaker's self-accusations in 35, this phrase seems to introduce some such *bewailèd guilt* as is referred to in line 10; here the completed line reduces the sense to "I grant," "I must admit."   *twain* (1) separate; (2) separated, parted (with a play on the proverbial idea of "being twain," "being at odds," "being unfriendly"; see Tilley, T640 and *T&C* III.i.95: "She'll none of him; they two are twain"). The word also has witty overtones of its here tautological meaning "two" and of a substantive meaning that states the opposite condition to the one described here: "a twain" is "a couple," "a married pair" (see *Temp* IV.i.104–05: "To bless this twain, that they may prosper-

ous be, / And honour'd in their issue"; for further word play on *twain*, see 39.13
and *Phoenix* 25–26, 45–46).

3. *So shall those blots* Both in construction (*So* denotes consequence), and in
substance (*blots* means "disgraces"), this phrase confirms the first, now rejected,
impression evoked by *Let me confess* in line 1.

4. *by me . . . alone* (1) by me . . . only; (2) by me . . . in solitude, without company. *borne* (1) endured; (2) carried, worn, shown. The speaker's
account of his relationship with the beloved and his selfless manner of sacrificing
himself for the sake of the beloved's reputation echo situations in which a mistress consents to keep secret her relationship to a lover for whom their alliance
might be an embarrassment. The diction of this line enhances that likeness by
suggesting the situation of a girl left pregnant to have her baby in solitary disgrace. (See 68.3, note.)

5–6. These lines exemplify Shakespeare's habit of using language with a
special precision that both gives a precise meaning not quite demonstrable in the
syntax and a wealth of additional meaning as well. Compare 16.9–12. Lines 5
and 6 obviously convey the meaning demanded by their context: "Our love
makes us one person, though unfortunately we must live separately." Such a
restatement, however, is not strictly a gloss on the lines but a free translation,
a paraphrase that does unavoidable violence to the lines, diminishing them in
the name of sanity. The paraphrase suppresses a lot of undeniable but not
easily accommodated meaning and gives solid form to the simple and appropriate statement which, although both context and diction suggest it, is engulfed
and obliterated by a syntax that acts not only to confirm, enlarge on, and in-
tensify the expected statement but also to make my paraphrase and any other
coherent restatement of the substance demonstrably impossible.

Consider the word *respect*, the only word in line 5 that needs glossing; no one
of its meanings quite makes sense of the line if it is put into the line to replace
respect: "In our two loves there is but one reference"? "but one focus of attention"? "one physical appearance"? "one consideration"? "concern"? "care"?
"motive"? "aim"? "esteem"? "state of being esteemed"? "rank"? Elsewhere
Shakespeare uses *respect* with all these meanings, and all these meanings are in
one way or another pertinent to the particulars of this sonnet. So too are the
meanings to which *respect* contributes in its commonest uses, the stock idiomatic phrases in which its sense is derived from its alliance with auxiliary words
that are not present here or appropriate to this syntax, e.g. "to have respect
to" means "to have relation to (or connection with, or reference to)," "to give
attention to," and "to take into account." All in all, the word *respect*, both in
its common uses and in its particular use here, is an emblem of the poem's
substance and the means by which the poem leads its reader's mind to enact a
demonstration that what is true about something looked at one way—seen in
one of its aspects—may be the opposite of what is true of the same thing seen
in another respect. Since the syntactical relationship of *respect* to the rest of the
line is imprecise—since *respect* is not heard "in respect to" one limited construction, all the relevant configurations in which the word commonly functions are available. They are audible because the line contains fragments of such

constructions as "in respect to" and phrases that suggest a variety of uses of *respect* pertinent to the present context. For example, in context of *undivided loves* in line 2 and the disgraces mentioned in line 3, *but one respect* suggests that the lovers share a common reputation and have one social rank, and anticipates the last lines of the poem by suggesting that the honor of one is the honor of both. The obvious, but imperfectly demonstrable, meaning "we are one person," "we are 'but one,'" is delivered by the presence of *but one* in spite of the alien "there is" construction in which it appears. Although *respect*, the key word in that construction, denies the implied "we are" construction by making *one* an adjective, it also tends to confirm the expected sense because *respect* is a word used in describing, and a word that could label, the general topic of the preceding quatrain. Moreover, the expected restatement of the first quatrain is heard because the stock phrase "in respect" is suggested by the context, is physically present (though interrupted by the full length of the rest of the line), and is pertinent to the developing, evident, but never quite developed statement, "In respect to our loves we are one, but in respect to our lives we are separate." As lover and beloved are a single being and also separate individuals, so the construction "in respect" is both intact as a unit of meaning and physically fragmented, its two elements participating in other syntactical relationships where its parts are seen in respect to other meanings and constructions.

Separable spite in line six is similarly meaningless and similarly overcharged with meaning. The phrase is particularly worth discussing because its effects can so easily seem to be voided by scholarship. Shakespeare and his contemporaries often use adjectives that are now exclusively active passively and now-passive adjectives actively (e.g. "sightless" in *Macb* I.v.46 and I.vii.23—see Abbott, par. 3). Shakespeare also occasionally reverses the relationship of noun to adjective (as in 9.14; 51.1,6; and 77.7). Here *separable spite* means "separating spite" (a vexation that separates) and / or "spiteful separation" (a separation that vexes). However, a student must remember that those glosses are derived not from a rule about Renaissance grammar or about Shakespeare's special variations on it but from a compromise between what the context demands and what the words would otherwise say. The relationships of *separable* to *spite* and of both to the sentence at large remain unfixed, even though common sense tells us what must be meant; as a result, the usual meaning of the noun colors a reader's sense of the unfortunate separation with a suggestion that lover and beloved have been separated by mutual ill will or by a dispute or by the ill will of one of them.

6. *separable*   = four syllables.

7. *sole*   (1) only; (2) of singleness; (3) unique (see *Phoenix* 2: "the sole Arabian tree" where *sole* suggests "lonely," "isolated," as it does here). (Shakespeare often puns on "sole" and "soul"; his contemporaries might have heard "effect on the soul" in *sole effect*.)

8. *hours*   = monosyllabic.

9. *not evermore*   not always, not continually (or, perhaps, "nevermore," "never again").

12. *Unless thou take . . . name* (1) without thus dishonoring yourself; (2) except by sharing your honors with me.

13–14. See 96.13–14, note.

13. *in such sort* in such a way.

14. *As* that. *report* reputation.

SONNET 37

1. *decrepit father* A metaphor of sexual impotence is dimly apparent throughout quatrain 1.

3. *made lame* rendered ineffectual (for biographical inferences from orthopedically literal readings of this metaphor, see *Variorum* I, 105–07, 223–24). *dearest* most grievous (but with overtones of its more usual meanings [see 30.4, note]; in the context of a love sonnet the word inevitably has an ironic echo of "most cherished"; it also carries traces of the meanings "most costly" and "of greatest worth," meanings developed in the succeeding lines). *spite* (1) injury; (2) malice.

4. *of* from. *truth* (1) genuineness; (2) honesty; (3) fidelity.

4,6. See 26.1–14, note (on possible sexual innuendo in *all*).

7. *Entitled* Although Q's "Intitled" and "ingrafted" (line 8) are only variant spellings of *Entitled* and *engrafted*, the Q spellings can distort a modern reading by making the plays on *in* in lines 7–13 (plays still audible in some modern dialects) more ostentatiously artful than they would have been for a Renaissance reader. *Entitled* (in any spelling) was probably pronounced as if it were "in tight led." *Entitled in thy parts* (1) enrolled, listed (*OED*: s.v. *entitled*, I.3) among your good qualities; (2) given authority (*OED*: s.v. *entitled*, II.4) over or among your (other) qualities. *thy* Q reads "their"; the emendation is standard, although arguments have been made for the Q reading. The best meaning derivable from "Intitled in their parts" is "Entitled by virtue of their good qualities"; but since the "thy" / "their" error is so common in Q (see 26.12, note), and since the Q reading requires that we conceive of good qualities as themselves having good qualities, the emendation is probably justified. (A theatrical sense for the Q version of line 7 has been suggested: "Given noble titles by their roles, wear a crown and set on a throne," but the reading is not invoked by the lines that precede and follow it, and is not any way relevant to them.)

8. (1) "I fuse myself to (and thus draw strength from) your abundance of virtues"; (2) "I add my love to your store of valuable things." Shakespeare may be playing on the fact that "stock" is a synonym for *store* and grafts are made to the "stock," the trunk, of a tree. (See 134.9, note—on "ideational puns.") *store* See 11.9, note.

10. *shadow, substance* = a traditional pair for contrasting concept and actuality (or, often, the valueless and the valuable); see 53, headnote. The wit of this line derives from its reversal of the causal relationship of the two: here the shadow creates the substance.

12. *part*   portion (for plays on "part" similar to the one here between this use and *parts* meaning "qualities" in line 7, see 31.11 and 151.6, notes).

13. *Look what*   whatever (see 9.9, note).

SONNET 38

In much the mock-literal way that sonnets 36, 37, 39, and 40 probe the traditional hyperbolic metaphor by which lover and beloved are a single being, this sonnet investigates the implications both of the idea that the worth of a poem is determined by the worth of its subject and of the metonymy by which a writer *is* his works.

1. *want subject*   lack a subject.   *to invent*   to treat in literary composition, to write about.

3. *Thine own sweet argument*   The meaning of this phrase is obvious but not demonstrably present in it (compare 16.9–12 and 36.5–6, notes). The *argument* (i.e. the theme or topic) of love sonnets is traditionally some beloved "thou." This phrase is preceded by the rhetorical question, "How can I lack a topic while you are alive?" The phrase must mean "your own sweet self as subject." The construction does not quite say that or anything that one can pin down. As if Shakespeare took his basic meaning as automatically established from context, the energy of the phrase goes to expanding and intensifying the hyperbole of the compliment that is its assumed content. By making the beloved the possessor of *argument*, the syntax both implies the beloved's active generosity in offering himself as a topic and approaches the suggestion that the beloved really deserves an author's credit for Shakespeare's poems—their arguments are the beloved's, the beloved thinks up Shakespeare's topics for him. Moreover, the imprecision of the construction lets *sweet* act twice in a reader's understanding—"you, who are sweet, are the sweet theme of my verse." (For other instances of *argument* meaning "subject" or "theme," see 76.10, 79.5, 100.8, 103.3, and 105.9.) Shakespeare may have been drawn to this locution by the obscene potential of *argument*. John S. Farmer gives the French *l'argument* as a slang term for either male or female sex organs (*Vocabula Amatoria*, 1896); Ellis (pp. 35–37) notes two Shakespearian uses of *argument* to mean "vagina": *T&C* IV.v.26–29 and *R&J* II.iv.94–96: ". . . I was come to the whole depth of my tale, and meant, indeed, to occupy the argument no longer." Compare the similar phrase *thy lovely argument* in 79.5; see 76.10, 79.5–6, 100.8, 103.3, and notes.

4. *vulgar*   (1) ordinary, commonplace (as in *Ham* I.ii.98–99: "as common / As any the most vulgar thing to sense"); (2) public, generally disseminated (see 112.2, note); (3) base, low (see 112.2, note).   *vulgar paper*   ordinary literary productions (*paper* is used figuratively for what is written on it; the effect is to suggest that writing—and writers—are commonly worth no more than the paper they fill—see 17.9).   *rehearse*   set forth, give an account of (but see 21.4, note).

5. *thyself*   Q gives "thy selfe." Renaissance printers ordinarily print "thyself," "myself," "yourself," etc. as two words; the practice is conventional and would have been insignificant to Renaissance readers. Some editors retain the Renaissance form because for modern readers it can function as a convenient (though rhetorically distorting) means to point up the double sense: (1) yourself (the

simple reflexive); (2) your person. (Compare 37.7, note—on *Entitled.*) *in me* in my writings. (Compare *Thine own sweet argument*, a construction that fuses and confuses the beloved's identity as a living human being with his identity as a mere function of poems written about him. Here in an unusual, i.e. first-person, use of the common metonymy by which, for example, "in Shakespeare" or "in Virgil" says in Shakespeare's or in Virgil's works, the poet speaks of his writings as if they were himself but in a context that does not restrict *in me* to its figurative sense; the phrase thus sounds pathetically self-deprecatory, reducing the poet's identity and value to that of a sheaf of poems—or, rather, as a result of the taint infused by *vulgar paper*, a sheaf of scribblings.)

6. *stand against thy sight* This is another phrase in which an obvious primary meaning ("meet your eye"), is determined largely by context and modified by the imperfectly neutralized particulars of the actual construction: *stand against* means "take arms against" or "hold out against," and the complete phrase must suggest "withstand your inspection" (see *curious* in line 13); the phrase thus simultaneously finishes out the benign and humble statement begun in line 5 and gives it contradictory overtones of antagonism and resentment (see line 14, note). *sight* See 123.14, note.

7. *dumb* (1) incapable of speech; (2) insensible, incapable of feeling (see Tilley, D56: "As dumb as a doornail"). *to thee* This construction echoes a pattern abandoned after quatrain 1, each line of which ends with a phrase containing a version of the word "to": *to invent, into my verse, too excellent, to rehearse*; see also line 12.

8. *invention* inventiveness, creative power (but with an echo of line 1 and a gentle play on the pertinent technical sense of "invention"—the first of the five traditional parts of rhetorical theory, the discovery or selection of a subject, an argument; compare the interrelation of *argument* and *invention* in 103.3,7).

11. *bring forth* give birth to (a traditional metaphor for poetic creation; see 76.8, note).

12. *numbers* verses (but note the gratuitous wit resulting from the proximity of *ten* and *nine* in the preceding lines; see 17.6; the conjunction of the numbers, *Eternal numbers*, and *date* makes the line suggest the idea of arithmetical infinity). *long* a distant (see Spenser, *Prothalamion*, line 17: "Against the Brydale day, which is not long").

13. *these curious days* these fastidious times, this age of connoisseurs. *curious* = dissyllabic, by syncopation.

14. *pain* pains, effort. (Although Renaissance writers occasionally use the singular of *pain* in this sense, the plural was more usual and would have more efficiently prevented a reader from momentarily hearing a reference to the speaker's suffering. By choosing to use the singular, Shakespeare gives the line a bitter undertaste.)

SONNET 39

1–4. "A friend is a second self" was proverbial (Tilley, F696); see 36, head-note, 42.13, 104.2, note, 133.5–6, and *RIII* II.ii.151: "My other self."

1. *O how thy worth* This construction turns out to be parallel with the open-

ing phrase of sonnet 38, and *worth* turns out to be the direct object of an inter-rogative sentence in which *how* means "in what way," but the phrase first sounds like the beginning of an exclamatory declaration in which *how* means "to what great degree" and in which *worth* is the grammatical subject (the last lines of sonnet 38 prepare a reader for some such sentiment as "O how thy worth enriches my poor verse"). *with manners* decently, politely 'see the implied explanation in line 2; to praise oneself is unmannerly).

2. *the better part of me* Golding (XV. 989) uses this phrase to translate Ovid's *parte . . . meliore mei* in the closing lines of *Metamorphoses* where its meaning is "my soul" (see 74.8 where Shakespeare uses the phrase in context of the theme of immortality through verse, the context in which he found the phrase in Golding's *Ovid*). In addition the phrase suggests "my better half," a term already current in its modern sense, "my wife," or "my husband" (see *CofE* II.ii.18–145, III.ii.61–62, 66, and *JC* II.i.272–74: "By all your vows of love, and that great vow / Which did incorporate and make us one, / That you unfold to me, your self, your half" and *OED*, s.v. *Better*, 3c); also see 36, headnote. The phrase also suggests ideas initiated in Plato's *Symposium* (which, like Ephesians 5, is a *locus classicus* for assertions that a pair of lovers becomes a single individual), particularly the myth that accounts for lovers as the divided halves of spherical hermaphrodites trying to return to their original form.

3. Ingram and Redpath say, "The most evident meaning is: 'What benefit to myself can blowing my own trumpet bring?' . . . But is there also a play on 'mine own self' as 'you' . . . ?" See 62.13. The suggested wordplay gives the line this undersense: "What good can praise of myself (or my praise—i.e. the praise I give) do you?"

5. *Even for* precisely because of.

6. *dear* (1) precious; (2) heartfelt. *lose* See 18.10, note.

9. *absence* separation (see 97.1, note). *torment, prove* See 110.8 and 11, notes.

10. This line is metrically problematic. My text is essentially Q's, and, since *sour* is regularly monosyllabic, that reading is adequate; however, the meter invites "Were't not" and a dissyllabic pronunciation for *sour*. *leave* permis-sion, liberty (perhaps with an abstruse play on "to leave" meaning "to depart").

12. *doth* Q has "dost"; the emendation is standard. It allows two different readings of the line: If *Which* is read as a pronoun, then its antecedent is *love*, and the line says, "which deceives time and thoughts." In the syntactically less probable event that *Which* is understood as a demonstrative adjective (see Abbott, par. 269), then *time and thoughts* are the grammatical subjects of *doth*, and the line is a parenthetical comment that says, "The aforementioned time and thoughts was sweet deceivers" (the second reading is possible because singular verbs were commonly used with plural subjects as well as singular—compare 112.1 and 123.11). Some editors have justified "dost" by seeking out *thou* in line 9 and calling it the antecedent ("Thou, absence, who deceive time and thoughts"). *deceive* (1) delude; (2) while away (*OED* gives this from 1591: "Let us do something to deceave the time, and that we may not thinke it long").

13. *to make one twain* As the line is read, this phrase echoes the earlier statements about the effect of absence: to split a pair of lovers (a unit, *a single one*) in two. The next line establishes the sense as "to double one person," "to give one person existence in two places at once." (The doubleness and contrariness of the phrase is augmented by the relevance here of *twain* in the sense of "a married pair"; see 36.1, note.)

14. *here* (1) in the poem; (2) at the place where I am as I write. The meter suggests a third (and illogical) sense which results from stressing *him* rather than *here* as logic requires (compare "she here" in *A&C* III.xiii.98).

SONNET 40

See 133.2, note, and compare the apparent situations in 40–42 with those in 133, 134, and 144.

1. *Take all my loves* This phrase includes three different senses of "my love" and thus includes three statements: (1) accept all the kinds of affection I can give; (2) deprive me of the affection I possess, your love of me; (3) steal my mistress (my love, my beloved).

2. *then . . . than* = a modernization of Q's "then . . . then"; see 16.4, 8, note. *then* (1) in that case; (2) at that time.

3. *No love* (1) no affection; (2) no beloved. *true love call* (1) call genuine love (not mere infatuation or lust); (2) give the title "true-love" (faithful lover and lover faithfully loved—see *MND* II.ii.28–29: "Do it for thy true-love take; / Love and languish for his sake").

4. *All mine* (1) all my true, my genuine, love; (2) all my affection; (3) all my loves—the affection I give, the affection I receive, my mistress. (For the potential sexual suggestiveness of *all* in *all mine* ["my 'all' "?] and throughout the poem, see 26.1–14, note.)

5. *Then* Both senses *then* has in line 2 occur again here. *if for my love thou my love receivest* For, love, and receivest each has several appropriate and syntactically available meanings here; some of their many combinations are these: (1) if, out of affection for me (for love of me), you take my mistress; (2) if, because of my affection for you, you courteously welcome my mistress; (3) if, for yours (as your possession—you being *my love*, my beloved), you take my mistress; (4) if, in place of my affection, you take my mistress; (5) if you understand my mistress to be my true-love; (6) if you understand what I feel for my mistress to be love; (7) if, because of my affection for you (or yours for me), you accept (or suffer) my affection. Overtones of two pertinent special contexts of *receivest* reflect dishonorably on the transaction: (a) such agents as tax collectors, toll takers, and stewards were called "receivers" (see *OED*, s.v. "receive," I.1 and "receiver"); (b) "receiver" was also used as we use "receiver of stolen goods" (*OED*, s.v. "receive," I.1.c and "receiver").

6. *for* because. The meaning of *for* is clear, but its relation to the clause is double: it typifies the substance and style of the whole sonnet by presenting a single action as simultaneously grounds for guilt, a reason for blaming ("for the crime of using," "because you use") and grounds for innocence ("the reason

that I cannot blame you is that . . ."). (Q puts a comma between *blame thee*
and *for*; if one takes the comma as valid testimony on the poet's intent, the
logical action of *for* is limited to modifying the whole phrase, *cannot blame thee*;
even so, the identity and effect of the pertinent though syntactically irrelevant
standard idiom "blame for" is at least as strong as the punctuation that seems
to deny the meaning.) *my love thou usest* (1) you have sexual intercourse with
my mistress (a common meaning for "use"—*OED* gives this from 1584: "Manie
are so bewitched that they cannot use their owne wives"; see also *Oth* V.ii.72);
(2) you accept my affection (but see 4.7, 6.5, and 20.14; the idea of utilizing
affection, turning it to account, carries an unpleasant suggestion of the poet's
affection for the friend as capital put out at interest, or of the mistress as the
friend's profit from investing the love he should expend on the poet).

7. *thyself* This is the traditional emendation for Q's "this selfe," which some
recent editors have retained, arguing that "this self" refers to the poet, one of
the two persons who are one self in 39.1–4. *deceivest* (1) cheat, betray; (2)
delude.

8. *wilful* (1) stubbornly self-willed, heedless of advice; (2) willing, intentional; (3) lustful (see "will" meaning "lust" in 134–136). *taste of* (1) test of
(see *Lear* I.ii.44: "as an essay or taste of my virtue"); (2) sampling of; (3)
tincture of, taint of (as in *T&C* V.ii.125: "my negation hath no taste of madness"); (4) liking for, enjoyment of. *what thyself refusest* (1) what you deny
to yourself (i.e. abstain from); (2) what you yourself (or what you when you
are yourself) decline to take; (3) what you decline to give or grant.

10. *steal thee* take for yourself (an ethical dative; see Abbott, par. 220).
all my poverty (1) my poor all, what little I have (this meaning, rightly given
by the majority of editors, is not literally present in the phrase but results from
the expectations aroused by the context of the construction, "I forgive you,
although you . . ."); (2) the whole extent of my lack of wealth and/or of my
feebleness; (3) nothing but my worthless things (for *all* meaning "only," "nothing but," see 76.5 and *Much Ado* II.i.297: "I was born to speak all mirth and no
matter"; for *poverty* meaning "worthless things," "inferior matter," see 103.1).

11. *love knows* the spirit of love—and those under its influence—know; the
echo of such phrases as "Heaven knows," "Lord knows," and "God wot"
suggests a mock oath upon the god of love, upon Cupid.

12. *love's wrong* (1) the profanation of affection; (2) injury inflicted by a
friend; (3) injury related to or resulting from affection. *than* = a modernization of Q's "then" (see 16.4,8, note). *known* recognized, expected (but see
129.13, 151.1, notes and *love knows it* in the preceding line.

13. *Lascivious* = trisyllabic, by syncopation. *all ill well shows* every evil
appears virtuous (Shakespeare's reader may have heard a pun on "ill will" ["only
ill will, spite, appears"], or on "ill William" ["in whom William demonstrates
all ill" or "in whom all William's ill appears"]; for the probable phonetic
similarity of "well" and "will," see 112.3, note; for the potential sexual suggestiveness of *well*, see 154.9, note.)

14. *spites* injuries, vexations.

SONNET 41

See 40 and 139, headnotes.

1. *pretty* In Renaissance usage this word is similar to the modern "cute"; it was applied only to inconsequential objects (a limitation probably assisted by its phonetic likeness to "petty"), and includes the ideas of "comely," "artful," "sportive," and "apt"; it is inevitably colored by the subjects to which it was habitually applied: children and childish behavior, young gallants, handsome soldiers, and knickknacks. "Little things are pretty" was proverbial (Tilley, T188); in *LLL* Armado explains that Moth is properly called pretty because he is little. The ironic use of *pretty* (as in the modern "a pretty kettle of fish") was already commonplace. *liberty* license, freedom of behavior, unrestrained action.

2. *sometime* sometimes (see 18.5, note).

3. *befits* befit. (The subject is *wrongs*; third person plurals in "s" are common in Renaissance English; see 95.12, 101.3, 112.1, and 123.11.)

4. *still* continually, always (as in 9.5; 126.6,10; etc.).

5, 6. *to be* (1) can be; (2) should be.

5–6. An intensified (not "woo" but *assail*) and significantly perverse variant on the topic (woman) and order (first woo then win) of a popular proverb used twice by Shakespeare: "She's beautiful, and therefore to be woo'd; / She is a woman, therefore to be won" (*1HVI* V.iii.78–79); "She is a woman, therefore may be woo'd; / She is a woman, therefore may be won" (*Titus* II.i.83–84). Here the inverted echo of a proverb in which the man is the aggressor and the woman his beautiful and pliant object prepares for the sudden reversal of roles at the end of line 8 (*till he have prevailed*).

6. *Beauteous* = dissyllabic, by syncopation.

8. *sourly* = dissyllabic. *he* So Q; in the name of consistency most modern éditors emend to "she" (thus removing the wit of the statement). They follow Malone, who said, "The Lady, and not the man, being in this case supposed the wooer, the poet without doubt wrote . . . *she*" (edition of 1780). Dover Wilson commented: "Nearly all editors agree with Malone, but male readers, except those who know less about sex than Shakespeare, will agree, I think, with Q" (edition of 1966).

9–14. "When love puts in, friendship is gone," was proverbial (Tilley, L549).

9. *my seat* the place that belongs to me (used like "the chair" or "the throne"—a symbol and perquisite of authority; *Variorum* cites J. A. Fort, who called this "a reference to the time-honoured courtesy of not occupying the chair most used by the owner of the house"). Here the reference is specifically sexual; see *Oth* II.i.289–90: "I do suspect the lustful Moor / Hath leap'd into my seat."

10,11. These lines play on the tone and diction (*youth, lead, riot*) of such commonplace moral injunctions as the proverb "Youth riotously led breeds a loathsome old age" (Tilley, Y47).

11. *riot* wanton, loose, and wasteful living, debauchery, dissipation.

12. *truth* troth, allegiance, covenant (note "I plight thee my trouth" in the

English marriage service [*The Booke of the Common Prayer*, 1549; "troth," 1552, 1559]).

13. *to thee*   This is the last in a series of travel metaphors for emotional and spiritual motion and change: *absent* (line 2), *follows* (4), *straying* (10), *lead thee . . . there* (11); the metaphors are commonplaces but are so concentrated here that they are revivified and suggest actual travel. Here *to* indicating direction is wittily balanced against *to* indicating the recipient of action in *to me* (14).

SONNET 42

See 40 and 139, headnotes.

2. *dearly*   fondly, earnestly, deeply (but with plays on "grievously"—see line 1 and 37.3, *dearest*—and "at great cost").

3. *of my wailing chief*   i.e. the principal cause of my wailing (the strange and elliptical construction may have been prompted by Shakespeare's wish to echo the already common term "chief mourner," the nearest relative present at a funeral.

4. *nearly*   intimately, pressingly (*nearly* also meant "with close kinship"; compare "near" in *RII* III.i.17: "Near to the King in blood, and near in love").

5. *Loving offenders*   *Loving* describes their offense (making love); it also describes their relationship to the speaker; and it echoes standard salutations, common in royal proclamations, in which *loving* was used like "gracious" or "noble" or "faithful"; see *RII* I.i.21: "My gracious sovereign, my most loving liege," and *John* II.i.204: "You loving men of Angiers."   *excuse*   (1) make excuses for, justify; (2) pardon.

7. *ev'n*   See 15.6, note.   *ev'n so*   just so, by the same token.   *abuse*   (1) wrong; (2) deceive; (3) dishonor (see *1HVI* IV.v.41: "your renowned name; shall flight abuse it?").

5,7. *excuse, abuse*   Note the presence of "use" in both words; see 2.9, 121.10, notes.

8. *approve her*   (1) put her to the proof, try her out (sexually); (2) commend her (this sense complements sense (3) of *abuse*; the activity of each member of the triangle is described in a word related to speech: *excuse, abuse, approve*).

9. *my love's*   (1) my mistress's; (2) my affection's; (3) your (my beloved's, my friend's).

9,11. *lose*   See 18.10, note.

12. *lay on me this cross*   give me this vexation, thwart me (the phrase inevitably suggests that the speaker is Christ-like in his innocence, in his suffering, and in the patience with which he loves his persecutors, abets them, forgives them, and, in the pattern of Christian paradoxes, sees loss as gain, grief as joy, etc.).

13. On the unity of lover and beloved see 36, 37, 39, and 40.   *one*   Note *loss, lose*, etc. in lines 4, 9, 10, 11 and the presence here of the logically irrelevant but contextually pertinent sound of "won"; compare 135.13, 14, note.

14. *flatt'ry*   (1) delusion (see 33.2, 87.13, 114.2, 138.14, and *Oth* IV.i.128–29: "she is persuaded . . . out of her own love and flattery"); (2) palliation, failure to blame (note *excuse* in line 5, and see Proverbs 28:23: "He that rebuketh . . .

shal finde more favour . . . then he that flattereth with his tongue"). The word thus describes the speaker's preceding extenuation, and the idea that two lovers are one being, and the idea that the mistress loves only the speaker.

SONNET 43

The recurring themes of this sonnet—things that are the opposite of what they would normally be expected to be, and the distinction between images or shadows of objects and the objects themselves—are played out stylistically in an intense display of antithesis and a range of rhetorical devices of repetition that make the language of the poem suggest mirror images. The rhetorical devices are these (some examples qualify for more than one label): antithesis: *wink, see* (line 1); *bright, dark* (4); *shadow, form* (5,6); *living day, dead night* (10,11); antistasis (repetition of a word in a different or contrary sense): *bright* the adjective, *bright* the adverb (4); *shadow shadows* (5); *form form* (6); *clear, clearer* (7); epizeuxis (repetition of a word with no other word between): *shadow shadows, form form*; diacope (repetition of a word with one or a few words in between): *bright, are bright* (4); *see till I see* (13); polyptoton (repetition of·words from the same root but with different endings): *darkly, dark* (4); *shadow, shade* (5,6,8,11), etc.; antimetabole (inversion of the order of repeated words): *darkly bright, are bright in dark* (4); and rhetorically unclassified word plays: a sort of fusion of antithesis and an antistasis of ideas (compare 134.9, note—on ideational puns): *dark* meaning "darkness," "night" (4), with *fair* meaning "beautiful" (11) and the noun *light* (7) with the adjective *heavy* (12); and words that in combination suggest oxymoron (miniature paradox) but are used in senses that are logically compatible: *shade shines* (8) where *shade* means not "darkness" but "image."

1. *wink*   shut my eyes, sleep (*When most I wink* is curiously unidiomatic in its use of *most*; perhaps the construction was dictated by the context of the preceding sonnet; for a reader following the Q sequence, this line first seems to continue the theme of studied refusal to recognize evil: "to wink" meant "to shut one's eyes to—connive at—a fault"; see *Macb* I.iv.51–52: "Let not light see my black and deep desires. / The eye wink at the hand" and the proverb "Although I wink, I am not blind" [Tilley, W500]).

2. *unrespected*   ignored, unheeded (with overtones of "not held in respect," "not prized," "held in contempt," and with a play on "unseen").

4. In considering this calculatedly confusing line, it is some help to remember that in the Renaissance eyes were generally thought of as giving off light.   *darkly* (1) in secret (see *AW* IV.iii.9–10: "I will tell you a thing, but you shall let it dwell darkly with you"); (2) frowningly, gloomily, ominously (see *RIII* I.iv.165: "How darkly and how deadly dost thou speak"); (3) blindly, sightlessly (*OED* gives this from 1576: "dimme and darke eyesight"); (4) dimly, obscurely. *bright* (1) shining, emitting light; (2) beautiful (see 28.9); (3) cheerful (see *Macb* III.ii.28: "Be bright and jovial among your guests"); (4) clear.   *darkly bright*   A reader's understanding of this phrase is dictated by what it must mean: (1) shining in the dark; (2) seeing clearly though closed. However, the phrase also acts as an oxymoron (thus continuing the paradoxical vein of lines 1 and 2): the qualities—

"emitting light" and "in a dark way"—seem incompatible. As in all oxymorons, compatible senses of the words (senses by which a phrase designed to suggest an impossibility comes to describe an apprehensible condition) come into play almost immediately; here, however, they present not only compatible combinations ("shining in secret" and "shining dimly") but further oxymorons ("obscurely clear" and "gloomily cheerful"). *bright in dark directed* No paraphrase quite fits both the syntax (in which *bright* is used adverbially) and the sense demanded by the possibilities of the context; *Variorum* records these efforts: (1) "clearly directed in the darkness"; (2) "guided in the dark by the brightness (of thy 'shadow' or apparition)"; (3) "directed toward that which is bright in the dark (*bright-in-dark* having the effect of an adverb)." Ingram and Redpath, straining toward the modern use of *bright* to mean "quick-witted," say " 'alertly directed in the darkness' (i.e. heedfully, contrast line 2)."

5. *Then* (1) at that time; (2) in that case. *Then thou* seems to introduce a straightforward "then" clause on the model of the one in the first line, but the construction breaks off before predication, and a new, substitute construction begins in the next line.

The reader's mind will presumably have set off into the construction signalled by the context of the preceding lines; such a reader's own, real (though merely syntactic) experience can make him a genuinely (though casually) engaged participant in the speaker's sudden desire for certainty, solidity, and a precise distinction between image and actual object. *shadow* image produced by the imagination (see 27.10). *shadows* darkness.

6. *shadow's form* the model for the image, the reality of which the shadow is an image, body, self. *form happy show* create a joyous spectacle, be a pleasing sight (note the choice of *show*, a word that connotes illusion, to describe its opposite; see also *form* meaning "mere external appearance" in 125.5).

6–7. As line 6 is read, *form happy show* does not invite its reader to understand *show* as a verb or the whole phrase as a contorted inversion of "show a happy form," "present a delightful appearance"; but the last word of line 6 is *show*, and line 7 begins *To the clear day*, which sounds like the indirect object of the verb *show*: "show to the clear day."

7. *clear day* (1) bright day; (2) full day (see *Measure* IV.ii.202: "it is almost clear dawn"). *clearer* (1) brighter; (2) more illustrious (as in the Latin *clarus* —see *Lear* IV.vi.73–74: "the clearest gods, who make them honours / Of men's impossibilities"); (3) purer, more innocent (see *Lucrece* 382: "In his clear bed might have reposed still"); (4) more clearsighted, more perspicacious (see 46.12 and *CofE* III.ii.62: "Mine eye's clear eye"); (5) more evident, more visible; (6) more perfect, more complete. *light* (1) brightness; (2) sparkle in the eyes (see *Lucrece* 1378: "eyes gleam'd forth their . . . lights"); (3) eyesight (*OED* gives this from 1607: "lift up thine eyes . . . They were not borne to loose their light so soone"); (4) mental illumination or enlightenment, mental sight (see *2Gent* II.iv.206: "that hath dazzled my reason's light"); (4) glory (see 100.4).

8,12. *so!* and *stay!* Q reads "so?" and "stay?" (see 97.2,4, note).

11. *thy* Q reads "their"; see 26.12, note. *imperfect* deficient, wanting a part or parts necessary to full form (note *clear* and *clearer* in line 7). *shade*

Here the word means simply "image," but in the context of *dead night* and of nocturnal visions, a commoner meaning of *shade*, "ghost," may well impinge on a reader's understanding (see 18.11, note).

14. *show thee me* The sense here must be "show thee to me," but the rhythm (accent on *me*) and the idiom ordinarily dictate "show me to thee" (compare *Temp* II.ii.150, 131: "I'll show thee the best springs"; "My mistress show'd me thee, and thy dog and thy bush"); the phrase thus presents a final abnormality in a poem that is a succession of paradoxes and reversals of the norm.

SONNET 44

This poem is specifically linked with 45; this pair, in turn, is recalled by a later pair, 50 and 51. Both pairs share topics and conceits with *HV* III.vii.11–79, the Dauphin's praise of his horse.

1–10. Compare Donne's "Sapho to Philaenis," lines 7–8: "Thoughts, my mindes creatures, often are with thee, / But I, their maker, want their libertie."

1. *dull* sluggish, inert, heavy, slow of motion. *were thought* were made of thought (instead of material substance); Shakespeare regularly uses *thought* as a metonymy for "the swiftest of all possible things"; Falstaff, chidden for arriving late, says: "Do you think me a swallow, an arrow, or a bullet? Have I, in my poor and old motion, the expedition of thought?" (*2HIV* IV.iii.30–31); see also *HV* III.Prologue. 1–3.

2. *Injurious* (trisyllabic, by syncopation) spiteful. *stop* block. *way* (1) act of passing (see *Shrew* III.ii.230–31: "I'll bring mine action on the proudest he / That stops my way" and *CofE* IV.iii.86: "shut the doors against his way"); (2) path (see *2Gent* IV.iii.24: "the ways are dangerous to pass"). (Here Shakespeare may intend a quiet play on *way* meaning "distance"—as in *Oth* III.iv.200: " 'Tis but a little way that I can bring you").

3. *despite of* in spite of.

4. *limits* districts, regions (see *1HIV* III.i.72–73: "The Archdeacon hath divided it [the nation] / Into three limits"). (The context of "stop my way" in line 2 activates overtones of *limits* meaning "barriers"—as in *R&J* II.ii.67: "stony limits cannot hold love out"). *where* to where. *stay* (1) abide, sojourn; (2) tarry, linger (with a probable play on *stay* meaning to hold [something] back, "stop the progress or passage of").

7. *nimble thought can jump* The personification of *thought* developing here is complete in line 8 and continues through line 10.

8. *would be* wishes to be.

9. The first *thought* in this line has not only the meaning it has elsewhere in the poem (intellectual action and its products, that which exists in the mind but has no physical substance) but also (1) contemplation (i.e. the act of thinking—of realizing, of remembering, what I actually am); and (2) melancholy (see 30.1, note).

9–10. *thought / To* Most editors put a comma at the end of line 9 to indicate the logically self-sufficient unit "thought kills me because I am not thought." The substance of the preceding lines and the inevitable line-end pause do the work of a comma in any case, and by foregoing the editorial comma one includes ". . . that I am not thought, which can leap . . . " and the mystical overtones inherent in the syntactically possible ". . . that I am not believed to leap. . . ."

11. *so much*   being so much.   *earth and water*   The reference here (and in the following sonnet) is to the doctrine of the four elements. Shakespeare probably thought of *Met.* XV.239–44—probably specifically of Golding's version (lines 263–67—see Appendix 2). (Brent Cohen points out to me that "the echo of *earth and water* with *sea and land* [line 7] embodies the paradox of the poem— that 'we are made of the same stuff that separates us from what we desire.' ")

12. Ingram and Redpath note that "the image appears to be that of a petitioner waiting on a great man."

13–14. These lines may intend a play on *elements* meaning "the heavens"; in both singular and plural "element" was used to mean "sky" (see *Lucrece* 1588–89: "These water-galls in her dim element / Foretell new storms").

13. *naught*   Q reads "naughts"; the emendation is made by all modern editors. "Naughts," though rare, was used to mean "worthless things" (see *OED*, 3a); *OED* (3b) gives two examples of "naughts" as a synonym for "nothing" (the meaning required here for the "nothing but" construction), but both *OED*'s instances provide a needed rhyme.

14. *heavy*   sorrowful (but with a play on "of great weight").   *either's*   (1) of earth (*heavy*) and of water (wet, like *tears*); (2) your and my.

SONNET 45

1. *The other two*   Sonnet 45 continues from 44, and this syntax makes them indivisible; on the four elements, see 44.11, note.   *slight*   insubstantial, not heavy (*OED* gives this from 1594: "He that could make a garment slightest and thinnest carried it away"; the word inevitably carries overtones of "unimportant," "of little worth," "trifling").   *purging*   cleansing, purifying ("to purge" also meant "to issue forth"—*OED* gives this from 1610: "When parting from the body, forth it [the soul] purges"). The word *purging* suggests and anticipates a topic that does not emerge openly until line 7: medicine. The commonest use of "purge" was as a medical term; as the foundation of traditional natural philosophy, the doctrine of the four elements was the basis for traditional medicine. Disease resulted from an imbalance among the four elements of which the body is composed; the standard means of righting the balance was a purge.

1–2. See 44.1–10, note.

3. "The first being my thought, the other being my desire."

4. *present-absent*   (1) simultaneously both present and absent; (2) now present—now absent, alternately here and away. The hyphen is a standard editorial addition. These words—themselves an oxymoron, a capsule of contraries—act to harmonize a variety of logically incompatible conceits and, thus, to facilitate the reader's "swift slide" from one to another. Lines 1–3 have turned a commonplace hyperbole ("my thoughts and desires are always with you"; "half of myself is always with you") into a paradox by equating *thought* and *desire* with

air and *fire*; the equation invites consideration of the hyperbole as if *with* (line 2) were intended literally; but 50 percent of a human body cannot be anywhere but with the other 50 percent. In sense (1), *present-absent* capsules the paradox: "physically present, spiritually absent." Sense (2) capsules the conceit introduced by *with swift motion slide*; this new conceit, which takes up the rest of the poem, is logically incompatible with sense (1) and with the assertion in lines 1–3 that *thought/air* and *desire/fire* are always with the beloved, always absent from the speaker.

5. *quicker* (1) swifter, livelier (more capable of fast motion and rapid travel); (2) more alive, livelier (endowed with more life—compare the phrase "the quick and the dead" in the Apostle's creed, and see *life*, line 7, and *death*, line 8). The word is especially apt here because "quick" had specialized meanings when applied to fire ("burning strongly," *OED*, 11b) and—when used by Shakespeare—to air ("sharp," "piercing," *OED*, 18c—see *Per* IV.i.28–29: "the air is quick there, / And it pierces and sharpens the stomach").

6. *to thee* The phrase both indicates the object of the embassy ("embassy to thee") and modifies *love* ("love to thee" = "affection for you"—compare *2Gent* III.ii.48: "She shall not long continue love to him").

7. *being* = monosyllabic (see 52.14, note).

8. *Sinks down* and *oppressed* The wit here consists in using common metaphors in a context pertinent both to their figurative meanings ("declines" and "afflicted") and their literal meanings (*Sinks down*: "becomes submerged in water," "subsides into the earth," "is weighted down"; *oppressed*: "is weighted down"). *melancholy* In the composition of a human body, the four elements were said to manifest themselves as the four humors, the four primary bodily fluids; each combined the qualities of two elements; an individual's humor (his temperament, physical and emotional disposition, his "complexion" [see 132.14, note]) was determined by the particular humor dominant in his constitution: blood, wet and hot, sanguine (ardent, optimistic) temperament; phlegm, wet and cold, phlegmatic (sluggish, calm) temperament; choler (i.e. yellow bile), dry and hot, choleric (irascible) temperament; melancholy (from the Greek for "black bile"), dry and cold, melancholy temperament. Disease resulted when the dominance of one humour became absolute. Note that Shakespeare's primary attention is to the tenor of his statements not to their vehicle—the technical details of traditional physics and medicine: a rigorous understanding of his conceit of the four elements demands that, being made up of earth and water, the speaker should be oppressed with phlegm, but melancholy—extreme depression, brooding—is traditional to lovers separated from the beloved and makes sense where "phlegm" would be ridiculous. (Shakespeare probably intended a play on the fact that "thought"—see 44.1, 45.1–3—was potentially a synonym for dull *melancholy*—see 30.1.) Note that the word *melancholy* is metrically oppressive—particularly so, since its unstressed final syllable rhymes with the stressed final syllable of line 6.

9. *recured* restored (this word is especially apt in this context of medicine and repossession because the word "recure" represents a pair of homonyms that have related and easily confused senses: one is derived from a contraction of

"recover"—"to get back." "repossess"; the other comes from the Latin "re-curare"—"to cure"; "recure" carried either meaning or both.

11–13. *assured . . . joy* See *R&J* V.i.15–17: "How fares my Juliet? That I ask again, / For nothing can be ill if she be well." The conceit of the absent elements gives the life and wit of literalness to what might have been only a standard hyperbole like Romeo's—an assertion that the lover's health depends upon his assurance that the absent beloved is well.

11. *ev'n* See 15.6, note. *ev'n but now* just this moment. *assured* In context of *messengers, assured* carries overtones of its formulaic use as a closing to a letter; see 92.2, note.

12. *thy* Q gives "their"; see 26.12, note.

14. *sad* sorrowful (but with an abstruse play on "heavy" meaning "sad," "sorrowful"; meaning "slow," "sluggish," "dull" [as in 56.9]; and meaning "weighty"—i.e. being again constituted only of the two heavy elements). *straight* immediately.

SONNET 46

Both 46 and 47 play on distinctions and confusions between images made by art (pictures, paintings) and the image (the idea, the essence, of the beloved) kept in the heart of the lover. This sonnet presupposes a reader familiar with the endlessly reiterated Renaissance distinction between true love—from the heart—and mere infatuation—inspired by the sight of beauty; see *R&J* II.iii.67–68: "young men's love, then, lies / Not truly in their hearts, but in their eyes."

1. Contests and legalistic debates between eye and heart were a commonplace fancy in Renaissance love poetry; *Variorum* lists examples; see also the note on "eye-heart" poems appended to the commentary on sonnet 141. *Mine eye and heart* The wit of this and the following sonnet is derived from extravagantly complex convolutions in the relationships between *eye* and *heart*. Both poems evoke a sense of futile waste, of barren ingenuity, and of neurotic diversion of energy on to trivia. In this sonnet that sense is largely generated by a tangle of overlapping instances of chiasmus (*Mine eye my heart* [line 3] and *My heart mine eye* [4], *heart–part* [the rhyme words in lines 10 and 12] and *part–heart* [the rhyme words in the couplet], *heart's part* [12] and *part . . . hearts* [13, 14]), and of related effects (line 4 begins *My heart mine eye*; line 5 begins *My heart* and concludes with *lie*, a word that rhymes with *eye*; the rhyme words in lines 6 and 8 are *lies* and *eyes*). The relationship betwen this sonnet (eye and heart at war), and the next (*Betwixt mine heart and eye a league is took*), presents a similar pairing by contrasting echoes on a larger scale.

2. *conquest* spoils of war, booty, captured territory; Ingram and Redpath add " 'acquisition' (by any means other than inheritance, as in the Scots law of real estate: cf. 6.14)." The two meanings thus make *conquest* a hinge on which Shakespeare turns from a war metaphor to one of real estate law. *of thy sight* which is the sight of you (with a play on "site"?).

3,8,13,14. *thy* In each case Q has "their"; see 26.12, note.

3. *bar* prohibit (in the specifically legal sense in which "to bar" meant "to

restrain [someone] from enforcing [some claim]," but with pertinent, though logically unharnessed, suggestions of barred prison windows).

4. *freedom* unrestrained exercise (here the word is colored by uses of "free" in real estate law to mean "held without obligation or restriction" as in "freehold" and "freeland").

5. *thou in him dost lie* This phrase reflects and fuses two commonplace concepts, one from law and real estate: to lie within the domains of and so legally belong to (see *R&J* II.i.20: "the demesnes that there adjacent lie"); the other a traditional expression of affection: to lodge someone in one's heart (see *LLL* II.i.173–74: "you shall deem yourself lodg'd in my heart, / Though so denied fair harbour in my house," and *Ham* V.ii.338: "If thou didst ever hold me in thy heart"). In addition, cultural habit suggests a reading (which the following lines make primary) based on the traditional Platonic/Christian preference for invisible, inner reality over mere visible, outward appearance: "the essential, the real, you is located in (known to, valued by) the heart."

6. *closet* (1) a small private room (see *Ham* II.i.77: "I was sewing in my closet"); (2) a box or cabinet for valuables (with a possible play on the medical term "closet of the heart," a synonym for "pericardium").

8. *fair* (1) beautiful; (2) clear, distinct; (3) pure; (4) superficially attractive (used in contrast to true value; *OED* gives this from 1568: "a fayre speaker, and a deepe dissembler"). *in him thy fair appearance lies* Inferences from the parallel claim in line 5 give these words greater clarity and substance than is demonstrable in them. The eye's argument appears to rest—appropriately—on common sense: the disputed object is a picture and so, being visually apprehended, must be the province of the eye. The phrasing suggests a reference to the beloved's reflection in the lover's eyes (see 55.14, note, and *John* II.i.502–03: "I beheld myself / Drawn in the flattering table of her eye"). The phrasing is also another example of Shakespeare's delight in words and phrases that support a particular position or evoke a particular response and simultaneously confound it (compare *melancholy* in 45.8): "thy fair appearance—as opposed to essence—lies—is a lie, is a delusion."

9. *'cide* decide; Q gives "side." (Since Shakespeare regularly coins similar abbreviations, and since *OED* records "dissyde" as a sixteenth-century spelling of "decide," *'cide* probably represents a simple modernization. As a meaning for the verb "to side," *OED* gives "to assign to one of two sides or parties" but finds no evidence for it. The verb "to side" did, however, mean "to take sides with"—as in *Cor* I.i.191–92: "[the people] side factions . . . making parties strong"; that meaning, impossible in this line, pertains to the poem at large and to *all tenants to the heart* in particular.) *title* legal right of possession.

10. *quest* jury (as in *RIII* I.iv.180: "What lawful quest have given their verdict up"). *all tenants to the heart* This information evokes conflicting responses depending on the terms in which it is evaluated: in terms of theories of love, the choice of jurymen is just because the only source of thoughts of true love is the heart; thoughts that are tenants of the eye would be thoughts of lust. In terms of the legal metaphor, however, this is a packed jury.

12. *clear* The word modifies *eye* and is appropriate to it: clarity is a virtue in

eyes. But *clear* also pertains to the legal context and recalls such constructions as "a clear case," "a clear right," and "clear title to." *moiety* (= dissyllabic, by syncopation) part, portion (not necessarily a half). *part* assigned portion, share. (Compare the proverb "The eye will have his part"; Tilley [E233] indicates that the expression was well established by 1640.)

13. *thy outward part* (1) the part of you that is external and visible; (2) your external qualities (see 17.4). (Both here and in 47.8, *part* is extrasyntactically colored by the context of bodily parts.)

SONNET 47

See the headnote to 46 and 46.1, note.

1. *a league is took* an alliance is made. (In context of *Betwixt, league* can carry a momentary suggestion of its homonym "league," a unit of measure [as in *Temp* III.2.14: "I swam . . . five and thirty leagues"]; distance becomes a topic in quatrain 3.) *took* (Renaissance writers often use the past tense where earlier and later writers use the participle—"taken"; see Abbott, par. 343).

2. *good turns* Note the same expression in a related context in 24.9.

2,5. *now, then* See 90.1, note.

3–8. These lines may be intended as witty expansions on such stock figures of speech as "to hunger for the sight of," "to feast one's eyes on," "to feed on shadows," and "to eat one's heart out"; see also the proverb "When shared, joy is doubled and sorrow halved" (Tilley, J89).

4. *Or heart* or when the heart (however, at first glance *Or* can appear to introduce an alternative to *look*—"famished for a look or for a . . . "). *himself* itself (but see 73.10, note).

4–7. "Or when the heart, which is in love, smothers itself *with* (i.e. by means of) sighs, then my eye feasts *with* (i.e. upon—see *Measure* IV.iii.149: 'to dine and sup with water and bran') my love's picture, and invites my heart to join him." (But as the lines are read—before the one reasonable sense is evident—other and commoner meanings of the standard constructions "in love with" and "feast with" invite pertinent and momentarily probable readings which the developing sentence immediately denies: (1) "or when the heart, which is in love with sighs [a symptom of love melancholy], smothers itself with [by means of] my love's picture . . . "; (2) ". . . smothers itself; then with [in company of] my love's picture my eye doth feast . . . ").

6. *painted banquet* The phrase suggests the coldness, artifice, and inadequacy of the substitute, "a painted show of . . . false blisse" (*FQ* VI.x.3); see *FQ* III.ii.44: "feed on shadowes, whiles I die for food."

8. "And shares in his love thoughts" (but the sequence of reading causes the line to include "in his thoughts [in imagination] shares a part of love"). *part* portion (but see 46.13, note).

10. *Thyself* Q has "Thy seife"; Rollins reports that "apparently the Rosenbach copy has the spelling *selfe*, all other copies *seife*" (II, 5); see 89.11, note. *are* = the Q reading (the majority of editors have emended to "art" for gram-

matical purity). *still* (1) always; (2) nevertheless (i.e. even though you are away).

11. *no* Q gives "nor"; some editors choose to read "not." Note that *move* activates a muted play on "motionless" in *still* in lines 10 and 12.

12. *still* always.

14. *heart to heart's* See 24.13–14, note.

SONNET 48

This sonnet appears to play on two proverbial expressions: "Love locks no cupboards" (Tilley, L520) and "Love laughs at locksmiths" (see *V&A* 575–76: "Were beauty under twenty locks kept fast, / Yet love breaks through and picks them all at last"). Although this poem cannot be said to employ sexual double entendre, it derives an aura of sexual innuendo from its concentration of words commonly used in sexual senses: for example, see "usest" in 40.6; "hand" in *LLL* IV.i.128; "ward" in *T&C* I.ii.250–62; "jewels" in *MofV* II.viii.18–24; and, on "locks," *Lucrece* 302–58, the passage from *V&A* quoted above, and *Cymb* II.ii.40–42 (quoted in 52.1–2, note). See 31.3, note and 98, headnote.

1. *took my way* set out on my journey. (Note that the rest of the poem concerns "taking" in its literal sense. Moreover, "to take" already had sexual meanings irrelevant to *took* in this phrase but relevant to the poem at large: (a) a female in sexual intercourse is said to "take" the male [*OED* gives this from 1577: "Neither can they suckle their young, till they have taken buck"]; (b) a male is said to "take" a woman [compare the analogous case of Latin *rapere*, "to seize," and the English "to rape"; see the proverb "A maid that laughs is half taken"—Tilley, M22—and *Tim* I.ii.146–48: "My lord, you take us even at the best." "Faith, for the worst is filthy, and would not hold taking . . ."].)

3. *to* for. *use, unusèd* See 2.9, note and the passage quoted from *R&J* in the note to line 12 below.

4. *hands of falsehood* perfidious hands (i.e. thieves). *wards* = a word meaning "guards" and used to describe places that can be locked for safekeeping; the range of its applications includes chests (see line 9) and prison cells (see lines 11 and 12). (There is probably a play on "the wards" of a lock, the metal ridges in a lock casing or keyhole that permit only the right key to enter. Compare the similar play in *Lucrece* 302–03). *of trust* that are trustworthy (see 21.5, note). *trust!* Q has "trust?" (see 97.2–4, note).

5. *to* compared to (see *Ham* I.ii.139–40: "a king that was to this / Hyperion to a satyr"). (At first glance, however, *to whom* is likely to be understood as "in whose estimation"—see 104.1). *jewels* = dissyllabic.

6. *Most worthy comfort* (1) [who are] most deserving of assistance, consolation, joy. (2) [who are my] most valuable joy.

7. *best of dearest* [who art] (1) best of best; (2) best of the most precious; (3) best of the best beloved. *mine only care* (1) my only grief; (2) my only concern (with a play on Latin *carus*, "dear": "my only beloved," "the only thing I care about"—compare Italian *cara mia*).

8. *every vulgar thief* any and all common thieves. *vulgar* (1) ordinary (see the example in 38.4, note); (2) base (with suggestions of "generally circulating"; see 112.2, note).

9. *chest* Shakespeare makes the same play on "coffer" and "ribs and breastbone" in *Lucrece* 761 and in *RII* I.i.180–81: "A jewel in a ten-times barr'd-up chest / Is a bold spirit in a loyal breast."

11. *closure* enclosure.

12. *at pleasure* at will (with a probable play on the sexual sense of *pleasure*; see 58.2, note, 20.13, note, and *R&J* II.iv.152–53: "I saw no man use you at his pleasure; if I had, my weapon should quickly have been out . . .").

14. See *V&A* 724: "Rich preys make true-men thieves" and the proverb "The prey entices the thief" (Tilley P570). *truth* honesty. *dear* (1) costly; (2) beloved.

SONNET 49

1. *Against* in anticipation of, in preparation for (it has the same meaning in lines 5 and 9, but in line 11 *against* means "in opposition to"; see 12.13, 13.3,11, and 63.1,10).

2. *defects* Although this word *means* only "failings," "deficiencies," "imperfections" here, three other senses have non-logical pertinence in context of three succeeding topics: (1) "defect" is a quantitative and mathematical term (although *OED* gives no example before 1660), meaning "the quantity by which anything falls short" or, in mathematics, "a part by which a figure or quantity is wanting or deficient"—see *sum* and *audit* in lines 3 and 4; (2) "defect" was used like Latin *defectus* to mean "eclipse," "failure (of a heavenly body) to shine" (*OED* gives examples from 1603, 1607, and this from 1692: "Prodigious and lasting Defects of the Sun, such as happened when Caesar . . . was slain") —see line 6 and note; (3) "defect" was a synonym for "defection," "falling away," "desertion" (*OED* gives this from 1540: "The king . . . made a defect from his purpose")—see *To leave poor me* in line 13. (Shakespeare may also be playing on the philosophical concept of "defective—or deficient—cause," which St. Augustine derived from his definition of evil as the absence of good; the term designates an omission that effects a result and was widely used in Renaissance theological controversies; in *Ham* II.ii.101–03 Shakespeare plays with both the term and the pedantic contortions in which it figured: "find out the cause of this effect: / Or rather say the cause of this defect, / For this effect defective comes by cause"—see *allege no cause* in line 14.)

3. *thy love* (1) your affection for me; (2) your beloved, I (for similar constructions, see 34.13, note). *cast* Here again a word that has a single simple meaning ("reckon up") reverberates with barely realized extra pertinences: (a) *cast his utmost* is a perverse echo of the stock phrase "at last cast," originally a metaphor from dicing, and meaning "in extremity," "near death," or "near ruin"; (b) in context of *frown*, overtones of "to cast"—meaning "to cloud," "to darken," "to become overcast"—assist in building toward the weather metaphor

in line 6; (c) "to cast" meaning "to defeat in a legal action" and "to find guilty" and "to condemn" (*OED*, 14, 16, 17) anticipates the legal language of lines 11–14. More significantly, *cast* could be an emblem for the poem at large: *cast* meant both "calculate or anticipate the future"—"forecast"—and "reject," "abandon," "cast aside" (*cast his utmost sum* can momentarily suggest "cast out, reject, his most precious possession," or, perhaps, "his other self"—see note on *the thing it was*, line 7). *his* (1) its (but see 73.10, note); (2) his (taking *thy love* as "your beloved").

    4. *audit* official examination of financial accounts (with verification by reference to witnesses as in a judicial hearing—see lines 11–14). *advised respects* judicious considerations, considered motives. (The phrase appears in *John* IV. ii.214, where it indicates the opposite of "humor," that is "whim" or "emotional inclination"—here it suggests "considerations of motives unrelated to simple affection and friendship"—see *reasons* in lines 8 and 12. Willen and Reed note that "respect" also meant "rank" or "high rank"; for *respects* here, they suggest "marks of deference for high rank.")

    5. *strangely* (1) like a stranger, as if you did not know me; (2) with cold, distant, or unfriendly bearing—for instance with eyes averted—see line 6 (for a similar use of *strangely*, see *2HIV* V.ii.63: "You all look strangely on me"). Here the word is colored by the now more common meaning "in an unusual or odd manner"; see line 7.

    6. *scarcely* (1) barely, only just; (2) scantily, inadequately. *that sun thine eye* See 20.6, note, 18.5, 33.5–8, 35.3, and 130.1. This phrase enlarges on and activates the metaphoric potential in *frown* and *cast*; in context of the *Against* construction it suggests the proverb "It is good to lay up somewhat against a rainie day" (Tilley, D89).

    7. *converted* (1) transformed; (2) changed for the better (see *Tim* IV.iii.140: "he whose pious breath seeks to convert you"); (3) turned away (see *eye* in line 6; for "convert the eyes from" meaning "turn the eyes away from," see 7.11–12). (Shakespeare may remember the astronomical and cosmological contexts of the Latin *convertere*, "to revolve"; he uses the verb "to convert" four times in the sonnets, three times in a context of heavenly bodies: see 7.11 and 14.12.) *the thing it was* (1) its former nature; (2) its former vile nature (for *thing* used in contempt to mean "mere object," "person unworthy of respect," see *WT* II.i.82–87: "O thou thing . . ."). (There may also be a play on *thing* meaning sexual organ; see 20.12 and note. In company with the poems that assert the shared identity of lover and beloved—see 36, 37, 39, 40, 42.13, and notes—*the thing it was* also suggests "*me*," and anticipates the speaker's confusion of role in line 11.)

    9. *ensconce me* fortify myself (a "sconce" was a minor fortification; see *HV* III.vi.68–70: "where services were done—at such and such a sconce, at such a breach").

    10. *desert* spelled "desart" in Q, and probably pronounced to rhyme with *part* (see 17.2, note).

    11. (1) "and raise my hand to swear in court as a witness against myself";

(2) "and raise my hand to attack myself in battle" (see the siege metaphor in line 9). Willen and Reed point out that *this my hand* refers literally to the poem: "this my handwriting."

12. *guard*   protect (Ingram and Redpath suggest "ward off," "parry"; *OED* gives this from 1661: "We . . . defended ourselves by guarding his blowes and repelling his injuries.")   *part*   Q has a comma after *part*; the dash given here comes as close as modern punctuation can to retaining Q's momentary parallel between *To guard* in line 12 and *To leave poor me* in line 13; as the syntax develops the apposition becomes impossible, but the rejected understanding of *To leave poor me* does in fact describe the speaker's action and the ultimate rhetorical action of the poem: abandonment of self.

14. This line echoes the traditional legal locution "show cause why."   *allege*   put forward as a legal ground, plead as an excuse.   *cause*   proper and adequate legal ground for action, reason (compare *Lear IV*.vii.75).

SONNET 50

See the headnote to 44.

1. *heavy*   (1) sadly, sorrowfully (see *LLL* V.ii.14: "He made her melancholy, sad, and heavy"); (2) sluggishly, slowly (see *MND* V.i.357: "The heavy gait of night"); (3) wearily (see *Temp* II.i.180: "laugh me asleep, for I am very heavy"). These glosses are those indicated by the clause in which *heavy* appears.

The diction of the rest of the poem echoes and develops these senses (*woe* [line 5], *heavily*—i.e. "sorrowfully"—[11], *grief* [14], *dully* [6], *loved not speed* [8], *weary* [2], *tired* [5]). The diction also expands on shades of metaphoric meaning irrelevant to the syntax of line 1 but pertinent to the situation as developed: *heavy* meant "grievous," "hard," "severe," "oppressive" (see *CofE* I.i.32: "A heavier task could not have been impos'd"); it also meant "annoying," "wearisome" (see *RIII* III.i.3–5 where the response to "The weary way hath made you melancholy" is "No . . . but our crosses on the way / Have made it tedious, wearisome, and heavy"). Moreover, the succeeding lines play on the literal meaning of *heavy*, "weighing a lot." Much of the wit of the poem lies in a burlesque of one variety of the rhetorical figure prosopopoeia, personification, the variety now called "the pathetic fallacy," by which a poet attributes human qualities—commonly sympathy with human suffering—to animals or the weather or objects: words that describe or relate to the idea of heaviness, a probable cause of sorrow in a saddle horse—the weight, the heaviness, of its rider— are used to describe a fanciful one—the sadness, the heaviness, of its rider. (The literary joke is elaborately introduced by the ostentatiously extravagant use of the same rhetorical figure in lines 2–4 where one imprecise abstraction teaches two others to speak. Compare 51.9–14 where the standard metaphor "keep pace with" takes on increasingly literal meaning until, in the last lines, a personified abstraction—*desire*—seems to be engaged in a foot race with a horse. In 51, note also that the slow horse remains a slow horse no matter what sympathies may be attributed to him.)

2. *my . . . travel's*   (1) my journey's; (2) of my painful labor (see 27.2, note). *end*   (1) termination; (2) goal.

3. *teach that*   The word *that* turns out to be a demonstrative adjective, but, since it has no antecedent, and since *teach that* is a standard construction (see *AYLI* I.iii.92–93: "the love / Which teacheth thee that thou and I am one"), *that* can momentarily seem a signal for some such construction as "teach that ease is unattainable." The construction revealed by the completed line is "what I seek teaches that ease and that repose to say"; *that ease* and *that repose* are thus metonymies for *what I seek* (*my weary travel's end*), and their effect is curious: they are urgently vague (because the nature of the construction is initially unclear and because neither *that* has an antecedent), and, by their syntactic nature, they function to particularize the significance of *what I seek* and *travel's end*. The use of demonstratives—particularly demonstrative pronouns—in gestures of specificity is common in the sonnets; see 73.13 (where the demonstrative pronoun *This* announces that the first three quatrains are summarizable, have been summarized, and are firmly within the reader's intellectual grasp) and the uses of imprecisely precise demonstrative pronouns in the couplets of sonnets 33, 45, 64, 95, 116, 123, 124, and 129. The value of such gestures is that they give a reader the sense that he is dealing precisely with precise things without incurring the limitation that genuine particularity would necessarily put upon the breadth and sweep of the poem's and the reader's vision; see the final general note on sonnet 116.

5–12. Contrast the proverb "The horse thinks one thing and he that saddles him another" (Tilley, H659).

5. *tired with*   (1) wearied by, worn out by; (2) sick of (hearing about), tired of (see 66.1); (3) dressed up in, attired in, adorned by (*OED* gives this from 1589: "But am not I a Gentleman, though tirde in a shepheardes skincote?"). (Shakespeare also puns on "tired" meaning "attired" and "wearied by" in *LLL* IV.ii.119–21 and, probably, *V&A* 177.)   *tired with my woe*   This phrase modifies *me* or *beast* or both.

6. *dully*   = Benson's reading (1640); Q gives "duly." The emendation, supported by and probably inferred from 51.2, is usual, but *dully* ("heavily," "slowly," "sadly," "drowsily," "stupidly"), and "duly" ("dutifully") are equally apt. (Although "duly" and *dully* were probably never homonyms, the likeness between the two vowel sounds may have been sufficient to allow Shakespeare's reader to understand both from either; *OED* gives "dully" as an obsolete spelling of "duly," and gives "dul" as an obsolete spelling of "dull"; note also that Shakespeare puns on "fool" and "full" regularly [Kökeritz, p. 108].)   *Plods . . . on, to bear*   The comma between *on* and *to* is in Q, but, in context of *journey, travel's end*, and a verb indicating motion, *to* can still momentarily seem to introduce the destination the *beast . . . plods . . . to*. The momentary error is reinforced by the syntactic impropriety, awkwardness, and vagueness of *to bear*, a curious construction in which *to* appears to indicate intention ("in order to bear") and from which any meaning that makes immediate sense in context (like "bearing," "while occupied in bearing"), can only be forced.   *bear*   (1) carry; (2) endure; (3) wear (see *AYLI* IV.ii.13–16: "Take thou no scorn to wear the horn; / It was a crest ere thou wast born. / Thy father's father wore it; / And thy father bore it"), wear as a mark of distinction (for the heraldic use of *bear* see 1.4), possess, be endowed with (see 13.8).   *that*

weight in me   (This is an instance of synesis: the semantic and syntactic signals do not firmly establish any of the senses the phrase suggests.) (1) the weight of my body; (2) my sorrow (that heaviness suggested in line 1 and called *my woe* in line 5; *weight* was not used to mean "sorrow," but, since "heaviness" was, and since the demonstrative pronoun points to the sorrows in lines 1–4, *that weight* is understood just as "that heaviness" would be [for similar equations, see 109.6–7, 142.13, 149.2, 152.11, and notes; for a punning variation on the same equation see Donne's "Goodfriday, 1613. Riding Westward," line 16: "That spectacle of too much weight for mee"; Donne was apparently generally influenced by the conceit of this poem when he wrote his own poem about riding in the wrong direction]); (3) my importance, consequence, dignity (see *HV* II.ii.34–35: "quittance of desert and merit / According to the weight and worthiness").

7. *some*   = the ordinary indefinite pronoun, but, perhaps, with a pun on "soume," "a horseload" (compare the French *somme*). *instinct*   To read this word with its modern accent ("ínstinct") deadens the rhythm of the line in a way invitingly appropriate to the word *Plods*, but, like *aspéct* (26.10), *Authóriz-ing* (35.6), *conténts* (55.3), *recórd* (59.5, 123.11 [but not 55.8 or 122.8]), and *envý* (128.5), *instinct* probably regularly retained the stress of its Latin root; see *Variorum* I, 16, and Abbott, par. 490.

8. *being*   = monosyllabic (see 52.14, note). *being made from*   In context of weight and slowness, this construction, standard in such phrases as "made from wood," can seem about to specify some heavy substance of which the rider could be thought to be composed; see 51.10. Some such false start is particularly likely from a reader coming to this poem fresh from 44 and 45 (the two sonnets on the heavy and light elements—see 45.7: *My life, being made of four*). Moreover, the completed phrase, *being made from thee*, need not wholly dispel the reading: in context of this collection and of Renaissance love poetry at large the idea that the beloved is the substance of which the lover is composed, that the lover could be said to be made from—made out of—the beloved, could be just another variation on the commonplace assertion that the lover and beloved are one being (see the poems listed in the headnote to 36 and, in context of *that weight in me*, 133.13–14 in particular). *being made from thee*   (1) when he is being carried away from you (limits the assertion); (2) because he is being carried away from you (explains why the rider loves not speed). This is a particularly dense phrase; in effect the passive construction conflates two senses of "make": "make" meaning "go" (see 60.1 and *Lear* I.i.142: "The bow is bent and drawn; make from the shaft") and "make" meaning "constrain" (see *3HVI* I.i.141–42: "He rose against him . . . / And made him to resign his crown perforce"); the senses fuse: one fits the particulars of the situation but does not fit the passive construction of the phrase (no one can "go" someone else); the other fits the syntax, but suggests a new fact about the speaker's situation (he was *sent* away, rejected). Moreover, the effect of the phrase is also necessarily ironic because when "make" was used as a verb of motion, it usually indicated forward motion, always indicated purposeful mo-tion, and carried strong connotations of *speed*. The phrase *being made from*

thee thus capsules the paradox from which the poem arises: the speaker's advance toward one goal is a retreat from—and delays achievement of—a greater one.

9–10,14. Note the proverb "Behind before, before behind, a horse is in danger to be pricked" (Tilley, H631).

9. *him*   Common sense says that *him* refers to the horse, but the grammatical antecedent is *His rider*; the vagueness of designation furthers the ongoing process of identifying the horse with the rider.

11. *heavily*   See line 1, note.

12. *sharp*   painful (with play on the literal meaning; see *spur*).

10,12. *into his hide, -ing to his side*   Since initial *h* and the *g* of *-ing* were customarily inaudible or nearly so, these two phrases—effectively the same in meaning—probably sounded nearly identical too.

13–14. The couplet recalls lines 2–4 in its substance, in its use of personification, in its lack of economy (line 13 is padded out with empty syllables, e.g. *that same, doth*), and in the way it imitates the factory-polished slickness of a poetic hack trotting out rhetorical clichés and putting them through their paces; the couplet is too neatly balanced; like the *that/that* pair in line 3, the *that/this* pair in line 13 suggests symmetry for symmetry's sake and thus advertises its rhetorical contortions and the underlying awkwardness of the situation and of the whole poetic contrivance that describes it.

14. *onward, behind*   (1) ahead of me (in space), behind me (in space); (2) in the future, in the past.   *my joy*   (1) my happiness (referring to the speaker's state of well-being, the opposite of *My grief*); (2) my beloved (compare Lear's use of the epithet to indicate Cordelia in *Lear* I.i.81–82: "Now, our joy, / Although our last and least").

SONNET 51

See sonnet 50 and notes.

1. *my love*   the affection I feel (but until line 3 a reader has no reason not to understand "my beloved" instead; see line 12 and 34.13, note).   *slow offence* (1) offensive slowness; (2) offense of slowness (note, however, that the gloss is derived from context of sonnet 50, from editorial foreknowledge of 51.2–14, and from the need to make sense of a nearly senseless phrase—of which the literal meaning is "offense that moves slowly," "offense given slowly"; the literal meaning could refer to the offensiveness to the speaker of his slow journey away from his beloved, but that reading also relies on reference to sonnet 50 and reflects it less immediately than the glosses given above; *swift extremity* in line 6 is another instance of the reversal of noun and adjective functions; compare 127.4 and 137.12, note, and see 13.12, note).

2. *my . . . bearer*   (1) the carrier of me (with a play on *bearer* meaning "sufferer"—see *Tim* V.iv.3–13 where Alcibiades says that the time of helpless suffering is past and that now "crouching marrow, in the bearer strong, / Cries of itself 'No more'"; on the senses in which the horse is a sufferer, see 50.1, note); (2) my messenger, the bearer of this piece of paper, my message (*posting*

in line 4 continues this play on the speaker's subject [a journey on horseback] and his mode [the poem is a letter carried back to the beloved by a post, a messenger]).   *dull*   See 50.6, note, and the proverb "A spur and a whip for a dull horse" (Tilley, S790).

3. The comma after *art* is in Q and points up the appearance of apposition between the two *from* constructions in lines 2 and 3; many editors remove the comma, but the apposition is momentarily apparent in any case.

4. *posting*   riding at high speed (the word was also used to mean simply "hasting," but it is basically a riding term; for the play on "to post" meaning "to carry letters on horseback" see the note to line 2 and *OED*, which gives this from 1560: "as messenger, that posteth with letters").

6. *swift extremity*   extreme swiftness (see the note on *slow offence* in line 1).

7. Q puts a comma after *wind*; most modern editors, a semicolon.

10. *being*   = monosyllabic (see 52.14, note).

11. *fiery*   = dissyllabic.

12. *thus*   (1) therefore; (2) in the following way.

9–14. The Q text of these six lines needs or seems to need substantial assistance in lines 10 and 11. Faced with the obvious grammatical faultiness of "perfects," an editor has his choice of emending to "perfect" or to *perfect'st* (the reading given in the present text). No argument for one or the other can be conclusive or, for that matter, very convincing (*perfect'st*, a contraction of "perfectest," is awkward; "perfect love," on the other hand, is a standard phrase and one used four times by Shakespeare [*1HVI* V.v.50, *RIII* II.i.16, III.vii.90, and *Shrew* IV.iii.12], but it does not account for the *s* in the Q text: "perfects" seems more likely to have resulted from the sloppiness of a printer with *perfect'st* or "perfectst" before him than from the positive error of one who imported an *s* from thin air). Such fussing is not only fruitless but foolish: *perfect'st* or "perfect" have the same sense and even the same intensity, and the difference in their phonetic effects on the line is not violent.

However, "naigh noe dull flesh" (or, in modern spelling, *neigh no dull flesh*) in line 11 is another matter; it does not appear to make sense, and it gives no simple sign of a way to bring sense out of it. The context does set up expectations toward which an editor can push his text: *Therefore* in line 10 signals that the following clause will announce some remedy for the insufficiency described in line 9. In the crucial phrase the apparent verb fails to fit the expected conclusion. The simplest and most radical editorial course is simply to guess that "naigh" is an error and replace it. Some scholars have suggested simply emending to "shall *need* no dull flesh," which makes excellent sense, but sacrifices all other probabilities to those of consistent substance: emendation to "need" ignores the last four letters of "naigh"; what suggested them to the printer? To accept "need" we must posit a printer who had "need" before him and then made a succession of errors to arrive at "naigh." Among less radical emendations, "wait" is slightly more probable; and so is "weigh," which is physically closest to "naigh" and has some support in the diction of the preceding poem (see the notes to sonnet 50), but both "wait" and "weigh" must be puzzled into sense: "wait" must be taken as "wait for," and "weigh" yields only the weak meaning "consider," "take account of." Moreover, all radical emendations for "naigh" ignore its obvious pertinence in a poem so much concerned about horses. We might, therefore, accept the emendation suggested by Edmund Malone in 1780; Malone suggested replacing "noe" with "to" (an emendation that would result in a line as weak as those in which "naigh" is replaced and one in equal need of vigorous glossing): "Shall neigh to dull flesh in his fiery race." Malone said the line thus meant that desire, in the ardor of impatience, would call to the sluggish horse to proceed with swifter motion.

It has also been argued that Q is correct as it stands, and needs only a reader prepared to understand "naigh" as "neigh to," "neigh after"—an intellectual effort no greater, but no more probable, than those demanded by "weigh" and "wait." The majority of editors have hoped to lick line 11 into shape by re-punctuating the Q text. The resulting texts have, however, retained all of Q's incomprehensibility, and therefore require explanations more ingenious, more extensive, and no more convincing than those of editors who substitute for one of Q's words. Repunctuation (adding a comma after *neigh* or isolating *no dull flesh* with brackets or commas) adds no clarity to the line, and all the glosses are variants on the one suggested by George Steevens in 1780: "Therefore desire, being *no dull* piece of horse-*flesh*, but composed of the most perfect love, shall neigh as he proceeds in his hot career." As Seymour-Smith points out, the Steevens reading and all others that take *no dull flesh* as an appositive to, or gloss on, *of perfect'st love being made* are as perceptible in the Q punctuation as in those substituted for it.

Therefore, since no suggested editorial improvements on line 11 improve it, the present edition reads *perfect'st* for "perfects" in line 10, but, except for modernizing the spelling, leaves line 11 alone. The difficulties presented by line 11 are, after all, atypical of Shakespeare's usual practice only in being immediately perceptible as difficulties. Over and over again in the sonnets we find words and phrases that are a bit awkward, that deviate slightly from clear idiomatic English in order to embody more meaning than a more usual and appropriate locution can have—often to make a phrase embody not only many meanings but meanings that contradict each other in substance, tone, or the response they elicit. Look again at the last six lines of sonnet 51.

In line 10, *desire, of perfect'st love being made* contrasts with the *dull bearer* (line 2); the suggested contrast seems to be between the heavy plodding horse and something light, ethereal, and swift. On the other hand, and simultaneously, in the Christian-Platonic tradition on which Shakespeare's readers from his own time to ours were raised, the phrase *perfect'st love* suggests the least physical love, the exact opposite of the love suggested by *desire*.

In line 11 itself, *in his fiery race* operates in three different local contexts and in three different ways: in context of a galloping horse, desire's *race* is "his course," "his career," "the race he runs"; in context of *of perfect'st love being made* and *no dull flesh*, desire's *race* is his "breed," "strain," "lineage"; the general context of the speaker's desires and the comparison between the temperament of a horse and that of personified desire suggests *race* meaning "natural disposition," "temperament" (see *Measure* II.iv.160: "now I give my sensual race the rein"). In the larger context of the poems that precede this one in the 1609 sequence, *of perfect'st love being made* and *no dull flesh in his fiery race* (like many other things in this and the preceding poem) recall sonnets 44 and 45 (on the light and heavy elements) where the speaker talked about elemental composition and equated desire with the light, swift element, fire.

In combination with lines 7 and 8 *no dull flesh* and *fiery race* suggest the hubris and punishment of Icarus and Phaethon.

In line 12 the first *love* in *love, for love* says all of these: "desire," "my affection" (personified), "Cupid," and—taking *desire* as subject of *shall excuse*—"my love" ("my beloved"); *for love* says "for love's sake," "in requital of love" (the love shown in sonnet 50 where the horse's slow pace is ascribed to sympathy with its rider's disinclination to travel further off from the beloved), "out of affection for the horse," "for the sake of the affection that awaits me," and "because I am a lover"; in addition to all these in their many combinations, the whole phrase *love, for love* echoes constructions like "tit for tat" and suggests an overall construction first noted by Tucker: "Therefore desire . . . shall neigh . . . but—love for love—shall also excuse . . . ."

Line 13 evokes two adverbial meanings of *wilful*: (1) "willingly," "intentionally" (i.e. with the generous and sympathetic intent attributed to the horse in sonnet 50) and (2) "stubbornly"; the first meaning sounds like the excuse line 13 is advertised to be, but the second meaning has a directly contrary thrust. Moreover, in context of *desire* the word also has overtones of "lustful" (see 40.8, note and 135, headnote).

Since *love* (desire) is the excuser, *love* is the only logical antecedent for *I* in line 14, but the context of *thee* makes it seem to refer to the speaker as it does in lines 2, 3, 4, 7, and 8. Line 14 thus contains not only a high, vague, poetic metaphoric sense for *I'll run* but a literal one that conjures up a ludicrously literal instance of the proverbial folly of "going before one's horse to market." The line also presents a context in which *go* means both "walk" (as opposed to *run*—see 130.11) and "depart" (the same basic sense *going* has in the preceding line and one that activates a play on *leave*, which here is a noun meaning "permission" but can be a synonym for the verb *go* [see 5.7 and note]): (1) "I'll run but allow him to walk at his own slow pace"; (2) "I'll run, and give him leave to leave, dispense with his services." The last line thus follows up on both the contradictory evaluations that line 13 makes on the horse: the generous intentions of a sympathetic horse are rewarded by tolerance—he is excused for walking when the rider's desire runs; conversely and simultaneously, the stubborn, uncooperative horse is excused—dismissed; one reading fits an announced intention to absolve (line 12); the other fits a conclusion inherent in line 9: if the fastest horse is insufficient for the return journey, surely this *jade* must be replaced.

The syntax and diction of these lines achieves a similar balance of force and counterforce: an overt function of the lines is to assert the differences between *desire* and a horse; at the same time the distinction between *desire* and a horse is

so carefully blurred that a reader is often unlikely to know which he is reading
about.

Given a profusion of constructions in which multiple relationships result in
multiple and often antipathetic meanings and responses, the following pure but
responsible speculations on the origins of line 11 take on some weight: the
awkward word in line 11 of the Q text, the one least easily assimilated into it, is
"naigh," which—whatever else it may be intended to be—has struck all commentators as an idiosyncratic transcription of both the sound and sense of
neigh. Neigh obviously pertains to a context of horses, but whinnying doesn't
seem pertinent to any of the particulars of the lines in which *neigh* appears.
Shakespeare may have brought in *neigh* for its potential as a pun on "nay"
(meaning "refuse," "say no to"—see Robert Greene's "The Sheapheards Ode"
[in *Tullie's Love*, 1589], lines 85–86; "The swain did woe, she was nice, / Following fashion nayed him twice"). The pun would have given *neigh no dull flesh* a
sense consistent with *desire*: "refuse no dull flesh," "accept any sexual partner."

The obvious and traditionally noted likeness between equestrian and sexual
activity is elsewhere overtly exploited by Shakespeare; the sexual undermeaning
is, of course, perfectly irrelevant to the overt assertion of the lines, but *neigh no
dull flesh* appears amid a steady succession of words that have a potential for
bawdy double meaning, potential that is not exploited in the phrases where they
appear but which gives both this and the preceding poem an aura of bawdy
innuendo from the mere fact of their profusion.

The following excerpt from the conversation about the Dauphin's horse
(*HV* III.vii.11–79) shares some of the ideas in sonnets 44, 45, 50, and 51, and
plays explicitly on several words that appear in sonnet 51 (see *bearer* in line 2,
and *jade*, which means "horse" or "worn-out horse" in the sonnet but has also
its common meaning "whore" in the last line of the quoted passage):

> *Dauphin*: . . . he is pure air and fire; and the dull elements of earth
> and water never appear in him, but only in patient stillness while his rider
> mounts him; he is indeed a horse, and all other jades you may call beasts.
> . . . I once writ a sonnet in his praise and began thus: "Wonder of nature"—
> *Duke of Orleans*: I have heard a sonnet begin so to one's mistress.
> *Dauphin*: Then did they imitate that which I compos'd to my courser;
> for my horse is my mistress.
> *Orleans*: Your mistress bears well.
> *Dauphin*: Me well; which is the prescript praise and perfection of a good
> and particular mistress . . . .
> *Constable of France*: You have good judgment in horsemanship.
> *Dauphin*: Be warn'd by me, then: they that ride so, and ride not warily,
> fall into foul bogs. I had rather have my horse to my mistress.
> *Constable*: I had as lief have my mistress a jade.

Sonnet 51 also contains *spur* and *mounted* (line 7), *motion* (line 8—see 149.12,
note), *posting* (which did not yet have the particular technical meaning it now
has as an equestrian term, but which, meaning "ride hard," "ride swiftly,"

presented an obvious sexual analogy), and the materials for a pun Shakespeare and his contemporaries use regularly: "horse"–"whore" (see *CofE* III.ii.84–87, *2Gent* III.i.260–75, and Kökeritz, pp. 115–16). (Compare 33.13 and note.)

In line 11 the pun, "deny no dull flesh," provides a counterweight to the assertion that desire is composed of love and *no dull flesh*; *neigh no dull flesh* would thus have continued the contradiction inherent in *desire, of perfect'st love being made*. The problem is that the syntax that puts *neigh* and *no dull flesh* together obscures the syntactic relation between *of perfect'st love being made* and *no dull flesh*; the syntactic structure provides no immediately comprehensible sense of any kind and no other sense that can be perceived except through editorial paraphrases in which *of perfect'st love* and *no dull flesh* are rejoined.

Perhaps a primary, immediate meaning of the line has been lost as a result of the passage of time and of the strange pronunciation and spelling Shakespeare demanded as the foundation for his play on "whinny" and "deny." Perhaps Shakespeare expected his reader to understand "naigh" as a form of the verb "to nigh" meaning "to approach," "to come close to," "to handle," or "to accept" (see *OED* and *English Studies*, XLII, 134; neither *neigh* nor "nigh" is known ever to have been spelled "naigh"; in the fifteenth century "neigh" had been among the spellings of "nigh," both as adverb and verb, and the sound presumably represented by *neigh* and "naigh" survives in "neighbor"); if indeed Shakespeare's readers heard the sense "nigh" in the sound *neigh*, then line 11 would have had the immediate meaning "shall come near no dull flesh in his fiery race."

SONNET 52

1. *So am I as the rich*   I am the same as the rich (until line 2 it is unclear whether *rich* means "a rich man" or "rich people"). (When the phrase "so am I" has an appropriate antecedent, it functions emphatically and idiomatically: it is usually used in response to an assertion, and means "so *too* am I," "I *also* am such as has been specified"; in such situations *so* carries both the pronominal meaning, "the same," and the adverbial, "also." *So am I* here suggests the common idiom, but, lacking an antecedent, does not function like it. On the other hand, the "so" construction in line 9 sounds like a simple repetition of this construction but is actually an instance of the more usual idiom—for which *So am I as the rich* furnishes the antecedent. Note also that the interplay of likenesses and differences is further complicated by the repetition in line 9 of *as* from this phrase but not in the "so" construction.)   *key*   here pronounced to rhyme with *survey*; the word appears to have had two common interchangeable pronunciations: Shakespeare elsewhere rhymes it with "bee," "thee," and "may."

1,5,9. *So am I, Therefore, So*   Since this sonnet is so much concerned with locks and enclosure, note that each quatrain opens with a potential but deactivated gesture of logical closure. In line 5, the sound of finality in *Therefore* is disabled by the inverted syntax signalled by *are*. In line 9, where *So* does act conclusively, the finality achieved at the end of the line is dissipated and finally vanishes as the syntax of three more lines unfolds from it.

1–2. The phrase *blessèd key* suggests the "keys of the kingdom of heaven" given to St. Peter in Matt. 16:19, but *rich* may remind us that "it is easier for a camel to go through the eye of a needle, than for a rich man to enter the kingdom of God" (Mark 10:25). There is also sexual innuendo in *key* and *sweet up-lockèd treasure*; see 20.14, 136.5, notes; 48, headnote; and *Cymb* II.ii.40–42: "this secret / Will force him think I have pick'd the lock and ta'en / The treasure of her honour"); see also the rest of the sonnet and in particular lines 4 and 12, *coming* in line 6, *Being had* in line 14, and, perhaps, *instant* in line 11 (Shakespeare appears to have seen potential for imprecise and abstruse sexual wordplay on the sound and the literal meaning of *instant* [from the Latin *instans*, a derivative of *in* and *stare*, "to stand"]; something of the sort seems to be working in *T&C* III.iii.151–54, IV.iii.32–53; *Tim* I.ii.101–07, IV.i.6–7; and *Lear* V.iii. 228–29; compare 151.12 and 16.5).

3. *hour* = monosyllabic.

4. See 56.2,4, note. *For blunting* for fear of blunting (see *2Gent* I.ii.136: "here they shall not lie for catching cold"); until the completed line makes the reading unreasonable, a reader may understand the more usual construction, "for the purpose of blunting." *seldom* infrequent (for Shakespeare's license in using adverbs as adjectives, see 7.2, note).

3–4. It was proverbial that "A seldom use of pleasures maketh the same the more pleasaunt" (Tilley, P417); compare 56.14 and 102.12.

5. *solemn* (1) festive, ceremonious; (2) impressive, awe-inspiring; Shakespeare may also intend a reference to its root, Latin *sollemnis*, "annual," or to French *solennel*, for which Cotgrave gives this gloss: "Solemne (not altogether as we doe commonly understand it, but) annuall, yearelie . . . ." *rare* (1) splendid (see *MofV* II.ii.100: "Bassanio . . . gives rare new liveries"); (2) uncommon; (3) widely separated from one another (as in *Paradise Lost* VII.460–61: "The cattle in the fields and meadows green: / Those rare and solitary, these in flocks . . .").

6–8. Many modern editors isolate *seldom coming* in commas, but the Q punctuation of line 6 (given here) allows *in the long year* in effect to operate twice; for Shakespeare's reader the operation of *Like stones* was presumably similar (the comma that separates lines 6 and 7 in Q would have seemed merely formal because in this poem Q puts a comma after every line except 4, 8, 12, and 14, which have periods): "Since seldom coming in the long year, set in the long year like stones of worth, like stones of worth or captain jewels in the carcanet they are placed at wide intervals."

8. *captain* chief (*OED* gives this from 1581: "sound sleepe, the captaine cause of good digestion"). *jewels* = dissyllabic. *carcanet* necklace or jewelled collar.

9. *So is the time* the time is also like the rich (see notes to line 1; until the completed line makes the reading impossible, *time* can seem to mean "occasion," and the phrase can seem to refer to *feasts*: "So is the occasion," "the occasion too is solemn and rare"). *time that keeps you as my chest* (1) time, that causes you to continue to function as my treasure chest; (2) time, that maintains you, preserves you, in your capacity as my treasure chest (see 126.7: *keeps thee to this*

purpose); (3) time, that, in its capacity as my treasure chest, preserves you.   *keeps*
The word has appropriate connotations of restraint—see *RII* V.ii.99–100: "He
shall be none; / We'll keep him here."

   12. *his*   its (but see 73.10, note).   *pride*   (1) splendor, ornament, fine clothes
(see 103.2); (2) best (i.e. that in which most pride can be taken). See also 151.10,
note, and 64.2; the sexual undermeanings of *unfolding* and *pride* make *imprisoned pride* a summary reprise of lines 1–4.

   13. *scope*   (1) opportunity, free range; (2) a target, aim (see 61.8, note).

   14. *Being*   often pronounced as one syllable (as in 50.8 and *Lucrece* 229),
and often as two (as in 57.1); there is no telling how a Renaissance reader would
have pronounced the two *being*'s in this line. See 86.5, note.   *had*   See 129.6
and 87.13, note.   *to triumph* and *to hope*   These constructions may be equally
well understood as infinitives or as preposition-noun phrases.

SONNET 53

In the work of Renaissance Platonists, *substance* and *shadows* were used as
technical terms. The poem is not in any way an exposition of the philosophic
ideas to which it alludes, but the mere presence of the two Platonic terms in lines
1 and 2 establishes the Platonic doctrine of "ideas" or "forms" as a basis from
which Shakespeare can expand. Plato and his Renaissance followers are vague
and inconsistent about his carefully paradoxical theory, but—roughly stated—
it is this: what we ordinarily take for reality is not reality; the particulars we
perceive are only *shadows* (images, reflections) of the *substance* (ideas, forms)
manifested in, and distorted by, the dross of physicality. Each particular thing,
each shadow, has something of reality, i.e. something of the form it approximates, but the particulars we perceive are impermanent and always changing,
while reality is unchanging, *constant* (see line 14). The most celebrated of the
Platonic forms is the idea of the good, of beauty, the disembodied *substance* of
which each particular beautiful thing is only a partial and flawed reflection.
Shakespeare here takes the Platonic idea of beauty and works his own paradoxes
upon it; the poem is a hyperbolic compliment in which the beloved, an instance
of *embodied* beauty, is said to be the form, the idea, the substance from which
all other particular beautiful things derive. (See 98.11–14 and 101.2–3.)

   1. *substance*   (1) material of which a physical object is composed; (2) essence
(in the Platonic sense).

   2. *strange*   (1) unusual, outlandish; (2) alien, not your own.   *shadows*   (1)
the shadows cast by objects in sunshine, silhouettes formed by a body that in-
tercepts the sun's rays; (2) images (both in the Platonic sense and—as in *Lucrece*
1457: "On this sad shadow [Hecuba's portrait] Lucrece spends her eyes"—likenesses, portraits, or reflections); (3) supernatural spirits, ghosts (a meaning made
forceful by the choice of *shade* in line 3 and suggested here by *tend*).   *tend*   attend, follow like servants.

   3. "Since everyone, each single person, has one shade."   *shade*   a synonym
for "shadow," but one particularly common in the third sense given above.

   4. *but*   only.   *every shadow lend*   (1) supply (cast) every shadow; (2) show

the likeness of all [other beautiful] creatures; (3) cause and share in the existence of every [other beautiful] creature (a Platonic form was thought of as both the source of each humanly perceptible particular shadow of itself and as a participant in its existence, a part of it—see line 13).

5–14. These lines have some vague overtones of the Pythagorean–Ovidian arguments for constancy in change. See the excerpts from Golding's translation of *Metamorphoses* in Appendix 2 (lines 221–35 in particular).

5. *Adonis* in classical mythology, an ideally beautiful boy with whom Venus becomes infatuated; Ovid tells the story in *Met.* X.298–559, 708–39, and Shakespeare tells it in *Venus and Adonis*. Adonis was particularly important in ancient rites of spring (see lines 9 and 10). *counterfeit* portrait (but with overtones of the scornful sense, "mere—fraudulent—imitation"; see 16.8, note). In view of the sexual ambiguity inherent in a love poem to a man and stressed by the casual equation of the male Adonis and female Helen, Shakespeare may intend an abstruse conflation of a play on *counterfeit* meaning a fraudulent imitation and a play on the bawdy potential in the first syllable of *counterfeit* (see 58.3; 26.1–14; 151.1, 2, 13, notes).

7. The context demands that a reader understand this line as "Paint the most skillful possible portrait of Helen," but the phrasing in this and the next line has unpleasant overtones of cosmetic deceit. *Helen's* The reference is to Helen of Troy, whose name is synonymous with perfect sensual beauty.

8. *tires* attire, clothes (the word was usually used of particularly ornate dress; a "tire" also meant an elaborate headdress). *are painted new* This phrasing of the idea that any effort to imagine any particular beauty must result in a portrait of the beloved calls attention to the fact that what is said of the beloved better suits Helen, the beauty from the lost past made visible in a painting—*painted new*; the line thus comes to embody the unspoken but appropriate corollary assertion that all lost beauty lives still and is again visible in the beloved (see 31.13–14).

9. *foison* rich harvest (as in *Temp* IV.i.110–11: "Earth's increase, foison plenty, / Barns and garners never empty").

12. (1) "And we know you (i.e. recognize you) in every . . . shape"; (2) "And you [appear] in every . . . shape known to us." (In effect *we know* acts twice.) *blessèd* favored with blessings (note that the word did not yet have the ironic and euphemistic use it now has as an intensifier in phrases like "not a blessed thing you can do about it").

13. (1) "you contribute to all external grace"; (2) "you share in all external grace." In conjunction with *blessèd* in line 12, *external grace* seems not only to introduce the commonplace distinction between external and internal beauty but also to introduce it in Christian terms as physical beauty on the one hand and spiritual beauty (blessedness, grace) on the other.

14. *like none, none you* (1) are similar to none and none is similar to you; (2) are similar to none and none is comparable to you (is your equal). (Note, however, that *like* can momentarily register as a verb: "you feel affection for no one and no one feels affection for you" [for a Shakespearian use of *like* in this sense, see *AYLI* V.ii.2]. The coincidence of the two *like*'s could invoke a fleeting

pun on *none* and "nun"; see 8.14, note). *for constant heart* This phrase may have been undercut by its pronunciation, which may have been hard to distinguish from "for constant art"; see 24.13–14, note. Also note that the second syllable of *constant* echoes that of *substance* in line 1 (the notes on *instant* [52.1–2, note] and *counterfeit* above might be dimly relevant here).

SONNET 54

"Sweet as a rose" was proverbial (Tilley, R178).

1,13. *beauteous* = dissyllabic, by syncopation.

2. *By* as a result of, through the agency of (with overtones of "to the amount of," a use of *by* that pertains to the quantitative comparison in line 1; *By* can momentarily register as "alongside of," "beside" [i.e. "as compared with"]). *truth* (1) constancy, fidelity; (2) genuineness, non-artificiality (see the cosmetic overtones in 53; for a similar use of *truth*, see *HV* IV.iii.14: "thou art fram'd of the firm truth of valour").

3,5,6,11. *rose, canker, roses, roses* = capitalized in Q; see 1.2, note.

4. *For* because of.

5. *canker blooms* dog roses, wild roses (which have next to no scent). (Following on *which doth in it live* in line 4, *canker* can momentarily have its commonest Shakespearian meaning: "cankerworm," "caterpillar"; see 35.4, note.)

6. *tincture* dye, pigment (particularly common as a word for cosmetic coloring agents). (In addition, the contexts of the Platonic allusions in 53 and the adjective *perfumèd* evoke the alchemical and chemical sense of *tincture*: "essence"; see lines 12–14.)

7. *play* (1) flutter and sway (*play* as used of inanimate objects—commonly used to describe the motion of leaves stirred by the breeze or rapid variations of color or the flickering of reflected light); (2) gambol, frisk, disport themselves (*play* as used of animate objects; the *canker blooms*, already personified by the context of moral judgment, are distinctly personified by *wantonly; wantonly* also evokes a suggestion of *play* as a standard euphemism for "have sexual intercourse"—see *V&A* 124; *Oth* II.i.110–16; *A&C* II.v.5–6; and *Paradise Lost* IX.1027–32: "now let us play . . . For never did thy beauty . . . so inflame my sense / With ardor to enjoy thee . . ."). *wantonly* frolicsomely, lightheartedly, playfully (but with a suggestion of *wantonly* meaning "lasciviously," "lewdly").

8. *discloses* opens up, unfolds (*OED* gives this from 1577: "It [a rosebud] discloseth it selfe and spreadeth abroad"; here *maskèd* evokes a pun on "disclose" meaning "reveal," "expose").

9. The context of this line requires one meaning ("But because their only virtue is their show"), but the word order suggests another and contrary one ("But because their virtue is the only thing they show"). (Compare *only* in 94.10.)

10. *unrespected* See 43.2, note.

11. *Die* perish (but with a pun on *dye*). *to themselves* (1) by themselves, alone; (2) for themselves, without effect on any other creature (compare 94.10;

Willen and Reed demonstrate this use of *to* with a quotation from Edward Clarendon, *Collection of Several Tracts* [written in the 1670's]: "They live to and within themselves"); (3) in their own opinion (i.e. *Die to themselves* = "consider themselves as good as dead," "give up hope"; compare the *to* construction in 81.6).

13. *lovely* (1) beauteous; (2) worthy to be loved, loveable (as in 126.1).

14. *vade* (1) depart (*vade*—derived from Latin *vadere*, "to go"; see Spenser, *Ruins of Rome*, 279–80: "Her power disperst, through all the world did vade; / To shew that all in th'end to nought shall fade"); (2) fade (*vade*, as a variant of "fade," was commonly used of colors [see Sidney, *A&S* 102.5: "How doth the colour vade of those vermillion dies"], and of flowers [see *RII* I.ii.20, in which the first quarto gives "summer leaves all faded" and the first folio gives "summer leafes all vaded"]). *by* This, the Q reading, is commonly emended to "my," which is idiomatic and accords with similar assertions in sonnets 16–19, 55, 60, 63, 65, 81, 100, 101, and 107; *by*, on the other hand, echoes the construction of line 2 and makes sense despite the effort needed to remember that *distils* is intransitive (as in the 1611 Authorized Version of Deuteronomy 32:2, in which "My doctrine shall drop as the rain, my speech shall distil as the dew" translates a passage rendered ". . . my speache shal stil as doeth the dewe" in the Geneva version of 1560 and ". . . my speache shall flowe as doth the deawe" in the Bishop's Bible of 1568): "by means of verse your truth distils, drops like dew"; if *by* is retained, the reader must forget that he understood *of you* in line 13 as "*out* of you," "from you"—as a parallel construction to *Of their sweet deaths* in line 12; retention of *by* requires that a reader behave as if he had understood *of you* as "with regard to you," "as to you." Since *by* has the authority of Q, the arguments for *by* and "my" weigh about equally, and no decision between them can be reasonable. *truth* reality, nature, essence (see the final rubric to the Communion service in the 1552 *BCP*: "For it is agaynst the trueth of Christes true natural bodye, to be in moe places then in one, at one tyme"); compare *truth* in line 2; its meanings there are included here, but the general topic of essences gives this *truth* a Platonic cast (see sonnet 53).

SONNET 55

The two preceding poems in the 1609 order build toward this one. In 53 artistic description is an incidental topic; the poet's verse suddenly becomes primary in the last line of 54.

Like 65, 81, 107, 123, Whitney's *Scripta manet* and *Penna gloria perennis* (*Choice of Emblems*, pp. 131, 196–97), and Chapman's dedicatory epistle to *The Iliads* (lines 62–70), this poem echoes two famous classical passages, passages so regularly echoed in the Renaissance that it is impossible and unnecessary to guess whether a poet who uses them had them at first hand or not: Golding's version of the famous last lines of Ovid's *Metamorphoses* (XV. 871–79) is reproduced in Appendix 2, and this is the Loeb translation of lines 1–8 of Horace, *Odes* III. xxx:

I have finished a monument more lasting than bronze and loftier than the

Pyramids' royal pile, one that no wasting rain, no furious north wind can destroy, or the countless chain of years and the ages' flight. I shall not altogether die, but a mighty part of me shall escape the death-goddess. On and on shall I grow, ever fresh with the glory of after time.

1. *monuments* This is the nearly universally adopted emendation of Q's "monument"; although the emendation is indicated both by the sense of the quatrain and by the necessities of a rhyme with *conténts*, the Q version may be Shakespeare's. The small obstacle to comprehension that arises if "monument," the singular, is left where the plural is called for occurs in company with two similar hazards to smooth reading: in line 3 *these conténts* seems to refer to *this . . . rhyme* (singular) in line 2, but the plural form makes the sense of the phrase hard to pin down; lines 3 and 4 seem to compare *unswept stone* and *you* ("you shall shine more bright than unswept stone"), but the probabilities of the context demand that *Than unswept stone* be taken as "than *in* unswept stone"— i.e. as an elliptical parallel for *in these conténts*.

1–2. See 81.8–9, notes.

2. *rhyme* poem (see 107.11, note).

3. *in these conténts* The word *in* and the idea of the poem as a receptacle make the phrase ominously reminiscent of *monuments*: the phrase carries a suggestion of "in this coffin," a suggestion given scope by the vagueness and imprecision of *these conténts* as a means of expressing "this poem" or "these lines." *conténts* = accented on the second syllable (see 119.13, note).

4. *besmeared with sluttish time* This phrase conflates three idioms: "smeared with . . . time" (*time* considered as a substance smeared on the stone— compare "smeared with grease"); "smeared by . . . time" (*time* considered as the smearer); and "smeared in the course of . . . time" (*with* indicating association in time—*OED* gives this from 1611: "Mans . . . skill wil faile with yeeres"). *sluttish* (1) dirty, careless, and slovenly (used of objects and of persons of both sexes); (2) lewd, morally loose, whorish.

5. *wasteful* devastating, destructive (with overtones of *wasteful* meaning "vain," "profitless").

6. *work of masonry* (1) products, creations, of the stonemason's crafts-manship; (2) structures built of masonry, work made of stone. (*Work* is particularly apt here because it was a military term for a fortification; see *HVIII* V.iv.55: "I was fain to draw my honour in and let 'em win the work.")

7. *Nor . . . nor* neither . . . nor (a standard construction—see 5.12 and 98.5, and compare 72.12, 75.14, and *MND* II.i.171: "Will make or man or woman madly dote"). *Nor Mars his sword* Syntactically this phrase is the first of the two subjects of *shall burn*; the equation suggested by the *nor . . . nor* construction, the phonetic likeness and mythological identification of *Mars* and *war's*, and the traditionally paired destroyers *sword* and *fire* (see *OED*, s.v. "fire," 5, and the flaming sword in Genesis 3:24), all contrive to make a reader oblivious to the fact that swords cannot literally burn anything. *Mars his* This kind of archaic genitive developed into a sixteenth-century literary mannerism, an affectation by which some language-conscious Elizabethans ap-

love); (3) your friend (*your servant* was a term of civility, similar to "at your service," and used rather as we use "glad to meet you"; see *TN* III.i.66–70 and *HVIII* V.i.54–55: *Gardiner*: ". . . good night, Sir Thomas." *Sir Thomas Lovell*: "Many good nights, my lord; I rest your servant"). *adieu* Shakespeare rhymes *adieu* and *you* a dozen times; there is no evidence that he ever gave *adieu* its French pronunciation.

9. *question with* ask by means of (but with inevitable overtones of the common Renaissance idiom "question with" meaning "discuss with" or "converse with"; see *Lucrece* 122–23: "after supper, long he questioned / With modest Lucrece, and wore out the night"). *jealous* (1) watchful, careful, fearful; (2) mistrustful; (3) apprehensive of being displaced in a beloved's affections, or distrustful of a lover's faithfulness; (4) eager, zealous (see I Kings 19:10: "I have bene very jelous for the Lord God of hostes").

10. *or your affairs suppose* or speculate on your activities ("affaire" was not yet a euphemism for "illicit sexual relationship").

12. "Except how happy you make those [who are] where you are" (the perverse word order, however, causes *think of nought / Save where you are* momentarily to say exactly what the preceding lines have denied: "think of nothing except *where you are*—where you may be, your whereabouts." Moreover, a Renaissance reader may have noticed that to think of *where you are* and of *nought* could be to think of the same place; see the notes on the sexual meanings of *nothing* in 20.12 and *no* in 135.13).

13. *true* (1) faithful, honest; (2) genuine, real. *fool* See 137.1, note. *will* (capitalized in Q) (1) wish, inclination, whim; (2) sexual desire, lust; (3) William. See 135, headnote.

13–14. The grammar of the couplet is multiple: (1) "Love thinks there is no ill in your will (i.e. in your whim), no matter what you do in your will (i.e. in your lust, when you are driven by desire)"; (2) "Love in your William (i.e. William's love, the love felt by William) is so true a fool [or makes William so foolish] that it [or he] thinks no ill, no matter what you do." See 89.7, 112.3, and 154.9, notes, and note the rhyme in 58.13–14.

SONNET 58

This sonnet is on the same topic as 57 and repeats much of its language; see 133, headnote.

1. "That god who first made me your slave forbade." (Note that the line echoes and thus carries overtones of the common deprecatory supplications "God forbid" and "God forbid that"; see Galatians 6:14: "But God forbid that I shulde rejoyce, but in the crosse of our Lord.") *forbid* = the standard Renaissance form for the past tense of "to forbid."

2. *in thought* The vagueness of this phrase and its proximity to 57.9–10 causes it to suggest all of the following: (1) in imagination; (2) even think of; (3) think to, expect to (see *2HIV* I.iii.27–30 where Hotspur is said to have "lin'd himself with hope . . . Flatt'ring himself in project of a power / Much smaller than the smallest of his thoughts"); and, perhaps, (4) in my melancholy (see

30.1, note). *control* (1) challenge, find fault with, object to (see 20.7, note); (2) regulate. ("Control" was originally an accounting term—as in the modern "comptroller"—and meant "to test the accuracy of," "to call to account," "to check accounts by comparison with a duplicate register, a counter-roll"; it thus anticipates the financial-legal overtones of *account* in line 3. "Control" also meant "restrain from action," "prevent," "check"; see *stay* in line 4 and *check* in line 7.) *your times of pleasure* (1) the occasions of your recreation; (2) the occasions of your lust, of your sexual activity (for the specifically sexual meaning of *pleasure* see 20.13, note and 97.2, note). This phrase thus repeats the full substance of *times of your desire* in 57.2; both phrases carry overtones of "your pleasure," "your will," "your whim," "your convenience"; see *2Gent* II.iv.112–17: —"Madam, my lord your father would speak with you."—"I wait upon his pleasure. . . . Once more, new servant, welcome. . . ."—"We'll both attend upon your ladyship."

3. *account* see 30.11, note. *hours* = pronounced as a monosyllable; *hours* probably includes a pun on "whores" (see *AYLI* II.vii.26–28: "from hour to hour, we ripe and ripe, / And then from hour to hour, we rot and rot; / And thereby hangs a tale." The proximity of *hours* may also activate the bawdy potential of *account*: "a cunt" (compare 75.7, 136.10, *HVIII* II.iii.41, and the arcane punning in *AW* II.ii.30: "From below your duke to beneath your constable" [next below a duke is a count]); also note *control* in line 2 and see 20.7, note). *to crave* = not grammatically parallel with *control* in line 2; Shakespeare and his contemporaries often changed constructions in passage; see Abbott, par. 416, and *AYLI* V.iv.21–22: "Keep your word, Phebe, that you'll marry me, / Or else, refusing me, to wed this shepherd."

4. *Being* = monosyllabic (as in 50.8; see 52.14, note). *bound* obliged. *stay* wait for. *bound to stay* This phrase is rich with puns irrelevant to the particular context of this sentence but relevant to the general context of the substance and diction of the poem—puns on: *bound* meaning "imprisoned," "kept fast in bonds" (compare the proverb "They that are bound must obey" [Tilley, B354]); *stay* meaning "take prisoner" (see *FQ* I.x.40: "Poore prisoners to relieve . . . From Turkes and Sarazins, which them had stayd"); *stay* meaning "refuse to cancel a bond" (*OED* cites *Promos and Cassandra* II.v: "Nay, marry, the same I would gladly, / But my bonde for the forfeyt he doth stay"); *stay* meaning "endure"; and *stay* meaning "stop," or "prevent," or "bring under control." The general effect of the puns is to blur the distinction between the speaker's duty (*to stay your leisure*) and its opposite (*to control your times of pleasure*).

5,7. *suffer, suff'rance* See 86.5, note.

5. *suffer* (1) allow, acquiesce in; (2) bear patiently; (3) endure the pain of.

6. *absence* (1) state of being away (i.e. the beloved's being absent); (2) separation (see 97.1, note); (3) lack (*OED*, 2). This line is a complex miniature paradox made possible because the necessities of the context indicate a clear and appropriate relationship among the general ideas contained in the line (your absence, which is of—results from—your liberty—your freedom from imprison-

ment and your licentiousness—is forced on me and is, since I am kept from you, an imprisonment to me, who am your slave, *bound to stay* and thus imprisoned, already), and because a literal understanding of the line is both meaningless (an absence cannot be put in prison) and in contradiction to the facts of the situation (*absence of your liberty* in any ordinary context would mean that the beloved had lost his liberty, was imprisoned). *Absence of your liberty* here also carries suggestions of "lack of the liberty of you," "lack of the privilege of unrestricted access to you" (compare 46.4 and such expressions as "freedom of the city" [*OED*, s.v. "franchise," sb.4]).

7. This is an instance where the modern practice of looking to punctuation for clarity unsupported by idiom and rhythmic habit can diminish the range of the line. Q punctuates the line this way: "And patience tame, to sufferance bide each check," and most modern editors repunctuate; each punctuation gives a slightly different syntax but none significantly alters the effect of the line. For a modern reader, the Q punctuation establishes "each check to sufferance" as a noun phrase, "each limitation on my privilege," and makes *patience tame* a compound adjective: "patience-tame," "made tame by patience" or "tame as patience." If the line is punctuated "And, patience tame to sufferance, bide each check," it says "And [let me, who am] docile to the point of acquiescence (or accustomed to suffering) endure each check." The most popular punctuation has been "And patience, tame to sufferance, bide each check" ("And [let] patience, which is tame to sufferance, bide . . ."). Ingram and Redpath hyphenate "patience-tame," but otherwise retain the Q punctuation; they gloss the line as "[Let me,] tame as patience itself, endure to the point of acquiescent indulgence, every . . . ." *tame* (1) docile, subdued; and perhaps (2) accustomed (see *T&C* III.iii.8–10: "all / That time . . . / Made tame and most familiar to my nature"). *to suff'rance* (1) to the point of acquiescence; (2) with respect to misery (*to* as in "inured to cold"; for *suff'rance* meaning "misery," "suffering," see *Tim* IV.iii.267: "Thy nature did commence in sufferance" and, for the same wordplay present here, *T&C* I.i.27–28: "Patience herself . . . / Doth lesser blench at suff'rance than I do"); (3) to my privilege of exercising my rights. *check* (1) rebuke; (2) hindrance, stop.

9. *where you list* wherever you want (with a probably intentional play on "list" meaning "boundary"; for another but more complex play on "list," see *TN* III.i.73: "I am bound to your niece, sir; I mean, she is the list of my voyage"). *charter* privilege, acknowledged right (a standard, nearly atrophied, metaphor from the written document by which a privilege, right, or pardon was legally granted; see 87.3).

10. *yourself* See 13.1–2, 7, notes. In the course of reading the line, *yourself* acts first as the object of *may privilege* ("you may privilege yourself") and then as an appositive to *you* when *time* is revealed as the object of *may privilege*. *privilege* (= trisyllabic) grant special rights, immunities, or freedoms to; charter.

11. *To* for (since Malone, several editors have needlessly emended *time* / *To* to some variation on "time: / Do").

12. *self-doing* (1) committed by yourself; (2) done to yourself; and perhaps (3) done to me (for lovers as each other's other selves, see the headnote to sonnet 36 and 39.1–4, note).

13. *wait* (1) await; (2) serve (see 57.1–2, note and 97.11).

14. See the note on *pleasure* in line 2 and the notes on *well* and *will* in 154.9, 112.3, and 135 (144.12, note [on *hell*] may also pertain).

13–14. Note the rhyme in 57.13–14.

SONNET 59

1. *but that* The fact that *that which is* turns out to be the subject of a second clause instead of an object of the first indicates that *but* and *that* here are a conjunction—meaning "and on the contrary"—and a pronoun. However, since the elements connected by *but* are not syntactically coordinate, the line at first glance invites the reader to take *but* and *that* as a preposition and a conjunction ("except the fact that"—as in *Ham* II.ii.235–36 where Hamlet asks "What news?" and Rosencrantz answers "None, my lord, but that the world's grown honest"), or to take *but* and *that* as a preposition and a pronoun ("nothing is new except for what exists"). The first of these potential constructions vanishes immediately because to make sense it would need two *that*'s: "but that that which is" (i.e. "except that what exists"); the second vanishes when the sentence continues into line 2, and *that which is* becomes the grammatical subject of a new clause. Nonetheless, a reader's progress may be complicated by the presence of one or both of these momentarily present constructions. (Note that the second, in which the line says "Nothing is new except everything," lets the first quatrain embody a vestige of an exact contradiction of the position it asserts.)

1–2. That "there is nothing new under the sun" was already proverbial (Tilley, T147); its best-known *locus* is Ecclesiastes 1:9–11, a passage which also embodies the ever-popular related notion (presented as literal truth by some stoic philosophers) that history is cyclical and each action and event duplicates a former one: "What is it that hathe bene? that that shalbe: & what is it that hathe bene done? that which shalbe done: and there is no new thing under the sunne. / Is there anie thing, whereof one may say, Beholde this, it is newe? it hathe bene alreadie in the olde time that was before us. / There is no memory of the former, nether shal there be a remembrance of the later that shalbe, with them that shal come after." These lines have also reminded many editors of Pythagoras's speech in *Metamorphoses* XV (see Appendix 2, lines 279–84); although Ovid stresses the constancy of change rather than the idea of eternal repetition, the influence of *Metamorphoses* XV here is made probable by similarly vague Ovidian echoes in lines 3 and 4 and by the clear Ovidian echo which begins the sonnet immediately following this one in the traditional order.

2–4. See 76.8, note.

3. *for invention* (1) to create something new; and (because *invention* is a rhetorical term meaning "the discovery and choice of topics and arguments"), (2) to achieve literary originality.

3–4. See *Met.* XV.255–56 (Appendix 2, lines 279–80—on "that which wee /

Doo terme by name of being borne"). *bear amiss* / *The second burthen of a former child* The primary sense is evident ("give birth a second time to a child that lived before"), but in the act of capitalizing on the potential birth metaphor inherent in *lab'ring*, the word *bear* presents a potential metaphor of oppression and endurance: *bear . . . / The . . . burthen*. A reader's understanding of the phrase is further complicated by the adverb modifying *bear*: taking *amiss* to mean "erroneously," "mistakenly," *bear amiss* both resembles and carries the same sense as the common idiom "take amiss" (which did not yet mean "take offense at"): "misunderstand"; taking *amiss* to mean "faultily," "defectively," *bear amiss* also suggests "miscarry."

4. *burthen* burden. *child!* Q has "child?" (see 97.2,4, note).

5. *recórd* memory (see *TN* V.i.238: "O, that record is lively in my soul"; for the accent, see 50.7, note; the inevitable overtones of *recórd* meaning "a written account of past events" (as in 123.11) anticipate and prepare the way for the *ántique book* discussed in lines 7–14; see 122.8).

6. Ingram and Redpath suggest that this is a reference to the "Great Year"— "the period (variously reckoned) after which all the heavenly bodies were supposed to return to their original positions. To those who believed in stellar influence on human affairs this would naturally seem to cause a corresponding recurrence in human affairs. The periods assigned to the Great Year included 540 years and 600 years as well as far longer periods. On these smaller estimates, if a cycle were in measurable distance of its end, a regression of five hundred years . . . would put the world back into a previous cycle." *Ev'n* See 15.6, note. *Ev'n of* (1) of fully (see *Temp* V.i.63–64: "Mine eyes, ev'n sociable to the show of thine, / Fall fellowly drops"); (2) of as much (or as little) as (for "even" used as an intensive particle, see *Measure* II.ii.84–85: "He's not prepar'd for death. Even for our kitchens / We kill the fowl of season"). *hundred* Q has "hundreth."

8. The general sense of the line is evident—"dating from (i.e. written at) the time when thought was first set down in writing," but precise paraphrase is impossible: *Since* does not indicate a logical relationship between this line and those that precede it. After verbs of recollection Shakespeare often uses *since* where we would use "when" (see *MND* II.i.148–49: "Thou rememb'rest / Since once I sat upon a promontory"); here, where *since* appears in context of the topic of memory, its idiomatic use with verbs of memory may well have colored the understanding of Shakespeare's reader and may have contributed to the implication in the line that the *ántique book* comes from the earliest recorded time, but Shakespeare's contemporaries are unlikely to have understood *since* as a simple synonym for "when." In any event, such a substitution would still not connect line 8 with *ántique book*; something like "written" or "from the time" still must be inserted before *since*. The same gap exists when *since* is understood in its ordinary sense: "after the time that." Whatever the cause of this difficult ellipsis, it results in a disjunction in continuity that—like the clumsy, unidiomatic, pseudo-primitive construction it introduces—mirrors the substance of the sentence. *in character* in writing, in letters, in characters (see 85.3; also see 78.3,7,11, note).

1-8. Compare 108.1-4.

9-12. To the idea of repeating cycles of history that is challenged in lines 1-8, these lines add a less specific and less direct challenge to another classical idea, that of the Golden Age and the world's decline from the perfection of the Golden Age (see Appendix 2, lines 103-20); that idea and the idea of human progress and the idea that history repeats itself—each incompatible with the others— coexist in these lines as they have in the minds of most people through the whole course of western civilization.

9. In addition to the phonetic wit of pairing *see* and *say*, Shakespeare may have expected his reader to perceive the wit of a line that is a sensible metaphoric concept (find out, learn, what the old world could report), a foolish literal one (use my eyes to perceive sound—see *MND* III.i.81: "he goes but to see a noise that he heard"), and a sensible synthesis of the two (look into a book and thus *see* what was said—written down, done in character).

10. *To* (1) in response to, about; (2) compared with. *composèd* well constructed, well framed (see *2Gent* III.ii.69-70: "wailful sonnets, whose composed rhymes / Should be full-fraught with . . . vows," and note *frame* below). This word pertains both to the stylistic peculiarities of the poem (*composèd* meant "made up of parts," and "to compose" meant "to bring together conflicting elements"), and to its substance (*composèd* meant "constructed in words," "written"; see *ántique book* and lines 13-14, and note that *this composèd wonder* suggests "*this* particular poem"). *of* which is (and, perhaps, "on the topic of"). *frame* constitution, bodily and/or mental nature, form.

11. *mended* improved (see *AYLI* V.iii.38: "God mend your voices"); *mended* also carries overtones of its other common meaning, "repaired," "patched up," and thus also embodies suggestions contrary to the idea of historical progress. *where* This, the Q reading, makes sense as "in what respects." *OED* also gives *where* as a sixteenth-century variant spelling of "were"; *or where better they* could mean "or they were better." Most editors take *where* to be a contracted form of "whether"; they print one or another variant on "whe'r"; the argument for emending is that only "whether" is compatible with *or*, but the coordination of non-coordinate elements is characteristic of this poem. (Whatever Q's *where* may have indicated, it is altogether probable that *whether* and *where* were pronounced alike in this line—as a monosyllable: "whe'r," or "where," or "were"—and that *whether* in line 12 was pronounced as a dissyllable; see 86.5, note.)

12. Here again the sense is evident from context: "or whether each new historical cycle (each *revolution*, full circuit, of the heavens), duplicates the earlier ones so that each change (*revolution*), is no change (results in leaving things *the same*)." But the words are not idiomatically suited to one another (*revolution be the same* carries no literal sense). Throughout the poem the syntax acts metaphorically: its studied opacity demands that the reader leap to uneasy comprehension of lines whose function is the assertion of similar uncertainty about the relation of things that precede them chronologically.

13. *wits* (1) intelligences; (2) clever men.

14. *subjects worse*   (1) less worthy persons; (2) inferior topics. (The figure—litotes, understatement—is usually hyperbolic in its effect; here it also undercuts the speaker's position by echoing idioms by which a speaker praises by comparison with something even less praiseworthy; compare the modern expression "you could do worse.")

SONNET 60

See *Met.* XV.176–227 (lines 196–251 in Golding's version, Appendix 2).

1. *Like as*   just as.

1–4. This quatrain echoes *Met.* XV.181–84 (lines 200–03 in Golding). Ovid accurately describes the physics of the progress of waves toward the shore. Shakespeare's third line does not; waves do not exchange places with one another. (However, Jocelyn Harris of the University of Otago has pointed out to me that as each wave ebbs from the beach it does appear to slide under the next.) Line 4 sweeps the whole problem away.

2. Some editors replace Q's comma after *end* with a full stop by which they attempt to signal the independent identity of lines 3 and 4—an identity that does not become apparent until one reaches *do contend* in line 4. Whatever the punctuation, however, a reader's experience of quatrain 1 presumably includes (a) accepting lines 1 and 2 as an independent, self-contained unit, (b) seeing the sentence apparently reopened by an adjectival appendage, *Each changing place with that which goes before,* and then (c) perceiving those same words as modifying *all,* the subject of a second independent sentence. The intermeshed syntaxes by which the two pairs of lines are at once independent of one another and at the same time joined in a third identity that overlies them is such that the physics of the quatrain approximate the physics the quatrain remarks in waves.

4. *sequent*   characterized by continuous succession, in unbroken series. *toil*   (1) struggle; (2) hard work (but overtones of *toil* meaning "net" or "snare" cause *In sequent toil* also to suggest "chained together in a line," "plodding like slaves").   *contend*   strive. The coincidence of *toil* and *contend* activates suggestions of other and otherwise related meanings of both words: "a toil" meaning "a dispute," "a fight" (the sense from which "struggle" and "hard work" metaphorically derived), and "contend with" meaning "fight against" give the quatrain overtones of armed conflict—of a battle or a duel (see *'gainst* . . . *fight* in line 7).

5. *Nativity*   (1) a newborn infant (an abstract noun—meaning "birth"—used for a related concrete one—what is born). This first meaning is succeeded by (2) the sun (suggested by *main of light,* of which it is the literal inhabitant); (3) "the moment of birth" considered in relation to astrological influences; and (4) a "nativity," the astrological chart in which a person's destiny is mapped. The four meanings come into and out of operation in response to the flow of contexts in the next eight lines.   *main*   the open sea (used metaphorically in *main of light*; see the French idiom *singler en haute mer* in 80.5–13, note).

6. *wherewith*   (1) with which; (2) whereupon (*OED* gives this from the early

sixteenth century: "As sone as the lady saw Gerames she knew him, wherwith she began to chaunge coloure"); *wherewith* also suggests "at which place," a suggestion inherent in the first half of the compound.

7. *Crokèd* malignant (this, the astrological sense, is made dominant by *eclipses* [see 107.5, note], but *Crokèd* also suggests the crookedness of an old man bent by age; see lines 9–12). *his* its (but see 73.10, note).

8. The line is reminiscent of a sentence at the beginning of the burial service: "The Lord geveth and the Lorde taketh away." This is Job 1:21, from which that sentence derives: "And said, Naked came I out of my mothers wombe, & naked shal I returne thether: the Lord hathe given, and the Lord hathe taken it: blessed be the Name of the Lord." *Confound* ("destroy," "demolish," and, in military contexts, "defeat") is, however, much more violent than "taketh away." Another passage from Job (14:1–2) follows this one in the burial service. This sonnet echoes its concern with birth, the passing shadow, the flower, and vertical and lateral motion: "Man that is born of a woman hath but a short time to live, and is full of misery: he cometh up, and is cut down like a flower; he flieth as it were a shadow, and never continueth in one stay."

9–12. See 19.1–2, note.

9. *transfix the flourish* In context the meaning of this phrase is clear (destroy the beauty), but *transfix* and *flourish*—each of which pertains to what precedes and follows this line—do not obviously pertain to one another and give no immediately apparent precise literal sense: *transfix* pierce through (see *fight* in line 7 and the suggestions of digging, pecking, and cutting in lines 10–12); *flourish* (1) blossoming, state of being in blossom (compare the verb "to flourish" in Golding's version of *Met.* XV.204: "Then all things florish gay" [line 225]); (2) highest degree of prosperity, perfection, prime (*OED* gives an example from 1612 that speaks of "The Romans . . . in the flourish of the empire"; see line 6); (3) blossom or spray of blossoms (the basic meaning of *flourish*—note *set*, and see the botanical/agricultural diction of lines 10–12 [compare 16.6 and note]); (4) a brandishing or ostentatious waving of a weapon (see line 7); (5) literary or rhetorical embellishment, florid expression, literary glorification (see *my verse* in line 13, and note that "to set" was used to mean "to put down in writing" [*OED* gives examples from 1450 on; see "The Coronet," where Andrew Marvell refers to his verses as "flow'rs"—line 6—and then, in lines 23 and 24, says "And let these wither . . . / Though set with Skill and chosen out with Care"; also see *OED*, s.v. "set up," where this 1607 example of "to set up" meaning "to compose" occurs: "Those which are able shall upon that daye sett upp verses"]); (6) flowing curves and similar flowery embellishments in penmanship (in 1593 in the dedicatory epistle to *Christ's Tears Over Jerusalem* Thomas Nashe referred to a "flourish with a Text-penne"; *transfix the flourish* could suggest "draw a line through a scribal flourish"). *the flourish set on youth* Compare the Latin idiom *flos aetatis*, "virginity," "maidenhead" (see 94.9, note; *Catullus*, LXII.46; and Suetonius, *Julius Caesar*, 49); compare the verb "to deflower"; note *confound, delves, nothing,* and *stand(s)* in lines 8, 10, 12, and 13; and see the notes on 151, and 20.12. (If *transfix the flourish* is taken as an arcane reference to defloration, it makes sense.)

10. *delves the parallels* digs the wrinkles. (Literally, *parallels* are military trenches; see 2.1–8 and 19.9–10. Mr. R. J. C. Wait points out to me that the image is of the parallel lines left by a harrow drawn across the devastated vegetation of a new ploughed field and that the whole quatrain and its Ovidian model present an image of "Time the Farmer.")

11. *rarities wonders.* *truth* (1) corresponding image, antitype; (2) reality, genuineness (compare 54.2).

12. *his scythe* The reference is to the traditional image of Father Time (as in 74.11, 100.14, 116.10, 123.14, and 126.2), but here (as in 12.13), revivified by the agricultural context.

13. *to* (1) until; (2) in opposition to (for the idiom "stand to" meaning "stand up to," "persist in the face of" see *T&C* I.ii.123: "Troilus will stand to the proof"). *in hope* (1) still to come, future; (2) hoped for (i.e. better); and— modifying *my verse shall stand*—(3) I hope (a sense only vaguely present and then largely because of an echo of the standard idiom "stand in hope"—see *WT* V.ii.98: "they say one would speak to her and stand in hope of answer").

14. *cruel* = dissyllabic; see 129.4, note.

SONNET 61

This sonnet is a perverse play on the proverb "One friend watches for [i.e. cares for, looks after] another" (Tilley, F716); compare 27, 43, and 57.6.

1. Until line 2 continues the sentence, this line sounds like a complete clause, whose meaning would be "Do you insist on showing yourself in public?"—a momentary suggestion that anticipates the topic of the couplet.

1,3. *open, broken* The same rhyme occurs in *V&A* 47, 48.

4. *shadows* images (see 27.10, note). *like to thee* (1) which look like you; (2) like you (i.e. as you do).

5. *Is it thy spirit* (1) Is it your disembodied essence, your soul (*OED* cites examples of *spirit* used "in contexts relating to temporary separation of the immaterial from the material part of man's being," e.g. the 1582 Rheims Bible version of Revelation 1:10 where St. John introduces his mystical vision by saying "I was in spirit"; here, where *spirit* occurs in company of *shadows* and where the bedside apparition echoes the tradition of Hector's appearance to Aeneas in *Aeneid* II.268 ff., the phrase has playful overtones of "Is it your ghost [come to haunt me]?"); (2) Is it your disposition, is it like you (this understanding of *spirit* requires that *send'st* be taken intransitively—as in *RIII* III.ii.15: "he sends to know your lordship's pleasure"; *OED* exemplifies *spirit* meaning "disposition," "temperament" with this from 1588: "There mette us another youth of less years, but no lesse gentle spirit"). It is not metrically obvious whether *spirit* is a monosyllable here (see 74.8, note) or a dissyllable (as in 129.1); see 86.5, note.

7. "To discover my shameful deeds and the time I waste" (with a play on "my time of rest"). *hours* = monosyllabic; see 58.3, note.

8. The line can be apposite either to all of line 7 ("finding out my shames, which activity is the *scope and tenor of thy jealousy*"), or to *shames and idle hours*,

or to *me.*   *scope*   target, object aimed at or desired (see Spenser, *Shepheardes Calender*,   November, 155: "shooting wide, doe misse the marked scope"). *tenor*   (Q's "tenure" is a standard sixteenth-century spelling of *tenor*) purport, meaning (see *Measure* IV.ii.189: "he . . . receives letters of strange tenour").

10,11. *my love, Mine own true love*   the affection I feel (but with plays on "my beloved"; the lines thus contain a reassertion of the very theory they deny).

10–14. *awake, watchman, watch, wake*   Ingram and Redpath give the following note, which is not to be improved upon: "These words involve a complex of puns, originating in the reference in the second quatrain to the Friend's spirit spying on the poet's actions. 'Watch' = (1) 'keep a look out,' (2) 'remain awake.' 'For' (line 13) correspondingly, means (1) 'in expectation of,' (2) 'on account of.' 'Wake' might naturally be taken to mean (1) 'remain awake,' (2) 'be on guard,' but both these meanings are here ingeniously excluded in favour of (3) 'sit up late for pleasure or revelry.' Cf. *Ham* I.iv.8: 'The king doth wake tonight and takes his rouse,' and, if there is a reference to the Friend's lasciviousness, (4) 'lie awake in bed too near a mistress.' "

14. *with others all*   For a possible play on "with other's 'all,' " see 26.1–14, note.

SONNET 62

1. *eye*   In this context, *eye* embodies a casual play on *I*:   *mine eye* = "my self."

4. *my heart*   See 24.13–14, note.

5. *Methinks*   it seems to me.

6. *true*   perfect (see *Lear* I.ii.8–9: "My mind as generous, and my shape as true, / As honest madam's issue").   *truth*   (1) perfection; (2) fidelity; (3) nature, essence (see 54.14, note). See the note on *indeed* in line 9.   *of such account*   so valuable.

7,9,13. *myself*   Q gives "my selfe"; see 38.5, note.

7. *for myself*   (1) on my own behalf; (2) in my own person, myself (i.e. I do it myself instead of having someone else do it for me).   *do*   I do (the subject is understood, derived from the impersonal construction *Methinks* in line 5).   *define*   state the nature of, describe, set the limits of.

8. *As*   The sense most readily available to the syntax is (1) "since," "in as much as" (introducing the reason why the speaker chooses himself to be his own definer), but that sense is not readily available in a context that prepares the reader to hear an account of the definition (e.g. "define as very great"); the context supports (2) "so that" (see *Shrew* Induction i.67–69: "we will play our part / As he shall think . . . / He is no less than what we say he is"); the sense that best fits the logical context is (3) "as if" (but that is least smooth grammatically because *surmount*, the indicative, follows and not "surmounted," the subjunctive).   *other*   others (a standard plural form; see *MND* IV.i.63: "he awaking when the other do").

9. *shows me myself*   (1) displays my features to me; (2) reveals me to be myself (and not someone or something else).   *indeed*   in truth (a) as in physical

fact I am (modifying *shows*); (b) really, actually (modifying *Beated* and *chopped*); (c) in fact (modifying the elliptically present "to be" in *shows me myself*); *indeed* activates reverberations between its sense, "in truth," and the unexploited basic senses of *true* and *truth* in line 6; the conjunction of the three words enriches the ideational fabric of the poem, making it feel as if it were bottomed in precise distinctions between truth and falsehood, reality and illusion, substance and shadow (*my glass*), and physical fact (*indeed*) and spiritual fact (*inward in my heart*).

10. *Beated*   beaten. (*OED* lists *beated* as a seventeenth-century weak form of the past participle of "beat." Many editors have suspected an allusion to "to beat" meaning "to slice sod from fallow ground" [*OED*, "beat," v.2]; from that they derive the sense "flayed" for *Beated*. Shakespeare was given to puns on "beat," "bate," and "bait" [see *WT* II.iii.90–92 and *Shrew* IV.i.179–80], and there may be wordplay here that is lost to us; although "bate" as a tanner's term appears to date from the nineteenth century, it is possible that both *beated* and *chopped* are—or pun on—now-forgotten tanner's terms; Shakespeare's father was a glover.)   *chopped*   (1) hacked (i.e. lined and cracked); (2) chapped.   *with tanned antiquity*   (1) by old age which tans the skin (for Shakespeare's habit of using adjectives signifying effect to signify cause, see 13.12, note); and, in effect (2) having the weathered look of old age (apposite to *Beated and chopped*—compare the adjectival *with* constructions in 12.8; 29.6; 33.6,10; 45.4,7; 63.2; etc.).

11. *read*   interpret. (This line reports two paradoxically compatible alternatives to the narcissism apparent in lines 1–8: (1) my self-love turns to self-loathing; (2) my self-love turns out to have been not my own, not love of my *own* self. The line cannot be precisely glossed. The roundabout phrasing may have been dictated by Shakespeare's desire to play on the fact that a mirror image is reversed, *contrary*. The phrase *contrary I read* may also have appealed to him because it embodies the reader's and speaker's sense that the speaker's self-image has been exactly contrary to the physical facts of his experience, and because it embodies a capsule description of the poem's process and the reader's experience of it—repeatedly shifting from one kind of truth to another and from one to another basis for perceiving the speaker's position as contrary to truth [the speaker is not the nonpareil of beauty, and he is not literally the beloved either].)

12. *Self so self-loving*   (1) loving such a self; (2) loving one's own physical self (as opposed to the other self specified in the next line).   *were iniquity*   (1) would indeed be sin (see line 1); (2) would be unjust (the root sense of *iniquity* is "inequality"; it is essentially the same word as "inequity"; both derive from the Latin *iniquitas*; *OED* gives this from 1587: "In the measuring of ten quarters, . . . they lose one through the iniquitie of the bushell").

13. *thee, myself*   For the idea of the unity of a pair of lovers, see 36, headnote.   *for myself*   (1) instead of myself; (2) as myself; (3) for my own benefit (playing on the meaning the same phrase has in line 7).

14. (1) "Describing my own aged state by means of a description of your youthful beauty"; (2) "Using your youthful beauty like a cosmetic to remedy

the defects in my own aged appearance"; (3) "Flattering my aged self by claiming your youthful beauty (for "to paint" meaning "to flatter," see *LLL* IV.i. 16–17, quoted in 82.13, note). (Compare sonnet 3.)

SONNET 63

The key word in this poem is *Against*. In both substance (the first eight lines concern a life that continues after beauty dies; the last six concern beauty that lives on after death) and fabric (see notes on *Against, traveled, Stealing away, black*, etc.), this is a poem of paradoxical oppositions, fused pairs of contraries that cancel each other out. The sonnet may thus be said to do stylistically what Ovid states overtly in *Metamorphoses* XV.252–58 (lines 276–84 in Golding's version—see Appendix 2), a passage echoed in this sonnet and intended by Ovid as evidence that "No kind of thing keeps ay his shape and hew. . . . Neyther dooth there perrish aught . . . in all the world . . . . Things passe . . . from place too place: yit all from whence they came returning, doo unperrisshed continew still the same."

1. *Against* in anticipation of (in preparation for) the time when (see 49.1, note).

2. *injurious* = trisyllabic, by syncopation. Shakespeare regularly pronounced suffixes like *-ious* as one syllable, "yus"; even so, the line sounds appropriately crushed metrically.

3. *hours* = monosyllabic.

3–4. Note the wit of the simultaneous parallelism and non-parallelism in the pairing of *drained* (which pertains only to liquids) and its antonym, *filled* (which can pertain to any substance and is applied to *lines* and *wrinkles*, which are not liquids but are conduit-like—could be filled with liquid).

4,5,8,12. *morn, night, spring, life* Like *Met.* XV.186–229 (lines 206–51 in Golding), this sonnet treats analogous time spans—a day, a year, a human life—focusing momentarily on one or another, but essentially treating them (as Ovid does) as merely different faces of the same thing. Compare sonnet 73.

5. *traveled* (1) journeyed; (2) toiled (Q gives "travaild"; Elizabethans made no distinction in spelling between "travel" and "travail"; see 27.2 and 50.2). The differing connotations of the two senses of *traveled* help Shakespeare conflate the images of the sun climbing, toiling, up to noon, and descending, traveling on, to night. He presents climb and descent not as two stages in passage but as a single progress in one fixed direction. Shakespeare's fascination with actions that are their own counteractions appears again in 64.8 and is most vividly expressed in 129. For a related effect, see also *lines* in lines 4 and 13, and *Against* in lines 1 and 10. *steepy* steep (as in line 249 of Golding's version of *Met.* XV).

8. *Stealing away* At first glance *Stealing away* seems to be a synonym for *vanishing* in line 7; it comes to mean "pilfering" only when the developing syntax of the line presents an object of theft: *treasure.* (See *steal* in 92.1 and 104.10.)

10. *Against* in opposition to. *confounding* destroying (see 5.6 and 60.8). *cruel* = dissyllabic; see 129.4, note.

12. *love's* (1) of my beloved; (2) of the affection I feel. *though my lover's life* (1) even though his life be cut off; (2) even though his life be forgotten, cut from memory. (On the kind of relationship indicated by "lover," see 126.4, note.)

13–14. See 65.13–14. *black, green* The primary meaning of *black* is literal; its funereal connotations and its opposition to *beauty* (see 127.1, note) are secondary. The primary meaning of *green* is metaphoric: "[be] youthful, lively" (see *spring*, line 8); its literal meaning, which is operative only because *black* precedes it, acts only to add a casual auxiliary paradox to those by which *black lines* preserve what *lines and wrinkles* destroy and by which the dead and forgotten beloved will live remembered forever.

14. *still* (1) even after that (i.e. after his death); (2) always, forever.

SONNET 64

1. *fell* See 74.1, note.

2. *proud* splendid. *cost* (1) expenses; (2) costly creations (see *2HIV* I.iii.58–61: "one that draws the model of a house / Beyond his power to build it; who, half through, / Gives o'er and leaves his part-created cost / A naked subject to the weeping clouds"). Compare 146.4–5. *outworn* (1) worn out; (2) worn away, obliterated; (3) out of date, obsolete; (4) exhausted, spent of vitality; (5) past. *age* (1) oldness, antiquity; (2) old men (see *WT* IV.iv.749: "Age, thou hast lost thy labour"); (3) era(s).

3. *sometime* once, formerly. *towers* = monosyllabic. *down razed* Note the paradox inherent in hearing "down raised." See 1–14, note below; also see 63.5, note.

4. *eternal* modifies both *brass* (*brass eternal* is a stock phrase, echoing the Horatian phrase *aere perennius* [quoted in the headnote to 55]) and *slave*; in effect *eternal* operates twice: "ever-enduring brass is forever the slave . . ."). *mortal* (1) non-eternal, subject to death; (2) deadly, death-dealing; (3) human. *rage* (1) fury and violence; (2) passion (see 13.12, note—on *rage* meaning "lust").

5–9. See *Met.* XV. 261–63; Golding's version is given in Appendix 2 (lines 287–90). (As a result of intense antiquarian and topographical activity during the last years of Elizabeth's reign, territory lost to and gained from the sea was of more than usual popular interest; see 65.1.)

6. *Advantage on* (1) profit at the expense of (with overtones of "advantage" meaning interest paid on a loan); (2) superiority over (often used in military contexts). (Note the enriching shadows of the standard phrases "on shore," "advantage ground" [meaning "high ground that gives superiority to a combatant"], and "advance on," "advance upon" [which inheres in its cognate].) *of* possessed by.

7. *of* from. *watery* = dissyllabic, by syncopation; Q gives "watry."

8. *store* (1) the quantity possessed; (2) plenty, abundance (as in 84.3—see also 11.9, note [on "store beasts"] and 14.12).

9. *state* condition. (Both here and in line 10 *state* presents a punning ideational echo of *kingdom* in line 6.)

10. *state* the pomp and splendor of power and high rank. *confounded* deteriorated (Willen and Reed cite *HV* III.i.12–13: "as doth a galled rock / O'erhang and jutty his confounded base").

11. Note the phonetic play of *Ruin* and *ruminate*. Meditations on architectural ruins were already a longstanding literary genre (e.g. the Old English poem *The Ruin*, Spenser's *Ruins of Rome*, and its original, Du Bellay's *Antiquités*).

12. *time will come* Time here is personified as in line 1, but note the logically irrelevant presence of the generally relevant stock phrase "time will come."

13. *which* The antecedent is vague: *death*, the nearest potential antecedent, cannot choose, but it cannot weep or fear either; *thought* makes better sense, but it is the thinker who does the weeping and fearing.

14. *to have* (1) that it has; (2) in order to have, in supplication for. *lose* See 18.10, note.

1–14. This poem is full of words regularly used with sexual connotations. No sexual sense is active at any given point in the poem, but the cumulative effect of the diction is to invoke a vague aura of reference to male helplessness to postpone the moment of sexual climax and the general collapse and sexual helplessness that follows sexual emission; note *proud* (see 151.10, note—sense 4), *buried, down razed* (and "down raised"), *rage* (see 13.12, note), *store, confounded* (see the notes to 26.1–14, 59.9–12, 60.9, and 151.1,2,13), *death* (see "dye" in the example quoted from Donne in 154.9, note), *which cannot choose, weep,* and *have* (see 87.13, note).

SONNET 65

See 55, headnote.

1. *Since* Since there is no (for examples of similar ellipses in Shakespeare, see 111.11, 141.6, and *RIII* IV.i.84–85: "no man in the presence / But his red colour hath forsook his cheeks"). *earth, sea* See 64.5–9 and note.

2. *But . . . mortality o'ersways* except such as . . . mortality overrules (surpasses). *sad* See 107.6, note. *power* strength (but, since "a power" can mean "an army," anticipating the military metaphor of quatrain 2).

3. *with* against. *rage* See 64.4, note (in support of the secondary meaning "sensual appetite," Willen and Reed cite *RIII* III.v.83 where the quarto text gives "lustful" and the folio substitutes "raging"). *hold a plea* successfully argue its case ("to hold a plea" is a legal phrase that does not make sense in this context because its precise meaning is "to try an action"—i.e. to have jurisdiction, to be judge, to decide between adversaries in a law case; the gloss given here is a conflation of the metaphor introduced by the legal phrase and the sense dictated by the context: *hold out / Against,* "withstand").

4. *action* (1) law case; (2) active operation against an enemy (see *Oth* II.
iii.178–79: "would in action glorious I had lost / These legs").

6. *wrackful* wreckful, destructive.

10. *jewel* = dissyllabic (see 129.4, note). *chest* coffer, jewel casket (*time's chest* would be a coffin).

11. *hand* The casual wit in juxtaposing *hand* (in its literal sense) with *foot* (in a figurative sense) results in an incidental image of a person hobbled or tripped up. In calling attention to *hand* the juxtaposition can reduce the suddenness of the introduction of the miraculous *might* of *black ink* in the couplet, which in turn can realize a hitherto unexploited potential reference to handwriting in *strong hand*; see 49.11, note. *his* (1) time's or (2) the beloved's.

12. I retain the Q reading. All modern editors have, perhaps justly, emended *spoil or beauty* to "spoil of beauty." The emendation simplifies the line, but removes a typically Shakespearian richness and complexity. Undoctored, the line is no more difficult than dozens that no responsible editor would tamper with. *his spoil* (1) his (time's) plunder, the loot he takes (see *1HIV* I.i.74–75: "is not this an honourable spoil? / A gallant prize"); (2) the despoliation wreaked by him (by time); (3) the decay, ruin, undergone by him (by the beloved—for a similar use of *spoil*, see *1HIV* III.iii.10: "villainous company hath been the spoil of me"). *forbid* (1) prohibit, deny possession of (compare *LC* 164: "To be forbod the sweets"; the line would thus be a rhetorical question asserting that no one can deny time the right to take the beloved's beauty or to have the despoliation of the beloved—that no one can put the beloved or the beloved's beauty off limits to time); (2) prohibit, decree the nonexistence of (the line would thus say that no one can stop the despoliation of the beloved or order him to cease being beautiful, to cease being a desirable prey for time). (Although any simple paraphrase of this line must be so strained as to seem to justify emendation, a casual reading of the line can supersede the implied syntactic unity of *his spoil or beauty*, by taking *his* in *his spoil* as "time's" and the implied *his* of [*his*] *beauty* as "the beloved's," and taking the construction as a zeugma: "no one can prohibit time's ravages or exclude the beloved's beauty from time's ravages." The potential of *his spoil* to mean "the beloved's ruin" and the suggestion of forbidding the beloved to be beautiful would inhere as further extrasyntactical implications of the line.)

13. *might* power, efficacy (the strength of the word is appropriate to the metaphors of violent attack in the preceding lines, but *might* is idiomatically ill-suited to its clause; the usefulness of *might* as a rhyme presumably recommended it, and so, perhaps, did its homonym, the verb "might," which enables the line to embody the shadow of an alternate construction: "except if this miracle might occur"; note the presence of *may* in line 14).

14. See 63.13–14. *black* For black as the opposite of beauty, see 127.1. *my love* (1) my beloved; (2) the affection I feel. *still* See 63.14, note.

SONNET 66

1. *Tir'd with* sick of, fed up with (see 50.5).

2. *As* Such as, for instance. *desert* worthiness, merit (i.e. meritorious persons; this is the first of many instances in this poem, 67, and 68 of a species of metonymy by which qualities [*faith, virtue,* etc.] act as indefinite collective nouns meaning "those who are faithful," etc.).

2–3,10. Compare Ecclesiastes 10:6–7: "Folie is set in great excellencie, and the riche set in the lowe place. / I have sene servants on horses and princes walking as servants on the grounde."

3. *needy nothing* (1) those who are without advantages (i.e. (a) those who are so downtrodden that they are "nobodies" whose needs and merits are ignored, or (b) those who are mere ciphers, entirely wanting in merit and ability); and, if one accepts Dover Wilson's dubious extrapolation from the standard idiom "needy *of*," (2) those in need of nothing (i.e. (a) those who possess every material luxury, or (b) those who possess every desirable quality).

If its context did not so obviously identify line 3 as another item in a continuing list of social abuses, it would make its reader pause to puzzle. As it is, a reader simply moves on down the list. The list format releases Shakespeare from the obligation to make a solid statement and frees him to augment his indictment by making a line that mirrors stylistically the paradox he is pointing out in the societal distribution of rewards, a line that can include suggestions and echoes of a persuasively vast range of related vices.

This line is so composed that its reader confuses the deserving with the undeserving. The confusion occurs because the line relates to and pairs with line 2 in several different and contradictory ways. Coming so immediately after *beggar born, needy* appears to attribute poverty to the noun it modifies, *nothing,* which, being under the influence of *needy* and in a line that is apparently a reprise of line 2, suggests "people who have nothing and are treated as if they were nothing, did not exist"; at the same time, however, "a nothing" does not connote one of the deserving poor but a cipher, a person useless and worthless (like Cloten, the Queen's cloddish son in *Cymbeline,* who is called "that harsh, noble, simple nothing"—III.iv.131). The final words of the line, *trimmed in jollity,* mean "decked out in fine clothes" (Ingram and Redpath note that Cotgrave glosses *Iolieté* as "trimness," "fineness"); the phrase also carries overtones of the careless happiness associated with the commoner sense of *jollity. Trimmed in jollity* thus completely cancels the original effects of *needy,* and turns the line from an apparent restatement of line 2 into a contrasting complementary corollary to it (the worthy are beggars; the worthless are rich). The reader, who now perceives that "needy nothings" are wealthy fops, now understands the line as he would have had he read "in need of" instead of *needy,* or as he would have had he read *needy* with foreknowledge of the completed line and had therefore limited its meaning to "lacking ability."

While the word-by-word sequence of line 3 makes *needy nothing* seem first to be a restatement of *desert a beggar born* in line 2 and then to present its antithesis, the completed pair of lines can also suggest a simpler antithesis: *needy nothing* could be another label for a *beggar born.* The two lines thus embody all of the following commonplace complaints about false values and inequitable rewards in Elizabeth's London: "Able and deserving men who are born without wealth and position are unappreciated while men who lack not only money and position but also personal ability as well can succeed at court by making a great show of finery they cannot pay for." "Able and deserving gentlemen of good family are passed over while social and economic upstarts are influential at court and get positions of trust for which they are qualified only by their fine clothes."

4. *unhappily* (1) regrettably (the most usual meaning); (2) maliciously (*OED* gives this from 1509: "what man on live can use suche governaunce . . . but right pryvely Behinde his backe some sayth unhappely"); (3) wretchedly, evilly (*OED* gives this from 1509: "these lewde catifs . . . , living unhappily, In shame they live, and wretchedly they dye." *forsworn* (1) abandoned, betrayed; (2) perjured, guilty of faithlessness.

5. The operation of this line is a variation on that described in the note to line 3: *gilded honor* parallels *purest faith* in the preceding line and so seems to be the fourth in a list of metonymies for types of people; only when the line is completed is it evident that *honor* means "honors"—ceremonial signs of respect, titles and dignities. *misplaced* conferred on unworthy recipients.

6. *strumpeted* (1) falsely accused of being a strumpet (*OED* gives this from 1632: "durst with his untrue reports strumpet your fame"); (2) made a strumpet, debauched. "To strumpet" was never a standard verb, and *strumpeted* so resembles "trumpeted" that it can color the line with suggestions of "hawked in the street"; compare the advertising campaign in *Per* IV.ii when the bawds have a virgin to vend.)

7. *right* true, genuine (with a play, invoked by *wrongfully*, on *right* meaning "just").

8. *sway* those who have authority and hold sway, commanders, leaders (perhaps with a play on a limping man's gait). *disablèd* (perhaps pronounced "disable-ed" [four syllables]; perhaps pronounced "dis-abe-led" [three syllables]; the topic of the line—*limping sway* and disability—makes a decision doubtful) crippled, prevented from acting.

9. This line could refer specifically to censorship.

10. *doctor-like* with professorial pomposity ("doctor-like folly" differs from the other metonymies in the poem; it recalls a particular and traditional personification of folly, the most notable instance of which is Erasmus's *Praise of Folly* [trans. 1549], a scholarly lecture by Folly, who wears academic robes for the occasion). *controlling* (1) in authority over; (2) restraining, hindering; (3) refuting, arguing against (as in *Temp* I.ii.437–40—see 58.2, note). *skill* (1) sagacity (i.e. those who are wise); (2) ability, expertise (i.e. those who are able).

11. *simple* plain, pure (see 76.4, note). *truth* (1) straightforwardness, honesty; (2) accurate information. *simplicity* simplemindedness, stupidity, foolishness, naïveté.

12. *attending* (1) servant to, thrall to; (2) listening to, taking instruction from. *captain* (1) the military title (as in "Captain Pistol" [*2HIV* II.iv]; note that Captain was the rank commonly appropriated by confidence men pretending to be war veterans); (2) predominant, chief (see 52.8).

14. *to die* in dying, if I die. *I leave my love alone* I leave my love solitary—without a companion. (Richard Sylvester suggests to me that "I leave only my

love" is also possible; that reading would reinforce the otherwise inherent notion of the beloved as the only earthly thing worthy of regret.)

SONNET 67

1. *wherefore* why. *with infection* (1) in the company of corruption, among the corrupt, in a corrupt society (see 66.2, note on *desert*); (2) having infection, being corrupted (for the use of *with*, see *V&A* 147: "like a nymph, with long dishevelled hair"). *live* (1) dwell, abide; (2) continue to exist, go on living (sense 2 is underscored by its pertinence to sonnet 66, in which the speaker weighed the desirability of his own continued existence; note *living* [line 6] and *lively* [10]).

2. *with* by means of. *grace* (1) adorn, embellish; (2) honor; (3) sanctify.

3. *That* with the result that. *by* (1) by means of; (2) being in proximity to, next to. *advantage* (1) benefit; (2) favorable circumstance, a chance to prosper.

4. *lace* embellish, trim, *grace* (the metaphor is of lacework used for ornamentation; "to lace" was also used to mean "to diversify with streaks of color," "to streak with color" [*OED*, 6], and thus prepares the way for *painting* in line 5).

5. *false painting* (1) portraiture (called "false" because a painting is only an imitation of life); (2) the use of cosmetics. (In his edition of 1898, George Wyndham argued that the phrase contains allusion to "the 'false art' of other 'eternizers,' viz. the Rival Poets"; see 21, 68.14, 82.9–14, and 83.)

6. *dead seeing* lifeless semblance (with suggestions of [a] the blank, lifeless eyes of bad portraits; and [b] the fact that a portrait preserves its subject's appearance after the subject is dead, and preserves its subject's youthful beauty after the subject is old and faded; and [c] the use of cosmetics and of hair purchased to revivify lost beauty or compensate for ugliness—see 68.3–8). As a sense for *seeing*, "semblance" is inferred from context; it has that meaning in no other of Shakespeare's many uses of *seeing* as a noun. Some editors have therefore concluded that *seeing* resulted when a printer overlooked the nunnation mark (see 33.14, note) in "seēing"—i.e. "seeming"—in his copy. That emendation, however, robs the phrase of the suggestion in *dead seeing* of "a look at—a sight of—that which is dead" (which carries morbid overtones of "a viewing of the body"). *of* (1) from; (2) belonging to, pertaining to; (3) of (indicating *hue* as the object seen). *hue* (1) appearance, form, shape; (2) complexion; (3) color (compare 20.7).

7. *poor* (1) unfortunate (used as a term of tenderness and compassion as in *2Gent* I.ii.124: "Poor forlorn Proteus"); (2) inferior. (A play on "pure" is also present; see 125.10, *1HVI* IV.vi.21–24, *Macb* IV.iii.53, and *Lucrece* 692–93: "Pure Chastity is rifled of her store, / And Lust, the thief, far poorer than before.") *indirectly* (1) by means of an intermediary (*OED* gives this from 1590: "Whereof any person is not capable directly or by himself, he is not capable thereof, indirectly or by any other"); (2) dishonestly, wrongfully (see

HV II.iv.93–95: "he bids you then resign / Your crown and kingdom, indirectly held / From him").

7–8. On the Platonic echoes in these lines, see 53, headnote.

8. *Roses of shadow* (1) imitation roses, roses imitated in paint; (2) the ghosts of dead roses (see 53.2, note).

9. *bankrout* = a variant spelling of "bankrupt"; *bankrout* is the older form and probably indicates the usual Renaissance pronunciation.

9–14. These lines suggest the myth of the Golden Age. For the best known account of it, see *Met.* XV.96–103 (lines 103–11 in Golding; see Appendix 2).

9–10. The syntactical relationship of the phrases is multiple and gives multiple senses; no punctuation can quite obliterate any of them (the internal punctuation given here is Q's): (1) Why should he continue to live, now that nature has so degenerated (now that she is *Beggared of blood*, is destitute of blood) and has not enough vitality to give the look of health to living things? (2) Why should he (i.e. it is unfair that he should) live now, in an age when nature is bankrupt (instead of in an earlier and better age)? (3) Why should he go on living now that nature is bankrupt (i.e. now that his vitality is gone), and he has not blood enough to color his cheeks (and must do so with cosmetics)? (4) Why should he live to blush (i.e. to be the only source of vigor, or, perhaps, to blush with shame) now that nature is otherwise bankrupt, otherwise destitute of blood?

11. *For* (1) because (introducing an answer to *Why should he live . . .*?); (2) just because, only because (introducing and belittling an account of his function); (3) since (introducing further details of the bankruptcy). The Q punctuation, which puts a comma after line 10 and the question mark after line 12, allows a modern reader only senses (2) and (3).

12. *proud of many* No satisfactory explanation has been offered for this phrase; these are some possibilities: (1) swollen with many offspring (for *proud* meaning "swollen," see *OED*, 7.d, and *RII* III.iv.59, where the gardener speaks of trees "over-proud in sap and blood"; also see 151.10, note); (2) falsely proud of many creations that do not justify pride; (3) proud of having created so many things; (4) made splendid by her abundance, graced with and laced with her multitudes, spangled with creatures (see 2.3 and 25.7, notes). *lives upon* (1) lives off, nourishes herself by draining the substance of; (2) continues to exist by virtue of (see line 1). *his gains* the interest he earns (= a financial metaphor of investment for profit; note *Advantage* [see 64.6, note], *bankrout*, and *exchequer* in lines 3, 9, and 11).

13. *stores* keeps, preserves. (This use of "store" is not idiomatic; the sense, dictated by the context, is an extension of "store" meaning "keep in store," "keep in reserve for future use." Shakespeare may have used *stores* here because of its overtones of "store" as an agricultural term meaning "breed livestock," "continue or improve the breed" [see 11.9, note], and of "store" meaning "stock with people," "populate" [as in *HV* III.v.31: "To new-store France with bastard warriors."])

See 68.1, note.

SONNET 68

This sonnet shares some elements with 127.1–6 (e.g. *In the old age* in 127.1 and the idea of "bastard" beauty).
1. *Thus*   This sonnet continues from 67; like 67 it suggests and plays on the classical myth of the Golden Age (see 67.9–14, note).   *map*   (1) the embodiment, the incarnation (*OED* gives this from 1591: "What were man if he were once left to himself? A map of misery"); (2) a detailed representation in epitome (a figurative use common in the seventeenth century; see *OED*, 2). (The context of *cheek* evokes overtones of the already commonplace comparison of the human face to a map, a chart of the earth's surface; Rollins gives several examples, and see *Lucrece* 1712–13: "The face, that map which deep impression bears / Of hard misfortune, carv'd in it with tears." The phrase *map of days outworn* develops the comparison by suggesting a face worn by age, as full of lines as a map.)   *outworn*   See 64.4, note; the word has special pertinence to the talk of wearing apparel that follows (compare 15.8, 55.12, and notes).
1–8. See 141.13–14, note (on unexpressed phonetic links between topics).
2. *as flow'rs do now*   (1) i.e. without cosmetic aids, unpainted; (2) i.e. flowers die when their beauty does; (3) i.e. the beauty of flowers dies with them and is not reused.
3. *bastard signs of fair*   counterfeit or illegitimately borrowed trappings of beauty, cosmetics (for *fair* used as a noun meaning "beauty," see 18.7; for *bastard* used as an adjective meaning "artificial," "counterfeit," see *CofE* III.ii.19: "Shame hath a bastard fame [if it is], well managed"; here *bastard* also carries the idea of "debased," "adulterated"—like "bastard," a wine to which extra sugar has been added).   *borne*   (1) carried, worn (with heraldic overtones; see 1.4, note, and 50.6); (2) born, brought into existence (note the context of *bastard*; Renaissance writers and printers made no regular distinction in spelling between "borne" and "born." See 36.4, note and *AYLI* IV.ii.13–16, quoted in 50.6, note); (3) endured, tolerated (note *durst* in line 4).
5–8. Compare *MofV* III.ii.72–101, which includes reference to "golden locks," "the dowry of a second head— / The skull that bred them in the sepul-- chre."
6. *The right of*   properly owed to, by rights the possession of.
9. *ántique*   For the pronunciation, see 17.12, note.   *hours*   = monosyllabic. (Note the incidental presence of the sound or approximate sound of "wholly [or holey] antic whores"; see the notes to 127.7, 153.5, and 58.3; also see 69.6– 7,14.)
10. *all*   any (as in 74.2; but, in context of *holy . . . hours*, with a possible incidental play on a sexual sense of *all* [see 26.1–14, note]; *all ornament* would then mean "pubic hair," or "merkin" [the Renaissance found pubic baldness very funny]).   *itself*   The antecedent is doubtful—perhaps *holy ántique hours* (understood as singular, the Golden Age); perhaps *beauty*.
11. (1) "Not making a summer out of someone else's youth," "not using someone else's beauty to eke out its own"; (2) "Not making someone else's

summer green," "not used to beautify someone else (who is younger but ugly)."
(Note the metaphoric link between hair in quatrain 2 and the implied image of
green flourishing grass here.)

    12. *old, new*   See 30.4 and 76.11 and notes; *old* is a noun here.

    13. *store*   (1) stock (with beauty); and, given the context of 67.13, (2) pre-
serve, keep.

SONNET 69

    1. *parts*   (1) portions; (2) qualities, attributes, talents (see 17.4).

    2. *Want*   lack (with an incidental play on "wish to have," "desire," a sense
that heightens the probability that the conjunction of *parts* and *nothing* will
be colored by their logically irrelevant sexual senses [see 20.12, 151.6, notes]).
nothing   Since the rest of this sonnet concerns "noting," the pronunciation of
nothing as "noting" is pertinent to a reader's general experience of the sonnet
(see 20.10,12, note).   *thought of hearts*   (1) hearts' desire or imagination; (2)
deepest thought; (3) love melancholy (for *thought* meaning "melancholy," see
30.1, note).   *mend*   improve upon.

    3. *tongues*   As the poem progresses *tongues* are gradually personified into
their possessors (see *By seeing* in line 8); the resulting slight confusion accords
well with the random display of parts (*eye, hearts, tongues*) in lines 1–3.   *due*   Q
gives "end"; presumably the printer picked up the "b" rhyme *end* from *mend*
or *commend*; his copy (in Elizabethan secretary script, in which *d* looked like
e, and *u* looked like *n*, would have encouraged the error.   *the voice of souls*
This phrase seems gratuitous. The purpose of its introduction into a poem
concerned with inner and outer essences may be to evoke St. Paul's famous
distinction between the outward man (the body) and the inward man (the
soul): ". . . thogh our outwarde [*uttwarde* in Tyndale's version of 1534, *ut-
warde* in Cranmer's of 1539] man perish, yet the inwarde man is renewed daily
. . . loke, not on the things which are sene, but on the things, which are not
sene: for things which are sene, are temporal: but the things which are not sene,
are eternal" (2 Cor. 4:16,18).

    4. *ev'n*   See 15.6, note.   *ev'n so as foes*   (1) in the same [grudging] way as
foes; (2) in the same way as even his foes (in effect *ev'n* acts twice; one sense—
"exactly," "just"—inheres in the construction; the other—*ev'n* as an intensive
particle emphasizing identity as in 35.5 and 115.2—is evoked by the substance:
"his enemies themselves," "his very enemies").

    5. *Thy*   Q prints "their," which is confusing, but for which a case could be
made. However, since this sonnet is sloppily printed throughout, and since the
"thy" / "their" error occurs so often in the collection (see 26.12, note), this,
the usual, emendation is probably justified.   *Thy outward*   = *Those parts*
specified in line 1 (for *outward* as a noun, see 125.2).   *outward praise*   (1) praise
of your external appearance; (2) public praise, praise in public (to your face),
as opposed to in private (behind your back); (3) external praise, what appears
to be genuine praise. (Ingram and Redpath suggest the possibility "that the

similarity in Elizabethan pronunciation of 'outward' and 'uttered' might afford an additional play." Note the context of *Utt'ring* in line 4, and see the
variant spellings of *outward* in the note to line 3.)

7. *other accents*   language different in both tone and meaning (see *OED*, 5).
confound   (1) destroy (see 63.10, 5.6); (2) confute (*OED* gives this from 1555:
"The plain words . . . which . . . confound this fantastical invention").

8. *the eye hath shown*   (1) your eye has revealed; (2) the eye (the eye of the
public) has revealed (to them); (3) your eye has shone, did shine ("shone" =
"was visible" as in 135.8; and/or "sparkled," "gleamed," "emitted light" [see
20.6, note]). (*Shown* also carries overtones of "mere show" as opposed to what
is genuine; see line 13. In support of the supposition that "shown" and "shone"
were already homonyms in the sixteenth century, see *Ham* II.ii.76, in which Qq
print "shone," and Ff print "shewne" [always pronounced "shown"]; note that
Shakespeare rhymes "own" and "shown" here and in *MND* III.ii.458–59, and
that Sidney rhymes "own" and "shone" in *A&S* 22.10–11. Here the pun embodies a pertinent fusion of the idea of a purposefully presented surface image
and a favorite Renaissance idea, the idea that a person's true nature, good or
bad, shines through; see *Macb* III.i.128: "Your spirits shine through you,"
and *2Gent* II.i.29–36—a passage generally pertinent to the devices of this sonnet.

10. *in guess*   by guess, by rough estimation.

11. *Then, churls, their thoughts*   The commas are not in Q; they are required
to provide a subject for *add*, the verb in line 12. Some editors prefer to put the
commas around *their thoughts*, thus making it apposite to *churls*, and making
churls the subject of *add* instead of an abusive epithet for "them," the public.

12. *thy fair flow'r*   The wit of the line derives from the way this phrase,
which first presents itself in two stock, lifeless, metaphoric senses (the flower of
anything means its "most desirable and attractive part"—see lines 1 and 2;
one's "flower," the "flower" of one's age, is one's prime, the time of youth and
vigor), gradually revives as the sentence progresses and the phrase comes into
company with *weeds, odor, soil,* and *grow*—words that evoke *flow'r* in its literal
sense.

13–14.   Compare the substance, diction, and wit of 93.13–14.

14. *soil*   This is the most widely accepted of the proposed emendations of
Q's "solye"; apparently the printer transposed the third and fourth letters of
"soyle" in his copy. Many editors have proposed "solve," but its use as a noun
meaning "solution" is unknown. Ingram and Redpath have concisely and sensibly summarized both the problem and the arguments for *soil*; picking up from
their consideration of "sully" as a reading of "solye," they say this:

> The reading *soil* seems to us the best. It has the following attractions: (1)
> that it was already adopted by Benson in 1640, which is some evidence that
> Q's reading already appeared unsatisfactory; (2) that it does not involve an
> extra syllable; (3), and most important, that the word 'soil' was in current
> use between the fourteenth and early sixteenth centuries *as a verb* meaning
> 'to resolve, explain, answer (a question)' (*OED*, v.²3). It was, moreover,
> often spelt 'soyle'. A good instance, from Harsnet, *Popish Impostures*, 77,
> reads: 'Now a few questions I must soyle, and then I will proceede to your

holy grace.' Moreover, although *OED* quotes no instance, except this line, in which 'soil' is used as a *noun* meaning 'the solution of a problem' (sb.5), 'assoil' was used as a noun, with the meaning 'solution', 'explanation', e.g. by Puttenham, *Arte of English Poesie* (Arber reprint, 198): 'By way of riddle (Enigma) of which the sence can hardly be picked out, but by the parties owne assoile.'

To that may be added the argument that in being multiply relevant to its context, *soil* represents Shakespeare's usual practice in the sonnets: the meaning "explanation" fills the requirements of the sentence, and the commoner meanings of *soil* resonate generally: *soil* meaning "stain," "blemish" is generally pertinent to the topic of corruption; *soil* meaning "earth," "ground," "land," pertains to the botanical image in which corruption is described (moreover, "ground" as a synonym for "reason" pertains to explanation); and *soil* meaning "a field" is auxiliary to the succeeding pun on *common*.

　　common　　(1) always to be seen, familiar, "common-hackneyed in the eyes of men" (*1HIV* III.ii.40); (2) ordinary, undistinguished, inferior (like a weed); (3) available for public use (like a whore—see "commoner" in *Oth* IV.ii.74 and *AW* V.iii.192), community property (like a *common*, common land, fields [soils], which, by Shakespeare's time, were usually uncared for, allowed to grow wild, and used as common pasture—see 137.9,10, notes).

SONNET 70

This poem complements the preceding one, to which it directly contrasts.

1. *art*　(Q gives "are").　*thy defect*　your flaw (i.e. considered a fault in you, counted against you).

2. *mark*　target (with a play on *mark* meaning "blemish," a *defect* in appearance). Compare 35.3, 34.4, and the proverb "Smoke follows the fair" (Tilley, S571).

3. *The ornament of beauty*　(1) the embellishment that beauty is; (2) beauty's ornament, an embellishment to beauty. (When line 4 glosses *suspéct* and severely limits the meaning of line 3, it belatedly erases sense (1) from our understanding.) *suspéct*　(1) suspect, an object of suspicion; (2) suspicion, being suspect. (Here again sense (1) is cancelled after the fact. The word order of line 3 and the obvious pertinence to line 2 of an assertion that beauty makes people suspicious of those who have it combine to invite the reader to take *suspéct* for the adjective and to understand it as "suspected," "an object of suspicion" (*OED* gives this from 1576: "An age suspect, because of youthes misdeedes"). Line 4 demands that the reader find another meaning for *suspéct* because the adjectival reading would make *The ornament of beauty* the antecedent for *crow*. Although crows make good marks, targets, "*beauty* is a *crow*" does not seem reasonable; "suspicion is a *crow*" does.)

4. Since the black *crow* is to the *air* as *slander's mark* is to *the fair*, *crow* and *fair* interact to invoke a muted play on *fair* meaning "beautiful" (as it does in line 2) and *fair* meaning "light colored" (for explicit exploitation of the pun, see

sonnet 127). Since *fair* was already used to mean "clear," "sunny," "not cloudy," its proximity to this line about a crow that is a blot on the sky helps to generate the vague suggestions of "light," sunlight, that run through the poem; see the note on line 13.

5. *So* as long as, provided that (as in 112.4, 134.3, and 136.11). *doth but approve* only proves, just acts to demonstrate (for *approve* meaning "prove," see *RII* I.iii.110–14: "Here standeth Thomas Mowbray . . . to defend himself, and to approve / Henry of Hereford . . . disloyal"). ("To approve" meaning "to sanction" is generally pertinent here and colors the phrase; "to approve" meaning "to commend" also pertains here—although such a reading requires that *the greater* in line 6 be understood adverbially, as "the more," "even more" [for examples of these two senses of "to approve," see *MofV* III.ii.78–79: "What damned error but some sober brow / Will bless it, and approve it with a text" and *Ham* V.ii.131–32, where Osric begins a sentence with the periphrasis "I know you are not ignorant," and Hamlet interrupts: "I would you did, sir; yet, in faith, if you did, it would not much approve me"].)

6. *Thy* Q gives "Their"; see 26.12, note. *being wooed of time* being wooed by time. The phrase is full of vague meaning: (1) since *wooed* tends to personify time, a suggestion of Time seducing the beloved toward his inevitable marriage with Death; (2) a suggestion of "being mortal" and thus of both the brevity of human life and the frailty of human flesh; (3) a suggestion of "tempted by your time of life"—by the fact that you are young (see line 7) or by the fact that time is passing you by (see line 9); (4) a suggestion of "being the beloved of the time(s)," "being popular and sought after"; (5) a suggestion of "being open to the influence of this age, of current mores," "tempted by the bad examples of your contemporaries"; (6) a suggestion of "being wooed by 'history' " (i.e. that the passage of time will vindicate you, that the future will reveal your innocence).

7. *canker vice* vice, like a canker; see 35.4 and note.

8. *unstainèd* See 33.14, note (on *stain*). *prime* (1) prime of life; (2) springtime (see 3.10 and 12.3).

10. This line is metrically unusual; it appears to have eleven syllables of which six are stressed. *Being* is often monosyllabic (as in 50.8), but the rhythm here invites dissyllabic pronunciation. *Either*, however, is sometimes monosyllabic— even where it begins a line and its syllabification is not immediately signalled in reading (see Kökeritz, p. 322). Here the metrics are only academically interesting, since the pronounced logical and syntactic pause before *or* lets a modern reader pronounce all eleven syllables just as he would in modern prose. *charged* attacked (with overtones of the generally pertinent sense "accused").

11. *so* (1) so much; (2) therefore.

12. *To* as to. *envy* maliciousness. *evermore* (1) forever (modifying *tie up*); (2) at all times (modifying *enlarged*); the emergence of sense (2) cancels sense (1). *enlarged* (1) set at liberty, at large (like a beast or criminal uncaged); (2) increased, spread further.

13. Compare the last four words of 69.13, and see the note on *shown* in 69.8; *masked not thy show* is the last in a series of muted references to the sun and

clouds that begins in line 4 and continues in *unstainèd* in line 8; see *masked* in
33.12.   *masked*   (1) hid; (2) disguised.
    14.   *alone*   (1) only, uniquely; (2) without sharing [possession] with anyone
else.   *owe*   own, possess (see 18.10, note).

SONNET 71

1,2,3. The end of each of these lines is potentially the conclusion of the clause;
three times a following line continues and thus obliterates the independent
identity of a sentence already fixed in the reader's understanding. Quatrain 1 is
thus an emblem of the speaker's self-mocking tactics in the poem at large: the
poem says "what is finished is finished; be done with it," but it defeats its espoused purpose by being a persistent reminder of its author. Compare line 5,
which is self-defeating in its substance, and line 9, which, in repeating that substance, does what the constantly reviving syntax of quatrain 1 does: make the
actual experience of reading the poem an experience of being unable to get on to
something new.
    2.   *Than*   = a simple modernization of Q's "Then" (but see 16.4,8, note and
the time-related context *Than* has in this line).
    3.   *Give warning*   Common sense requires that we understand this as we
would "give notice," but Shakespeare's actual words introduce the idea of
"memento mori," a reminder of mortality (see 77, headnote)—an idea that
undercuts the advice the speaker purports to offer by inviting a wider view of all
particular deaths than his mundane premises allow for; also see lines 7 and 8.
    4.   *vildest*   vilest. ("Vilde" was a common variant form of "vile." In *The
Garden of Eloquence* [1577], Henry Peacham cites the expansion of "vile" to
"vilde" as an example of the rhetorical figure paragoge [or proparalepsis], the
addition of an extra sound in a word for metrical convenience or simply "to
make the verse more fine"; see Sister Miriam Joseph, *Shakespeare's Use of the
Arts of Language*, pp. 51–52. The pairing of *vile* and *vildest* is thus an elaborated
polyptoton; compare 86.5, note. Shakespeare so commonly inserts the *d* that it
seems standard for him; see Kökeritz, p. 299.)
    6.   *so*   (1) so much; (2) in such a way.
    7.   *sweet*   modifies both the *thoughts*, and the thinker (whose thoughts are
sweet because he is).
    8.   *make you woe*   cause you woe *or* make you woeful (see *Temp* V.i.139: "I
am woe for't").
    6–8. These lines give the basis for the imperatives in lines 1 and 5: "do not
mourn for me or even remember me; doing either will only depress you." The
speaker's stance in the first two quatrains makes him a comic caricature of a
reneging or departing lover who says "try to forget me"; such charity derives
from and advertises self-conceited assumptions (in this case the narcissistic
smugness of the speaker's gesture of selflessness is made ridiculously apparent
by the logic of the situation he evokes: a survivor rereading a poem about forgetting the deceased speaker must necessarily be reminded of him). These lines also

open the way for the couplet's surprising but hardly more grotesque argument for forgetting the speaker.

11. *rehearse*   repeat, utter (as in 21.4).

12. *your love*   (1) your beloved (a sense that vanishes immediately under logical pressure from its effective synonym, *my life*, later in the line); (2) the affection you feel.   *ev'n*   exactly, at the same time (with a play on "even" meaning "of the same length"); on the pronunciation of *ev'n*, see 15.6, note.

14. *with me*   (1) by means of me (i.e. mock you on account of your association with me); (2) along with me, as well as me (the same general sense *with* has in lines 4, 10, and 12).

See 72, headnote.

SONNET 72

This sonnet continues from sonnet 71.

1. *task you*   (1) command you, oblige you; (2) challenge you (see *1HIV* V.ii. 45–52).

2. *lived*   was, was contained. (In choosing the verb "to live" as a synonym for "to be," Shakespeare chose a word that does double duty in this particular context: *lived* here includes "while I was alive" as well as "was." Note the reappearance of "to live" in line 12, where *live* means "continues to exist," "continue living.")   *that*   = either (1) which (the relative pronoun with *merit* as antecedent) or (2) to account for the fact that (the conjunction; modern practice is to precede the conjunctive use with a comma).

2–3. Some editors put a comma after line 2, thus limiting the reference *After my death* has for punctuation-bound modern readers. *After my death* acts twice, first indicating the time when *you should love*, and then the time to *forget me quite*. These lines thus present something like the comic self-contradiction of sonnet 71 (see the notes on 71.1,2,3, and 6–8).

4. *you in me can nothing worthy prove*   (1) in associating with me you show yourself in no way worthy (this reading is suggested by the word order); (2) you can demonstrate nothing worthy to have existed in me; (3) you can find (see 153.7) nothing worthy in me. (Note the casual pun on "worth thee" in *worthy*; see 150.14, and compare *Delia* 34.5–8: "Then take this picture which I heere present thee, / Limned with a Pensill not all unworthy: / Heere see the giftes that God and nature lent thee; / Heere read thy selfe, and what I suffered for thee." There is obscene potential in the juxtaposition of *in me* and *nothing*; see 20.12, note and line 14 below.)

5. *virtuous*   (= dissyllabic by syncopation) (1) morally good; (2) potent, efficacious (see 81.13 and the still standard expression "by virtue of"). (The word is particularly appropriate here because it describes two qualities of the lie and also indicates its substance: the beloved will generously and successfully attribute virtues to the speaker.)

6. *desert*   = pronounced to rhyme with *impart*; see 17.2, note.   *than mine own desert*   (1) than is warranted by my own deserts (by what I deserve); (2) than my own deserving (my own merit), does.

7. *hang* = probably an allusion to the practices of hanging epitaphs on the tombs of the recently deceased (see *Much Ado* V.iii.1–10) and hanging trophies and other badges of honor on the tombs of valiant men (see *2HVI* IV.x.66–67 and 31.10). *I* me (Shakespeare often sacrifices grammar to euphony; here he uses the nominative because it fits his rhyme; see Abbott, par. 209.)

9. *true love* (1) faithful affection; (2) faithful beloved; (3) actual beloved. (See 40.3; and note the wit in juxtaposing *true love* with *truth* in line 8 and with *false*.)

10. *of me untrue* (1) untruly about me (the adverbial use is uncommon; *OED* gives this from 1622: "Some fooles would say I flatter'd, spake untrue"); (2) about imperfect me; (3) about unfaithful me.

10,11. *well, My name* See 112.3, note.

11. *My name be* let my name be.

12. Double negatives for intensity are common in Renaissance literature. *nor . . . nor* neither . . . nor (as in 55.7).

13–14. This kind of hyperbolic modesty about their literary offspring was conventional with Renaissance writers; see 76.8, note, and compare 103.1.

14. *should you* (1) would you be (referring to a future time); (2) ought you to be (referring to the present). *things* (1) what the speaker brings forth, these poems; (2) objects of affection (like the speaker). For a bawdy sense of *thing*, see 136.11, note. *nothing worth* worthless (bear in mind, however, that, since *nothing* and "noting" were pronounced alike [see 20.10,12; 108.5, and notes], Shakespeare's reader heard the appropriately counterproductive "noting worth," "worth noting").

SONNET 73

1–8. J. Dover Wilson compares Ovid, *Met.* XV.199–213, 186–98 (lines 213–35, 206–07 in Golding; see Appendix 2).

4. *ruined choirs* Q gives "rn'wd"; the word was presumably pronounced dissyllabically ("rue-ned" or as in modern English); *choirs* is presumably a drawled monosyllable. *choirs* The choir of a church is the area where services are sung. Although the architectural meaning is primary here, the fact that *choirs* can also describe groups of singers (*sweet birds*), gives an extra-logical solidity both to the image and to the very vague assertion that the speaker (a poet, a singer), is like a season. (Tilley heard an echo here of the proverb "Destroy the nest and the birds will flee away" [N124].) Also see 73.3–4, note on pp. 579–80.

8. *Death's second self* = a stock Renaissance epithet for sleep, here applied to *night* (but note *rest*, and see the following note on closed eyelids). *seals up* closes up, shuts up (as in a coffin). In this context of seeing, the expression carries auxiliary overtones of "seels up" (see Ingram and Redpath); to seel a hawk is to stitch its eyelids shut; see *Macb* III.ii. 46–47: "Come, seeling night, / Scarf up the tender eye of pitiful day."

10. *That* as. *his* its. (In sixteenth-century English "his" was still often used, as it was in earlier English, as a possessive form of the neuter pronoun "it," but, since it was already usual to use "its" and "his" as they are used in later

English, *his* does tend to personify the *fire* and, thus, collaborates with *youth* and *death bed* [line 11] to cause the tenor [a human life] to overwhelm the metaphor [a fire].)

12. *with* (1) by; (2) simultaneously with, at the same time as. The use of *Consumed* lets the line enact a paradox that reflects the one it describes: "consume," already the commonest verb for indicating the action of fire upon fuel, is here used to describe the action of the fuel upon the fire (choked by ashes); *nourished* further complicates a reader's understanding by leading him into another common context of "consume"; the line could be paraphrased as "Eaten up by that which it ate up" (compare Ovid, *Met.* XV.234–36 [lines 258–60 in Golding]).

14. *that* (1) me or my love; and, perhaps, secondarily, (2) your youth or life. *that well* Although I cannot believe that in this otherwise solemn poem Shakespeare intended or any reader ever heard a pun on "that well" as adjective-plus-noun, that reading is syntactically possible; see 154.9, note. *leave* (1) depart from; (2) give up, forego. The meanings were equally common and are equally appropriate here: a series of descriptions of things departing prepares us for sense (1); the same context, however, demands sense (2) after *thou* (the speaker is departing, not the beloved). The conflict has no effect on the meaning of the line, but the double action of *leave* is a stylistic metaphor or emblem for the contrariness that the poem manifests throughout. The contrariness, overt in line 12, is inherent in the presence, in a poem about old age, of a dimly perceptible metaphor of a child taken off to sleep (lines 7 and 8) by *black night*, a sinister nursery maid or (line 12) wet nurse; also note the stylistic metaphors of contrariness in the poem (e.g. in line 2, *none*—suggesting the last phase of leaf-fall, the bare tree—comes before *few* [compare 77.10–12, 97.9–10, and the construction of line 227 of Golding's translation of *Met.* XV: "And vertue small or none too herbes there dooth as yit belong"]; and in lines 5–6 and 9–10 *of such day* / *As* and *of such fire* / *That* are complexly and pointedly alike and as complexly and as pointedly different). *Leave* also contributes to a reader's sense of wrongness, of things that are backwards or are their own opposites, by presenting a phonetic but logically insupportable echo of the *leaves* in quatrain 1; the likeness is presumably not often brought to consciousness, but a reader who did test for a third sense of *leave* would be led to the verb "to leaf," "to put out leaves as a tree does in spring," which would merely duplicate and change the dimension of the sense of paradox evoked by the unexamined but inevitably heard phonetic equation that *leave* must introduce into even a casual reading (compare 5.7, 77.3, and 97.14).

See 74.1, note.

SONNET 74

1. *But* This poem continues from 73. *be contented* do not be upset, be tranquil (the succeeding financial language [*bail, interest*] can activate overtones of "to content" meaning "to pay in full," "to remunerate" as in *Oth* III.i.1: "I will content your pains"; see 32.1, note). *fell* cruel, painful, ruthless, deadly

(with pertinent overtones of the verb "to fell" meaning "to strike down" or "to kill"). *arrest* (1) stay, stop (i.e. act of halting); (2) apprehension and restraint (as by a policeman—see *Ham* V.ii.328–29: "this fell sergeant Death / Is strict in his arrest").

1–2. The Q punctuation is this: "But be contented when that fell arrest, / Without all bail shall carry me away, / My life hath . . . ." Aside from deleting the comma at the end of line 1, I retain Q's punctuation, which does not fix the relationship between the *when* clause and those that precede and follow it, but which should not seriously disturb a modern reader's progress through the poem. An editor who feels that his reader's possible confusion justifies emendation has two choices. He can put a period or colon after *away*, so that the *when* clause modifies the opening injunction and makes it future. Or he can add a colon, semicolon, or period after *contented*, so as to make the *when* clause modify line 3: "But be contented. When that fell arrest / Without all bail shall carry me away, / My life hath . . . ." There is little reason to favor either over the other.

2. *Without* with no possibility of (see *OED*, 10c; "held without bail" was already a standard legal phrase—see *OED*, s.v. "mainprize," sb. 2, and *An Act for the Uniformity of Common Prayer* [1559], par. 3: "imprisonment . . . without bail or mainprise"). *all* any (see 68.10).

3. *line* line of verse (with a play on "line of life"—from classical mythology [the measure of one's time on earth, spun by the Fates], or from palmistry [the life line]. Hugh Holland appropriated the conceit for his sonnet on Shakespeare, prefaced to F1: "For though his line of life went soone about, / The life yet of his lines shall never out"). "Therse lines" would have more clearly indicated that the speaker referred to his writing, but the singular allows the pun and also suggests "family line." There may also be a pun here on "loin"; see the note on 16.9 on p.579. *interest* (trisyllabic here; contrast 31.7) (1) shares; (2) legal right of possession, title (for the same wordplay, see *RIII* II.ii.47–48: "so much interest have I in thy sorrow / As I had title in thy noble husband"). Line 3 is presenting two reasons, one serious, one comic, why the beloved should bear the speaker's death with patience: (a) since the speaker's life is part of, has a share in, the verse, a part of him (specified in lines 6–9) lives on; (b) the verse, spoken of as if it were an entailed estate (property settled on one man and his lineal heirs), on which the speaker has a legal claim, is suggested to his potential heir as cause to see a brighter side to the impending bereavement. (The use of *interest* to mean "concern for" or "curiosity about" does not occur until the eighteenth century.)

4. *for memorial* (1) as a reminder; (2) instead of a monument or other more usual sort of memorial. *memorial* = trisyllabic, by syncopation. *still* always (modifying the verb *stay*, but coloring the noun *memorial* with a suggestion of "eternal"). *stay* remain (note the play on *arrest*; the two words are synonyms and are here opposed; see 134.9, note).

5. *When thou reviewest* when you look over, reexamine. *review* see again, behold once more. ("Review" already had a specialized literary sense: "to look over in order to revise" [*OED* gives this from 1603: "Dionysius had put into his

hands a tragedy of his owne making, commanding him to review and correct the same"]; but I find no trace of "to review" meaning "to write a criticism of" before the middle of the seventeenth century.)

6. *part* (1) talent; (2) portion, piece (see 17.4 and 69.1). *consecrate to* sacred to, consecrated to, reserved for.

6–14. The metaphoric use of *consecrate* establishes a religious frame of reference. The speaker then proceeds to echo the burial service (line 7) and to develop a secular parody of traditional Christian consolations to mourners for the dead (lines 8–14). In conflating two traditional ideas (the immortality of art [see 55, headnote] and the immortality of the soul), Shakespeare's speaker is typical of courtly lovers; there is no sacrilege here, or hint of contempt for Christian doctrine; the religious language merely acts as a hyperbolic metaphor to vivify the speaker's assertion that his spirit is in his verse and is immortal with it.

7. This line echoes the burial service ("earth to earth, ashes to ashes, dust to dust"), and alludes to common proverbial ideas: "to owe God a death" (Tilley G237), and "to pay one's debt to nature" (Tilley D168). *his* its (but see 73.10, note).

8. *spirit* = often slurred or monosyllabic in pronunciation; "spear't," or "sprite," or "sprit," or "spurt" (see 56.8, 80.2, 85.7, 86.5, 144.4). *better part* See 39.2, note; here the expression is apposite to *spirit*, but also describes the beloved, the "thou" latent in *thine*.

11. *The coward conquest* the cowardly captive. (The wit of the phrase derives from the common denominator by which both cowards and dead bodies are defined: both lack spirit. The context provided by *wretch's knife* gives the phrase non-grammatical overtones of "the cowardly-won prize"). *wretch's knife* See 60.12, note.

12. *of* by. *rememb'red* = Q's "remembred" (three syllables), which is metrically satisfactory. The four syllable alternative "rememberèd" recommends itself more to a reader counting beats on his fingers than to one listening to the verse.

14. *remains* (1) stays (see line 4); (2) endures. (*OED* records no use of the noun, "the remains," as a euphemism for "the corpse" before 1700; the modern currency of that idiom can give this line a perverse wit that Shakespeare's reader probably could not hear.)

SONNET 75

1. "You are to my thoughts as food is to life." *So are you* Compare *So am I* in 52.1. *to my thoughts* for my thoughts, in relation to my thoughts (with overtones of "in my opinion," "to my thinking," "to my mind").

2. *sweet seasoned* (1) sweet and seasonable, gentle and appropriate (with a suggestion of "of the sweet season," "of the spring"—compare *2HVI* III.i.337: "Faster than springtime show'rs comes thought on thought"); (2) sweet-seasoned, made temperate by sweetness; and, in the context of *food*, (3) sweet-flavored.

3. *for* (1) for the sake of; (2) in order to achieve; (3) because of; (4) instead

of, in exchange for. *the peace of you* (1) your tranquility (i.e. the peacefulness you experience or with to experience); (2) the contentment you bring to me. (This line passes all understanding. Shakespeare seems to have sacrificed expository content in order to achieve the balanced antithesis of *peace* and *strife* and to include a logically and syntactically inadmissible pun on "the piece of you I hold," "the part of you that I possess"—as one would a piece of *ground* [line 2] or a piece of money, a coin [lines 4–6].)

4. Context and common sense dictate that the line mean "as is exemplified in a miser's attitude toward his wealth," but the literal sense of the construction gives the line an appropriate suggestion of strife between lover and beloved.

5. *Now . . . and anon* (1) at one moment . . . and then immediately; (2) sometimes . . . and sometimes. *proud as an enjoyer* vaunting as a possessor (but with a play on the sexual meanings of *proud* [see 151.10 and *all full* below] and *enjoyer* [spelled "inioyer," i.e. "*in*joyer," in Q; see 129.5, 15.14, 37.7,8, and notes; also see the notes to sonnet 52]).

6. *Doubting* fearing that, suspecting that (see *Ham* II.ii.117: "Doubt truth to be a liar"). *the filching age* these dishonest times we live in (in the context of sonnets like 63, this expression carries a suggestion of old age stealing youthful beauty and, perhaps, sexual potency).

7. *counting* counting it, thinking it (with plays on the traditional occupation of misers—counting money—and on "cunt" [see 58.3, note]).

8. *bettered* made better, made happier. *my pleasure* (1) that which pleasures me, that which is my joy; (2) that I am happy (for a specifically sexual sense of *pleasure*, see 20.13, note).

9. *Sometime* sometimes (as in 18.5,7).

10. *clean* wholly.

12. "Except what is had from you or must be taken from you." (*Must . . . be* carries two ideas: that of futurity ["will in future be," "is still to be"], and that of exclusiveness or uniqueness ["cannot be had except"]; note the ideational echo of *Possessing or pursuing* in *had or must . . . be took*. The use of the past tense [e.g. *took*] instead of a participle in *-en* [e.g. "taken"] is common in Renaissance English; see Abbott, par. 343.)

13. *pine* (1) languish with longing; (2) starve (see *V&A* 602: "surfeit by the eye and pine the maw").

14. *Or . . . or* either . . . or (a standard Renaissance construction; see 55.7, note). *all away* possessing nothing. (The general meaning is obvious and is largely determined by the construction, which leads a reader to assume that, as *gluttoning* mirrors the substance of *surfeit* in line 13, *all away* mirrors that of *pine*; Shakespeare may have chosen the imprecise expression because *all away* suggests "all *put* away," "all hidden"—as by a miser—or in order to activate a pun on a sexual sense of *all* [see 26.1–14, note; the same pun may operate in *alone* in line 7 and *all full* in line 9].)

SONNET 76

1. *barren of* destitute of, lacking in. (The clothing metaphor introduced by *of new pride* activates overtones of a sense of *barren* that is usually conveyed by

"bare"; "without clothing," "naked." The conjunction of *verse* and *barren* anticipates the introduction in line 8 of the traditional idea of poems as poets' children and helps to give the poem that tradition's mannered modesty from its beginning.) *pride* adornment, ornament, fine or extravagant dress (see *Lucrece* 1809–10: "[Brutus] Began to clothe his wit in state and pride, / Burying in Lucrece' wound his folly's show"). In the context of *barren*, *pride* carries overtones of its various sexual senses (see 144.8, 151.10, and notes)—notably *pride* meaning sexual desire in female animals, "heat" (see *Oth* III.iii.408: "As salt as wolves in pride"); see also *proud* in 98.8 (where it means "swelling," "pregnant"), and compare 103.1–2; note also that *pride* occurs in context of *wit* (see 26.1–14, note), *burying* (see 64.1–14, note), and *wound* (see 133.2, note) in the foregoing quotation from *Lucrece*.

2. *quick*   (1) rapid, sudden; (2) lively (see 113.7, note).

3. *with the time*   (1) as is usual now, in the currently fashionable manner; (2) with each change of fashion.

4. *methods*   modes of procedure ("method" was used as a specifically literary term; *OED* cites Puttenham's assertion [1589] that "Poesie" was not an art "untill by studious persons fashioned and reduced into a method of rules and precepts"). *compounds*   (1) mixtures; (2) compound words (a verb without prefix was called a "simple," one with a prefix was called a "compound"; *OED* gives this from 1530: "*je prens* is a symple which hath for his compoundes *je reprens*, etc."); (3) compositions, literary compositions. (The juxtaposition of *methods* and *compounds*, in the context of a possible need for a cure for barrenness, activates the specifically medical meanings of both words: a "method" was the specific systematic treatment proper to a specific disease; *OED* gives this from 1541: "Every kynde of dysease hath his owne Methode." A "compound" was a compound drug, a remedy made by mixing two or more "simples," two or more pure herbs or elements. The three schools of classical medicine were called the Dogmatic, the Methodic, and the Empiric, but *OED* notes that in the seventeenth century the term "methodist" was "sometimes applied to the regular or orthodox medical practitioners of the day, in contradistinction to those who favored the use of new remedies." The longstanding dispute between physicians who prescribed simples and those that favored compounds is also relevant here. The chemists and physicians' distinction between simples and compounds was much used metaphorically; see 125.7 and *Phoenix* 41–44: "Reason, in itself confounded, / Saw division grow together, / To themselves yet either neither, / Simple were so well compounded.")

5. *Why write I still*   (1) why do I always write; (2) why do I continue to write.   *all one*   only one way (for *all* meaning "only," see 40.10, note; *all one* meaning "the same" was already idiomatic in such phrases as "all is one with her," *MWW* II.ii.70).

6,7,11. See 15.3–6, note.

6. *invention* literary creation (a rhetorical term; see 38.1).   *noted weed* familiar garb (for a similar use of *weed*, see 2.4; Shakespeare's reader may have heard a casual pun on the botanical senses of "knot" and *weed*; see 8.2,3,12, note and *know* in line 9 below).

7. *That* so that. *tell* Q gives "fel."

8. *their, they* The antecedent is *every word*, treated as if plural (compare 78.3–4, note). *Showing their birth* The conceit by which the poet speaks of himself and his poem as mother and child dates from classical times and was particularly popular in the Renaissance; see 17.13–14, note; 26.8, note; 32.10–11; 38.11; 59.2–4; 72.13–14; 77.11; 78.3,7,11, note; 103.1; the example from Donne in 21.8, note; Montaigne's essay "Of the Affection of Fathers for their Children"; *A&S* 1; and *Amoretti* 2; also note *barren* in line 1 above. *where* whence (see *HV* III.v.15: "where have they this mettle?"). *proceed* issue, come forth (see the Nicene Creed in the Communion Service: "And I believe in the Holy Ghost . . . who proceedeth from the Father and the Son"; see also Matt. 4:4: "Man shal not live by bread onely, but by everie worde that proceadeth out of the mouth of God").

1–8. Note the syntactic jerkiness that results from this succession of appositives and appositive-like pairs; it comically testifies that, although the speaker protests that his verse lacks the virtues of witty substantive variation, his verse— at least this example of it—is capable of the vices of one kind of quick change: although the ideational reiterations obviously witness the truth of the speaker's description of his verse, its syntax glances aside spastically.

9. *O know* Shakespeare probably knew that his reader might momentarily mistake this for "O no," a common idiom, and one appropriate to the beginning of a new quatrain; see 61.9 and 116.5. (Shakespeare elsewhere puns on "known"/ "none" and "knot"/"not"; see Kökeritz, p. 305, *noted weed* in line 6 above, and 8.2,3,12, note.)

10. *argument* topic (but colored by the sexual senses; see 38.3, note).

11. *all my best* the best I can do. (In the company of so many clothing metaphors, a modern reader may perceive a witty echo here of "one's best" meaning "one's best clothes"; but that idiom appears to be of eighteenth-century origin.) *dressing* arranging (compare the French *dresser*, which Cotgrave defined as "To straighten, set right, make straight . . . erect; . . . set . . . up; . . . fashion, frame, build, make"; and see the substantive use in 123.4). *dressing old words new* arranging old words anew (with suggestions of "putting new clothes on old words" and "dressing old words up as new ones" [compare 30.4 and 68.12, and note *new and old* in line 13 below]—and with a play on "to dress" meaning "to address" [*OED* gives this from the early sixteenth century: "A knyght . . . dressed hys wordes toward her & said . . . "]).

12. *again* See 13.6–7, note. *spent* (1) paid out, dispensed; (2) worn out (see 107.14).

12–14. Line 12 invites a reader to hunt for witty extra meanings in it and in the lines that immediately precede it; but, although the line gestures toward several strange compounds, its sum is as simple and dull as its immediately obvious surface meaning would lead us to expect any lines by this speaker to be: "In just the same way my affection consists in (is expressed in) forever saying over again what has already been said." That is all the substance there is to the line. However, the sun simile (in line 13), which line 14 ultimately identifies as an emblem of monotonous repetition, is also a potential emblem of glorious and

eternally Phoenix-like rejuvenation; and, in the construction *For as the sun . . . /
So is my love*, the simile invites the reader momentarily to take *my love* as "my
beloved" (compare 23.7–8, 34.13, and notes)—"my sunlike beloved" (compare
33 and 34). The completed line then tells the reader that the simile can be applied
only to the speaker's plodding demonstrations of affection. Aside from investing
our final understanding of the line with some of the noble connotations of
still ("eternally," "unfailingly") to complement its derisive ones ("unremit-
tingly," "ceaselessly," "interminably"), the momentarily perceived comparison
of the sun and the beloved only takes the reader on a fool's errand, a semantically unproductive wild goose chase.

The potential oxymoron *still* (silent) *telling* is not quite realizable either; nor
is the muffled pun on "a gain" in *again* in line 12 (see 13.6–7, note).

A further sense of yearning but muffled wit is evoked by the conjunction of
two words that regularly cohabit in financial contexts—*Spending* in line 12 and
telling here (spending money, counting money), and by the careful parallelism
between *Spending . . . spent* and *telling . . . told*; but neither potentially
meaningful link has an apparent meaning. (Compare the equally gratuitous
parallelism between *So . . . is dressing* [line 11] and *So is . . . telling*, and
between *old words new* [11] and *new and old* [13].)

Telling what is told also feels as if it had some witty undermeaning: *telling*
and *told* echo *tell* in line 7, and, even as the monotony of the diction illustrates
the speaker's point, just the opposite can seem to be indicated by pregnant-
sounding repetition, the variation in form (the polyptoton in *telling* and *told*),
and the potential variation in sense (*telling* could mean "counting" [as in 12.1],
and, *told* could be a pun on "tolled"). A reader who follows out this line of
thought will not arrive at any extra dimension for the line ("my beloved is
eternally counting what is already counted"? " . . . what has already been
rung"?). If one searches the line for the kind of poetic ingenuity it promises and
that the speaker so pointedly says it and his poems lack, one can find oneself
mired in notions of counting, bells, clocks, and time (see 77.1–2); one can find
oneself asking "what it is o'clock," asking the proverbial example of a fool's
question, one that need not be asked (see *1HIV* I.ii.1ff. and *AYLI* III.ii.282;
Tilley, O9a, gives this explanatory example from 1666: "To ask in what month
Twelf-tide falls in, viz. to ask an absurd question, to ask what's a clock when it
strikes").

SONNET 77

This sonnet alludes to and plays on the *memento mori* tradition. A *memento
mori* was a symbolic object (often a ring with the figure of a skull or a "death's-
head at the feast," an actual human skull placed amid the finery of a banqueting
table), kept as a reminder of human mortality and the impermanence of worldly
things. In *1HIV* Falstaff says this about Bardolph's red face: "I make as good
use of it as many a man doth of a death's head or a memento mori: I never see
thy face but I think upon hell-fire, and Dives that lived in purple; for there he is
in his robes, burning, burning" (III.iii.28–29).

1. *glass* mirror (but see 3.1, note). *wear* (1) diminish, waste away, fade; (2) last, endure, hold up. (Q gives "were," a reasonably common variant spelling of *wear*. The "were"/*bear* rhyme is not useful evidence for guessing how Shakespeare's reader would have understood this line [see 98.11, 140.5–7, and notes]; but "were" meaning "used to be" is not immediately meaningful here, and *wear* is. Meaning can, however, be inferred from "show thee how thy beauties were": "remind you of the beauty you had," "remind you of the way you used to look," and, although the chain of thought that leads to that reading is too long to allow "used to be" to register with the immediacy of *wear*, recollection of lost beauties is a corollary to an inspection of the current state of one's appearance; thus the orthographic and aural interchangeability of the words now distinguishable in the spellings "were" and *wear* presumably enriched Shakespeare's reader's understanding of *show thee how thy beauties wear*.)

1,5. *show, show* Q gives "shew," "show." The two spellings were interchangeable, and the variance here signifies nothing (see 69.8, note and the long final note on 129).

2,7. *dial, dial's* = dissyllabic.

2. *dial* timepiece (a watch or clock—as in 104.9—or a sundial; *dial's shady stealth* in line 7 seems to specify a sundial. *waste* pass away, are used up (with a suggestion both of "are wasted," "are used unprofitably [because you waste your time]," and of "waste you," "destroy your beauty"; for similar plays on timewasting and the wasting inflicted by time, see 9.11, 12.10, 30.4, and notes.

3,4,10,14. *The vacant leaves, this book, these waste blanks, thy book* Most readers and editors have agreed with George Steevens's inference (1780), that "probably this Sonnet was designed to accompany a present of a book consisting of blank paper," a "table-book" like the one Hamlet mentions (I.v.98–107); see 122.

3. *The* So Q. Several editors follow Malone's suggestion that *The* is an error for "These"; the emendation, which makes the apparent topic of the poem clearer sooner, is helpful but unnecessary. *vacant* empty (but with play on the fact that *vacant* is a synonym for *waste* meaning "empty"—a sense irrelevant to *waste* in line 2, but its primary meaning in line 10. Note also that *vacant leaves* is a chiasmic echo of a relevant stock expression (see "left . . . vacant" in *Much Ado* I.i.264) for indicating a counteraction to the one the line assumes. Compare 5.7, 73.14, and 97.14.

4. *of* from.

6. *mouthèd* gaping, devouring, mouth-like (literally *mouthèd graves* would mean "graves which have mouths").

3,5,6. *imprint, wrinkles, mouthèd graves* See 81.7, note (on *grave* and "to grave").

7. See 104.9–10, note.

7–8. The primary meaning of *shady stealth* is "stealthy shadow," but a reader derives it from his knowledge of sundials rather than from the syntactical construction before him. Shakespeare counts on context and the reader to establish the idea of a shadow stealing slowly across the face of a sundial; he uses the actual phrase to augment that idea with a construction calculated to stress the idea of theft in *stealth* more than that of hardly perceived motion; the possessive construction makes the dial responsible for shady stealth, makes time seem guilty of stealing; the adjective *shady* applied to *stealth* carries the sinister connotations of ghosts, where the straightforward evocation of a shadow passing across a sundial would not. The ultimate effect of the careful imprecision of *dial's shady stealth* is to give the phrase, the three words, the capability the sentence attributes to what the three words describe: *dial's shady stealth* in line 7 anticipates, lets a reader know, *Time's thievish progress* in line 8. (Note that *shady* meaning "disreputable" [as in "shady character"] is not found until the mid–nineteenth century. Of course it always had the metaphoric potential from which that usage developed; see Falstaff's description of thieves as "gentlemen of the shade" [*1HIV* I.ii.25].)

9. *Look what*   whatever (see 9.9, note).

10. *waste*   empty, unused.   *blanks*   blank pages. (Q gives "blacks," which probably resulted when the printer overlooked the nunnation mark [see 33.14, note] in blācks in his copy; the same error appears in *Ham* II.ii.322 where Ql and the folios have "blanke verse" and Q2 has "blacke verse.")

10–12. See 76.8, note. Roughly, the sense of the lines is this: "Commit your thoughts to these blank pages as one puts children out to nurse, and, when you look at them in the future, you will seem to be meeting them for the first time; like children who have matured in absence, they will seem both new and improved by maturity." (The sense is obscured by the logically inverse order of *delivered from thy brain* and *nursed*: "Those children who were delivered from thy brain, having been nursed, will take a new acquaintance . . . " The inversion may have been prompted by Shakespeare's desire to stress the idea that what the mind gives it also receives, an idea akin to the one expressed in 16.13: "To give away yourself keeps yourself still"; both ideas are distant relatives of a crucial Christian paradox: "whosoever will save his life shall lose it: and whosoever will lose his life for my sake shall find it.")

13. *These offices*   these duties, these actions (see 101.13); the antecedents of the phrase are perfectly imprecise and can include all the actions implied or specified in the first 12 lines. The proximity of lines 9–12 implies reference to writing in the book and rereading it later; that would make *much enrich thy book* in line 14 an implied assertion that looking over what one has written will make what one will write better. In the logic of lines 1–8, *These offices* would be looking at the glass and dial.   *look*   (1) look at what you have written; (2) look in thy glass and at thy dial; and, perhaps (3) look to them, i.e. attend to these duties. (Contrast *Look* in line 9.)

13–14. These lines are another example of Shakespeare's efficient use of syntactic imprecision. The lines mirror the fusion (or confusion) of past and future time that the poem generates; the lines sound very precise, but the syntax does not allow separation between any of the *offices* that *profit* the beloved and those that *enrich* the book, or among *offices* performed in the past, in the near future, and in the distant future. The lines thus also mirror a poet's victory over invincible time. The poem is full of such fusions and confusions of incompatible objects, actions, states, and responses—e.g. *wear* (which in line 1 sums up the poem in its two meanings), *waste* in lines 2 and 10, and *vacant* in line 3—fusions by which incompatible and contradictory truths are voiced simultaneously. The syntax does for a reader what practical defenses against time cannot do; it supersedes the concept of time.

SONNET 78

This sonnet and the ten sonnets that follow it all play to some degree on the word *in* (e.g. *invoked, in, influence*, and *In* in 78.1,2,10, and 11); moreover, the idea of inherence figures in each of them. See 79–88, notes (and the notes to 81.2, 82.14, and 83.13–14 in particular).

1. *for* (1) as; (2) to be; and, perhaps (3) in support of, to assist.

2. *fair* (1) kindly; (2) promising (see 26.10, note). (Some of the words and ideas that follow the phrase evoke suggestions of other meanings. Although *fair assistance in* means "kindly help with," *in* suggests locality; it thus activates the sense "beautiful presence in my poems" [for this Frenchified sense of *assistance*, *OED* cites this from Milton: "His sumptuous burial . . . solemnized with so great an assistance of all the University"; Shakespeare regularly uses the verb "assist" to mean "attend"]. The word *pen* in line 3 cannot be said to add to the meaning of *fair*, but the coexistence of the two words colors the passage with unharnessed but belittling overtones of the expression "a fair hand"—a stock phrase for describing neat and legible handwriting [*MofV* II.iv.12]. Similarly the suggestions in line 3 of dishonesty in the rival poets give pertinence to *fair* meaning "honorable," as in the already current expression "fair and square.")

3. *As* that (a gloss dictated by the logical necessities of the completed line, but not evident until the reader reaches *my use*, an unexpected direct object for *hath got*; until then this seems to be an ordinary "such . . . as" construction in which *As every alien pen hath got* would specify the nature of the *fair assistance*). *alien* (= dissyllabic: "ale-yen") stranger's, outsider's. *use* habit (*hath got my use* means "has taken up my habit of addressing you in verse"; but *use* also carries suggestions of "right of possession" [*OED* gives this from 1596: "They conveyed their full estates of their lands in their good health, to friends in trust . . . and this trust was called, the use of the land"] and "privilege of using"—in a sexual sense [see 2.9, and note the potential for sexual innuendo in *pen* and in line 4]).

3–4. *every . . . pen, their* The pronoun treats *every . . . pen* as if it were grammatically as well as effectively plural; compare *every word* in 76.7.

3,7,11. *pen, feathers, style* These three words, each the key word in line 3 of a quatrain, are complexly related: The word *pen* derives from Latin *penna*, "feather," and, in the Renaissance, not only indicated a writing-quill but also was still occasionally used to mean "feather." *Style* in line 11 refers to literary style, the way a writer expresses himself. The word derives, however, from Latin *stilus*, a writing instrument, and—as a symbol of literary composition—was loosely used as a synonym for *pen* (*OED* gives this from 1579: "Suche as for the gravitie and fidelitie of their penne and style were cherished"). The root meaning would be irrelevant here except for two things: *mend the style* repeats the substance of the metaphor of repairing a hawk's wing by imping feathers to it; and *mend* and *pen* were regularly used together in the stock expression "mend a pen" (cut a worn quill to make it sharp and serviceable again). (Shakespeare seems to rely on the familiarity of the phrase in *MofV* V.i.237 where Gratiano's "I'll mar the young clerk's pen" contains both an obvious sexual play on "pen" and an abstruse play on "mend" which depends equally on "mend a pen" and the familiar proverbial phrase "mend or mar" [see 103.9–10, note].)

Such wordplay as this is so tenuous and its effect is so insubstantial, that even to call it wordplay is to exaggerate its weight. Such logically extravagant and substantially gratuitous webs of pertinence contribute to a poem in much the way rhyme, rhythm, and alliteration do. A reader who recognizes them must resist any temptation to read substance into them, and, however much he may insist on his sense of proportion, an editor who points them out can become a Satan tempting his readers to ingenuity and may himself be charged with ingenuity. I have therefore refrained in many cases from spelling out or trying to spell out imperfectly realized connotative networks such as those that inhere in most of the other sonnets where Shakespeare mentions pens and penmanship (look, for example, at *outstripped, pen,* and *style* in 32, *character* and *mended* in 59, *quill doth come too short* in 83.7, 84.5, and *write* in 134.7). For a further discussion of pens, see 85.3–4, note. On Shakespeare's uses of *pen* in a sexual sense, see Hulme, pp. 133–43 and this curious triad in *Lear* III.iv.94–96: "Keep thy foot out of brothels, thy hand out of plackets, thy pen from lenders' books." Also note the sexual suggestiveness of *pen* in *AW* II.i.74–77 (where Shakespeare probably also plays on the medical sense of "simple," on "Pepin" and "pee pen," and, by a studiously false etymology, on "-main" and "hand"): "[a physician] whose simple touch / Is powerful to araise King Pepin, nay, / To give great Charlemain a pen in's hand / And write her a love-line."

The sense of coherence given a poem by a logically irrelevant common denominator like the sharpening of pens in 32, 59, and 78 can give the rhythm-like effect I suggest above, but that is not to imply that such substantially irrelevant networks of pertinence are more than or other than subconscious for either writer or reader. The cluttering of words randomly related to pens in the poems listed above is comparable to the "linked images" demonstrated by critics who note that candy relates to dogs in Shakespeare's mind, birds to beetles, geese and strawberries to unpleasantness, and so forth (see E. A. Armstrong, *Shakespeare's Imagination*); indeed 32, 59, and 78 each present the pen-sharpening language in company with the traditional conceit by which poet and poem are described as parent and child (see also 77.9–12 and 76.8, note).

4. *under thee* under your protection. *disperse* (1) scatter about, spread around; (2) publish, put into circulation (*OED* gives this from 1555: "which is nowe printed and dispersed throwghowte Christendome"). This line is a source of the belief that, if these poems refer to a real relationship, the beloved was a patron of poets (like Southampton and Pembroke—see Appendix 1).

5–8. *the dumb, ignorance, the learnèd's* ("the learneds," Q), *grace*   These four words are insistently parallel: all four describe qualities; each is used as a noun; any or all of them could, since each is singular, indicate one particular possessor of the quality indicated (*the dumb* and *ignorance* could refer to the speaker himself; "the learnèd" and *grace* could refer to a particular rival of the speaker's) or indicate the whole class of possessors of a quality ("persons incapable of speech," "ignorant persons," "of learned men," "gracious person"). They are also insistently nonparallel: the first two are paired against the second two (and thus break the parallelism of the four entities with a superimposed parallelism of pairs); the first and third are adjectives used as nouns (again two superimposed patterning systems counter one another); the substantive opposites balanced in *ignorance* and *the learnèd's* give the middle pair an identity of its own; *grace*, which appears after the reader has adapted to the idea that words indicating qualities will be used to indicate persons who possess those qualities, acts as a synecdoche only to the extent that the pattern makes the reader expect one; otherwise, *grace* asks to be understood simply as "the quality of grace." The reader's incidental exercise in the different kinds of relationships among the four words mirrors the effectively similar mental actions by which he follows a diversely linked chain from singing, through *on high*, to *aloft*, to flying, to *feathers*, to the heights of *majesty*, and by which he recognizes the diversely achieved recapitulation of all the elements of the second quatrain in the third.

5. *on high*   (1) aloud; (2) loudly (*OED* gives this from 1519: "If we call any thing on high, The taverner will answer"; compare the adverbial use of *high* in *A&C* I.v.49 where a horse is said to have "neigh'd . . . high"). Here the completed phrase *on high to sing* causes *on high* to anticipate the wit of *aloft* in line 6 and *high* in line 14 by suggesting the location and nature of the singer and the song: aloft and in exultation like a bird or an angel (compare *FQ* I.xii.39.3–5: "an Angel's voice, / Singing . . . / In their trinall triplicities on hye").

6. *heavy*   (1) weighty; (2) dull-witted, sluggish (see 50.1, note).

7. This is a metaphor from falconry and refers to the practice of imping, engrafting extra feathers in the wing of a bird so as to mend it and improve its ability to fly high.

9. *compile*   compose, construct, make. (Shakespeare probably chose the word in order to play on its Latin root, *compilare*, "to steal," "to snatch up and carry off"; Virgil's jealous rivals called him a *compilator* because he imitated Homer; *compile* thus embodies and undercuts the underlying proposition of quatrain 1: the poems of the thieving poets are to the speaker's as the speaker's poems are to the beloved.)

10. *Whose influence is thine*   whose nature is wholly determined by you (the metaphor is from astrology—see 15.4). *and born of thee*   is your child (see 76.8, note). The two metaphors in this line pertain to one another in that each pertains to a source of a child's essence; but the sentence is logically coherent only through the common utility of the metaphors as vehicles for the poet's assertion that the poems are the creations of their subject, the beloved.

12. *graces gracèd*   The repetition of words from the same root is a com-

monplace rhetorical figure called polyptoton; here the figure is a metaphor for the assertion its clause embodies; it presents a verbal demonstration of the assertion in line 8.

12–13. *arts . . . art . . . art* = another common figure, antanaclasis (homonymic pun, the repetition of one word in different senses); again the effect of the figure (which contrasts with that of the one described above) is a metaphor for the substance of the clause: the beloved's being and the speaker's art are one and the same thing.

13. *all*   In this context *all* might have been sexually suggestive; see 26.1–14, note.   *advance*   (1) aid in the success of, help on; (2) lift up (compare its literal use in *Temp* I.ii.408: "The fringed curtains of thine eye advance").

14. If, as is probable (Kökeritz, pp. 306–08 and Ellis, pp. 170ff.), initial *h* and *g* were commonly silent in *high*, then its incidental likeness to *I* would have made it an extralogical, extrasyntactical (and probably inefficient) capsule demonstration that what the couplet says is true: the speaker (*I*) actually is " 'igh." (Note *eyes* and *on high* in line 5.)

SONNET 79

1. *alone*   The word contains the potential for idle and syntactically unexploitable wordplay on "own all" (see line 2 and line 14, note) and "a loan" (see *aid* and, in line 9, *lends*).   *call upon*   (1) invoke (as one does a deity, a muse, or a patron); (2) make application for (as one "calls upon" someone for a certain sum of money); (3) claim (as in *Tim* II.ii.25, quoted in 117.3, note).

1–2. Note that *alone did call / alone had all* effect a rhyme in the third through sixth syllables of the two lines; and see 78.13, note (on *all*) and 87.13, note (on *had*).

2. *had all thy . . . grace*   (1) possessed all your favor (compare *Measure* IV.iii.131–32: "you shall have . . . Grace of the Duke"); (2) embodied all your personal charm, beauty, elegance (i.e. owned it all and was sufficient to contain and express it); (3) was as graceful as you are. (In the context of *muse* in line 4, Shakespeare may intend a gratuitous play on the Graces; in classical mythology the three Graces are regularly associated with the nine Muses, whom they assist in serving and honoring poets; see *SC*, "April," 100–16, Spenser's dedicatory sonnet to the Earl of Ormond and Ossory, and *A&S* 80.4–5.)

3. *gracious*   (1) graceful; (2) fortunate, prosperous (as in *AYLI* I.ii.168: "if I be foil'd, there is but one sham'd that was never gracious"); (3) worthy to have favor (as in *Titus* I.i.428–29: "if ever Tamora / Were gracious in those princely eyes").   *numbers*   verses (as in 17.6, 38.12, and 100.6—with a play on the contrast between *numbers*, "many," and the "one" of *alone* ["all"-plus-"one"]; the phrase *numbers are decayed* may also play on "all one" meaning "at one," "in harmony" [for which *OED* gives this from 1548: "the Frenche kyng and the erle of Warwicke wer al one"]).   *are decayed*   (1) are reduced in quality; (2) are reduced in prosperity; (3) have lost their health and strength (compare *2HIV* I.i.164–65: "your health . . . must perforce decay," and note *sick* in line 4); (4) are in ruins (with a possible play on "to decay" meaning "to decrease [in num-

ber]"; *OED* gives this from 1600: "he had decaied the number of the nobles").

4. *my . . . muse* my poetic powers (however, for a reader fresh from 78 where the speaker said that the beloved was his muse, this phrase accuses the beloved of giving [the speaker's] place—office and employment—to another). *give another place* make way for another, yield to someone else. *another* Q gives "an other"; see 1.8, note.

5. *thy lovely argument* the lovely theme of you, you who are a beautiful topic. (For *argument* meaning "topic" see 38.3 and note; here, however, that sense does not emerge until line 6 reveals itself to be an unexpected syntactic continuation of line 5—a potentially complete sentence, which initially presents itself as the familiar idiomatic statement meaning "I concede the justice of the reasons you offer in support of your position." Compare 82.1.)

5–6. The sexual senses of *argument* (see 38.3, note) and *pen* (see 78.3,7,11, note) color these lines with suggestions of sexual *travail*, copulation; compare the similar conjunction in 100.8.

6. *worthier* = dissyllabic, by syncopation.

7. *of thee* concerning you, on the subject of you (the meaning "from you" is momentarily possible, is rejected, and then—in its chiasmic echo, *thee of*—is revealed in the next line to have been an accurate description of the poet's invention). *invent* = a rhetorical term, it originally meant "to find and elaborate arguments" and later came also to mean "to compose," "to write" (as in *AYLI* IV.iii.28–29: "she never did invent this letter: / This is a man's invention, and his hand"); (1) devise, create, construct by original ingenuity; (2) find, come upon, discover (the word thus blurs the distinction between making and taking that is the topic of the next seven lines).

7,11,12. *invent, in, in* See 78, headnote.

8. *pays it thee* pays it to you. *again* See 13.6–7, note.

9. *lends thee* credits you with, attributes to you.

9–11. *lends, beauty, cheek* Compare 53.4–7.

11. *can afford* is able to give (with a play—evoked by the context of paying and lending—on the financial sense: "is rich enough to bear the expense of").

14. *owes* is under obligation to pay. (The word has its usual modern meaning and no more, but in this context of robbery, lending, and possession *owes* carries some resonances from "to owe" meaning "to own" [as in 18.10 and 70.14]; on the relevance of the word "own" to this poem, see 141.13–14, note.) *thyself* As usual Q gives "thy selfe." There is some wit in the fact that what the beloved pays is in fact his self, but the wit is not orthographically signalled; see 1.8, note.

SONNET 80

This sonnet contains many words used elsewhere in sexual senses (see *use*, 2.9, note; *will*, 135, headnote; *pride*, 151.10 note; 26.1–14, note [on *all*]; 129; and 137.5–10); none of them is fully activated here, but their concentration gives the poem vague sexual overtones.

1. *faint* lose courage; and, perhaps, (2) feint (i.e., "feign," "deceive").

2. *spirit* (= monosyllabic by syncopation; see 74.8, note) person (used with regard to the extent to which the person is mentally or physically "spirited," vigorous, courageous, mettlesome; compare *JC* III.i.164: "The choice and master spirits of this age"; and note *faint*, line 1).

3–4. The logic of these lines is straightforward: "and spends all his might in praise of your name with the result that I am made tongue-tied"; the speaker's discomfiture is an accident of his rival's success in praising the beloved. However, the word order and *To make* shift the emphasis of the assertion; the lines end up presenting the rival as a petty and malicious creature whose main concern is to make the speaker tongue-tied.

5–6. The tongue-tied syntax is contracted: *worth* is the subject of both *is* and *doth bear; wide as the ocean is* must be understood as if it were "which is wide as . . ." line 6 = "bears the humble [sail] just as it [bears] the proudest sail."

3,7. *in, inferior* See 78, headnote (also note the related sounds contained in *since* and *ocean* [line 5], and see 83.13–14, note [on the pronunciation of *-ing*]).

5–13. Compare Martial VIII.lxx (on the modesty of Nerva, a poet content *famae nec dare vela suae*, "content not to hoist sail to his fame". The metaphor of the poet as sailor is traditional, but here and in 86 it may play macaronically on "sail" in the English pronunciation of the French *saillir* ("to issue forth," "to protrude," and, in Cotgrave's words, "to leape one another, as the male doth the female"), and/or "sing" in the French *singler* ("to sayle," "to cut the water with a full wind" [Cotgrave translates the expression *singler en haute mer* as "to sayle in the Mayne"; "to have stuffe enough to worke on or the world at will"]).

7. *saucy* (1) impertinently bold; (2) lascivious (as in *AW* IV.iv.23 and *Measure* II.iv.45: "Their saucy sweetness that do coin heaven's image"; see 118.6, note). *bark* boat. (*Bark* too may contain some sort of sexual innuendo; see *Lear* III.vi.25–28: "Come o'er the bourn, Bessy, to me." / "Her boat hath a leak . . . .") *My saucy bark* is the subject of *doth . . . appear* in line 8, but, after syntactic confusion of lines 5 and 6, the phrase can momentarily register as the object of *bear*: "your worth doth bear my saucy bark." *inferior* = trisyllabic, by syncopation: "in-feer-yer."

8. *wilfully* (1) stubbornly, perversely; (2) at will, freely (*OED* gives this from 1475: "thys hors so went wylfully here and there over all where at hys lust wold"); and, perhaps, (3) lustfully (compare *wilfulness* in 117.9 and *wilful* in 40.8). (The word may have been chosen for its pun on the poet's name: the saucy bark is full of Will; see 135, headnote.)

9. *shallowest* = dissyllabic by syncopation: "shall'west" or "shallow'st."

8–9. Note the incidental wit inherent in the conjunction of *wilfully* and *shallowest*: the first syllables of the two words are potentially synonymous in senses that those two syllables do not have or pertain to here (note *will* in line 9, and compare *Shall will* in 135.7); the "full" of *wilfully* pertains casually to *shallow-*. See 134.9, note (on ideational puns).

10. *soundless* unfathomable (with a play on "silent"?).

11. *wracked* wrecked.

12. *tall building* grand and sturdy construction (said of ships). *pride*

splendor (as in 99.3—but with overtones of "haughtiness," "arrogant self-esteem," and of "exuberance of animal spirits," "mettle"—as in *1HIV* IV.iii.22: "their [the horses'] pride and mettle is asleep").

13. *cast away*   (1) spurned, rejected; (2) shipwrecked.

14. *love*   (1) affection; (2) beloved.   *decay*   ruin, the cause of my ruin.

SONNET 81

1–2. *Or . . . Or*   Whether . . . or (as in *MofV* III.ii.63–64: "Tell me where is fancy bred, / Or in the heart or in the head"). This pair of lines starts the poem off in an ostentatiously alternative mode, and—by virtue of the tone inherent in the *Or . . . Or* construction and of the logical relation of these lines to line 3—says that it makes little difference which alternative comes to pass. A similar stress on and indifference to pairs of paralleled opposites is of the essence of this poem (on simultaneous mortality and immortality) and occurs repeatedly in its formal and semantic particulars. Look, for example, at *From hence* in lines 3 and 5 and the three pairs of lines that follow this one: line 3 (on the beloved's memory) and line 4 (on the speaker's) are echoed by lines 5 and 6, but a variation on the same pair reverses their order in line 7 (on the speaker's grave) and line 8 (on the beloved's); all three pairs echo the neatly balanced alternatives of lines 1 and 2, but do not do so neatly because one cannot say whether one perceives line 1 as being about the speaker and line 2 about the beloved (as the syntax—*Or I shall live / Or you survive*—suggests) or perceives line 1 as being about the beloved (whose demise is the urgent fact conveyed by line 1), and line 2 as about the speaker (whose death is the substantively urgent fact behind line 2). The experience of understanding lines 1–8 (as opposed to what is understood from them) is one of so many simple alternations and alternatives to pairs of alternatives that the actual experience of plodding through them is like a physical experience of relationships that are literally metaphysical—an experience of perceiving stolidly physical patterns (of paired lines and pairs of paired lines) that are both reductively simplistic in their interrelation and too multifariously complex to think about. For similar relationships and effects in other dimensions, see below (and the note on *epitaph* in particular).

1. *epitaph*   The word is derived from the Greek preposition *epi* and *taphos* (a tomb); since *epi* means both "upon" ("on top of") and "at" (and, by extension, "on the occasion of" and "on the topic of"), the word is inherently capable of simultaneously indicating location and topic (compare "epithalamium"). Ben Jonson played on the similarly dual capacity of the English *on* in "On My First Daughter." Here there is no such overt wordplay, but *epitaph* does occur in a poem that persistently probes the distinctions between literal, physical truth and figurative truth (see the following note); the two senses of "upon" inherent in *epitaph* make it a fit companion and auxiliary to the many words (discussed below) that fuse and confuse physical and a nonphysical reality by designating both at once.

2. *survive*   The context of *in earth* evokes a play on the Latin roots of *survive* (*super*, of which one sense is "above," "over," and *vivere*, "to live" ["to exist"

or "to dwell"]); this poem makes a casual but persistent investigation of the various ways "superiority to earth" has meaning: being above ground (alive, not buried—note the double sense of *o'er-read* ["read over"] in line 10); being in heaven (consider the Christian implications of *immortal life* in line 5); being buried in a raised tomb (line 8); and being superior to physical mortality.   *in* This word, which pertains urgently to the substance of the poem, appears three more times (lines 4, 8, and 14) in slightly varying senses. Moreover, an assimilated form of the sound "in-" (meaning "not") appears as the first syllable of *immortal* (line 5); *en-* in *entombèd* (line 8) is a variant form of the prefix "in-" (in fact Q spells "entombed" as "intombed" [see 37.7, note]); also see the note on *ev'n in* below. (Compare the operation of *in* in 15, 25, 35, and 93; and see 78, headnote.)

2–8.   These lines only spell out implications already inherent in lines 1 and 2.

2,6,7,12.   *in earth, all the world, The earth, all the breathers of this world* These four related and independent expressions are a good example both of the urgent and inefficient parallels and alternatives discussed above and of the way the diction of the sonnet passes back and forth effortlessly between literal and figurative meaning and between one figurative or literal meaning and another. *Earth* and *world* are potential synonyms. But *earth* means "soil" in line 2 and *world* means "human society" in line 6. (See 134.9, note.)

At the beginning of line 7 (which is a good emblem of the semantic metempsychoses that characterize the sonnet at large), *earth* means "this planet"—as opposed to the metaphysical locale implied in *immortal life*. But the influence of *yield* and *common* draws *earth* toward meaning "human society" ("earth's inhabitants"—who do not value the speaker). And the coexistence of *earth* and *grave* reactivates "soil" as a supplementary reference of *earth*, while the combination of those two words with *yield* evokes vague but pertinent reference to the Last Judgment—when the earth shall yield up her dead. The idea of the Last Judgment—in which *earth* and *grave* (which in context of burial would ordinarily be thought of as "takers"), are "givers"—is strengthened by an idea evoked by the phrase *earth can yield* and simultaneously related (the Last Judgment is a fulfillment of earthy potential) and foreign (the Last Judgment is frightening and irrevocably associated with destruction, death, and the withering of every tangible human good) to the idea of the fruitfulness of the soil. Moreover, the tone and context of the line suggest still another variation on the idea of giving: the speaker's stance is that of a yielder, someone giving up. The ideas and traces of ideas in the line and their relations with other elements of the poem (e.g. *take* in line 3), are so many and so various that the line conflates a logically incompatible mass of outlooks on, and responses to, the still simple elements of a line that is straightforward to the point of seeming pedestrian.

In line 12, *all the breathers of this world* is an enlarged reflection of *all the world* in line 6, one in which *this world* at first seems to mean only "this planet" (and thus to echo line 7), and then, when line 13 reveals that line 12 did not refer to the Last Judgment (the end of the world), turns out not to distinguish *this world* from others spatially but in terms of time—to distinguish the world of the present from the world of the future.

3. *From hence* away from here (this world? this poem?) *your memory* memories of you (a potential second sense, "what you remember" or "your ability to remember," is presumably overwhelmed by the parallelism of this line and line 1).

4. *in me each part* (1) every part of me; (2) every one of my good qualities (see 17.4 and 69.1); the syntactically most obvious sense of lines 3 and 4 ("death cannot remove the memory of you, even though in me—in my memory, inside me—all your good qualities [and/or everything about you] will be forgotten") probably never registers at all because the model of lines 1 and 2 makes it unthinkable.

5. *from hence* (1) henceforth, from this time forward; (2) as a result of this [poem] (as in *Measure* IV.ii.105: "Hence hath offence his quick celerity"); (3) [you] being away, once gone. (These meanings do not emerge until dictated by the completed line; *from hence* at first seems to repeat the sense it had in line 3.)

6. Note the syntactically irrelevant presence of the standard construction "gone to" and the gratuitous complexity whereby *once gone* is used metaphorically to mean "once dead," while *die*, whose literal sense echoes the metaphorical meaning of *gone*, is itself used metaphorically to mean "be forgotten." *to all the world* as far as everyone in the world is concerned (compare the use of "to" in *WT* II.i.131–32: "the Queen is spotless/ I' th' eyes of heaven and to you"). (This phrase carries appropriate overtones from constructions like "to a man" and "to the skies" where "to" indicates extremity of extent; it also echoes contextually impertinent constructions in which "die to" means "become insensible to," "become as good as dead with respect to," notably Romans 6: 11—which appears in a chapter generally relevant to this sonnet about mortality and immortality: "ye are dead to sinne, but are alive to God in Jesus Christ our Lord.")

7. *but* only, nothing more than. *common* ordinary, undistinguished. *grave* an excavation in which a corpse is buried. (In this special context, however, *grave* can carry a faint and syntactically irrelevant trace of "to grave" meaning "to incise" [as in 100.10], "to cut letters into" [as in *MofV* II.vii.36: "this saying grav'd in gold"]. Compare *epitaph*; see the interplay of ideas of incising and graves in *RII* III.iii.167–69; consider the triple pun on "to grave" in *TNK* V.iii.45–46: "his brow / Is grav'd, and seems to bury what it frowns on"; also see 77.3,5,6).

5,7. *have, grave* This rhyme appears a dozen times in Shakespeare, who also rhymes *have* with "cave," "crave," "gave," etc.; Shakespeare's pronunciations of *have* and the second syllable of "behave" were apparently identical (see Kökeritz, pp. 177, 446, and 448).

8. The allusion here is to one of the two common kinds of monuments erected over the graves of important persons: one, a brass plate with the lifesized portrait of the deceased incised upon it, lies flat at floor level to mark the grave of a notable person buried under a church aisle; the other is an elaborate box-like stone tomb with a lifesized figure of the deceased cut in high relief lying flat on the top, as on a bed or bier (see 17.4, note). *in men's eyes* i.e. in a prominent place (although the phrase does have a literal sense capable of indicating the

physical place of entombment and thus of anticipating the conceit of line 14). (Line 8, like the *when* clause in line 12, modifies both what precedes it [*The earth can yield*], and what follows it [*Your monument shall be*]; that is effectively true in any punctuation; to retain the Q punctuation would distort the experience for a modern, punctuation-sensitive reader [see Preface, pp. xiv–xvi].)

9. *monument* The wit of the poem depends largely on this word. It derives from Latin *monere*, and its root sense thus is "a reminder." It not only meant a grave marker but also was used to mean a carved effigy of the sort described in the preceding note (see *Cymb* II.ii.31–33: "O sleep, thou ape of death, lie dull upon her! / And be her sense but as a monument, / Thus in a chapel lying"), and to mean a written record, a document (as in John Foxe's *Actes and Monuments of these latter and perillous Dayes*—1563). *my . . . verse* (1) this poem; (2) my poems (with a play on *epitaph*, verse cut into a grave marker). *gentle* (1) tender, meek, weak; (2) amiable, kindly meant; (3) noble, "well-born" (as opposed to *common*—see line 7).

9–14. The thrust of the octave is to proclaim the worth of the beloved and the worthlessness of the speaker; the last six lines still proclaim the beloved's superiority, but in a way that includes the worthiness of the speaker whose verse makes him immortal. Note that line 9 presents the beloved (*Your*) and the speaker (*my*) together for the first time since lines 1 and 2. The speaker's self-assertiveness reaches its height in *such virtue hath my pen*, which illustrates his new attitude stylistically by abruptly obtruding itself into the syntax of the couplet.

10,12. *o'er-read, dead* The rhyme, imperfect in modern dialects, may or may not have been so in Shakespeare's. The evidence suggests that individual Elizabethans varied the vowel sounds in *read* and *dead* arbitrarily and at will (much as individual modern Americans may sometimes say the first syllable of "either" one way and sometimes another; the same is true of "tomato" and "vase"); see Kökeritz, pp. 194–203. Whatever the particular sounds may have been, the intricate music of *earth, verse, created, o'er-read, rehearse, breathers, dead, breath*, and *breathes* must always have been as complex phonetically as it is ideationally (Kökeritz [p. 252] offers evidence of Elizabethan rhymes between *earth* and "death" and *earth* and "breath").

11. *rehearse* (1) recite; (2) recount (with a play on the verb "to hearse," meaning "to enclose in a coffin"—"to rehearse" suggests "to hold another funeral for," "to bury again").

12. *breathers of this world* In this context the phrase probably had a witty extra dimension by virtue of the fact that it would have sounded just like "breathers of this word" (see 138.4, note).

13. *still shall live* (1) shall continue to live; (2) shall live forever (for *still* meaning "forever," see *Temp* V.i.214–15: "Let grief and sorrow still embrace his heart / That doth not wish you joy"); (3) shall live nevertheless; (4) when dead, when motionless, you shall be living. (The context of *tongues* and *mouths* gives a perverse pertinence to "silent" as a meaning for *still* [see 85.1].) *virtue* power (as in *MofV* V.i.199: "If you had known the virtue of the ring").

14. *ev'n in the mouths* in the very mouths (*ev'n*, here, is an emphatic particle

emphasizing identity; on its pronunciation, see 15.6, note: *ev'n in* may have been pronounced "in in"—and, as an exercise in agnominatio, would thus complement *breathers, breath, breathes* [polyptoton] and the many other examples of simultaneous likeness and difference in the poem).

10–14. Note the partial but urgent parallelism between lines 10 and 11: *eyes* and *tongues* are ideationally related, particularly in *eyes not yet created* and its twin, *tongues to be*; *shall* occurs at the same point in both lines; and *o'er-read* and *rehearse* are approximations of one another in both sound and sense. The likeness of the lines is so persuasive that they act like nearly physical evidence that the poem's final assertion is more than the genteel hyperbole it so obviously is—that, as the two nonparallel elements in the two lines, the grammatical objects of *o'er-read* and *rehearse*, are equated by the effective interchangeability of the other elements in the two constructions, so *my gentle verse* and *your being* could be in fact what they are syntactically: interchangeable entities so much alike that having one is just as good as having the other.

The syntax of lines 11–13 is similarly demonstrative of the almost supernatural "virtue" of the speaker's pen; the lines expand as they are read so that each in effect speaks twice:

The sense of line 11 starts out to parallel that of line 10, and *rehearse* confirms the parallel (*my gentle verse* shall be read by future eyes, shall be rehearsed—recited—by future tongues); line 11, however, provides its own object for *rehearse—your being* (future tongues shall rehearse your being, i.e. recount your life, tell about you).

Q puts commas after each of lines 9 through 12; a modern punctuation would require a decision—a full stop is needed either after line 11 or after line 12—which would diminish the poem. If the noncommittal commas are retained, line 12 acts twice, first to modify line 11 by indicating when the tongues will rehearse, and then to modify line 13 by indicating when *You . . . shall live*.

You . . . shall live says you shall go on living, shall survive, continue to exist; line 14 adds to and changes the meaning of *live*—you shall dwell where breath most breathes.

SONNET 82

2. *attaint* dishonor. *o'erlook* read over (see *o'er-read* in 81.10), read through, survey (this sense is made exclusive by the lines that follow, but the discordant relationship implied by line 1 evokes other and contrasting senses: "to o'erlook" also means both "to look down upon contemptuously," "treat with contempt," and "to disregard," "ignore," "take no notice of"—see *OED*, 3, 5; in context of the marriage metaphor Shakespeare may intend a play on *o'erlook* meaning "look over," "give the once over to"—compare *MWW* I. iii.55: "Page's wife . . . gave me good eyes too, examin'd my parts with most judicious oeillades").

3. *dedicated* (1) devoted (i.e. devoted to you as to a deity and devoted to

writing about you, *their fair subject*); (2) in author's dedications (see *V&A*, Dedication: "I know not how I shall offend in dedicating my unpolisht lines to your Lordship").

4. *blessing every book*   Syntactical proximity suggests that the phrase modifies either *their fair subject* (the beloved blesses any book of which he is the topic), or *writers* (who can be thought of as blessing their books—making them happy, doing them a service—by dedicating them to the speaker's beloved), but, since the substance of dedications ordinarily is to ask blessings of a patron, the phrase also modifies "thou" (understood as the subject of *mayst*). (*Every book* suggests that the beloved indiscriminately allows himself to be used as *fair subject* for, and gives his patronage to, many books and any *book*—whether it has merit or not.)

5. *hue*   (1) appearance; (2) complexion. (See 20.7, note.)

6. *Finding thy worth*   in deciding (or discovering) that thy worth is (in this reading, the one made exclusive by the syntax of the next two lines, line 6 presents the occasion and supporting evidence for the assertion in line 5; however, line 6 can at first be mistaken for, and understood as, an anticipatory modifier to a following clause beginning *I*: "Finding thy worth to be . . . I do such and such").   *limit*   region, an area defined by established boundaries (as in 44.4; much of the effect of *a limit past my praise* is derived not from its own sense but from its echo of the common constructions "past the limits of"—"beyond the boundaries, restricted scope, of" —and "past the limit of"—"beyond the capacity of").

6–7. *Finding, seek*   Note the incidental wit in the use of related words; the first is used metaphorically, the second literally.

7. *art enforced*   Thou art enforced. (However, although the syntactic parallel with line 5 overrides it, the phrase carries overtones of its potential as a pertinent noun phrase meaning "art that is enforced," "strained touches lent by rhetoric" [see line 10], *gross painting* [line 13].)   *enforced*   = a modernization of Q's "inforc'd" (see 37.7, note); the fifth syllables of lines 5 and 7 are nearly identical in any case.   *anew*   newly (an adverb; note, however, that *anew*'s potential for being read as article and adjective—"a new [praise]"—anticipates the actual object of *seek: Some fresher stamp*).

8. *stamp*   (1) instrument for making impressions, marks, or imprints (here used figuratively to mean "writer"; compare 81.7, note); (2) impression, mark, or imprint made by such an instrument (here used figuratively to refer to the writer's creations). (Being a printer's term, *stamp* has a special pertinence to the preceding lines; in this context the word also carries suggestions of other meanings: *stamp* may already have been used to mean "value derived from suffrage or attestation"; *OED*'s earliest example is from 1632 and from an author's dedication: "Your auspicious Favor, shall leave a greater stampe to the Worke"; *stamp* also meant "physical appearance" as in *Cor* I.vi.22–23: "Who's yonder / That does appear as he were flay'd? . . . / He has the stamp of Marcius"— compare lines 13 and 14.)   *the time-bett'ring days*   this present advanced and progressive period (compare 32.5; the ironic tone of the phrase derives in part from its likeness to scornful expressions like "time-serving" and "time-pleaser"

—see *Cor* III.i.44–45: "call'd them / Time-pleasers, flatterers"—and in part from our previous experience of the speaker as someone who considers himself old and time as a decayer).

10. See 17.12, note.

11–12. These lines play variously on adverbial and adjectival forms of *true* meaning "genuine," "accurate," "faithful," and "sincere."

11. Note the ideational echoes of line 1. *truly fair* Q puts a comma after *fair*; some editors mark the apposition by adding a comma between *Thou* and *truly*. The Q punctuation, which is rhetorical, accurately dictates the rhythm, but can be logically misleading to a modern reader; but a modern logical punctuation can distort the rhythm of the line. *sympathized* matched (i.e. depicted accurately, so that your portrait corresponded to your actual appearance and character; compare *Lucrece* 1112–13: "True sorrow then is feelingly suffic'd / When with like semblance it is sympathiz'd," and see "sympathize with" in *HV* III.vii.145; *sympathized* also carries overtones of its more usual uses and thus suggests not only correspondence between portrait and subject but fellow feeling between poet and subject).

12. *plain* (1) frank, honest; (2) simple, ordinary, lowly; (3) clear.

13. *painting* (1) description, depiction (compare *Much Ado* III.ii.97: "The word is too good to paint out her wickedness"); (2) decoration; adornment (i.e. extravagant praise; Ingram and Redpath suggest a play on the "colors" of rhetoric, rhetorical figures); (3) flattery (as in *LLL* IV.i.16–17: "Nay, never paint me now; / Where fair is not, praise cannot mend the brow"); (4) application of cosmetics.

14. *in* on (but the use of *in* suggests the commoner construction [where *in* indicates inherence] and thus gives the phrase overtones of accusation; compare *LLL* IV.iii.111: "Do not call it sin in me"). (Note *in* in lines 5 and 12; see 78, headnote [on continuing incidental play on *in*], 83.13–14, note, and the present participles in this poem.) *abused* misused (Shakespeare may have chosen the word because of the general pertinence of several senses irrelevant to this line but generally pertinent to the poem: "to abuse" meant "to misrepresent," "to cheat," "to deceive" [compare the modern word "disabused"], and "to malign").

SONNET 83

1. *painting* See 82.13, note.

2. *fair* (1) beauty (as in 16.11); (2) fair face (see 18.7, note).

3. Compare 82.6. *did exceed* (1) were beyond the capacity of; (2) were superior to.

4. *barren* (1) valueless, worthless; (2) sterile, incapable of bearing fruit (for the conceit by which a poet's works are his children, see 76.8, note). *tender of* (1) offer of (a legal phrase for which *OED* gives this from 1560–63: "All such persons shall bee compellable to take the Othe upon the second Tender or Offer of the same"; it was also used for general senses; *OED*'s first example is from an author's dedication in 1577: "I dare presume to make tendour of the protection

thereof unto your Lordship's hands"); (2) offering which is, object offered which is (compare *Ham* I.iii.106: "You have ta'en these tenders for true pay"); (3) regard which is, tenderness which is (compare *1HIV* V.iv.49—where *of* = "for": "show'd thou mak'st some tender of my life"). (Empson notes that "the meaning 'person who looks after' [i.e. 'one who tends'—see 57.1] may be fancied in the background"—*Seven Types*, p. 135. For similar plays on *tender* see *Ham* I.iii. 99–109 and *MND* III.ii.85–87. Note that *tender* meaning currency, "legal tender," did not come into use until the mid–eighteenth century.)   *a poet's debt* (1) what a poet owes, is obliged to furnish; (2) what is owed to a poet (the beloved can be thought of both as superior to receiving the offerings of a poet— i.e. of the speaker or of a rival poet—and as superior to paying for them with money, praise, or affection).

5. *in*   with regard to.   *your report*   (1) telling about you; (2) your reputation (as in *Measure* II.iii.10–12: "A gentlewoman . . . / Who . . . / Hath blister'd her report").

1–5. Lines 1 and 2 imply that the speaker has been writing about the beloved (although without exaggerating his virtues). Lines 3 and 4 can be regarded as amplifying the first two by stating a reason for the modesty of the speaker's claims for the beloved, but, as a result of the multiple inferences available from line 4, there is also a suggestion that the speaker has ceased to write at all. Line 5 confirms that suggestion ("I have slept in your report" = "I have neglected to write about you"), but it also fits the situation indicated in lines 1 and 2 ("I have slept in your report" = "I have insufficiently emphasized, have not done justice to, your virtues").

6. *that*   so that.   *being*   = monosyllabic (as in 50.8; in lines 10 and 11 *being* is dissyllabic; see 52.14, note).   *extant*   alive, still existing (with a play on the root senses [from Latin *exstare*]: (a) prominent, conspicuous, to be seen publicly, standing forth to view—see *well might show*; (b) "projecting," "protuberant"— see line 7; since *extant* appears here in context of *saw* in line 1 and *eyes* in line 13, note that the word was related to eyesight—as in the phrases "extant to be seen" and "extant to the eye" [for which *OED* gives this example from the 1570's: "There are yet extant to the eie, the ruined walles of an auncient fortification"]; also see the note on *modern* in line 7).

7. *modern*   (1) of the present (see *extant*, of which another meaning was "present"—as in *T&C* IV.v.168: "in this extant moment"); (2) ordinary, commonplace, trite (the usual Shakespearian meaning—see *AYLI* IV.i.7: "betray themselves to every modern censure").   *doth come too short*   falls short, is inadequate (as in *AW* V.iii.174: "Your reputation comes too short for my daughter"; the line also prepares for the stylistic joke in line 8 and also contains some sort of joke—probably sexual [note *come*]—about short pens—see 78.3,7, 11, note).

8. *Speaking of worth*   in speaking about value.   *what worth*   of the value that.

7–8. The syntax of these lines is appropriately and wittily elliptical; it "comes short" in two senses—in leaving "of" out of "come too short of what . . . ," the syntax is inadequate, and is so because it is not long enough.

9. *for* as. *impute* consider, regard (*OED* gives this from 1611: "[He] was imputed a Saint").

10. *being dumb* I being dumb (the participle is dependent on a pronoun, "I," that is only present by implication [in *my glory*]; such constructions are not unusual in Shakespeare; see Abbott, par. 379).

12. *When* whereas (as in *V&A* 984: "Who is but drunken when she seemeth drown'd"). *bring a tomb* Compare 17.3 and, for a different attitude toward poetic entombment, 81.8–9. *tomb* The rhyme with *dumb* in line 10 appears to have been a true one; Shakespeare uses the same rhyme three other times, including 101.9,11. In "Shakespeare's Word-play on *Tombe*" (*MLN*, 64 [1944], 235–41), T. Walter Herbert successfully argued the historical and artistic probability of a *tomb*/"tome" pun here and in 17.3 ("[my verse] is but a tomb"), 86.4, 101.11, and 107.14. Kökeritz dismissed Herbert's suggestion crankily but without reason (pp. 86–87); see Ellis, pp. 197–98.

14. *devise* The word derives from Latin *dividere*, which is unrelated to *videre* ("to see"); in this context, however, *devise* presumably suggests the whole range of "vision" words—even to scrupulous twentieth-century etymologists.

13,14. *in, in* within, by way of. (These two uses of *in* conclude the poem's ongoing exercise in contrasting meanings of *in*; see lines 5 and 8. For a Renaissance reader the incidental harmony in *in* probably included the second syllables of *painting, Speaking, being* [probably = "bin" in line 6 and "be-in' " in lines 10 and 11; see Kökeritz, pp. 312–14], and *silence* [see 35.8–9, note]; also note *barren, tender, sin, impute,* and *impair.* Relatively intense play on the sound and meanings of *in* continues in 84.3 [*In . . . immurèd*], 5 [*within*], 10, 12 [*making*], 13 [*blessings*]; in 85.1,9 [*Hearing*], 10 [*something*], 11, 14 [*speaking in*]; 86.3 [*in . . . inhearse*], 4 [*Making . . . wherein*], 8 [*Giving*], 10 [*intelligence*], 11 [*silence?*], 12 [*thence?*], 13 [*countenance*], 14 [*enfeebled*]; 87.1 [*possessing*], 3 [*releasing*], 4 [*in . . . determinate*], 7, 14 [*In . . . waking*], and the rhyme words of lines 5–12; and in 88.2,5 [*being*], 7 [*whérein*], 8 [*in losing . . . win*], 10 [*bending . . . loving*], 11 [*injuries*], 12 [*Doing*]. None of these repetitions of the sound of *in* is more than incidental, but inherence is a theme of all these poems. See 78, headnote.)

SONNET 84

1–4. "Not even those who say most [in quantity and/or quality] can say anything more in your praise than that only you have the distinction of being you. No one has it in him to think of something with which you can be compared [because the qualities your equal would have to possess are possessed only by you]."

Q punctuates lines 1–4 with commas after *most, more, praise, alone, are you, store,* and *grew*; Q's first full stop is a period at the end of line 8. The Q punctuation is unsatisfactory, but no modern punctuation is quite satisfactory either. Here the four lines are punctuated in a way calculated to save as much of a Renaissance reader's experience of Q as possible for a modern reader (who, if given the Q punctuation, would presumably act as his own editor and furnish restrictive modern logical punctuation of his own). The dash recommends itself only because it is the one logically noncommittal punctuation mark left to us. As line 1 is read, *which* seems first to be an interrogative and parallel with *Who*. Malone and many editors after him made that first impression permanent by punctuating thus: "Who is it that says most? Which can say more / Than this rich praise, that you alone are you?" However, as one reads lines 1 and 2, they come to make sense as the single rhetorical question indicated by the Q punctuation: "Who is it among those that say most who can say more than this . . . ?" Most of the best recent editors therefore sensibly reject Malone's question mark after *most*. Having done so, they also reject the question mark at the end of line 2, taking *whose* in line 3 as a relative pronoun with *you* as antecedent; they then paraphrase—but cannot precisely gloss—3 and 4 as something on the order of this by Harbage: "in whom are locked up all the qualities needed to provide an equal example" or this by Barbara Herrnstein Smith: "i.e., within whom is locked up the entire supply of those qualities which your equal (if any such existed) would have to possess." Some such sense is undeniably in the poem; the juxtaposition of *you* and *In whose* makes it at least an undermeaning. But, if a punctuation comprehensible to a modern reader must be chosen, then one may salvage more of the poem by taking *whose* as an interrogative introducing a new question: "Who has it in him to provide a creature to whom you can be likened?" Or, more literally, "In what poet's (sayer's) confine (enclosure, pen, place for keeping valuable things) is immured (walled up, penned in, enclosed, confined) the stock from which could be produced an analogue for you?" The confusion over *which* (resolved in favor of the relative) and *whose* (probably best resolved in favor of the interrogative) could be continued in line 4, where *Which*, although clearly a relative, is potentially the beginning of yet another new question.

The confusion and awkwardness of the syntax of lines 1–4 is so extreme—and so regularly patterned—that it seems studied. Such a stylistic palimpsest—a sentence in which two sets of signals, the punctuation and the apparent parallelism of the pronouns, give a reader different instructions on how *which* and *whose* function—is consistent with Shakespeare's practice elsewhere and is an appropriate auxiliary to a series of propositions that are ridiculous if taken literally: there cannot be more than most; only one person can be that person; and it is unproductive to use one's subject as a simile for itself.

2. *you alone are you*   only you are you (Seymour-Smith hears a suggestion of "you are only yourself when you are alone").

3. *In*   See 78, headnote and 83.13,14, note.   *store*   (1) abundance (as in 37.8, 64.8, 135.10, 136.10, and *Cymb* I.iv.93: "I do nothing doubt you have store of thieves"); (2) supply stock (the context of *confine* and *immurèd* invokes a casual play on "store beasts," livestock kept for breeding purposes; see 11.9, note).

4. *example*   exemplify (the word is particularly appropriate here because it is a technical term in rhetoric).

5. *Penury* plays on *rich* in line 2; *pen* plays on *penury*; both *penury* and *pen* play on *confine* and *immurèd* in line 3; *dwell* plays on *where . . . grew* in line 4.

8. *so*   thereby, thus.   *story*   Note *store* in line 3.

9. *but* only (compare the conjunction in line 7).

10. *clear* (1) bright, shining, beautiful (*OED* gives this from 1578: "The cleare and pleasant Venus"); (2) illustrious, glorious (as in *Lear* IV.vi.73: "The clearest gods . . . have preserved thee"; note *fame* in line 11); (3) free from guilt (as in *Macb* I.vii.16–19: "Duncan / . . . hath been / So clear in his great office, that his virtues / Will plead like angels"; compare lines 13–14); and, in context of this discussion of literary skills, (4) free from obscurity (i.e. in no need of comparisons, metaphors, or illustrative examples; *OED* gives this from 1615: "The words are cleare and plaine").

11. *counterpart* copy (see 82.11; *OED* ignores the present instance of *counterpart* meaning "copy"; the earliest *OED* example dates from 1617). *fame* make famous.

12. *style* For the probable play on *pen* in line 5, see 78.3,7,11, note.

11–12. There is considerable (but substantively irrelevant) obscene potential in the coincidence of *counterpart, wit,* and *style*—each of which could be a synonym for "phallus." See 58.3 and 136.10, notes (on *account*), 151.6, note (on *part*); 26.1–14, note (on *wit*), and the note cited above on *pen* in sonnet 78. The joke in *counterpart* would be outlandishly elaborate: (a) "complementary organ"; (b) "organ that encounters"; and, via a fanciful verb extrapolated from the pun on "cunt," perhaps even (c) "organ that 'counters,' " " '[in] cuntering' organ"; see 86.13, note. (Also note *nature* in line 10, and see 109.9,10,12,14, note.)

13. *beauteous* = dissyllabic, by syncopation. *blessings* (1) your good qualities, the blessings of nature, your good parts; (2) the blessings, the patronage, you bestow (see 82.1–4). *add* The word has no specifically arithmetical denotation here, but it is the fourth term in the poem that has an unexploited arithmetical sense; the others are *equal* in line 4, *tell* in line 7 (for *tell* meaning "count," see 12.1; also see 86.10, note—on *intelligence* and *countenance*), and *counter-* in line 11. (Also note the language of wealth [*rich, penury, lends*], and the poem's general concern with quantity.)

14. *Being* = monosyllabic (as in 50.8; see 52.14, note). *Being fond on* (1) since you love; being fond of; (2) since you are desirous of (for *on* used for "of," see *MND* II.i.266 and *Cor* IV.v.166: "Worth six on him"); (3) having been rendered simpleminded by (see 3.7).

SONNET 85

1. *in manners* out of politeness (see *TN* II.i.9–12: "I perceive in you so excellent a touch of modesty that you will not extort from me what I am willing to keep in; therefore it charges me in manners the rather to express myself"). *holds her still* keeps quiet, keeps herself silent. (The phrase also carries overtones of *still* in its adverbial meanings: the proximity of 84 activates "nevertheless" as a meaning for *still; still* meaning "always"—as in 41.4 and line 6 below —also pertains, as does *still* meaning "now no less than before"—a sense that activates overtones latent in *-tied* and *holds* and makes the phrase *in manners holds her still* carry faint suggestions of "continues to restrain herself in the bounds of politeness." [Note that *in manners* also appears among words of re-

straint in the foregoing quotation from *TN*; both contexts probably derive from Shakespeare's apparent pleasure in the etymology of *manners* (from Latin *manus*); he (perhaps alone) seems to have heard a pun on "to hold in the hand" in *in manners holds* and an interplay among "touch," "extort," "keep in," "in manners," and "express" in the passage from *TN*. See 111.7, note.]) *in* See 78, headnote, and 83.13,14, note.

2. *comments* expositions, expository treatises. (*OED* gives this from 1513: "I have . . . a schort comment compild, To expon strange historeis and termes wild." "A comment" meaning "a systematic exposition" ordinarily pertained to scientific, theological, or philosophical topics; here *comments* is used with a wry sense of its impropriety and suggests both that the encomiums are labored and pedantic and that they misrepresent their subject to be other than mortal. *OED* also records that, like the Latin *commentum*, "comment" was "sometime . . . taken for a lie or fayned tale." In context of sonnet 84 and line 1, *comments* meaning "criticisms" also pertains: "unfavorable remarks about the extravagant and mannered encomiums written about you." In addition "comment" is a technical term in rhetoric, a synonym for enthymeme, and therefore has extra, though incidental, pertinence to this context of literary jewelry.) *of* The word first appears to mean "on," "about" ("treatises on"), but in the completed construction it comes to mean "consisting of" ("treatises made up of praise of you"). *richly compiled* The phrase modifies *comments*, *praise*, or both. *compiled* See 78.9, note.

3–4. The topic of pens regularly evokes apparently studied imprecision from Shakespeare (see sonnet 78). When he talks about pens he sacrifices immediate clarity to often subtle or intricate wordplay on one or more of the meanings of "pen." Here (and in line 8) Shakespeare plays on *filed* meaning "polished" and the fact that quill pens must be sharpened, filed sharp, but the regularity with which pens appear in semantically obscure contexts suggests the presence of some lost pun or now forgotten use of the word "pen." These "rival poet" sonnets are full of sexual innuendo, but, although Shakespeare regularly makes comic references to the phallic quality of pens (see 78.3,7,11, note), something else—or at least something more—appears to be operating here.

The difficulty in the present lines is the phrase *Reserve their character*. Two senses of *character* pertain: *Comments* are preserved in *character*, by means of writing letters of the alphabet (compare 59.8). On the other hand, although *character* did not yet have its modern sense of "mental or moral constitution," Shakespeare uses *character* to mean personal appearance, particularly personal appearance as an indicator of inward qualities (see *TN* I.ii.50–51: "I will believe thou hast a mind that suits / With this thy fair and outward character"); richly compiled praises might be expected to preserve the beloved's character. Here, however, the pronoun is *their*, not "your" or "thy." Both *Reserve* and *their* have been popular targets for editorial emendation; *Variorum* I,215 gives details. *Reserve*, which commonly meant "preserve" (as in 32.7), does not appear to need the editorial repairs suggested for it, but *their* may well be another instance of the commonest printer's error in Q, "their" for "thy" (see 26.12, note). "Reserve thy character" makes better sense than *Reserve their character*, but that may well be the best reason for retaining the Q reading, in which the discrepancy between the pronoun we expect and the one we get mirrors the distinction between writers whose purpose is to display the merits of their subjects and those who write principally to display their own elegance and learning.

4–5. It may be helpful to remember that self-consciously learned and fashionable Renaissance writers imitated the ancients scrupulously and were much concerned about *good words*: "good Latin" (e.g. Ciceronian vocabulary) and, by analogy, good English. Here *filed* is a literal translation of *limatus*, which along with the other forms of the jeweler's word *limare* is a favorite Ciceronian term for praising rhetorical and oratorical skill. Thus, the use of *filed* here both describes and demonstrates the carefully polished writing with which the speaker must compete.

3. *golden*   (1) aureate; (2) precious (the word describes not the quill but its products).

5. *other*   others (a standard plural form; see 62.8).

6. *like unlettered clerk*   like an illiterate clerk. (In this context the phrase evokes four different uses of *clerk*: (1) The parish clerk, a lay assistant to the clergyman, led the congregation in response and amens—see *RII* IV.i.172–73: "God save the King! Will no man say amen? / Am I both priest and clerk? Well then amen." (2) *Clerk* was still used as a synonym for "cleric," "clergyman"— compare the "priest that lacks Latin" in *AYLI* III.ii.300–03—an *unlettered clerk*, who has nothing to do "because he cannot study." (3) *Clerk* is a synonym for "scribe," a professional penman—as in *MofV* V.i.181–82 and 237; and for (4) "scholar"—as in *Per* V.Prologue.5; both these latter senses make *unlettered clerk* a paradox, a contradiction in terms.)   *still cry amen*   Compare *holds her still* in line 1, and the paradox of *speaking in effect* in line 14.

6–7. Rollins (*Variorum* I,216) notes an echo of 1Cor.14:16: "When thou [who speak in an unknown tongue] blessest with the [Holy] spirit, how shal he that occupieth the roume of the unlearned, say Amen, at thy giving of thanks, seing he knoweth not what thou saiest."

7. *hymn*   song of praise. (The word implies religious praise specifically; see 29 and 105. Here *every hymn* may include a play on "every him," [see 21.8, note], "every rival poet," thus giving a sense comparable to that of "every alien pen" in 78.3).   *that able spirit affords*   (1) which [any] able spirit furnishes; (2) furnished by that [particular] able spirit, by the *better spirit* mentioned in 80.2. (For a similar use of "afford," see 79.11; but, also note the context of material wealth, a context that lets *affords* carry overtones of "is rich enough to be able to bear the cost of." *Spirit* is a monosyllable here; see 74.8.   *able spirit* better poet—or, as the context provided by the echoes of Paul on inspired prophets suggests, a better muse.

8. See 3–4, note.   *form*   literary style, orderly method of expression (*OED* gives this from 1551: "The faulte that is in the forme, or manner of maryng"; compare *Ham* III.i.163: "what he spake . . . lack'd form a little"; *form* is not quite idiomatic here, but recommends itself for its overtones of "mere form"— lacking both substance and personal commitment—and for the ambiguity by which *In . . . form of* seems to mean "in the shape of" and *well-refinèd pen*

seems to be a dehumanizing metonymy for the penman, the rival poet). *well-refinèd* There may be a pun here on a sexual sense of the noun "well"; see 154.9, note.

10. *most* utmost. *add* See 84.13 and note.

12. *his* its (see 73.10, note). *before* at the fore, in front of all others (with pertinent overtones of "as formerly": *his rank before*," his former rank; see 79.1–2).

13. *Then* therefore. *respect* (1) take notice of, care for (as in *2Gent* III.i. 89: "Win her with gifts, if she respect not words"); (2) regard with reverence (as in *Oth* I.iii.183–84: "learn me / How to respect you"); compare 149.9.

14. *in effect* in fact, in reality (*OED* gives this from 1600: "In shew, a senate . . . was to govern, but in effect one only man should . . . do all in all"; the expression usually indicated contrast to "in show" or "in words"; here, coupled with *speaking*, it presents an apparent paradox (being dumb but speaking), and also says (1) speaking by signs, by showing my love (since *effect* also meant "manifestation," "sign," "appearance," as in *2HIV* I.ii.151–52: "not a white hair . . . but should have his effect of gravity"); and (2) speaking in my actions (rather than by mere protestations of love, mere *breath*).

SONNET 86

See 80.5–13, note.

1. *proud full sail* Compare 80.6. *proud* (1) stately and splendid; (2) swollen and vainglorious (see also 151.10, note). *proud full* (1) proud, full (i.e. proud and full); (2) proudful (i.e. "prideful"; *OED* gives a Scottish example from 1578: "proudfull ambition"). *his* the rival poet's.

2. The metaphor is of an expedition in quest of treasure. *all* See 26.1–14, note.

3. *inhearse* coffin up, entomb (as in *1HVI* IV.vii.45: "See where he lies inhearsed").

4. For the conceit whereby poet and poem are mother and child see 76.8, note. *tomb* See 83.12, note.

1–4. The likeness Shakespeare saw between sails and pregnant women is presented overtly in *MND* II.i.128–29: "the sails conceive, / And grow big-bellied with the wanton wind." The speaker's humility combined with metaphors of a *proud full sail* and childbearing may bring to mind the standard idiom "to bear low sail" meaning "to demean oneself humbly"; see *3HVI* V.i.52. See 76.8, note.

5–12. These references to ghostly familiars seem too sinister to describe a rival muse. They sound as though they allude to some specific details about some specific rival poet (see Appendix 1, page 549). The lines remain puzzling and obscure. (Shakespeare may have been attracted to the word *compeers* [7] by its likeness to the word "compare"; see his comments on poetic comparisons in 84.3–4, 18, 21, and 130.)

5. *spirit* (1) mental vigor; (2) vivacity, mettle, spirited temperament. *spirits* supernatural beings. The meter suggests that *spirit* is monosyllabic here

("sprite" or "spear't" or "spurt," as in 74.8 and 85.7), and that *spirits* is dissyllabic (as in 129.1). Abbott (pars. 474–76) cites this line among instances in which
Shakespeare uses a word twice in a single passage, once as a monosyllable and
once as a dissyllable. The practice may have had aesthetic appeal similar to that
of rhyme or of rhetorical figures of simultaneous likeness and difference (such
as polyptoton [*night, nightly*], and punning) or of unlabeled effects like the one
achieved in 115.9–14 by the two *might I not* constructions. See 71.4, note; and
compare *heav'n/heaven's* in 21.3,8 and 29.3,12; *burièd/buried* in 31.4,9; *Being/
being* in 52.14; *suffer/suff'rance* in 58.5,7; *Whether/where/whether* in 59.11–
12; *flattery/flatt'ry* in 114.2,9; *flow'rs/flowers* in 124.4; and *spirits/spirit* in
144.2,4.

    6. *pitch*   level of attainment (*OED* gives this from 1608: "Raysing the valour
. . . to a farre higher pitch"; the general context and the use of *Above* evoke
overtones of *pitch* as a technical term in falconry: a falcon's *pitch* is the height
to which it soars before swooping to catch its prey; the higher the pitch, the more
effective the falcon).

    8. *astonishèd*   (1) stunned with terror; (2) struck dumb, made stonelike (see
Lucrece 1730: "Stone-still, astonish'd").

    9. *He, nor*   neither he nor (compare 141.9). *familiar* compliant, servant-
like ("a familiar" is a demon in the power of a conjurer whose bidding he does;
OED gives this from 1565: "A familiar spirit which hee had . . . in likeness of
a Catte"). *ghost* spectre (with a play on the fact that *ghost* and *spirit* are
synonyms in all their relevant senses—compare "Holy Ghost").

    10. *gulls*   deceives, fools (compare *HV* II.ii.121: "that . . . demon that hath
gull'd thee"). (Ingram and Redpath note the existence of another verb "to gull,"
which, like the French *engouler*, meant "to cram," "to gorge," "to stuff"; *OED*
gives this from 1604: "Let us gull ourselves with eating and quaffing"; in any
case, although "cram" makes good sense, "gull" meaning "cram" was so rare
that, even in context of *full* and *filled up*, its common homonym would surely
have registered in a Renaissance reader's mind.) *intelligence* reports, information. (Note that the second syllable of *intelligence* and the first syllable of
countenance [in line 13] echo a pair of synonyms; see 12.1 and 84.13, note—on
tell and *counterpart*, which appear in context of the same sort of rococo wordplay that this sonnet appears to indulge in.)

    11. *cannot*   can (double negatives for emphasis are common in Renaissance
English; see 134.5 and Abbott, pars. 406 and 408).

    12. *of*   from (note *of* meaning "about" in line 11).

    13. *countenance*   (1) appearance, face (i.e. your beauty); (2) patronage. (A
variant on the same pun occurs in *1HIV* I.ii.27: "our . . . mistress the moon,
under whose countenance we steal.") Q gives "countinance," which may indicate the usual pronunciation; Shakespeare's reader may have heard a bawdy
joke in the conjunction of "count" and "in" (see 78, headnote and 83.13–14
and 84.11–12, notes).

    filled   Q gives "fild," which some editors have read as "filed," polished (see
"fil'd" in the Q text of 85.4), but "filed up" is idiomatically improbable; Q gives
"fild" for *filled* in 17.2 and 63.3, and *filled up* here echoes line 1. *filled up*   (1)

became the subject matter of; (2) supplied the deficiencies in; (3) inflated. Here *line* may play on "loin" (see the note on 16.9 on page 579). *Line* may also play on the rare use of *line* to mean "ship"; *OED*, sb. 3, compares the Old French *lin*.

14. *lacked I matter* I had no subject to write about (with a play on "I was deprived of physical substance" which in one sense would indeed be enfeebling [would make him a disembodied spirit], and, in another, echoes the miscarriage in lines 3 and 4 [note the phonetic likeness of *matter* and the Latin *mater*]). *that* that fact (although *that* can momentarily seem to refer to *matter*: "matter which enfeebled mine"). *enfeebled* Q gives "infeebled"; see 37.7, note (there may be another bawdy *in* joke here; for the sexual sense of *matter*, see 87.14, note).

SONNET 87

Only this sonnet and sonnet 20 use feminine rhymes throughout.

1. *dear* (1) precious (i.e. beloved); (2) costly; (3) grievous (see 37.3, note).

1,9. *Possessing* in line 1 and *Thyself thou gav'st* in line 9 are colored by ideas of sexual possession and sexual submission; see *had* in line 13.

2. *like enough* very probably. *estimate* value.

3. *charter of thy worth* (1) the special privilege which is yours because you are personally worthy (see 58.9, note); (2) the official document that confers high rank and special privilege on you. *gives thee releasing* (1) sets you free; (2) grants you special exemption from legal obligation (*releasing* includes a pun: "the right to lease again").

4. For a similar metaphor, see 18.4. *bonds in thee* (1) ties upon you; (2) legal covenant with you, the deed by which you are legally tied and obligated to me (and/or I am tied and obligated to you). *in* See 78, headnote, and 83.13,14, note. *determinate* ended (compare *RII* I.iii.150–51: "The . . . hours shall not determinate / The dateless limit of thy dear exile"). The meaning "ended" is dictated by the context and by the likeness between *determinate* and the related words "terminated" and "determination" (a legal term meaning the expiration, at a stated date, of rights of ownership [see 13.6, note]), but *determinate* ordinarily had the more general sense "limited," "bounded," "restricted." It therefore both provides a play on *bonds* and gives the quatrain extra pathos in overtones of "my world is circumscribed by you," "you are my world."

5. *hold* In this context the word acts as a legal metaphor: "hold title to" (but with overtones of "embrace"—see line 13). *granting* permission (with a play on "a grant," "a charter," "a deed of possession").

6. *for that* of that. The construction is unusual and can momentarily seem to mean "because" and, since *for* here echoes *For* meaning "because" in line 5, seem to be continuing the preceding construction: "how do I hold you except because . . ." (compare *MWW* III.iv.77–80: "for that I love your daughter . . . I must advance the colours of my love"); compare 89.13–14. *riches* wealth, treasure (*riches* derives from the French *richesse* and was still often used as a singular—as in *Oth* II.i.83: "The riches of the ship is come ashore").

7. The context dictates that *in me* go with *cause* and/or *wanting*: "The cause

in me (the quality of mine), that would justify my possession of your favor (*this fair gift*) is lacking in me." But the construction *fair gift in me* embodies a contradiction to the assertion in which it assists: "a good quality in me" would be a cause why the speaker should receive the gift of the beloved's favor (for the construction, compare *AW* I.i.35: "her dispositions she inherits, which makes fair gifts fairer" and *LLL* IV.ii.68: "The gift is good in those in whom it is acute"). Similarly, if *wanting* could be taken in the sense of "desire," it too could be a cause in the speaker that would account for his good fortune. *fair* (1) desirable, valuable; (2) kind; (3) beautiful (the beloved is the gift and is beautiful). Note the phonetic echo of *Farewell* in line 1.

8. *patent* privilege, right of possession (conferred by a legal document called a patent; compare *charter* in line 3).

8,12. *again* See 13.6–7, note.

10. *Or me* The phrase includes and anticipates the full substance of the completed construction *Or me . . . else mistaking*: as lines 9 and 10 are read, *Or me* can momentarily register as an appendage to the preceding construction: "then not knowing thy own worth or me." *mistaking* (1) having an erroneous view of the character of; (2) taking in error, wrongfully taking (*OED* gives this from 1550: "make restitution of that ye have misse taken"; this second sense introduces a logically gratuitous contrast to *gav'st*). For a similar pun, see *TN* V.i.251: "So comes it, lady, you have been mistook."

11. *misprision* (1) contempt, undervaluation; (2) error, misprizing, mistaking of one thing for another. *upon misprision growing* (1) error having increased; (2) contempt having increased; (3) being grounded in error; (4) (modifying *gift*) increasing, growing greater, on the basis of error.

12. *on better judgment making* [you] having changed your mind, having made a better judgment (compare the expression "on second thought").

13. *had* possessed, held title to (with a play on "possessed sexually," "embraced"; see 52.14, 129.6,10, and 110.9–12, note). *flatter* See 33.2, note. (Sexual dreams were a common Renaissance topic; see *FQ* I.i.47–49, Jonson's "The Dream," Herrick's "The Vine," and *Oth* III.iii.416–32. Compare Gascoigne's *Supposes*, I.ii.133: "Erostrato shall never have her—unless it be in a dream.")

14. *a king* (1) I am a king; (2) you are a king. *no such matter* nothing of the sort (with plays on *matter* meaning real substance as opposed to illusion and on the sexual sense of *matter* [as in *Ham* III.ii.111: "country matters" and *JC* I.i.23: "women's matters"; see 86.13,14, notes; and compare 151.12: *stand in thy affairs*]).

SONNET 88

Compare sonnet 49.

1. *disposed* Q has "dispode." *set me light* value me lightly, hold me in low esteem (as in *RII* I.iii.292–93: "Sorrow hath less power to bite / The man that mocks at it and sets it light").

1–6. Note the play inherent in the differently used metaphors of physical location: *set* (in line 1), *place . . . in* (2), *Upon* (3,6), and *set* (6); also note the potential physical metaphor in *against* (3) and the atrophied metaphor inherent in *disposed* (from Latin *ponere*, "to place"—1). See 78, headnote, and 83.13,14, note.

2. "And hold my merits up to ridicule."

4. *virtuous* = dissyllabic, by syncopation.

6. *Upon thy part* on your side, in support of your case (the logic of the situation requires that the phrase modify *I* [as the like phrase does in line 3], but it could modify *faults* or *concealed* or both; lines 6 and 7 thus incorporate a muffled contradiction of the self-sacrifice they assert: "I can tell about faults on your part, concealed by you, of which I am accused").

7. *attainted* (1) tainted, corrupted, dishonored; (2) accused (*OED* gives this from 1586: "How processe ought to proceede against those that are attainted of it, and how such as are convicted thereof are to be punished").

8. *That* so that. *losing* destroying, ruining (*OED* gives many examples including *Ham* III.ii.190, *Lear* I.i.233, and this from 1591: "Lest heat, wet, wind, should roste, or rot, or lose it"; *win* plays on two other senses of "lose": "be defeated" and "forfeit"; *belong* in line 13 plays on "lose" meaning "cease to have possession of"). Q reads "loosing" here; Renaissance spelling made no distinction between "lose" and "loose" (see 18.10, note); the wordplay in *win* testifies that *losing* is meant, but "releasing" also makes some sense (see 134.12).

9. *a gainer* Note the incidental phonetic echoes of *against* (line 3), *acquainted* (5), and *attainted* (7).

10–11. This is the Q punctuation; an editorially inserted comma after *For* would clarify the sense, but it would remove the ambiguity by which the present punctuation momentarily suggests that the speaker is a gainer as a result of (i.e. for) bending his thoughts on the beloved.

10. *bending all my . . . thoughts on thee* As it is first read, this phrase registers as "turning . . . all my thoughts to consideration of you," "giving you my full attention," but subsequently, in the light of the reminder provided by line 11, *bending* seems less metaphoric, and the phrase carries implications of truth bent (twisted, perverted), for the benefit of the beloved.

12. *vantage* advantage, benefit (the first *vantage* is a noun, the second a verb; note that *vantage* is a military term [see 64.6, note]). *double* doubly (some editors hyphenate "double-vantage"; the effect is the same).

13. *so* so entirely.

14. *for thy right* (1) to attain what is due to you; (2) to attain justice for you; (3) in behalf of your claim, title, privilege; (4) to establish that you are in the right, to put you in the right. *bear all wrong* (1) endure all injustice and injury; (2) take the guilt; wear all the signs of guilt (for *bear* meaning "wear," see 50.6, note); (3) misrepresent everything, report everything incorrectly; (4) reveal, lay bare, all faults and crimes. (Renaissance spelling made no consistent distinction between "bear" and "bare.")

SONNET 89

1. *Say that thou* assert that you. (The meaning can at first seem to be "sup-

pose you should"; that sense is erased when line 2 begins with *And I will* instead of with "I would," but it exists long enough to establish the hypothetical mode. The confusion about *Say* contributes to an artful confusion about mode and tense: here and throughout the poem one cannot—as apparently the speaker cannot—be quite sure whether he has already been forsaken by the beloved or only fears that he will be. (See 90.1, note, and compare 92.14.)

2. This line is prose; see line 3 and note.

3. People desperate for biographical titbits have been known to take this line as confirming the evidence of Shakespeare's physical lameness supposedly provided by 37.3 (see *Variorum* I,105–07, 223–24.) Presumably the line is only one of the many stock witticisms that derive from juxtaposing traditional idioms (metrically clumsy verses are called lame or said to halt) with the fact that metric units are called feet. Compare Ovid, *Amores* III.i.8, *AYLI* III.ii.154–59, *Ham* II.ii.322, Webster's *White Devil* IV.i.125–26; "My suite / Thus haltes to her in verse," and Marston's *Scourge of Villainy* V.18: "Rude limping lines fits this lewd halting age." *I straight* I shall immediately (with a play on "I who am straight," i.e. not crooked and lame). *halt* limp.

1,3. *fault, halt* Both words were probably pronounced to rhyme with modern "caught"; see 138.14, note.

4. *thy reasons* (1) Your statements (as in *LLL* V.i.2: "Your reasons at dinner have been sharp and sententious"); (2) your grounds for action (i.e. the reasons for forsaking me). (For a possible play on "thy raisings," see 129. 6,7, note.)

5. *disgrace* (1) disfigure, deprive of beauty (*OED* gives this from the mid–sixteenth century: "The flower . . . Whose glosse and beauty stormy winds do utterly disgrace"); (2) discredit, disparage, dishonor; (3) dismiss from favor, put out of grace (*OED* gives this from 1600: "Although . . . without lands, and disgraced by Henry, yet being favoured by the people, he supposed that Henry dying, he shoulde . . . be crowned"; see also 33.8, note).

6. *To set* (1) in order to set; (2) in the course of setting. *set a form upon* (1) give shape and order to (as in *John* V.vii.26–27: "set a form upon that indigest / Which he hath left so shapeless and so rude"); (2) give beauty to, make attractive (for this use of *form*, see *MND* I.i.232–33: "Things base and vile . . . / Love can transpose to form and dignity"). These two senses combine with inherent suggestions both of phrases like "set a good face on," "set a gloss upon" (as in *1HVI* IV.i.102–03: "with forged quaint conceit / To set a gloss upon his bold intent"), and of *form* meaning "empty show." *desired change* the change you desire (with a suggestion that the desire for change is prompted by the beloved's new desires).

7. I retain Q's punctuation. In providing modern logically restrictive punctuation, editors are divided on whether to put a full logical stop after *disgrace* (thus fixing *knowing thy will* as a modifier for *I* in line 8), or after *will* (thus tying the phrase to *I'll* in the preceding clause). The rhyme scheme (which has its full stop at line 8), and the play on *thy will* and *I will* recommend the first alternative; the rhythm of the line recommends the second. Either decision diminishes the poem, and the need to decide is not urgent. *knowing thy will*

(1) being aware of what you want; (2) being aware of your lust, your sexual desire (see 135.1 and 135, headnote). There may be a play on "your William" as in 57.13, 112.3, 135, 136, and 143; the sense of the phrase would thus echo 88.5. Since "to know" was regularly used to mean "to use sexually," "to know carnally" (as in *V&A* 525 and throughout AV), and since *will* is used in 135 and 136 to mean not only "lust" but both the male (135.6,12; 136.3) and female (135.5,12) sex organs, Shakespeare's reader may have heard an incidental bawdy joke in *knowing thy will.*

   8. *acquaintance*   My acquaintance with you; the fact that we know each other (with a quiet play on *knowing* in line 7: "even though I know, I will pretend not to know"). *strangle*   Several meanings of *strangle*—"stifle," "smother" (as in *R&J* IV.iii.33–35: "be stifled in the vault . . . And there die strangled"), "suppress," "choke," and "conceal" (as in *1HIV* I.ii.195–96: "mists . . . that did seem to strangle him [the sun]")—combine to convey the idea of a violent and painful struggle to keep from speaking a word of greeting. *look strange*   The gloss provided by *acquaintance strangle* and the link emphasized phonetically by *strangle* and *strange* dictate that this phrase be understood in its commonest Renaissance sense: "behave as if we were strangers" (see the note on *strangely* in 49.5), but, in context of the speaker's promises to disfigure himself, *look strange* also suggests "appear unusual."

   8,12. *acquaintance*   Shakespeare's reader might have heard bawdy overtones of "quaint" here; see 20.3, note.

   9. *walks*   the places where you walk. (See 90.6, note.)

   11. *profane*   Ingram and Redepath say, "Probably playing on (1) 'outside the sacred circle of your intimacy,' cf. Lat. *profanus*; and (2) 'blasphemous.' " Two of the thirteen known copies of Q give "proface"; the rest have "prophane" (see *Variorum* II,5; other evidence that Q was revised in the press is one copy that numbers sonnet 116 correctly and, perhaps, the one copy in which there is a semicolon and not a comma after *deeds* in 150.6; also see 47.10, note).

   12. *haply*   (1) perhaps; (2) by chance.   *our old acquaintance*   our former friendship (but with momentary potential to suggest "our mutual friend"; compare line 8 where *I will acquaintance strangle* carries overtones of the literal murder of *an* acquaintance, a friend).

   13. *For*   on behalf of.   *debate*   combat (but, for a reader fresh from sonnet 88 and lines 1 and 2, with strong overtones of its specialized meaning "combat in words").

   14. *For*   because (compare line 13, and see 87.6, note).   *ne'er*   never (but see 118.5, note).   *hate*   See 90.1, note.

SONNET 90

   1. *Then*   means "therefore" here and indicates an extension from a preceding argument; the repetition of *hate* from 89.14 confirms the relation of this sonnet and 89. A submerged play on the correlatives *Then* (the first word of line 1) and *now* (the last) echoes the confusion in 89 between the present and the hypothetical future (see 89.1, note), a confusion that persists throughout this

sonnet. (Compare the incidental play between *best* in 91.8 and *worst* in 92.1 and 5, and the play on *now* (the sixth syllable of 47.2) and *then* (the sixth syllable of 47.5).

    2. *bent*   intent, resolved (the line is also colored by *bent* meaning "twisted," "turned awry"; *bow* in line 3 activates a quiet and incidental play on *bent* meaning "bowed in submission"; see *Temp* I.ii.114–15: "Subject his coronet to his crown, and bend / The dukedom, yet unbow'd . . ."). *cross*   thwart (as in 133.8 and *John* III.i.91: "Lest that their hopes . . . be cross'd").

    1–3. I retain the Q punctuation, which lets line 2 modify both *hate* and *Join*.

    4. *drop in for an after-loss*   The general meaning is obvious, but the phrase has resisted scholarly efforts at precision: *for* can indicate either "as" ("in the capacity of"), or "to achieve"; *after-loss* ("after losse" in Q), is evidently a nonce word on the model of "after-taste," "after-pain," "after-thought," "after-love" (*2Gent* III.i.95), and "after-clap" ("an unexpected blow, struck after an affair is apparently ended"—exemplified by *OED* from More's *Richard III*). The allusion might be to the "after-game" in Irish, a backgammon-like board game; *OED*'s examples suggest that the after-game was commonly employed in similes for sudden losses after something has apparently been decided (e.g. this from Milton's *Ready and Easy Way to Establish a Free Commonwealth*: "Losing by a strange after-game of Folly, all the Battels we have won"). The game is sketchily described in Charles Cotton's *Compleat Gamester* (1674). The problem is *drop in*. In apparent desperation, *OED* cites this line as an improbably early instance of an idiom not current until a century later: "pay an unexpected or casual social call," a sense uninvited by—and ridiculous in—this context.

    The phrase *sounds* metaphoric. It might allude to some game where a ball or a marble or a playing card could incur a retroactive penalty. Compare *Cymb* II.i.1–2: "Was there ever man had such luck! When I kiss'd the jack, upon an up-cast to be hit away!" Like *drop in*, the precise meaning of "up-cast" is doubtful (see J. M. Nosworthy's note in the New Arden *Cymbeline*), but Cloten is obviously lamenting a potential winning cast that was invalidated by the next player's bowl; Nosworthy explains: "The 'jack' or 'mistress' is the small ball at which the players aim in the game of bowls, and to kiss the jack is to lay one's bowl alongside it." Bowls are ordinarily weighted so that they do not run true; such a bowl can seem to have missed the jack and then curve in toward it. (If the reference in sonnet 90 is to bowls, then it involves a play on the fact that to be left by other players' bowls is an advantage.) A more inviting possibility is the croquet-like variety of pocket billiards that Cotton describes in the second chapter of *The Compleat Gamester*:

> . . . watch all opportunities to hazard him [i.e. strike his ball so that it drops into one of the holes in the table], or king him; that is, when his ball lyeth in such manner that when you strike his ball may hit down the king, and then you win one.
>
> Here note, that if you should king him, and your ball fly over the table, or else run into a hazard, that then you lose one notwithstanding.

Beware when you jobb your ball through the port with the great end of
your stick that you throw it not down, if you do it is a loss, but do it so
handsomly that at one stroke without turning the port with your stick
you effect your purpose; it is good play to turn the port with your ball,
and so hinder your adversary from passing; neither is it amiss if you can
to make your adversary a Fornicator, that is having past your self a little
way, and the others ball being hardly through the port you put him back
again, and it may be quite out of pass.

Or *drop in* might have had a specific military sense which would anticipate
the language of lines 6, 8, and 11. However, I can find no similar military context for *drop in* earlier than this passage from Defoe's *Farther Adventures of
Robinson Crusoe* in 1719 (*Works*, ed. G. H. Maynadier, II [N.Y., 1903], 205):
"Our men . . . came dropping in some and some, not in two bodies, and in
form, as they went, but all in heaps, straggling here and there in such a manner
that a small force of resolute men might have cut them all off."
    The weather metaphor in line 7 suggests that *drop in for an after-loss* might
might be a Shakespearian elaboration on "after-drops," drops of rain that fall
after a storm has apparently passed; *OED's* single example is from Sidney's
Arcadia (Book III, chapter 18, p. 320^r in the 1590 edition).
    Whatever lost reference the phrase may have had, some of its peculiarities
were probably designed to complement the paradoxical texture the poem gets
from a perversity inherent in its diction. For Shakespeare the attraction of *drop
in* may have been the word *in*: subsequent lines equate the "come in" constructions (lines 6 and 11) with *linger out* (8), *leave* (9), and *loss* (14). (Shakespeare
puns elsewhere on "fall out" meaning "quarrel" and "fall in" meaning "join,"
"be on friendly terms"; see *Shrew* IV.i.46–49 and *T&C* III.i.95–97: *Pandarus*:
"He! No, she'll none of him; they two are twain." *Helen*: "Falling in, after
falling out, may make them three.") Moreover, *for an after-loss* embodies the
sound of the standard phrase "fore an' aft" in a poem that confuses one time
with another, one direction with another, and time and direction with one another (see the note on *rearward* in line 6).
    5. *'scaped this sorrow*   (1) recovered from the present sorrow; (2) avoided
the sorrow of being the object of your hate.
    6. *in the rearward of*   "Ward," from Old English words meaning "guard,"
and the suffix "-ward," indicating direction, are hopelessly fused in *rearward.*
Thus: (1) in the rear of, behind, after; (2) as a member of the rearguard of
(Ingram and Redpath explain: "like a reserve following up earlier waves of
troops [i.e. *woe*] whose attack has been repulsed [i.e. *conquered*]"). The interrelation of the ideas of "after," "behind," and "guard" here with *after-loss* in
line 4 gives a gratuitous density to both lines.   *a conquered woe*   vanquished sorrow (i.e. a grief from which the speaker has recovered or to which he has become
resigned). Note that *woe*, which pertains to the tenor of the line, rhymes
with "foe," which would fulfill the military metaphor (and which one editor
actually proposed as an emendation—see *Variorum* I,225); the presence of *woe*
and the contextually inferred presence of "foe" combine to strengthen both

lines of thinking. (Compare 89.9, where *walks* intrudes into a context of talking, and 91.5–8, where both the substance of the lines and the rhymes (*pleasure, rest, measure, best*) invite "treasure chest"; see 141.13–14 and 134.9, notes—on other examples of abstruse interplay between sound and sense.)

7. This line echoes two contrary tenets of folk meteorology: (a) rain follows and is the means of calming high winds (see *T&C* IV.iv.52–53, and *Lucrece* 1788–90; (b) "A blustering night [presages] a fair day" (proverbial—Tilley, N166, citing this line).

8. *linger out*   prolong, protract (as in *2HIV* I.ii.223–25: "I can get no remedy against this consumption of the purse; borrowing only lingers and lingers it out, but the disease is incurable"). *purposed* intended. *overthrow* (1) victory over sorrow (i.e. the speaker's mastery of his own grief); (2) victory over the speaker (by the beloved and the world [line 2]).

10. *other petty griefs*   The context provided by the speaker's previous estimates of the beloved demands that the phrase be understood as "other and—by comparison—petty griefs"; see lines 13 and 14.

11. *in the onset* (1) as one of the first wave of attackers (i.e. not *in the rearward*); (2) at the beginning (for a similar use of *onset*, see *Titus* I.i.237–40: "[I] will with deeds requite thy gentleness; / And for an onset . . . / Lavinia will I make my emperess." *shall*   Q has "stall," an obvious misprint.

13. *strains* (1) kinds, sorts; (2) stresses (a similar play on "strain" occurs in *MWW* III.iii.162: "I would all of the same strain were in the same distress").

SONNET 91

Dover Wilson (pp. 195–97) describes and evaluates a suggestion (by K. A. Svensson) that this sonnet echoes Xenophon: "What first struck Svensson were the following words . . . in the *Memorabilia*, I.vi.14: 'Some delight in good horses or dogs or birds; / I delight even more in good friends.' And their likeness to . . . 11.4–5, 8 of 91 is certainly striking. . . ."

1–4,8,14. *Some* and *All*   The poem presents a running play on two traditional (and traditionally confused) expressions: "all and some" ("each and every one") and "all and sum" ("the whole sum, the entirety").

1. *skill* (1) cleverness; (2) knowledge, understanding (*OED* gives this from 1587: "the tree of the skill of good and evil").

2. *force*   strength (as in 56.1 and *2Gent* III.ii.72: "Much is the force of heaven-bred poesy").

3. *though new-fangled ill*   although they are bad examples of bad fashions (in effect *new-fangled* acts twice—both as an adjective indicating a bizarre novelty valued for its oddity and as the past participle of the verb meaning to manufacture such aberrations).

4. *horse*   This may be plural like *hawks* and *hounds*; for similar plurals see *Shrew* III.ii.201 and *1HIV* II.i.3, and IV.iii.19–20: "certain horse / Of my cousin Vernon's are not yet come up."

5. *humor*   temperament (see 45.8, note—on *melancholy*). *his* its (see 73.10, note). *adjunct* related, accompanying, corresponding.

7. *these particulars* (1) the things I have listed, the foregoing particular sources of joy (*particulars* as opposed to the *general best* in line 8; the phrase is colored by "particular" meaning "private," "personal," "peculiar"; by "particulars" meaning "individuals"; by the idea of "partiality" for something or someone; and by suggestions of the pettiness of mere parts, mere particles); (2) means of particularization; (3) single things (things that are less than everything). *my measure* (1) the standard for comprehending my nature; (2) the standard I use [for measuring happiness]; (3) enough for me (for *measure* meaning "sufficiency," "enough to satisfy," see *Cor* II.ii.121–22: "He cannot but with measure fit the honours / Which we devise him"; here the word is colored by *measure* meaning "temperance," "moderation").

8. *better* surpass, outdo (as in *Per* IV.vi.160: "they do better thee"). *best* Note *worst* in 92.1, 5.

5–8. See 90.6, note.

9. *better* Q has "bitter," probably a misprint, although "bitter" represents a usual pronunciation for *better* (see Kökeritz, pp. 186–90 and the notes on 111.11 and 119.10).

10. *cost* pomp (see 64.2 and note).

10,12. *cost, boast* Apparently a perfect rhyme in Shakespeare's pronunciation. Peter Levins's *Manipulus Vocabulorum* (1570, O4ʳ) lists "cost" and "frost" as rhymes for "coast," "ghost," "host," and "post." Such rhymes are common in Shakespeare, but we cannot now be certain what their vowel sound was.

13. *Wretched* (1) unhappy; (2) contemptible, worthless.

14. *wretched* (1) unhappy; (2) poverty-stricken. See 92.1, note.

SONNET 92

2Gent V.iv.108–20 employs many themes and words that also appear here.

1. *But* acts to link this sonnet to 91 syntactically, and the substance of line 1 seems to continue from 91.13–14. Line 1 points toward a rhetorical stance similar to that of sonnet 90, which is similarly related to the sonnet that precedes it (see 90.1, note), but line 2 abruptly revises the speaker's premises, and line 3 changes them again. *do thy worst to steal* The infinitive results in a conflation of two stock expressions: "to do one's worst" (an idiom that does not ordinarily govern an infinitive), and "to do one's best" (which commonly does govern an infinitive—as in *MND* II.ii.145–46, *TN* I.iv.39–40, *WT* II.i.27–28, and *T&C* I.iii.274); the following crude play on the two expressions illustrates the syntactic distinction: "doe your best to doe your worst" (cited by *OED* from 1639). The phrase participates in the ongoing play on *better* and *best* in 91.8, 9 and on *worst* and *better* in lines 5 and 7 below; it also quietly exploits the paradoxical similarity of meaning between "best" in "do one's best" and "worst" in "do one's worst" (the thrust of both is "do one's utmost"); that paradox is emblematic of the whole sonnet and anticipates the qualitative likeness of opposites asserted in lines 11–12. (See 94, a sustained exercise on the indistinction between "the best" and "the worst.")

to steal thyself away to rob me of you (but colored by the standard phrase "steal away," meaning "depart secretly," and by common use of "steal" and of "steal away" to indicate "elope with" (see *Ham* IV.v.170; *2Gent* III.i.11,15 IV.i.48; and *MWW* IV.iv.72–74: "And in that time / Shall Master Slender steal my Nan away, / And marry her at Eton"). *thyself* As usual, Q gives "thy selfe"; see 1.8, note.

2. *For* during (compare line 4, where *For* means "because"). *term* the duration, the length. *For term of life* is a legal phrase used with regard to set periods of possession (*OED* gives this from 1544: "The husbande hath Estate in the speciall tayle, and the wife but for terme of lyfe"); Shakespeare presents the phrase with careful imprecision so that until line 6 a reader is not sure whether the lifetime is the speaker's or the beloved's. Other—and logically irrelevant— senses of *term* are dimly reflected in (a) *end* (line 6—for *term* meaning "end," "termination," see Spenser, *Shepherd's Calendar*, December, 127: "now my yeare drawes to his latter terme"); (b) *state* (line 7—"a term," as an abbreviated form of "a term of life" or "a term of years," also indicated both "a legal right of temporary possession" and the estate so possessed [*OED* gives this from 1592: "A particular estate which is but onely a terme, is an estate determinable by limitation of time"]); and (c) *title* (line 11). Note also that "terms" and "state" are often synonyms meaning "condition" (*OED* gives this from 1580: "He found the common-wealth turmoiled with seditions . . . and . . . the house of Ægeus in very ill tearmes also"), and that "term" can mean "title," "name" (as in *MWW* II.ii.260–64: "I shall not only receive this . . . wrong, but stand under the adoption of abominable terms. . . . Terms! names! Amaimon sounds well; Lucifer well. . . . But cuckold! Wittol! Cuckold! the devil himself hath not such a name"). *assurèd mine* (1) certainly mine; (2) legally mine, signed over to me, conveyed to me by deed (*OED* exemplifies the specifically legal use of "assure" by quoting a decree from 1572: "All such Houses and Grounds may bee granted dimised and assured"); (3) pledged to me ("yours assured" was as common in closings of sixteenth-century letters as "Yours sincerely" is now [for examples see John Cheke's letter to Thomas Hoby, dated 1557 and prefaced to Hoby's *Courtier* in 1561, John Lyly's letter to the scholars of Oxford prefaced to *Euphues* in 1581, and the catalogue of model subscriptions Angel Day offered aspiring letter writers on pages 27–29 of *The English Secretorie* in 1586; for Shakespeare's contemporaries this phrase may well have had the mocking tone that "you are sincerely mine" would have today). The phrase is colored by the specialized use of "assured" meaning "betrothed," "engaged for marriage" (see *John* II.i. 534–35 and *CofE* III.ii.137–38: "this drudge . . . laid claim to me . . . swore I was assur'd to her")—and thus gives an echo of "till death us depart" (see 11.2, note) to *For term of life* and suggestions of the marriage service to the line at large.

3. *stay* remain (note, however, two senses of "stay" that are irrelevant to this line but relate to the diction of the sonnet at large: "stay" was already a legal term—as in "to stay an execution," and "to stay upon" meant "to rely on"—as in Isaiah 48:2: "They . . . staie them selves upon the God of Israel").

4. *depends upon* (1) is contingent upon (the most usual modern sense, as in "it all depends on the weather"); (2) is entirely sustained by, is dependent upon

for support—like a servant or other retainer. (The expression has extra pertinence here because "depend" is also a legal term (compare "pending"; *OED*
gives this from 1523: "Every matter, cause, and contention now dependyng
. . . before any of the sayde archebishops . . ."), and because the context of
assurèd activates overtones of *depends upon* meaning "is confident of," "relies
on" (as in *JC* III.i.217–18: "Will you be prick'd in number of our friends, / Or
shall we on, and not depend on you?")

5–8. This quatrain is so constructed as to seem more straightforward and
more obvious than it is. *Then* suggests that the assertion it introduces follows
logically from the assertions in quatrain one. In fact line 5 is indeed a reasonable
summary conclusion from lines 1 and 2, and the substance of line 6 restates the
essence of lines 3 and 4. But line 5 does not follow logically from lines 3 and 4,
the lines it follows physically and syntactically (if loss of the beloved leads
inevitably to loss of life, then there is need to fear). *To fear the worst* (already a
stock phrase—as in *RIII* II.iii.31 and *T&C* III.ii.70) suggests "to fear death," to
fear the specific danger presented in the two lines immediately preceding; on the
other hand, *the worst of wrongs* echoes the apparent situation and the key word
in *do thy worst*, the phrase that began line 1, and thus refocuses the reader's
attention on *wrongs* like the one specified in line 1. Line 6 presents a new way of
evaluating the diagnosis in lines 3 and 4, and thus justifies the assertion in line
5 (an assertion which *Then* had signalled as already self-evident). However, in
the process of adding logic to the freefloating pertinences in line 5, line 6 itself
requires that its reader take sound for substance: a reader can neither be sure
what sort of wrongs *the least of them* might be, nor, as he reads through the
smooth and neatly echoing syntax and diction, can he feel any call to stop and
guess that, if *the worst of wrongs* is the abandonment of the speaker by the lover,
then *the least of them* might be some lesser slight. He is not even called upon to
reject "death" as a sense for *worst*, although it no longer makes sense. Lines 7
and 8 leap to yet another new attitude: *I see a better state to me belongs* introduces a metaphor of religious awakening (continued in *happy to die* in line 12 and
vestigially echoed in *blessèd* in line 13). The same lines at the same time sound
like further explanation and justification of the earlier assertion of fearlessness;
they also continue the metaphors of quatrain 1 (see the notes on *state* below),
and echo its diction: the "depend on" construction in line 8 repeats the one in
4; *better* (7) contrasts with and balances *worst* (1,5); *belongs* (7) echoes and
plays on *longer* (3); and *Than* (8) echoes and contrasts with *Then* three lines
earlier (Renaissance spelling made no regular distinction between "then" and
"than"; Q gives "then" in lines 3,5, and 8; see 16.4,8, note). The reader's
experience of this quatrain is accidentally summed up in the first line of the next:
the minds of both speaker and reader are inconstant and perfectly unvexed by
that fact.

7. *state* condition (manner of existing—as in 29.2 and 64.9; state of health
(as in 118.11); and spiritual condition (as in the expression "state of grace").
The general context of possession, property, and law and the particular context
of *belongs* evoke strong suggestions of "state" as a common variant on "estate"
(as "tayle" is on "entail" in the first quotation in the notes to line 2), and mean-

ing "legal title to property" (as in *FQ* V.xi.3) or "property," "estate" (as in *MWW* III.iv.5–6: "My state being gall'd with my expense, / I seek to heal it only by his wealth"). *State* meaning "social status," "rank" (as in *Lucrece* 1006) also pertains. *to me belongs* (1) is my rightful possession; (2) is appropriate for me (compare 23.14 and 58.11). The juxtaposition of *belongs* with *state* in this context of dependency activates further overtones of both words: "to belong to" meant "to be a retainer of, a dependent of" (as in *TN* V.i.7: "Belong you to the Lady Olivia, friends?") and a great man's retinue of attendants was called his "state" (*OED* gives this from 1617: "Our new lord keeper goes with great state, having a world of followers put upon him").

8. *humor* (1) temporary state of mind, mood (as in *MWW* II.iii.71: "See what humour he is in"); (2) whim, caprice (as in *V&A* 850: "the humour of fantastic wits"); (3) nature, temperament (as in 91.5; see 45.8, note).

9. *vex* harass, afflict, annoy. *inconstant* vacillating (with contextual overtones of inconstancy in love). *mind* (1) attitude (as in *2Gent* I.ii.33: "I would I knew his mind"); (2) manner of thinking; (3) disposition, humor (as in *2Gent* V.iv.108–09: "It is a lesser blot, modesty finds, / Women to change their shapes than men their minds"; and III.ii.58–59: "You are already Love's firm votary / And cannot soon revolt and change your mind"); (4) intention, purpose, desire (as in *JC* II.ii.95–96: "If you shall send them word you will not come, / Their minds may change"). *vex me with inconstant mind* afflict me by means of—or by virtue of—your inconstancy of mind. Note, however, that, although *OED* does not record it, *vex* seem to have had a special legal sense: "accuse falsely" or "accuse maliciously." In 1611 Cotgrave gave this gloss for *serment de colomnie*: "An oath taken . . . both by the plaintife that he sues not, and the defendant that he answers not, with any purpose to calumniate, or vex his adversarie, but because he imagines himselfe in the right." And this is Thomas Hobbes in Chapter 26 of *Leviathan* (1651), "Of Civill Lawes": "he that supposeth himself injured, . . . if he complaine before he consults with the Law, he does unjustly, and bewrayeth a disposition rather to vex other men, than to demand his own right" (p. 142). Shakespeare seems at least to allude to this special legal sense in *HVIII* V.iii.107 (where *vex* is used with reference to unjust charges against Cranmer) and in *RII* III.i.2–34; moreover, his ordinary uses of *vex* to mean "afflict" regularly occur in context of unjust accusations (see *TN* IV.ii.23, *Much Ado* II.ii.27, *RII* I.i.138, and *2HVI* I.iii.72.) (*OED* does cite related senses for "vexation" and "vexatious.") In context of the many legalisms in this sonnet, the logically unharnessed pertinence of *vex* in its special legal sense conjoins with the wanton inconstancy of the speaker's premises and the structural likeness of *vex me with* and "charge me with" to give overtones of "charge me with vacillation" ("charge me with having an inconstant mind"), to *vex me with inconstant mind*.

10. *Since that* in as much as. *on . . . doth lie* is staked on, depends on (as in *FQ* I.iii.12: "she fled as if her life upon the wager lay"). *revolt* change of allegiance or opinion (see *2Gent* III.ii.58–59, quoted above for *mind*).

11. *happy* (1) pleasing, delightful (i.e. joy–giving); (2) fortunate, lucky. *title* legal right to possession (usually used of real estate). *find* discover,

perceive the existence of (but with overtones of the various legal uses of *find* with reference to verdicts).

12. *Happy*   contented, willing. The word has special pertinence to *to die* and *blessèd-fair*: *happy* was a synonym for "blessed" (where Wiclif, the Bishops' Bible, Geneva, the Rheims Bible, and AV give "blessed" in James 1:25, Tyndale and Cranmer give "happy"); this sense of *happy* often described the souls of the virtuous dead (as in *RII* II.i.128–29: "My brother Gloucester . . . / Whom fair befall in heaven 'mongst happy souls"). (See also Shakespeare's plays on the Beatitudes in *Cymb* I.vi.6–9 and III.ii.57–60: "[Say] how far it is / To this same blessed Milford. And . . . / Tell me how Wales was made so happy as / T'inherit such a haven.")

13. *blessèd-fair*   (1) supremely endowed with beauty; (2) fairly blessed, well endowed with—lucky in—happiness, fortune, and worthiness. (The expression resists a precise gloss; the hyphen is a nearly standard editorial emendation, but it is minimally helpful in specifying the relation of *blessèd* and *fair*. See 53.12, note.) Note that *fair* was used substantively to mean "happiness" (see the lines from *RII* quoted for *happy*), and was often used specifically to indicate purity, spotlessness, the absence of blots (see *OED*, III, 7, 9). Note also that *fair* and *fear* apparently sounded enough alike for Shakespeare and Lyly to pun on them; see Kökeritz, p. 106—citing *V&A* 1083–86.

14. Ingram and Redpath note that the syntax here imitates the uncertainty it asserts by being unclear whether it refers to a possible future situation or a chronic one. (Compare the uncertainty of tense in 89, 90, and 97; and see 93.3, note.)   *yet*   (1) nevertheless; (2) as yet. See 93.1 and note.

SONNET 93

The thematic common denominator of this sonnet—simultaneous constancy and change, fixed identity and lack of it—is imitated in a sort of stylistic double life that is evident throughout the poem: in its diction (*live* means "behave," "conduct one's life" in line 1 and "dwell," "exist," and "survive" in line 5; note also the juxtaposition of *ever* in line 10 and *Whate'er* in line 11); in its sounds (note, for instance, the phonetic plays of *live* and *love* in lines 1–3—play which reaches an attenuated climax at line 10 in the baroque relationship of *love* with *dwell*, a phonetically irrelevant synonym for the phonetically relevant "live"; or the *v* sounds in the fourth syllables of lines 1–3, 5, 13 [though technically the *v* in *Eve's* is part of the third syllable, it slurs into the fourth], and 14); in its structure (many lines and phrases modify what precedes them and subsequently act separately as new beginnings; similarly, the quatrains simultaneously are and are not distinct syntactic units [lines 7–10 are as distinct a syntactic unit as lines 5–8 or 9–12]); and in the responses it evokes from a reader (the courtly compliment begun at line 9 follows a smooth track marked by the word *sweet*, but emerges in the couplet as a stern moral warning against hypocrisy; note also the perfectly neutralized conflict, contrast, and contradiction inherent in *still* and *altered* in line 3). Summary examples are provided by *For there*, the first two syllables of line 5, and *Therefore*, the same syllables reversed at the beginning of line 6; and by a similar chiasmic echo of the next two syllables of line 6, *in that*, by *That in* in line 10. In line 5, *For* seems to introduce an explanation of something in lines 1–4—particularly since it is coupled with *there*, which momentarily echoes the topic of place in line 4 (*For there can live no hatred*, "For no hatred can live there"). However, *in thine eye* fixes *there* as a substanceless anticipatory subject found in idioms like "there is—" (compare "There dwelt a man in Babylon"—*TN* II.iii.75—where "There" carries no substance whatever, although it appears in a context of place). In the next line *Therefore* both renders *For* superfluous ("Since no hatred can live . . . , therefore . . ."), and dictates that the assertion introduced by *For* must pertain only to what follows it. Line 6 continues: *Therefore in that*; ultimately *know thy change* makes "by means of your eye" ("by your expression"), the only admissible meaning for *in that,* but the phrase can be synonymous with *For* (compare *2HVI* III.i.257: "Let him die, in that he is a fox") and, like *there* in line 5, is a potential indicator of "place where" (as in *Much Ado* II.iii.235: "there's a double meaning in that"). Play on place continues quietly through the next four lines, in each of which *in* has a slightly different meaning, and culminates in a return to the tonic in *That in thy face . . . dwell* in line 10, the line that mirrors *in that* in line 6 and in which *in* finally does indicate place for the first time since line 5. (Compare the operation of *in* in 15, 25, and 35; and see 78, headnote.) Line 10 is both a reprise of line 5 and a function of the new and still developing creation-Eden theme initiated at line 9. Everything changes and nothing does.

1. *So*   in the following manner (momentarily, however, *So* can seem to mean "therefore"—see *so*, line 2, and *Therefore*, line 6—and to introduce a conclusion based on 92.14).   *supposing thou art true*   The phrase describes the lifestyle indicated by *So*, but, as Ingram and Redpath observe, it can momentarily "mislead, by suggesting the sense 'if we assume you are true.' "

2. *so*   (1) in consequence; (2) so that, in order that.   *love's face*   the appearance of affection, [your] loving facade, the show of love (see *thy show*, line 14). (Ingram and Redpath say, "The image is of the face of the beloved; the idea is of the outward show of love.")

2,3. *husband, altered*   See 115.6, note.

3. *May*   (1) can; (2) might perhaps. (In its imprecision about whether the beloved's defection is a fact or a fear, this poem duplicates the effect derived from confusion of tenses in 89, 90, and 92: the reader's semantic uncertainty is similar to the lover's uncertainty about the beloved.)   *still*   (1) always, forever; (2) nevertheless, even so; (3) continue to (see 81.13).   *seem love to me*   appear to me to be affection toward me. (In effect, *to me* acts twice.)   *though altered new*   though newly changed [into something] new. (In effect, *new* acts twice; the syntax makes the adverbial sense dominant, but the content and context of the phrase invoke the elliptical addition in which *new* describes the necessary effect of change; compare *Temp* I.ii.81–83: "new created / The creatures . . . / Or else new form'd 'em." As to the phrase at large, the logic of the described situation dictates that it modify only *love*; in the logic of the syntax, however,

the phrase modifies *face* at least as much as it does *love*. The momentary uncertainty about what is and what is not altered epitomizes both the style and substance of the poem.)

4. *Thy looks* (1) your loving glances; (2) your outward appearance (i.e. your physical presence—what appears to be your real self—as opposed to your thoughts and feelings). (The context of *love's face* sustains the first meaning, which would ordinarily call for "toward me," "directed toward me"; the second is called up by *with*.)   *heart*   affections (but with overtones of the familiar paradox inherent in the literal sense of *heart*: no bodily organ can literally negotiate in physical independence of the body it sustains and that sustains it; see 22.5–14, 24.2, and notes).

5. *in thine eye* (1) within your eye (*in* used in its simplest literal sense and indicating the *eye* as a potential dwelling place); (2) in the expression of your eyes, in your appearance (*in* meaning "as an adjunct of," "as a quality of"). (The phrase also contains a momentary and flattering suggestion of "in your presence"—as in *Ham* IV.iv.6: "We shall express our duty in his eye"; in context of *to me*, "in my judgment," *in thine eye* also carries unharnessed overtones of "in the eye of" meaning "in the opinion of"—see 55.11 and *CofE* II.ii.114: "pleasing in thine eye"; note also the gentle but complex play of relationships between *eye* and *looks*.)

7. *looks* (1) facial expressions; (2) appearance.   *false heart's*   See 24.13–14, note.

8. *moods* (1) facial expressions, visible signs of a person's actual state of mind; (2) looks of moodiness—of irritability or depression. (The sense is clear and, in effect, specific, but only because the context requires that *moods* be understood as if it were "signs of moods.")   *wrinkles*   facial wrinkles like those made by a smile or a frown. (Wrinkles, of course, are also signs of age, and thus the word carries an additional incidental complementary counterweight to the generally negative drift of the lines; Shakespeare plays with both meanings in *MofV* I.i.80: "With mirth and laughter let old wrinkles come." "Wrinkle" also meant "trick" or "cunning device," a sense obviously pertinent to the hiding of *the false heart's history*; *OED* gives this example from the mid–sixteenth century: "Every wrynkle they have to cover and worke disceit with al." In this context, where an accusation of hypocrisy lurks behind the compliments, one further sense of "wrinkle" is pertinent, although it does not affect the immediate meaning of this line: "Wrinkle" meant "moral blemish." That sense appears to originate in the Pauline phrase "without spot or wrinkle" in Ephesians 5:27 [quoted in the headnote to sonnet 36], and, as the *OED* examples testify, does not appear to have achieved much independence of its Biblical context. Ephesians 5:22–23 concerns the proper relations of husbands and wives, a context pertinent to the opening simile of this poem. On Shakespeare's mastery of Ephesians 5, see 36, headnote.)   *strange*   unfamiliar (in all its common senses; see the notes on *strangely* in 49.5 and *look strange* in 89.8; and, since *strange* appears here in context of "looks," note that "to look strange" meaning "to look at a person as if one did not know him" was a very common idiom).

9. *heav'n in*   = pronounced "hev nin."

11. *workings*   activities, deeds.

10–11.   I retain Q's punctuation. Line 11 acts twice: first it modifies lines 9 and 10; then it modifies line 12.

12. *should*   would (as in line 10).   *thence*   (1) from there (i.e. from the face *or* from the mind and heart); (2) from that [reason], therefore (as in 111.5–6). *but*   except (contrast the conjunction in line 9).

13–14.   Compare the substance, diction, and wit of 69.13–14.

13. *Eve's apple*   The external appearance of apples was proverbially deceptive; see Tilley A300 and *Mof V* I.iii.96–97: "A goodly apple rotten at the heart./ O, what a goodly outside falsehood hath." The apple in Genesis, which came of a tree that "was pleasant to the eyes" (3:6), exemplifies that truth in a metaphysical dimension. The story of Adam and Eve is broadly pertinent to the general context provided by *heav'n in thy creation, deceivèd husband*, and the problem of knowing good from evil.   *grow*   become (but enhanced by the pertinence of its literal meaning to the botanical context inherent in *apple*).

14.   Contrast 94.1–2.   *virtue*   (1) inherent quality, essence; (2) goodness, virtuousness (compare the juxtaposition of the two senses in *Tim* III.v.7–8: "I am an humble suitor to your virtues; / For pity is the virtue of the law").   *answer not*   does not match, does not correspond to (as in *3HVI* V.vi.78–79: "Since the heavens have shap'd my body so, / Let hell make crook'd my mind to answer it").   *show*   appearance (as in 70.13).

5–14.   These lines embody the commonplaces of a familiar Neo-Platonic dispute; for example, in the last conversation of Castiglione's *Courtier* one of Bembo's companions points out that there are "many wicked men that have the comlinesse of a beautifull countenance, and it seemeth nature hath so shaped them, because they may bee the readier to deceive, and that this amiable looke were like a baite that covereth the hooke." Bembo, however, replies that "beautie commeth of God, and is like a circle, the goodnesse whereof is the Centre. And therefore, as there can be no circle without a centre, no more can beautie be without goodnesse. Whereupon doth very seldom an ill soule dwell in a beautifull bodie. And therefore is the outwarde beautie a true signe of the inward goodnesse, and in bodies this comelines is imprinted more and lesse (as it were) for a marke of the soule, whereby she is outwardly knowne: as in trees, in which the beautie of the buddes giveth a testimonie of the goodness of the fruite" (tr. Thomas Hoby [1561], pp. 308–09 in the Everyman's Library text [London, 1928]).

SONNET 94

Like 93, this sonnet is a stylistic mirror of the speaker's indecision. Here, however, the effects are grosser and have so impinged on the consciousness of readers that this is the most frequently interpreted of the sonnets. The sentences wander from attribute to attribute in such a way that a reader's response to "them" who are the subject of lines 1–8 swings repeatedly back and forth between negative and positive: *They that have pow'r to hurt* invites a negative response; the addition of *and will do none* invites a dramatically opposed positive response. The chilliness of *thing* and *show* in line 2 leads into a list of repellent qualities: *as stone, Unmoved, cold*, in lines 3 and 4; but being slow to temptation (line 4) can be an admirable quality and becomes one when the next line delivers the reader into a Biblical context . . . , and so on.

1. *Posse et nolle, nobile*, " to be able to do [harm] and to be unwilling to do it is noble," was proverbial (Tilley, H170). *will do* choose to do. *none* no hurt (the reader abstracts the pronoun from the verb; compare *HVIII* III.i.171–72: "The King loves you; / Beware you lose it not"; and see Schmidt, p. 1421).

2. *the thing they most do show* what their appearance suggests they are most likely to do.

1–2. Contrast 93.14 and the couplet of this poem.

3–4. Martin (pp. 34–35) notes that these lines suggest not only that "they" are cold as stone but also that they are like a lodestone: "others are drawn to them as metal to the magnet, 'they' like the magnet remain motionless." Compare the play on "adamant" used to mean as impenetrably hard stone and "adamant" used to mean "magnet" in *MND* II.i.195: "You draw me, you hard-hearted adamant." (The now-atrophied metaphor in which we refer to "personal magnetism" and "attractive qualities" was already traditional.)

4. *cold* The Q spelling is "could"; see the supplementary note on p. 580.

5. *rightly* (1) truly, indeed; (2) in proper manner; but, in the context of an ongoing evaluation, the dominant sense is (3) rightfully, justly, by right (as in *FQ* II.ii.1: "rightly . . . reprove / Of rudenesse"). Ingram and Redpath reject this third sense on the curious ground that Shakespeare does not elsewhere use "rightly" to mean "justly." Neither Shakespeare nor his reader can be supposed to have known or recognized such an argument for limiting the sense of a word. Moreover, if there were reason to believe that uniqueness argues the nonexistence of unique instances, one might note that two of Shakespeare's twenty-five other uses of "rightly" pun on "justly" (*1HIV* II.iv.315–16; *2HIV* V.ii.65–66), and that seven others appear in suggestive contexts of justice.   *inherit* come into possession of (the sense it has in Matt. 5:5, the famous sentence that this line so inappropriately echoes: "Blessed are the meke: for they shal inherite the earth"; however, usage was already narrowing toward the limited context of property, particularly real estate, received as the result of a death—see 146.7).   *heaven's graces* (1) heavenly qualities of attractiveness; (2) God-given good fortune, the favor of the gods. (In context of an echo of Christ's Sermon on the Mount, the juxtaposition of "heaven" and "grace" would suggest Christian grace, but the plural, *graces*, has only secular meaning. By Shakespeare's time the metaphoric nature of "grace" in love sonnets was so nearly forgotten that, even juxtaposed to "heaven," its sense is secular. Moreover, since lines 2 and 3 are an excellent description of courtly "daunger," the reader is prepared to take *heaven's graces* as an atrophied courtly love metaphor —one for which *nature's riches* in line 6 is an exact substitute.)

6. *husband* guard, protect. (The "husband from" construction is an extension of "to husband" maening "to manage with thrift" as in this *OED* example from 1574: "The office of the husband is, to husband the goods and of the wife to governe the familie." Note that the context of a love poem invokes

unharnessed overtones of "to husband" in its marital senses, "to marry" and "to get a husband for" [see the noun use in 93.2]; also note that, since "to husband" is ordinarily used in reference to tilling and managing agricultural land, *husband* joins *inherit* to prepare the way for the estate metaphor of lines 7 and 8.)   *nature's*   In context of *husband* and *expense* the obvious primary meaning of *nature's riches* may have been colored by the sexual senses of *nature*; see 109.9, 10,12,14, note.   *expense*   (1) expenditure; (2) waste (see 129.1, note).

7. *their faces*   (1) their visages (faces in its simplest sense); (2) the appearance they present, their *show*, their "facades" (see *love's face* in 93.2, and note the *face/place* rhyme in 93.2–4).

8. *but stewards*   only custodians, mere hired managers. (Note that, in keeping with the self-contradictory spirit of the poem, the lords and owners husband riches and thus are characterized by exactly the defining function of stewards, the group with which they are contrasted; in fact the noun "husband" was a synonym for "steward"—*OED* quotes a letter from 1475 in which Sir John Paston offers to act as his mother's "hosbonde and balyff.")   *their*   Shakespeare leaves the antecedent unclear: the syntax of the line and the logic implied by *faces* as the objects possessed favor *Others*, and the logic of the estate metaphor favors "them," *the lords and owners*.   *their excellence*   In his extended discussion of this sonnet (*Some Versions of Pastoral*, revised ed. [New York: New Directions, 1968], p. 93), William Empson pointed out an echo of "your excellence" (i.e. "your excellency"), a title of honor by which a steward might refer to *lords and owners*; compare *1HVI* V.i.4: "They humbly sue unto your Excellence."

9. *The summer's flow'r*   Although *flow'r* must be understood in its simple literal sense, note that this phrase is a literal translation of the Latin *flos aetatis*, "virginity," "maidenhead" (see 60.9, note; Catullus, LXII.39–48; and, perhaps, 21.7). All commentators properly equate the singular, inanimate, frail, transitory *summer's flow'r* with the plural, animate (though, in another sense, *Unmovèd*), steadfast, cold "them" that have pow'r; Shakespeare makes the equation by rhyme: *They that have pow'r/The summer's flow'r*. (The rhyme sound reappears in *sourest* [dissyllabic] in line 13.)   *to*   with respect to its relation to (compare the use of "unto" in Romans 10:12: "For there is no difference betwene the Jewe & the Grecian: for he that is Lord over all, is riche unto all, that call on him"). (The general idea is that the summer benefits, but *to* carries suggestions of "in the estimation of" [as in *JC* II.i.289: "dear to me"], and perhaps "to the length of," for the duration of" [*OED*, 6]; compare the use of *Above* in 86.6.)

9–10. Contrast sonnet 54 and *V&A* 166: "Things growing to themselves are growth's abuse."

10. *to itself*   (1) by itself, alone; (2) for itself, for its own benefit (see 54.11, note). Willen and Reed suggestively exemplify the usage with Romans 14:7–8: "For none of us liveth to him self, nether doeth anie dye to him self./For whether we live, we live unto the Lord: or whether we dye, we dye unto the Lord." The whole of Romans, which, in the English translations, is particularly rich in unusual and confusing "to" constructions, is curiously relevant to this sonnet.

Paul there discusses justification by faith as opposed to justification by works: "Now to him that worketh, the wages is not counted by favour, but by dette, / But to him that worketh not, but beleveth in him that justifieth the ungodlie, his faith is counted for righteousnes. . . . the promes that he shulde be the heire of the worlde, was not given to Abraham, or to his seed, through the Law, but through the righteousnes of faith" (4:4,5,13). Like the Sermon on the Mount (Matt. 7:1,16–20), Romans is much concerned with judgment and the bases for judgments. Moreover, the topic of justification invites a reader to judge among lifestyles. However, Paul, who acknowledges the confusions and mis-conceptions he engenders (e.g. 7:6–13, and Chapter 3), denies his reader the possibility of judging. The denial is both specific ("But why doest thou judge thy brother? or why doest thou despise thy brother? for we shal all appeare before the judgment seat of Christ . . . Let us not therefore judge one another anie more . . ." [14:10,13]), and stylistic ("He that observeth the day, ob-serveth it to the Lord: and he that observeth not the day, observeth it not to the Lord. He that eateth, eateth to the Lord: for he giveth God thankes: and he that eateth not, eateth not to the Lord, and giveth God thankes" [14:6]).   *only* This word first modifies *to itself* (Ingram and Redpath cite *Measure* II.ii.209: "Novelty is only in request"), and then modifies *live and die*: "Though it do no more than merely live and die by itself alone." (There is also a play—visible in Q, which gives the common Renaissance spelling "onely"—on "solitary"; *OED* exemplifies this adjectival sense with this from 1500: "Hit is not good man onely to be"; see also *FQ* IV.viii.28.7; 1.10; and 141.9, note.

12. *basest* humblest (but see line 11 and 96.6, note). *weed* The primary sense is botanical, as in 124.4. However, *outbraves* was as commonly used to mean "surpass in fine array" as it was to mean "oppose valiantly" (compare 12.14) or simply "surpass" (see *brave* in 15.8 and *bravery* in 34.4; *OED* gives this from John Gerard's *Herball* of 1597: "The Lillies of the field outbraved him"). The pun on "weed" meaning "garment" (see 2.4, note, and 76.6) is also sus-tained by the context of the Sermon on the Mount established in line 5; lines on the self-sufficiency of flowers suggest a later section of that sermon, Matt. 6:28–29: "And why care ye for raiment? Learne, how the lilies of the field do growe: they labour not, nether spinne, / Yet . . . even Solomon in all his glorie was not arayed like one of these." Here the flower in its corrupted finery is to the humbly dressed weed as Solomon is to the uncorrupted lilies in the Sermon on the Mount. (The Sermon on the Mount is also reflected in sonnet 96.)   *his* its (see 73.10, note).

11, 12. *base infection, basest weed* Martin (p. 32) suggests that the repetition of *base* implies a degree of equation between *infection* and *weed*, and that the flower thus becomes corrupt by associating with the weed.

13. The line echoes the post-classical Latin proverb *optima corrupta pessima* (Tilley, C668), which Owen Feltham glossed as "the best things corrupted, become the worst" (*Resolves*, XXX—"Of Women," 1st edition, [1623?], 2d, 1628).   *by their deeds* Martin (pp. 38–39) notes that the only deeds suggested for "them" in lines 1–8 and the flower in lines 9–12 are "non-deeds," acts of omission, "these too, like vigorous action, have their consequences."

14. The difficulties inherent in comprehending this ostensibly simple line make it an emblem of the whole poem: (1) The line acts as a metaphoric restatement of line 13 and presents *Lilies* as an example of "the best"; "once corrupted and rotting, the most admired of flowers are inferior to healthy weeds." (2) This line echoes, and thus includes the idea expressed by a proverb on uncorrupted lilies (Tilley, L297), a proverb incompatible with the premises implied in *optima corrupta pessima*: "The lily is fair in show but foul in smell" (it does not do the thing it most does show). (3) The line also invites its reader to understand it as saying that rotting lilies smell worse than rotting weeds (anyone who has been around a church in the week after Easter knows that, however fresh lilies may smell, rotting lilies smell worse than other rotting plants); the line thus includes the idea that a vicious and corrupt creature that once surpassed others in virtue will to the same degree surpass others in vice (and culpability —*noblesse oblige*). (Line 14 appears verbatim in *The Reign of King Edward the Third*, an anonymous play printed in 1596. Some scholars have claimed all or part of the play for Shakespeare; Rollins gives details, *Variorum* 1, 234–35.)

SONNET 95

1. *lovely* (1) beauteous; (2) worthy to be loved, loveable (see 54.13).

2. *canker* cankerworm (see 35.4, note). *rose* Q has "Rose" (see 1.2, note).

3. Q's question mark presumably occurs because the exclamatory sentence beginning *How* is structured like a question (see 97.2,4, note). Q is not consistent about using question marks for such sentences; Q puts exclamation points after lines 4 and 12, both of which conclude interrogative-like exclamations.

2–4. Cankers attack roses in the bud—when they are still immature and show promise of greater beauty to cóme. Cankers destroy buds from within; the extent of devastation is not visible until the matured rose opens. A cankered bud is as beautiful and as promising as a healthy one; only a small hole, a small *spot*, betrays the presence of the worm. Compare 93.13–14.

4. *sweets* (1) perfumes, sweet odors (*OED* cites sonnet 25 of Drayton's *Idea's Mirrour* [1594]: "the ayre . . . exhald refined sweet"; see also 99.2); (2) sweetnesses, pleasing qualities, delights (in general). *enclose* Q gives "inclose"; for a justification of the modern form, see 37.7, note.

4,9. *sins, vices* See 112.5,8,10,14, note.

6. *lascivious* = trisyllabic by syncopation: "la-sive-yus." *sport* (1) merrymaking, diversions, high jinks; (2) sexual exploits, amorous sport (see "act of sport" in *Oth* II.i.226 and "intercepted in your sport" in *Titus* II.iii.80; the sense is very common in Shakespeare; compare *sport* in 96.2 and *sportive* in 121.6.

7. *but* except.

7–8. Q punctuates thus: "Cannot dispraise, but in a kind of praise, / Naming thy name, blesses an ill report." Most editors adopt the punctuation given in the present text. Since Renaissance punctuation is a reliable guide to neither an author's nor a Renaissance reader's perceptions of the logical relationships among sentence parts, there are no sure grounds for preferring either punctuation. Ingram and Redpath analyze the alternative effects. The Q punctuation, they say,

> antithesizes 'dispraise' against 'bless' (i.e. censure against sanctification), and oversteps the more obvious antithesis of 'dispraise . . . kind of praise', though without destroying the paradox. The usual punctuation gives a reading of line 8 immediately acceptable to a modern ear, and eases the involution of the syntax by breaking the quatrain into 3 + 1. It leaves line 7 somewhat cryptic, but explains it by the syntactically isolated line 8. With the [Q] punctuation . . . , the sense is: 'The tongue that tells rich stories of your amours cannot really besmirch your reputation, but in effect only sanctifies the scandal by attaching your name to it.' With the usual [emended] punctuation the sense is: 'The tongue . . . can only censure your deeds by in a way praising them. To bring your name into such a story sanctifies the scandal.'

9. *mansion* dwelling place, house (with a play on "man"; see 146.6, note; compare *R&J* III.ii.26 and the elaborate plays on "manner"–"manor-house"– "man" in *LLL* I.i.200–06).

10. *for their habitation* for their abode. (Lines 9 and 10 echo the physics of the canker/bud simile: the canker inhabits the bud; the vices inhabit the beloved. However, the generous injustice by which the speaker's comparisons make the beloved a victim is more evident here because vices, having no will of their own, do not adopt but are adopted. Brent Cohen points out to me that, in a poem about "bad habits," *for their habitation* has suggestions of "as their habits [i.e. the *vices*, the bad habits, have habits]," or, by synesis, "to be the habits of." [Note that several of habitation's cognates had double reference to dwelling and to custom; *OED* gives Renaissance examples of "habit" meaning "dwelling place," "to habituate" meaning "to inhabit," and "to habitate" meaning "to habituate."] The general context of evils wrapped in beauty and *veil* in line 11 give extra pertinence to the first two syllables of habitation; for "habit" meaning "clothing," see 138.11 and note.)

11. *Where* The antecedent is *thee* in line 10; by speaking of a person as one would of a place Shakespeare confirms and gives energy to the metaphor initiated with *mansion*. *beauty's veil* The completed line requires understanding the phrase as "the veil provided by beauty," but "the veil that obscures beauty," the sense suggested by the construction, is momentarily possible.

12. *turns* Many editors emend to "turn," but the change is unnecessary and robs the syntax of its imitative qualities. At the beginning of the line *And* suggests that line 12 will parallel line 11, that—as *beauty's veil* was the subject of *doth cover*—*all things* and *turns* will be subject and verb of the new clause; such a reading is quite possible; third person plurals in *s* are reasonably common in Shakespeare; Abbott (par. 333) cites more than a dozen examples including *befits* in 41.3. On the other hand, plurals in *s* were never the norm, and, when *turns* appears, Shakespeare's reader, like a modern reader, may have found the sentence he seemed to be reading suddenly transformed into one where *all things* parallels *every blot* and *veil* is the subject of *turns*: "beauty's veil covers

every blot and turns all things to fair." *that eyes can see* The phrase acts primarily to stress the inclusiveness of *all* (compare such hyperbolic formulas as "everything in sight"); but it also acts restrictively and contains a reminder that all that is visible is not all there is: the cankered bud is beautiful to the eye but corrupt within.

13. *large* (1) great; (2) extensive, unrestricted; (3) licentious (as in 135.5 and *A&C* III.vi.93–94: "th' adulterous Antony, most large / In his abomina-tions"). Compare *R&J* II.iv.92: "Thou wouldst else have made thy tale large"; in both the line from *R&J* and the present line *large* also carries suggestions of publicness (as opposed to privateness; note the potential for insignificant word-play in the fact that "private" and *privilege* are cognates).

13,14. *privilege, ill, edge* Note that line 14 echoes not only the last syllable of *privilege* but its second syllable as well (*privilege* is trisyllabic).

14. Compare 94.14. Landry (p. 195) describes this line as "a phallic proverb," and cites *Ham* III.ii.244–45 where Hamlet's reply to Ophelia's "You are keen, my lord," is "It would cost you a groaning to take off mine edge" (see also "hard" in *HV* V.ii.294, *knife* in *R&J* II.iv.195, and *usest* in 40.6; note *all things* in line 12, and see 26.1–14, 20.12, notes). Shakespeare's homemade proverb resembles the traditional "Everything is the worse for the wearing" (Tilley, W207), and "Iron with often handling is worn to nothing" (Tilley, I92). *his* its (but see 73.10, note).

SONNET 96

1. *wantonness* (1) capriciousness, high-spirited playfulness; exuberance, extravagance (as in *John* IV.i.15–16: "Young gentlemen would be as sad as night, / Only for wantonness"); (2) sexual promiscuity, lechery.

2. *gentle* aristocratic, suitable for and usual in a gentleman (and thus not dishonorable). *sport* (1) amusement, recreation, diversion, wantonness (in the first sense above); (2) wantonness (in the second sense above); compare *sport* in 95.6.

3. *Of more and less* by the great and by the humble, by all classes, by "gentle and simple" (for examples of this last synonymous phrase, see *OED* s.v. "sim-ple," B.1).

4. "You make the faults that resort to you into graces." (The gloss reflects the sense inherent in the clarifying analogy in lines 5 and 6. However, as line 4 is read its contorted word order complicates comprehension by opening the way for consideration of the syntactically possible but idiomatically improbable read-ing, "You make the graces that resort to you into faults." The line may have been further complicated by the sound of "false graces" in *Thou mak'st faults graces,* a momentary misapprehension that would anticipate the concern with *truth* and falsehood in the next two quatrains; see 138.14, note—on the pronun-ciation of *faults* and "false.") *to thee resort* See 95.9–10.

6–12. Like sonnet 94, these lines reflect themes and metaphors from the Ser-mon on the Mount: "Enter in at the streicte gate: for it is the wide gate, and broad waye that leadeth to destruction. . . . Beware of false prophetes, which come to you in shepes clothing, but inwardely they are ravening wolves" (Matt. 7:13,15).

6. *basest* (1) least valuable, lowest in worth; (2) falsest, least genuine (for "base" meaning "counterfeit" see Hulme, p. 284; also see 100.4, note—on "base" meaning "dark"). *jewel* = dissyllabic; see 129.4, note. Also note the incidental harmony of -*wel, will,* and *well* (see 112.3, note).

7. *errors* Prefaced by *those, errors* refers to the youthful peccadilloes of the first lines and has a meaning close to that of its Latin root: "wanderings," "deviations from the straight and narrow path of sober virtue." However, as one moves on into line 8, *truths* translates the sense of *errors* to "falsehoods," the proper opposite of *truths.* The second half of line 8 invokes another shift in one's understanding of *errors*, a paradoxical shift in two logically incompatible directions at once; the first 6 lines of the poem suggest two pertinent opposites to *true things*: the previous contrast between youthful high spirits and truly wicked behavior suggests that the opposition of *errors* and *true things* is between apparent and real viciousness (that the beloved's innocent behavior will be mistaken for the true evil it resembles); the contrast previously implied between base jewels and valuable ones suggests that *true things* contrast with *errors* as genuine jewels do to imitations or cheap deceptive substitutes (that the beloved's evil ways will look like virtue). The signification of *errors*, thus, meanders from "mistakes made by the beloved" toward "mistakes of judgment by those who watch his behavior"; *errors* describes both the actions judged and the judgments. Our understanding of *errors* is further complicated because the lines permit no distinction among peccadilloes mistaken for true crimes, faults mistaken for true graces, and shams mistaken for what is genuine.

8. *translated* transformed (as in *MND* III.i.109: "Bless thee, Bottom, bless thee! Thou art translated"). *for* to be.

9–12. The thinking behind this quatrain is traditional; see the first of the excerpts from *Courtier* in 93.5–14, note.

9. *stern* i.e. not wanton like the frisking youth described in lines 1 and 2 but grim in both appearance and intent.

10. *If like a lamb he could* This construction appears to be other than it is; syntactic habit momentarily causes a reader to mistake the nature of the clause (in much the way he might be fooled by a wolf in sheep's clothing): the syntax indicates that the action to be designated will be lamb-like (compare the standard use of the construction in *Ham* II.ii.200: "If, like a crab, you could go backward"); however, since lambs have no power to transform themselves, and since any reader knows the relation of wolves to lambs and all about the proverbial wolves in sheep's clothing (Tilley, W614), common sense dictates that *like* be understood as if it were "unto those of" and translates the line to "If he could transform his looks so as to look like a lamb."

11–12. These lines present still another example of simultaneous equation and distinction. Line 11 carefully parallels line 9, and the likeness of line 12 (*If . . . -ate*), to line 10 (*If . . . -ate*), seems to continue the parallel. The various structural and phonetic equations encourage a sense of exact analogy in which the logical distinction between *could* and *wouldst* (paired phonetically and by their identical grammatical functions) is overwhelmed; *wouldst*, thus, muffles the crucial distinction it signals: unlike the wolf, the beloved has the power to mislead, has that "power to hurt," and can use it at will; contrast 94.1–2.

11. *lead away* (1) lead astray, seduce; (2) deceive.

12. *the strength of all thy state* Ingram and Redpath gloss this phrase as "all the glamour at your command," and that is indeed the general sense a reader receives. The phrase does not, however, have any solid content; a variety of meanings of *state* pertain here (see 64.9,10; 92.7, and notes), but *state* is a neutral word that takes its specificity from its context. This phrase has none to give; the inscrutability of the word *state* here is emblematic of the whole poem; the poem offers no reliable way to know or evaluate the beloved's state. Q puts a question mark at the end of line 12; see 95.3, note.

14. *being* = monosyllabic, as in 50.8.

13–14. These lines are also the couplet to sonnet 36. Most editors have speculated that their presence results from some sort of accident—either a printer's error or a printer's effort to find a conclusion for a sonnet incomplete in his copy text. (Rollins summarizes the speculation, *Variorum* I, 238.) We will probably never know for certain how the lines came to be used twice. Some editors argue that the couplet is inappropriate here, but sudden changes of approach are characteristic of sonnets. In his edition of 1936 Tucker Brooke suggested that the repetition was intentional. Brooke based his faith in the hypothetical narrative he was concocting from the sonnets. One may more safely argue that Shakespeare here purposely repeated the couplet of another sonnet on the grounds that this final repetition merely enlarges on the thematic and stylistic common denominator of the first twelve lines and extends it into another dimension. From the first two lines, this poem has presented a succession of antonyms that are synonyms, synonyms that are antonyms, equations stated as distinctions, and distinctions stated as equations—a succession of variations on the principle of mirror images, which are in some sense identical to and in another the reverse of their originals. Explanatory notes for these lines would not differ at all from those given for 36.13–14 where they conclude another exercise on and in simultaneous likeness and difference (one that is like this one and very different from it). Here, however, the couplet relates entirely differently to the poem it concludes; the assertions are identical, but their philosophic basis, the human relationship they imply, the implied natures of speaker and beloved, and the understood motives for the request are completely different.

SONNET 97

1. *absence* separation. *OED* does not distinguish this common Shakespearian use of "absence" from its standard use to indicate "a state of being away." Since Shakespeare so often uses "absence" and "absent" in contexts where they are not idiomatic and "separation" and "separated" are, it is evident that he and, presumably, his contemporaries were accustomed to use and understand them that way. Schmidt recognizes the distinction in usage and gives many examples including 39.9, 57.7, and 58.6. Here the need to distinguish vanishes in

line 2 because, although in modern usage "absence" and "separation" are not interchangeable in the potentially self-contained clause that ends with line 1, "absence *from*" and "separation *from*" are effectively synonymous. Note, however, that, since the Shakespearian use of "absence" to mean "separation" easily conveys the non-geographic idea of "estrangement," it adds a metaphoric dimension to the separation discussed.

1–4. Compare 5.5–8.

2. *thee, the pleasure of the . . . year* (1) you, who are the pleasant time, the pleasurable season, of the year (compare 18.1 and *WT* IV.iii.3, where "the sweet o' the year" describes spring and summer). (2) you, who delight the year, are that which gives the year pleasure (*year* is personified in *WT* IV.iv.78–80: "the year growing ancient, / Not yet on summer's death nor on the birth / Of trembling winter" and in *2HIV* Induction, 13–14: "The big year, swoln with some other grief, / Is thought with child"). (*Pleasure* was also used to mean specifically sexual pleasure; see 20.13, note, and 1Timothy 5:6 [in a section "concerning widowes"]: "she that liveth in pleasure, is dead, while she liveth.") *fleeting year* The sense, indicated grammatically, is "the swiftly passing year," but the situation described and the diction invoke suggestions of other ideas. The adjective *fleeting* modifies a word it does not well fit in this context: the fact that English winters and lovers' separations both seem endless combines with an uneventful rhythm (in effect, each of the first two lines has three unstressed syllables in the middle) to suggest that the year in question is long and dreary rather than *fleeting*. The context does, however, invite reflection on the brevity of life; the idea expressed by "fleeting year*s*" is present in the line by means of—and as well as—*the fleeting year* (see 19.5–6, note). Similarly, the proverbial transitoriness of pleasure (see 129), springtime, and youth gives the line the added richness of "the fleeting pleasure of the year."

3. *freezings, dark days* Both expressions describe winter weather, but they carry strong metaphoric overtones of the coldness of an estranged friend and a period of despair.

4. *everywhere* Q gives "every where"; see 98.3, note.

2–4. Q puts a question mark at the end of each of these lines. Question marks and exclamation points ("admiration points") are easily mixed up in a printer's font, and many Renaissance texts interchange them. Here, however, the Q punctuation was dictated by the Renaissance practice of sometimes retaining interrogatory punctuation in sentences which, like these, are exclamations structured like questions; compare 43.8,12; 48.4; 59.4; and 96.12; see 95.3, note.

5. *this time removed* (1) the aforementioned period of separation, this *absence*, this time of my removal [from you] (Ingram and Redpath follow Schmidt in citing the analogy of *RII* II.iii.79: "take advantage of the absent time"); (2) this now-past time, this time which now is distant from the present (*TN* V.i. 80–83 presents a somewhat similar use in a context generally similar to the situation suggested by *freezings*: "his false cunning . . . Taught him to face me out of his acquaintance, / And grew a twenty years removed thing"). See the following note. *summer's time* (1) the time, the part of the year, that belongs to summer (personified); and, therefore, (2) summertime. The next three lines

are in apposition to *summer's time*, and they transform a reader's understanding of *time*: (3) summer's time to give birth (for a woman's "time" meaning the time when she is due to begin labor, see Luke 1:57 and 2:6 [Geneva], *WT* II.i.20, and II.ii.25: "She is, something before her time, deliver'd"). The change worked upon *time* by the three appositive lines that follow it extends back to *this time removed*, which now takes on suggestions of the various periods and occasions when women were segregated from society and from intercourse with their husbands. The Bishops' Bible (1568), like the Authorized Version (1611), reads "lyke the uncleannes of a removed woman" in Ezek. 36:17 where the Vulgate gives *iuxta immunditiam menstruatae* and Geneva gives "as the filthines of the menstruous." The principal female bodily function specified in Leviticus (Chapters 12 and 15) as requiring purification by separation is childbirth. The "churching of women" is a Christian derivative of the ceremony prescribed in Lev. 12:6 for each mother "when the daies of her purifying are out." A woman's "confinement" is an eighteenth-century expression, apparently a euphemistic reincarnation of the medieval "Our Lady's bonds," but the association of sequestration with pregnancy and childbirth is traditional. Shakespeare plays on it elaborately in lines 67–82 of *Cor* I.iii (a scene studded with literal and metaphoric variations on loneliness, motherhood, confinement, and children); see also *RII* II.iii.79–80 and the topics and diction of II.iii at large.

  5–8. The structure of this quatrain reflects its substance in its proportions (one word, *time*, is enlarged into 3 appositive lines), and in the way it presents seasonal change (the transition from summer at the end of line 5 to autumn in line 6 is fluid—like changes of season themselves), and—when the appositive nature of the construction reveals itself in its failure to provide a verb, and "summertime" and *autumn* are, at least momentarily, confused for one another (see line 5, note)—in syntactically evoking a sense of dismay at paradox in the reader's experience of the poem, a sense of dismay that corresponds to the speaker's supposed response to the paradoxical situation described in the winter-summer conceit on which the poem is based.

  6. *teeming*   delivering (the root senses of "to teem" are "to empty," "to pour out"), fruitful, pregnant. (As the preceding glosses indicate, "teem" and its derivatives were used to refer either to a state of fullness—readiness and ability to deliver—or to the action of delivery. *Bearing* in line 7 has similar and similarly paradoxical qualities; in many contexts one cannot tell—and one does not feel obliged to know—whether "bearing a child" or "bearing fruit" refers to the carrying (holding, being full of) or the delivery of offspring. Here the inherent ambiguity of *teeming* and *Bearing* as designators of point in time and stage in process provides another manifestation of the theme that permeates the whole poem: the difficulty of knowing where in time one is.

  7. *Bearing*   Note that *Bearing* echoes the sound and contrasts with the sense of *bareness* in line 4.   *wanton*   Ingram and Redpath provide a gloss that cannot be improved on: "(1) 'frolicsome' (of children—the 'wanton burthen'); (2) 'luxuriant', cf. *MND.* II.i.99: 'the quaint mazes in the wanton green'; (3) by hypallage [= a kind of synesis in which a construction is understood in an extragrammatical logic—e.g. *wanton burthen of the prime* as "burthen of the

wanton prime"], referring to 'the prime' (= the spring), 'amorously sportive', cf. *MND*. II.i.128–9: 'To see the sails conceive / And grow big-bellied with the wanton wind'. For 'wanton spring' see *R2*. I.iii.214: 'Four lagging winters and four wanton springs'." *burthen* burden. *of the prime* (1) belonging to, fathered by, the spring; (2) which is the spring (*of the* indicating that of which the burden consists); (3) which is the state of full perfection, the period of greatest perfection. (For the senses of *prime*, see 3.10, 12.3, and 70.8.)

9–10. These lines present the extreme of confusion about position in time; *this* points back to lines 5–8 and suggests, as *issue* does, that, at the time of seeming, the offspring were already born; *But hope of orphans* ("only the promise of orphans, a sign that some orphans [children who have lost one or both parents] would be born") seems to present an event already apprehended as complete in line 9 as having been still anticipated at the time it was perceived by the speaker: *hope of orphans* appears to refer to the future, an anticipated birth, although it is apposite to *abundant issue*, which implies a birth completed. (Compare 73.2, 77.10–12, and 98.3; and see 73.14, and 92.14, notes.) Ultimately, a reader must understand the lines as saying "Nevertheless what has since proved to be abundant issue then seemed to me no more than . . . ," but, whether he stops to figure the lines out or just skims across them without precise understanding, the reader must go through a personal confusion about time.

An additional density derives from another dimension of complexity; in these lines it becomes practically impossible to remember whether one is thinking about harvest in terms of childbirth or childbirth in terms of agricultural harvest; three noun phrases are equated in lines 9 and 10: *abundant issue, hope of orphans,* and *unfathered fruit*; as one reads from one to another, they simultaneously destroy and increase one's sense of distinction between agricultural and human increase. In line 9 *issue* enlarges on the straightforward human simile in the preceding line, but *abundant* pertains not to the birth metaphor but to agriculture itself. *Hope of orphans* has literal relevance only to human existence, the metaphor. The third phrase, *unfathered fruit*, is like *abundant issue*, but here the noun is agricultural and the adjective human. "Fruit" is regularly used to indicate human offspring, but its agricultural sense is by so much its commonest that that sense has come to seem its "real" one. "Fruit" feels (and presumably would have felt to Shakespeare's reader) like a metaphor in any but agricultural contexts. Here the context of harvest forcefully asserts the agricultural sense. As a result, *fruit* acts here as a metaphoric botanical substitute for metaphoric human substitutes for the botanical subject that is the speaker's topic. At the same time, however, neither the participial sense of *unfathered* ("conceived without a male parent"), nor the sense dictated for it by the context of orphans ("fatherless," "left without a father"), can pertain literally to the botanical sense of *fruit*; *unfathered* thus asserts that *fruit* is a metaphor *from* rather than *for* human childbirth, just as *abundant* had asserted the opposite about *issue*.

11. *his* its (but see 73.10, note). *wait on thee* are your servants (and therefore travel with you, are never found except where you are; *OED*, 13. j, k, m). The general context invokes overtones of *wait on* meaning "await," "wait for" (see *OED*, 14.f,i and 57.1, note). Moreover, the proximity of *hope* in line 10 may

activate a suggestion of "wait on" meaning "place one's hope in," "have faith in." Since what one has faith in is often also both something one looks ahead to—waits for—and something one serves, the senses are often hard to distinguish; the English Bibles demonstrate the extent to which the ideas of serving, trusting, and governing one's behavior on the basis of expectation are tangled together in *wait on*: for example, the Vulgate phrase *dum spero in Deum meum* is rendered as "whiles I waite for my God" in the Geneva translation of Psalms 69:3, and, three verses later, *qui exspectant te* is translated as "them that trust in thee." The Bishops' Bible translates the two phrases as "through the long attendaunce that I have geven upon my Lord" and "them that trust in thee." AV gives "while I wait for my God," and "them that wait on thee." Geneva gives "Hope in the Lord" for Psalms 27:14; Bishops' gives "Attende thou upon God" and AV has "Wait on the Lord." One construction, *exspectare* plus accusative, appears in Isaiah 42:4, 51:5, and 60:9; Geneva gives "wait for" all three times; Bishops' gives "look for," "hope in," and "wait for"; AV gives "wait upon," and "wait for."

12. *thou away*   you being away, when you are away (contrast *my absence* in line 1).

13. *dull*   (1) faint, spiritless, woebegone (see *2HIV* I.i.70–71: "so faint, so spiritless, / So dull, so dead in look, so woe-begone"), listless, gloomy, melancholy; (2) depressing, dulling (compare *A&C* IV.xv.60–62: "Shall I abide / In this dull world, which in thy absence is / No better than a sty?").   *with so dull a cheer*   so gloomily. (The root sense of *cheer* is "face" [as in *MND* III.ii.96: "All fancy-sick she is and pale of cheer"]; from that sense grew "face as an indicator of disposition," and then "mood" [as indicated by demeanor], and "good cheer," "welcome"; here *cheer* partakes of all these senses.)

14. The context of *near* and a poem on absence gives *leaves* some resonance of "to leave" ("to depart" or "to abandon"); compare 5.7, 73.14, and 77.3.

SONNET 98

The language of this sonnet and of sonnet 99 is full of unexploited relevance to sexual love: for example, see *proud* in 151.10; *thing* in 20.12; "leaping-houses" meaning "brothels" in *1HIV* I.ii.7; "laps" in *Oth* IV.iii.86 ("[husbands] pour our treasures into foreign laps"); "pluck" and "pluck a sweet" meaning "deflower" in *LLL* IV.iii.110; "rose" meaning "maidenhead" in *AW* IV.ii.18; "play" in *HVIII* I.iv.45–47 and in the examples listed in 54.7, note; "Summer songs" in *WT* IV.iii.11–12 ("Summer songs for me and my aunts, / While we lie tumbling in the hay"); and *Per* IV.vi.33–41, a conversation among a bawd, Boult his henchman, and Lysimachus their customer (what is omitted at the end of the first speech is "a thorn"—i.e. "a pricker," "a penis" [see 35.2 and note]):

> *Boult.* For flesh and blood, sir, white and red, you shall see a rose; and
> she were a rose indeed, if she had but—
> *Lys.* What, prithee?
> *Boult.* O, sir, I can be modest.

> *Lys.* That dignifies the renown of a bawd no less than it gives a good report to a number to be chaste.
>
> *Bawd.* Here comes that which grows to the stalk—never plucked yet, I can assure you. [*Enter Marina.*]

(Compare sonnets 31 and 48.) All these senses remain dormant throughout the poem; they function only to the extent that such a concentration of potentially suggestive terms gives a vague aura of sexuality to the poem and thus, like the presence of the lily and the rose in lines 9 and 10, reinforces the persistent and essential analogy Shakespeare draws between the speaker's relationship with a beloved and the traditional courtly love poet's relationship with a mistress.

1. This sonnet appears to continue comment on the circumstances that occasioned sonnet 97 (as sonnet 99 appears to continue from this one).

2. *proud-pied* Q gives "proud pide." The hyphen, adopted by almost every editor since the eighteenth century, is justifiable more as a reflection of the intended rhythm than as an indicator of logical intent or syntactic limitation. The compound adjective established by the hyphen means "splendidly dappled," "magnificently variegated in coloring," but that sense is there with or without the hyphen, as are all the relevant senses that the simple adjectival sequence "proud, pied" would carry: *proud* suggests that April is "exultant," "arrogant," "vain," "vain-glorious," "smug," "grandly dressed," and "swollen" (see 104.4, note); *pied* suggests that April is dressed *in* piedness, and "proud *of*"—"proud because of"—his piedness. *his* April is personified by the adjectival phrases joined to it, not by the pronoun (see 73.10, note). *trim* fine array, elaborate clothing (as in *1HIV* IV.i.113: "They come like sacrifices in their trim").

3. *Hath put* The tense appears to be present perfect (i.e. it indicates a present of completed action); since the tense of all the other verbs in the poem is perfect, two nineteenth-century editors emended to "had put"; the change is unwarranted but not unreasonable: this is another of Shakespeare's many evocations of uncertainty about time (see the examples cited in the notes to 92.14 and 97.9–10). (To a lesser degree, "have been" in line 1 is also confusing; editors have quarreled over whether line 1 refers to habitual absences or one specific absence [see *Variorum* I, 241 and Ingram and Redpath, p. 224]; the relative validity of the various opinions is of little significance, but the existence of the debate testifies to the typically Shakespearian minor doubt the poem generates.) *everything* Q gives "every thing"; a Renaissance reader would have seen no distinction between the two forms, and it thus seems less distorting to give the usual modern form than to invite a modern reader to mistake standard idiom for a self-conscious and self-assertive play on that idiom. Compare "every where" in the Q text of 97.4, and see 37.7, note.

4. Compare *PP*, 12 ("Crabbed age and youth cannot live together"). *That* To such a great extent that. *heavy* (1) ponderous; (2) grave, solemn. *Saturn* The point of the line is that *even* Saturn feels the power of spring. The Roman god Saturn (who is the Greek god Kronos and the model for our "father time" [see Ben Jonson's *Time Vindicated* in Orgel, *Masques*, p. 391]), is generally represented as a bent, infirm old man. In astrology the slow, cold planet Saturn

"rules" two winter signs, and is associated with heaviness (the metal proper to Saturn is lead), with gravity of manner, seriousness, dullness, sorrow, and melancholy, and with old age and death (see Shumaker, pp. 4–6, and note that "figure" is an astrological term, a synonym for "horoscope"; although *figures* in line 11 has no logical pertinence to astrology, the word asserts a continuity in the poem at the same time that it is semantically independent of the astrological diction it echoes). *laughed* See 25.4, note (on "Joys of the Planets").

5. *Yet* even so. *nor . . . nor* neither . . . nor (as in 55.7). *lays* songs (but, since the word usually describes carefully composed works of art, the cavalier indecorum of its application to bird songs gives the speaker a tone of witty self-confidence and artistic self-consciousness; see line 7 and note).

1–5. Compare *The General Prologue to the Canterbury Tales*, lines 1–11.

6. *different* = dissyllabic, by syncopation; contrast 105.8, where *difference* is trisyllabic. *different flow'rs* various flowers (with a suggestion, sharpened in the lines that follow, of "other flowers," "flowers other than you"; for the phonetic likeness of *hue* and "you," see 20.7, note); (2) flowers different, flowers that differ from one another. (In effect, *different* acts twice: first as in *Tim* I.i. 256–57: "We'll share a bounteous time / In different pleasures"; then in the relationship to *odor* and *hue* demanded and first indicated by *in* ["in respect to"]. Compare *RII* III.i.9: "A happy gentleman in blood and lineaments"; Abbott [par. 419a] discusses and gives other examples of the Elizabethan habit of splitting adjectival phrases into their adjectival elements, placed before the noun, and their adverbial elements, placed after it.) Note that this line is an expansion on the variegation theme indicated by *pied* in line 2.

7. The sense of the line is clear though general: "could put me in harmony with the season, make me join the rest of creation in its joy." The idea of telling a story invites a reader to think of the speaker as writer; lines 9 and 10 (*wonder at, praise*) continue our sense of the speaker's self-image as one whose participation in the awakening and productivity of spring and summer would have been literary, would have been that of a love poet wondering at beauty and praising it (see the note on 9–10 below).

Shakespeare uses the expression *summer's story* as one uses stock proverbial expressions to which a reader may be expected to respond precisely, but *summer's story* does not appear elsewhere. What precision it has derives from its identity as the opposite of "winter's tale," a genuinely proverbial expression. A similar extrapolation occurs in another sexually suggestive passage, *2Gent* II.iv.155–59 (where the conjunction of "proud" and "summer-swelling" gives the passage extra suggestions of foolhardy presumption and unnaturalness derived by analogy to "winter-proud," a standard expression for describing grain that sprouts prematurely [*OED* gives this from 1601: "When either corne is winter-proud, or other plants put forth and bud too earely, by reason of the mild and warme aire . . . ."]):

> . . . bear my lady's train, lest the base earth
> Should from her vesture chance to steal a kiss
> And, of so great a favour growing proud,

Disdain to root the summer-swelling flow'r
And make rough winter everlastingly.

(See also *summer's pride* in 104.4.) "Winter's tale" seems to have had two not-quite-compatible connotations; one contrasts with the implied nature of a *summer's story*: a "winter's tale" suggests a solemn one appropriate to the season when it is told; the other shares some of the probable attributes of a *summer's story*: it is an idle, frivolous tale, an old wives' tale, a superstitious story told and credited only by the gullible. Malone cited both *Cymb* III.iv.11–13: "Why tender'st thou that paper to me with / A look untender? If't be summer news, / Smile to't before; if winterly, thou need'st / But keep that count'nance still . . ." and *WT* II.i.25–26, in which Shakespeare capsules the two senses: "A sad tale's best for winter. I have one / Of sprites and goblins." As defined by its antithesis, *summer's story* takes on extra pertinence to the rest of the poem: a speaker unmoved by a season that makes even Saturn youthful would be loath to tell a cheerful tale or a "young men's tale," and line 14 suggests that the story the speaker does tell is to be taken with a grain of salt.

8. *their . . . lap* The antecedent is *flow'rs* in line 6 (compare *MND* II.i.107–08: "hoary-headed frosts / Fall in the fresh lap of the crimson rose"), but the "pluck from" construction dictates an anatomical logic incompatible with the one implied by *their*: a reader is first directed to think of *their . . . lap* as a metaphoric reference to petals or some other flower parts, but, since flowers cannot be plucked from their own laps, a reader must come to understand *their . . . lap* as the place where they grow, the ground ("the lap of mother earth" is a traditional and obvious conceit; see *RII* V.ii.47 and III.iii.47: "The fresh green lap of fair King Richard's land"). *proud* (1) gorgeously dressed, splendid (compare 2.3 and 64.2); (2) swelling, luxuriant, pregnant (see 67.12, 76.1, 103.1, 104.4, and notes; also see *OED*, 7d., and the note on *summer's story* in line 7 above).

9. *lily's white* Q gives "Lillies," which in Renaissance spelling could indicate any and all of these modern spellings: "lilies white" (i.e. "lilies which are white," "white lilies"); "lilies' white"; and the reading given here (which is the choice of most editors but is nonetheless entirely arbitrary).

9–10. "White as a lily" and "red as a rose" were proverbial (Tilley, L296 and R177). Lilies and roses were a traditional pair in courtly-love tributes to the ideal complexions of idolized ladies. (See 106.5, note, and Song of Songs 2:1: "I am the rose of the field, & the lilie of the valleis." Shakespeare improvises on the tradition in 99.6–11, *Lucrece* 1–77, and *LLL* I.ii.96–99.)

11–14. These lines allude to the Platonic doctrine of forms; see the headnote to sonnet 53; here again Shakespeare doubles the Platonic paradox—this time by using the word *figures*, which can substitute for both Platonic reality (form), and its earthly approximation (mere images and shadows).

11. *but . . . but* (1) merely . . . merely (the whole of the second *but* phrase is apposite to the whole of the first); (2) merely . . . mere (the second *but* phrase is apposite to *sweet*). *were* Q gives "weare"; "weare" probably represents a printer's whim rather than an indication that Shakespeare meant

(or meant to pun on) the word we now spell "wear." The pun is not impossible (for instance, the quarto text of *MWW* I.iii.73 gives "wer" for "wear," and the evidence from rhymes is contradictory and inconclusive; see 140.5,7; 77.1; and notes). But, since Renaissance spellings in general indicate pronunciation no more accurately than the modern "tear" indicates our pronunciations of "tear" meaning "rip" and "tear" meaning "liquid shed from the eyes," one cannot suppose that any spelling of "were" or "wear" would signal a pun more readily than any other. *figures of delight* (1) delightful forms, shapes that give delight to the eye; (2) images, representations (pictures or statues) of (real) delight. (Apposition to the first half of line 11 initially makes sense (1) primary; line 12 makes sense (2) primary.)

12. See 101.3, note. *after* on the model of.

14. *shadow* image (see 27.10 and 53.2; note, however, that *play* suggests playing with a shadow, playing with a silhouette formed on the ground when a body interrupts the sun's rays; children play games where they leap about trying to pounce upon one another's shadows. Note also that, since the shadow of a person walking into the sun seems to trail after him, *shadow* can activate a belated play on *Drawn after you* meaning "pulled behind you." And, finally, note that in context of line 13, which repeats the opening conceit of sonnet 97, *shadow* also suggests the dark sunless days of winter [97.3], and, perhaps, the idea of winter as summer's ghost). *I with these did play* When a reader comes upon it, *these* is a substitute for the flowers in the preceding lines (and, as a result, the clause casts doubt on the veracity of the speaker's examples of his devoted indifference to flowers other than the beloved). If the reader goes on immediately to sonnet 99, *these* can seem to have been pointing ahead to the flowers the speaker teases there. (Many editors have concluded the poem with a colon to signal that line 14 refers to what follows, but since *these* has obvious antecedents, no punctuation can deny even a modern reader a first understanding of the line in relation to the assertions that precede it.)

13–14. "A good friend is as the sun in winter" was proverbial (Tilley, F700).

SONNET 99

See the headnote to sonnet 98.

This is the only fifteen-line sonnet in the collection. There are other fifteen-line Renaissance sonnets (Barnabe Barnes wrote several), but no other surviving sonnet expands the form by adding an extra alternatively rhymed line to a quatrain (Barnes puts the extra line between line 12 and the final couplet and rhymes it with line 12). Formally, Shakespeare's extra line is number 5, but it is syntactically indispensable; substantively, line 1 is introductory and thus distinct in function from 2–5, but, since it identifies the object of the following four lines, it cannot be considered extra either. Hyder Rollins (*Variorum* I, 244–46) details the wanton scholarly speculations the anomalous form has prompted. Rollins also cites some of the many Renaissance poems that use the traditional conceits of this poem.

1. See 98.14 and note. *forward* (1) early blooming, precocious (as in

2Gent I.i.45, quoted for lines 12–13 below); (2) presumptuous, pert, brash (as in *2Gent* II.i.11, where "You'll still be too forward" is a reprimand to a perversely clever boy).   *violet*   = trisyllabic (as in 12.3).

2–5. Some editors put these lines in quotation marks.

2. *Sweet thief*   This epithet echoes thousands of oxymorons like "sweet foe," traditionally applied to disdainful or unfaithful ladies by love-sick courtly lovers. (Compare *sweet thief* in 35.14, *gentle thief* and *Lascivious grace* in 40.9,13, and "fair cruelty" in *TN* I.v.272.) Here the wit consists in applying the traditional conceit in its traditional context of Petrarchan praise, but applying it where it pertains literally: *sweet* is here not a word of praise but a simple descriptive adjective (all violets are sweet by kind), and *thief* is not the conventionally general hyperbolic epithet for an "attractive" person, but introduces a fanciful accusation of real pilfering. In effect the epithet reverses the traditional assertion ("You are flower-like") that underlies the poem; the speaker doubles his compliment by using a convention that implies that the violet is the object of flattery in being compared to the beloved ("flowers are like you"). The inversion presents the speaker to us as one who actually believes the pointedly incredible assertions he goes on to make.   *steal thy sweet*   A chiasmic and complicated echo of *Sweet thief*: *steal* is a verbal equivalent for the noun *thief*; phonetically, *sweet* is simply repeated, but the second *sweet* is not an adjective but a noun, and its sense is not parallel with the general sweetness reported by the adjective but is narrowed by *that smells* to the particularized Renaissance sense "perfume," "sweet smell" (compare *Macb* V.i.50: "All the perfumes of Arabia will not sweeten this little hand," and see line 15 below).

3. *purple*   The word indicated not only the violet-mauve-magenta range of colors, but also bright reds (compare Donne's "The Flea," line 20: "Purpled thy naile, in blood of innocence"); the fact that the term "purple" could indicate both the color we visualize for the violet and the red we visualize in a human complexion lets Shakespeare stress difference (we cannot comfortably visualize a person with a violet-colored face), in the same assertion that insists on likeness between the violet and the beloved.   *pride*   splendor (as in 80.12).

3–5. *The purple pride . . . thou hast too grossly dyed.*   A reader presumably understands this sentence to mean that the violet gets its color from the beloved. But that understanding derives entirely from inference. What the sentence actually does is to assume such a statement has been made; it then goes on to comment that the deepness of color in the violet is the result of overlong immersion in the beloved's veins. The reader is helped to infer the missing statement in part by analogy with the preceding sentence, which tells him what to expect from a sentence on color. The general silence of editors and commentators on this sentence suggests readers do in fact assume the content they expect. They have apparently also been untroubled by the potential logical and imaginative difficulties presented by *pride* as a solid object that can be dyed, by the standard idiom "dwells in"—presented in fact but logically inoperative, by the improbability of dyeing anything *in* blood vessels, by the failure of the sentence to evoke the inappropriate but more available image of something dyeing something else in the blood of a wounded man, or by the idea of dyeing purple pride purple. The reader's unawareness of these details may in part result from the sustaining action of some reassuring details: "Vein" can mean "rivulet" (*OED* gives this from 1601: "These mountaines are full of bathes and veins of warme water"); and the sentence can evoke a vague metaphoric image of a human being dipping something in a stream. The conjunction of *in, veins,* and *dyed* may sound clearer, more usual and straightforward, and more meaningful than it is because it echoes the idiomatic phrase "dye in the vein," meaning "bleed to death" (*OED*, 2a, gives an example from the mid–sixteenth century). "Vein" meaning "disposition," "temper," "personal manner," pertains to this context of stolen characteristics, and the presence of *veins* thus carries extra-logical overtones of rightness to the sentence at large.

    4. The rhythm of the verse requires that *soft* be more heavily stressed than *cheek*. The rhythm of idiomatic prose invites just the opposite. The metrical awkwardness results in a line that sounds as if it refers to the violet's soft cheek as opposed to its hard one. *for complexion* (1) as a source of color, as color-giver (for "complexion" meaning "color," see *2HIV* II.ii.5 [pun], and *RII* III.ii. 194–95: "Men judge by the complexion of the sky / The state and inclination of the day"); (2) corresponds to (is the floral equivalent of) facial coloring and texture in human beings; (3) as a cosmetic (*OED* gives this from 1601: "They are called at this day complexions, whereas they be cleare contrarie; for the complexion is natural, and these altogether artificiall").

    6–11. See 98.9–10, note.

    6. *condemnèd* = pronounced "con-dem-ned." *for* for stealing (compare the construction of the proverbial "hanged for a sheep").

    8. *on thorns* (1) in a painful state of anxiety (*OED* exemplifies the idiom with this from 1561: "The poore gentilwoman stood upon thornes, and thought an houre a thousand yeare, till she were got from him." "To stand upon thorns" was proverbial; see Tilley, T239 and *WT* IV.iv.577); (2) on their thorn-covered stems (Shakespeare regularly calls rosebushes "thorns," see 54.7 and *MND* I.i.77).

    9. Several editors point out that, since one cannot "blush white despair," blushing is not a participle here. Logically enough, they conclude (with Ingram and Redpath) that *blushing* "is an adjective. The red rose is 'blushing shame' personified, and the white rose 'white despair' personified." That all makes excellent sense, but all the denials and substitutes testify authoritatively that readers *do* (and, since there is no evidence that the idiom has changed in 400 years, presumably always did) follow the habitual patterns of English syntax and read this line as a pair of participial modifiers for *stand*: semantic logic is easily overwhelmed by common sense; readers presumably simply generalize *blushing*, understand it in the second phrase as "changing facial coloring," and take the line as if it were "one reddening in shame, another paling in despair." Compare *LLL* I.ii.96–99. *One* Q gives "Our," an obvious misprint.

    10. *nor . . . nor* neither . . . nor.

    11. *to his robb'ry . . . annexed* added to his robbery—to his booty, to what he had already stolen (*annexed* also suggests "appropriated," and thus, despite the syntactic limitation of the "annexed to" construction, *annexed thy breath*

meaning "stole thy breath" may also impinge on a reader's consciousness to enrich the line by presenting a syntactically unharnessed extra description of the same theft).

12. *But for* however, in punishment for; however, because of (although the construction can be momentarily understood as "except for" [as in *V&A* 504; compare *But* in line 15 below]). *in pride of* (1) in the prime of; (2) at the height of his self-satisfaction about; (3) at the time of the fullest splendor of (see 25.7, note); see 104.4, note.

11,12,13. *his, him* See 73.10, note.

13. *canker* cankerworm. *ate* did eat. Q's "eate" is retained by most editors, but, since Shakespearian spellings of the past tense of "eat" are indistinguishable from his spellings of the present tense (*Shrew* IV.i.181: "She eat no meat to-day, nor none shall eat"), and since the two were pronounced alike as well ("et"? "ate"? see Kökeritz, pp. 203, 103–04 for evidence of identical pronunciation of the words we now spell "eat" and "ate" and speculation on what that sound was), to retain the old spelling here is to create a quaintness rather than report one. (Retention of "eate" is particularly misleading here because the childlike redundancy of *ate him up to death* has genuine coyness, a nursery-tale ring, that a reader allowing for quaint archaisms can lose. This poem—perhaps intentionally—sounds like a parody of its kind; it is grossly uneconomical; the speaker sounds like someone who is "pouring it on," and, in this line, he sounds conscious of the listless, stale perfunctory nature of such an exercise in traditionally appropriate fancies; in short, he sounds contemptuous of the role he is playing and of himself for playing it.) *death* Note *dyed* in line 5, and see the note on lines 3–5.

12–13. Line 12 suggests a full-blown rose, one that has achieved *all his growth*. Cankers, however, attack buds. There is no reason to assume that Shakespeare's reader would have demanded botanical precision here any more than he would have demanded semantic precision in line 9. Shakespeare does, however, assume and exploit a reader's precise knowledge of cankers and buds in 95.2–4; he also plays on *pride* meaning phallic tumescence (see 151.10, note, and *proud* in 75.5) and uses *pride* in reference to children in the womb (see 76.1, *proud* in 98.8, 103.1–3, and notes). One may, therefore, note that the discrepancy between the evident reference of *in pride of all his growth* and the actual victims of cankerworms is wittily reconciled in the word *pride*, which, on the one hand, pertains to blown roses in the three senses given in the note on line 12 and, on the other hand, also pertains to rose buds, which are phallic in appearance (a fact to which line 11 may also allude), and can also be said to be pregnant, about to open and give birth to the full beauty of the rose (compare 25.7). (Note also the context established by *forward violet* in line 1: for the association of "pride" and prematurity, see the note on "winter proud" in 98.7.)

15. *But* except. *sweet* scent, sweet smell.

SONNET 100

3. *Spend'st thou* (1) do you use; (2) do you use up (as in 105.11). *fury*

poetic fury (a casual allusion to *furor poeticus*, a standard Renaissance term for poetic inspiration. The term originates with Marsilio Ficino, who, in 1482, gave the subtitle *De Furore Poetico* to his Latin translation of the *Ion*, in which Plato expounded the already traditional idea that poetic ability is a supernatural gift, a divinely inspired madness (see 17.11 and *MND* V.i.7–16: "The lunatic, the lover, and the poet . . ."). Here *fury* carries the idea of great power, the idea of a god-given gift (which should not be frittered away), and (paradoxically in the context of accusation) the idea that the poet can be neither credited nor blamed for his actions.

4. *Dark'ning* (1) sullying, disgracing; and, in context of *Spend'st*, (2) burning up, expending the fuel of. *thy pow'r to lend* (1) your ability to lend, your lending power; (2) your poetic power in order to lend (i.e. for the purpose of lending). *base* low, inferior, worthless (with a play on "base" meaning "dark" [*OED*, 5]; Shakespeare makes similar puns in *Titus* IV.ii.71: "Is black so base a hue," and many other times—e.g. 33.5, 34.3, *RII* II.iv.19–21, III.iii.176– 83, *1HIV* I.ii.191, and *Cymb* I.vi.107–08; note particularly the amazing ideational interplay in *Tim* IV.iii.28–29: "this will make black white, foul fair, / Wrong right, base noble . . ."). *lend base subjects light* give luster to subjects (persons written about) who have no luster of their own (as opposed to the beloved, who gives luster to poems—see lines 2 and 8 and 84.4–10).

5. *straight* immediately.

6. *gentle* noble, not base (as in 96.2; also see *gentle verse* in 81.9). *numbers* verses (as in 17.6). *so idly* (1) in such idleness, so indolently; (2) so frivolously, so wastefully.

5–6. *redeem, time* See the note on *wrinkle* in line 10 below.

8. *argument* subject matter (but colored by the sexual senses; see 38.3, 79.5– 6, and notes).

9. *resty* This word has caused considerable scholarly controversy (summarized by Rollins, *Variorum* I, 249). *Resty* is a horseman's term (see Tilley, H684: "A resty horse must have a sharp spur"); it describes the various characteristics of horses that have been idle for some time: such a horse may be lazy, sluggish, stubborn (hard to manage), perverse, or so full of energy as to be liable to bolt. Ordinarily, whether *resty* is applied to animals or metaphorically to human beings, the particular symptom of inactivity is indicated from context; thus *OED* gives this example (1571) of *resty* meaning "sluggish," "indolent," "lazy": "Thyne enemies surmyze thee to be restie and ydle bycause thou bestirrest thee not"; and this example (1603) of *resty* meaning "unmanageable": "Which restie growne, with your much Power, withdraw Your stiff'ned Necks from th' yoke of Civill Awe"; and this (1605), which demonstrates connotations of eagerness to expend pent up energy: "Th'Ox, over-fat, too strong, and resty, leaps About the Lands, casteth his yoke, and strikes." In this sonnet charges of idleness and truancy, the speaker's hortatory tone, and the word *Rise* provide a context that actively supports all the usual senses of *resty*; they all operate together with a paradoxical, and paradoxically easy, concision typical of Shakespeare. *survey* When it is read at the end of line 9, *survey* means simply "look at," "gaze upon" (as in 52.3), but *If* in the next line makes a reader understand

survey a second time and in a second sense: "examine in order to ascertain the condition of." (Note that *Rise* activates overtones of "to survey" meaning "to look at from above" and thus also activates implications of mastery in the surveyor [*OED* gives this from the 1580's: "From sea to sea he shall survey All kingdoms as his own"].)

10. *If* to see whether (Abbott, par. 382, gives many examples of similar ellipses). *have* The mood is subjunctive (Abbott, par. 361). *wrinkle* facial wrinkle. (Like *redeem* and *time* in lines 5–6 above, *wrinkle*, meaning "visual blemish," is part of a bundle of associations from Ephesians 5 [see 93.8, note and the headnote to sonnet 36]; however, although Shakespeare may have heard a play on the moral sense of "wrinkle" here, he could not have expected his reader to hear it; therefore my observation of the image cluster here pertains not to the poem but to the poet.) *graven* incised, cut (the verb "to grave" is ominous here because it includes an echo of the noun "grave"; see 81.7, note).

11. *be a satire to decay* make a mockery of decay, be a satirist of decay (for "satire" meaning "satirist," see Rollins [*Variorum* I, 249]; he cites W. S. Walker as the source of various examples, including this from Ben Jonson's *Time Vindicated* [1623]: " 'Tis Chronomastix, the brave satyr— / The gentleman-like satyr, cares for nobody" [53–54; Orgel, *Masques*, p. 393; some details of *Time Vindicated* are intriguingly reminiscent of the sonnets; see 98.4, and note that the name "Chronomastix" can be translated variously as "scourge of the time," "scourge of time," or "scourge of Kronos"—i.e. of Saturn, Father Time]).

12. *time's spoils* (1) the plunder taken by time; (2) the acts of spoliation done by time (for a similar play, see 65.12).

13. *faster* more quickly (an adverb, modifying *Give*, but with a grammatically unsustained play on an adjectival use of "fast" meaning "firmly fixed": "more permanent fame"). *wastes* destroys (but with punning overtones of "to waste time" [see line 6 above], invoked by the juxtaposition of *time*; compare 12.10, 15.11, 30.4, 106.1, and *RII* V.v.49: "I wasted time, and now doth time waste me").

14. *So* thus. *prevent'st* (1) thwart (as in *Lucrece* 220: "this vile purpose to prevent"); (2) get the start of (*OED* gives this from 1556: "I should prevent him, and take frome him the flower and grace of the noveltie"); (3) outstrip, surpass (*OED* gives this from 1540: "Be not onely even with them . . . but . . . prevente them whan thou mayst"). *and crookèd knife* Although this phrase only repeats *scythe* (a hendiadys), *crookèd* also carries syntactically unharnessed suggestions of "crooked age," of Father Time and his effect on his victims (see 60.12, note).

SONNET 101

1. *what shall be thy amends* (1) what reparation will you make; what payment will you give in satisfaction of your offense; (2) how will you recover from your lapse; what will cure you (compare *Shrew*, Induction, ii.95: "Lord be thanked for my good amends"). Later, lines 5–9 proceed as if this phrase had

included the sense "what will you do to amend the beloved's condition," "what improvement will you make in the beloved" (compare *mend* in 103.9).

1-2. Note the wit of the *truant/truth* jingle.

2. *truth* (1) fidelity; (2) moral perfection; (3) eternal verity, disembodied essence of things, the Platonic ideal (see the headnote to 53).

3. This reverses the Platonic relationship of the eternal disembodied ideal and its temporal, physical approximations; sonnets 53 and 98 make the same kind of flattering inversion. *my love* (1) my beloved; (2) the affection I feel. *depends* Third person plurals in *s* are not unusual in Shakespeare; see 41.3, 95.12, notes.

4. *therein dignified* (1) that is the source of your worth and title to respect (see 84.8); (2) that is the source of your office as muse and of the high title, muse, that goes with it (i.e. you would otherwise be an unemployed nobody; for "dignify" meaning "give high office to" and "confer a title upon," see *OED*, 2, which gives this from 1660: "The Earl . . . now with much merit dignifyed with the great office of Lord High Treasurer," and *OED*, s.v. "dignity," 3: "an honourable office, rank, or title"). If, as several sonnets (e.g. 26 and 82), suggest, these sonnets were addressed to a titled nobleman, then this phrase carries the suggestion that the muse shares in the honor of the patron-subject.

5. *haply* perhaps (but with suggestions of "happily," "fortunately," as in 29.10; the word carries appropriate overtones of casualness, offhandedness).

6. *Truth* (1) virtue, honesty; (2) veracity, "the simple truth"; (3) reality, genuineness. *colour* (1) cloak of falsehood (*OED* gives this from 1592: "You carry your pack but for a colour, to shadow your other villainies"); (2) excuse (as in *Lucrece* 267: "Why hunt I then for colour or excuses"); (3) cosmetic aid (the context of *muse* gives the work specific suggestions of "colors of rhetoric" [*OED*, 13], and the context of *dyed* invokes a play on "color" in its simplest sense, "hue"). "Truth needs no colors" and "truth has no need of rhetoric" were proverbial (Tilley, T585 and T575; Tilley's two sixteenth-century examples of the former proverb indicate that it refers to rhetorical devices, and that it uses "colors" as an exact antonym for "truth," as a synonym for "lies": "Treuthe nedeth no peynted or colored termes." "Truth needes noe cullors though I mean to lye"). *with his colour fixed* (1) in addition to his natural ingrained coloration, his complexion (which will not smudge and needs no fixative; compare *TN* I.v.222: " 'Tis in grain, sir; 'twill endure wind and weather"); (2) Since he has natural ingrained color (taking the phrase as modifying *Truth*: "Truth with his color fixed needs no color"; compare *V&A* 1-2: "the sun with purple-colour'd face / Had ta'en his last leave . . ."); (3) affixed to—i.e. joined with, grafted onto—his [own] color (taking "to need fixed" as the verb).

7. *pencil* artist's brush (not "pencil" in the modern sense; see 16.10, note). *lay* (1) apply, lay on (i.e. achieve with cosmetics); (2) lay on (i.e. fix on canvas with colors), portray (*OED* gives "to laie colour on a picture" from 1570; compare Donne's "A Valediction: of Weeping," lines 11-12: "A workeman that has copies by, can lay / An Europe . . . ," and *TN* I.v.223-24: " 'Tis beauty truly blent, whose red and white / Nature's own sweet and cunning hand laid

on"). *Lay* resonates with other contextually pertinent meanings: (a) "to lay" meaning "to abase," "to humble," "to lay low" (as in *John* II.i.399: "Lay this Angiers even with the ground")'; (b) "to lay" meaning "to allay," "to cause to subside," "to neutralize the force of," "to suppress" (as in *T&C* IV.iv.52: "to lay this wind"). See also the notes on *intermixed* in line 8 and *for't lies in thee* in line 10. (Moreover, although there has never been a verb "to lay" meaning "to hymn," "to sing about," the existence of the noun "lay," "song," gives *lay* logically irrelevant extra pertinence to its general context here; see 21.8, note— on "to hymn.")

8. *best is best* This has a proverbial ring, and it brings three real proverbs to mind: "Truth is truth" (Tilley, T581—used five times by Shakespeare); "Better is better" (Tilley B330); and "The best may amend" (Tilley, B321—a logical paradox to which Shakespeare's axiom provides precise correction, and to which lines 6–8 present general opposition; the context of *amends* in line 1 points up the casual clash between the two undeniable but incompatible truisms). *never intermixed* never adulterated, never alloyed, left pure. Line 8 relates to line 7 by means of a sense of *lay* that is dormant in line 7 and only activated when the logic implied by *But* presents "to intermix" as a synonym for *to lay* and thereby instructs the reader to read line 8 as if he had previously understood *to lay* as "to allay," "to alloy," "to mix" (*OED* gives only Scots examples of "to lay" as an abbreviated form of "to allay," but the noun form was common; Shakespeare puns on "to allay" meaning "to mitigate" and "to allay" meaning "to alloy," "to mix," in *MofV* II.ii.171 and *Cor* II.i.44). (The idea of intermixture is traditional in discussions of complexion, and its presence gives this line a sound of rightness; on the other hand, intermixture has only good connotations in such contexts [see *TN* I.v.223–24, quoted above in the note to line 7], and, although the speaker's objection is limited to mixtures of real and artificial color, any objection to intermixture of colors in a context of complexion is likely to sound somehow unorthodox and create a vague tension in a reader's mind.)

10. *for't lies in thee* for it depends on you (note line 3)—it rests with you, is in your power. This phrase is a central point in a network of incidental and variously established relationships which conveys no substance but joins with the similarly uncommunicative network of echoed proverbs to give the poem quasi-organic density and the undeniability a natural organism has in being so complexly and variously organized that its identity supersedes and overwhelms the identities of its elements. A sense of felt but unidentified system makes the poem's assertions and their logical interrelation feel certain, obvious, self-evidently true. *Lies* and *lay* have perfectly different functions and significances here, but the two verbs are related phonetically and in the likeness of their often confused root senses. Similarly, *lies* is not, but could be, a form of the verb "to lie" meaning "to speak falsely"; it thus pertains to the idea expressed in *colour*; and the theme of falsehood can evoke a suggestion—distant but syntactically sustained by the availability of *silence* as antecedent for "it" in *for't lies*—of the meaning "to be silent is to lie" in this line (where *Excuse* also echoes an idea invoked in line 6 [see the foregoing note on *colour*, sense 2]). Another potential

sense that *lies in* does not convey in line 10 relates to a potential sense that *lay* did not convey in line 7; in suitable syntaxes "to lie" can mean "to be in a recumbent position," or "to lie dead" (*OED*, 1d), and "to lay" can mean "to lay in the grave," "to bury" (as in *R&J* V.iii.73); line 11 activates this unrealized and previously irrelevant potential (and sharpens the mortal implications of line 3) in *outlive a gilded tomb*, in which *gilded* ("beautified by application of artificial color") pertains to *dyed* in line 2 and to "laying" colors in line 7, and in which *tomb* pertains to *dyed* through the intermediary of a pun on *die* that is never called into a reader's consciousness at all.

1. *make him much*   Note that until *outlive* limits and fixes their function ("make him outlive by many years"), these words carry a scrambled echo of "make much of him" in a poem that has making or not making much of the beloved as its topic.   *tomb*   See 83.12, note.

11–14.   These lines establish the second element in a distinction vital to the argument of the poem, the distinction between two kinds of permanence: the beloved's beauty is permanent (*fixed*, line 6) as opposed to beauty achieved with cosmetics or claimed by hyperbolic flattery; but it is not eternal: " 'twill endure wind and weather," but not the passage of time. See 55, headnote (on immortality through verse).

13. *Then*   therefore (but, in context of *ages yet to be*, with a fleeting incidental play on "at that time").   *do thy office*   do your duty (meaning *both* "perform the particular function that is yours by nature," and "perform the function that is yours only because of the fortunate circumstances described in lines 3 and 4").

13–14.   Q puts a comma after *how*. Neither the Q punctuation nor any other can indicate all—or effectively deny any—of the multiple relationships among the parts of this sentence: (1) "Then, muse, do thy office [which is] to make . . . ; I teach thee how [to do it]"; (2) "Then do thy office, muse; I teach thee how to make . . ."; (3) "Then do thy office, muse; I teach thee how, [and that is] to make. . . ."

14.   Note that, now that the distinction has been made between misusing artifice and using it properly, *seem* and *shows* bring back connotations of deceit, pretense, and vanity in the very line that defines the honorable action of telling the plain truth (see *seeming* and *show* in 102.1–2).

SONNET 102

1. *My love*   the effection I feel.   *in seeming*   in appearance, apparently. (The preceding glosses reflect the sense line 1 conveys if the poem is read in isolation; line 2, which acts as a gloss on line 1, dictates that reading in any event. However, for a reader coming directly from sonnet 101, *in seeming* can carry overtones of "with respect to my output of flattering embellishments and rhetorical exaggeration." Moreover, since lines 1 and 2 echo key words from 101.14, *My love* can momentarily mean "my beloved," *strengthened* can suggest the poetically sustained vitality prescribed in 101.11–14, and the second half of line 1 can refer to the beloved's future physical condition as opposed to the eternal youth and beauty he has in the speaker's poems.)

2. *less . . . appear* (1) may seem less; (2) is less in evidence. *show* (1) outward manifestation; (2) ostentatious display.

3. *love* (1) affection; (2) instance of mutual affection, loving relationship (as in line 5 and in line 7 of Donne's "A Valediction: forbidding mourning": "T'were prophanation of our joyes / To tell the layetie our love"); (3) beloved. *merchandised* (1) treated like merchandise, reduced to the level of a mere commodity; (2) hawked for sale. *whose rich esteeming* of which the high value (the use of "whose" for a non-human antecedent is common in Shakespeare; it does, however, heighten the latent metaphor of prostitution and pimping here—see 66.6, note).

4. *publish* make generally known, advertise, proclaim (with a play on "to publish" specifically meaning "to offer printed matter for public sale").

3–4. See 21.14, note.

5. *but in the spring* only in its springtime, just beginning, just beginning to grow.

5,10. *then, Than* Q gives "then" for both; see 16.4,8, note.

6. *greet* (1) salute; (2) welcome. *it* (1) *Our love*; (2) *the spring*.

7. *Philomel* the nightingale (here used simply as a poetic name for the species, with no active reference to the myth of Philomela). *front* beginning, forefront.

8. *his* its (see 73.10, note; although the use of "his" for the modern "its" tends to personify an antecedent, the personification is not specifically masculine. Since Philomela was a female, since Shakespeare—following traditional folk ornithology—ordinarily thinks of the singing nightingale as the female, and since he says *her* in lines 10 and 13, many editors change *his* to "her." The confusion, though gratuitous, may be deliberate; see *hymns* in line 10 and the note on *hems* in line 8 of sonnet 21—a poem of which this one is otherwise reminiscent).

9. *Not that* I do not mean to imply that I act as I do because.

9–10. (1) "Not that the present season, late summer, is less pleasant than early summer was"; (2) "Not that summers are any less pleasant now than they were when our love was new." (The literal and metaphoric senses are totally conflated. A reader's knowledge that English nightingales stop singing in late July leads him to understand *the summer* as any individual summer and *now* as indicating a time late in that summer. In the analogous situation time is measured in years; *the summer* means "summers," "summertime"; and *now* indicates "this year" as opposed to an earlier year when the speaker celebrated his love in verse.)

11. *But that* The action of this construction is odd. It parallels *Not that* in line 9, and thus might be expected to strike a reader as an ellipsis for "I *do*, on the other hand, mean to imply that I act as I do because." In fact the parallelism is probably only phonetically perceived; since *mournful hymns* in line 10 provides an antecedent, *that* asks to be read as a demonstrative pronoun indicating what *wild music* this line concerns. But, moving on in the line, the reader learns that the *wild music* now *burthens every bough*; that music cannot be the music of the nightingale, which sang alone in the hushed night and which we know no longer

sings. Presumably the reader now understands line 11 as offering a reason why the nightingale and the speaker choose to be silent now: in the late summer lost of inferior birds sing, and, at the present stage of the speaker's relationship with the beloved, *every alien pen* (78.3) is celebrating the beloved. That is to say that the reader now understands the line just as the *Not that/But that* pair dictated before the gratuitous confusion of *that wild music*. That understanding, however, is derived more from the logic of the situation than from the potential syntactical signal in *But that*. (Note that one available sense of *burthens*, "becomes a burden to," prepares the way for lines 12–14.)

12. This sounds like a proverb; see 52.3–4, note; Tilley points out a likeness to "Familiarity breeds contempt" (F47). *lose* See 18.10, note. *dear delight* (1) cherished faculty for giving pleasure; (2) precious (with overtones of "high priced" [see line 3]) faculty for giving pleasure; (3) the capacity for giving pleasure that they have when scarce (for *dear* meaning "scarce," Willen and Reed cite Coverdale's Bible, 1Samuel 3:1: "The word of the Lord was dear at that time"; Geneva gives "precious" for the Vulgate's *pretiosus* and a marginal gloss that says "Because there were very fewe Prophetes to declare it"). The proverb "The thing that is rare is dear" (Tilley, T145) plays on the fact that in one sense of *dear* the equation is a truism.

13. *sometime* sometimes (as in 18.5,7).

14. *duall you* (1) bore you (*OED* gives this from 1576: "My desire is not to dull you, if I cannot delight you"); (2) diminish your value by making people tired of hearing you praised, render you common and thus less delightful (see line 12 and compare 52.4: *blunting the fine point of seldom pleasure*).

SONNET 103

1. *Alack* The context of the words that follow generates a delayed pun on "a lack." *poverty* paltriness, poor stuff. *brings forth* The metaphor, which is traditional (see 76.8, note), is of giving birth. (Note that the metaphor of pregnancy and childbirth is faintly sustained in lines 2 and 3 where the conjunction of *pride* and *bare* ["bear"] relates them to *brings forth* through birth-related senses that are inactive and inadmissible in the syntax; see the notes of *proud* in 98.8 and *barren of new pride* in 76.1; for a similar play, see the lines from *HVIII* quoted in the note on *pride* in line 2.)

2. *That* in that (introducing a justification for the label *poverty*; Ingram and Redpath compare *R&J* I.i.213–14: "O, she is rich in beauty; only poor / That, when she dies, with beauty dies her store"). (Until the syntax of line 3 reveals the actual grammatical subject of the clause, *That* asks to be understood as a relative pronoun substituting for muse: "who, having such a scope . . . "). *having* although she has. *scope* See 29.7, 61.8, notes. *show her pride* (1) display her splendor (i.e. how good she is); (2) display her pride and joy (i.e. show off the beloved, her favorite, what she is proud of); (3) display her offspring (see the note on *brings forth* above). In line 3, *bare* activates the special sense, "fine clothing," that *pride* has in 52.12 and *HVIII* I.i.23–25: "The madams too, / Not us'd to toil, did almost sweat to bear / The pride upon them."

3. "The unadorned argument is worth more." (The preceding gloss, which recognizes *argument all bare* as a noun phrase, reflects the sense dictated by a construction not evident until the reader comes to *Than* in the next line. Until then the line seems to be a self-sufficient syntactic unit meaning "The argument is entirely wanting in more worth"; compare the similarly inverted poetic word orders in 7.11, 48.5, and 52.7.) *The argument* the theme, the subject written about (with appropriate overtones of a specialized literary sense: "the argument" of a chapter or poem or book is like a table of its contents, a brief prefatory summary; see "The Argument" prefaced to *Lucrece*). *The argument all bare* Compare 26.4–8, and see 26.1–14, note; for the bawdy senses of *argument*, see 38.3, note. Those senses can retroactively color *her pride* with casual suggestions of "in pride" meaning "in heat" (see 151.10, note); *argument* can also give a vaguely bawdy cast to *my blunt invention* (from *in* and *venire*, "to come") in line 7 and to *well* in line 10 (see 154.9, note).

4,9,12,13,14. *Than when, then, Than, than, when* See 16.4,8, note.

3–4. It was proverbial that "truth shows best being naked" (Tilley, T589).

5. *no more* (1) no longer; (2) nothing additional (to what is inherent in the topic); (3) nothing of greater worth (than what I do write and/or than what I write about [i.e. I do not exaggerate your virtues]).

7. *overgoes* (1) goes beyond, outdoes, surpasses; (2) overwhelms, defeats. *blunt* (1) plain, unceremonious (as in *John* I.i.71: "A good blunt fellow"); (2) clumsy, awkward, not adroit (as in *Shrew* II.i.45: "You are too blunt; go to it orderly"); (3) rough (as in *V&A* 884: "the blunt boar, rough bear, or lion proud"); (4) dull, stupid (like "blunt Thurio" in *2Gent* II.vi.41); (5) blunted, worn dull. *invention* (1) power of imaginative creation; (2) imaginative creations (see 59.3, 38.8, notes).

8. *Dulling my lines* making the lines I write seem dull (i.e. both uninteresting and mere shadows of the real thing, diminished and distorted crude approximations). *doing me disgrace* shaming me (with a play on the fact that the speaker's disgrace is in doing disgrace to the beloved, obscuring, distorting, and failing to capture the beloved's graces; for "disgrace" meaning loss of beauty, see the notes on 33.8 and 89.5).

9. *mend* improve.

9–10. *to mend, To mar* The antithesis was proverbial; see 78.3,7,11, note; *OED*, s.v. "mar"; and Roger Ascham, *The Scholemaster* (1570), ed. E. Arber (London, 1870), p. 31: "They . . . rather marre him, then mend him." Tilley (W260) hears an echo of "Let well alone" in these lines.

11. *pass* end, effect (*OED* gives this from 1542: "[He] shall easily bryng the same to suche ende, and to such passe and effecte, as he would dooe"). *tend* aim (compare Proverbs 10:16: "The labour of the righteous tendeth to life: but the revenues of the wicked to sinne"; in context of the speaker's general tone of subservience, *tend* can color the line with syntactically irrelevant overtones of servility [see 53.2 and 57.1–2, note].

12. *tell* In this context of measurements and evaluations, *tell* can carry syntactically incidental suggestions of "to tell" meaning "to count" (note *added* in line 4, and see 84.13, note).

9–12. The substance of these lines and the conjunction in them of *mar* and *tell* combine to evoke an echo of the proverb "A good tale ill told is marred in the telling" (Tilley, T38—echoed in *Lear* I.iv.32).

13. *sit* have its seat, have place, be enthroned (compare 37.7, *seat* in 105.14, and *Lucrece* 288–89: "Within his thought her heavenly image sits, / And in the selfsame seat sits Collatine").

14. *shows you* (1) reveals to you; (2) reveals you to be.

SONNET 104

This sonnet and sonnet 107 have figured largely in circularly argued attempts to read the sonnets as autobiography. Rollins (*Variorum* II, 59–61) summarizes both the theories in terms of which 104 has been read and the evidence the sonnet has therefore provided for those theories.

2. *your eye I eyed* I saw you. (This phrase is a showy combination of pun [*eye, I*], polyptoton [*eye, eyed*], and epizeuxis [repetition of a sound without any intervening sound]. The wit of the construction can never have been subtle, but it is now unfortunately made gross and puerile by the semantic strain a modern reader must feel in the use of "eye" as a general synonym for "see" or "gaze upon." Shakespeare's reader probably would not have found that use unusual or noteworthy. According to Schmidt, "to eye" has such a meaning fourteen times in Shakespeare; in the thirteen other instances the word appears in contexts where a modern reader presumably understands it just as matter-of-factly as Shakespeare's reader would; the distortion here arises because the context of a play on words automatically alerts a reader to his expectations about usage. As a result of the modern reader's need to fight off suggestions of "to peer at acquisitively" or "to leer" in the verb "to eye," the play on *eye* and *eyed* is now so ostentatious as to swamp both the comparatively graceful triple pun by which Shakespeare achieved a clause in which grammatical object, subject, and verb are all expressed in one sound—"eye," "I"—and the stylistic tension between the simultaneously paired and unpairable *your* and *I*. Moreover, for Shakespeare's reader—accepting *your eye I eyed* more casually than we can—the phrase would have had the capacity to introduce witty and pertinent suggesions of a conceit it approximates structurally, the fusion and/or exchange of the identities of lover and beloved [see 22, 36, 39.1–4, 42, and notes]: "A *friend* is another *I*" [my italics] was proverbial; see Tilley's examples from 1539 and 1578 [F696].)

3. *Such* such as it was (the reader is called upon not only to fill in the ellipsis but also to extrapolate "it was" from *you were* in line 2). *still* to this time, yet (lines 9–12, on unperceived motion, act as a punning echo of *still* meaning "motionless"; see the plays on *yet* in lines 8 and 9 and on *still* in line 11).

4. *shook* shaken. *pride* splendor (particularly "splendor in dress," "fine clothes"; see 52.12 and 103.2, notes). (*Pride* here is metaphoric—likening leaves to clothing—but it has logically unharnessed special botanical pertinence as well: trees are said to be "proud" when the sap rises in them in the spring; compare the similar conflation of the ideas of splendid dress and rising sap in *RII* III.iv. 55–60:

> O, what pity is it
> That he had not so trimm'd and dress'd his land
> As we this garden! We at time of year
> Do wound the bark, the skin of our fruit trees,
> Lest, being over-proud in sap and blood,
> With too much riches it confound itself . . . .

See *proud-pied April* in 98.2 and 98.7, note; also note the pertinence here of *pride* meaning "prime," as in 99.12.)

    5. *beauteous* = dissyllabic, by syncopation: "beaut-yus."

    6. *process* the progression.

    7. *Three April pérfumes* The sweet smells of three Aprils. *burned* The precedent set by the withering indicated in the preceding clauses dictates that *burned* be understood as "dried out," "evaporated," "burned away." However, the non-idiomatic figurative use of "burn" retroactively evokes an incidental play on the etymological roots of "perfume" and "to perfume" (from the French *parfumer*, which derives from Latin *fumare*, "to smoke," and *per*, "thoroughly"); some commentators overread the wordplay and take the whole line as a metaphor of incense burning (see *Variorum* I, 256).

    8. *fresh* full of life and vigor, blooming, youthful, bright and clear of color. (Compare the proverbial phrases "As fresh as flowers in May," "As fresh as May," "As fresh as a rose" [Tilley, F389, M763, and R176], and—in context of *fair friend* in line 1—the proverbial phrase "fair and fresh" [as in *Shrew* IV.v.36; *T&C* IV.v.1; *FQ* I.xii.21 and 22, II.vi.3 and 15, ix.36, etc.]. Here there is also a play on the adverbial sense of *fresh*, "newly," which duplicates the action of *first*.) *yet* to this time, still (in the sense *still* has in line 3). *green* fresh (not faded in color as the *beauteous springs* were in line 5. However, this line carries disconcerting overtones of "green" meaning "naive," "inexperienced," "gullible," as in *John* III.iv.145: "How green you are and fresh in this old world").

    3–8. *Three winters . . . green* The structures of this sentence make it a model of simultaneous constancy and change and a model for the last line of the poem where the speaker at once changes his position entirely and reasserts his former spirit, metaphors, and diction. The elements of this long second sentence of the poem are pointedly like and pointedly unlike one another. In line 4 *summers' pride* is and is not a parallel to *winters cold* (i.e. "cold winters") in line 3. The three apposite "three" clauses (*Three winters cold . . .* , *Three beauteous springs . . .* , and *Three April pérfumes . . .*), are urgently similar and urgently dissimilar to one another. *Three beauteous springs*, the opening phrase of the second clause (line 5), repeats the basic structure of *Three winters cold*, the opening phrase of the first, but reverses the noun-adjective sequence; *Three beauteous springs* thus corresponds to *Three winters cold* in logical structure and position in its clause, but its substance corresponds to *three summers' pride*. The essential structure of line 5 seems on its way to duplicating that of the preceding clause (noun, prepositional phrase, transitive verb, object), but the parallel ends abruptly in the intransitive verb that ends the line. *Three summers' pride*, "the finery of three summers," suggests green leaves, but, since the particular context of this line demands that *summers' pride* describe the leaves as they were when shaken from the trees (withered and yellowed with age), *yellow autumn* echoes the phrase to which it contrasts; what is more, *yellow autumn* can also suggest the gaudy colors of autumn foliage—particularly in tandem with *summers' pride,* a metaphor of sartorial ostentation. In the third "three" clause (line 7), *April* echoes the idea of *springs* in the second, and *burned* both rhymes with *turned* and relates ideationally to the dryness suggested by *yellow autumn.* Like *shook three summers' pride,* the syntactically very different *three hot Junes burned* suggests dry autumn foliage more than it does the season it purports to describe. Each of the three clauses makes the same general statement about the whole three-year period, but, since the number of clauses is the same as the number of years, each clause in the succession of similar clauses suggests and seems to represent one of the three separate years, and, although each of the three makes the same inclusive statement, the time spans which express a year's passage from vitality to destruction become progressively shorter: in the first clause the season of vitality is not finally ended until winter; in the second it ends in autumn, and in the third, June.

Moreover, the never-resting syntax of the sentence is a stylistic model of the seasonal process it describes. When the first clause concludes at the end of line 4, the next line begins a similar clause that duplicates the function of the first. When that second clause has apparently concluded in *turned,* the last word in line 5, the next line continues it, transforming *turned* from an indicative verb into a past participle, and turning the whole of line 5 into the grammatical object of "have seen." Once lines 5 (direct object) and 6 (subject and verb) are established as a syntactic unit, line 6 turns out to be also and simultaneously the first half of an overlapping chiasmic duplicate of that unit: line 6 (subject and verb) and 7 (direct object). (Note also that, in perceiving summer as autumn in lines 4 and 7, a reader participates in a literary analogue to the inexorable flow of seasonal changes.)

Finally, having presented a syntactic approximation of the substance of its first three clauses, the syntactic structure of the sentence imitates the final paradox expressed in it. The syntax dwindles away into its fullest vigor: in line 8, the *Since* clause, which is grammatically only a subordinate afterthought, changes the physics of the whole sentence by lumping the first three clauses into a single intensifying gesture in support of the fifth, last, and weakest clause of the sentence, the one that delivers the paradox for which the sentence was written, *which yet are green.*

(Leishman [p. 161], crediting L. P. Wilkinson with the observation, notes that lines 3–8 echo Horace, *Epodes,* xi.5–6: "The third December, since I ceased to lust after Inachia, now is shaking the glory from the forests.")

9–10. "To move as the dial hand, which is not seen to move" was proverbial (Tilley, D321); see 77.7.

9. *yet* (1) nevertheless, even so, still (in a sense *still* does not have in line 3); (2) now no less than before, still. *dial* (= dissyllabic) clock or watch (see 77.2).

10. *Steal from* depart unseen from, slip away from (but with strong—though syntactically and logically freefloating—overtones of "steal from" meaning

"rob," "stealthily take from"; compare 63.8 and 92.1).   *his*   (1) its, the dial's
(see 73.10, note); (2) his, the beloved's.   *figure*   (1) number (i.e. character
denoting a number on the clock face); (2) form, shape, visual appearance. (By
the time a reader reaches *figure*, he is understanding two coexistent and inseparable things; "beauty departs like a clock hand" is the one overt assertion of the
clause until *his* gives equal authority to what has been only a syntactically unsupported shadow sense suggested in the context: "the dial's hand [i.e. time] takes
beauty from the beloved's appearance": *his* makes excellent sense with *figure*,
if "he" is the beloved and "his figure" is the beloved's appearance, but, since no
one number on a clock face is ordinarily thought of as the special property of a
clock hand, and since to infer the firm meaning "a number belonging to a dial
face" from *his figure* requires more time and conscious effort than a reader is
likely to spend, "its number" makes no immediate sense, and the action of the
dial hand on a clock becomes secondary to the action of time on beauty.)   *and no
pace perceived*   without any perceptible motion.

11.   *hue*   (1) complexion, coloring; (2) appearance (see 20.7, note—which also
considers the possibility of Shakespearian puns on "hue" and "you"; compare
eye I in line 2).   *methinks*   it seems to me.   *still doth stand*   (1) does not move
(as in *AYLI* III.ii.293: ". . . who Time gallops withal, and who he stands still
withal"); (2) survives to this time (for "to stand" meaning "to remain intact,"
"to survive," "to persist unconquered," see 60.13); (3) survives forever, is eternal
(compare *still* in 9.5 and 126.10).

12.   *deceived*   Like *seems* in line 3 and *seasons* in line 6, *deceived* casually
embodies the sound of the word "see," a word that could act as common
denominator for the poem; also note *perceived* in line 10.

13.   *For fear of which*   to provide against the chance that my eye may indeed
be deceived [I say the following].   *age unbred*   (1) future time; era not yet
begotten (see *bred* in 108.13); (2) ignorant, ill-bred, boorish period of time (*OED*
gives "Borish unbred upstartts" from 1622; for "bred" meaning "trained,"
"educated," see *AYLI* I.i.10). (In context of the topic of old age, a reader may
perceive a play here on two meanings of *age*; compare 108.10,13.)

14.   *you*   any of you (who live in the *age unbred*).

SONNET 105

The wit of this playful experiment in perversity derives from the false logic
resulting from the speaker's studiously inadequate understanding of idolatry.
Idolatry has traditionally been almost synonymous with polytheism: in Shakespeare's England its commonest occurrence was in self-righteously puritan
attacks on Roman Catholics; it referred not so much to *substituting* worship of
idols or other false gods (such as the golden calf in Exodus) for worship of the
Christian god as to real or apparent worship of other gods (e.g. the saints—
Mary in particular—and relics), *in addition to* the Christian god (see, for example, "An Homily against Peril of Idolatry," quoted below). However, although all polytheism is idolatrous, it does not therefore follow that any and all
monotheisms are orthodox as the speaker here pretends. In the narrow and

misleading sense of *idolatry*, the poem makes its case, but the diction of the argument is ostentatiously reminiscent of Christian doctrine (lines 12–14 cap the
litany-like repetition of the suggestively triple *Fair, kind, and true* with a specific
echo of the doctrine of the Trinity [compare 8.9–13, and see 8.13, note]), and of
the forms of Christian devotion (line 4 echoes the *Gloria Patri*: "Glory be to the
father, and to the sonne, and to the holy ghost. As it was in the beginning, is
now, and ever shal be: worlde wythout ende"). Thus the same rhetoric that
strengthens the argument for innocence of idolatrous polytheistic beliefs not
only testifies to the idolatrous nature of the speaker's allegiance to the beloved
but sharpens the evidence with overtones of active sacrilege.

Compare 21.3 and 130.11–13, and see 29, headnote.

1. See 108.5–8, note.

2. *show*   seem, appear (compare the similarly intransitive use of *shows* in
40.13).

3–4. The "since" clause is potentially complete at the end of line 3 and momentarily says what sonnet 76 says: "Since my songs and praises are all the
same." Line 4 reopens the syntactical unit and transforms *all alike* from an
adjective to an adverb: "Since my . . . are all equally (in effect, 'are unani-
mously') written for one [person], about one [person], constantly, of that sort,
and will always be so." (Line 4 also carries a suggestion of "to one and of one
who is always the same [or is constant] and always will be.")

4. A similar echo of the *Gloria Patri* occurs in the obviously related context
of the "Homily against Idolatry" but to strikingly different purpose: ". . .
images in temples and churches be indeed none other but idols, as unto the
which idolatry hath been, is, and ever will be committed" (1852 ed., p. 182).
(The two books of homilies, 1547 and 1563, reissued together in 1623 as *Certain
Sermons or Homilies*, are quoted here from an 1852 edition of the 1623 text by
the Society for Promoting Christian Knowledge. Article 35 of the Anglican
"Thirty-nine Articles of Religion" specifically required that the homilies be
regularly read aloud in the churches; Shakespeare's contemporaries presumably
heard each of the homilies over and over again all their lives.)   *still*   always (as
in 41.4).

1–4. Compare Donne's "Sapho to Philaenis," lines 25–28: "Such was my
Phao awhile, but shall be never, / As thou, wast, art, and, oh, maist be ever. /
Here lovers sweare in their *Idolatrie*, / That I am such . . ."

5. *Kind*   (1) gentle, generous, benevolent; (2) affectionate. (The theme of
constancy also activates the root sense of *kind*, "natural"; the second use of the
word suggests "constant to his nature," "of the same kind as always"; see 134.6,
note.) Note that line 5 is a model of constancy in finishing on the same word it
began with (epanalepsis).

6. *Still*   (1) always, constantly (as in line 4); (2) to this time, yet (as in 104.3).
constant   (1) the same; (2) faithful.

7. *constancy*   (1) sameness, being always the same; (2) the theme of faithfulness in love (and the beloved's faithfulness in particular).

8. *leaves out difference*   The general context dictates that this phrase be
understood as (1) "does not attempt to achieve variety [in either topic or style]

(see sonnet 76)" and (2) "leaves out everything else, anything different"; for "difference" meaning "diversity," Willen and Reed cite *Per* IV.ii.76–79: "Indeed shall you . . . taste gentlemen of all fashions. . . . You shall have the difference of all complexions"). However, since the phrase is so unidiomatic and relies so much on context for its meaning, it is possible that Shakespeare chose it for the supplementary commentary inherent in *difference*: the word meant "mark of distinction" (as in *Ham* V.ii.107: "an absolute gentleman, full of most excellent differences"); this phrase thus embodies a submerged but pertinent criticism of verse that lacks variety. *Difference* is also a term in logic and means "That characteristic which distinguishes a thing from others of the same class" (*OED* cites this from Thomas Wilson's *The Rule of Reason* [1551], a textbook on logic: "When the propertie or difference is granted, then the kinde straight foloweth"); *leaves out difference* thus pertains obliquely and ironically both to the comic fallaciousness of the speaker's argument about idolatry and to his theme, the nature of the beloved. A *difference* is also a "disagreement," and *difference* is "hostility" (see *MofV* IV.i.166–67: "the difference / That holds this present question in the court"); both disagreement and hostility are in regular evidence in the sonnets, and the speaker denies or ignores both as regularly as he reports them.

9. *Fair* (1) beautiful; (2) pure (as in *2Gent* IV.ii.5–6: "Silvia is too fair, too true, too holy, / To be corrupted with . . . gifts"); (3) honorable (compare "fair play" in *Temp* V.i.175); (4) kind (compare *Cor* III.iii.91–92: "I would not buy / Their mercy at the price of one fair word"). *true* (1) constant, faithful; (2) honorable, honest; (3) natural (see *truth* in 54.14 and note). *argument* topic (as in 76.10 and 103.3). Note, however, that, although the context dictates "is my only topic" for the focal phrase of this line, the line can be read as (and in any case carries overtones of) "All of my reasoning is honest, natural, and accurate."

10. *varying* = dissyllabic, by syncopation. *varying to other words* The overall sense of the phrase is "diversified only to the extent of sometimes being expressed differently." The phrase conflates three uses of "to vary," each of which is either logically or syntactically inefficient for its task: (a) "to diversify" or "to change" ("diversifying to other words" and "changing to other words" make sense, but each is a long logical and syntactic step from fully meaningful union with *Fair, kind, and true*); (b) "to express in other words" (which makes *varying* syntactically incompatible with—and logically unnecessary to—*to other words* [*OED* exemplifies the use with this example from 1580: "I gave him this Theame out of Ovid, to translate, and varie after his best fashion"]); and (c) "to spin out variations [on a theme]" (a reading by which *varying* would be logically and syntactically incompatible with *to other words* [for this use of "to vary," see *HV* III.vii.30–33: "the man hath no wit that cannot . . . vary deserved praise on my palfrey"]). Here again the sense of the phrase is clearer from the requirements of context than from the construction; like *difference* in line 8, *varying* (which generally imitates its sense by being a variation on the word *difference*), comments on the argument by means of senses of "to vary" that do not pertain to the sentence where *varying* appears: (a) "to vary from" meaning "to depart from standard practice" (*OED*, 3) is generally pertinent to the context of

idolatrous practices; (b) "to vary" meaning "to be logically inconsistent" (*OED*, 7a) pertains to the speaker's inept defense of his orthodoxy; and (c) "to vary," like "to differ," meant "to quarrel" (*OED*, 5b). (The awkwardly elliptical phrase could also have been prompted by Shakespeare's desire to point up a trivial and insignificant, but also undeniable, conflict between constancy and variation of any kind; the syntactic awkwardness of the phrase invites thought and thus opens the way for a reader's mind to stray into the clownish absolutism of perversely applying strict logic to idiomatic speech; compare the gravedigger in *Ham* V.i.115–32.)

9–10. The "Homily against Idolatry" gives an extended and etymologically ornamented demonstration that "idol" and "image" are exact synonyms (pp. 181–82).

11. *this change*   this variation. (The usage here suggests that *change* refers to a fixed, limited cycle of possible permutations; a *change* in dancing apparently was one cycle of changes of partners, ending when each pair of original partners were reunited in their original positions [see *LLL* V.ii.209: "in our measure do but vouchsafe one change"; the same general sense underlies "changes" as a term in bell-ringing meaning "the different order in which a set of bells may be rung"]; *change* here is also colored by its use as a musical term meaning "variation" or "modulation" [as in *2Gent* IV.ii.66–69:

> *Host.* Hark, what fine change is in the music.
> *Julia.* Ay, that change is the spite.
> *Host.* You would have them always play but one thing?
> *Julia.* I would always have one play but one thing.]

Note also that when *spent* appears later in the line it activates the commercial context common to both "spend" and "change" [= "a place where business is transacted," "an exchange"], and thus introduces a submerged punning sense in the whole line: "And in this trading center is my invention paid out.") *invention*   (1) power of literary creation (see 38.8, note, and 59.3); (2) inventiveness. *spent*   (1) used, employed; (2) used up, exhausted (i.e. capable of no more; compare 107.14).

12. The point of the line is that, paradoxically, limitation to one theme is not a limitation in this case because the speaker's one theme is multiple; indeed, the echo of the Trinity suggests that the one theme is infinite, is all themes.   *in one* (1) subsumed in one theme, unified; (2) embodied in one person. (Note that the dwelling metaphor that starts to develop in *scope* and emerges clearly in the couplet expands from this, the third *in* of the poem—from its root sense as an indicator of physical location.) *scope*   See 29.7, note. *affords*   allows, furnishes (this word also has financial senses [*OED* gives this from 1514: "I may not aforde nowe for to spende out all"], which, although syntactically and logically irrelevant here, continue the commercial subtheme incidental to the preceding line).

13. *lived alone*   existed singly in individual persons.

12–13. Note the play between *in one* and *alone*; compare 79.1–3 and notes.

13–14. The observation that "beauty and honesty seldom meet" was proverbial (Tilley, B163); see *AYLI* I.ii.33–36: "those [women] that she [Fortune] makes fair she scarce makes honest; and those that she makes honest she makes very ill-favoredly."

14. *seat*   residence (see *sit* in 103.13 and note). The line is nearly prose; whether by accident or design, its rhythmic awkwardness suggests the difficulty of retaining three in one.

SONNET 106

1. *of wasted time*   The essential sense of the phrase is "of the past," "of past times," and is derived from a reader's awareness that a chronicle is necessarily "from and about the past." (Compare *JC* II.i.59 and *Oth* I.iii.84 where the context similarly dictates "past" as a sense of *wasted*.) *Wasted* does not interfere with that sense, since "to waste" commonly meant "to consume," "to use up," and since what is "consumed" is "past." However, much of the energy of *wasted* and *time* in combination goes into suggestions of time as waster, as destroyer. The sum total of the phrase is in effect "of past ages destroyed by time," "of the time-withered past." (The phrase also carries an inevitable suggestion of "time spent fruitlessly"; see 100.13, note.)

2. *wights*   persons, men and women. (The word would have carried the tone of self-consciously affected archaism that made it a favorite with Spenser and that it later has in Romantic poetry; Shakespeare uses the word eight other times: once in the context of witchcraft, once in a mock-proverb by Iago, once in Iago's ballad of King Stephen, once by Gower, once to describe Armado, and three times in the mouth of Pistol.)

3. *beauty*   The completed line makes *beauty* the syntactic parallel and equal of *descriptions* in line 2, but it can momentarily act as a continuation of the *of* phrase: "I see descriptions of the most beautiful beings and [descriptions of] beauty."   *rhyme*   verse (see 107.11, note).   *making beautiful old rhyme*   (1) making old verse beautiful, giving beauty to old verse; (2) creating beautiful old verse; making old verse that is beautiful.

4. *In praise*   The phrase indicates both beauty's purpose in beautifying old rhyme and the kind of old rhyme beautified.   *ladies dead*   ladies now no longer living.   *lovely*   (1) beauteous; (2) worthy to be loved (as in 54.13 and 126.1).

5. *blazon*   catalogue of properties, list of admirable qualities. ("Blazon" is an heraldic term derived from a Middle English word for "shield" and meaning "coat of arms." The use here is one influenced by "to blaze" meaning "to trumpet forth." The context of a love poem and the list of bodily parts in line 6 suggest a particular kind of literary blazon, the sort of exercise in *effictio* referred to in sonnet 130 and descended from the anatomical inventories in Song of Songs [e.g. 5:10–16: "My welbeloved is white and ruddy. . . . His head is as fine golde, his lockes curled, & blacke as a raven. His eyes are like dooves. . . . His chekes are as a bed of spices . . . , & his lippes like lilies . . . "]. This is sonnet 39 in Bartholomew Griffin's *Fidessa* [1596]:

> My Lady's hair is threads of beaten gold,
>   Her front the purest Chrystal eye hath seen:

> Her eyes the brightest stars the heavens hold,
>   Her cheeks red roses such as seld have been:
> Her pretty lips of red vermillion dye,
>   Her hands of ivory the purest white:
> Her blush Aurora, or the morning sky,
>   Her breast displays two silver fountains bright,
> The Spheres her voice, her grace the Graces three,
>   Her body is the Saint that I adore,
> Her smiles and favors sweet as honey be,
>   Her feet fair Thetis praiseth evermore.
> But ah the worst and last is yet behind,
>   For of a Gryphon she doth bear the mind.

of sweet beauty's best of the best that beauty possesses. Q's "beauties" allows for the reading fixed by the modernization, and the word order, the model of *beauty* in line 3, and the adjective *sweet* presumably encouraged Shakespeare's reader to understand "beauties" as "Beauty's," i.e. "possessed by the personified abstraction 'Beauty.' " However, the modern spelling denies the range inherent in the Q spelling, which would have included the senses now indicated by the spellings "beauties" (which would give "of sweet beauties best" the sense "of the best of sweet beauties"), and "beauties' " (which would give the sense "possessed by 'beauties' of the past, by beautiful persons now dead," and/or "possessed by the beauties, by the qualities of loveliness, visible then"). The ambiguity results in a fusion of the disembodied ideal and its particular manifestations.

7. *I see* I perceive that (compare line 2, where *I see* means "I behold"). *their* The antecedent, the authors of *the chronicle of wasted time*, is only present by inference. *ántique pen* See 17.12, note. *would have* was trying to.

8. *Ev'n* See 15.6, note; if *Ev'n* is pronounced "in," it is the fourth monosyllabic "in" sound in the octave. (Note that no two of the three preceding *in*'s have the same sense [lines 1, 4, and 5]; compare the various uses of *of* in lines 1, 2, 4, and 6.) *Ev'n such* just such. *master* are master of, possess (as in *MofV* V.i.173–74: "the wealth / That the world masters").

9. *their praises* (1) the praises written by ancient authors (see *their*, line 7, note); (2) writings that belong to—are in praise of—*the fairest wights* of past ages.

9–11. These lines suggest a mock-sacrilegious equation between the beloved and Christ (compare sonnet 105); they echo the Plato-like thinking by which the church fathers from Paul on perceived the Old Testament typologically—as a series of prefigurations of the Gospel story; for instance Abraham's sacrifice of Isaac was to God's sacrifice of his only son as the shadowy approximations of truth perceptible to human beings are to their Platonic ideals (see 53, headnote).

11. *but* merely (contrast the conjunctive use in line 14. *divining* prophesying (as in *3HVI* IV.vi.69).

11–13. *for they . . . For we* because they . . . because even we.

12. *skill* Q gives "still." The emendation has been generally accepted since the eighteenth century. A case can be made for "still"; for instance, Sisson

(II.213) argued that "still" here means "as yet," and that the emendation cancels the contrast between skillful poets of antiquity, who lacked the ideal topic, and modern poets, who have the beloved to write about but are unable to express his beauty. There are arguments against Sisson's defense and others like it (the retention of "still" provides no reference for *enough*; Sisson's sense of "still" is not recorded before 1632), but the best argument for emendation is that with "still" in it the line does not *seem* meaningful; it pulls a reader up short, and the sonnets rarely do that; Shakespeare's locutions often turn out to be logically wanting when carefully examined, but they usually sound simple and clear as a reader goes along. Rollins (*Variorum* II, 262) and Ingram and Redpath (pp. 240–42) summarize arguments for and against *skill* and "still." Tucker suggested "style"; *OED* gives "still" as a spelling of "style" in the fourteenth through sixteenth centuries; note *pen* in line 7.

14. *to wonder*   for beholding with amazement.

13–14. Note that the whole poem has a common denominator in different kinds of "seeing."

SONNET 107

Like sonnet 104, this sonnet figures in attempts to date the sonnets and to locate them in relation to one or another of the supposititious biographical explanations of their occasion. The theorizing was presumably originally prompted by line 8, which is clearly political, which *may* have a specific reference, and which *might* have more than metaphoric significance. The bulk of the theorizing, however, has been directed toward explaining the eclipse of the mortal moon (line 5), finding specific identities for the *sad augurs* and their *preságe* (line 6), and explaining *cónfined doom* in relation to the other two. All the theories are inconsequential, but scholars have been producing them for so many years, that the questions about this poem are not now *whether* it alludes to a specific event in Shakespeare's lifetime and *whether* it provides a clue to dating but *which* date the poem gives for its writing. Thus, in his edition of 1963, Martin Seymour-Smith both demonstrates the flimsiness of the theories he summarizes and assumes that he must pick one to espouse:

> There is no doubt that this sonnet contains a specific reference; the difficulty lies in discovering it. Leslie Hotson (*Shakespeare's Sonnets Dated*) develops Butler's earlier suggestion that the defeat of the Armada is the event referred to: the 'mortall Moone', according to Hotson [who understands 'mortall' as 'deadly' and/or 'subject to destruction'] is the familiar [crescent-shaped] formation of the Spanish fleet. . . . Dr. G. B. Harrison claims that the reference is to the genuine anxiety caused by the Queen's entrance, on September 6th, 1595, into her Grand Climacteric (her sixty-third year, representing the association of the mystic numbers seven and nine) . . . . Sir Edmund Chambers favours 1599, when the Queen was ill; but his reasons are less convincing than those Harrison puts forward for 1596. Another popular but unlikely date is 1603, when Elizabeth died and James

VI of Scotland came to the English throne. There is a theory for almost every year, from 1588 to 1609. . . .

Rollins (*Variorum* I, 263–67) summarizes most of the theories, and Ingram and Redpath summarize the less obviously nugatory among them.

1–2. Q puts commas after *fears, soul, world,* and *come.* Modern editors customarily delete the comma at the end of line 1; some remove one or more of the other commas as well. None of these punctuations would deny a seventeenth-century reader either the limited sense indicated to a modern reader by the modern punctuations (*mine own fears* and *prophetic soul | Of the wide world* are parallel noun phrases), or the limited sense that the Q punctuation indicates to a modern reader accustomed to logically directive punctuation ("Not mine own fears of the wide world nor the prophetic soul of the wide world"). No punctuation is likely to put an efficient limit on the modification of the *dreaming* phrase, even for a modern reader. The punctuation adopted here is the least unsatisfactory of the possible available choices.   *the prophetic soul | Of the wide world* speculative forebodings by the world in general. (The stock expression *wide world* causes the phrase to act principally as a sweeping, all-inclusive gesture [compare 19.7, 137.10, and *Much Ado* IV.i.288: "not for the wide world"]; however, the phrase gets a note of philosophic solemnity from its vague and unharnessed suggestions of *anima mundi,* "the world soul," the universal animating spirit which various classical philosophers [e.g. Plato and the Stoics] posited for all creation. Shakespeare habitually used *soul* to indicate the seat of intuition; see 136.1, *Much Ado* IV.i.325: "Think you in your soul the Count Claudio hath wrong'd Hero?" and *Ham* I.v.40–41: "O my prophetic soul! / My uncle.")

1–4. For a reader coming directly from sonnet 106, which concerns accounts of the past, this quatrain on speculations about the future seems to introduce the second of a pair. Note too that for a reader of the sonnets in the 1609 sequence 106.9–11 will have already introduced the topic of prophecy, and that the fears mentioned here can acquire some specificity from the context of the particular fear expressed in 104.9–14.

2. *dreaming on*   predicting (less particular senses—"thinking about," "musing upon," "speculating on"—are also possible, but the context evokes the specific meaning; compare Shakespeare's use of "dreamer" to mean "soothsayer" in *JC* I.ii.24 and *1HIV* III.i.150: "the dreamer Merlin and his prophecies").

3. *yet*   Here the word is nearly meaningless because the indicators of meaning (i.e. the relevance of the word to the general train of thought in which it appears and the significance implied by its syntactic position) work at cross purposes. *Yet* used for emphasis and meaning "even" pertains to the preceding construction ("Not . . . nor yet . . . "; *OED* gives this from 1581: "Neither he, ne yet his parentes can forsake their prince"); *yet* does have some extrasyntactical emphatic effect on lines 1 and 2, but its syntactic position in line 3 mutes the effect and suggests another idiom entirely. The standard construction " 'X' cannot yet 'Y' " invites a reader to understand *yet* as "so far," "as yet," "up to this time," but that sense is not readily meaningful where the particular

grammatical subjects are those of lines 1 and 2 and the verb is *control*. *Yet* meaning "hitherto" (as in *Lucrece* 366) pertains to *Supposed* as in line 4 ("hitherto thought to be"), but, again, the word order allows only the vague suggestions inherent in any context that couples *yet* and a contrast between past and present conditions. The sense that best fits the completed quatrain is "now" (as in *HV* III.iii.1: "How yet resolves the Governor of the town?"), but since the context that invokes that sense does not emerge until line 4 and since that sense of "can yet" would have been as foreign to idiomatic Renaissance English as to modern, one cannot suppose that such a reading suggested itself to Shakespeare's contemporaries.

    lease (1) term of duration; (2) right of possession and/or a certificate of that right (compare 18.4, and see 87.3–5,8). (Willen and Reed note an incidental play in "the opposition between *true* and an archaic meaning of *lease*, that of 'falsehood' "; see the examples in 124.10, note.) *of* (1) on; (2) belonging to, possessed by. *my . . . love* (1) my beloved; (2) the affection I feel (see 34.13, note). *true* See 105.9, note. *control* (1) have authority over, restrict; (2) overpower, defeat (as in *Lucrece* 678–79: "with her own white fleece her voice controll'd / Entombs her outcry"); (3) deny the value of. Note that *control* is an accounting term (see 58.2, note).

    4. *Supposed as* which was thought to be (the antecedent is doubtful; see below). *forfeit* forfeited (the past participle). *forfeit to* (1) subject to, in the control of, regulated by; (2) surrendered into the possession of ("forfeit to 'someone' " was a common construction [see "forfeit unto the crown" in the *OED* example below]; here the idiom indicates a sense that must immediately be rejected because *doom* cannot describe a possessor); (3) surrendered in adherence to. The three senses are invoked by different stimuli; each pertains to the general assertion of the quatrain, but no single paraphrase can hold them all. Because of the syntactical relationship indicated by *as*, and because of the logical necessity that results from the semantic limitations of *doom*, and because of the context of *lease* and *control*, the primary sense of the line must be "thought to be subject to a cónfined doom." In effect *forfeit* acts as a synonym for "controlled." However, *forfeit* also carries overtones of the ordinary meanings it has in non-restricting contexts (what is forfeited is surrendered as a penalty) and in less restrictive contexts of real estate law (*forfeit* here carries syntactically unincorporated suggestions of "possessed in reversion by the lessor [or by the original owner]"; compare this *OED* example from 1594: "Forfeit and confiscate unto the crowne" and this example from a law of 1495 of a use of "forfeitable": "All Castels . . . be not . . . forfeitable . . . to the Kyng"). *cónfined* restricted, limited (and, by inference, "already established," "preordained," "fixed"). The stress is indicated by the meter; Abbott (par. 492) gives other examples of Shakespearian stress on prefixes derived from Latin *cum*. *doom* (1) law, decree (as in *FQ* I.ix.41: "The term of life is limited, / Ne may a man prolong, nor shorten it; / . . . Who life did limit by almightie doome, / . . . knows best the termes established"); (2) judgment, sentence of punishment (as in 145.7); (3) fate, destiny (as in *John* III.i.311–12: "alter not the doom / Forethought by heaven"); (4) ruin, destruction, death (as in 14.14). Although the logic of the

sentence presents the whole of line 4 as a modifier for *lease* in line 3, *my true love* is a nearer antecedent and can activate suggestions of "the fate of being confined (imprisoned—as in a tomb of brass)" in *a cónfined doom* (for analogous syntactical inversions, see 13.12, note).

5. *The mortal moon* (1) the moon, which (though apparently immortal) has mortal characteristics (the impermanence of the moon's condition—its susceptibility to eclipse and its repeating cycles of birth, growth, maturity, and decay—made it a traditional emblem of the perpetual transience and the eternal constancy in eternal change of all life on earth); (2) that mortal (i.e. that person) who has the characteristics of the moon (which is to say, is bright, exalted, and chaste like the virgin goddess Diana in her various manifestations [e.g. goddess, the moon] and under her various names [e.g. Diana, Delia, Cynthia, Phoebe; compare Ben Jonson's hymn to Diana in *Cynthia's Revels*: "Queene, and Huntresse, chaste, and faire, / Now the Sunne is laid to sleepe, / Seated, in thy silver chaire . . . "]). By Shakespeare's time the obvious likeness between Elizabeth, the virgin queen, and Diana had been exhaustively exploited in almost half a century of hyperbolic compliments and philosophic analogies. The equation of the moon and Elizabeth necessarily looms larger for modern specialists in Elizabethan history and literature than it would have for Elizabeth's contemporaries for whom the word "moon" had after all to fulfill its day-to-day function of indicating a heavenly body; to take *mortal moon* as a reference to the queen is not unreasonable, but one cannot assume absolutely that Shakespeare's audience understood it that way. *her* The moon was generally thought of as feminine (as death was thought of as masculine; see lines 10–12). *eclipse* The context does not indicate whether *eclipse* is meant literally (eclipses of the sun or moon are traditionally bad omens; see *Lear* I.ii.99–142) or metaphorically (the "eclipse"—the physical or moral decay—of a person influential in either a private or public sphere bodes ill to others within that sphere; see *A&C* III.xiii. 153–55: "Alack, our terrene moon [i.e. Cleopatra] / Is now eclips'd, and it portends alone / The fall of Antony"). *endured* (1) undergone without succumbing, survived; (2) submitted to, allowed without opposition (compare *Temp* III.i.61–62: "endure / This wooden slavery"); (3) suffered the pain of.

6. *sad* (1) solemn, grave, serious (unlikely to mock or be mocked); (2) sorrowful, dejected. *augurs* augurers, prophets. *mock* (1) deride, laugh at; (2) set at naught, despise, defy (as in *MofV* II.i.30–31: "[I would] mock the lion when 'a roars for prey, / To win thee, lady"). *preságe* (1) prognostication, prediction (as in *John* III.iv.158); (2) intuition, foreboding (as in *RII* II.ii. 142).

7. Compare 115.11–12. *Incertainties* uncertainties. *crown* This use of "to crown" is metaphoric, but the mere presence of the word *crown* would tend to strengthen the assumptions of any reader who heard a reference to the queen in *mortal moon*.

8. *olives of endless age* everlasting peace. (Olive branches are a traditional symbol of peace; here *olives* stands for "peace" by synecdoche. Horace also used "olive," *oliva*, to mean "olive branch," or "a crown of olive branches" in *Odes* I.vii.8, and in 1622 Ben Jonson uses "olive" similarly in *The Masque of*

Augurs [line 332, Orgel, *Masques*, p. 387].) Shakespeare likes to rhyme and pun on pairs of sixth syllables; *olives*, the fifth and sixth syllables of this line, is echoed by *I'll live*, the fifth and sixth syllables of line 11.

1–8. H. C. Beeching (edition of 1904) called 107 "the most difficult of the sonnets"; Dover Wilson agreed and perhaps hit on the source of our difficulty when he quoted Beeching's estimate and coupled his own comment to it: "though it seems at first sight a simple and natural allusion to a well-known historical event." The combination of apparent simplicity and demonstrable difficulty is perhaps the commonest trait of the sonnets. This one, however, exaggerates that paradox—perhaps because of its initial theme: prophecy. Although the poem does not imitate the mannerisms of prophecy, the first two quatrains have the kind of effect on a reader that prophecies have. They feel full of important and valuable meaning that seems potentially available to a reader but always remains just beyond his reach. The two quatrains have evoked great quantities of interpretation because, like dreams and prophecies, they require it; for instance, *hath her eclipse endured* (line 5) is like Calpurnia's prophetic dream of Caesar's statue spouting blood (*JC* II.ii.76–90); it signifies triumphant survival, and just as clearly signifies final defeat; similar, though less obvious, in its prophecy-like demands for assistance from its audience is the syntax of lines 1 and 2 in which *fears* (what is felt) is structurally parallel with *soul* (which feels). The syntax of quatrain 1 also contributes to an impression of mystical and majestic superhuman pronouncement: the opening negation has no object until line 3, and the dangling modification that constitutes line 4 attaches to *world* as well as *lease* and *love*. Another characteristic of prophecies is specificity that fails to specify. The syntax of quatrain 2 is flat-footed in its simplicity; in lines 5 and 6 straightforward nouns and verbs are in straightforward relationship to one another; the lines seem not only specific but as though they must be successfully delivering their meaning to any but the densest readers (indeed, the easy precision apparent in the lines may account for the scholarly presumption that they can be made to divulge highly particular specific meaning). The two clauses of lines 7 and 8 make a structural and formal pair with those in lines 5 and 6; the likeness vouches for continued simplicity and holds out the promise that the simplicity will now be real as well as apparent. However, lines 7 and 8 also advertise a clarity they lack; both clauses have personified abstractions as grammatical subjects, but the effect of the personification is, on the one hand, to insist that the actions described are designed so as to be immediately available to the reader's imagination and, on the other, to preclude visualization of any kind. Moreover, although the association of olive branches with peace is familiarly meaningful, their normal relation is reversed (olives signify peace; in line 8 *peace proclaims olives*). Similarly the reader's sense of rational continuity is both maintained and diminished by the relationships between the two quatrains and among the lines of quatrain 2. Line 7, on *Incertainties*, follows naturally from the topic of unjustified faith in predictions in line 6, but the frustrated *augurs* exemplify and underscore the folly of just such confidence as the speaker cheerfully announces in line 7, an inherently self-contradictory assertion that uncertainties can be certain. Line 8 is extra-syntactically linked to line 7 by *crown* and *olives*, which unite to suggest the classical practice of honoring victors with crowns of olive branches; the connection simultaneously testifies that passage from line to line follows some rationally based program, and, since crowns of olive branches are never assimilated into the exposition, suggests that the speaker's thinking is random, unfocused, and rambling; in addition, the extra link to line 7 annexes the insecurity necessarily inherent in any action by *Incertainties* to the proclamation of eternal peace and casts doubt on its validity. Lines 5 and 6 and lines 7 and 8 insist on a distinction between past insecurity and present confidence, but they also blur the distinction and, since it is *Incertainties* which now are assured, deny absolutely that certainty is possible, that anything can be of *endless age*. All in all, the first eight lines both present grounds for and completely undercut the informed optimism of the last six.

9–10. *Now . . . fresh*   Ingram and Redpath point out that "the image is of invigorated plants."

9. *with*   as a result of, by means of (= the limited sense fixed by the completed clause; when a reader first gets to *with*, it can seem to be indicating simultaneity—as in *Cor* I.i.180: "With every minute you do change a mind"). *drops*   In the logic of the completed clause *drops* seems to indicate "rain drops" or "dew," but *balmy* invokes suggestions of drops of sap (rising in a tree in springtime [note *olives* in the preceding line]).   *balmy*   (1) revitalizing, refreshing, softly restorative; (2) delightful, deliciously mild. The various senses of "balm" and of the words derived from it retain elements of its root sense: a tree resin valued for its fragrance (see "balmy slumbers" in *Oth* II.iii.250).

10. *My love*   (1) the affection I feel; (2) my beloved.   *fresh*   See 104.8, note.   *to me subscribes*   submits to me, gives allegiance to me (compare *Shrew* I.i.81: "to your pleasure humbly I subscribe"). (The context of legal documents in lines 3 and 4 invokes a gently unifying, though non-signifying, play on "to subscribe" meaning "to sign one's name"; the idea of writing inherent in "subscribe" also provides a link to the speaker's new topic in line 11, his own actions as a writer.)

11–14. See 55, headnote.

11. *spite of*   in spite of.   *rhyme*   poem. (The word appears five other times in the sonnets [16.4, 17.14, 32.7, 55.2, 106.3]—each time in this sense, never with reference to words paired by likeness of sound, but each time in a rhyme-pair [with *time*]; that may be mere coincidence or may result from Shakespeare's sense of the wit inherent in rhyming the word *rhyme*. Also note the potential but unexploited play on *him* ["hymn"] and *rhyme* ["hymn"]; see 21.8, 102.8, and 134.9, notes.)

12. *insults o'er*   triumphs over in an insolent and scornful manner (see *mock* in line 6).

13. *find*   Note the echo of *cónfined* in line 4.

14. *crests*   The word simultaneously suggests a battle helmet (and thus the martial glory of tyrants) and heraldic crests, coats of arms (commonly used to ornament and identify great men's tombs).   *tombs*   See 83.12, note (on the likelihood of a pun on "tome").   *spent*   wasted away, gone, consumed. The word gets various extra resonances from the contexts of *lease* and *forfeit*, of

endless, and (since "spend" was used to mean "speak" [as in *Oth* I.ii.48: "I will
but spend a word here in the house"] and figured in the standard idiom "to
spend one's mouth" meaning "to bark" [as in *T&C* V.i.89: "He will spend his
mouth and promise, like Brabbler the hound"]), of *dull and speechless tribes*.

SONNET 108

1. *character*   inscribe, write (as in 122.2 and *Ham* I.iii.58: "these few precepts
in thy memory / Look thou character").
2. *figured*   portrayed, represented (but with suggestions of other senses of
"figure": (a) the context of literary invention [compare 59.1–8] gives pertinence
to "to figure" as an extension of "rhetorical figure" and meaning "to express
metaphorically" or "to adorn with rhetorical figures" [*OED*, 9, 10]; (b) the context of prophecy in 106.9–10 and 107 does the same for "to figure" meaning "to
prefigure" [as in *3HVI* II.i.32: "In this the heaven figures some event"]; (c) the
coincidence of *figured* and *character* can activate a gentle and incidental play on
their common denominator in nouns meaning "a letter of the alphabet."   *true*
(1) constant, faithful; (2) genuine, unfeigned, honest; (3) real, actual (as opposed to "literarily approximated").   *spirit* = dissyllabic (as in 129.1);
Kökeritz (p. 212) notes that Spenser rhymed *spirit* and *merit*, and that *spirit*/
"inherit" occurs as a rhyme in Marlowe and throughout the seventeenth century.
3. *what now to register*   what now remains unrecorded. (A majority of editors
unnecessarily emend *now* to "new" in order to simplify the parallelism of the
two apposite phrases [a parallel complicated in any case by the change from
What's in the first to *what* in the second], and to balance *old . . . old* in line 7.)
4. *my love*   the affection I feel (= the sense dictated by the model of *my true
spirit*. But "my love" meaning "my beloved" is inherent in *my love*—just as the
fact that poetic expressions of affection usually include poetic descriptions of the
beloved is inherent in the topic of the quatrain; *my love* thus both contrasts with
and is duplicated by *thy dear merit*, which thus anticipates the interchangeability
of lover and beloved implied by *thou mine, I thine* in line 7; see 109.3–4 and 36,
headnote).   *dear*   (1) endearing; (2) precious.
5. *Nothing*   Since "nothing" and "noting" seem to have been pronounced
alike (see Kökeritz, pp. 132 and 320, and the rhyme between "a-doting" and
"nothing" in 20.10,12), Shakespeare's contemporaries may have heard a pun
here where *Nothing* follows upon *character, figured, speak, register*, and *express*—five synonyms or near-synonyms for "to note" (Shakespeare puns overtly
on "nothing" and "noting" in *Much Ado* II.iii.50–53, the title of that play, and
WT IV.iv.603).   *yet*   nevertheless (with a play on "yet" meaning "now as
formerly" [as in 104.8]).   *sweet boy*   Compare *lovely boy* in 126.1, and see 126.4,
note.
7. *Counting*   accounting, thinking (but, as a result of the context of prayers
repeated daily, with a possible play on "counting one's beads"—i.e. "saying
one's prayers," "saying the rosary"; compare *3HVI* II.i.162: "Numbering our
Ave-Maries with our beads").   *thou mine, I thine*   The syntactic position of
these phrases indicates that they function as parenthetic examples from the

speaker's litany of love; Tucker put them in quotation marks. Ingram and Redpath note an echo of Song of Songs 2:16: "My welbeloved is mine, and I am his." (The unexploited bawdy potential of *Counting, no,* and *old thing* can give the line overtones of comic self-mockery; note *conceit* in line 13, and see 20.12, 53.5, 58.3, notes.)

    8. *Ev'n* See 15.6, note. *Ev'n as* just as. *hallowed thy fair name* Compare "hallowed be thy name" in the Lord's Prayer, and see 105.1.

    5–8. As in 105, the wit of this quatrain derives from the speaker's apparent self-betrayal in presenting evidence of sacrilege and in his apparent obliviousness to the implications of his words; here the self-mocking wit gets an extra twist because the sacrilegious echo appears in a context that reminds us that the Lord's Prayer, the most repeated of all Christian prayers, is prefaced by "when ye pray, use no vaine repetitions as the heathen: for they thinke to be heard for their muche babling" (Matt. 6:7).

    9. *So that eternal love* The apparently conjunctive phrase signals a firm logical relationship between the sentence it introduces and quatrain 2, but, since their substance and syntax do not sustain any particular understanding of their relationship, *So* and *that* are freefloating and effectively meaningless syllables. One can make sense of the construction: (a) "with the result that eternal love . . ." (introducing the effect of doing what lines 6–8 specify); (b) "thus, that eternal love . . ." (taking *that* as a relative pronoun referring to the love implied by the dedication described in lines 7–8). But both senses are more evident in an analysis than in a simple reading of the lines, where *So that* is a mere gesture of coherence. *in love's fresh case* (1) in the situation of being newly in love; (2) with regard to the matter of unwithered affection (with a play on "in love's [i.e. Cupid's? a lover's?] youthful skin"; Willen and Reed note a similar pun in *WT* IV.iv.802: "though my case be a pitiful one, I hope I shall not be flay'd out of it." Also note this adaptation of Job 19:25–27 at the beginning of the Burial Service: "I know that my Redeemer liveth, and that I shall rise out of the earth in the last day, and shall be covered again with my skin, and shall see God in my flesh: yea . . . with these same eyes"). *fresh* Compare 107.10, and see 104.8, note.

    10. *Weighs not* does not take account of, does not consider, ignores. (*Weighs* fulfills the legal metaphor latent in *case* and points up the legal root of *injury*.) *the dust and injury of age* (1) the disfigurement and harm inflicted by the passage of time (for dust as an emblem of that which destroys splendor, see *Lucrece* 944–45: "[Time's glory is to] ruinate proud buildings with thy hours, / And smear with dust their glitt'ring golden tow'rs"); (2) the decaying remnants left by and the harm inflicted by the passage of time (for this use of *dust*, see *Ham* V.i.199: "the . . . dust of Alexander"). (The syntax does not indicate the logical relationship of *dust* and *age* precisely; it must be inferred. The vagueness of the construction allows other senses pertinent to the general context to color the line: "dust" is emblematic of worthlessness, and transitoriness, and thus of all material things [as in *John* III.i.165], specifically, of the physical, mortal part of man, who was "made of the dust of the grounde" and returns to dust again [Gen. 2:7, 3:19]; the religious context established in quatrain 2 gives *Weighs*

nòt dust sanctimonious overtones of traditional Christian *contemptus mundi*; the senses of *dust* in this line are summed up in "we . . . commit his body to the ground, earth to earth, ashes to ashes, dust to dust" in the burial service. The line gets some incidental wit from the casual and irrelevant pertinence of the literal sense of *Weighs* to *dust*, an emblem of literal as well as figurative lack of weight.)

11. *gives to . . . place* (1) yields to the pressure of, gives ground before; (2) allows itself to be superseded by; (3) defers to, takes an inferior position to; (4) pays attention to (*OED* gives an example from 1578 and this from 1633: "If ye had given place to that saving word"). (The judicial context invokes overtones of "to give" meaning "to deliver judgment"; see *OED*, 18 and, in particular, 18b, "to give the case" meaning "to decide the case"). *necessary* inevitable, unavoidable (as in *JC* II.ii.36–37: "death, a necessary end, / Will come when it will come").

12. *makes antiquity . . . his page* (1) makes old age his servant (rather than yielding to it); and, since pages were always young, (2) turns old age into a young boy (in his edition of 1936, Tucker Brooke said that "the image is of a grave senior shifting roles with his boyish attendant"). (In context of *the chronicle of wasted time* in 106, of the last lines of 107, of the literary concerns of the opening of this sonnet, and of *Finding* in the following line, *page* carries punning suggestions of "the paper, the leaf [Latin *pagina*], where one can read about—see, find out about—the past." *for aye* forever, eternally (but see the puns on *eye* in 148.8,9). *his* its (but see 73.10, note).

13. *the first conceit of love* (1) affection unchanged from what it was when originally conceived, love in its first bloom (with play on "conception resulting from love," "conceiving a child"; compare *Lear* I.i.11–12: "I cannot conceive you." —"Sir, this young fellow's mother could"); (2) the first idea, the first inkling (or the initiating perception), of affection (perhaps with a play, invoked by the literary topic with which the poem began, on *conceit* meaning "an artful turn of wit or expression"; see also 26.1–14, note and 151.1,2,13, note—on the bawdy potential of *con-*). *there* (1) in *antiquity* (old age personified, the old yet ever young beloved); (2) in *antiquity* (in the past); (3) in the [always fresh and yet now wrinkled] skin (*case*, line 9) of the beloved. *bred* (1) still being begotten, still being generated; (2) was begotten. (The line allows for simultaneous assertion of miraculous youthfulness and for the attribution of the sentimental value of a relic, a reminder of its former self.)

14. *would* (1) want to, try to; (2) might be expected to. *show it* (1) make it seem to be, give it the appearance of being; (2) show it to be, reveal it to be. *it* (1) affection; (2) the beauty that engenders affection.

9–14. Ingram and Redpath note that these lines can also be read as a commentary on the speaker's admission that he repeats his poetic formulae, and thus as a clear continuation of the discussion of literary invention in lines 1–8. This is their paraphrase:

> And thus a love that is eternal, expressed in a form of words that never loses its vitality, sets no store by the dusty overlay and wear and tear of time,

and does not admit that words shrivel with age but makes an ancient phrase still his youthful and vigorous servant, finding the original idea of love still perpetuated in that formula which the passage of time and the pattern of the words might seem to render obsolete.

The paraphrase unavoidably exaggerates the purposefulness and continuity of this secondary train of thought, but the juxtaposition of lines 9–14 with the first two quatrains makes it probable that some of this meaning impinges on a reader's consciousness.

SONNET 109

2. *flame* (1) passion (as in 115.4 and *AW* I.iii.202); and, in context of the speaker's apology for his verse in sonnet 108, (2) creative power, poetic vigor (as in the Poet's speech on his art in *Tim* I.i.25: "our gentle flame"). *qualify* lessen the force of (as in *Lucrece* 424: "His rage of lust by gazing qualified; / Slack'd, not suppress'd").

3. *myself* Q gives "my selfe"; see 38.5, note.

4. *soul* essence, spirit (with two casual plays on *false of heart* in line 1: (a) literally speaking, it is the heart that *doth lie*, resides, in the breast; (b) "to lie" is "to be false").

3–4. These lines allude to the idea (familiar from Ephesians 5 and the marriage service) that lover and beloved are one flesh (compare 22.6–7 and 62.13; see 36, headnote); note also that *depart* (in a sense other than the one it has here) figured prominently in the marriage service (see 11.2, note).

5. *ranged* (1) roamed, wandered (literally); (2) strayed (figuratively, as in "stray from the straight and narrow").

6. *him* one, a person. *return again* See 13.6–7, note.

5–6. Whether Q's comma after *ranged* is or is not retained, *Like him that travels* modifies both *I have ranged* ("I, like a traveler, have ranged") and *I return* ("I, like a traveler, return").

7. *with* (1) by; (2) in the manner of.

6–7. The evident sense of the clause is "Like a traveler I return right on time and unchanged by the passage of time." Shakespeare's purpose is presumably to display Falstaff-like gall in solemnly making a logical-sounding equation between two non-comparable things: the journeys of a traveler and the promiscuous sexual liaisons of an unfaithful lover. The grossness of the speaker's logical fraud is emphasized by the suddenness with which the virtue of punctuality is introduced into the argument; the false equation is stylistically mirrored in the double use of *time* (first to mean "appointed time" and then to mean "the passage of time," "the time that has passed"), and further underscored by a collection of incidental verbal tricks and anomalies tucked into the clause: (a) In *Just to the time*, "faithful to my appointed hour," *Just* presents a potential antithesis to *false* in line 1 (see *JC* III.ii.85: "He was my friend, faithful and just to me"), and thus accentuates the flimsiness of the speaker's defenses against the charge of falseness. (b) Although "just" meaning "precisely," "exactly," is idiomatically standard in references to times of occurrence (as in *MWW* IV.vi.19: "just twixt twelve and one"), adverbial "just to" constructions ordinarily occurred only in spatial contexts and meant "as far as" (*OED*, adv. 1a, gives this from 1568: "The Englishe Marshalles ranne abroade even just to Parys"); here *Just to* refers to *time*, but in a syntax that aggravates its idiomatic difficulty by including the standard spatial phrase "return to" (*I return again | Just to*: "I return again as far as"). (c) Similarly, the clause requires its reader to circumvent an echo of the equally standard phrase "just time," meaning "correct musical measure" (*OED* gives this from 1598: "A marvellous sweete concert keeping just time and measure"; see also the pun in *Much Ado* II.i.57–58: "The fault will be in the music . . . if you be not wooed in good time"). (d) *Exchanged* is used in a context that requires that it be understood as "changed," "altered"; *OED* cites two other uses of "to exchange" in place of "to change," but both of those appear in sentences that can accommodate—and indeed benefit from—the idea of reciprocity, interchange, inherent in the usual uses of "to exchange." In any event, the usage is rare; and here, where the word *with* is a reminder of the familiar idiom "exchange with," *exchanged* is one more obstacle to easy comprehension and thus to easy conviction. (Compare *TN* II.v.140: "She that would alter services with thee"—a phrase in which the use of "alter" to mean "exchange" is made meaningful by its context [i.e. by synesis], informed by a pun on "altar" [see 115.6, note], sustained by the relevance of both the liturgical and sexual senses of "service" [see 141.10, note], and smoothed over by an implied logic which says that, since "exchange" and "change" are synonyms and "alter" and "change" are synonyms, "exchange" and "alter" must also be synonyms.)

8. The essential idea of the line is the implied argument that since the speaker's crime was his departure, his return cancels it; here, again, the joke is in the speaker's opportunistic misapplication of a partially apt analogy: water can wash away a stain, but the periodic returns of a promiscuous lover do not wash away the crime of his infidelities (see 34.5–12). The metaphor of water and stain has a comically inappropriate and yet affecting sound of philosophic solemnity and winning sincerity: it has vaguely Christian overtones of holy water and of the coming of Christ to cancel the sin of Adam (see the verb "to stain" in 33.14); *water* also suggests tears of repentance (particularly when the solemnity of this line is undercut in the next by the frivolous pun on "rained" in *reigned* [for other puns on "rain" and "reign," see *WT* V.ii.55 and *RIII* IV.iv. 52–53: "tyrant of the earth / That reigns in galled eyes of weeping souls"; the pun also lurks behind the metaphors of sonnets 33 and 34]).

9. *reigned*   prevailed, held sway over (said of qualities [as in 31.3 and *2Gent* I.ii.15: "folly reigns in us"], of diseases [as in *LLL* IV.iii.91–92: "a fever . . . / Reigns in my blood"], and of heavenly bodies as sources of astrological influence [as in *WT* I.ii.363: "Happy star reign now"]).

10. *All*   any and all.   *kinds of blood*   sorts of temperament, natures (compare 121.6 and *Much Ado* I.iii.22–25: "I had rather be a canker in a hedge than a rose in his grace; and it better fits my blood to be disdain'd of all . . . ").

9,10,12,14. *in my nature reigned, All frailties, all kinds, nothing all, my rose, my all* Clustered as they are, these words and phrases might once have carried vague (and logically chaotic) sexual overtones; see 20.12, note (on *nothing*), 26.1–14, note (on *all*), and *AYLI* III.ii.101–02 (where *rose* means pudendum—see Partridge and 35.2, note).

The bawdy possibilities of *in my nature reigned* are strong—particularly in view of the pun on "rain" and the potential *in* has for indicating location: *nature* was used as a term for the female sex organ, for semen (Farmer and Henley give an example from 1547), and for genitalia generally (compare the similar use of Italian *natura* and Latin *natura* and *naturalia*, and see *OED*, 7a and 8; for a Shakespearian example see *R&J* II.i.23–26 [quoted in 129.1, note]); *in my nature reigned* suggests comic reference to buggery.

11. *it* The antecedent is *my nature* in line 9. *preposterously* (1) absurdly; (2) unnaturally, perversely. The word has now come to be a simple synonym for "ridiculously," but for Shakespeare's contemporaries it was an "ink-horn" term—a new word dredged up out of another language with a self-conscious scholarly flourish; it still carried the precision of its Latin root *praepostere*, "in a reversed order"; "preposterous" meant "reversed," "inverted," "backside to," "arsy-versy." Compare this from Thomas Nashe's *Anatomie of Absurditie* (1589, *Works*, ed. R. B. McKerrow, I.36): ". . . their discredit, which endevour to turne our day into night, and our light into darkenesse, . . . those that are called *Agrippae* . . . being preposterously borne with their feete forward." Note that in the next three lines preposterousness, getting things backwards, is both the theme (line 12 describes an inversion of values), and the method (the hyperbolic compliment in lines 13 and 14 depends on reversing the common sense judgment that the universe—the sum, the whole—is greater than any one of its constituent parts in worth as well as bulk; the "nothing-all" contrast in the couplet both duplicates the evaluation in the "nothing-all" contrast in line 12 and reverses the relative values of the greater and the less; in line 13 *For nothing* must mean "because nothing," but it plays on—and can momentarily be mistaken for an apposite repetition of—the same phrase in the preceding line; the mistake the reader is invited to make about the word *nothing* is a miniature analogue to the misvaluation of nothing—of what is worthless—described and rejected in the preceding line. *stained* (1) defiled; (2) obscured (see 35.3).

12. *for nothing* (1) for the sake of something absolutely worthless; (2) as worthless, on the grounds that it is nothing (i.e. mistaking "all" for "nothing"); (3) for no reason (as in *CofE* IV.iv.124). *sum* vast quantity (as in 4.8). (The currency of the standard idiom "all and some" [see 91.1–4,8,14, note, and *FQ* III.xii.30: "they . . . vanisht all and some"], and the context of *nothing* and *all* can combine to invoke a substantively incidental play on *sum* and "some." The phrase *all thy sum of good* also carries the suggestion that the beloved possesses the sum of good, all the goodness that exists; moreover, as a macaronic echo of the stock expression *summum bonum, sum of good* anticipates the couplet by suggesting that the beloved is "the highest good.")

13. "Because I call this wide universe nothing" (i.e. I consider everything worthless). Shakespeare may intend a complex phonetic and ideational play on "you" (i.e. *thou*) and *universe*; see line 14 and 141.13–14, note.

14. *my rose* = a common appellation of affection in which *rose* is emblematic of perfection and understood as "the best"; see *RII* V.i.8 where Richard's queen calls him "My fair rose" and *Ham* IV.v.154–55: "O rose of May! / Dear maid, kind sister, sweet Ophelia"; see also the quotation from *Much Ado* in the notes to line 10 above.

13–14. Compare 110.8 and 13. (Q capitalizes *universe* and *rose*; see 1.2, note.)

SONNET 110

1. When read in the 1609 sequence, this opening can indicate a continuation of the nimble apologia in sonnet 109; this line combines simple remorse (*Alas*) with the scoffing tone of *here and there*, and thus, like line 5, suggests the tactical concession of a skilled pleader disarming his opponent's best arguments by granting them so as either to imply that they are trivial as compared with his own arguments or to turn them from arguments against him to arguments for him (see lines 6–8: *But . . .*).

2. *a motley* a fool, a clown (i.e. a wearer of motley, parti-colored cloth of the sort traditionally worn by professional jesters; compare *AYLI* III.iii.68: "Will you be married, motley?"). *to the view* (1) in appearance, to all appearances (compare *MofV* III.ii.131: "You that choose not by the view"); (2) in public, on exhibit for all to see (as in *Ham* V.ii.369–70: "give order that these bodies / High on a stage be placed to the view"). This line has been the source of most of the considerable commentary on this sonnet. The line is an elaboration on the standard but complex metaphor "play the fool," which uses one pair of meanings for "play" and "fool" ("perform the role of professional clown") to indicate another ("behave like an idiot"). Here *made myself a motley* echoes "made a fool of myself," an expression that contains no theatrical allusion but does the same job as the metaphor "play the fool." If this poem were not by a professional actor, the line would simply say, "I have made myself a public laughingstock" (with an echo, noted by Gerald Massey in his edition of 1888, of Saul's confession in 1Samuel 26:21: "I have done foolishly, and have erred excedingly"). However, Shakespeare's profession is—and presumably always was—known to his readers (see 111.3–4), and this line therefore is colored by (and colors the following lines with) its pertinence to the particular circumstances of its author's life. The fact of Shakespeare's profession operates—much as the accident of his first name does in the "Will" sonnets (57, 89, 135, 136, 143)—to give witty, pun-like extra dimension to statements complete and meaningful in themselves. Unfortunately, scholarly craving for biographical insight into William Shakespeare has led to readings of this poem as an expression of Shakespeare's opinion of his profession and to correspondingly extravagant counterdistortions which deny that the poem refers at all to Shakespeare's theatrical career (see *Variorum* I, 275–78).

1–2. Note that, although one relates to color and the other to space, *motley* is an ideational echo of *here and there*.

3. *Gored* (1) wounded (as in *T&C* III.iii.228: "My fame is . . . gor'd" and *HV* IV.i.170: "gored the gentle bosom of peace"; the basic sense of "to gore" is

"to pierce" and, specifically of horned animals, "to pierce with horns"; in this context of a lover's offenses *Gored* can thus carry suggestions of "horned," "cuckolded"; see "horning" in *Titus* II.iii.67); (2) besmirched, sullied (usually used with reference to dried blood, but the noun "gore" was still used generally for "filth" of any kind; see *OED*, sb.1). In context of *motley, Gored* plays on "to gore" (*OED*, v.3), meaning "to furnish with gores" (i.e. with wedge-shaped or triangular pieces of cloth such as those by which the motley, patchwork effect of a jester's costume may be achieved), and suggests that the speaker has made his own thoughts parti-colored. Ingram and Redpath note that "in heraldry . . . a 'gore' was a shaped area interposed between two charges, and was used as a mark of cadency or abatement of honour." *dear* (1) costly; (2) precious; (3) beloved (compare 48.14).

4. *offences* (1) injuries inflicted; (2) resentments, dislikes (Willen and Reed cite an *OED* example from 1580: "To have incurred her Majesties greate offence"). The principal action of line 4 appears to be to echo the antithetic pairing of *cheap* and *dear* in line 3; it thus suggests the idea of chronic infidelity more by its style than its substance. What specific meaning the line does have must be inferred from context: "turned new affections—new attachments to new acquaintances—into fresh occasions to do and give offense of the kind usual with me—into chances to be unfaithful anew' " (for *old* meaning "accustomed," "usual," see *1HIV* II.iv.188: "Thou knowest my old ward"). For a reader moving quickly through the poem the substance of the line probably has greatest effect as another (though vague) instance of sullying, of reducing value, turning something new and bright into something old and stale.

5–8. Compare 119.9–12.

5. *looked on* beheld, looked at (*Askance* and *strangely* in line 6 give this phrase suggestions of the sense "look" has in 89.8 where it indicates the facial expression of the beholder and thus his estimate of what is beheld; note, however, that any echo a modern reader hears of "looked on as," "considered as," "judged to be," in *looked on . . . Askance* is probably anachronistic; *OED*'s earliest example is from 1629). *truth* (1) the real thing, actual as opposed to apparent or imitation reality (commonly used in religious contexts to indicate revealed truth; see 1John 2 : 21–22: "I have not writen unto you, because ye knowe not the trueth: but because ye knowe it, and that no lye is of the trueth. / Who is a lyer, but he that denyeth that Jesus is Christ?"); (2) fidelity, constancy (as in 54.2); (3) truthfulness, veracity, honesty (compare *V&A* 804: "Love is all truth: Lust full of forged lies").

5–6. The end-of-line pause after *I have looked on truth* allows it momentarily to register as a self-contained assertion; the addition of the two adverbs at the beginning of line 6 causes *I have looked on truth* in effect to act twice: "I have seen truth, but I have not properly regarded it."

6. *Askance* (1) disdainfully (compare *Shrew* II.i.240: "Thou canst not frown, thou canst not look askance"); (2) sideways, asquint (*OED* gives this from the 1540's: "as she lookt a scance, Under a stole she spied two stemyng eyes"). *strangely* See 49.5, note. *by all above* by heaven (an oath).

7. *blenches* (1) swervings, inconstancies, deviations (compare "to blench"

in *Measure* IV.v.4–6: "hold you ever to our special drift; / Though sometimes you do blench from this to that / As cause doth minister"); (2) stains, blemishes, and/or offenses (*OED* records "to blench" as a fifteenth-century variant of "to blemish"); (3) side glances, turnings aside of the eyes (*OED* gives only the present example, but the reading is justified by the connection there demonstrated among "to blench," "to blink," and "to blenk"). *gave my heart another youth* (1) gave me another time of being young (i.e. rejuvenated me and gave me another chance to learn by trial and error); (2) rejuvenated my love (for you). In context of the speaker's infidelity and the relative ages of the lover and beloved (see *sweet boy* in 108.5), *another youth* carries incidentally self-incriminating suggestions of "a different boy" (Q, as usual, gives "an other"; for a justification of the modernization, see 37.7 and 38.5, notes).

8. *worse essays* (1) experiments with inferior materials; (2) less virtuous experiments. *proved thee* demonstrated you to be (with a play, continued by *proof* and *try* in line 11, on "tested you," "made essay of you"). *best of* best (compare *Measure* III.i.17: "Thy best of rest is sleep" and the use of "of" to mean "with regard to" in idioms like "fleet of foot").

9. *Now* (1) as of the present moment; (2) since, now that. *Now all is done* The context suggests that *all* refers to the loose behavior discussed in lines 1–8: "Now that all of that is over and done with." However the absolute sense, "everything" (which is played on in the paradoxical conjunction of *all is done* and *what shall have no end*) can also impinge on a reader's consciousness and give the phrase a note of despair. (*Now all is done* echoes the common expression "when all is done," meaning "all things considered," "in the last analysis" [compare *MND* III.i.14, *TN* II.iii.29, and *Macb* III.iv.67], and thus carries reverberations of the assertion in line 8.) *have* Malone took *have* to be a misprint, and replaced it with "save," giving the reading "Now all is done except my love which is eternal." A few editors have accepted this emendation, but it is unnecessary. (Moreover, by retaining the Q reading one retains a chiasmic echo of the generally pertinent standard imperative "have done," meaning "cease," "be done" [see *R&J* III.v.72 and *RIII* I.iii.215,279].) *have what shall have no end* This expression has the ring of verbal gesture like—and to the same effect as—"come what may" (compare the substantively related oath in line 6). It can also be read as an imperative in which *have* means "take," "receive," "accept": "take what is eternal" (i.e. my love for you). Q puts a comma after *end*; most modern editors put a full stop; I have adopted the logically noncommittal dash in order to retain as much as possible of the expression's double nature as verbal gesture and imperative clause. (Note, however, that in any reading its paradoxical union with *all is done* gives *what shall have no end* strong suggestions of "heaven," "eternal reward," and "posthumous bliss." See line 13 and note.)

10. *Mine appetite* The full stop with which most modern editors conclude line 9 reflects editorial awareness of the grammatical function of *Mine appetite*, awareness a reader does not gain until he meets the subject and the verb of which *appetite* is the object. Regardless of punctuation, however, *Mine appetite* momentarily seems to be an explanatory apposite for *what shall have no end*.

9–12. In context of *appetite* and a love poem about promiscuity, these lines can be colored by the sexual senses of *done* (see Donne, *Satyres* II.32: "To out-doe Dildoes" and *Titus* IV.ii.75–76: —"Thou hast undone our mother." / —"Villain, I have done thy mother"); *have* (see 87.13, 129.6,10, *R&J* I.iii. 95–96, and *1HIV* III.iii.129: "thou or any man knows where to have me"); *grind* (see Cotgrave, s.v. *Pierre*: "Mettre toutes pierres en oeuvre. . . . *applyable unto a wench, that suffers any mans stones to grind at her Mill*" and Milton's *Doctrine and Discipline of Divorce*, I.vi: "to grind in the Mill of an undelighted and servile copulation"); and—perhaps—*all, welcome* (in line 13), and *confined* (see 26.1–14, note [on *all* and *con-*] and the notes on *will* in 135 and 136, *well* in 154.9, *Came* in 154.13, and *conscience* in 151.1).

10–11. *grind / On . . . proof* The metaphor is of sharpening on a grindstone; it is a witty revivifying extension of the atrophied traditional metaphor "sharpen the appetite," "whet the appetite." (These lines are vaguely suggestive of two proverbs on friendship: "He is my friend that grinds at my mill"; and "Prove your friend [or assay your friend or try your friend] ere you have need" [Tilley, F705 and F718].)

11. *proof* (1) experimentation, trial; (2) experience (as in 129.11 and *Much Ado* IV.i.44–46: "if you, in your own proof . . . made defeat of her virginity"); (3) evidence. *try* (1) afflict (as in Hebrews 11:36: "And others have bene tryed by mockings and scourgings" [Geneva Bible, 1560; the separately published 1557 text of the Geneva New Testament gives "Other suffred mockings . . ."]); (2) test. (The conjunction of *proof* and *try*, words that have special pertinence to one another in a special context of the law, gives *try* overtones of "bring to trial for judicial examination.") *newer . . . older* Compare the antithesis in line 4.

12. *A god in love* who is godlike with respect to, as regards, love (with a flattering suggestion of *in love* meaning "infatuated"; "who resembles one of the classical gods engaged in a love affair with a mortal"). *confined* Although the sense of *to whom I am confined* is obviously "to whom I confine myself," *confined*, "limited," is not quite idiomatic with *to whom*. One can explain the use of *confined* as a compromise dictated by the need to rhyme *grind*, but Shakespeare may have chosen it because it relates variously to so many of the various elements of the poem: the word *confined*, "limited," relates to the "finished/endless" paradox of line 9. The "confine to" construction suggests "to confine oneself to," a quasi-medical expression apparently common in the later seventeenth century but unrecorded before 1649 (from which year *OED* gives this example [7b]: "As a man . . . apt to be mis-carried by his appetite confines himself by his vow to one dish"); if the expression was known to Shakespeare and his contemporaries, the use of *confined* in context of *appetite* could have evoked a fleeting metaphor of dietetic self-regulation (note the medical metaphor of 111.9–11, 14). Moreover, the non-idiomatic phrasing of *to whom I am confined* does not immediately restrict a reader's understanding of *confined* to senses appropriate to the speaker's clear intent and allows the phrase to carry dissident qualifying overtones of "*by* whom I am restricted, imprisoned" (compare *Macb* III.iv.24–25: "I am cabin'd, cribb'd, confin'd, bound in / To saucy doubts and fears").

13. *Then give me welcome* Note the summary effect inherent in the non-

signifying antithetical complements that inoperative potential senses of the components of this phrase provide for elements prominent at the beginning of the poem and in the new beginning at line 9: -*come* balances *gone* in line 1; *give* balances *sold* in line 3 and *have* ("take"), the imperative in line 9; *Then* balances *Now* in line 9. *next my heav'n the best* you, whom I consider the next best thing to heaven (a vocative epithet). Here again a non-idiomatic phrase is so constructed that a reader understands the sense demanded by its context and is also invited to respond to other considerations suggested by its constituent elements. Although *my heav'n* resembles the standard hyperbolic epithets of courtly lovers who use "heav'n itself for ornament" (see 21 and 130, and compare *A god* in line 12 above, *my sun* in 33.9, and "goddess," "heavenly love," and "paradise" in *PP*, 3.5–14), and although *my heav'n* is here part of what is clearly just such an hyperbolic epithet, the beloved is not called *my heav'n* but next best to it. The model of *my best* in line 8, the speaker's attitude in lines 6–12, and previous acquaintance with the ways of love poems presumably lead any reader to understand *my* as if it went with *best* ("next to heaven my best") and to extrapolate the idea that the beloved is the speaker's heaven and inferior in delight only to the heaven he hopes to enter after death; but, since *my* in fact modifies *heav'n*, which is distinguished from its nearest secular approximation, the construction of the epithet supports its substance by making the phrase a piece of evidence for the literal truth of the hyperbolic metaphor it asserts: the construction actually confuses the beloved and heaven and is comprehensible only after a reader has actively refused to mistake the beloved ("my heaven") and heaven (*my heav'n*) for one another. The epithet does not assert the speaker's idolatry but demonstrates it (see 105, 106.9–11, and 108.8). The construction also calls a reader's attention to the broad implications of what would otherwise register as a mere hyperbolic gesture. The strangeness of the phrase makes a reader pay attention to the word *heav'n*, and—particularly in context of *welcome*—makes it difficult for him to keep the rhetorical gesture and the passion it expresses safely isolated from the perspective of philosophically higher goals—notably reception into heaven (into Abraham's bosom); moreover, when a reader's understanding momentarily stumbles over *my heav'n*, the religious pertinence and the common religious context of many of the ideas and some of the language of the preceding lines is activated—at least to the extent of being perceptible as a structural theme: for instance, *by all above* in line 6, *what shall have no end* (9), which echoes "world without end" in the Christian liturgy, and line 12, which has reminded many commentators of sonnet 105 and of the first commandment (Ingram and Redpath note that, by removing the pause between *in love* and *to whom* and reading "in love to whom" as one phrase, one gets a meaning that amplifies the metaphoric pertinence of the sin forbidden in the commandment to the one renounced here, "viz. that the poet has passed from amorous polytheism to amorous monotheism"). Note also that the logic of quatrain 2 bears some likeness to that of the paradox of "the fortunate fall" of Adam (compare 119.4–14).

13–14. Note that the idea of an embrace in line 14 relates to—and can seem to develop from—*next*, even though it indicates relative value in line 13 rather than physical proximity. *heav'n, Ev'n* See 15.6, note.

14. *Ev'n* See 59.6, note. *most most loving breast* Presumably a reader's primary understanding of *most most* is as a self-conscious, precious, but essentially simple hyperbolic synonym for "very very." But *most most* also caps a running exercise in comparatives and superlatives (*worse, best* in line 8, *most, Most, more* in lines 3, 5, and 10), and in tests of the finality of ultimate statements (statements of definition like *old* and *new* in line 4; statements of absolute limit like *all* and *done* in line 9, *I am confined* in line 12, and *next my heav'n the best* in line 13; statements of absolute limitlessness like *what shall have no end* [which carries conviction in line 9 when the speaker's love for the beloved is measured against casual flirtations but not when line 13 thrusts it into the perspective of human mortality and Christian immortality]). Moreover, by virtue of the attention the illogical and non-idiomatic doubling of the superlative calls to the phrase, *most most loving breast* carries perverse overtones like those embodied in so many of the phrases that precede it: *most most loving* suggests "most most-loving," "most many-loving," "most promiscuous," and thus simultaneously contradicts and complements *pure* (which the literature of virginity had long established as an antonym of one sense of "loving"), and presents the uniquely superior beloved as the champion practitioner of the particular vice charged to the speaker.

SONNET 111

Like sonnet 110, this sonnet derives extra precision from its reader's knowledge that William Shakespeare, actor, provided for himself by public means; see 110.2, note. The poems are linked by similar subject matter (see 110.1–6 and *my harmful deeds* in 111.2); by likenesses of minor detail (see *god* in 110.12 and *goddess* in 111.2; *Ev'n* begins the last line of each; both poems open with exclamations, and each is dominated by imperatives [see 110.9, 111.1, 111.8, and the thirteenth lines of both]); by likenesses of incidental wit (see 110.14, note [on superlatives and comparatives in 110], and *better, bitterness, bitter* in 111.3, 11; see 110.13, note [on the punning relationship of *Then* to *Now* in 110.9] and *Than, Thence, thence, then, then* in 111.4–13); and—perhaps—by use of medical metaphors (see the note on *confined* in 110.12).

(The language of this sonnet appears to have influenced Milton when he wrote the sestet of his sonnet 15, "Fairfax, whose name in arms . . . .")

1. *do you . . . chide* = an imperative. (The word order could suggest that the construction might be briefly mistaken for an interrogative or an inverted indicative, but the rhythm probably precludes all intonations but the imperative.) *wish* This, the Q reading, is usually changed to "with" and was so emended in the first printing of this edition. I have belatedly changed my mind. The case against emendation is outlined in a supplementary note (pp. 580–82).

2. *The guilty goddess of* the goddess guilty of. (Many editors capitalize *fortune* in line 1, and thus give a reader foreknowledge that the goddess Fortuna is meant (see *AYLI* I.ii.27ff.).

3. *That* The logic of the sentence indicates that the antecedent is *goddess* and the meaning is "who." (The syntax, however, presents *my . . . deeds* as the most likely antecedent; the sentence thus embodies implications that contradict

its gesture toward transferring responsibility to an external force; for similar
self-defeating locutions, see 110.14, note, and *another youth* in 110.7). *better*
(1) more adequately (a comparative adverb); (2) something better (a substantive,
paralleled by *means* in the next line). *my life* (1) my lifestyle, my way of
living (as in *1HIV* I.ii.93: "I must give over this life"); (2) my continued existence, i.e. keeping me alive (compare *Lucrece* 141–42: "The aim of all is but to
nurse the life / With honour, wealth, and ease in waning age"). *better for . . .*
provide (1) more adequately take care of (compare *2HIV* V.v.99–100: "his
wonted followers / Shall all be very well provided for"); (2) supply something
better in support of (*OED* cites the 1552 *BCP*: "The bread and wine for the
Communion shall be provided by the Curate . . ."); (3) more providently anticipate the needs occasioned by (compare *CofE* I.i.80–81: "a small spare mast, /
Such as sea-faring men provide for storms"). Note that "to provide" retains suggestions of all the ideas inherent in its real or apparent Latin roots (*pro* =
"ahead"; *pro* = "in behalf of"; *videre* = "to see," "to look"; *videre* = "to see
to," "to look to," "to take care of"); *provide* thus suggests not only supply and
nurture but foresight and advance preparation as well, and, in this context of
heavenly negligence, carries unharnessed reference to the complex matter of
heavenly providence.

4. (1) "Than . . . means which breed . . . manners"; (2) "Than . . . means
which are bred by . . . manners." Both nouns in this line are plural in form
but singular in sense; *means* (in various senses) and *manners* were commonly
treated as singular nouns (*WT* IV.iv.610,823: "by this means," "a means";
R&J V.iii.213 and *Lear* V.iii.234: "what manners is in this," "Which very manners urges"). Neither grammatical form, nor syntactical structure, nor the substance of the nouns indicates whether *means* breeds *manners* or *manners* breeds
means (in sentences of this sort, substance ordinarily indicates such relationships, e.g. "cakes that cooks make" and "cooks that cakes make" [compare *RII*
II.i.139: "them . . . that age and sullens have"]). The wit of the line, its complexity, and its capacity for illustrating the helplessness the quatrain asserts are
enhanced by the fact that *means* and *manners*, which, though etymologically
unrelated, sound somewhat alike (compare *Whilst, willing, will* in line 9, *bitter-*
ness, bitter in line 11, and *correct correction* in line 12), can be near synonyms
("means of achieving," "manner of achieving"), and can be nearly synonymous
with *life* ("lifestyle") in line 3. *Than* = a simple modernization of Q's
"Then"; see 16.4, 8, note. *means* (1) resources, wealth (the sense invited by
for my life provide and the idea of *manners* as a breeder [i.e. creator] of means, a
source of wealth; compare *Measure* II.ii.24: "Let her have needful but not lavish
means"); (2) method, way of getting "means" in sense (1), way of getting
wealth (the sense *means* has in 16.4, here invited by the idea of *means* as breeder
of *manners*). (Note that *means* was commonly used in medical contexts as a
synonym for "medicines" [as in *CofE* V.i.103, *3HVI* V.v.45, and *MofV* III.i.52:
"healed by the same means"], and thus gives an extra sound of pertinence to the
medical metaphor in the last six lines.) *public means* (1) wealth achieved in
public (as by performing publicly) and/or wealth dependent on public favor;
(2) a way of getting a livelihood that involves public action and/or is dependent

on public favor for its success. *public manners* (1) a lifestyle of easy and indiscriminate familiarity with everybody, lack of reserve; (2) habitual self-display (as on the stage). *breeds* (1) engenders, is the source of; (2) leads to, encourages. (The metaphoric use of *breeds*, a word from sexual contexts, gives the line particular reference to the sexual aspects of the speaker's lifestyle and particular pertinence to the inherent concern of love sonnets, to the *blenches* of 110.7, and to the implied nature of the *harmful deeds* in line 2.)

5. *Thence*   from that (i.e. from fortune's failure to provide better), for that reason, therefore (colored by the literal physical sense "from that place"—compare 93.12). *my name receives a brand*   This metaphor conflates the Roman practice of marking the names of persons guilty of immorality with a *nota*, a mark of censure, in lists of citizens, and the practice, still current in Shakespeare's England, of branding criminals—who thus could never live down their guilt—on the forehead (as the Romans had marked bad slaves with a *nota*, a brand). (*OED* gives this from 1628: "Are they not a public brand and blemish to our church"; see *Ham* IV.v.115–16: ". . . brands the harlot . . . between the . . . brow.") See 112.1–2.

6. "And for that reason my nature is almost subdued."

6–7. *is subdued / To*   At the end of line 6, *subdued* momentarily acts independently of *To* and means "is overpowered"; when the idiomatic unit "to subdue to" emerges, the completed phrase operates in two senses: (1) "is reduced to the nature of" (as in *Lear* III.iv.69–70: "Nothing could have subdu'd nature / To such a lowness but his unkind daughters"); (2) "is subjugated by," "is under the control of," "is submissive to" (compare "subdue my father / Entirely to her love" in *Oth* III.iv.59–60 and "his face subdu'd / To penetrative shame" in *A&C* IV.xiv.73–74).

7. *hand*   Line 7 echoes the substance of line 4; Shakespeare may intend—and many Renaissance readers would have been able to perceive—an abstruse additional link between *hand* and *manners*, a word ultimately derived from Latin *manus* (see 85.1, note).

8. *then*   therefore. *renewed*   restored to the same condition as when new. (In this prayerful line, *renewed* carries overtones of spiritual renewal [see 2 Corinthians 4:16, Romans 12:2, and Titus 3:5: "according to his mercie he saved us, by the washing of the new birth, and the renuing of the holie Gost"]; moreover, the currency of "to renew" as a medical term prepares the way for the metaphor that follows [see *MofV* V.i.13–14: "the enchanted herbs / That did renew old Æson"].)

10. *eisel*   vinegar. *'gainst*   (1) in opposition to; (2) as a provident precaution for averting (see the quotation below and 49.1, note). (Vinegar was traditionally used medicinally; a 1603 broadsheet titled "Sundrie Aprooved Remedies against Plague" [reproduced in F. P. Wilson's *The Plague in Shakespeare's London*] recommends vinegar potions both as "a remedie against the plague" and "a preservative against the plague." The usefulness of vinegar as a stain remover is generally pertinent to this sonnet. So is the fact that vinegar, an emblem of sourness, and gall, an emblem of *bitterness* [see line 11], were proverbially combined in an emblem of cruel punishment [see Psalms 69:20–21: "I loked for some

to have pitie on me, but there was none . . . For thei gave me gall in my meat,
and in my thirst thei gave me vinegre . . ." and Matthew 27:34: "Thei gave
him vineger to drinke, mingled with gall: and when he had tasted thereof, he
wolde not drinke"; see *penance* in line 12].)

11. *No bitterness* There is no bitterness (i.e. there is no taste so acrid; for a
similar ellipsis see 65.1). *bitter* (1) acrid (the literal sense of *bitter*); (2) injurious, painful (the metaphoric sense from which the next line proceeds). (Note
the echo of *better* in line 3; in pronunciation *bitter* and *better* were sufficiently
similar to invite punning—see 91.9, 119.10, notes.)

11–12. In effect these lines generalize the sense of *patient* in line 9 from
"person attended by a physician" to "person who bears grief calmly."

12. *to correct correction* = a hyperbole expanding from *double*: (1) to
punish and more than punish me; (2) to reform and more than reform me; (3)
to dose me and double-dose me (with a suggestion of "to cure the cure," "to
repair the damage done by the remedy"—see 118.4; for the special medical uses
of "to correct," see the Latin *corrigere*). Rollins (*Variorum* I, 282) reports a plau-
sible suggested reading which takes *to* as "too" and *correct* as an adjective. *OED*
records no adjectival use of "correct" before 1676, but in 1611 Cotgrave glossed
the French adjective *correct* as "correct, congruous, perfect; good, pure, neat."

13. *then* (1) therefore; (2) at that time.

14. *Ev'n* See 59.6 and 15.6, notes.

13–14. See 112.1–2.

SONNET 112

1–2. This poem continues from sonnet 111; see 111.4–5, 13–14. In his edition
of 1924, T. G. Tucker discusses efforts of branded criminals and ex-slaves to fill
in and thus hide their scars. (The process would be comparable to replacing di-
vots in damaged turf; see line 4.)

1. *doth* do (*doth* was a common plural form; see 123.11 and Wilhelm Franz,
Shakespeare-Grammatik, 2d ed. [Heidelberg, 1909], pp. 154, 173, 564–65; compare the plurals in *s* in 41.3, 95.12, and 101.3).

2. *vulgar* (1) public, general, widely disseminated (as in *Lear* IV.vi.212:
"Most sure and vulgar; every one hears that"); (2) base, low, common (as in
2HVI IV.i.128: "stand uncover'd to the vulgar groom"; compare the substantive use in "the base vulgar" in *LLL* I.ii.48). *scandal* (1) disgrace, shame
(and, in particular, "a mark of disgrace"—as in *1HVI* III.i.69: "what a scandal is
it to our crown"); (2) malicious gossip, detraction (*OED* gives an example from
1596).

3. *who calls me well or ill* The sense of the clause is obvious ("whether people speak well of me or ill"), but the use of this sense of "to call" ("to title," "to
address by the name of") with adverbs is not idiomatic. The unusual construction may be accountable to a pun on "who calls me Will" in *who calls me well*;
compare 72.10,11. (Shakespeare appears to rhyme "Jill," "ill," and "well" in
MND III.ii.461–64; he punned on "well" and "will" in *MWW* I.iii.46, and confused scribes, printers, and editors in doing so: the 1602 quarto gives "He hath

studied her well and translated her well out of honesty into English"; the 1623 folio gives "will . . . will"; modern editors follow one or the other or else mix them, e.g., Peter Alexander gives "well . . . will" [see Kökeritz, pp. 104–05, 153–54]. For "will" meaning "lust" and speculation on a bawdy sense of "well," see the notes to 135 and 154.9. In the foregoing line from *MWW* "English" probably plays on "ingle" ["a catamite"] and "to ingle" [which ranges in meaning from "to bugger" to "to fondle"—*OED* gives a 1595 reference to Venus's "ingling sparrowes"]; a similar pun probably underlies "English tailor" in *Macb* II.iii.12.) In context of *fill* in line 1 and *profound abysm* in line 9 (which begins a three-line restatement of this line), *well* can also carry vague, unharnessed, and substantively irrelevant overtones of "well" meaning "a hole dug to reach underground water." (Note the sound of "pit" in *pity* in line 1; for explicit exploitation of the "pit/pity" pun, see "pitiful rascals" and "fill a pit as *well* as better" in *1HIV* IV.ii.61,63 [my italics], Herrick's "Cherry Pit," and *AW* I.i.167–70 [which is quoted in 154.9, note.)

4. *So* as long as, provided that (as in 70.5, 134.3, and 136.11). *o'er-green* overgreen, cover over (as a patch can be returfed or reseeded, or become overgrown by neighboring plants; the word is apparently a Shakespearian coinage). *my bad, my good* what is bad about me (my badness), what is good about me (my good points). *allow* (1) acknowledge, admit; (2) approve (as in *T&C* III.ii.88: "Praise us as we are tasted, allow us as we prove").

4,5,7,9,14. *allow, all, None, none, alive, all, all* Compare 109, and see 109.9, 10, 12, 14, note.

5,8,10,14. *world, sense, voices, sense, world* Since this sonnet is generally concerned with distinctions and confusions among what is true, what is reported, what is perceived, and what is believed, it is well to remember that Shakespeare and his readers appear to have made no phonetic distinction between *world* and "word" (see 138.4, and note), or *sense* and "sins" (see 35.8–9, 141.13–14, notes), or *voices* and "vices" (see Kökeritz, pp. 151–52, 216–18; he cites *MWW* I.iii.43–45 [the speech that evokes the response quoted in the note on line 4 above]: ". . . I can construe the action of her familiar style; and the hardest voice of her behavior, to be English'd rightly, is 'I am Sir John Falstaff's' "). ("Sins" and "vices" occur in 95.4 and 9. The thinking in 95 resembles the thinking in this sonnet, but there the particulars of syntax almost entirely override the punning potential of "sins" and "vices.")

5. *my all the world* Q gives "my All the world"; many editors give "my all-the-world," thus signalling a grammatical unit that solidifies the hyperbole of *You are my all*; but the identity of *all the world* as a single substantive does not emerge until a reader has momentarily accepted *my all* as a unit and then, because *the world* is otherwise syntactically superfluous, been forced to take *the world* as an appendage of *my all*. (Compare the context of the phrase in *John* III.iv.104–05: "My life, my joy, my food, my all the world / . . . and my sorrow's cure," and see the couplets of 109 and 112.)

7–8. In his edition of 1780, George Steevens called lines 7 and 8 "purblind and obscure." He extrapolated a reasonable sense from the lines: "You are the only person who has power to change my stubborn resolution *either* to what is right, or to what is wrong." Subsequent editors have offered only slight variations and expansions on Steevens's explanation. Steevens's gloss is an act of desperation, but I have no more satisfactory explanation to offer. The problems presented by these lines and by line 14 make this a good occasion for some general comments on editing the sonnets and reading them, and, although I cannot clarify these lines or line 14, they are discussed below in a long final note on this sonnet.

9. *so* such a. *abysm* = dissyllabic.

10. *of* about. *others' voices* what other people say (a metonymy).

10–11. *my adder's sense . . . stoppèd are* Until *are* reveals *sense* to be a plural form, it appears to be singular (as in line 8); the uninflected plural was common (compare *Oth* IV.iii.92: "Their wives have sense like them; they see and smell"). Adders were proverbial for both physiological and studied deafness: see *T&C* II.ii.172, Tilley, A32, and Psalms 58:4–5: "the deafe adder that stoppeth his eare. / Which heareth not the voyce of the inchanter." (Note that the expression was traditionally used of those who refuse to hear truth.)

12. *my neglect* (1) my negligence, my want of attention (to *others' voices*); (2) inattention to me, neglect of me (by *you*, the beloved). *with . . . dispense* (1) excuse from penalty, condone, excuse (as in *Measure* III.i.136–37: "Nature dispenses with the deed so far / That it becomes a virtue"); and, on the other hand, (2) disregard (as in *MWW* II.i.41: "take the honour. . . . Dispense with trifles"). ("Dispense with" is not only generally but precisely self-negating: it can mean "put up with" [*OED* gives this from the 1580's: "I would and could dispense with these difficulties"]; it can also mean the exact opposite: "to put up with the want of," "do without.")

13. *in my purpose bred* cherished in my intention, established as my concern (a gloss dictated by context and derived by extension from various meanings of *purpose* ["that which one aims to achieve," "that for which one acts or exists," "one's intended meaning," etc.], and from *bred* meaning "brought up," "nurtured"). Since the construction is highly unidiomatic, Shakespeare might mean to play on *my purpose* meaning "my discourse," "what I say" (for *purpose* meaning "discourse," "conversation," see *FQ* III.ii.4 and "listen our purpose" in the Folio texts of *Much Ado* III.i.12—where it appears in context of *bred* and of the topics of this sonnet), or conceivably, on *my purpose* meaning "my riddle" (compare *FQ* III.x.8: "oft purposes, oft riddles he devysd").

14. The text adopted here is essentially only the Q text in a modernized spelling. There are obvious arguments for several emendations and a possibility that Q gives the line as Shakespeare left it. The matter is discussed in detail in the following general note on cruxes.

1–14. *A note on 112.7, 8, and 14, with comments on explications and emendations of unsatisfactory Shakespearian texts*:

Most commentators are agreed in understanding both *None else* and *none* in line 7 as "no one else" and in reading the whole line as an elliptical expansion on *my all the world* in line 5—one in which *alive* functions twice as a verb ("None else [is] alive as far as I am concerned, and I [am] alive to no one else") and also as an adjectival appendage of *to none*, a hyperbolic intensifier ("to

absolutely nobody else," "to no other living soul"): "No one else means anything to me, nor do I mean anything to anyone else alive." The telling point
in favor of such readings is the critical consensus that supports them. Other
logically possible readings would be far more convenient for a commentator
trying to find a coherent logical relationship between lines 7 and 8 and between them and the rest of the poem. One might point out that the syntactic
antecedent for *None* is *tongue* in line 6 and argue that the line should properly
be read "As far as I am concerned all other tongues are dead, and I am dead
to all other tongues." That reading of line 7 prepares the way for *steeled sense*
in line 8 and so far informs that phrase that a reader need not stop to puzzle
over it; to that extent the suggested alternate reading of line 7 makes lines 7 and
8 less anomalous, makes lines 10 and 11 more obviously an appositive gloss
on them, and makes line 14 in one way or another an echo of them.

One may grant that the alternate reading makes sense and provides some
degree of clarity and continuity for the poem at large, but that does not mean
that a commentator may legitimately make the logical step of legislating (or
trying to legislate) that reading. When a critic offers a "new reading" for a line
written in an earlier time, he is ordinarily doing one of two things: either presenting historical argument and evidence that the cultural and linguistic milieu
in which the line was written would have given it an effect different from the
one it has in the foreign context of the experience, values, and linguistic habits
of later readers, or demonstrating that the line has or had potential for saying
something that it is not now seen to say and that it could not have been expected
to say in any earlier time. My hypothetical alternate reading of 112.7 is of the
latter sort; to accept it—or rather to try to sell it—would be to presume that
what a line can say or logically should say is what it does (or did) say and to
assume that previous commentators, most of whom have been thoroughly
versed in Renaissance language and thinking, misread the line not from historical ignorance but from inattention—even though 112.7–8 are now a celebrated crux and have been attentively studied and discussed.

There are good reasons why *None else* is not understood as "no other
tongue(s)" and why *nor I to none alive* is not understood as "nor am I alive to
any other tongue(s)": *None else* and *none alive* so obviously echo the thinking behind *my all the world*, are so commonly found in protestations that lovers are
everything to one another, and, being in an elliptical clause, so clearly invite a
reader to abandon reliance on synatctic guidelines and to piece out its imperfections with his contextually evoked expectations, that line 7 cannot reasonably
be read otherwise than as the expansion on *my all the world* that commentators
have assumed it to be.

Having acknowledged that line 7 invites its reader to understand it as "No
one else means anything to me, nor do I mean anything to anyone else alive,"
one is still faced with the larger difficulties of understanding the relation of line
7 to line 8 and of simply understanding line 8. For a modern reader, the difficulty
can be compounded by the standard Renaissance use of *or . . . or* where we
would use "either . . . or" (see 75.14 and 55.7, note; and compare the word
order in *Lucrece* 874–75: "Opportunity / Or kills his life or else his quality").

But familiarity with that construction does not clarify *That my steeled sense or changes right or wrong*. Puzzling over the line does not help much either. The line remains vague even after one has rejected the syntactical possibility that *steeled sense, changes*, and *That* are subject, verb, and object, and has decided from context that *That* means "who," stands for *none*, and must be the grammatical subject of *changes*; the line remains vague even after one has decided that *steeled sense* must mean "hardened sensibility" (compare "the steeled gaoler" in *Measure* IV.ii.83), and must be the grammatical object of *changes*; the line remains vague even after one has been through the logical convolutions of recognizing both that *or changes right or wrong* makes sense if understood as "changes the way things are," "changes the values of things," and that it cannot be understood that way in a reading that accommodates *my steeled sense*— a phrase that displaces *right* and *wrong* as potential grammatical objects of *changes*, dictates that the line be read as "that changes my steeled sense either right or wrong," and therefore requires one to understand *right or wrong* adverbially ("rightly or wrongly") or as a prepositional phrase in elliptic form ("changes my steeled sense either for good or ill, for the better or for the worse" [or—as Pooler, who read *steeled sense* as "my fixed opinions," suggested, ". . . whether they are right or wrong"]).

All that puzzling and the need to fill in syntactic and logical gaps (see line 1), testifies that the line does not in fact deliver meaning. What is most interesting about this passage is not that it is in itself demonstrably meaningless; such phrases and clauses are all but commonplace in the sonnets. Usually, however, such constructions are as effectively meaningful as any others because of clear intent implied by context, or because of a syntactical momentum that carries a reader into clarity and thereby dispels puzzlement before the reader has a chance or the need to puzzle, or because of a clear and clearly parallel nearby phrase or clause that acts appositively as an instant gloss on the potential puzzle (see, for example, sonnet 115 and notes). What is remarkable in these lines is that they resemble Shakespeare's usual practice in all respects but the most vital one: whereas most potentially troublesome Shakespearian lines make effective sense as they are read and do not interrupt a reader's progress through the poem, these call attention to their faultiness.

The Q text of the sonnets is occasionally very sloppy (as in 146.2), but it would be as foolish to assume that the problems of 112.7–8 result from a printer's error as it would be to assume otherwise. One cannot assume that the lines as we have them in Q are a mutilated version of some clear lines that Shakespeare wrote (see 24.1, note—on "steeld" in the Q text of that poem). The strongest argument against that assumption is that lines 7 and 8 share so many of the peculiarly Shakespearian characteristics of other lines in other sonnets that do not seem faulty. To discuss those characteristics, I want to return to the previous discussion of line 7. In rejecting "no other tongue is alive to me, nor am I alive to any" as a gloss on line 7, I do not mean to dismiss it altogether from consideration. I suspect that, if the following line had a readily apparent surface sense, if a reader were not brought up short and forced to hunt for understanding, then the syntactic reference to *tongue* in *None* and the syntactic potential of *alive* to suggest that the speaker is dead to all other voices would function in the poem as so many similar secondary meanings and overtones of secondary meaning do in other sonnets (as, for example, the dormant noun potential of the adverb *well* in line 3 can make *profound abysm* feel like an already established metaphor when a reader reaches line 9). It may seem ridiculous to discuss line 8 as it would be if it made sense, but I think that doing so might be generally informative about—or at least suggestive of—Shakespeare's methods in constructing his sonnets. As I said, what we have in lines 7–8 are lines that in all respects but the most important—capacity to communicate—are typical of Shakespeare. It is hard to explain the lines, but easy to guess why they are as they are. Shakespeare appears to have done all the work of furnishing these lines with ties to those that precede and follow them. The ideational echo in line 7 of *my all the world* in line 5 and the groundwork laid for lines 9–14 have already been mentioned. These further effects may be pointed out as well: (a) The *to . . . to* construction in line 7 is repeated in a substantively related context in line 11. (b) *Right or wrong* in line 8 is the fourth element in a train of variants that begins from *well or ill* in line 3, continues in *my bad, my good* in line 4 and *shames and praises* in line 6, and reappears in *critic and . . . flatt'rer* in line 11. (c) Each vagary of diction and construction that impedes comprehension of line 8 (i.e. makes line 8 incoherent in the usual sense in which the word is applied to writing), functions to give the poem coherence of another sort (i.e. functions in one or more of the non-signifying patterns that tie the poem together in a way analogous to the action of alliteration, rhythm, and rhyme). In *That my steeled sense, That, steeled,* and *sense* are insufficiently precise for their primary duty, telling a reader what is being related to what, what is being talked about, and what is being said about it; but the phrase performs its typically Shakespearian secondary activities superbly. *That my steeled sense* "rhymes" with *that my adder's sense* (as *dead* in line 14 is an ideational rhyme for *alive* in line 7, or *ill* is for *well*, or *well* is for *good* and *right*); the two phrases begin and end alike, but the first *that* is a relative pronoun and the second is a conjunction introducing an effect clause; the first *sense* is apparently singular and the second is suddenly revealed as a plural when line 11 ends with *are; my* is constant in function and position; *steeled* (one syllable) is replaced by *adder's* (two syllables) in the echoing phrase; *adder's* also glosses *steeled,* pins it down to one kind of meaning, but not before the nondirective context of *steeled* has allowed the mind of a reader progressing toward understanding *steeled* as "hardened" to touch on various other connotations of *steeled* (e.g. "armed in steel," "steel-bound" [as in *RIII* I.i.148]; and "stolen" [see *OED*, s.v. "stealed," an obsolete past participle of "to steal"]). Moreover, *steeled* functions in an alliteration in *st* that runs from *stamped* in line 2, through *else to* in line 7, to *sense / To, stoppèd,* and *strongly* in lines 10, 11, and 13. In *or changes right or wrong, changes* is an ideational echo of the remedial change described in lines 1 and 2, as *right or wrong* is of *well or ill* and *my bad, my good.* The *or. . . or* construction follows upon a juxtaposition of the sound "or" in two phrases where it has two different meanings (*well or ill / So you o'er-green,* lines 3 and 4; one commentator went so far as to suggest reading *or changes* as "o'erchanges" [*Variorum* I, 112]). Lines 7 and 8 do not seem right, but they do not seem accidental either.

Before speculating further about lines 7 and 8, it will be well to look at the more grossly faulty line 14 and include it in the discussion. Line 14 appears to present a very different sort of crux; the Q text, "That all the world besides me thinkes y'are dead," does not make ready sense without emendation and, what is most important for this discussion, offers several inviting possibilities for emendation.

The easiest and most popular of the emendations is merely to unify Q's "me" and "thinkes," strike off the *y'* from *y'are* and thus produce one or another variation on "That all the world besides methinks are dead," i.e. "that every one in the world seems dead to me except you." That reading follows the lead offered by the echo of line 5 in *all the world* and by the complement *dead* provides for *alive* in line 7; it also allows line 14 to end the poem on a simple restatement of the essential assertion of lines 5 and 7. A second sort of editorial emendation—which has also had distinguished supporters—retains *y'are* and takes *y'* to be an unusual instance of the common practice of abbreviating the initial *th* or *th-plus-vowel* in some common words by using *y* (the character early English printers used instead of the Old English character "thorn," which was lacking in their imported continental type fonts). Taking *y'* as *th'* and *th'* as "they" gives one or another variant on "That all the world besides methinks they are (or they're) dead," a reading that can give the same general sense as the "methinks are dead" reading discussed above ("they" is taken as a redundant substitute for *all the world* [compare *1HIV* III.ii.60: "The skipping King, he ambled up and down"]; or the line is taken as an elliptic form of "it seems to me that, as regards all the rest of the people in the world, they are dead [compare *Ham* I.ii.112–14: "For your intent . . . It is most retrograde to our desire"]). A reading of *y'are* as "they are" also allows for the potential in Q's "besides me thinkes" for "besides me, thinks" as well as "besides methinks," and thus allows a reading that includes "that all (the people in) the world believe in addition to me (i.e. agree with me, believe as I do), that they are dead" and, perhaps, ". . . believe that they are dead as well as I."

A third kind of reading leaves line 14 essentially as it is in Q and understands it as it would be understood if its context were unknown: "That, except for me, all the world thinks you are dead" (a reading which, like the "they are" reading, allows for the ambiguity of *besides me*—"except me" or "in addition to me"— by which the assertion would include its own contradiction, "not only I, but all the world thinks you are dead"). This third way of reading the line is in some ways more satisfactory than the others: it makes no major change in the line; it requires no puzzling out of *y'are* as a contraction of "they are"; it takes *y'are* as an obvious contraction of "you are"; it provides an appropriately startling conclusion instead of a mere restatement of lines 5 and 7. On the other hand, this straightforward acceptance of the meaning on the page demands that a reader spin out the argument by which this obvious sense of the Q line relates to the poem, a task so difficult that it is the source of the whole controversy about the

line; this is Martin Seymour-Smith's strenuous effort to justify taking the line
at face value:

> The sense [of lines 13–14] is: "The world (which does not understand
> anything about my love for you, or about my desire for the ideal personage
> that you could become), imagines you as dead, i.e. ordinary and vulgar as
> it is itself." He [the speaker] has already said (l.5) that the Friend is his
> "All the world," and here he clearly shows that he knows he is addressing
> one (the Friend as he actually is) who, like "all the world besides me," has
> no understanding of his poetically inspired "purpose."

No emendation or reading of line 14 recommends itself to the exclusion of
others. In fact, the various arguments balance each other out with remarkable
precision. Again, line 14 does not seem right, but it does not seem accidental
either.

I suspect that what we have in sonnet 112 is an unfinished poem or one that
Shakespeare abandoned in frustration. I do not pretend that I can prove my
suspicions, but examination of their grounds may give some perspective on the
substantively incidental verbal patterns and tricks I point out in other sonnets
and help a reader to believe that, when I use words like "overtones" and "echo,"
I mean no more than I say and have no intention of denying or offering a substitute for the immediately available sense that most of the sonnets make.
Consideration of my reasons for thinking sonnet 112 is not damaged but unfinished may also open the possibility that Shakespeare went about constructing a sonnet with less emotion and more concern for fashioning a literary artifact
than Ben Jonson's famous comment would lead us to believe or than our habitual sentimentality about unfettered poetic furor makes us comfortable in believing. Essentially, I suppose this poem to be unfinished or abandoned because
it is atypical of Shakespeare's sonnets *only* in being incomprehensible. It is full of
verbal effects of the sort I point out as incidental in other sonnets. For example,
the sonnets regularly present occasions where a dormant sense of a word is
recalled in a later line by a synonym or near synonym, or is called to mind by a
new topic or metaphor irrelevant to the earlier word in the earlier context but
relevant to the dormant sense, or where a sense dormant in a later word will
relate to and thus casually recall an earlier topic, metaphor, or word; sonnet 112
is particularly rich in such effects, which range from the commonplace and non-
evocative pairings of the verb *care* in line 3 and the noun *care* in line 9 and of *So*
meaning "provided that" in line 4 and *so* indicating degree in lines 9 and 13,
through the shadowy interactions between *well* in line 3 and *profound abysm* in
line 9, between *strive* in line 5 and *purpose* (meaning "intention") in line 13,
among *world*, "word," *sense*, "sins," *voices*, and "vices" in lines 5,8,10,14, and
among *allow, all, none*, and *alive* in lines 4,5,7,9,14, to the unobtrusive but complex exploitation of the potential inherent in *impression*, which means "indentation" in 112.1, relates to a dormant sense of *steeled* (= "engraved"—see 24.1,
note), and is echoed in two of its own dormant senses: in line 1 *impression*
refers to a mark of shame like the *brand* referred to in 111.5, and that referent is

echoed in *shames* (112.6) and, complexly, in *Mark*, which, though it appears in 112.12 as an imperative verb meaning "pay attention to," has a syntactically irrelevant noun sense synonymous with *th' impression*, the scar, the mark of shame, in the opening metaphor; the topic of reputation (*scandal, calls me well or ill*, etc.) relates to "impression" meaning "effect upon the mind" (as in *RIII* I.iv.63· "Such terrible impression made my dream"). Another sort of typical Shakespearian by-action is exemplified in the pun on "Will" in *well* in line 3; Shakespeare habitually conflates structures, doubles the sense of his assertions by making them do double duty, and often, as in the case of *calls me well*, achieves his extra meaning at the cost of idiomatic smoothness in the obvious immediate assertion, producing a sentence with clear meaning that is a little awkward, does not squarely strike the sense its context and general content indicate.

As sonnet 112 is among the most densely patterned of the sonnets, so the problem passages in it, lines 7–8 and 14, participate more ways in more patterns than the other lines of the poem. I have already mentioned the patterns that have seemed to point the way for glosses and emendations. There are several others; for example, the substance of both passages contributes to the sonnet's potential for alluding to the literally unique lovers in the Eden myth and its traditional accretions; the allusion is obviously unrealized but is well prepared for in a poem that refers to snakes, flatterers, greening over, and a *profound abysm*. In addition, in line 14 *me thinks* subsumes an echo of the topic of reputation: "thinks me," "thinks that I am"; line 14 also restates the essential statement of *my all the world* in line 5, but repeats *all the world* in a sense that pertains to connotations inherent in *vulgar* and thus both relates to the topic of public shame and, by acknowledging that there is an all the world besides the beloved, undoes the hyperbole of the phrase it echoes.

In short, it is possible and seems to me probable that the problem passages in sonnet 112 exist because, after Shakespeare had worked all the various subordinate effects into lines 7–8 and 14, he could not in this case manage to retain all the verbal by-play in the lines and make them carry simple expository meaning as well. (Compare 113.14 and note.)

The commentary I offer in this edition is designed to counter a tendency in editors, critics, and students to assume that an obvious expository coherence precludes other less important or unimportant coherences, i.e. coherences that import very little or, being non-syntactic, non-logical, make no specific or establishable assertion at all. Most people who talk about poetry will not admit secondary senses or overtones or invasions of logically impertinent contexts unless the presence of such ideational static is capable of promotion to the distinction of full-fledged, syntactically admissible ambiguity and therefore capable of interpretation—usually as an irony; they want to dismiss elements in poems that are demonstrably present but just as demonstrably doing nothing that can be harnessed in a critical exposition of what a poem says or what a poet wanted to say. Since language obviously exists to convey substance, we are uncomfortable in talking about actions of language that cannot be related to what the poem conveys about its subjects or its author; that is perhaps the reason why poetic elements like verse form, meter, and rhyme are rarely talked about except in instances where they can be said to act as rhetorical auxiliaries to the substance a poem conveys. In the sonnets Shakespeare uses more of the ideational potential in words than the logic of their exposition needs or can admit. He often uses words that have a common pertinence to a context other than the one in which he uses them; sometimes the words relate to one another through senses entirely foreign to the ones that relate to the assertions in which they appear. I mean to suggest in my commentary that Shakespeare uses syntactically and logically impertinent ideas, ideas latent in words because of their habitual uses in other contexts, in rather the way he uses rhythm and rhyme— that he "rhymes" ideas, and "rhymes" ideas with sounds, and makes rhythm-like patterns in which extra-syntactical meanings link to sounds or to other extra-syntactical meanings or to meanings active in the syntax to give his sonnets extra-logical coherence. Shakespeare plays to the mental faculties that under cruder conditions cause us to make and understand puns; the language of the sonnets ordinarily limits its reader's mind to the terms of specific assertions while at the same time suggesting room and direction for vast and multi-directional expansion.

My commentary attempts not so much to demand serious attention to the incidental mental events Shakespeare's sonnets take us through as simply to acknowledge them, to admit they exist and are a part of poems we admire. There are two difficulties about the notes I write. The first is that readers— particularly those who have encountered the wanton ingenuity of disciples of the new criticism—will believe or fear that, in pointing out the logically incidental verbal effects I examine, I mean to invite interpretations that ignore, or deny, or diminish the clear and effectively straightforward sense all but a few of the sonnets so obviously make. The second problem is related: I worry that someone somewhere in a graduate seminar will welcome the ideational rhymes I talk about and undertake to do exactly what I insist on not doing: seize on overtones, suggestions, auras, reminders, and puns and—reading the poems as puzzles, clever devices for hiding their real meaning—reduce the poems to coded assertions as thin as, but far more misleading than, the assertions turned out by traditional editors who, though they brushed aside everything that did not sustain the overt intent of a poem, were at least demonstrating meanings that *are* overt. The great danger in discussing the subtleties of poetry is that, since their description almost inevitably exaggerates their relative effect upon a reader, one can seem to invite critical interpretations that reverse the priorities but imitate the methods of their predecessors and explain poems by fleshing out ideational incidentals and insisting on unlikely simplifications and reductions instead of the likely ones apparent to everyone.

Although I have taken pains to keep suggestions and echoes and wordplays in perspective by labeling them as such, I still fear that I will seem to be a crazy advocate of crazy interpretations. I have dwelt at length on the two incomprehensible passages in sonnet 112 in the hope of forestalling misinterpretation of my purposes in the notes to the other sonnets. Since the Q text of sonnet 112 does not make sense as it stands, editors, deprived of immediately coherent assertions in lines 7, 8, and 14, have attempted prosthetic substitutes extrapolated from one or another of the sets of terms offered by the poem. I hope that one effect of discussing the various signals and countersignals of meaning in sonnet 112, a poem which drives any reader to look hard at its makeup, will be to reassure such readers as are made nervous by my comments on muted patterns in other sonnets—sonnets where there is no temptation to press incidental patterns into expository service. Incidental verbal patterning can enrich poems by making them feel as though they encompassed the broad range of attitudes and topics that any word, sentence, or paragraph is designed to exclude. However, such verbal side effects *cannot* displace or substitute for the clear expository intentions that are ordinarily obvious in the sonnets and happen to be missing in sonnet 112.

SONNET 113

The topic of this poem continues in sonnet 114.

1. The fact reported in this line is that, absent from the beloved, the speaker sees the beloved in his "mind's eye" (compare "In my mind's eye" in *Ham* I.ii. 185); that sense is supported by the phonetic likeness between *mine eye* and the traditional metaphor "mind's eye," but is largely derived from a reader's commonsense awareness that the reference of the speaker's whimsical assertion ("since I left you, my eye has also left its natural position and moved into my mind"), must be the same as that of "mind's eye," the commonplace metaphor it echoes phonetically. (See the note on line 14 below.)

2. *that*   the one, the eyesight. The gloss given is the one demanded by the logic of lines 3 and 4. As a reader comes upon line 2, *that* can seem to refer to *mind*, its most convenient antecedent. (The mind can certainly be said to "govern one to go about," and Shakespeare's contemporaries, not conditioned to rely on punctuation for logical direction [see the Q text of 64.13: "This thought is as a death which cannot choose"], would presumably have been prepared to read line 2 as a modern reader would read it if *which governs me to go about* were isolated in commas.) *Partly blind* and *Seems seeing* make it clear that *that* refers to an eye, and that the *that which* construction indicates a syntactically unsupported distinction between "the mind's eye" and a real one—or rather between the mind's eyesight and ordinary eyesight. That reading, which emerges as the quatrain is read, finally clarifies line 2 completely, but the *that which* construction does embody a reminder that, although *eye* must mean "eyesight" and have the effect the plural would have, eyes come in pairs; the distinction between two differently functioning *eyes* thus initiates a grotesque image of a person who looks cockeyed because one of his eyes looks out and the other is literally turned round in its socket and looks in. The idea of inversion, of things turned inside out, permeates the poem, and is supported stylistically by a series of complex chiasmic patterns (i.e. patterns evoked by a series of elements stated and then repeated in reverse order, in a sort of mirror image); for example, see the *abba* rhyme scheme of the opening syllables of lines 5–9: *For, Of, Of, Nor*; or see the two "of" constructions in which the end rhymes of lines 5 and 7 function, and in

which *heart | Of* is in ordinary syntactic order and "part of" is inverted—*Of*
. . . *part*; or see *day, night, crow, dove* in lines 11–12 (a sequence organized in
two different kinds of lightness and darkness [i.e. degree of illumination in the
contrasted halves of a day, and degree of color in the two contrasted birds], and
running "light thing beginning with *d*," "dark thing," "dark thing," "light thing
beginning with *d*"); see also *true mind, m'eyne* ("mine" in Q) *untrue* in line 14 (a
sequence in which *true* and *untrue* present one sense of "true" balanced against
the negation of a different sense of "true," and in which *mind* and *m'eyne* are
nearly identical in sound and contrasted in sense).   *governs*   guides (*OED* cites
BCP: "governe thy holy Churche universall in the right waye").

3. *Doth part*   (1) divides (as in *HVIII* V.ii.27–28: "I had thought / They had
parted so much honesty among 'em"); (2) leaves, departs from, abandons (as in
Per V.iii.38: "When we with tears parted Pentapolis"—note *I left you* in line 1
above); (3) does part of, partly does (compare the use of *part* in *Oth* V.ii.299:
"This wretch hath part confess'd his villainy").

4. *effectually*   (four syllables, by syncopation of "-tual-") in effect.   *out*
blinded, extinguished (for the idea that the eyes emit light, see 20.6, note; in
context of line 1 *out* carries incidental play on *out* as an indicator of position, the
opposite of *in*, and *is out* suggests "has left," "has departed").

5. *heart*   center of intellectual activity, mind (Shakespeare uses *heart* similarly in *Ham* I.v.121: "would heart of man once think it?").

6. *latch*   = the generally accepted emendation for Q's "lack" (for "latch"
meaning "apprehend," see *Macb* IV.iii.193–95: "words / . . . howl'd out in the
desert air, / Where hearing should not latch them"). The emendation is dictated
only by the need to rhyme *catch* in line 8; "which it doth lack" meaning "which
the heart lacks," "which the heart goes without," makes sense—a fact that
probably accounts for the printer's misreading.

7. *quick*   (1) lifelike, vivid (*OED* cites this from 1533: "Als quyk as thai war
led afore your Ee"), active, busy (as opposed to the static unchanging mental
image of the beloved); (2) rapidly passing, fast fleeting (as opposed to the permanent mental image of the beloved). The word also carries generally pertinent but
syntactically unharnessed overtones of *quick* as applied to the senses or to the
mind to mean "keen," "capable of ready perception" (as in *FQ* I.ii.26: "busying
his quicke eyes, her face to view").   *part*   portion, share.

8. *catch*   apprehend (compare "catch sight of").

7,8. *his, his*   its, its (but see 73.10, note); the antecedents are deeply, perti-
nently, and illustratively ambiguous. Both instances of *his* make sense both as
"the eye's" and as "the mind's." As one begins reading line 7, the logic of the
described situation favors *eye*, which has been the grammatical subject in the
preceding constructions (assuming that "lack" was wrong in line 6 and *latch* is
right); when one reaches *hath the mind no part*, however, *mind* is established as
the grammatical subject of an inverted clause: "the mind has no part of *his* quick
objects." In line 8 the nearest potential antecedent for *his* is *mind* in line 7; *his
own vision* can momentarily seem to indicate "the mind's own object," the
beloved, the vision beheld by the mind's eye. However, in the instant that "Nor
does [the mind] apprehend even its own proper object" is taking shape as a

reading for *Nor his own vision holds*, that reading (which fits neither with the
apparent contrast between *his quick objects* and *his own vision* nor with our
previous understanding of the beloved as constant object of the mind's eye),
dissolves; the completed construction makes *vision* the grammatical subject of
holds, and dictates that *vision* be understood as "capacity to see" and that *his
own* is "the eye's own." One finally understands line 8 as an assertion that the
eye is so distracted by the remembered image of the beloved that its own capacity
to see is impaired. (Compare 114.11–12.)

9–10. *rud'st, deformèd'st*   Both words demonstrate their sense; they are contorted alternatives for "rudest" and "most deformed" (contrast *gentlest* and
most sweet).

10. *favor*   (1) face (*OED* gives this from 1581: "My favour is harde, my body
croukte"); (2) appearance, aspect (as in 125.5 and *JC* I.iii.128–30: "the complexion of the element / In favour's like the work we have in hand, / Most
bloody, fiery, and most terrible").

12. *feature*   form, shape, appearance (as in *AYLI* III.iii.3: "Doth my simple
feature content you?").

14. *true*   constant, faithful, unchanging, devoted.   *untrue*   (1) guilty of
false reports, untruthful; (2) unreliable (with suggestions of "not genuine eyes"
and "crooked").   *m'eyne*   my eyes ("eyne," an archaic plural for "eye," appears several times in Shakespeare; e.g. *Lucrece* 643,1229). The Q reading,
"mine," has been supported unconvincingly on the ground that *untrue* is here
intended as an (otherwise unknown) substantive; most editors make the line
accommodate the obviously necessary reference to "eye" or "eyes" by simply
reading "maketh mine eye untrue" or, in deference to mechanically regular
metrics, "makes mine eye untrue"; *m'eyne* and its variants were suggested
several times in the nineteenth century (see *Variorum* I, 286 for details). The best
argument for choosing to read Q's "mine" as an anomalous contraction of "my"
and "eyne" is that the improbability of *m'eyne* is in keeping with the kind of
experimentation that apparently engaged Shakespeare in the preceding poem:
sonnet 112 concludes with a line made confusing by *y'are*, which—like *m'eyne*—
appears to be a contraction; in both sonnets Shakespeare seems more concerned
for verbal and ideational gymnastics than for sense; see the preceding notes and
the incidental play of *governs* and *go* in line 2; *part* and *partly* in line 3; *Seems
seeing* in line 4; *For, form, For*, and *deformèd'st* in lines 5, 9, and 10; *vision* and
sight in lines 8 and 9; also note the various kinds of relationship among *form,
shape, favor, feature, part, heart*, and *mind* (e.g. *favor* means "face" in line 10, but
can be used to mean facial "feature" [as in *1HIV* III.ii.136], but *feature* means
form in line 12; a face is a bodily *part*, as is the *heart*; *feature* can also be used
to mean "a quality"—as can *part* [as in 81.4]). Line 1 shows, and to a degree
begins, the playful exploitation of the potential *mine* has as an intermediary for
simultaneously comparing, contrasting, equating, and differentiating *mind* and
eye by means of arbitrary and erratic substitutions of language for logic: in one
respect—the phonetic—*I* and *eye* are interchangeable, but, in another, *eye* is
only a part of *I*, of an individual body, and, in yet a third respect, they are comparable and contrast with one another (*I left*, but *eye is in*—a conceit continued

and further complicated by *part* in line 3 and *is out* in line 4); *mine eye* is contrasted to *my mind*, but *mine* and *my* are identical in sense, genitive forms of *I; mine*, in one member of the contrasted pair, is so similar phonetically to *mind* in the other that they are easily confused in speech, while *eye* in the first half of the contrast rhymes with *my* in the second. In a poem that begins with such a line as line 1 is, the syntactic outrage of *m'eyne* ("mine" in Q)—the final violent unification of *mine, my, I, eye, eyne*, and *mind*, a capsulation of everything the poem has logically distinguished in the course of reporting a fanciful collapse in distinctions of function—is all but inevitable.

Both the last line and the poem as a whole are daring attempts at poetic concentration that fail (or at least fail to be more than contortionists' tricks) because Shakespeare cannot quite transmit the energy or semantic clarity of his verbal mathematics to the simple surface substance asserted by the speaker; see 112 and commentary.

SONNET 114

This sonnet expands upon sonnet 113.

1,3. Or whether . . . Or whether Willen and Reed explain: "an Elizabethan construction used for alternatives in a question; modern usage would retain only the second *or* and eliminate all else." See Abbott, par. 136, and compare the related constructions in *Cor* I.iii.63: "or whether his fall enrag'd him, or how 'twas" and *MofV* III.ii.116–18: "Move these eyes? / Or whether riding on the balls of mine / Seem they in motion."

1. being See 52.14, note; here *being* is probably monosyllabic. *crowned with you* (1) made glorious, made king-like, by the honor of possessing your friendship (compare 87.13–14); (2) fulfilled, brought to the peak of success, by your friendship (compare *HVIII* V.v.58: "no day without a deed to crown it"). The phrase also carries the suggestion that the beloved's friendship is to the speaker as the crown of laurel, the traditional badge of poetic success, is to other poets. (The phrase derives playfulness of tone from the incidental relationship the mind and crowns have by virtue of their common locality, the head.)

2. Drink up eagerly accept (the traditional, nearly petrified metaphor, repeated in line 10, is elaborated and revivified in lines 12 and 13). *flattery* gratifying illusion, delusion (as in *Oth* IV.i.128–29, quoted in 42.14, note). Since kings are traditionally susceptible to insincere praise (see 28.5–12, 33.2, and 87.13–14), this context activates suggestions of the commoner sense of *flattery*— the flattery that follows monarchs and can destroy them like a poison. As a result, *this flattery* simultaneously refers to the illusion discussed in sonnet 113 and colors a reader's understanding of *crowned with you*—suggesting that the beloved's friendship is feigned or is only the speaker's illusion.

2,9. flattery, flatt'ry See 86.5, note (and compare the comparable—and comparably gratuitous—effect of *I say* and *eye saith* in line 3).

4. your love (1) your love of me, your friendship for me; (2) the love of you, my love for you (sense 1 is invoked by a reader's expectations about the purport of the idiom *your love*, which usually refers to affection felt by "you"; sense 2

is invoked by commonsense diagnosis of the symptoms of lovesickness described
in 113 and repeated in the following lines). *alchemy* magical power to transform inferior objects into valuable ones (as alchemists tried to transform base
metals into gold; see 119, headnote).

1–8. Q puts question marks at the ends of lines 2 and 4, and a colon at the end
of line 8. That punctuation has the advantage of emphasizing the identities of
lines 1 and 2 (on the mind), and lines 3 and 4 (on the eye), as balanced alternatives phrased in a pair of direct questions. The parallelism of the two pairs of
lines is maintained by the *Or whether . . . Or whether* construction and by the
likeness of the similarly placed *this flattery* and *this alchemy*. However, since it is
offset by the structural dissimilarity of *doth my mind . . .* and *shall I say mine
eye saith . . .*, the parallelism of the two momentarily equal pairs undergoes
unwarranted diminishment when the question mark that indicated a full stop
after *alchemy* is removed in order to recognize the syntactic function of quatrain
2 as auxiliary to lines 3 and 4. Moreover, although the sequential relationship of *this alchemy* and *To make* tends to limit quatrain 2 to specifying the
reference of *this* in *this alchemy*, and although ultimately *his beams* in line 8
absolutely limits the reference of quatrain 2 to the eye's alchemy, lines 5–7 can
be understood as specifying the nature of *this flattery* ("this delusion") as well
as that of *this alchemy* ("this power of magically transforming"). A modern
directive punctuation endorses the implications of syntactic sequence and
instructs a reader to take *this* in line 2 as pointing back to the delusion described
in 113.9–12, and *this* in line 4 as pointing ahead to the explanation in quatrain 2.
As a reader moves through the poem in Q's punctuation (and, I hope, in my
compromise punctuation), the parallelism of *this flattery* and *this alchemy* is
complete until line 8; *this flattery* and *this alchemy* both point backward to
113.9–12, and both point forward to quatrain 2, which explains *this alchemy* and,
for three lines, *this flattery* as well.

5–6. *To make of . . . Such* (1) to transform . . . into such (explaining *this
alchemy*); (2) to consider . . . as such, take . . . to be such (explaining *this
flattery*; compare *Temp* II.ii.156: "to make a wonder of a poor drunkard").

5. *indigest* shapeless, chaotic (a pertinent echo of *chaos rudis indigestaque
moles*, a much imitated phrase from the opening of *Metamorphoses* where Ovid
announces his intention to speak of bodies changed into new forms and begins
with the divine creation of the world from chaos, a crude and shapeless mass
[I. 7]; note also the construction of *Metamorphoses* I.78–81: *sive hunc divino
semine fecit | ille opifex rerum . . . | sive recens tellus seductaque nuper ab alto |
aethere cognati retinebat semina caeli*, which the Loeb editor translates as
"whether the god who made all things . . . made man of his own divine substance, or whether the new earth, but lately drawn away from heavenly ether,
retained some elements of its kindred sky"; six lines later Ovid says that "the
earth, which had lately been a rough and formless thing [*rudis et sine imagine*],
was changed and clothed itself with forms of men before unknown").

6. *Such . . . as your . . . self resemble* (1) like those whom you resemble;
(2) like those that resemble you; (3) that resemble you.

7. Tilley (B316) heard an echo here of "Bad is best." The echo is purely ver-

bal, however; the gist of the proverb (that even the best is bad) is not evoked by or immediately relevant to the topic of metamorphosis. *perfect best* See 115, headnote, and 113.13, a gloss on the literal sense of *perfect*.

8. The most immediate sense of the line is "As quickly as objects come within the eye's gaze." However, the diction of the line pertains not only to the speed and occasion of the transformations, but also (extra-syntactically) to the process of creating objects out of chaos: *As fast as objects* carries a suggestion of "just as firm as objects are," a sense that the overall syntax cannot accommodate, but which pertains to—comes from, is native to—the topic on which the syntactically evident sense comments. Something similar is true of *his beams assemble*, which has syntactically irrelevant potential for saying "the eye's beams put together (construct, make, create)" and thus embodies an incidental extra-syntactic reassertion of the general proposition of the quatrain. Ingram and Redpath attempt to harness some of the special pertinence inherent in the diction; they strain syntactic probability to suggest that the line be understood as saying " 'As fast as things on which the beams of his vision fall gather themselves into ('perfect,' cf. line 7) shapes.' " It seems more probable that, for a reader not engaged in studying the way the sonnet works, the potential of the line's component words and phrases to say things that the syntax does not readily accommodate is felt rather than understood. The fact that the diction used to express "As quickly as objects come within the eye's gaze" is chosen from the traditional vocabulary of "making" testifies rhetorically to the veracity of the speaker's general assertion. (The logically illegitimate effectiveness of the pertinence of the diction to the general topic is roughly analogous to that which Henry Ford would have as a witness to a traffic accident.) Here diction doubly qualified for its task gives the conceit of the eye's alchemy a validity, a measure of quasi-physical reality, that momentarily surmounts the preciousness of a poem that is always in danger of being dismissed as fancywork because it makes its reader uncomfortably conscious that the poem is an inevitably barren, self-consciously cute, basically frivolous exercise in intellectual ingenuity. *his* its (but see 73.10, note). *beams* See 20.6, note.

9. *O 'tis* O the answer (to *Or whether . . . Or whether*) is. *'tis flatt'ry in my seeing* it is a delusion caused by my eyesight, a delusion of the mind (see lines 1 and 2, the first alternative) caused by my deluded eyesight. (The imprecise construction relies on context for its meaning; the clause can, however, allow "in my seeing [i.e. in my view, my opinion is that] it is delusion" to register in the mind of a reader of this line, which is, after all, reporting the speaker's decision between two possibilities.

10. *great* (1) grandiose, pompously self-assured, newly aggrandized (see line 1); (2) highly estimable (as compared with the eye; see the note on lines 10–14 below). *most kingly* (1) in very king-like fashion (an adverbial phrase modifying *drinks*); (2) which is very king-like (an adjectival phrase modifying *mind*).

11. *gust* taste. *is greeing* agrees (*OED* gives examples of the verb "to gree" from the fourteenth century through the nineteenth).

12. *to* to suit.

11–12. *his* . . . *his*   its . . . its (but see 73.10, note). The logic of the situation (in which the eye deceives the mind), and the implications of the butler-king
metaphor suggest that *his* refers to the mind. The logic of the syntax (in which
eye is the most convenient antecedent), and the couplet (which reports that the
eye loves it), suggest that *his* refers to the eye. (Since this poem is entirely devoted to efforts to make difficult decisions between the mind and the eye, the
perfect ambiguity of the reference of *his* is appropriate and constructive.)
Compare 113.7,8.

10–14. The metaphor here is of the eye as servant (a butler in lines 11 and 12,
an official taster in lines 13 and 14) to the mind (the king). In terms of the
metaphor, the argument of the couplet is that the eye's guilt in offering poisoned
wine (misapprehended truth) to the mind is lessened because the eye too is
deceived, it too is eager to drink up the apparently wholesome poisoned wine,
and, as taster, is a victim too. That sense is clear, simple, and an appropriately
fanciful conclusion to the intellectual confection this poem is. However, these
lines also invoke the Platonic tradition and ask to be seen against a background
of Platonic values. The solemn theorizing typical of that tradition is, of course,
a far cry from this philosophically naive sonnet—which more than anything
else reflects the traditional observations that everything reminds lovers of their
beloveds and that everything looks good to a person in love. However, both the
topic and diction of this sonnet are familiar in philosophic investigations of the
kinds and morality of love. In the couplet the phrase *the lesser sin* opens the
way to understanding not only that the eye's sin is less than it would be if it
were not a co-victim but also that its sin in loving misvalued objects is less than
the mind's. The reader is thereby invited momentarily to remember Neo-
Platonic and Christian-Platonic analyses of the psychological condition this
sonnet plays with and to remember that, because of the obligations imposed on
the mind by its nobility of function and capacity, the mind—like a king—is more
culpable when it errs than are the senses, its inferior subject faculties (compare
the traditional arguments for considering Adam's sin greater than Eve's; and
see the implied argument in *LC* 183–84 and 195–96: "All my offences that
abroad you see / Are errors of the blood, none of the mind" and "[I] kept
hearts in liveries, but mine own was free, / And reign'd commanding in his
monarchy").

SONNET 115

This sonnet and 116 cooperate to demonstrate an inconsistency in traditionally approved attitudes toward mutability in love. When—as in 116—one is
considering a diminishment of love, one agrees that a love that alters with the
passage of time is no true love, is an imperfect love. On the other hand, a love
that increases with time is generally considered not only true but ideal, even
though by definition a perfect love, one that is complete, pure in the Platonic
sense (see the note on 114.10–14), can neither decrease nor increase. John Donne
stated the purely theoretical problem in "Love's growth":

> I Scarce beleeve my love to be so pure
>   As I had thought it was,
>   Because it doth endure
> Vicissitude, and season, as the grasse;
> Me thinkes I lyed all winter, when I swore,
> My love was infinite, if spring make'it more.
>
> But if this medicine, love, which cures all sorrow
> With more, not onely bee no quintessence,
> But mixt of all stuffes, paining soule, or sense,
> And of the Sunne his working vigour borrow,
>
> Love's not so pure, and abstract, as they use
> To say . . . .

Shakespeare's sonnet 115 can be described as deriving its energy from a sustained quibble on "perfect" in its literal sense ("complete," "incapable of augmentation"), and "perfect" less precisely used to mean "most excellent." (The word "perfect" does not appear in this poem [see 141.13–14, note], but see 113.13 and 114.7, note.) In sonnet 115, Shakespeare uses a series of philosophic commonplaces for belittling the attractions of physical, time-bound love to express a mock-solemn despair over a love which betrays its imperfection by growing greater (lines 1–2, 5–8), and defends himself against being held at fault for his earlier misrepresentation of his love as perfect on the grounds that for all he knew at the time his love might indeed have reached its highest point and would decline thereafter (lines 3–4, 9–12). (Compare 124.14, which tempts its reader to condemn a change for the better.)

2. *Ev'n* See 15.6, note. *Ev'n those* (1) the very ones (as in 55.11); (2) not even excepting those (for "even" as an intensifier indicating the unexpected, see 59.6, note). Note that *Ev'n those* may have sounded like "In those" (see 15.6, 81.14, notes).

3. *Yet* (1) however; (2) as yet.

4. *most full* (1) very abundant, very intense; (2) perfect, complete, increased to its limit, incapable of further growth. *flame* passion (as in 109.2). *clearer* (1) brighter; (2) more visibly; (3) more perfectly, more purely. (Compare *HVIII* III.ii.96: "This candle burns not clear. 'Tis I must snuff it." The example from *HVIII* illustrates the general metaphoric usefulness of flames in discussing constancy and Platonic purity: the clarity of a flame increases with the purity of its fuel; "to snuff" a candle is to remove unconsumed remnants of burnt-out wick that, by reducing the purity of the fuel, reduce the flame's brightness and steadiness; *OED* gives this figurative use of "to snuff" meaning "to purify" from 1577: "The ministers of Christ must be . . . snuffed from all affections of the flesh.")

5–8. *But reck'ning time . . .* As a reader comes from the full stop at the end of line 4, he is likely to take the opening phrase of quatrain 2 as the grammatical subject of a new independent clause (understanding *reck'ning* as an adjective modifying *time*: "time which reckons"—"time that counts, that adds up the number of things" or "time which settles accounts" or "time which makes speculative estimates" [*OED* 5]); that independent clause, apparently interrupted by the list of time's activities, is left still incomplete at the end of line 8, where the exclamatory fresh syntactical beginning in line 9 gives the impression that the speaker's erratic syntax reflects the intensity of his feelings.

A reader disturbed by the fragmentary nature of quatrain 2 (or by the imprecision *reck'ning* has as a modifier for *time*) might, as some commentators have, reason the quatrain into a syntactic relationship with the clauses that precede and follow it. Pooler, for example, suggested that *But* be construed as an adverb meaning "only" and that *reck'ning* be read as modifying *judgement* (line 3) or *I* (lines 1 and 2 and inherent in *my* in lines 3 and 4)—a logically possible reading, which, being idiomatically improbable, can be accepted only as a reader's remedial rationalization of lines that confused him as he read; Pooler would substitute a comma for the period after *clearer* and read lines 3–5 thus: " 'I saw no reason why love should grow, for I took nothing into consideration but time [i.e. taking only time into consideration] . . . . ' " One might (as Beeching seems to suggest) attempt to reason the lines into submission by reading *reck'ning time* and its long modifying "whose" clause as parallel with *fearing of time's tyranny* in line 9; that would be to legislate a reading of lines 5–10 that, though it takes *But* as the conjunction it appears to be, does not otherwise reflect the reading experience of a reader attuned to the habitual patterns of English syntax: "But, alas, why, taking account of time, whose . . . , [and] fearing of time's tyranny, might I not . . . ."

In any event, the relationship of quatrain 2 to the syntaxes that precede and follow it will have presented a reader a complicated job of comprehension no matter how he decides to work it out. Moreover, the vagueness of the relationship increases a reader's susceptibility to the further complications evoked by pertinent but syntactically irrelevant "accidental" significances inherent in *reck'ning time*—which can suggest both "telling what time of day it is" (compare 12.1, *When I do count the clock that tells the time*) and "the time of reckoning," "the time for settling accounts," and which is immediately followed by *millioned* ("reckoned in the millions") and by three and a half lines that are, in one sense of the word, a "reckoning," a "list," an "enumeration" (*OED* gives this from 1561: "God kepeth a rekoning of all the days of our calamitie"). (The apparent use of *reck'ning* as an epithet for *time* can also cause a reader's understanding to be colored by the phonetic likeness of *reck'ning* to "wrecking," which indicates a principal activity of "injurious time.")

5. *millioned*   reckoned in the millions, which number in the millions.   *accidents*   (1) unforeseen events, chance occurrences; (2) events (as in *Temp* V.i.304–06: "the story of my life, / And the particular accidents gone by / Since I came to this isle"); (3) mischances, misfortunes (as in *RIII* I.iii.214: "by some unlook'd accident cut off"); (4) incidental qualities (as a logician's term, "accident" describes an attribute not of the essence, a property nonessential to one's conception of a substance).

6. *Creep in 'twixt vows* intrude between times of promising and the times of fulfilling the promises, change conditions under which vows were made and thus cause them to be broken (with overtones, invoked by the context of a love sonnet, of "come between vowers, between those who have vowed to be constant," particularly "cause man and wife to break their marriage vows," "come between man and wife" and, more particularly, "come between them by creeping into the marriage bed with one or the other partner"; reference to the marriage service, which becomes prominent in 116.1–4, is only dimly present here, sustained by *sacred* in line 7 and, perhaps, by the sound of "altar" in *alt'ring* in line 8 [note *alters* in context of the marriage ceremony in 116.1–4, *husband* and *altered* in 93.2–3, and *TN* II.v.140: "She that would alter services with thee"]).

7. *Tan* darken and make look like leather (compare 62.10). *sacred* (1) held to be holy, worshipped (courtly lovers traditionally compared the physical and/or spiritual beauty of their beloveds to divine beauty; see also the husband's final response in the marriage service: "With this ring I thee wed: with my body I thee worship"); and, perhaps, (2) entitled to respect, worthy of the respect promised in solemn vows of eternal love. *sharp'st* The use of "sharp" to mean "eager" or "urgent" is not quite idiomatic with *intents*, "purposes"; Shakespeare probably chose *sharp'st* in order to complement *blunt*. He may also be playing on "in" and the surgical term "to tent" meaning "to probe" (compare *Macb* I.vii.26 and the cruder play on the idea of piercing in *WT* I.ii.138: "Affection! thy intention stabs the centre").

8. *to th' course of alt'ring things* The following explanation by Ingram and Redpath cannot be improved upon: "Primarily (1) 'into the *direction* dictated by things as they change'; but probably also (2) 'into the *current* of changing circumstances,' fusing the two distinct and well-established senses of 'course'."

7–8. The contractions of "sharpest" and "altering," and the slurred article in *th' course* appear to result from the necessity of accommodating extrametrical syllables in regular lines. The lines do sound crowded; the metrical strain in line 8 is particularly audible. However, for a modern reader the metrical tyranny exhibited here and the words' struggle against metrical considerations accidental to their own nature are more strikingly emblematic of the substance the lines express than they would be for Shakespeare's contemporaries, who met such contractions constantly in both spoken and written language; for example, in *WT* IV.iv.391 the only other Shakespearian use of "altering" is also syncopated. On the other hand, I have replaced Q's colon after *alt'ring things* with a dash, indicating the syntactical break that *Alas, why* makes immediately evident at the beginning of line 9; Shakespeare's reader presumably felt an unfulfilled need for an "and" to signal the final element in a series: "tan . . . , blunt . . . , and divert . . ."; the lines were therefore probably always suggestive of the violent and arbitrary manipulation to which they testify.

9. *fearing of* fearing (a common Shakespearian construction; compare 150.5, and see Abbott, par. 177).

10. *then* (1) at that time (as in line 3); (2) therefore (the context specifically invites both meanings). *Now I love you best* Many editors indicate the obvious nature of this clause by putting it in quotation marks.

11. *When* (1) at the time that; (2) since, in as much as. *I was certain* (1) I was fully confident of the validity of my sense of things; (2) my nature was firmly and finally established, not liable to any variation; (3) I was steadfast, resolved (a combination of senses (1) and (2); this Latinate use of *certain*, not recognized by *OED* before Milton, is established here from context). *o'er incertainty* over uncertainty (see 107.7); the signification is imprecise: (1) beyond uncertainty (giving *I was certain o'er incertainty* the meaning "I was more certain than even uncertainty [which is the surest thing in life]," "my certainty exceeded uncertainty's"); (2) beyond doubt. Shakespeare could rely on context to indicate the general sense of the construction (which is immediately glossed by line 12 in any case); he may have chosen the vague and unusual locution because the wordplay in *certain o'er incertainty* (like the interaction of *then* and *now* in line 10) embodies a reminder of the futility of any certainty about anything still in mortal process, and/or because *certain o'er incertainty* is colored by its echoes of constructions like "victorious over" and "triumph over."

12. *Crowning the present* (1) glorifying the present; (2) taking the present to be the ultimate and treating it as such. See 114.1, note—on *crowned*. *doubting of* (1) uncertain about; (2) fearful of, fearing, *fearing of* (line 9); (3) fearing for (*OED* gives this from 1577: "Every one doubted of his owne life"). (This line is gently and casually ironic in that *the present* refers to a past time and in that *doubting* both participates in a restatement of the substance of line 11 and directly contradicts it.)

13. Compare 151.1. *so* (1) that Cupid is a baby; (2) what I previously suggested could be said: "Now I love you best."

9–14. Although no punctuation can effectively diminish the potential of these lines, no punctuation can testify to their full potential either. The punctuation given here is the least unsatisfactory of the arguable alternatives to the Q punctuation. Q puts a colon after line 12, but *why . . . / Might I not* in lines 9 and 10 makes it obvious that the whole third quatrain is a question and must be concluded with a question mark. Q ends the poem with a period, which, like many recent editions, the present text retains. In line 13, however, *then might I not say* echoes *Might I not then say* in line 10 so closely that it too looks like an interrogative (as the inversion of subject, *I*, and verb, *might*, suggests in any case), and invites one to read the couplet as a question. Almost all nineteenth-century editors replaced Q's final period with a question mark—and had good reason to do so. However (most appropriately in a poem that asserts the transforming power of passing time), *then*, a word that indicates both the time referred to and the relationship of a premise (*Love is a babe*) to a conclusion based upon it, changes its position between the first use of the phrase and the second. That change changes the rhythm of the second *might I not*, in which *not*, unstressed in line 10, is stressed. Thus, on the one hand, the *might I not* construction in line 13 indicates that the couplet is another rhetorical question like the four preceding lines ("Love is a baby; therefore, was I not at that time justified in saying 'Now I love you best'?"). On the other hand, the rhythm of the same phrase simultaneously indicates that this second *might I not* is declarative, the speaker's

retort to the rhetorical question he posed in quatrain 3 ("Love is a baby; therefore I was *not* justified in saying as I said"); moreover, the signals of a question—
idiom and the model of the preceding question—are countered not only by
rhythm but by the fact that *Love is a babe* does not reasonably lead to the conclusion inherent in the earlier rhetorical question, namely that saying that a
love has reached its peak is justified.

The stalemate between interrogative and declarative indications continues in
line 14. *To give,* "in order to give," is syntactically suited to introduce further
justification for saying "Now I love you best": "in order to assure full growth
to (i.e. not to stunt the growth of) that which still doth grow (i.e. both is as *yet*
growing, and goes on growing *forever*)." That reading emerges smoothly from
the syntax but is logically unsatisfactory because it is difficult to imagine how
saying "Now I love you best" would have such a result. *To give,* "in order to
give," makes logical sense in a declarative reading of *might I not* but is syntactically unsatisfactory because it entails an interpolated syntactic step between
line 13 and *To give*: "I was unjustified in saying that; [that statement is for-
bidden] in order to assure . . . ." The assumption that *To give* is to be read as
"in order to give" is, however, *only* an assumption (encouraged by the model of
quatrain 3 where the *Might I not* construction in line 10 was followed in line 11
by an auxiliary further justification for declaring that the speaker's affection had
reached its peak). *To give* can be understood as explaining the speaker's objection to saying "Now I love you best": "I was not justified in saying that, [to say
that is] to attribute full growth to that which . . . ." That reading requires some
syntactic patchwork, and is not immediately evoked by the idiom of *say so* /
To give, but it does relate clearly to the announcement that *Love is a babe,* the
fact on which the logic of the rest of the couplet depends.

The entire problem is further complicated by the reading of line 13 that is
most evident, a reading that would be the only one if lines 13 and 14 stood alone:
"Love is a baby; therefore would I not be justified in saying so, saying that love
is a babe?" In context of lines 1–12 that reading is to some extent invited by the
logical sleight of hand in *Love is a babe,* which abruptly changes the topic from
"love," meaning "affection," to "Love," "Cupid," and thus prepares a reader
for further trickery; after *Love is a babe,* the speaker can sound like an unscrupulous pleader capping the defense offered in quatrain 3 with an irrelevant argument, one based on an irrelevant premise and presented with lawyer-like triumph
as if it demonstrated that the supposed crime is actually a virtue (compare the
tone and lack of logic in 116.13–14). Following on the conclusion that there can
be no objection to saying "Love is a baby," line 14 can be read as an explanation
of the advantages of the label "baby," given love "in order to assure full growth
. . . ." (i.e. if one says that love is a baby—if one makes *that* statement of fixed
identity—one makes a definitive statement which, by virtue of the incomplete
condition that "baby" describes, is also a statement that is final and simultaneously not final because what is labeled "baby" is *still* [is as yet] progressing
toward its final larger form). In the particular case of *Love,* however, the non-
final final statement *Love is a babe,* which is only true because Cupid is commonly portrayed as a baby, is actually final, definitive, both as a sentence and

in the implications of the definition: Cupid, who never grows up, is a baby *still,* "forever."

The ramifications of the couplet and their contradictions of one another might be continued indefinitely. The logical conclusion the sonnet reaches is not expressed in the particular assertion embodied in its last sentence; the point the couplet makes is not in what its words express in relation to one another but in what is demonstrated about all human assertions by its syntactic completeness, its sound of finality, its position at the end of the poem, and its ultimate incapacity to make a final, a definitive, an ultimate, statement. It is impossible to make an absolute statement at any moment in—or about anything that exists in—time.

SONNET 116

See the headnotes to 115 and 117.

In twelve of the thirteen surviving copies of Q, sonnet 116 comes between 115 and 117 but is numbered 119, presumably as a result of an easy confusion by which a *9* was misplaced in sorting and put with the *6*'s in the printer's font. The Folger-Mildmay copy numbers 116 correctly (see 89.11, note).

Some glosses are omitted from the line-by-line commentary because they occur in the final general note on the poem.

1–2. In context of *marriage, Admit impediments* evokes a strong specific echo of the marriage service: "I require and charge you (as you will answer at the dreadful day of judgment, when the secrets of all hearts shall be disclosed) that if either of you do know any impediment why ye may not be lawfully joined together in matrimony, that ye confess it." Note that, although both the marriage service and this sonnet are principally concerned with truth—being true, being faithful, being constant—this first sentence of the sonnet and the section of the marriage service it echoes are concerned with speaking the truth, confessing what is true (see lines 13–14).

1. *Let me not* May I never. (The tone is that of a vow, but the imperative use of *Let* also suggests prayerful beseeching and gives the poem psalm-like overtones; compare Psalms 31:17–18: "Let me not be confounded, o Lord: for I have called upon thee: let the wicked be put to confusion, & to silence in the grave / Let the lying lippes be made dumme . . .").

2. *Admit* (1) concede the existence of, acknowledge; (2) permit consideration of. (The idiomatic implications of the construction "admit to the marriage" give the sentence overtones of a metaphor in which the speaker is like a doorkeeper or usher admitting or not admitting wedding guests, allowing or impeding their passage; compare *Measure* IV.iii.116: "You shall not be admitted to his sight.") *Love is not love* that so-called love is not true love, is not real love. Note that, although the word "true" is not physically present here, this phrase implies the idea of genuineness—an idea expressible in the word "true." See the note on lines 1–2 above; the substance of this phrase relates to a third sense of "true."

2–12. Compare the proverbs "A perfect love does last eternally" and "Love without end has no end [i.e. has no ulterior motive]" (Tilley, L539, L533).

4. _with_ (1) in the company of, along with; (2) like.   _the remover_   (1) one who goes away; (2) one who takes something away (as time takes away beauty). _to remove_ to depart, to change position. John Doebler ("A Submerged Emblem in Sonnet 116," _Shakespeare Quarterly_, XV (1964), 109–10), argues that this line "makes implied use of the compass emblem, a commonplace symbol for constancy during the period in which Shakespeare's sonnets were composed." The compass (which, since its function is to draw a circle, "the ancient symbol of eternity," relates generally to the topic of 116), demonstrates constancy in change because its fixed foot _bends with_, leans toward, its spreading foot, _the remover_, but does _not_ alter its own position, does not _remove_. Compare the final metaphor of Donne's "A Valediction: forbidding mourning." (For two more obviously relevant senses of _compass_, see the general note below.)

5. _ever-fixèd_ permanent, eternal, established forever.   _mark_ seamark (e.g. a beacon or lighthouse). Dover Wilson compares _Cor_ V.iii.74–75: "Like a great sea-mark, standing every flaw, / And saving those that eye thee."

7. _star_ Compare _JC_ III.i.60–62: "I am constant as the northern star, / Of whose true-fix'd and resting quality / There is no fellow in the firmament." _bark_ boat.

8. _Whose worth's unknown_ whose value remains unknown (because a star is too far above us to be measured with the precision possible for earthly, palpable things), whose precise nature is unknowable (like the pure, disembodied Platonic "idea" of love; note that the antecedent of _Whose_ can be momentarily taken to be _bark_).   _height_ Q gives "higth," which may have resulted from the printer's omission of the second _h_ in "highth" or from his reversal of final _t_ and _h_ in "hight"; "highth" and _height_ are variants of the same word.   _height be taken_ "To take the height of a star" is to calculate its altitude in order to steer by it. B. G. Kinnear cited this from Hakluyt's _Third and Last Volume of the Voyages_ (1600): "Where having taken the height of the pole-starre, they found themselves to be in 37 degrees and 1/2 of Northerly latitude" (_Cruces Shakespeariane_, 1883, p. 501, quoted in _Variorum_ I, 295). ("Worth" is imprecisely used in this line; its general sense is dictated by context. Shakespeare may have chosen the word in order to play on "worth" meaning "high value" [as in 52.7]; _worth's_ thus emphasizes a distinction between kinds of measure that is inherent in the simultaneous pertinence of both the literal and the figurative meanings of "high," one referring to physically perceptible altitude, the other to degree of value; compare 21.3 and the similar wordplay in _Much Ado_ I.i.147: "[Leonato's short daughter is] too low for a high praise." The North Star and ideal love— which is the highest rung on the Platonic ladder and the highest kind of love— are both beyond human estimation, too high to be measured. This line also assists in a general echo of Ephesians 3, where Paul says that his mission is to preach "the unsearcheable riches of Christ" [3:8] and prays that the gentiles, once they are "rooted and grounded in love, / May be able to comprehend with all Saintes, what is the breadth, and length, and depth, and height / And to knowe the love of Christ, which passeth knowledge . . ." [3:17–19].)

5–8. This quatrain echoes the tradition of Petrarch's _Poi che per mio destino_ and _Passa la nave mia colma d'oblio_ and Thomas Wyatt's "My galley charged with forgetfulness."

8,10,11. *his*   its (but see 73.10, note).

9. Compare Ephesians 5:14–16: ". . . Christ shal give thee light. / Take hede therefore that ye walke circumspectly, not as fooles, but as wise, / Redeming the time . . . ." (These verses come just before the long passage from Ephesians 5 that is part of the marriage service; that passage is given in the headnote for sonnet 36.) *time's fool* mortal, circumscribed by the finite limits of finite things (compare 124.3 and *the fools of time* in 124.13). (The allusion seems to be not only to the dependence, servility, and trifling occupation of court jesters, but also to their habit of trailing after their masters; jesters commonly mimicked their patrons, giving a flattering and amusing testimony to the great man's grandeur by contrasting it to their own feebleness and exaggerated incapacity for the lordly mannerisms they aped. There was also a kind of jester called a zany, who mimicked the actions of a principal clown, repeating each action in follow-the-leader fashion.) *rosy* (1) rose-colored; (2) rose-like, flower-like (and thus temporary, seasonal, and vulnerable; note *sickle's* in line 10).

9–12. Compare 55.9–12.

10. *his bending sickle's*   Compare *crookèd knife* in 100.14; for other references to "Father Time," see 60.12, note.

11. *with*   The sense is a conflation of *with* indicating accompaniment and *with* indicating simultaneity (as in *Temp* IV.i.164: "Come with a thought"); *with* can also seem momentarily and illogically to indicate instrumentality: "by means of." *his* (1) time's; (2) love's (see 73.10, note). *hours* = a monosyllable.

12. *bears it out*   endures. (Dover Wilson compares *AW* III.iii.4–6: "A charge too heavy for my strength; but yet / We'll strive to bear it for your worthy sake / To th'extreme edge of hazard." He also notes the echo of "St. Paul's hymn to Charity . . . ['Love' in the Geneva and Bishops' Bibles], 1Cor. xiii, which Shakespeare surely had in mind." This is the Geneva version of verses 6–10: ". . . [Love] rejoyceth in the trueth. / It Suffreth ['beareth' in AV, 1611, but not earlier] all things: it beleveth all things: it hopeth all things: it endureth all things. / Love doeth never fall away, thogh that prophecyings be abolished, or the tongues cease, or knowledge vanish away. / For we knowe in parte, and we prophecie in part [Bishops' Bible: 'For our knowledge is unperfect, and our prophesiyng is unperfect']. / But when that which is perfite, is come, then that which is in parte [Bishops': 'is unperfect'] shalbe abolished.") *ev'n* See 15.6, note. *to the edge of doom* (1) until doomsday, until the last judgment, until the end of time (see the parenthesis in the quotation from the marriage service in the note on lines 1–2); (2) until the moment of death (compare "to love and to cherish, till death us depart" in the marriage service; for *doom* meaning "death," see 14.14 and the proverb "Death's day is doomsday" [Tilley, D161], and note the proverbial idea of being "upon the edge of one's grave" [Tilley, E57]).

13. *this* See 50.3, note (on the constructive vagueness of Shakespeare's use of demonstratives). *error* Tucker noted that *error* is a legal term; *OED* gives an example from 1495 and this from 1641: "Errour is a fault in a judgement,

or in the processe, or proceeding to judgement, or in the execution upon the same in a Court of Record." Since the commonest use of this legal sense is in the phrase "writ of error" (a legal order for the reexamination of a case in which a judge is thought or known to have made or allowed an error in the proceedings), there is incidental and logically gratuitous wit in the juxtaposition of *error* with the verb *writ*—the past tense of "to write"—in line 14. *upon me proved* proved against me. (The legal metaphor recurs to the one implicit in *Admit* and *impediments* in line 2.)

1–14. *A General Note on Sonnet 116:*

Sonnet 116 is the most universally admired of Shakespeare's sonnets. Its virtues, however, are more than usually susceptible to dehydration in critical comment. The more one thinks about this grand, noble, absolute, convincing, and moving gesture, the less there seems to be to it. One could demonstrate that it is just so much bombast, but, having done so, one would have only to reread the poem to be again moved by it and convinced of its greatness.

A major problem about literary art is that abstract general assertions do not feel any truer than their readers already believe them to be; they carry no evidence of their truth and very little of the life (and thus very little of the undeniability) of the physically extant particulars from which they derive. Descriptions of those particulars, or exempla, or metaphoric allusions can bring life and conviction to a generalization, but they also limit its range and its value to the reader. The attraction of abstract generalizations is the capacity they offer us to be *certain o'er incertainty* (115.11), to fix on a truth that allows for and cannot be modified by further consideration of experience or change in our angle of vision. One means of achieving universality and vividness at once is bombast: high-sounding, energetic nonsense that addresses its topic but does not indicate what is being said about it, and thus rises free of human intellectual limitations like a hot-air balloon. Bombast, however, is rarely satisfying for long or to any listener who pays attention to the signification of the words he hears strung together. Bombast overcomes the difficulties of language by abandoning its purpose; a general, noble, vibrant utterance that conveys no meaning operates like a bureaucracy that functions perfectly so long as it ignores the purpose for which it was established.

Sonnet 116 has simple clear content; indeed, its first clause aside, it is one of the few Shakespeare sonnets that can be paraphrased without brutality. That alone excludes it from classification as bombast, but much of its strength and value is of the same sort that bombast has. Sonnet 116 achieves effective definition unlimited by any sense of effective limitation. One obvious source of that success is that its positiveness is achieved in negative assertions (a definition by negatives is minimally restrictive because the thing so defined may be thought to possess all qualities but those specifically denied). Some of the means by which negative definition is made efficient, convincing, and satisfying in this sonnet are those that can be used to give grandeur to nonsense.

The sonnet combines extreme generality—even vagueness—with locutions that imply some degree of personification and thus invest abstract statements with the urgency, vividness, and apprehensibility of concrete particulars.

That occurs in obvious fashion in the straightforward navigation metaphors of quatrain 2, but the equation of *love* with a seamark or a star only *explains* the speaker's meaning, is a chosen substitute for the speaker's topic, a substitute that acknowledges by the necessity of its use that the actual topic remains a distant impalpable essence, sensorily apprehensible by imperfect proxy. Other, less openly supportive effects do more toward achieving the special grandeur of this poem than the navigation metaphors. Consider the effects of *the remover, looks,* and *bears it out*; each operates differently, but they have a common denominator in giving effective concreteness to the identity of ideal love, in at the same time reasserting that that essence is indeed disembodied and incapable of comprehension in images, and in insisting that what is here encompassed and made apprehensible is nonetheless too big, too grand, too spiritual to be grasped. In line 4, *the remover* presents an embodied characteristic left free of any specific body or kind of body; it suggests all—but specifies none—of "people who are inconstant," "time (which is the remover of beauty, the alterer)" and "a departed lover (one who has ceased to requite the love given him, or one who has literally gone to another place, or one who is dead)." The shadowy personification of *the remover* lets us do something like visualize an actor and action without knowing at all what they are.

Similarly, *bears it out* in line 12 means only "persists," "endures," but suggests positive particular action, allowing a reader to visualize action, motion, and power, without visualizing any actor, mover, or wielder of power; *it* suggests specific objectivity, but has no antecedents and therefore no more particularity than in the modern phrase "stick it out," meaning "endure." *Bears it out* suggests an heroic striding forth, but no visualizable strider; it is not limited or diminished, and, not being ostentatiously figurative, does not advertise its identity as a mere translation of the unknowable into knowable terms.

Lines 5–7 present another instance of abstract statement that has the vividness of sensually perceived action. The assertion that love *is an ever-fixèd mark* is simple metaphor; it explains. The statement that a seamark *looks on* is another matter. The sense is clear enough; the focus of concern dictated by *ever-fixèd* makes *looks on* an effective synonym for "endures," "persists in the face of." That a seamark should be said to "look" also makes sense (as does the same action by a *star* in line 7); the most effective seamark is a beacon (see *OED* examples from 1566 and 1617); a Renaissance reader would recognize the aptness of the image both from the way a beacon looks at night and because Shakespeare's contemporaries were used to speaking of eyes as if they emitted the light they reflect and see by (see 20.6, note). The statement that a seamark *looks on tempests and is never shaken* is also apt; a tiny distant flame that withstands the wind and water of a tempest is as fitting an emblem of steadfastness as the ever-fixed North Star in the next line. None of that is poetically remarkable. What is remarkable is that the logic in which *looks on* indicates "persists," the logic in which a seamark is eye-like and can be considered capable of looking, and the logic in which a feeble but constant flame is emblematic of steadfastness are independent of one another; each supports the assertion without reference to its relation to the other two. As a result the statement gets all the validity of the seamark's concreteness but remains mystic and wonderful, made as resistant to comprehension as available to it—and by the same locution. Moreover, whatever else it does, *looks on* personifies the insensate seamark as a beholder, although the function of seamarks is exactly opposite. On the other hand, the beholders, the sensate mariners who are guided by seamarks and stars, are presented (by metonymy) as *every wand'ring bark*, i.e. as boats.

None of that is at all complicated until it is explained. The lines do not demand any explanation; they are immediately clear, but they derive much of their power from being both simple and straightforward and simultaneously so complexly wondrous that beholder and beheld are indistinguishable from one another in a statement that makes their ordinary relationship perfectly clear.

A similar blend of substantial and insubstantial fabric occurs on a larger scale in *Love is not love* (line 2) and in *I never writ, nor no man ever loved* (line 14). In those two cases the speaker's meaning is clear and immediate, uncolored by the incidental supernaturalness inherent in metaphoric perception; at the same time, both assert absolute nonsense. *Love is not love* is a traditional (and traditionally pleasing) kind of incidental paradox in which a straightforward assertion (in this case "That kind of love is not genuine love") is phrased so as to be meaningless if taken literally. Similarly, the hyperbole of the couplet is so extreme that it merely vouches for the speaker's intensity of feeling; it gives no evidence to support the validity of his statement because on a literal level it is ridiculous (we cannot doubt that what we read was written). Moreover, though the special meaning "truly loved" is obvious in *no man ever loved*, that assertion, like *Love is not love,* gets its rhetorical power from the ostentatious falsehood of its unmodified literal sense.

The discussion of Shakespeare's devices for simultaneously emphasizing particularity and vagueness, substance and emptiness, brings us to a related technique in sonnet 116 that has related effects: the poem is both singleminded, presenting constancy as the only matter worth considering, and heterogeneous in ways that do nothing to diminish or intrude upon its singlemindedness. In examining the special appeal of sonnet 116, it may be well to remember that in saying anything—no matter how general—one advertises the fact that one has *not* said everything else—everything else pertinent to one's topic and everything else impertinent to one's topic. That may sound less simpleminded and more worth saying if one considers the related proposition that the literary creations we value most are works like *Hamlet, King Lear, Paradise Lost,* and *Ulysses,* works so full—so full of matter, so full of different kinds of matter, and so open to being viewed from so many angles of vision—that their particulars seem to include all particulars, and the experience of them seems to take in all experience and all attitudes toward it. Sonnet 116 is overlaid with relationships established in patterning factors that do not pertain to or impinge upon the logic and syntax of the particular authoritative statement it makes. The most obvious of them, of course, are the formal iambic pentameter rhythmic pattern and the sonnet rhyme scheme. This sonnet, however, also contains patterns of a kind that falls between the ideational structure (what the poem says) and the substantively irrelevant phonetic patterns of the sonnet form: patterns established by the relationship of the meanings of its words—in this case meanings that are irrelevant to, and do not color, the particular sentences in which they appear here but which do pertain generally to the topic about which the sentences isolate particular truths in particular frames of reference:

Let in line 1 and Admit in line 2 both have the general sense "allow," but Let can mean "stop," "prevent," "impede" (as in Ham I.iv.85: "I'll make a ghost of him that lets me" and in this marginal gloss to the Geneva text of Psalms 115: "No impediments can let his worke, but he useth even the impediments to serve his wil" [gloss (c); Shakespeare echoed gloss (f), which says that the makers of idols are "As muche without sense, as blockes & stones," in JC I.i.36; he echoes the Psalm itself in 137.2]). Similarly, "to admit," meaning "to allow to enter," and impediments, as things that prevent entrance, also have an extra-syntactic relationship. (Also note O no in line 5; the exclamation not only contains the sound of the casually auxiliary imperative "O know [that]" but also presents a logically incidental example of a suitable prefatory exclamation introducing an impediment volunteered by a parishioner responding to the injunction in the marriage service that "if any man can show any cause, why they may not lawfully be joined together, let him now speak . . . .")

The meanings of true in line 1 are "faithful" ("constant to one another") and "steadfast" ("constant in intent," "unwavering"), but, since marriage of true minds has overtones of the Christian and Platonic ideal of purely spiritual love, of true minds can also suggest "which is truly of minds (or souls) rather than merely of bodies"; true meaning "not a lie" pertains generally to truth-telling, the topic of this sentence, even though that sense of true is not evoked by the syntax or admissible in it; true meaning "straight," "not bent," implies the rightness, the spiritual health, of constant minds and is balanced by the idea of "becoming bent" inherent in bends in line 4.

Bends, which is used to mean "turns aside," "changes its direction," contains untapped potential for nearly contrary meanings irrelevant to its use in line 4 but relevant to the general topic of constancy: "to bend to" means "to apply all one's energy, attention, and concern on one object"; the "to bend to" construction here adds the idea of fixed intent on removing to the contrary idea of turning aside (see bent to . . . cross in 90.2 and bent / To follow in 143.6–7); bends also suggests stooping (as opposed to the staunch uprightness of the seamark in the following line) and submission (as opposed to the steadfastness required to withstand time's bending sickle in line 10—a line in which bending echoes bends but describes the curving blade of a sickle, the curving stroke with which a sickle is wielded, the bending of the grass before it, and the submission of grass to blade). In line 11, alters echoes alters and alteration in line 3 where they follow immediately upon a precise echo of a church service performed at an altar (see the notes to 115.6 and 116.1–2).

In line 10, the reference of his is specified by sickle (because Father Time has traditional association with a sickle, and the other available antecedents do not). In line 11, the same reference for his is dictated by the model of the previous his, by the obvious substantive link between time and hours and weeks, and—most importantly—by the context of the poem's general argument that love is permanent. However, the line includes—and thus acknowledges within the poem's triumphant sweep—the altogether arguable proposition which the whole poem denies, the proposition that love is fleeting, the proposition which *Love alters not with his brief hours and weeks* would imply if those words stood alone as a paradox in which the syntactic norm prevailed, *Love* were the antecedent for *his*, and the line presented this paradox: "Love, with its brief hours and weeks (love, which is characterized by its brevity), alters not." As read in context the line says, "Love alters not with *time's* brief hours and weeks," and that straightforward and single-minded sense is absolute—is absolutely undiminished, is absolutely unmodified, and is, in fact, absolutely strengthened by the self-contradiction engulfed within it.

Compass means "encircling reach" and "sphere of influence" in line 10, but appears in context of a quatrain-long metaphor of navigation to which "mariner's compass" pertains.

One sense of *error* in line 13 is a synonym for one sense of *wand'ring* in line 7. As one comes upon the word, *error* suggests "that which is erroneous," "not true," and thus recurs to the specific concern of the portion of the marriage service echoed in lines 1 and 2: telling the truth; *upon me proved* is an obvious legal metaphor, and its juxtaposition with *error* narrows the meaning of that word to "heresy," "a false creed," and makes the whole line a specific metaphoric allusion to formal accusations of false belief (see sonnet 105) and inconstancy in religion. The completed line, however, still refers back to the marriage service echo but takes another ideational route to get there: the passage echoed in lines 1 and 2 comes from the general section of the service where the congregation is asked to present evidence that the marriage cannot morally or legally go forward. The idea of doomsday (introduced by *to the edge of doom* in line 12) is also abstrusely relevant to matrimonial impediments; the priest asks the bride and groom if they know any impediment why they may not be lawfully joined together and charges them to answer as they "will answer at the dreadful day of judgment."

That tangle of incidental relationships surely never enters into a reader's understanding of the lines; presumably it never touches his consciousness even to the extent that rhythm, rhyme, and alliteration do; every habit of purposefully used and purposefully comprehended language leads a reader to ignore the ideational static in what he hears. In this sonnet, however, the denseness of incidental meaning patterns and their close ideational relevance to what the speaker is saying are sufficient to make the poem's assertions sound as if they took cognizance of all viewpoints on all things related to love and were derived from and informative about every aspect of love.

The best example of effective expansion of the scope of a narrowly based generalization is the undercurrent of frivolous sexual suggestiveness in the poem. High-principled definitions of true love are ordinarily inefficient because they exclude not only sexuality but the human habit of taking the topic of sexuality lightly, joking about it. Many of the metaphors and ideas of this sonnet seem just on the point of veering off toward puerile joking about temporary male impotence—loss of tumescence—after sexual climax and about temporary abatement of female sexual desire; quatrain 2, for instance, is always ready to turn into a grotesquely abstruse pun on "polestar." Most of the sexually suggestive elements in the poem are obvious and in more danger of being exaggerated than missed (but see 80.7, note [on *bark*], 137.1, note [on *fool*], *mark* in *LLL* IV.i.123–29, and *rose* in *AYLI* III.ii.101–02; with reference to *looks* in line 6, see Eric Partridge, *Shakespeare's Bawdy*, s.v. "eye" and "naked seeing self"). That is not to say that sonnet 116 is an elaborate dirty joke masquerading as a grand statement of grand principle (any more than sonnet 115, which in technique and effect is the mirror image of this one, is a solemn philosophic statement masquerading as a toy); here one cannot find a coherent sexual undermeaning as one can in schoolboy jokes like "My dame hath a lame tame crane" or even Drayton's "Since there's no help," but the poem does offer a substratum of random bisexual references that suggest preposterous teasing based on the ridiculously logical argument that a male lover is inconstant, not faithful, untrue in love, if his sexual potency is not constant, and a female is likewise inconstant if she is temporarily sated.

Sonnet 116 is probably valued not because it asserts the value of absolute fidelity, but because it is itself so absolute, so "certain o'er incertainty," that it can both recommend and successfully demonstrate singleminded allegiance to one governing principle. The poem testifies by example that singlemindedness, authority, and certainty can exist—or seem to exist—without a fanatic narrowness of reference.

The triviality, irrelevancy, and baseness of the sexual innuendo in sonnet 116, its indecorum, is a source of the poem's value, its success, and its grandeur. As with the incidental complexities, contradictions, and by-meanings discussed previously, the very pettiness of the sexual overtones contributes to the impression the poem gives that its general, all-inclusive, absolute, grandly simplistic moral imperative is genuinely general, that it presents a genuinely definitive definition, one that excludes no particulars or attitudes that might modify or challenge it, one that has been tested by all exceptions that might prove its rule wanting, one that is both absolute and absolutely true.

SONNET 117

This sonnet is something like a pun on sonnet 116. It picks up on 116's topics (e.g. constancy, departure, accusation, proof, value, writing, ties between people, measuring worth), its metaphors (e.g. navigation, trials at law, the range of weapons [116.10: *Within . . . compass*, 117.11: *within the level*]), and its language (e.g. *minds* and *unknown* in 116.1,8 and *unknown minds* in 117.5; *error* in 116.13 and *errors* in 117.9); but 117 uses them to entirely different effect (in 116 the speaker is grand, noble, general, and beyond logic; in 117 he is petty, particular, and narrowly logical). Note the phonetic and ideational relationship between the fourth lines of the two, the repetition of "alter" in 116 and *all* in 117, and the strikingly urgent likeness and correspondingly urgent difference between the two couplets.

1. *scanted* stinted on, inadequately performed, came short of, neglected (as in *Lear* I.i.278: "You have obedience scanted").

1–2. *all / Wherein* everything by which. (Q marks the line end with a logi-cally irrelevant comma; in any event, however, the break between lines delays the modifying clause long enough to give temporary identity to the absolute as-sertion "I have stinted on everything" as a syntactically complete whole.)

2. *deserts repay* The combination of these two words effectively conflates two duties: rewarding merit (giving what is due), and repaying favors (paying debts); the conflation thus suggests that the beloved does the speaker a benefit by merely existing. *deserts* = a capsule summary of the poem: the noun *deserts* presents a locally irrelevant shadow of the verb "to desert"—"to abandon"—in a poem whose chief topics are deserving and desertion. (Note that the consonant sounds of *dearest* in line 3 make it a scrambled echo of *deserts*.)

3. *upon your . . . love to call* "Affection" is not readily meaningful as an object for "to call upon." The vagueness of the phrase lets it carry all pertinent senses of both verb and object and invites a reader to understand the line without much concern for the logical strictures implied by the grammatical functions of *your* and *love*. The phrase contains fragmentary signals of (1) to invoke you (as one would a deity or as a poet does his muse—compare 38.11); (2) to invoke you (as a poet does a patron—i.e. to write poems for you—see 79.1); (3) to call upon you to aid me for the sake of your love for me (i.e. to call upon you for the aid to which I am entitled because of your love for me—see 79.1, note); (4) to ask for your love, to make appeals for, plead for, your love; (5) to claim my rights of love, to avail myself of your [physical?] love (compare *Tim* II.ii.24–25: "My master is awak'd by great occasion / To call upon his own"); (6) to visit you (as in *JC* II.ii.122: "Remember that you call on me to-day"). *dearest* (1) very precious; (2) best beloved; (3) best (compare *best of dearest* in 48.7).

4. *Whereto* to which. *bonds* (1) moral and spiritual ties; (2) obligations, duty (as in *Measure* V.i.8–9—note the relationship of obligations and merits: —"You make my bonds still greater." —"O, your desert speaks loud . . ."). *day by day* (1) more and more firmly each day; (2) for daily service.

3–4. Note the special pertinence *bonds* has to the context of *Accuse* and *repay* in lines 1 and 2 because of its legal and financial uses. "To call upon" (which could be used to mean "to call as a witness" [see 124.13]), and *dearest* (which can mean "most costly"), have similar extra-logical pertinence to *Accuse* and *repay* respectively.

5. *frequent . . . with* often in the company of, familiar with. (This line is *OED*'s earliest example for *frequent* meaning "familiar"; the next is this from 1615: "A talkative Barber: with whom he is the more frequent"; the sense appears to be reasonably common in the early seventeenth century. Here *fre-quent* also carries the adverbial implication that the speaker has been with strangers often—"frequently." A reader's understanding of *frequent* may also be colored by its relationship to the verb "to frequent," "to visit often"; over-tones of the verb here reinforce both the syntactically indicated adjectival meaning of *frequent* and its adverbial implications and also make *frequent* echo one sense of "to call upon" in line 3.) *unknown minds* strangers. (The in-convenient synecdoche by which *minds* substitutes for "persons" requires that a reader scramble a bit to understand the phrase; in doing so he may gather

supplementary modifying suggestions of "who knows how many people" ["incalculable numbers of strangers"], "people of a sort one would not want to know," "un*knowing* minds" ["ignorant dolts"], and "people whose ideas and values are strange and suspect." Note the echo of *Whose worth's unknown* in 116.8.)

6. *giv'n to time*   wasted (the commercial nature of *dear purchased* activates the contrasting idea of profligate generosity, giving as opposed to selling, in *giv'n*).   *dear purchased*   dearly purchased, acquired at great cost (in money and/or in effort). Editors ordinarily indicate the relationship of *dear* to *purchased* by hyphenating: "dear-purchased"; the hyphen makes perception of the adjectival unity of *dear purchased* a split second quicker for a reader and thus, to that small extent, diminishes his probably momentary syntactic misapprehension of *your own dear* as the first part of a construction that will be completed by some specified object that is "dear," is precious or beloved (note *dearest* in line 3): "your own dear 'something.' " The hyphen also diminishes the extent to which *dear* colors a reader's understanding of *right*; even after syntactic necessity reveals *dear purchased* as a single adjectival unit, *dear* still has some residual independent modifying effect on the direct object and supplements the idea that the beloved's *right* is dearly bought with the idea that, just by virtue of being the beloved's, the *right* is precious to the speaker.   *right*   Shakespeare may intend a pun on "rite" (compare 17.11 and 23.6); since the speaker registers his love by writing verses, the line can be colored by the sound of the syntactically irrelevant "write" (compare 116.13, note).

7. *hoisted sail to all the winds*   Shakespeare uses "hoist sail" rather as we use "drop everything"; it suggests sudden abandonment of all previous concerns and loss of self-control in a frantic dedication to a new purpose (compare *A&C* III.x.14–15: "The breese upon her, like a cow in June— / Hoists sails and flies"). The present phrase means "surrendered myself to be driven by every idle whim, temptation, or influence," "gone off [from you and/or fidelity to you] on the slightest provocation." (The phrase is also sexually suggestive; see 137.6, *all* and *all bonds* in lines 1 and 4, and 26.1–14, note.   *winds*   The rhyme with *minds* indicates Shakespeare's usual pronunciation.

9. *Book . . . down*   write down, record (as in a list of charges).   *wilfulness* (1) perverse self-indulgence; (2) lustfulness (compare *wilful* in 40.8); (3) purposeful actions (i.e. "intentional misdeeds" as opposed to "mistakes," "unintentional misdeeds"; Schmidt [s.v. *wilfulness*] compares *LLL* V.ii.471: "forsworn in will and error").   *errors*   (1) mistakes, unintentional misdeeds (with pertinent overtones from lines 7 and 8 of the root sense, "wanderings"—from Latin *errare*, "to wander," "to go astray"); (2) moral errors, faults, sins (as in 119.5).

10. Tucker Brooke paraphrased this line as "Pile on top of what you can prove all that you may suspect."   *just*   founded in fact, reliable.

11. *level*   line of fire, range and aim (compare *WT* II.iii.5–6: "quite beyond mine arm, out of the blank / And level of my brain, plot-proof").

13. *my appeal*   my plea (i.e. my defense against the preceding charges; *appeal* is a legal term).   *prove*   (1) test; (2) demonstrate.

14. *virtue* (1) strength (compare 81.13 and Latin *virtus*); (2) moral goodness; (3) worth (as in *FQ* V.i.10: "[the sword] was of no lesse vertue then of fame"). *of your love* of your affection for me (with a possible play on "of your beloved," i.e. "my," "of me").

13–14. See 110.9–12 and the rhyme words of 116.13–14.

SONNET 118

1. *Like as* just as. *appetites* desires (line 2 specifies *appetites* as "desires for food," but, even with *our*, the plural is unusual for that sense of "appetite" [see *our palate* in line 2], but usual for other senses. The probability that appetite for food is a metaphor for fleshly appetites in general and sexual lust in particular is implicit in the context of a collection of love sonnets and confirmed in line 5 when the similes are applied; the delay in limiting the reference of *appetites* and the habits of the expression *our appetites* anticipate the logical expansion introduced by *Ev'n so* in line 5).

2. *eager compounds* pungent concoctions (e.g. appetizers, hors d'oeuvres; compare *bitter sauces* in line 6; for *eager* meaning "bitter," see *RII* I.i.49, and for *eager* meaning "sharp," "sour," see *Ham* I.v.69). *urge* stimulate (as in *RIII* I.i.147: "I'll in to urge his hatred . . . ").

3. *As* just as. *prevent* forestall, provide beforehand against, take advance steps to preclude, ward off (with plays, activated by line 4, on "to prevent" meaning "to bring about prematurely," "to hasten" [*OED* gives examples from 1548 and 1553, and this from 1654: "Such as are of this nature, prevent the Worlds Doome, and their own, not staying for the general Conflagration, but beginning it"], and "to prevent" meaning "to surpass," "to outdo" (see *prevent'st*, 100.14, note, sense 3). *unseen* (1) not evident (i.e. only imagined); (2) not yet evident (i.e. only expected or feared).

4. See 111.12.

5. *Ev'n* See 15.6, note. *Ev'n so* just so. *being* = monosyllabic, as in 50.8. (Although *Ev'n* and *being* are syncopated, they do help make the line sound appropriately full.) *ne'er-cloying* never-cloying. *Ne'er-cloying* is the usual rendering of Q's "nere cloying." This is one instance in which unavoidable modernization demonstrably diminishes a poem. Both *ne'er-cloying* (i.e. "never-cloying") and "near cloying" make sense here, and their paradoxical amalgamation in a single self-negating expression constitutes an emblem of the whole poem; a seventeenth-century reader would not have known which of the two opposing ideas was meant or which of two lines of argument (one explaining why the speaker changed, one explaining why that change was foolish) "nere cloying" served. The phonetic confusion of "ne'er" and "near" is well demonstrated in Shakespeare's puns on "ne'er," "near," and "nearer" in *RII* V.i.88: "Better far off than near, be ne'er the near" (i.e. "It is better that we be far from one another [in different countries] than near [both in England], if we would then still be no nearer [still be separated, still prevented from living together]"). As to the spelling, "nere" is Q's apparent spelling for "ne'er" (17.8, 89.14, 144.13), but is never used for "near" (spelled "neere" in all five certain

instances); however, *OED* records "nere" as a common Renaissance spelling for "near" meaning "nigh," for "near" meaning "nearer" (i.e. "nigh-er"), and for "ne'er." The phonetic confusion of "ne'er," "near," and "nearer" presumably helped establish the proverbial phrase "ne're the near" ("never the nearer"); Tilley (E27) lists many examples, including two from James Howell's *Proverbs . . . in the English Toung* (1659), which illustrate the flexibility of the spelling: on page 4 Howell's printer used "nere" to indicate "ne'er," in the proverbial phrase, and on page 11 he used "nere" for "nearer" in the same phrase.

5–8. This quatrain plays on—and with—several common proverbs: "Sweet meat must have sour sauce" (Tilley, M839—which Shakespeare also plays on in *R&J* II.iv.75–78: ". . . very bitter sweeting . . . sharp sauce . . . "); "Sweet sauce begins to wax sour" (Tilley, S97); and "A surfeit of the sweetest things / The deepest loathing to the stomach brings" (*MND* II.ii.137–38, Shakespeare's version of Tilley, H560, "Too much honey cloys the stomach"). In light of lines 1 and 2, one may also remember that "A good appetite needs no sauce" (Tilley, S870).

6. *bitter sauces   = eager compounds.* (Since the metaphoric reference must be to inferior company, Shakespeare may intend some sort of play on "sauce" meaning "an impertinent fellow" [*OED*, sb. 6a]; compare "saucebox" and "saucy jack," and note that Shakespeare uses "saucy" to mean "lascivious" [see the examples cited in 80.7, note, and the complicated punning of *Cymb* I.vi.149–51: "If he shall think it fit / A saucy stranger in his court to mart / As in a Romish stew"]. Saucy fellows would presumably be eager [i.e. not "bitter" but "ardent"] compounders [see *Lear* I.ii.125: "My father compounder with my mother"].)   *frame*   adjust, adapt (*OED* gives this from the mid-sixteenth century: "Unto his teaching your life ye will not frame").

7. *sick of* (1) made ill as a result of; (2) weary of, no longer pleased by (as in *2HIV* I.iii.87–88: "The commonwealth is sick of their own choice; / Their over-greedy love hath surfeited").   *welfare*   (1) good health (as in *MofV* V. i.114: "praying for our husbands' welfare" ["husband health" in Q2, 1619]); (2) prosperity, happiness,well-being; (3) feasting, high living, sumptuous fare (*OED* gives this from 1577: "Those that are given much unto wine and such welfare")—with a play (visually emphasized by the Q spelling "wel-fare"), on "fare that makes one well," "healthful food" (compare *SC*, "January," 43–44: "feeble flocke . . . / Whose knees are weake through fast [i.e. fasting] and evill fare"); and perhaps—since both the situation described and such words as *shun* and *purge* suggest that the speaker refers to abandoning the beloved—with an additional play on "farewell," "goodbye" (compare the similar pun in *PP* XIV.5–6: " 'Farewell,' quoth she 'and come again to-morrow.' / Fare well I could not, for I supp'd with sorrow"; and see *OED*, s.v. "fare," *v.*1, 9 [1582]: "Well fare the life . . . I ledde ere this"). (*Welfare* may also contain some sort of sexual pun related to those discussed in 154.9, note [e.g. "traveling in the well" or "such fare as a well has to offer"]; the probability of such a pun being effective is increased by the pun [discussed below] on *meetness*: "meat" was and is a slang term for "whore's flesh," "whore" [as in *R&J* II.iv.—or in some editions iii.—131–32: "An old hare hoar, / Is very good meat in Lent"].)

found a kind of meetness saw a certain fitness, a kind of propriety (with a play on "meat" meaning "food" [not just animal flesh, but food in general], and on "kind" meaning "natural").

7–8. Line 8 is the object of *found* in line 7: "found to be diseased . . . [to be] a kind of meetness"; see Abbott, par. 354.

8. *diseased* (1) ill, sick; (2) deprived of comfort, dis-eased.

9. *policy* (1) prudence (as in *RII* V.i.84: "That were some love, but little policy" and *Lucrece* 528–29: "A little harm done to a great good end / For lawful policy"); (2) cunning strategy, scheming (as in 124.9 and *2HVI* IV.i.83: "By devilish policy art thou grown great"). *t'anticipate* to forestall (as in *Macb* IV.i.144: "Time, thou anticipat'st my dread exploits")—with a play on "to accelerate," "to cause to happen earlier" (*OED* gives an example from 1534 and this from 1625: "The funerall . . . is anticipated, and shall be on Thursday"). Compare *prevent* in line 3.

10. *ills* (1) diseases, symptoms of illness; (2) evils. *faults* disorders (*OED* gives this from 1538: "The commyn fautys and mysordurys of the same")—with pertinent overtones of "fault" meaning "dereliction of duty," "neglect," "misdeed." *assured* certain, indubitable, real. (Shakespeare may be playing on "policy of assurance," "insurance policy"; see 124.9, note.)

9–10. The syntax of these lines is very confusing (it surely confused the Q printer, whose punctuation consists of a comma after *were* and one after *assured*). The lines may be read in several ways, none of which is perfectly satisfactory and each of which must ignore some signals of syntactical relationship: *policy in love* = "policy with regard to love"; *in love t' anticipate* = "lovingly— out of generosity—to anticipate"; *t' anticipate / The ills . . .* = "in order to anticipate the ills . . . "; *ills that were not grew to* = "imaginary ills grew into"; *policy in love t' anticipate / The ills that were not grew to faults assured* = policy, which was to anticipate (or in order to anticipate) . . . , grew. . . . " The last of these readings, the only one that makes overall sense and the only one that can accommodate the syntactic parallelism of *grew* in line 10 and *brought* in line 11, takes everything from *policy* through *not* as a noun phrase, the subject of *grew*, and is the least satisfactory because it makes *policy* (singular) grow into *faults* (plural). Context and common sense reveal what the lines must be saying; the energy of the actual construction is effectively adjectival, emphasizing the paradox, irony, and perversity of facts it only suggests. (Note the nonparallel uses of *to* in the parallel phrases *grew to faults* in line 10 and *brought to medicine* in line 11. If *faults* and "false" were phonetically confusable [see 138.14, note], then the juxtaposition of *policy* [which connotes falseness] and *faults* would have added a further incidental complexity to the lines.)

11. *brought to medicine* (1) treated, used medical skill to heal (i.e. something like "took to the doctor"); (2) caused to arrive at a condition that required doctoring, brought to the state of needing medicine. *medicine* = trisyllabic.

10,12. *assured, cured* The pronunciation might be "assurèd," "curèd"; the Q spelling is no indication; the printer usually indicated syncopation of *-ed* with *'d* (as in line 8: "diseas'd") but did not do so always (see 85.6 and 120.4); *r* commonly canceled a following vowel in any case (see Abbott, par. 463).

12. *rank of goodness* Editors often set this phrase off in commas, thus

fixing *rank* as adjectival and the sense of *Which rank of goodness* as "which, being rank of goodness." The phrase thus echoes one sense of *sick of welfare* in line 7 and yields several shades of meaning in *rank of*: (1) made sick as a result of (as in *2HIV* IV.i.64: "To diet rank minds sick of happiness"); (2) overgrown (note *grew* in line 10), in need of pruning, as a result of (as in *HV* V.ii.50: "wanting the scythe, all uncorrected, rank"); (3) made lustful by (as in *MofV* I.iii.75–76: "the ewes, being rank, / . . . turned to the rams"); (4) abounding in, full with (*OED* gives this from 1575: "I never heard one so rancke of rudeness" and "rank of success he was so puft with pride" from 1652). However, since *a healthful state* is a *rank of goodness*, "a particular degree of goodness," *rank* may be read as a noun and *Which rank of goodness* may be read as a single pronominal unit replacing *a healthful state*: "The aforementioned healthful state would by ill be cured." *goodness* (1) prosperity, good fortune, happiness (*OED* gives this from the mid–sixteenth century: "After trouble and adversite foloweth all manner of goodnes and felicite"); (2) excellence (moral or material, the speaker's or the beloved's). *ill* (1) unpleasantness; (2) inferior things, things not excellent; (3) wickedness (with a play on "illness," "disease"; also see 119.9, note).

14. *so* in that way (i.e. by taking steps to forestall the sickness, by trying to avoid becoming weary of the beloved). *sick of* ill as a result of (with a play on "weary of"). (The unflattering harshness of the suggestion that the speaker no longer finds the beloved appealing is somewhat softened by its kinship with the traditional—and in a way flattering—courtly-love conceits by which love or the beloved is likened to a disease (e.g. Spenser's *Amoretti* 50 and Sidney's "Like those sicke folkes, in whome strange humors flow" [Ringler, p. 74], which ends "Sicke to the death, still loving my disease." See sonnet 147, a gross expansion on the same tradition.)

SONNET 119

This sonnet presents variations on the themes of sonnet 118. It is largely constructed of metaphors and analogies from alchemy and medicine; these are fused in lines 1 and 2; as the title page of George Baker's *The Newe Jewell of Health* (1576) illustrates, alchemy and medicine were generally thought of as the single science of "creating every bad a perfect best" (114.7)—of transmuting imperfect things (base metals, diseased minds and bodies) to perfect ones (gold, healthy minds and bodies); the "philosopher's stone" after which the alchemists vainly sought was to be both the means of turning every metal to gold and an elixir which would be a universal panacea. Aside from the metaphor of line 2 and its punning echo in line 10, alchemy is not prominent in the sonnet, but alchemical implications are present throughout. Although the metaphor of line 3 is primarily medical, the idea of judiciously countering hopes with fears and fears with hopes suggests not only the medical aim of achieving a balance among the body's four constituent elements (see the headnote to sonnet 44), but related alchemical principles (e.g. a perfect balance of pure mercury and pure sulphur produces gold). Lines 4–6 suggest the inevitable last minute failures of

¶ The newe Iewell of Health, wherein is
contayned the moſt excellent Secretes of Phiſicke and Philo-
ſophie, deuided into fower Bookes. In the which are the beſt ap-
proued remedies for the diſeaſes as well inwarde as outwarde, of all the partes
of mans bodie : treating very amplye of all Dyſtillations of Waters, of Oyles,
Balmes, Quinteſſences, with the extraction of artificiall Saltes, the vſe and preparation of Antimonie, and potable Gold. Gathered out of the beſt and moſt ap-
proued Authors, by that excellent Doctor *Geſnerus*. Alſo the Pictures, and maner
to make the Veſſels, Furnaces, and other Inſtrumentes therevnto belonging. Faithfully corrected and publiſhed in Engliſhe,
by George Baker, Chirurgian.

Printed at London, by Henrie Denham.
1 5 7 6.

alchemists and the traditional explanations for failures: errors of execution and the alchemist's lack of moral purity (an alchemist whose soul was impure could not succeed in purifying matter; God's grace was necessary for that; see Shumaker, p. 191). Line 7 concerns some sort of transmutation; so does line 8 where, as in distillation, the cause is heat (*fever*). The triumphant exclamation of line 9 is in the spirit of (and contains an incidental echo of the sense of) the alchemists' "Eureka" ("I have found it"). Lines 11 and 12 are particularly suggestive of alchemy, in which the essential operation was to break down matter and then reconstitute it in altered and superior form. Line 13 may allude to the proverb "Content is the Philosopher's stone, that turns all it touches into gold," although Tilley (C625) records no example before 1642. The last line introduces a note of avarice and, although it can be considered simply to refer to the necessity of using natural gold in the alchemical process and to the vast multiplication of wealth that theoretically ensued, its tone is that of a successful confidence man; that tone acknowledges the most salient fact both of popular practical alchemy (as illustrated in Jonson's *The Alchemist*) and of the speaker's mock-serious defense of his infidelities: both are transparent frauds.

1. *potions* medicinal drafts. *siren* alluring, deceiving, and dangerous—siren-like. (The sirens are mythological monsters—part bird, part woman—who lure sailors to destruction by the irresistibly enticing sweetness of their singing; compare *CofE* III.ii.45–47: "O, train me not, sweet mermaid, with thy note. / To drown me in thy sister's flood of tears. / Sing, siren, for thyself, and I will dote"; the word *siren* also gives *potions* a magical coloring.) ("Potion," particularly in figurative uses, suggests something unpleasant but beneficial [see *benefit of ill* in line 9]; *potions* thus presents an incidental contrast to the harmful sweetness implied by *siren*. The contrast, however, is muddied by the fact that "potion" meant "poison" as often as it did a curative medicine [e.g. Hamlet calls the poison he forces upon Claudius a "potion"—*Ham* V.ii.318]. The resulting confusion between harmful good and beneficial bad becomes the topic for the rest of the poem.)

2. *limbecks* alembics, stills (like the one pictured just below the left elbow of the goddess "Alchemy" on the title page of *The Newe Jewell of Health*); see *still* in line 10.

1–2. The sirens in classical mythology are female, and that may account (along with wishful thinking) for the widespread assumption of commentators that the speaker is referring to an infidelity with a woman. Adjectival uses of *siren*, however, do not necessarily imply reference to feminine allure; *siren* was often applied to speech. Although lines 1 and 2 are suggestive of perverse sexual activity (which mirrors the morally perverse action of infidelity and the logically perverse action of abandoning a worthy beloved for unworthy ones), the suggestions of male homosexual fellatio are—as is obvious from the shape and interrelation of the parts of alembics—at least as strong as those of cunnilingus (see the notes on *hell* in 129.14 and 144.12).

3. *Applying* administering (as a medicine—compare *WT* III.ii.149–50: "apply to her / Some remedies for life").

4. *Still* (1) always; (2) even so, nevertheless (as in 5.14, where it also occurs

in context of distillation; see line 10 below). *losing* See 18.10, note. *losing when I saw myself to win* (1) failing at the moment when I thought I had succeeded; (2) losing [the fight against illness?] when I thought to win out; (3) gaining victories (making conquests in love?) that were actually losses.

4,6,8. Q puts a question mark at the end of each of these lines. The reason is presumably the one given in the note to 97.2–4—except that in the case of lines 1–4, 5–6, and 7–8, the sentences are not merely exclamations structured like questions but have some interrogatory force (compare such exclamatory questions as "What have I done!"). All such sentences are problems for modern directive punctuators, but could not have troubled Renaissance writers, readers, or printers because they were not in the habit of relying on punctuation for logical instructions.

5. *errors* moral offenses, sins (note that the idea of wandering, of straying, inherent in "error" prepares the way for ideas in lines 7, 8, and 13; see 117.9, note).

6. *so blessèd never* never so blessed, blessed in the highest degree (an inversion of the standard idiom "never so . . ."). (Both here and in sonnet 120 Shakespeare seems on the point of exercising the traditional pun on the common verb "to bless" and the rare one derived from French *blesser* and meaning "to wound" [*OED* cites *Gammer Gurton's Needle*, III.iii: "Tarry, thou knave . . . I shall make these hands bless thee"; also see the last two lines of Henry Vaughn's "Jesus Weeping"]. Note the medical metaphor of line 3, the interplay of salvation and wounds in 120.12, and the paradoxical theme of both poems.)

7. *spheres* (1) sockets (as in *Ham* I.v.17: "Make thy two eyes, like stars, start from their spheres" [i.e. make your eyes bulge out, make you "bug-eyed"]); (2) proper orbits (see "like stars" in the preceding quotation), proper areas of activity, the range of activities to which they are *fitted* (for related figurative uses of "sphere," see *AW* I.i.83 and *A&C* II.vii.14). *been fitted* The usual gloss for *fitted* is "forced by fits," the definition *OED* gives for this, its one recorded instance of "to fit" used to indicate an action caused by "fits," "paroxysms." That gloss ultimately proves justified, but a reader cannot have the understanding reported by the gloss until he gets to the poem's first references to mental unbalance—*distraction* and *madding* in the following line; as a reader comes upon the "fitted out of" construction, its contextually obvious general sense is explicable only as the product of a comic logic that assumes that if "to insert" is "to fit in" then "to expel" or "to extract" must be "to fit out." A reader might attempt to derive a coherent reading based on *fitted* meaning "made to fit"; that understanding is likely to be the first to suggest itself because *fitted* appears in a context of "proper spheres"; but, although overtones of that sense surely inhere in *fitted*, the syntax of the line must be both twisted and supplemented to accommodate "made to fit" or any of its variants (e.g. Ingram and Redpath appear to suggest "adapted to fit objects in lower spheres"—i.e. "made suitable for gazing upon objects in lower social spheres," "turned away from the sphere to which they should confine their gazing"). Whatever the sense one puzzles out may be, the fact remains that, although *been fitted* can be explained, its need of an explanation is glaring. The quasi-alchemical shift from a laboriously earned

understanding of "fitted out of" as "expelled" (or as "adapted") to the equally improbable "forced by fits" is a typically Shakespearian effect, but its worth does not seem sufficient to balance out the disadvantages of so gross a stumbling block to understanding. Similarly, any small play on "putting out the eyes," "blinding," inherent in the juxtaposition of *eyes* and *out* is likely to be lost in the reader's scramble for a surface sense of the line and does not in any case provide a persuasive clue to the poetic motives behind the awkward and disconcerting nonce use of *been fitted*. Shakespeare more probably sacrificed the expository flow of his poem for *been fitted* because, in its Q spelling, "bene fitted," it includes and can be mistaken for "benefited" (the word elaborately played on in line 9); "In what way have my eyes, which are out of their spheres, profited . . ." ("benefit" is usually trisyllabic as in line 9 below, but the syncopated pronunciation "ben-fit" occurs in *A&C* V.ii.127, *Cor* V.vi.67, and *1HVI* V.iv.106 [Kökeritz, p. 390]).

8. *distraction*   (1) separation, forceable pulling apart (Latin, *distrahere*, to pull asunder); (2) madness, mental derangement; (3) turning aside of attention, change from one object of concern to another (i.e. infidelity of affection). *madding*   (1) raging; (2) maddening, delirium-producing. (On the metaphoric use of *madding*, see 129.8 and the note on *rage* in 13.12.)

9. *O benefit of ill*   Oh, how wonderful the benefit of ill is! (The exclamation also includes the materials for an answer to the question latent in lines 6 and 7: "What benefit have my eyes . . .?") This phrase—if not the whole poem— seems designed as a vehicle for a variety of contrived, arbitrary, logically extravagant puns on the sounds and primary senses of *benefit* and its Latin root, *bene fit*, "it is well made" (i.e. "it is well constructed"—see *made better* and *built* in lines 10 and 11): (a) a wittily wrongheaded equation of Latin *bene fit*, "it is well made," and the English "it is made well, it is cured" (a pun to some extent sustained by the Latin idiom *melius esse*, "to be better"); (b) macaronic puns on Latin *bene* and English "fit" which echo the ideas of propriety (what is well fitted and what fits well, in line 7), and support the conceit about the curative powers of disease ("good fit" = "healthy paroxysm"). If, as "dram of eale" in *Ham* I.iv.36 could suggest, "oil" (and/or its variant "ele"), *ill*, and "evil" were all capable of pronunciation as monosyllables sufficiently similar for punning, then it is possible that Shakespeare's reader heard a pun on "benefit of oil" in *benefit of ill* (for "oil" as a medical/alchemical term, see *FQ* I.v.41, lines 25–27 of Donne's "To Mr Rowland Woodward," and *Alchemist*, II.iii.190ff.). There may be a similar pun (in a nest of obvious ones) in *2HIV* I.ii.155–56 (an exchange that occurs in context of discussion of physical and moral corruption, of fat, and of medicine; "oil of angels" was a cant term for money paid as a bribe; for "angel" meaning a coin, see 144.14, note):

> *Chief Justice.* You follow the young Prince up and down, like his ill angel.
> *Falstaff.* Not so, my lord. Your ill angel is light; but I hope he that looks upon me will take me without weighing.

It is also possible that *hell* (pronounced without the *h*) could be confused with *ill*, "evil," and "oil"; consider *MWW* V.v.32–33: "I think the devil will not have

me damn'd, lest the oil that's in me should set hell on fire. . . ." (For the likeness
of the sounds spelled "-ill" and "-ell," see 112.3, note.) All of this, of course, is
grossly speculative. *ill* (1) evilness, wickedness; (2) evilness, unpleasantness,
what is displeasing; (3) illness, sickness. *find true* find it true, discover it is
true.
    9–12. Compare 110.5–8.
    10. (1) "That superior things are always improved by evil (i.e. by the action of
evil upon them, by evil done to them, or by doing evil)"; (2) "That superior
things are always cured by means of evil things (foul medicines)"; (3) ". . . always improved when they are by—next to, compared with—foul things"; (4)
". . . are improved by the action of [an] evil still, of an alembic *foul as hell*"
(the reference is simultaneously to the process of distilling medicinal substances
and to the alchemists' practice of getting an increasingly refined substance by
repeating the distilling process several times so that each "better" substance
becomes better *still*). A pun on *better* and "bitter" (which were commonly
pronounced similarly, see 91.9, 111.11, and notes), gives two additional readings
of the line: (5) "that superior things are always made bitter by the action of evil
on them (or by doing evil)," and (6) "that what is bitter is always cured by evil
things (like medicines)." (Reading (1) is the most obvious, but does not make
sense; readings (3), (4), and (5) indicate three ways by which reading (1) is paradoxically true.)
    11–12. These lines echo a very popular proverb that goes back at least to
Terence (*Andria* III.iii.23): "The falling-out of lovers is a renewing of love."
Tilley (F40) gives many Renaissance examples; they fall into two groups: one
group appears to take the proverb as a simple formulation of the universal
observation that the love of reconciled lovers is heightened by their relief that
the estrangement has not been permanent and by their pleasure in escaping the
general emotional discomfort that accompanies strife (e.g. this from the 1580's:
"What if she cast thee of? the falling out / Of lovers doth renewe and strengthen
love"); the other sort makes the proverb carry the implication—useful in
the speaker's attempt to justify his infidelity—that lovers fall out on purpose to
increase their love by making up again (e.g. this from 1577: "A proverb olde I
beare in mynde / . . . / The fallyng out of lovers kynde, / Is fayned wrath love
to renewe").
    13. (1) "Therefore, chastened, I come back to what satisfies me, what contents
me" (with a suggestion of "to a state of contentment" as opposed to madness);
(2) "Therefore I return to that which is my 'argument,' that which provides the
contents of my verse" (for the beloved as poetic subject, see 38; for *content*
[singular] meaning "contents," "that which fills a container [e.g. the glassware of
an alchemist]" or "that which is the substance contained in a book, poem, or
other document," see *OED*, which gives many Renaissance examples); compare
the similar plays on *content* meaning "contents" in 1.11 and *2HVI* I.i.35: "the
fullness of my heart's content." (The convention by which the two senses are
accentually differentiated—"cóntent," "contént"—is a mid–nineteenth-century
development; in the Renaissance the stress was always on the second syllable.)
In this context the ideational relationship of contents and container (the asser-

tion that "the content is always less than the continent" appears to have had near-proverbial currency) can give *my content* a semantically improbable suggestion of "that which contains me" (for the stock fancy by which the lover lives in the beloved's body, see 22 and notes); moreover, the obscene potential inherent in *con-* can give that suggestion a literal reference (see 151.11, note). (A modern reader may hear "rebuked sufficiently" in *rebuked to my content*, but the quantitative sense of phrases like "to his heart's content" is a recent extension of an idiom by which "to my content" would mean "in a way satisfying to me"; compare line 5 of Herrick's "To Dean-bourn" and *MWW* IV.v.114: "You shall hear how things go, and, I warrant, to your content.")

14. *ills* evil things (i.e. unpleasant things and/or wicked ones—with a play on "illnesses"). Since Malone many editors have arbitrarily substituted "ill"—presumably to achieve a match with *ill* in line 9. *spent* The word may have been sexually suggestive here; see 129.1, note.

4–14. The thinking and some of the language in these lines echo the traditional notion of *felix culpa*, the "fortunate fall" of Adam; see 110.13, note.

SONNET 120

This sonnet approaches the paradox of beneficial ill from another angle; it uses the medical metaphor and some of the diction of sonnet 119, but its particulars also invite comparison with 34.5–14.

1. *befriends me* does me a kindness, is a kindness to me, benefits me (*befriends* has special resonance in a poem about friendship and need).

2. *for* because of (with a suggestion of "in exchange for").

3. The diction of this line and the next acts in effect to demonstrate the truth of its assertion; the context dictates that the line refer to the speaker's acknowledgment of his heavy guilt ("I cannot do otherwise than humble myself, prostrate myself, as a sign of shame and repentance"), but the diction suggests a man helplessly suffering injury, not weighed down with guilt but bent by and bent under a rain of blows that falls upon him as upon metal in a forge. (Compare *how hard true sorrow hits* in line 10.)

4. *nerves* (1) sinews (as that in which bodily strength is constituted—the usual Shakespearian sense, as in *Temp* I.ii.484–85: "Thy nerves are in their infancy again, / And have no vigour in them"); (2) feelings, faculties for feeling, sensibilities (*OED* cites the first line of Ben Jonson's *Poetaster* [1601] where "Envy" rises from hell to speak a prologue and complains that the daylight hurts her eyes: "Light, I salute thee, but with wounded nerves, / Wishing the golden splendor pitchy darkness").

6. *a hell of time* a seeming eternity of pain (the phrase stresses the idea of hell as a place of endless suffering, but *passed a hell of time* suggests something more like purgatory. The idea of suffering as atonement relates to the theme of the sonnet: evils that cancel each other out, wrongs that ultimately prove to be benefits).

7–8. These lines can evoke a mental uneasiness in a reader: although *I . . . have no leisure taken* must logically be understood to include "until now when my thoughts are those just expressed," the unmodified assertion we actually read contradicts the facts of quatrain 1, in which we just heard the speaker do what he says he has not done. The effect is a curious one; the discrepancy is both real and unreal; as a mental experience, a reading of these lines is analogous to the speaker's paradoxical double view of his own and the beloved's suffering.

8. *weigh* think about, consider (with pertinent overtones of "to weigh" meaning "to care about" and of "to weigh" meaning "to see value in," "ascribe high value to"; compare the battle of puns between Katherine and Rosaline in *LLL* V.ii.25–28: ". . . you are a light wench." / —"Indeed, I weigh not you; and therefore light." / —"You weigh me not? O, that's you care not for me." / —"Great reason; for 'past cure is still past care'." In addition, "to weigh" meaning "to have heaviness" has logically gratuitous pertinence to "bow under," the metaphor in line 3; moreover, the idea of measuring by literally balancing a pair of scales—as Shylock means to do in *MofV* IV.i—embodies the principle of offsetting measures of pain that is the poem's theme).

9. *O that . . . might have* Would that . . . had. *our night of woe* It is never clear whether this phrase refers to the recent occasion when the speaker injured the beloved or the earlier occasion when the beloved injured the speaker. The ambiguity is a stylistic metaphor for the analogy the speaker proposes.

9–10. *rememb'red / My deepest sense* The syntax dictates that the primary meaning of *rememb'red* be "reminded" ("to remember" meaning "to remind" is standard Elizabethan usage; compare *Temp* I.ii.243: "Let me remember thee what thou hast promis'd"); however, "to remind a sense" is not immediately meaningful and is made less so by *deepest*. The construction indicates that *My deepest sense* must be understood as "me"; any reader will see what the words must mean—and scholars have managed to fashion glosses that incorporate both the necessary meaning and the actual words (e.g. Pooler: "Perhaps 'deepest' goes in meaning with 'remember'd'; impressed deeply on my heart the memory . . ."; Tucker: "re-awakened my deepest feeling of pain and made me remember . . ."; Ingram and Redpath: "put me in mind in my deepest feelings"). However, *My deepest sense* makes an excellent direct object for "to remember" in its other—now its only—usual meaning, "to recall"; moreover, as a reader is responding to the realization that a *night of woe*, the grammatical subject of *rememb'red,* cannot be thought to have a memory, he meets *My deepest sense*, a phrase that must appear to allude to the preceding eight lines on what and how much the speaker felt when he was the sufferer. The two sets of related but syntactically incompatible signals probably act to conflate the two potential sentences and cause the reader to understand the lines as he would if he had read "our night of woe might have reminded me of my very deep sense of how hard . . . ." (For Shakespeare's reader the passage was probably further complicated by the sound of "my deepest sins" in *My deepest sense*; see 35.8–9, 141.13–14, 112.5,8,10,14, notes.)

11–12. The syntax is drastically truncated. Strictly speaking, the grammatical subject of [*have*] *tend'red* is *night of woe* in line 9, but the logic of the situation leads a reader to understand the construction as if it were "would that our night of woe had caused me to tender."

11. *to you as you to me then tend'red*   (1) to you, as you to me, then offered
(i.e. at the time when the beloved first knew himself injured by the speaker);
(2) to you, as you to me then, offered (i.e. on the earlier occasion when the
speaker was the injured party). Ingram and Redpath summarize the problem of
punctuating the line: "Q has a comma after the first 'you', and . . . several . . .
editors follow . . . [but] a number of modern editors . . . [put] commas after
the first 'you' and after 'then'. . . . the remaining editors have commas after
the first 'you' and after 'me'. Certainly either a further comma is required besides that after the first 'you' or else none at all. Both . . . readings make good
sense. . . ." I follow Ingram and Redpath in saving both meanings by omitting
commas altogether. (Note that, although *tend'red* means "offered," it contains
pertinent echoes of the adjective "tender" and the verb "to tend" [see 83.4,
note].)

12. *humble salve*   salving humbleness, the healing balm of a humble apology
(the sense is dictated by context, but is colored by the sense *humble salve* would
have if it stood alone, "simple household remedy," and thus by the implication
that the speaker is particularly culpable in failing to use a remedy so easy, obvious, and available; in context of *hell of time* in line 6, *salve* can be colored by a
suggestion of "means of salvation" and in turn heighten the vague suggestions
of Adam's sin and Christ's sacrifice inherent in the diction of lines 13–14; see
119.6 and 119.4–14, notes). *fits*   is proper to, is suitable for. The construction
"which fits wounded bosoms" is not quite idiomatic, and its inverted word order
increases the gap between the words and a reader's comprehension; the implied
construction "*The . . . salve* + verb + *wounded bosoms*" leads one to expect
the verb to indicate healing, the action a medicine properly has on a wound. It
may be, therefore, that Shakespeare intends *fits* to include both "suits" and (by
metaphoric extension of "to fit" meaning "to make fit," "to make serviceable"
—as one "fits a ship") some suggestion of "restores," "repairs," "makes well";
that is, he may be exploiting the same potential in "to fit" from which the modern idiom in which "to be fit" means "to be healthy" later derived. (Shakespeare may also anticipate that idiom in *Ham* V.ii.210 where Horatio offers to
"forestall their repair hither, and say you are not fit." As sonnet 119 illustrates,
Shakespeare liked to play on the various forms and meanings of "fit"; in another quibbling exercise on the word, Cloten's soliloquy in *Cymb* IV.i, "woman's
fitness comes by fits" [IV.i.6] approaches the use of "fitness" to mean "good
health.")

13–14. It is hard to know what relationship *But that* signals between the previous sentence and the substance of the couplet. It sounds like a conjunctive
phrase—"except that"; but "Would that such-and-such had happened, except
that . . ." makes no sense—except to Seymour-Smith, who wrenches the construction into arbitrary meaningfulness by fabricating a parenthetical explanatory clause from the materials of lines 11 and 12 and including it in his paraphrase of the couplet: " '(Except I cannot tender the balm you tendered me)
because what you did to me is reason enough for your excusing my offence
against you now.' " Most commentators, therefore, choose to understand *that*
as a demonstrative pronoun referring to *your crime* in line 8, and to understand

But that your trespass as "However, that trespass of yours" (compare *But that wild music* in 102.11). That reading, which yields a syntactic harmony between quatrain 3 and the couplet, is the best one available, but a reasonable and relatively smooth syntactic transition does not guarantee a coherent train of thought: "Would that I had apologized on the spot. However, that trespass of yours now turns out to be *a fee* (payment, compensation)." Thus, having rejected the immediate sense apparent in *But that* because "except that" is syntactically incompatible with the previous clause, and having found a syntactically possible reading, one still has lines that require a patchwork of logical and syntactical additions to make sense: "Would that I had apologized. However, [I can stop wishing that because] that trespass of yours . . . ."

When one comes to *But that*, one has nothing to sustain one's sense of rational progress except the sound of logic, the recurrence of topics and ideas from the preceding twelve lines, and, perhaps, the substantively dormant echo of *fits* in *becomes* (which obviously means "turns into," "takes on the nature of," but has the capacity to mean "is suitable to," "is becoming to"). However, the poem has been building toward the reader's miniature crisis through a series of minor effects that one is unlikely to pause over or bring to consciousness but which involve a reader in perceiving two natures in one thing and/or engage him in trying to maintain his awareness that different things are not the same. Consider, for example, the two pairs of "that's" (lines 1 and 2, 9 and 13), and their variations in meaning, or note that the speaker requires that we cope with two "now's" (the time of writing—when he has realized that he doubled his guilt by not immediately begging forgiveness for it—and the present general period in time—as opposed to an earlier time when the beloved was the transgressor) and two "then's" (an occasion in the immediate past—a *night of woe*, when the beloved confronted the speaker with accusations—and the earlier time when their roles were reversed). *But that*, its problems, and the unsatisfactory solutions to them make explicit a curiosity of the poem that is present from the beginning but to this point unobtrusive: the poem's logical structure contributes to and is an illustrative analogy for the oddities of perception it reports and evokes. Line 1 introduces the beloved's previous unkindness, and everything that follows refers to that. On the other hand, the next line, casually attached by *And*, does not relate logically to the central point of line 1. The beneficial nature of the beloved's past unkindness is forgotten for eleven lines and then returns in the couplet, which, in the terms and scale of one's sixty-second experience of reading the poem, is as surprising a conclusion as the speaker's perception that the beloved did him a favor in breaking his heart. As one comes upon it, *But that* in line 13 makes the same sort of arbitrary conjunction that *And* made in line 2, but this time the conjunction, *But that*, is one which signals that the clauses it connects are related not only syntactically but logically (the difference is that between "Thursday I had the day off, and the King of France ate beans," and the same clauses connected by "but.")

If the couplet followed immediately after the first quatrain we would have a smooth, reasonable six-line poem: "Your past unkindness now benefits me, and, because of what I felt then, I would, unless I were insensitive, have to feel your present pain myself, except that your trespass now becomes a fee. . . ." The hypothetical six-line poem neatly controls and strictly maintains the opposition between a service and an injury; its justification of the paradox of line 1 is just a comfortable exercise in wit. By neglecting to invoke the governing power of *But* for twelve lines and then incapacitating it when he finally does use it, Shakespeare gives his reader a literary experience (i.e. an experience of successive words on a page), that corresponds with the mental experience the speaker is trying to organize: the poem makes two separable but still intertwined statements and does not effectively mediate between them: "I feel your pain because my own was once as great"; and "I do not feel your pain because my own was once as great." (Compare the similar disjunction between 123.1,13,14 and the rest of the poem.)

14. *ransom(s)*   pay(s) for; redeem(s).

SONNET 121

1. *vile esteemed*   (1) considered to be wicked, deemed so; (2) considered to be worthless, deemed so (*OED* gives examples from the fourteenth century on; compare the Italian *vile* and Florio's gloss: "vile, base, abject, to be scorned, contemptible, of no worth or value . . ."). Note the proverb "There is small difference to the eye of the world in being nought and being thought so" [Tilley, D336]; and contrast 1Peter 3:17: "For it is better (if the wil of God be so) that ye suffer for wel doing, then for evil doing."

2. *When*   since, as long as it is the case that.

3. *just pleasure*   (1) legitimate pleasure, innocent pleasure; (2) pleasure that is mine by rights (i.e. that I am entitled to because, if I am to suffer for a sin, I should at least have the pleasure of committing it). For the specifically sexual sense of *pleasure*, see 20.13, note.   *lost*   is lost (by ellipsis).   *so deemed*   (1) judged vile, *vile esteemed*; (2) judged just, considered legitimate.

4. "Not in our opinion but in the view of others" (indicating: (1) we do not consider our action *vile*; only others, who do not know what they are talking about, consider it so; and (2) we do not consider the actions we are falsely accused of committing to be *just*, though others justify such action). The line also has cynical overtones of the quite different moral standard by which sinfulness consists only in being seen to sin, in getting caught; compare the proverb "It is an ill thing to be wicked but a worse to be known so" [Tilley, T140]). A muted pun on *seeing* acts to effect a punning transition between "taking a view of something" (lines 1–3) and literally looking upon it (line 5).

3–4. The comma after *deemed* is Q's and is retained because it allows a reader's understanding of the obvious and logically primary construction "which is not so deemed by our feeling" to be colored by "pleasure not lost by our feeling."

5. *adulterate*   The word is trisyllabic by syncopation and is synonymous with *vile*—in all senses: (1) stained by adultery, adulterous (implying both that the lookers are themselves sexually depraved and that their eyes are like adulterers in violating the privacy of the relationship of speaker and beloved); (2) deceptive

(implying both that the eyes deceive the viewers, mistake what they see for something else, and that the viewers themselves are liars and hypocrites—*OED* cites Daniel's *Complaint of Rosamond* [1592]: "Th' adulterate Beauty of a falsed Cheer, Vile stain to Honour . . .").

6. *Give salutation to* (1) greet (as in fellowship); and, perhaps, (2) take notice of (Ingram and Redpath suggest "greet it with knowing glances") and/or (3) look upon (on the model of "greet" as it is used in *LLL* V.ii.374–76: "when we greet / With eyes best seeing, heaven's fiery eye, / By light we lose light"; the quotation from *LLL* occurs during an extensive investigation of the differences among what one is, what one appears to be, and what value one has in the estimation of others; moreover, the speech that uses "greet" to mean "look upon" is followed immediately by a verbal emblem of the scene's topic in Rosaline's answer—"This proves you wise and rich, for in my eye . . ."—in which "in my eye" has the same sort of transitional function that *seeing* has in line 4 of this poem). *Give salutation to* defies a precise gloss, but it carries suggestions of the ceremony, hypocrisy, backbiting, and gossip of courtiers (note that in Latin *salutatio*, "a salutation," was used to mean "a paying of respect" or "a ceremonial courtly visit" by a *salutator*, "a courtier"; see Martial's contemptuous pun on *salutatio* and contemptuous use of *salutator* in I.lxx.1, 18). Shakespeare is idiosyncratic in some of his uses of "salute" and "greet" (see Schmidt), but those uses, which are no easier to account for than this use of *salutation*, are no help in understanding how Shakespeare would have expected his contemporaries to understand this line. For instance, Shakespeare appears to use "salute" to mean "stir" or "move" in *HVIII* II.iii.102–04 ("Would I had no being, / If this salute my blood a jot; it faints me / To think what follows"), but, although that use, like *salutation* here, is coupled with *blood* and appears in context of gossip, tale bearing, and a discussion of courtiers' tactics, "stirs my sportive blood" does not help us much with line 6. Since Shakespeare's unusual uses of words that relate to greeting occur in contexts that have other elements in common as well (see *3HVI* III.i.14,18–20, *John* II.i.589–98, *Lucrece* 112, 85–111, and the passages cited from *LLL* and *HVIII*), we may guess that Shakespeare's reader was familiar with some now-lost idiom or conceit involving salutation, but, although all the idiosyncratic uses are easily understood from context, no one has yet explained what prompted Shakespeare's idiosyncracy. *sportive* wanton (see the note on *sport* in 96.2). *blood* nature, temperament (see 109.10, note).

7. *frailties* weaknesses, moral weaknesses, weaknesses of the flesh (compare *1HIV* III.iii.164–68: "in the state of innocency Adam fell; and what should poor Jack Falstaff do in the days of villainy? . . . I have more flesh than another man, and therefore more frailty"). *frailer* people even frailer than I, people of even less moral strength than I.

8. *Which* who. *in their wills* (1) in their lusts (see 135, headnote); (2) arbitrarily. Shakespeare may also intend a farfetched pun on "in their Williams," i.e. "who consider what I consider good to be bad in those whose relation to them is the same as mine is to you." (I would not want to argue that Shakespeare did intend the pun or that his readers would have perceived it in any case, but,

considering that the next line is overtly concerned with the singularity of the speaker's identity, I would not want to argue the opposite either. Note too that the conjunction of *wills* and *I am that I am* contains potential for a pun on "William," "Will-I-am," and that God's "I AM THAT I AM" in Exodus 3:14 is the response to Moses' question ". . . if thei say unto me, What is his Name? what answere shal I give them?".) *in their wills count* This phrase has unexploited, substantively irrelevant potential for bawdy innuendo. Although this syntax does not invoke any play on "cunt" in *count*, it incidentally juxtaposes two words, "will" and *count*, that elsewhere have synonymous sexual senses (note *in*; and see 135, headnote; 58.3, note; the plays on "encounter" and "tale" in *Much Ado* I.i.287 [quoted in 134.7, note]; Partridge, s.v. "tail" and "tale" [for "tail" meaning "penis"]; and "I was encountred by a wench" and "In a wenches counter!" in the 1607 quarto of *The Faire Maide of the Exchange* [p. Dl^r]).

9. *I am that I am* Dover Wilson commented: "Taken out of its context, much has been made of this. Crookback's 'I am myself alone' (*3HVI* V.vi.83) and Iago's 'I am not what I am' (*Oth* I.i.66) have both been quoted. Alden (*ap.* Roll.) comments: 'All Sh. says is, "I have an independent standard of character, and where others do not find theirs fitting it, the crookedness (line 11) may be theirs"' —and that is obviously all it means." One cannot be other than sympathetic with Alden's and Wilson's irritation at efforts to read the Biblical echo as a solemn assumption of divine authority, but, though the statement *means* no more than Alden said it does, the echo is unmistakably present and does make the speaker sound smug, presumptuous, and stupid. *level* (1) point, aim, shoot (see *the level* in 117.11 and *OED*, 6); (2) guess (as in *A&C* V.ii.333: "She levell'd at our purposes"). The glosses reflect the limitation put on *level* by *At* in the next line; but *level* stands alone long enough for the pertinent idea of "leveling"—"putting everything on one plane"—to impinge on a reader's consciousness (see *OED*, 2). (Note also that both aiming and equalization of heights pertain to straightness and lead a reader's mind into the metaphor of line 11; consider the noun "level" meaning "a tool for measuring straightness" and its figurative uses [*OED*, 1] to mean "standard of behavior.") See the following note for an additional sense of *level* invoked by *my abuses* in line 10.

10. *my abuses* my misdeeds, my corrupt practices, the injuries I do (colored by the specifically sexual uses of "to abuse" to mean "to seduce" or "to ravish" [*OED* cites this from Sidney's *Arcadia*: ". . . to have deceived me, and through the deceit abused me, and after the abuse forsaken me"]). The context of the speaker's complaints about the false opinions of his critics can make *my abuses* suggest "injuries done to me" (see 134.12)—a sense that would retroactively activate another meaning of "to level at": "to intend," "to aim toward" (*OED*, 6b, cites this from 1576: "All our actions are leveled . . . unto two ends"). *Abuses* has a special pertinence to this context because "abuse" is regularly used to refer to insults, libels, injurious speech, and reviling (as in *2HIV* II.iv. 301–05: —"No abuse, Hal . . . no abuse." —"Not—to dispraise me, and call me pantler . . ."), and because *my abuses* also contains suggestions of "lies" —deceits or deceptions practiced by or on the speaker (compare *Ham* IV.vii.49,

where Claudius doubts the genuineness of Hamlet's letter and the truth of its report: "is it some abuse?"). *reckon up* name, list, enumerate (colored by syntactically irrelevant senses of "to reckon" that are excluded by the syntactic limitations of the idiom "to reckon up" but which are generally pertinent to this context: e.g. "to reckon" meaning "to estimate the nature of," "to value" [as in *AW* V.iii.90–91: "she reckon'd it / At her life's rate"], "to attribute [qualities *to*]," etc. *Reckon up* also combines with *count*, which means "account," "consider to be" in line 8, to evoke substantively incidental plays on their common denominator as words meaning "find the whole number of" and on the fact that the primary meaning of each in the poem is latent in the other).

11. *straight* morally straight, not twisted in perceptions, values, or behavior —with a play on "strait" meaning "strict or scrupulous in morality or religious observance," "scrupulous about following the rules"; see 140.14 and "straitest" in the Authorized Version (and the Tyndale, Cranmer, and Bishops' versions) of Acts 26:5: ". . . after the most straitest sect of our religion I lived a Pharisee." (The last chapters of Acts are curiously relevant to this poem: Paul answers charges against him by accusers who "laid many and grievous complaints against Paul, which they could not prove" [25.7]. The whole business of Paul's accusation and trial [Acts 21–28] is comically inept and is echoed several times in the trial of Conrade and Borachio in *Much Ado*.) *be bevel* are crooked. (The sense is clear from—and dictated by—context. *Bevel* is an heraldic term used to describe a line; it means "zigzag." Like "*a* level," "*a* bevel" is a builder's tool; it is used for setting off angles; by the late seventeenth century an adjective meaning "oblique" had developed either from the heraldic use or from the noun. Shakespeare presumably strains the sense of *be bevel* here in order to achieve a comically contorted play on "be vile"; *OED* cites the Renaissance spellings "beuile" [i.e. "bevile"], "bevil," and "bevile.")

12. *By* (1) through the agency of (the commonest use of *by*, see line 4); (2) by the example of, by analogy to, by the model of (as in "Don't judge me by them"). *rank* (1) lustful; (2) loose, unrestricted; (3) sick (see 118.12, note); (4) fetid, stinking, foul (as in 69.12). *must not* (1) should not, it is intolerable that; (2) cannot (because such minds are incapable of evaluating anything without debasing it). *shown* (1) exhibited to view; (2) revealed; (3) interpreted.

13. *this general evil* The phrase describes both the following line (an evil thing, a cynical and vicious philosophy), and its content (the assertion that evil is general, is universal). Shakespeare's readers may have heard substantively incidental plays on *level* (note the conjunction of the final *l* of *general* and *evil*) and on *be bevel*; on the pronunciation of *evil*, see 144.5,7; 9,11, note (on the rhyming of *evil* and "devil"). *maintain* (1) affirm, assert the truth of; (2) nourish, cause to flourish.

14. *in their badness reign* (1) flourish with respect to their bad qualities (*OED*, s.v. "reign," 2d: "Yet shal thei reigne in large benefites and great renoume"); (2) flourish while in an evil condition; (3) each man reigns by virtue of the bad quality that reigns in him, each man holds sway by virtue of whichever bad quality is particular with him (i.e. holds sway over him, *their* has the effect

of making *reign* act twice in the phrase; see 109.9, note); (4) all men hold sway (or flourish) by virtue of that particular kind of badness that belongs to the frail spies who maintain this proposition (the line thus says that the frail spies take everyone to be like themselves, both in general worth—bad—and in particular vices). There may be a play on "to rein" meaning "to behave," "to submit to direction and control (as a horse submits to being reined in)"; *OED* gives this from 1580: "Youth never raineth wel, but when age holdeth the bridell."

SONNET 122

The coherence of this sonnet depends on the ambiguity of *thy tables* in line 1 (an ambiguity that is echoed, with different emphases, in *thy record* in line 8). However, judging from the comments of the majority of editors, the ambiguity does not appear to make itself felt by all readers; without being conscious of any shift, one can slide from perceiving *thy tables* in line 1 as a notebook the beloved has filled with observations and cherished phrases to understanding the same *tables* as a blank notebook to which the pronoun *thy* applies because the tables were the beloved's gift to the speaker and because their contents would properly have been accounts of the beloved's nature, worth, and activities. (The notes on the early lines attempt to distinguish between the probable sense a word carries as it is read and latent possible understandings which, by the logic of later developments, come to be the only possible ones.)

The process that requires the reader to erase his early understanding of the object under discussion is mirrored on a larger scale: first in lines 3 and 4 by the speaker's casual contradiction of the traditional contrast—stated repeatedly in this sequence (e.g. sonnets 16–19, 54, 55, 60, 63, 65, 81, 100, 101, and 107)—between an individual's life and memory, which soon pass away, and the written word, which endures; and then, in quatrain 2, by the rhetorically suicidal tactic of effectively pointing out the error in his measurement of relative staying power in *Or at the least, so long . . .* (compare sonnet 105, which also takes pains to undermine its own argument).

(The lines may, moreover, have been further complicated if, as is possible, the pronunciation of *heart* was such that it could be confused with "art"; see 24.13–14, note. Any pronunciation that resembled "so long as brain and 'art' would have reasserted the staying power of the written word in the course of a phrase that participates in dismissing it.)

1. *tables*   notebook (a plural commonly used to indicate a single book of bound sheets—as in *2HIV* II.iv.257: "his master's old tables, his note-book, his counsel-keeper"). Dover Wilson suggests looking at *Ham* I.v.99ff. "for an account of what young men noted in their 'tables.'" *Thy tables* suggests tables used as a commonplace book by the beloved and then presented to the speaker as a gift. In context of the 1609 sequence, the beloved's gift to the speaker seems to have previously been his gift *from* the speaker; it seems at first to be the same notebook that occasioned sonnet 77—but now "enriched" (77.14) by the thoughts the beloved has recorded in it. Pooler maintained that impression throughout the poem; he suggested that this book was "perhaps 'the vacant

leaves' of lxxvii. filled with his friend's thoughts in prose or verse, read and remembered by Shakespeare and now given away." However, before we learn in
line 11 that the speaker has given away the tables, line 10 has made it clear that
the speaker is talking about a blank notebook which he himself was expected to
fill. That does not, however, mean that one can dismiss Pooler's reading as
simple error; at this point in the poem every signal of syntax and usage invites it (see the following note). Pooler's error was only in manfully ignoring the
poem's subsequent contradiction of those signals.

    1–2. (1) "The contents of your notebook are imprinted in full on my brain,
are fully copied in my brain" (i.e. "I have them by heart"); (2) "I imagine myself
filling the empty notebook you gave me; in my mind the notebook is fully written
on, filled with letters" (see *character* meaning "writing," "letters" in 59.8 and
85.3). Unless one has just finished the whole poem and gone back to examine
the logic behind its placid progress toward the couplet, sense (1) will probably
be the dominant—if not the only—sense one gets from these lines: line 1, which
momentarily stands alone as a complete assertion, does not invite a reader to
take it literally, and the readiest alternative to imagining a sheaf of papers physically implanted in the speaker's brain is to understand *thy tables* as a metonymy
for "the contents of your tables," "what you said in your tables." When *are* is
transformed into an auxiliary verb by the addition of *Full charactered* in line 2,
the new construction reinforces one's understanding of *tables* as a notebook
already filled; the commonest sense of "to character" is "to inscribe," the sense
it has in 108.1 and in Polonius's speech to Laertes (*Ham* I.iii.59), where its object
is what is written *down*, not the surface *on* which it is written (*OED* gives one
example of the past participle used to mean "written on," "marked with characters," but no other instances of anything like "to character a writing surface"
meaning "to put writing on it"). Sense (2) occurs after the fact; it has presumably
never been registered except as a reinterpretation dictated by information received later in the poem. (On the metaphoric uses of *tables*, see 24.1, 24.2, and
notes.)

    2. *with* (1) by (presenting *memory* as if it were a scrivener or a pen); (2) in,
by the medium of (presenting *memory* as if it were ink); (3) by (indicating what is
written about, what is recorded, what fills the pages—they are *Full* of enduring
memory, filled with memories).

    3. *Which* The poem does not require that its reader puzzle over the antece-
dent; he will probably take both *Which* and *rank* as substitutes for *thy tables*—
Which indicating the contents and *rank* indicating the book itself. However,
Which can be taken as indicating *memory*, and *brain* is the syntactically probable antecedent for *that idle rank*. *above* (1) superior to; (2) longer than.
idle (1) worthless; (2) trifling, not taken seriously (compare the modern expression "idle jottings"); (3) inert and therefore ineffectual (*OED* gives this from
1522: "Mans mind is never ydle, but occupied . . . with good or evil"). *rank*
(1) status, place in the scale of relative value; (2) list, series of things (*OED*
gives this from 1576: "a ranke and rowe of litigious causes . . . hange one
uppon another, as linkes in a long chaine"; keepers of commonplace books
customarily organized their observations and such quotations as they wished to

remember under headings by topic; *rank* also suggests lines of letters [characters] written in rows on a page—see 32.12); (3) series of leaves (Beeching's suggestion). (*Rank* is the only word in the poem that a reader has to strain to understand; Shakespeare probably chose it for the sake of its capacity to register both "status" and "series" at once.)

4. *date*   limits of time, time.   *ev'n*   See 15.6, note.

6. *faculty*   capacity, the power.   *by*   (1) from, given by (*faculty by nature* = "natural faculty"); (2) by means of (*by nature to subsist* = "to continue to exist, maintain life, in the natural way, continue to exist in nature"); (3) according to, in accordance with.

4–8.   Q puts a period at the end of line 4 and a comma at the end of line 6; I have replaced them with dashes in order to retain the double syntax of the lines: although line 8 subsequently reveals lines 7 and 8 as a syntactically independent clause ("Thy record never can be missed until each has yielded his part to razed oblivion"), *Till* can first act in parallel with *Beyond* and *so long as* (". . . shall remain beyond all date . . . or . . . [for] so long as . . . , till . . .").

7. *razed oblivion*   (1) obliterating oblivion, oblivion which erases, wipes everything away (for Shakespeare's use of adjectives indicating effect to indicate cause, see 13.12, note); (2) blank oblivion, nothingness, the state of nonexistence. (Note the extra incidental general pertinence of *razed* to the context of blank pages and of *oblivion* to the context of *memory*; see the note on *forgetfulness* in line 14 below. There is also quiet wit in the echo of the stock metaphor *tabula rasa* ["a clean slate," "a blank"], an echo evoked by the use of *razed* in a poem about *tables*.)   *oblivion*   = trisyllabic, by syncopation.   *his*   its (but see 73.10, note).   *part*   share, share of memories (with casual play on the oddity of bodily parts—*brain and heart*—parting with parts of the beloved; for the specifically sexual use of *part*, see 151.6, note). (If one hears a pun on "raised" in *razed*, then yielding to *razed oblivion* can carry suggestions of sexual climax similar to those that operate in sonnet 64 [see 64.1–14, note]).

8. *thy record*   (1) memory of you (see 59.5, note); (2) what you wrote and/or the book you wrote in (compare *registers* and *recórds* in 123.9,11 and *record* in 55.8); (3) the book in which my memories of you are (or might have been) written down (*record* ultimately derives from the Latin *re-* and *cor, cordis* ["heart"]; here where *heart* is one of the recorders of memory the metaphor is revivified as a conceit).   *missed*   lost, lacked, missing.

9. *That poor retention*   that inadequate capacity for retaining (in effect, "that inadequate receptacle," "that inferior retainer"). The construction echoes *that idle rank* in line 3 and has the same reference: the *tables*.

10. The use of a notebook to record what one wishes to remember is here scornfully compared to the use of a "tally," a stick in which notches were cut ("scored") to keep account of debts; the practice connotes distrust between parties (when a debt had been notched, the stick was split lengthwise; each party took half, and, if the two strips did not "tally," the debt could not be collected); the use of "the score and tally" also suggested pettiness, ignorance, base values, and crude sensibilities (see *2HVI* IV.vi.21–43).

11. (1) "Therefore I took the liberty of giving them away" (this sense, derived

from taking *to give . . . was I bold* as an inverted form of the idiom "be bold to," "dare to," is demanded by the logic of the speaker's defense and is signalled by *Therefore*); (2) "Therefore in giving them away I was impudent, presumptuous" (compare *Lear* I.iv.241: "Men so disorder'd, so debosh'd and bold"; this sense reflects the charge against which the poem is a defense). (In the next line *To trust* activates an incidental pun on *bold* meaning "trusting," as in *AW* V.i.5–6: "Be bold you do so grow in my requital / As nothing can unroot you," and—in the welter of infinitives with which the poem closes—presents a syntactically difficult extra infinitive for another "be bold to" construction: "Therefore, in giving them away I took the liberty of trusting. . . ." Q puts a comma after *bold*, but since Renaissance readers could not rely on punctuation as a guide to logic, the presence or absence of a comma at the line-end pause does not signify.)

12. *To trust* so as instead to trust (but see the preceding note). *those tables* "the tables of my mind," my memory. *that receive thee more* (1) which can contain more of you; (2) which preserve [my memories of] you better. (This sonnet is full of materials for sexual innuendo that is never developed. For example, *tables*, being that to which a man put his "pen," was a comic epithet for the female sexual organ [that is, in fact, Poins's meaning when he calls Mistress Quickly Falstaff's "old tables" in the passage cited from *2HIV* in the note on line 1 above—see Hulme, pp. 136–37; Cotgrave, s.v. *Jouer de la navette*, "a wench to enter a man into her Tables"; and "constable" in the phrase quoted from *AW* in 58.3, note]. The bawdy potential of the topic of capacity to receive is demonstrated in 135.5 and 136.7; also see 8.3–4 and note. Also note the unexploited genital sense of *nature* in line 6.)

13. *an adjunct to remember* an auxiliary for remembering, an assistant.

14. *Were to import* would be a sign of. *forgetfulness* a poor memory. (The word *forgetfulness* capsules the matter of the poem: it plays on *forgetfulness* meaning "neglect," "indifference," "disrespect"—i.e. the very qualities that giving away a friend's gift would imply [see *Tim* V.i.142 and *2Gent* II.ii.9–12: "And when . . . / . . . I sigh not, Julia, for thy sake, / . . . some foul mischance / Torment me for my love's forgetfulness"], and, by virtue of the fact that *forgetfulness* can mean *oblivion* [as in *RIII* III.vii.128–29: "the swallowing gulf / Of dark forgetfulness and deep oblivion"], it also echoes line 7 and the meaning *oblivion* has there—thus allowing the couplet to carry the flattering implication that it is impossible to believe the speaker has forgotten or neglected the beloved without also believing the speaker dead or unconscious. Note too that the third syllable of *forgetfulness* is the final element in an eccentrically linked chain that includes *Full* in line 2 and the discussion of capacity in quatrain 3.) *in me* as one of my qualities (but echoing the previous metaphor of location, *within my brain* in line 1).

SONNET 123

1. *No* See 76.9 and note.

2–4. Compare 59.1–2, and see the passages from Ecclesiastes and Ovid cited in the notes on those lines.

2. *Thy pyramids* Taken metaphorically, the reference is to anything grand made by man and anything in nature that has evolved with the passage of time; Dowden's gloss captures the thrust and tone of *Thy pyramids* perfectly: "all that Time piles up . . . , all his new stupendous erections," and Beeching's is helpful too: "any modern marvels which seem to defy change." The pyramids are particularly efficient for Shakespeare's purpose because they are not only a traditional but a traditionally paradoxical emblem for (1) human efforts to withstand human mortality (the Egyptian pyramids are tombs designed to preserve human remains intact); (2) successful human efforts to create something eternal (the Egyptian pyramids are still there); (3) the folly of believing anything mortal or man-made can last (see the headnote to sonnet 55, the quotation from Horace, *Odes* III.xxx in particular; here the negative connotations are invoked by *Thy*: anything that belongs to time is temporary by definition). The reference to pyramids might be to some specific recent architectural event, and, although knowledge of the identity of the structures in question is neither available to us nor likely to add much to our experience of the poem, there have been some sensible guesses (e.g. Tucker's: St. Peter's at Rome; Leslie Hotson's: a number of Egyptian obelisks dug up, cleaned up, and set up in Rome by Sixtus V during the period 1585–90 [*Shakespeare's Sonnets Dated and Other Essays* (1949), pp. 21ff.]; and Alfred Harbage's: some pyramids erected in 1603 for the celebration of the accession of King James ["Dating Shakespeare's Sonnets," *SQ*, I (1950), 62–63]; and one entirely foolish effort to date the sonnet on the basis of a good guess (i.e. Hotson's assumption that *if* the sonnet refers to the obelisks it had to be written when the Pope was placing them around Rome). *with newer might* (1) by more modern means; (2) by the labor of persons of a later time; (3) so that they have new strength, newly strengthened.

3. *nothing . . . nothing* These may be read as substantives or adverbs (= "in no way," as in 130.1).

4. *dressings* reconditioned versions, reworkings (see 76.11, note; *dressings* here carries scornful suggestions of "mere trappings and outward shows," "representations").

5. *dates* lifespans (compare 18.4). *admire* (1) wonder at, marvel over (as in *TN* III.iv.143: "Wonder not, nor admire not . . . why I do call thee so"); (2) value highly, venerate (as in 59.14—nearly the modern sense but with stronger suggestions of awe).

6. "The used (or shopworn) goods you palm off on us as new." (*Foist*, originally a dicing term meaning literally "to palm," "to cheat by surreptitiously substituting false dice for true," has extra pertinence to this context because of its homonym "to foist"—a common variant of "to fust," "to become stale or mouldy"—*OED* gives this from 1583: "And what becomes of the Corne . . .? It foysteth and rotteth.")

5–6. "We were born yesterday and so are easily cheated."

7. *them* the things time brings forth (the plural antecedent is inferred from line 6). *make them born to our desire* take them to be things made to order for us (the metaphor = "our children," i.e. born to us, the products of our own passion; the figure is a version of "brainchild"; compare 59.3–4, and see the Ovidian passage cited in the note on those lines). *born* = the standard mod-

ernized spelling of Q's "borne" (which was a common spelling of, and could
be understood as, "bourn"; Ingram and Redpath explain the case for that reading and reject it; although reading "bourn to our desire," "the limit of our ambition," makes sense in this context, the context so strongly invites *born* that other
potential meanings and overtones are overwhelmed).

8. *Than* The usual modernization of Q's "Then" is obvious and necessary
(see 16.4,8, note); however, the pertinence of "Then" to a sonnet on time might
momentarily have flickered in the minds of Shakespeare's readers. *think* (1)
believe; (2) call to mind, remember. *told* told about. (Compare "to tell"
meaning "to proclaim" in *Ham* I.ii.125–26: "No jocund health that Denmark
drinks today / But the great cannon to the clouds shall tell"; the present slightly
awkward use may have been prompted by Shakespeare's desire to balance the
idea of birth in the preceding line with a pun on "tolled" in this one; for "to
toll" meaning "to announce the death of," see *2HIV* I.i.102–03: "a sullen
bell / . . . tolling a departing friend.")

9. *Thy registers* = *thy recórds* (line 11), time's record books, chronicles,
recorded history (compare *Thy pyramids* in line 2; *thy registers* can also include
ancient objects like the pyramids which are marked by time and are themselves
historical documents). *defy* despise, scorn, care nothing for (as in *1HIV*
IV.i.6–7: "I cannot flatter; I do defy / The tongues of soothers . . ."; the
word carries a tone of braggadocio).

10. *wond'ring* marveling.

11. *recórds* = *registers* (line 9); on the accent, see 50.7, note. *what we see*
the objects and events of current experience. (The paired subjects of *doth lie*
are a chiasmic echo of *present* and *past*, the paired objects of *wond'ring at* in
line 10.) *doth* a common Renaissance plural; see 112.1, note. (Tucker
suggested that *doth* might be a printer's error for "both," which, he says, "makes
a complete and effective correspondence with 1.9.")

12. *Made more or less* (1) built up and worn down; (2) made more or less
important (or valuable). *continual* = trisyllabic, by syncopation.

13–14. Ultimately, a reader has no choice but to conclude that *This* in *This
I do vow* points forward to line 14: aside from line 1, the first twelve lines contain
no vow for *This* to refer to, and line 14 *is* a vow, a solemn promise. However,
"to vow" can mean "to assert earnestly," "to asseverate" (as in *CofE* II.ii.
113–14: " . . . wouldst vow / That never words were music to thine ear . . . ");
This I do vow, "this I assert," thus first points backward to the assertions in
lines 2–12; similarly, *and this shall ever be* can mean "and what I have said will
always be true." Line 14 retroactively fixes "promise" as the meaning of *vow*;
it presents itself as the reference for *This* in *This I do vow* and presents *true* as
the antecedent for *this* in *this shall ever be*. Even so, the idea that both "this's"
point back is not erased entirely because the solemn promising indicated by
vow comes from the same experiential category as the solemn boasting and
blustering of the first twelve lines. The confusion is slight and brief, but it marks
the one point when the poem gives any sign by which its reader might become
conscious of the great but nearly imperceptible logical disjunction between
lines 2–12 and lines 1,13–14.

The disjunction is hard to talk about because it can be made to evaporate in a justifiable critical description, i.e., one can say that the topic of the first line and the last two lines is the speaker's changelessness, and that the topic of lines 2–12 is the changelessness of all things; looking at the potential in the poem's materials one might even describe the whole poem as a witty exercise in chop logic: "I will never change because nothing changes." However, such summaries imply a calculated logical balance not apparent in a line-to-line reading. On the other hand, a different analytic focus can lead to an equally reasonable, equally persuasive, and equally misleading account of the poem: line 1 is optimistic about human potential; lines 2–8 stress human helplessness and sound cynical and defeated. Line 1 challenges the general belief that change is irresistible; by the middle of the first quatrain the challenge is to the very idea that change exists. As one moves from line 1 to line 2, however, the poem does not invite one to perceive any contrast or change of topic: line 1 boastfully brands time as a boaster, and that tone continues in line 2. Line 1 concerns resistance to chronological change, and the pyramids in line 2 appear to be an example of the possibility of such resistance. As the poem drifts from the topic of the speaker's vow of changelessness to the argument that all change is illusory, the poem suppresses a reader's awareness that a change of focus and assumption is occurring or has occurred: the lines that deny the existence of change are composed of elements which assert that change is inevitable (e.g. *Our dates are brief*), and which assert the power of time (e.g. *What thou dost foist upon us*). As the poem progresses, obvious opposites blend into one another; change looks like constancy and constancy like change. Quatrain 3 continues logically from quatrain 2; its spirit is that of line 1; its final line supports an argument that change is only an illusion with an assertion hard to distinguish from "since everything changes so fast." The couplet returns to the vow of line 1, but does so in a way that simultaneously effects yet another disjunction in the speaker's train of thought: in line 1 only the context of a series of love sonnets suggests that *change* is to be understood specifically as a reference to fickleness in love; the next eleven lines concern the general concept of change; in the couplet, however, *I will be true* transforms the speaker's topic to constancy in love. In short, the logic, structure, and diction of the poem repeat the effect of the logically unaccommodated inherent paradox of the pyramids (which connote both independence of time and slavery to it).

   In transforming the meaning of *This* . . . *this* from "what I have said . . . what I have said" to "the following" and "true" (*and this shall ever be* = "and I will be true forever"), line 14 repeats the poem's typical action one last time: line 13 depends on a following clause for the revelation of its final syntax and meaning; it relies on time for its identity, and—*Made more or less by* the passage of time—comes to have meaning by coming to have been something it never was while read. Although the poem does nothing to evoke consciousness of the analogy between its substance and its style, a reader's actual experience of the couplet is an actual experience of the transforming power of time. (Compare the similar disjunction between 120.1,13–14 and the rest of that poem; and see 125.13–14, note.)

   14. Compare 152.1.   *scythe*   See 60.12, note. Perhaps Shakespeare's reader

heard a pun on *sight* (line 4) in *scythe*. The same pun may occur in 12.12,13 and 38.6. Marvell appears to pun extravagantly on the two words in "Damon the Mower" (e.g. lines 51–52 ["This sithe of mine discovers wide / More ground than all his Sheep do hide"], lines 57–60 ["Nor am I so deform'd to sight, / If in my Sithe I looked right; / In which I see my Picture done, / As in a crescent Moon the Sun"]). For Renaissance examples of *th* pronounced as *t*, see Kökeritz, pp. 319–22. On the other hand, the evidence from rhymes suggests that *scythe* and *sight* were easily distinguished (Spenser, Herrick, and Milton ryhme "scythe" and "blithe," and I find no Renaissance examples of any word now rhyming with "scythe" and "blithe" used to rhyme with a word that now rhymes with *sight*).

SONNET 124

This sonnet is the most extreme example of Shakespeare's constructive vagueness. Tucker said that "though the general purport of the piece is clear— viz. that the poet's love does not vary with the circumstances of the beloved—its individual expressions and their connections have perplexed every reader." The sum of this sonnet is so much greater than the sum of its parts that even the most scrupulously open-minded glosses on its particulars do very little to explain how it achieves its grandeur. The poem is as little influenced by the circumstances its particulars evoke as the speaker's love is said to be by the circumstances in which he loves. The key to the poem's power may be in the word *it*, which, like all pronouns, is specific, hard, concrete, and yet imprecise and general—able to include anything or nothing. The word *it* occurs five times; appearing regularly amid successive waves of subjunctives, negatives, and vaguenesses composed of precisely evocative words in apparently communicative syntaxes which come to nothing and give a sense of summing up everything, the word *it* stands sure, constant, forthright, simple, and blank.

Fortunately the operation of this poem is the subject of the most illuminating single comment on the sonnets, Arthur Mizener's "The Structure of Figurative Language in Shakespeare's Sonnets" (*Southern Review*, V [Spring, 1940], 730–47, revised in 1962 for inclusion in Willen and Reed [pp. 219–35]).

1. *If my dear love were but*   (1) if only my . . . were; (2) if my . . . were merely.   *dear*   Compare 30.4.   *love*   (1) beloved (the sense evoked by *dear* and *child*); (2) affection, feelings of love (the sense to which *love* is subsequently limited by *It* in line 2); see 34.13, note.   *the child of state*   Like the meaning of *love*, the meaning of this phrase is limited after the fact; the following lines indicate that *child of state* is to be understood as "the product of circumstances," "*Made more or less* (123.12) by changes of condition." However, for as long as the subject, *my dear love*, still appears to be the beloved, *the child of state* suggests "highborn, influential, and rich" (i.e. the offspring of "the stately," of those who have power, high rank, and pomp—or a child who has "state," who is possessed of pomp, power, etc.), and "a politician," "a courtier" ("someone motivated by personal expedience but at the mercy of other people's whims," "a self-serving and precariously situated toady"). Since the human

metaphor continues in *bastard* and *unfathered*, the various courtly connotations continue to color one's understanding of the speaker's subject even after *my . . . love* is revealed to be the speaker's affection and not beloved. (Mizener: "For no single one of the meanings of *state* will these lines work out completely, nor will the language allow any one of the several emergent figures to usurp our attention; it thus becomes impossible to read the lines at all without attention. . . . the purpose is to make the reader see them all, simultaneously, in soft focus; and the method is to give the reader just enough of each figure for this purpose" [p. 225].)

2. *for* as. *be unfathered* (1) be without status under the law and have no right of inheritance; (2) be disavowed, be disowned.

3. "Because entirely dependent upon the circumstances of the moment," "because at the mercy of the caprices of time" (note the pertinence of the traditional idea of the wheel of fortune; compare *3HVI* IV.iii.46–47: "Though fortune's malice overthrow my state, / My mind exceeds the compass of her wheel," and, for contrast, *Lear* V.iii.174, the words of the bastard adventurer Edmund in defeat: "The wheel is come full circle; I am here").

4. The relation of this line to line 3 is doubtful. Its function here is proverb-like—a summary statement in terms of some universal particulars whose relationship can be thought of as analogous to those of the situation in which the proverb is invoked. Here the connection between lines 3 and 4 would be clearer if Shakespeare had written "A weed among weeds, or a flower with flowers . . . "; the advantage of the plural, proverb-like form is that the syntactical leap from *It*—the particular, singular topic of the preceding lines—to the general categories *weeds* and *flow'rs* gives the line a tone that acts as a metaphor for the sort of casual dismissal the quatrain is concerned with. The reference of Shakespeare's homemade proverb appears to be "volunteers" in flower gardens, the offspring of species like johnny-jump-ups and some daisies that seed themselves freely; "volunteers" are treated as weeds when the gardener happens to be weeding and are his first choice when he gathers blossoms for a bouquet; their status is determined by what the gardener has in mind at the moment. *gathered* Mizener (p. 226) points out that the suggestions of harvest inherent in *gathered* evoke the idea of Father Time and his scythe (see 123.14 and 60.12, note). *flow'rs . . . flowers* See 86.5, note. Q gives "flowers . . . flowers." However spelled, "flower" (like "hour," "power," "shower," etc.) is ordinarily monosyllabic in Renaissance pronunciations. The inconsistent spellings adopted here are intended only to approximate the slightly differing pronunciations the rhythm would have dictated to Shakespeare's contemporaries; the two-syllable Renaissance pronunciations might be more accurately represented by "flowres," the spelling it has in the F text of *TN* I.i.40 (compare *numb'red* in line 10, but contrast "showres," the Q spelling of what was probably read as a monosyllable at the end of line 12).

5. *builded* = a standard Renaissance alternative to "built." (The word implies sizableness and durability in what has been built and purposefulness in the builder. The incipient real estate metaphor continues in *far from* and is reasserted in lines 10 and 11 by *leases* and *stands*; also note *in, falls, Under,*

Whereto . . . calls, and the "call to" construction in lines 6–13.) *far from accident* beyond the influence of chance. (The word *accident* both reflects and mediates between the metaphors of cutting in the preceding line and of falling in the following line: *accident* is from the Latin *accidere,* "to happen," which derives from *ad + cadere,* "to fall"; however, *accidere,* "to happen," is superficially identical with another *accidere,* which means "to cut something so that it falls" or "to ruin" and derives from *ad + caedere,* "to cut.") The metaphor of a building far from accident gives the poem overtones of the many Latin poems in praise of the independent country life far from the follies and dangers of Roman politics and society (e.g. Horace, *Epistles,* I.x.12–33, *Satires,* II.vi.; Juvenal, *Satire III*).

6. *suffers* (1) undergoes pain; (2) endures, persists in spite of, does not sink under. *in* (1) decked out in; (2) in the midst of. *smiling* (1) propitious (as in *Lear* II.ii.168: "Fortune, good night; smile once more; turn thy wheel"); (2) happy, cheerful (with suggestions of "false-smiling," "hypocritical"— suggestions extra-logically reinforced by the last word in the line, which embodies the sound of "false" in the word *falls; OED* gives "fals" and "falls" as Renaissance spellings for "false" as well as "falls").

7. *the blow of thrallèd discontent* (1) the injury that being in a state of *thrallèd discontent* is; (2) the injury inflicted by those who are in a state of *thrallèd discontent. thrallèd discontent* (1) discontent caused by oppression or enslavement (Abbott, par. 374, gives *thrallèd* as one of several Shakespearian instances where "passive participles are used as epithets to describe the state which would be the result of the active verb"); (2) discontent which is enslaved, enforced to act against its will.

3–8. Note that the implied distinction in line 3 between *time's love* (which would presumably benefit time's subject) and *time's hate* (which would presumably give him pain) is largely dissolved by the metaphor of line 4 in which both the pitiful *weeds* and the fortunate *flow'rs* are *gathered* by time. Lines 6 and 7 allow no basis for preferring *time's love* to *time's hate*; to be subject to time is painful under all circumstances. The distinction is finally denied absolutely in line 8 by *Whereto,* which capitalizes on the latent potential of *in* and *under* for indicating location and lumps *smiling pomp* with *thrallèd discontent* as a single place-like condition that is the opposite of the one *far from accident* in line 5.

8. *th' inviting time* (1) time which beckons us onward (compare 5.5–6); (2) this present attractive period (compare *Oth* II.iii.23–24: —"What an eye she has! Methinks it sounds a parley to provocation." —"An inviting eye . . . ") —with overtones of "this time of courtly socializing." (The phrase can be colored by ironic echoes of the Latin adverb *invite,* "against one's will"—evoked by the context of *thrallèd discontent*—and/or words derived from Latin *vitiare,* "to corrupt" [*OED,* s.v. "invitiate," cites Florio's 1598 edition of his Italian dictionary: "*Invitiare,* to growe vitious or wicked; to corrupt, to invitiate"].) *our fashion* the current modes (in everything from philosophy to dress), our ways. (*Fashion* is proverbially temporary and was proverbially contrasted to true friendship—see Tilley, H509: "There is no more hold of a new friend than of a new fashion." Ingram and Redpath suggest something on the

order of "our kind" or "our sort," and cite *2Gent* V.iv.61 [in which "fashion" means "kind" in a play on the proverb quoted above]: "Thou friend of an ill fashion"; their reading of *fashion* makes sense but is not likely to have been evoked by this context.) Line 8 can be read three different ways: (1) "Whereto time calls fashion"; (2) "Whereto fashion calls time"; and, as Willen and Reed presume, (3) "Whereto time, which is our fashion, calls" (i.e. *our fashion* = appositive to *th' inviting time*).

9. *fears not* is unafraid of. (Tucker took Q's "feares" as a form of "to fere," which means "to make a partner of," and for which *OED* records "to feare" as a seventeenth-century spelling. The verb "to fere" does not appear ever to have been common enough to have competed with "to fear" in a reading of "It feares" in line 9, but, although Tucker's reading must be rejected as benevolent ingenuity, the noun "fere"—meaning "companion," "mate," "partner"—was quite common, and associations between the sound of "feares" and the idea of companionship may have been one among many elements that would have eased a Renaissance reader's passage from the topic of policy's impotence and evanescence in lines 9 and 10 to the distinction implied in line 11 between *policy* and the speaker's affection, which is *all alone*. Note the earlier distinction embodied in *among* and *with* in line 4 and *far from* in line 5.) *policy* scheming strategy (particularly the sort of machination that aims at getting or keeping governmental power; see the example in support of sense (2) in the note on *policy* in 118.9). In this context *policy* appears as an emblem of all that is governed by selfish considerations of temporary expedience; being politic suggested not only being prudent and clever, but also being ingratiating in the manner of a calculating courtier. The roots and relatives of the word *policy* echo earlier elements in the sonnet (e.g. *policy*, which is ultimately derived from the Greek *politeia*, has the morally neutral sense of "statecraft," "political science," and thus sustains the reference to government present in the poem since *child of state* in line 1); *policy* is also echoed in the language of the following lines (e.g. "policy," a word derived from Romance words meaning "schedule," "bill," "bond," "written obligation," was already used with reference to "policies of assurance," "insurance policies" [see *policy* and *assured* in 118.9–10], which have a general kinship with *leases* in line 10; like the various Greek words relating to cities, citizens, building cities, etc., *policy* implies community, gregariousness, and contrasts with *all alone* in line 11 where *hugely politic* carries pompous and faintly comic suggestions of "a city in itself," "a community of one"). *heretic* This word, which acts to personify *policy*, connoted inconstancy, error, and—in an age when many people were shifting religious allegiances in accordance with political expediency—unreliability, false values, and timorousness. Compare the proverb "Policy with his long nails has almost scratched out the eyes of religion" (Tilley, P463).

10. *works on* operates within the terms of (with overtones of "to work on" meaning "to influence [someone's] mental state by subtle means"—*OED* gives this from 1595: "For friends, opinion, & succeeding chaunce, which wrought the weak to yeld, the strong to love"). *leases* contracts by which lands are held

for some fixed period of time. (For Shakespeare's reader, *on leases* would have carried a supportive echo of "on leashes" ["leash" was often spelled "lease" and the two appear to have been pronounced alike; see *OED* and Kökeritz, p.123]. In context of policy and heresy this line may also have been colored by the syntactically incidental echo of "a lease" meaning "a lie," "a falsehood" [*OED* gives sixteenth-century examples of the noun form, but it appears to have been rare; the verb "to lease" was common; see "leasing" meaning "lying" in *TN* I.v.91, *Cor* V.ii.22, and the proverb "When one's prick stands, his womb is full of leasing"—Tilley, M407.]) *short numb'red hours* (1) short-numbered hours, brief hours; (2) short hours which are numbered, a limited supply of brief units of time. *hours* = a monosyllable.

11. *all alone* (1) in solitude; (2) without support (with the suggestion that it alone, only it, stands so). *hugely* immense (big) and immensely (very). *politic* (1) wise, prudent (see the examples given for sense (1) of *policy* in 118.9); (2) well-governed—self-controlled, self-contained, independent (compare *Much Ado* V.ii.53–56: "maintain'd so politic a state of evil that they will not admit any good part to intermingle with them"). Presumably, Shakespeare's primary purpose is the play on the fact that *politic* represents both an echo of and a contrast to *policy* as used in line 9 (compare the similar but now forgotten wit of the proverb "Honesty is the best policy").

12. *That* (1) in that; (2) so that. *nor . . . nor* neither . . . nor (as in 55.7). This line recurs to the botanical metaphor of line 4, and in conjunction with line 11 presents a chiasmic echo of lines 4 and 5—lines which are only now revealed to have embodied a contrast between growing things, which are frail and inconstant, and buildings, which are static. (It is curious—and typically Shakespearian—that this sonnet assumes the validity of impressive architectural structures as symbols of the power to withstand time, is blandly oblivious to the contrary symbolism of evidence from both real and literary experience [see 55 and 125.3–4], and also invites its reader to recognize the speaker's blindness. Compare the use of *pyramids* in 123, where they are emblems of things that come and go as if with the seasons of history. Note also the similar mental inconvenience of condemning the artificiality of politic behavior and also valuing man-made things, things built, over natural growing things. Compare the inherent difficulties of perceiving *all alone* in line 11 as a trait in contrast with those of *policy, that heretic* in line 9; a heretic is by definition someone whose faith isolates and differentiates him from his society. Also see line 14, note.)

11–12. These lines have a vaguely phallic cast (see 26.1–14, note—on *all*) which reflects back on the earlier lines (possibly activating a pun on *hours* [see 58.3, note]), and colors those that follow (possibly activating the bawdy senses of "wit" in *witness* [see 26.1–14, note], of *fools* [see 137.1, note], and of *die* [for "to die" meaning "to reach sexual orgasm," see Partridge, the last speech of *Much Ado* V.ii, and—in Donne—line 26 of "The Canonization" and line 16 of "The Flea"]). Compare 151.9–14.

13–14. The pertinence of the couplet to the body of the poem is established as much by sound as logic: *To . . . call* echoes *Whereto . . . calls* in line 8; the

Which construction in line 14 echoes the *Which* construction in line 10 and
assists in the equation of *the fools of time* and *policy, that heretic*; line 14 repeats
the dominant device of the poem, the contrasting pair. See 125.13–14, note.

13. "I call the fools of time to bear witness to the truth of what I have said."
The metaphoric effect of *call* is to present *the fools of time* as witnesses called to
testify in a court of law; in effect, however, since the reference is not to a group
of persons but to a kind of person known by a general pattern of behavior (*die*
rather than "died"), one is asked to think of *the fools* as the evidence, as exhibits
rather than witnesses. As the line is read, *To this I witness* can momentarily
register as "to this which I see" and/or "to this to which I testify" (or perhaps
"to this eye witness" [i.e. "to the foregoing report"] or "as eye witness to the
foregoing"), and *call* can momentarily seem to be an imperative: "Call the fools
of time to this [place]." Moreover, *die for goodness* activates a retroactive play on
witness—which translates the literal sense of "martyr" and was used as a synonym for it: the Wyclif, Tyndale, Great, Geneva (1557), Bishops', and Rheims
Bibles translate the Greek *martyros* as "witness" in Acts 22:20; Geneva (1560)
and AV give "martyr"; the Collect for Innocents' Day played on two senses of
"witness": "Almighty God, whose praise this day the young Innocents thy
witnesses hath confessed and shewed forth, not in speaking but in dying . . . . "
the fools of time   (1) timeservers (see 116.9); (2) everyone subject to time's love
and hate (called fools because they do not recognize the ultimate frivolousness
of their ambitions and accomplishments; the modification introduced in the
next line narrows the reference to one group among the fools, particularizes
their folly, and specifies one kind of folly as particularly telling negative evidence
that what the speaker has said is true). In context of *child of state* in line 1, *fools*
can carry ironic overtones of "a fool" meaning "an innocent" (as in *Shrew* III.ii.
153: "she's a lamb, a dove, a fool, to him"); the Epistle for Innocents' Day was
(and is) Rev. 14:1–5, a vision of innocents freed from bondage to mortality,
"redeemed from the earth" because they "were not defiled with women . . . .
These were redeemed from men, being the firstfruits unto God, and to the Lamb;
and in their mouths was found no guile: for they are without spot before the
throne of God."

14. The poem has developed a contrast between what is (literally) secular—
temporal, time-bound—and what is immortal and unchanging; in that context
and in context of the metaphoric use of *heretic* in line 9, this line asks to be
understood as a reference to one or another kind of response to one or another
kind of crisis of conscience brought about by clashes between practical considerations and religious conviction. The problem is: what kind of response to
what kind of crisis? The largest difficulty is that the line does not sound like a
problem; its rhetoric suggests that its reference and our view of its reference are
self-evident. The couplet is an efficient and sufficient gesture; it does not need to
be or ask to be understood precisely; a reader can leave the poem without ever
noticing or caring that he does not know what kind of behavior he scorns or why
he scorns it. (An editor or student of the poem can easily respond to the couplet's
sound of transparent simplicity by casting about for a specific group that Shakespeare might refer to; a century of reformation and counterreformation provides

any number of specific candidates [in England, Jesuit conspirators, Protestant martyrs under Mary, Roman Catholic martyrs under the other Tudors, etc.], but a choice is arbitrary.)

Another difficulty springs from *this* in line 13; it points back at all that precedes it, and therefore gives no indication of the specific assertion *the fools of time* support, how dying for goodness is foolish, or where the ideological stress is in line 14 (compare *it* in lines 1–12). If one focuses on the contrast between *for goodness* and *for crime*, then *the fools* would seem to be martyrs of some sort—people who, having spent their lives in secular machinations to advance themselves or a cause in church or civil politics, finally refuse to budge on a point of doctrine or allegiance and become martyrs; such people can be considered *fools* because they wasted their lives seeking after temporary power and wealth, but if one considers living for crime foolish, one cannot reasonably consider dying for goodness foolish too. If one takes the politic position condemned by the speaker, then martyrs are foolish to die for a belief when they could just be practical and live; such people can be considered *fools of time* because their time-tested constancy to crime finally fails, but that leaves us in the unreasonable position of condemning change even if it is change for the better (see the headnote to sonnet 115). Aside from the difficulty of reconciling the many local logics within the couplet, a reader is also put in the improbable position of taking martyrs as emblematic of inconstancy, policy, and expediency.

If one focuses on the contrast between *die* and *lived*, then one can see every mortal as a fool of time, but to condemn mortals for their mortality is unreasonable. In his edition of 1898, George Wyndham glossed line 14 thus: "Who are so much the dupes of Time that they attach importance to the mere order or sequence in which events occur, and believe that a death-bed repentance can cancel a life of crime"; in terms of mundane justice Wyndham's attitude toward deathbed repentance is altogether reasonable; on the other hand, an important strain in Christian doctrine states precisely what Wyndham considers foolish (see Matt. 20:1–16, and note that the Order of Morning Prayer in *BCP* began with these words: "At what time soever a sinner doth repent him of his sin from the bottom of his heart: I will put all his wickedness out of my remembrance, saith the Lord"). Although Wyndham's reading is both reasonable and unreasonable, the line's potential for suggesting radical deathbed transformations is certain; the line might have struck Shakespeare's reader as a reference to the many instances—some real and some fabricated for purposes of crude propaganda—in which militant Roman Catholics were rumored to have admitted on their deathbeds that they always recognized that Calvin was right, or in which lifelong Protestants asked for the last rites of the Roman Church (see the proverb "to live a protestant and die a catholic," cited by E. M. Wilson in "Shakespeare and Christian Doctrine . . . ," *Shakespeare Survey* 23 [Cambridge, England, 1970], p. 87). If one reads line 14 with deathbed conversions in mind, one cannot know whether the change is *from* a doctrine one considers true or *to* such a doctrine, and one cannot know in any case whether to disapprove of conversion as inconstancy or as policy (an effort to save one's soul at the last minute), or to approve such conversion and take it as evidence that even the most practical, worldly, and unprincipled of men often realize that spiritual values outweigh temporal ones.

The poem presents two evils, inconstancy and expediency. Any reading of the couplet relates to both, but, unless one takes the practical way out by dismissing the problem, a reading of line 14 allows one neither to retain one's contempt for expediency without espousing an instance of inconstancy nor to retain contempt for inconstancy without espousing an instance of expediency.

crime   Mizener (p. 234) says this: "*Crime*, not ordinarily a very strong word among the Elizabethans, is here roughly equivalent to 'worldly success.'" The context of false values and religious language does indeed cause *crime* to include reference to "worldly success," but, as even a casual survey of sixteenth-century literature will demonstrate, *crime* was ordinarily as strong a word among the Elizabethans as it is for us.

SONNET 125

Landry (pp. 121–22, 167) points out marked similarities in theme and diction between this sonnet and lines 36–38, 42–66 of *Oth* I.i (a scene in which Iago acts as an informer against Othello). Landry's whole account of this sonnet is particularly helpful (pp. 120–28, 135–37).

1. *Were't ought to me*   (1) Why should it matter to me; (2) What good would it do me. *I bore*   (1) that I bore; (2) if I were to bear. *canopy*   a cloth covering, carried tent-like over the head of a dignitary in a ceremonial procession (*OED* gives this from 1576: "They beare the foure staves of the Canapie over the Kings head at . . . his coronation").

2. "Doing external honor to external worthiness."

3. *laid great bases*   (1) laid massive foundations (see the headnote to sonnet 55, and note the architectural references in 123.2 and 124.5,11); (2) set up pedestals. *for eternity*   (1) to last forever; (2) on which to enshrine eternity.

4. *Which proves*   (1) which turns out to be (taking *eternity* as the antecedent to *Which*, and taking the apparent illogicality as mocking irony); (2) which turn out to be (taking *bases* as the antecedent and *proves* as a plural like *befits* in 41.3, *turns* in 95.12, *depends* in 101.3, and *doth* in 112.1 and 123.11).

5. *dwellers on*   people who care about (a play on *dwellers* meaning "residents" is activated subsequently by *rent* in line 6). *form*   (1) external appearance; (2) ceremony, formality, decorum. *favor*   (1) external appearance (see 113.10, note); (2) the good will of superiors.

6. *Lose all and more*   (1) lose everything and more than everything; (2) lose their all and more than their all (i.e. go into debt?). Sense (1), the literal sense, is a contradiction in terms and therefore gives way to sense (2); compare the oxymoron *Pitiful thrivers* in line 8, the paradox in line 9 of being *obsequious in thy heart* (where show of duty must be unseen), and the unreasonable relative use of an absolute in lines 3–4 (which assert the existence of things that last longer than eternity).

6–7.   Q puts no punctuation after *rent*, a semicolon after *sweet*, and a comma after *savor*, thus inviting a reader to take *compound sweet* as that for which *rent* is paid. That, however, leaves *forgoing* [capitalized in Q] *simple savor* both logically and syntactically unrelated to its context; moreover, the emergence of the antithetic pairing of *compound sweet* and *simple savor* transforms the whole of line 7 into an adjectival comment on *dwellers*: "Forgoing simple savor in order to have compound sweet." No modern punctuation retains the chronological change in syntactic function that *For compound sweet* undergoes as the lines are read.

7. *compound sweet* (1) a sweet compound, sweet compounds (taking *compound* as noun and *sweet* as adjective: the phrase takes in a range of meaning from "delightful exotic mixtures" to "heavily sugared compotes"); (2) compound sweetness, concocted perfumes and/or sweetmeats (following the signal of the word order, and taking *compound* as adjectival and *sweet* as a substantive [compare 8.2]: "composite, complex pleasures"). *simple savor* unalloyed pleasure, natural flavors and/or perfumes. (Although *simple* is an adjective here, its conjunction with *compound* gives the antithesis metaphoric overtones of medicinal "compounds" as opposed to medicinal "simples"; see 76.4, note.)

8. *Pitiful* (1) evoking pity, eliciting compassion; (2) contemptible, pathetic. (In conjunction with *thrivers, Pitiful* also suggests "unsuccessful," "inadequate"; compare the use of "ill" in the proverb "Ill tithers, ill thrivers" [Tilley, T358]. Brent Cohen points out to me that *Pitiful* contains an anticipation of the specifically religious language of the following lines; although *Pitiful* meaning "pious" was rare [*OED* gives one example from 1570], "pity" and "piety" were interchangeable throughout the sixteenth century.) *thrivers* (1) successes, prosperous people; (2) people who attempt success (see the proverb quoted above). *in their gazing spent* used up on what they look on (with a play on "who spend all they have, waste all their substance, on externals, mere show").

9. *obsequious* (= trisyllabic, by syncopation) (1) servile, fawning, a slavish member of your entourage; (2) dutiful. (The ultimate Latin root of *obsequious, obsequi*, "to follow near," is audible in its phonetic likeness to the related word "sequence"; *obsequious* thus recurs to the procession suggested in line 1 and to the idea of being a follower in a literal sense. Through its relation to "obsequy," "funeral," *obsequious* had the specialized meaning "dutiful in performing funeral rites" [compare *Ham* I.ii.92: "To do obsequious sorrow"], and invites a reader to think of *the canopy* as borne in a funeral procession and to think back on lines 2–8 in relation to the distinction between mortal externals and immortal essence.) *in* Following *obsequious, in* momentarily appears as an element meaning "with respect to" in the idiom "to be obsequious in" (as in *MWW* IV.ii.2: "you are obsequious in your love"). The syntax of the completed construction *in thy heart* suggests that *in* indicates location and is used metaphorically. The sum of the various signals is likely to be a vague understanding of the line that includes being cherished in the beloved's heart and being concerned with inner essence rather than external physical incidentals. (Note the phonetically parallel and logically nonparallel echo of the *in* construction that concludes the preceding line, and see the *in thy* construction [which ends the poem by

introducing yet another sense of *in*] and *informer* in line 13. The poem's incidental exercise in different kinds of *in* has a non-signifying pertinence to the ongoing contrast between externals and inner essense.)

10. *oblation*   offering (specifically, offering to the deity; see sonnet 105; Landry [p. 126] notes an echo of Leviticus 1 : 9 and 13 in the conjunction of *oblation* with *sweet* and *savor* in line 7).   *poor but free*   Note the ideational echo of, and contrast to, *Pitiful thrivers* in line 8. In Renaissance pronunciations "poor" and "pure" were enough alike for wordplay (see 67.7, note); here *poor* would have included a phonetic anticipation of the topic of line 11.   *free*   freely given. The line suggests the standards of value embodied in the story of the widow's mite (Mark 12:41–44); the widow is contrasted to those "which love to go in long robes, and love salutations in the markets, / And the chief seates in the Synagogues, and the first roumes at feastes" (Mark 12:38–39).

11. *seconds*   stuff of inferior grade—a Shakespearian extension from the adjective "second" in its commercial sense, "not of the purest," "not of the best quality" (*OED* gives examples from 1577 and 1618; Landry [p. 126] notes that "second" was commonly used to describe an inferior grade of flour, and points to Leviticus 2:1: "his offring shalbe of fine floure"). Shakespeare's noun use of *seconds* anticipates *OED*'s next example of the modern commercial sense by a hundred years; the coinage may have been prompted by Shakespeare's desire to include the idea of "anything additional," "any secondary considerations" along with the idea of "anything inferior." (A modern reader may hear pertinent suggestions of "which has nothing to do with time" in *Which is not mixed with seconds.* "Second" meaning a fraction of a minute of time was not yet current; however, see the note on *seconds* on pp. 582–83.)   *not mixed with seconds*   The main idea appears to be that what is poor and pure is better than what is grand but padded out for show and thus adulterated. This phrase in combination with *knows no art* echoes the antithesis in line 7, but alters its focus by retroactively exploiting its latent potential as a contrast between pure and adulterated matter. *art*   (1) artificiality, adulteration; (2) artful purpose, craftiness. (Ingram and Redpath delete Q's comma after *art* and thus give dominance to a neutral extra meaning for *art* in "no art / But mutual render": "no skill *except* mutual render.")

9,11. *heart, art*   Since initial "h" was commonly dropped (see 138.12, note), these two words probably sounded almost alike here and may thus have given a paradoxical cast to the quatrain (see 24.13–14, note).

12. *But*   but is rather (although the reading accepted by Ingram and Redpath and described above is also present regardless of punctuation).   *mutual* = dissyllabic, by syncopation (as in 8.10).   *render*   exchange. Although the topic of mutual exchange relates to the commercial metaphors in lines 6 and 11, the topic seems new and sudden. The suddenness is somewhat tempered both by *only* ("simply"; "nothing more than"), which echoes the earlier concern for purity and simplicity as opposed to artful mixture and unnecessary extras, and by *me for thee*, which echoes and contrasts with the exchange of *simple savor*, for *compound sweet* in line 7.

13. *suborned*   bought, paid to bear false witness. (Note the phonetic echo of

bore [line 1] in *suborned* and of *on form* [line 5] in *informer*, and the ideational echo of *heart* [line 9] in *soul*.)

14. *control* power (with a logically casual play on "to control" meaning "to refute" [see 66.10, note]); *control* is an accounting term and thus has extra pertinence here (see 58.2, note).

13–14. The *informer* now addressed by the speaker may be inferred from the defensive tone with which the poem opens, but, although his sudden presence can be explained, the suddenness is real; like the closing platitude, the dismissal feels unrelated to the argument of the first twelve lines. In terms of the relationship between speaker and beloved, the *informer* would seem to be a straw man addressed in the character of a self-serving toady who has accused the speaker of some breach of the beloved's faith; however, since *thy* and *thee* in quatrain 3 indicate that the poem addresses the beloved, the couplet can also seem to be addressed to the beloved—which makes it even more disconcerting for a reader. (Note that this is the third of three successive couplets that pertain to solemn oaths and do not immediately pertain to the sonnets they conclude; see the notes on the couplets of 123 and 124. Here the gap between quatrains and couplet is to some extent bridged by the potential the word *informer* has as a punning epithet for "a dweller on form"—"an in-form-er," "one who cares that things be done in proper form.")

1–14. Various commentators have observed that many of the particulars of this sonnet pertain to Holy Communion (although they pertain to the Eucharist in ways that are independent of their relation to one another in the logic of the sonnet). For instance, a canopy was carried over the host in religious processions. There are some incidental likenesses between the diction of the service and that of the sonnet—e.g. the desired effect of communion is "that we may evermore dwell in him [Christ], and he in us" (*BCP*, p. 194); and those who do injury to God in refusing Communion are beseeched "that unto this unkindness ye will not add any more. Which thing ye shall do, if ye stand by as gazers and lookers on them that do Communicate" (*BCP*, p. 187). More significantly, just before the consecration of the host, the minister prays to God the Father, who gave his only son to suffer on the cross, "who made there (by his one oblation of himself once offered) a full, perfect and sufficient Sacrifice, Oblation, and Satisfaction for the sins of the whole world" (*BCP*, p. 194). In view of the *mutual render* of line 12, note that communion not only commemorates Christ's oblation on the cross, but is itself "a sacrifice"; the prayer just quoted is balanced by this prayer immediately after communion is received: "O Lord and heavenly Father, we thy humble servants entirely desire . . . [thee] to accept this our Sacrifice of praise and thanksgiving . . . [and] to grant that by the merits and death of thy Son Jesus Christ . . . we . . . may obtain remission of our sins, and all other benefits of his passion. And here we offer and present unto thee, O Lord, our selves, our souls, and bodies, to be a . . . Sacrifice unto thee . . ." (*BCP*, p. 195). Note also that the commercial use of "second" was particularly common in indicating grades of flour, and that the instructions appended to the text of the service go into detail about paying for communion bread and wine and specify that the parish purchase "the best and purest wheat bread, that

conveniently may be gotten" (*BCP*, p. 198). All in all, there is a great deal of
inviting evidence for seeing this sonnet in relation to Holy Communion. However, none of the evidence is such as would lead a reader to think about the
Eucharist while he reads the poem; the eating metaphor in the sonnet, for instance, can seem pregnant only after one has studied the poem. Allusion to Holy
Communion *could* have been highly efficient in the poem; the contrasts between
external accidents and internal essence and between mixed and pure substance
have an obvious analogy in the paradoxes of transubstantiation, consubstantia-
tion, and impanation, but, though the analogy is apparent if one totes up the
various potential Eucharistic references in the sonnet, the analogy is never applied or activated while the poem is in process.

Much the same can be said of a thin thread of potentially bawdy references
in the poem—a thread that could suggest frivolous reference to premature
ejaculation; see 26.1–14, note (on *all*), 118.6, note (on *compound*), 129.1, note
(on "spend"), 52.1–2 and 151.12, notes (on *stand*), and 20.7, note (on *control*);
also note the potential play on "in thy cunt roll" ("to stand in the roll of" would
mean "to be recorded in the books of"; compare "stands in record" in *Measure*
II.ii.40, and see 122.12, note [on *tables*]). Compare 116.1–14, note.

SONNET 126

The Elizabethans used the word "sonnet" as we do; in 1575 Gascoigne said
"I can beste allowe to call those Sonnets whiche are of fouretene lynes, every
line conteyning tenne syllables. The firste twelve do ryme in staves of foure
lines by crosse meetre, and the last two ryming together do conclude the whole"
(*Certayne Notes of Instruction* in *Elizabethan Critical Essays*, ed. G. Gregory
Smith [2 vols., London, 1904], 1, 55). However, they also used "sonnet" as a
label not only for poems "cross-rhymed" in various patterns (e.g. *A&S*), of
various lengths (e.g. sonnet 99 and Thomas Watson's eighteen-line sonnets),
and in various meters (e.g. sonnet 145), but also in the original Italian sense of
sonnetto, a little song, a short lyric poem of any sort. This sonnet, composed of
six rhymed iambic couplets, is not a sonnet in any technical sense; it is a sonnet
in that it is a short lyric (note, however, that its logical organization is by quatrains). The Q printer appears to have expected a sonnet to have at least
fourteen lines whatever its rhyme pattern; he bracketed two final blank lines,
apparently to indicate that he thought something was missing. (The poem's
sudden *quietus* after twelve lines is—probably accidentally—an illustrative
analogy that demonstrates the justice of the warning the poem offers.)

Although the sex of the beloved is unspecified in most of the sonnets, all those
that are specifically and exclusively addressed to a man precede this one in the
Q order, and all those specifically and exclusively addressed to a woman follow
it. In view of the poem's structural peculiarity, there is therefore some basis for
the widespread critical belief that sonnet 126 is intended to mark a division
between sonnets principally concerned with a male beloved and those principally
concerned with a woman. Dover Wilson calls 126 "an Envoy to the sonnet
series addressed to the Friend."

1. *lovely* (1) loveable; (2) beautiful (as in 54.13 and 95.1). *lovely boy* Compare *sweet boy* in 108.5. (The conjunction of *lovely, boy,* and *pow'r* can make the poem at first seem to be in the tradition of lovers' apostrophes to Cupid; *my* suggests an alternative possibility, that the poem is addressed to the beloved; that possibility quickly becomes the only one as the poem progresses and is more and more evidently addressed to a mortal.)

1–2. *who in thy pow'r / Dost hold* who have in your power (subsequent lines activate suggestions of "hold back" in *hold*). *glass* looking glass, mirror (said to be *time's* and *fickle* because its reports change with the passage of time; the next—and apparently appositive—phrase attracts and adds the sense of "hourglass" to *glass*). *his* its (but see 73.10, note). *his sickle hour* (1) which is his sickle hour (appositive to *time's fickle glass*); (2) and his sickle hour (syntax and the rhyme between *fickle* and *sickle* favor sense (1); logic favors sense (2)). *sickle* See 60.12, note; and compare *his . . . sickle's* in 116.10. (Q, of course, spells *sickle* with the now abandoned character for long *s*; thus *sickle* presents an ocular pun on *fickle.* The pun, the apparent but illogical syntactical equation of the two phrases, the *fickle-sickle* rhyme, the retroactively evoked hourglass, and the fact that glass can cut, all combine to effect an extravagantly elaborate confusion between two logically related but distinctly different things.) *sickle hour* (1) sickle which is hour (taking the words as appositive); (2) sickle-like hour, hour which cuts down growing things when they are ripe (taking the words as an adjective-noun pair like *fickle glass*). *hour* = a monosyllable.

3. *by waning grown* The phrase operates from the mortal paradox by which all growth toward perfection is also progress toward decay and death: everything by growing wanes; Shakespeare implies that paradox, assumes it, and presents a corollary to it—namely that the beloved grows more lovely as he grows older (which may be taken as a statement of temporary fact—i.e. the beloved has as yet grown more beautiful with time because he is not yet fully mature—or as a flattering absolute—i.e. age only makes him more beautiful; the "moral" the speaker develops pertains to both readings. Brent Cohen points out to me that *waning* can activate suggestions of the crescent moon, an image inherent in *sickle.* The image is logically casual but vaguely appropriate because the moon is a traditional image of constancy in constant change (see 107.5, note). *show'st* As the word is read it means simply "demonstrate"; its final sense, "demonstrate by contrast," "show up," emerges only under the logical pressure of line 4.

4. *lovers* So Q. Renaissance texts do not distinguish among the three different senses that are defined in modern English by the presence, position, or absence of an apostrophe: "lover's," "lovers'," "lovers." Usually the distinction is clear from context (e.g. Q gives "times fickle glasse" in line 2), but not here where "the withering of your lover" (i.e. "my withering"), "the withering of your lovers," "your withering lovers," and "that your lovers are withering" are equally probable. *withering* = dissyllabic, by syncopation.

The use of *lovers* here and the use of *lovely* in line 1 make this sonnet the ideal occasion to talk about the meaning of "lover" and, by extension, the meaning of "love" throughout the sonnets. Words like "lovely" and "lover" strike a modern reader as pertinent to and therefore suggestive of a sexual relationship. Ever since Malone, therefore, commentators have been at pains to point out that "lover" was used as an almost exact synonym for "friend" (e.g. Menenius tries to argue his way past a Volscian sentry by saying "I tell thee, fellow, / Thy general is my lover. I have been The book of his good acts . . . For I have ever verified my friends— / Of whom he's chief . . . " [*Cor* V.ii. 13–15, 17–18]; Ulysses concludes his advice to Achilles with "Farewell, my lord. I as your lover speak" [*T&C* III.iii.214]; "Your ever true lover," "Thy lover," etc. were commonly used as closings for letters and were as neutral sexually as the salutation "Dear Sir" is now [see *JC* II.iii.7; Rollins, *Variorum* I, 93, gives further examples]). Awareness of the existence and currency of the sexually neutral use of "lover" is vital to understanding the probable effect and intent of Shakespeare's use in the sonnets of the word "lover" and of the trappings of courtly love literature generally, but that awareness has tradition-ally been unjustly exploited—largely because most commentators have been concerned with finding our what Shakespeare was talking about, what the occasion of the sonnets was, rather than with the literary experience the poems evoke in us and/or evoked in a Renaissance reader. To take the abundant examples of the word "lover" used without suggesting "paramour" as evidence against automatically assuming that Shakespeare is talking about a real or imaginary homosexual relationship is logical and just. To argue that common use of "lover" to mean "friend" justified glossing "lover" here and in 31.10, 32.4, and 63.12 as "friend" is logical but foolish because in the sonnets "lover," "love," "lovely," etc., appear in contexts that carefully, constantly, and ostenta-tiously echo the manner, diction, and conccrns of love poems about sexual relationships between men and women. "Lover" meant "friend" in context of a friendship, and this is such a context; "lover" meant "paramour" in context of a love affair, and by literary kind this is such a context. The effective meaning of "lover" (and "love") in these sonnets is a dynamic and witty conflation of both meanings, which constantly and unsuccessfully strain to separatc from one another. (Compare the cruder, less complete, and therefore intellectually more manageable fusion of love of God and sexual love in Donne's *Holy Sonnets*.) In this sonnet the two senses of *lovers* are in almost perfect balance; the matter-of-fact tone suggests "friends"; the general context of the collection and the word *lovely* evoke the meaning "paramours"—at least to the extent where *lovers* acts as a hyperbolic intensifying metaphor of sexual passion.

    5. *nature* = capitalized in Q. Most editors retain the capital; however, since modern readers take capitalization to be meaningful, retaining the capital here acts to anticipate the personification that occurs in the next two words. Shakespeare's contemporaries would not have attached significance to Q's capitalization of *nature* any more than they would have attached significance to Q's capitalization of *boy* in line 1 or to the lack of capitalization of *time* in line 2 and 8 or, for that matter, of *minute*, which is also effectively personified. (See Preface, pp. xvii–xviii.) *mistress over wrack* (1) who is in charge of ruin; (2) who holds ruin in submission and so can check its course. (Line 6 limits a reader to understanding the phrase in sense (2), but both are momentarily

present as the phrase is read; the two contrary senses encapsule the argument of the rest of the poem.)

6. *still*   always, ever (with overtones of *still* meaning "even so," "anyway" [see 9.5, note], and with syntactically irrelevant but substantively relevant overtones of the adjective meaning "motionless" [compare line 10]). Editors commonly insert a comma between *onwards* and *still*, thus limiting the action of *still* to *nature . . . will pluck*. As the line is read, however, it first says "as thou goest onwards ever," and then says "[she] will ever pluck thee back"; the multiple action of *still* thus lets the line embody both nature's special acts of favoritism and their inevitable frustration.

7. *keeps*   (1) retains possession of, refuses to part with; (2) maintains for her own benefit (as one "keeps" servants [*MWW* I.i.250: "I keep but three men and a boy"], "keeps" a dog [*Tim* IV.iii.199], or "keeps" a whore [*T&C* V.i.94]; (3) guards, preserves, protects (as in *Measure* II.ii.42: "Heaven keep your honour," and *HV* V.i.62: "God bye you, and keep you, and heal your pate"); (4) holds back, detains (as in *A&C* I.iii.22–23: "Let her not say 'tis I that keep you here— / I have no power upon you"); compare 133.11.   *to*   for.

8. *disgrace*   discredit, make a fool of (with a play on "rob of beauty," "disfigure," see 89.5, note).   *minute*   Most editors take Q's "mynuit" as a misprinted plural and therefore emend to "minutes." They may be right, but, since it appears in company of the curious use of *hour* in line 2, of the echo and potential parallel provided by *minion* in line 9, and of the wholesale personification in the poem, *minute* is hardly odd enough to warrant emendation; personified as a threatening monster, *minute* (from Latin *minui*, "to diminish," "to weaken"), superficially echoes the Latin verb *minitor*, "I threaten" (in which, presumably, every schoolboy of every time has heard an etymologically wanton echo of the devouring Minotaur of Crete).

9. *minion*   (1) darling, favorite (as in *1HIV* I.i.83: "sweet Fortune's minion and her pride," but with overtones of its narrower sense, "paramour"—as in *FQ* II.ii.37 and *Temp* IV.i.98 where Venus is called "Mars's hot minion"); (2) servant, slave (i.e. "creature," "puppet"; compare *1HIV* I.ii.24: "let us be Diana's foresters, . . . minions of the moon . . . governed, as the sea is, by . . . the moon").

10. *still*   always, forever (with a play on "motionless"—i.e. not going *onwards*; compare 104.11; note the potential for further punning in *quietus* below).

11. *audit*   (= capitalized and italicized in Q, as also in 4.12) final summary accounting—as by a steward.   *answered*   satisfied by payment, made good on (as in *1HIV* I.iii.185: "To answer all the debt he owes"). The context of lines 10 and 12 dictates that *Her audit* be understood as "the accounting nature is obliged to render and satisfy" rather than as "the accounting she demands of you"; however, "to answer nature's audit" suggests the proverbial idea of "paying one's debt to nature" (Tilley, D168; see sonnet 4).

12. *her quietus is*   her means of settling her debts is (an ellipsis for "her means of getting her 'quietus,' her '*quietus est*,' her receipt for full payment").   *render*   give up, relinquish (with plays on "to render an account" [as in *Much*

Ado IV.i.331: "Claudio shall render me a dear account"], on "to render an answer" [as in *Measure* I.iii.48], and on "to pay a tax, or tribute, or other acknowledgment of dependence" [*OED*, 11; compare *Titus* I.i.159–60: "my tributary tears / I render for my brethren's obsequies"]).

SONNET 127

In the 1609 order this is the first of the so-called "dark-lady" sonnets, sonnets specifically concerned with the speaker's relationship to a brunette, who is, therefore, not "fair" in that she is not blonde, and who is also not "fair" in that she is morally foul (see 131.12). Not all of the last twenty-eight sonnets explicitly concern the dark lady (e.g. 128, 129), but, as the company of sonnets to a young man invites a reader to think of sonnets 1–126 as addressed to (or written about) a man and to assume that the beloved in those 126 is the same man throughout, so all unparticularized references to a beloved in the last twenty-eight sonnets invite a reader to assume the same female beloved referred to here. (Sonnet 127 resembles *LLL* IV.iii.228–70 in topic, logic, and many particulars of diction.)

1. *the old age* the "olden times." *black* The meaning of this word is established by its contrast to *fair*: (1) brunette; (2) ugly (Shakespeare and his contemporaries regularly use *black* as if it were a simple antonym for "beautiful"; compare 27.12, 63.13, 65.14, *AYLI* III.ii.83, and *2Gent* V.ii.12: "Black men are pearls in beauteous ladies' eyes"—a proverb for which Tilley [M79] gives several contemporary examples). *counted* accounted, thought to be. *fair* (1) blonde, light-colored; (2) beautiful. The logic of the line derives both from the pun on *fair* and on the traditional courtly-love ideal of blonde, blue-eyed beauty. (Actually, the self-consciously heretical practice of praising dark hair and dark eyes was an established part of the tradition it violated—e.g. Tasso played on *negra* and *alba* in praising Leonora, who is both *bruna* and *bella*; Sidney's Stella has black eyes—see *A&S* 7.10–11: "Whereas black seems Beautie's contrary, / . . . [Nature] even in blacke doth make all beauties flow." For a full discussion of the background, see Baldwin, pp. 321–25. Both the traditional ideal and its domesticated counter-tradition are anticipated and sustained by Song of Songs 1:4: "I am blacke . . . but comelie . . . . "

2. The logic of this line stresses the distinction between considering black beautiful and admitting to doing so; that improbable stress may be only a by-product of Shakespeare's desire to exploit the chop logic by which *beauty's name* is "blonde" (*fair*) and by which only blondes can be called "fair," and to set up the metaphor of bastardy in lines 3 and 4 (a bastard was not legally entitled to its father's *name*; compare *Lucrece* 522: "Thy issue blurr'd with nameless bastardy").

3. *successive heir* (1) successor in possession; (2) legitimate heir by succession (bastards had no rights of primogeniture). (*Heir* contains a quiet play on "hair"—compare *CofE* III.ii.122, and see 68.1–8.)

4. *a bastard shame* (1) the shame of being the parent of a bastard; (2) the shame of having its bastard (artificial beauty [see 68.3–8]) bear the name of beauty (be accepted as genuine); (3) the shame of being itself thought bastard

(because genuine, natural beauty may be taken to be cosmetically achieved; compare *LLL* IV.iii.259: "native blood is counted painting now").

5. *since* (1) from the time when, ever since; (2) inasmuch as, seeing that. *each* every (as in 7.2 and 48.2, but with a contextually derived implication of "any"). *each hand hath put on* everybody and anybody has usurped (taking *hand* as a synecdoche—as in "All hands on deck"; however, the phrase also carries a fleeting image of the particular usurpation in question: *nature's pow'r* indicates that *hand* and *put on* are used figuratively, but in this context their syntactically unharnessed literal meanings evoke a picture of hands putting on cosmetics, attaching hair pieces, etc.).

6. *Fairing* making fair, beautifying (compare the verb "to unfair" in 5.4). *the foul* those who are ugly, what is ugly (see 132.14 and note). *false* (1) deceiving; (2) artificial. (In this context, the ostentatious alliteration, consonance, and assonance in *Fairing, foul, false,* and *face* makes the line sound "beautified," artificially tricked out.)

7. *hath no name* (1) lacks a label, has lost its appellation (i.e. the word *fair*); (2) lacks fame, renown, honor (as in *1HIV* III.ii.108: "great name in arms"); (3) is without lineage, is nameless in the way a bastard is nameless (compare *Lucrece* 522 and *AW* I.iii.146: "I am from humble, he from honoured name"); (4) has lost its good name (as the parent of a bastard might; for *name* meaning "good name," "good reputation," see *CofE* II.i.112–13: "no man that hath a name / By falsehood and corruption doth it shame"). *holy bow'r* sacrosanct dwelling place (with a play on "holey"; compare the similar sexual pun in *Much Ado* III.iv.68–72, and see 68.9, 151.6, 153.5, notes, and Partridge, s.v. "hole," "holland," "holy," and "occupy").

8. *But is* (1) instead [it] is, on the contrary [it] is; (2) that is not (for similar uses of *but* after negatives, see 65.2,8 and *V&A* 526: "No fisher but the ungrown fry forbears"). *if not* (1) or even (as in *Temp* I.ii.475–76: "One word more / Shall make me chide thee, if not hate thee"); (2) or else (a sense derived from taking *if not* as an ellipsis for "or, if not profaned, it"). *lives in* exists in a state of (with a play, evoked by the context of *bow'r*, on "dwells in," "resides at"). *disgrace* ill repute (with a play on *disgrace* meaning "disfigurement," "ugliness," see 33.8, 126.8, and notes).

7–8. "Beauty hath no name and no holy bow'r; on the contrary beauty is profaned or reputed to have been profaned." The gloss is a summary guess at what a reader consciously understands from the two lines. That understanding is presumably achieved effortlessly and instantly, but it is complexly derived from and colored by a maze of pertinent and incidentally efficient signals of relationship. The lines could be difficult to understand; the two-line clause is an awkward syntactical/logical contraption, but its ill–fitted joints are effectively masked by effects that are accidental to—but which mediate between—the sense dictated by its syntax and the sense dictated by its context. The most obvious syntactical and idiomatic signals indicate that the clause be understood as "Sweet beauty has no name or sanctuary; instead it is profaned or even lives in disgrace." That reading is rhetorically essential to a reader's experience of the lines, even though it is logically unsatisfactory. "It is profaned or even lives in di.grace" does not make the kind of logical sense its syntax vouches for: "*x* or even *y*" presumes that *x* and *y* are related by degree; "to be profaned" and "to live in disgrace" are related ideas, but one cannot readily be thought of as a more or less extreme alternative to the other. Nonetheless, the syntactically and idiomatically straightforward surface sustains a reader's sense that he is reading an easy exposition of obvious facts, even while his understanding is actually directed by other signals to other senses.

Coming where they do, these lines present themselves as supportive testimony to the preceding assertions about the same matters (beauty, slander, shame); beauty profaned and beauty living in disgrace ask to be understood as, on the one hand, cosmetics (paint, powder, human hair worn in wigs, etc.), and, on the other, genuine natural beauty (a beautiful person's own hair, complexion, etc.), which is now assumed to be artificially enhanced. Moreover, although some potential syntaxes make line 8 a modifier for *beauty*, the proximity of *holy bow'r* and *profaned* and the dictional link between them invite a reader to understand "Beauty has no name; nor has it any holy bower that is not profaned"—a reading that cannot logically accommodate *if not lives in disgrace*, except through unwarranted syntactic ingenuity ("if there is a bower unprofaned, then beauty lives in disgrace anyway [because its holy bower will be assumed to have been profaned]"), but a reading otherwise supported by the substantively incidental common denominator among *bow'r, profaned* (from *profanus*: "before the fane," "before the temple"), and *lives in*. Similarly, *profaned* can modify *name* as well ("Beauty has no unprofaned name nor any unprofaned holy bower"); the idea of a *name* living in disgrace is readily meaningful and tends further to divert attention from the improbability of a *bow'r* living in disgrace.

Note that these lines—a clause that coheres in several systems but has no single natural identity in any of them—are generally emblematic of their topic—false identities that pass for real and real ones that seem false; and note that the confusion of negated negatives ("no name or bower that is not . . . if not . . .") makes a reader's experience of lines 7–8 comparable to the experience of sorting out and comprehending the distinction between deserved and undeserved infamy. (Note also that the combination of the metaphor of desecration and violation of sanctuary with the topic of misused beauty gives the lines suggestions of rape.)

9–10. *eyes . . . eyes*   The repetition of *eyes* has caused most commentators to find something wrong with these lines. The still unsolved and probably unsolvable problem has been to decide the nature of their faultiness. Shakespeare may simply have written a pair of lame lines: ". . . my mistress' eyes are as black as ravens (not 'as ravens' eyes are,' because ravens' eyes are not black); her eyes are so suited (i.e. 'dressed thus'), and seem to be mourners" (with the logical implication of "so that—with the result that—they seem to be mourners"). On the other hand, the repetition may have resulted from a printer's error in picking up *eyes* from line 10 and replacing it for the word Shakespeare wrote in line 9 ("hairs"? "brows"?) or, more probably, in repeating *eyes* from line 9 instead of "hairs" or "brows" or some other such word in line 10. An editorial emendation for *eyes* in one or the other line results in a smooth and idiomatic reading which realizes the double sense of *so suited* (i.e. "dressed thus" and "matched to it"), but no argument for emendation or for any particular emendation is sufficiently persuasive to overcome counterarguments (Ingram and Redpath, who tentatively adopt "Her brow" in line 10, efficiently summarize all aspects of the problem).

10–11. *mourners . . . / At such who*   mourners because of—at the behavior of—those people who (with actively rejected overtones of the vestigially present idiom "mourners for," an idiom overruled by the logic of *At* and the nature of its object; the conflict between the benevolent standard idiom and the actual construction gives the energy of irony to the scorn we feel for the pitiful creatures who beautify themselves with lifeless cosmetics).

12. *creation*   (1) nature's creations, things in the natural condition in which they were created; (2) nature's creative powers.   *Sland'ring creation with a false esteem*   The construction conflates several related ideas: (1) slandering creation by causing real beauty to be thought artificial—making it seem that *all* beauty is cosmetically achieved (by making artificial beauty indistinguishable from the real thing which is thus devalued) and that all beauty is equally undeserving of esteem; (2) slandering creation by appropriating the esteem properly due to nature and its creations; (3) slandering creation by taking remedial actions that imply that nature's power is insufficient; (4) slandering creation by implying that nature's achievement is inferior to art's and that nature does not deserve its high reputation. (The syntax of the line demonstrates the difficulty of distinguishing true from false and worthy from unworthy: a reader cannot fix on any one limited logical relationship between *false* and *esteem* or between them and the rest of the line; the wit of the line is heightened by its inclusion of the paradoxical assertion that creation is slandered by esteem [rather than by disgrace]: "slandering creation with an unjust accusation of worthiness, with the false charge that natural creation is estimable.")

13. *so*   (1) in that way (the way specified in quatrain 3); (2) to such a great extent, with such intensity (modifying *mourn* and/or *becoming*); (3) in such a way, in such fashion [as will now be specified]. Line 13 is not syntactically coherent, although its general sense is apparent from context. The line never quite makes an assertion in any one syntax, but it carries the sense of the three different assertions for which it carries fragmentary raw materials: (1) however, they mourn in a fashion that graces their woe (compare 150.5), makes their woe beautiful; (2) however, they mourn in a fashion so becoming *to* their woe; (3) however, they mourn in a way that transforms their woe—that makes their woe become (turn *from* grief into) beauty.

14. *look so*   (1) have such coloring; (2) have the appearance of being in mourning; (3) look like my mistress.   *so*   Contrast the related but different reference of *so* in line 13.

SONNET 128

The underlying conceit of this sonnet is of the traditional type in which a lover wishes he could be transformed into some object or creature used familiarly by the beloved. (See, for example, *R&J* II.ii.24–25: "O that I were a glove upon that hand, / That I might touch that cheek" and Robert Tofte's *Laura* II.xxv: "O that I were sly Proteus," where the poet wishes himself a lapdog; the ultimate example is sonnet 63 of Barnabe Barnes's, *Parthenophil and Parthenophe*, in which the speaker wishes he were his beloved's urine. Rollins cites several commentators who observe an analogue to this sonnet in Ben Jonson's *Every Man Out of His Humour*, III.ix "where Fastidious says of Saviolina, who is playing the viola da gamba, 'You see the subject of her sweet fingers, there? . . . Oh, shee tickles it so, that . . . she makes it laugh most divinely. . . . I have wisht my selfe to be that instrument (I thinke) a thousand times.' ") The intimate and affectionate relationship between a musician and the strings of a musical instrument was also commonly remarked by elegant love poets; Shakespeare exploited the conceit in *Titus* II.iv.44–46: " . . . lily hands / Tremble like aspen leaves upon a lute / And make the silken strings delight to kiss them." Rollins gives several other examples.

In this sonnet Shakespeare takes the conceit by which the lover envies an object and combines it with the conceit of the affectionate strings. However, the poem comes to grief because the loved and loving object he chooses is a keyboard instrument; the physics of keyboard instruments do not lend themselves to the hand-kissing conceit. Although keys rise when released and can be said to kiss the *fingers* (line 14) of the musician, *the tender inward* of the hand (line 6) best describes the palm. Moreover, since a "jack" in harpsichord-like instruments is "an upright piece of wood fixed to the key-lever and fitted with a quill that plucked the string as the jack rose when the key was pressed down" (Onions), jacks do not touch the player's fingers at all. (Rollins quotes E. W. Naylor to the effect that the jacks may "kiss" the palm of the hand while the instrument is being tuned, but here the beloved is playing the instrument, not tuning it.) One might conclude that Shakespeare merely uses *jacks* as a misnomer for "keys" or that he considers the whole key-and-jack mechanism as a single entity and calls it a "jack," but *jacks that nimble leap* clearly describes the frantic action one sees when one looks inside a keyboard instrument while it is being played.

Shakespeare's choice of an instrument physically uncooperative with his conceit was probably in part dictated by the sexual potential in the name of the instrument in question: a "virginal." ("Virginal" was the standard Elizabethan term for all the various harpsichord-like instruments in which keyboard-operated jacks pluck at wires to produce sound; the use of jacks, little pieces of wood, was probably the source of the name, derived from the Latin *virga*, "twig," and was presumably strengthened by the fact that playing on the virginals was a standard accomplishment of well-brought-up young women.) The sexual suggestiveness is crudely exploited in *TNK* III.iii.33–36: *Palamon.* "She met him in an arbor: / What did she there, coz? play o' th' virginals?" / *Arcite.* "Something she did, sir." *Palamon.* "Made her groan a month for't / Or two, or three, or ten." Shakespeare more subtly evokes the word's sexual suggestiveness in *WT* I.ii.125–26 when he has the jealous Leontes describe Hermione as "Still virginalling / Upon his palm." (Shakespeare seems to have regarded palm tickling as a telling sign of lasciviousness; see "paddling palms" in *WT* I.ii.115 and *Oth* II.i.245–49: —". . . she's full of most blest condition." —". . . Blest fig's end! . . . Blest pudding! Didst thou not see her paddle with the palm of his hand?" Compare *R&J* I.v.91–108, *LLL* V.ii.794: "by this virgin palm now kissing thine," and the curious phrase "the virginal palms of your daughters" in *Cor* V.ii.42.)

Shakespeare was presumably also eager to exploit the punning potential of *jacks*. "Jack" was a standard term of abuse for any worthless fellow and for impudent upstarts in particular ("Since every Jack became a gentleman, / There's many a gentle person made a Jack"—*RIII* I.iii.72–73); the pun in line 13 of this poem occurs in reverse in *Shrew* II.i.156–57: "she did call me rascal fiddler / And twangling Jack." The word "jack" also lends itself to sexual word-play; the general context, the surrounding diction (notably *leap*—see "leaping-houses" in *1HIV* I.ii.7), the shape and action of the jacks of virginals, and the fact that "Jack" is a man's name, that "jack" is used adjectivally to mean "male," and that "jack" is a slang appellation for a penis in erection (compare Rabelais' use of *Jacques*), all combine to suggest an analogy between the activity of the *jacks* described here and male sexual activity.

The poem is undeniably full of witty sexual innuendo, but Shakespeare works so hard for it and is so thwarted by the facts of harpsichord playing that the result is a mere labor at cleverness. (Compare the more effective musical-sexual metaphor in *Per* I.i.78–85 [quoted in 141.13–14, note].)

1. Compare 8.1.   *music music*   The first "music" is metaphoric, the second, literal. For a similarly self-conscious rhetorical gimcrack, see 104.2; the figure is antistasis, repetition of a word in a different sense.   *my music*   who art my music, who art music to me; or = a vocative ("thou, my music, music play'st").

1–4. The subordinate clause begun with *when* in line 1 is potentially complete at the end of line 1; the sentence is then syntactically ready for *Do I envy*. The subordinate clause reopens with *Upon* in line 2, is again potentially complete at *wood*, and then is augmented by its own subordinate clause, *whose motion sounds*, which is itself extended by *With thy sweet fingers* in line 3. Then in the middle of line 3 a new "when" clause begins; it is simultaneously a new start (a parallel appositive to the first "when" clause), and a further modification of the "whose" clause that modified the first "when" clause (i.e. *when thou gently sway'st* indicates the time when *motion sounds*).

2. *blessèd*   fortunate, happy (as in 16.4, 43.9, 52.1, 56.12, and 119.6).   *wood* (presumably) the keys of a virginal (*Upon that blessèd wood* carries accidental overtones of the crucifixion of Christ).   *whose motion*   (1) the movement of which (i.e. which, by moving); (2) the playing of which (i.e. which, by being moved; Willen and Reed clarify this second shade of meaning by reference to *Cymb* IV.ii.187–89: "My ingenious instrument! / Hark, Polydore, it sounds. But what occasion / Hath Cadwal now to give it motion?"); (3) the mechanism of which (*OED* gives an example from 1605 and this from the 1620's: ". . . curious Clocks; And other like Motions of Returne: And some Perpetual Motions"; compare the "movement" of a watch).   *sounds*   (1) makes sound, resounds

(intransitive); (2) causes to sound (transitive; the object, *The wiry concord* in line 4, is also the object of *sway'st* in line 3).

3. *With* (1) through the agency of, as a result of the action of; (2) simultaneously with [the action of], in consort with. *thou . . . sway'st* you govern, you control, you rule, you manipulate (as in *MND* I.i.193: "You sway the motion of Demetrius' heart"); with or without Q's comma after *sway'st,* the line-end pause, the context of *motion,* and the presence of *gently* invite a reader momentarily to understand *thou gently sway'st* intransitively as "you move gently from side to side" (*OED* gives an example from 1555 in which tree branches tossed by the wind are said to "swaye sumwhat from syde to syde"); that suggestion in *sway'st* introduces a logically and syntactically unharnessed by-reference to the virginal player's practice of producing tremulo sounds by vibration of the fingers after each key is depressed.

4. *wiry concord* harmony achieved by means of wires (the wires with which a virginal is strung); see 8.6, note. *confounds* stuns, dumbfounds, overwhelms with delight (with a play, evoked by the juxtaposition of *concord,* on "to confound" meaning "to bring to confusion," "to bring into discord").

5. *envý* = probably pronounced envýe; in Renaissance pronunciations both "envý" and "énvy" were common. *nimble* Shakespeare's contemporaries may have heard some wit in the juxtaposition of *nimble* and *jacks.* *OED* gives "nimble Jack" as a collocation meaning "an elusive person" (but its example is from 1682); compare "Jack be nimble, Jack be quick / Jack jump over the candlestick."

5,6. *jacks, kiss* Although these two words have technical senses in the game of bowls (see 90.4, note), this context does nothing to invoke an allusion.

7,8. *harvest reap, blushing stand* The first of these phrases—an atrophied metaphor impertinent to its context and efficient only because it is lifeless—is understood as an abstraction and evokes no image. Although the two phrases relate to one another by a contrast between harvested grain and grain still standing in the field, the effective action of the second phrase is as lifelessly abstract as the first; *blushing* pertains to the color of lips, but one cannot readily visualize lips standing except perhaps by imagining a pair of blushing page boys arbitrarily called *lips.* As in his use of the idea of harpsichord playing, Shakespeare disables his poem by ignoring the physics of the situation on which he works his witty embroidery. (In this case he may have done so in order to include the syntactically casual potential of *boldness by thee* to suggest "your boldness" and *by thee blushing* to suggest "beside you who are blushing.")

8. *by* alongside, next to.

9–10. *state / And situation* Ingram and Redpath say "Their 'state' is their position in the hierarchy of being, while their 'situation' is simply their physical position." (There is wit in the fact that the two words carry two distinct senses and are also synonyms; compare *expense* and *waste* in 129.1.)

11,14. *thy fingers, thy fingers* Q has "their" in both cases; see 26.12, note.

12. *more blest* (1) more fortunate, happier; (2) abler (i.e. blessed with more talent for making appealing sound; Rollins offers these often cited analogous lines by Constable from the early 1590's: "A lute of senseless wood, by nature dumbe, / Toucht by thy hand doth speake divinely well").

13. (1) "Since saucy jacks are so fortunate in the favors previously mentioned"; (2) "Since the favors previously mentioned are enough to satisfy saucy jacks" (sense (1) reflects the logic and attitude of lines 1–12; sense (2) introduces the sudden witty shift in logic made evident by the brash suggestion of line 14).

SONNET 129

The following were proverbial: "No extreme will hold long." "Hot love is soon cold." "Love is lawless." "Love is sweet in the beginning but sour in the ending." "Love is without reason." "Love's beginning is fear, middle sin, and end grief and annoyance." "Flee that present pleasure that bringeth afterward sorrow." "Short pleasure, long lament" (Tilley, E222, L483, L508, L513, L517, L555, P410, and P419). See also *T&C* I.ii.278–85: "Women are angels, wooing:/ Things won are done; joy's soul lies in the doing . . ." and *V&A* 799–804, 210–17.

1. *expense* (1) expenditure; (2) dissipation, consumption, using up (*OED*, 1.b,c); (3) loss (as in 30.8); (4) waste (the Folio text of *Lear* II.i.100 has "th' expence and waste of his Revenues"; the 1608 quarto, in its corrected state, has "wast and spoyle"). Partridge glosses "spend" as "to expend sexually," "to discharge seminally" (p. 191); he cites *AW* II.iii.272–74: "He wears his honour in a box unseen / That hugs his kicky-wicky here at home, / Spending his manly marrow in her arms."

spirit (= dissyllabic, as in 144.2, probably in 108.2, and perhaps in 61.5) (1) energy, vigor, ardor (as in *1HIV* IV.i.101: "As full of spirit as the month of May"); (2) non-physical energy (i.e. mental energy, emotional energy, and energy of soul), spiritual essence; (3) life force, that which keeps one alive, vital power (often indistinguishable from "life blood"; compare *A&C* IV.xv.58–59: "Now my spirit is going; /I can no more"; in line 2 *lust in action* reveals this to be a reference to the generally held notion that sexual orgasm shortened the lifespan of the male; see 6.6, note); (4) bodily fluid. (Renaissance medicine generally held that the body was permeated with three vaguely defined substances called "spirits." In the "exposition of strange terms" that he appended to his 1543 translation of *The most excellent works of Chirurgerie . . .* by Johannes de Vigo, Bartholomew Traheron says:

> A spirit is a subtle, fine, airy, and clear substance, produced of the thinnest and finest part of blood, that virtue and strength may be carried from the principal part to the rest. The physicians teach that there been [i.e. are] three kinds of spirits: animal, vital, and natural. The animal spirit hath his seat in the brain and is spread into all the body by sinews, giving faculty of moving and feeling. It is called animal because it is the first instrument of the soul. . . . The vital spirit is contained in the heart and is carried to the parts of the body to rouse natural heat. It is engendered of inspiration and of exhalation or outbreathing of blood. The natural spirit dwelleth in the liver and in the veins . . . [spelling and punctuation modernized].)

In connection with senses (2) and (3), note Cruttwell's assertion that *expense of spirit* is "a piece of contemporary sexual physiology. From the heart to the

sexual organs, was believed to go a vein, bearing in it the 'spirit generative'.
. . . what the phrase refers to is the loss of the 'spirit generative' in the act of
sex" (p. 14). In view of the speaker's subsequent references to the bad eyesight
that causes him to mistake the "foulness" of his lady for beauty (e.g. 137,
147.13–14, and 148), it may be worth noting that diminished eyesight was particularly associated with the diminishment of "spirits"; *OED* cites this from
Arthur Golding's completion of Sidney's translation of Phillippe de Mornay's
A Worke concerning the trewnesse of the Christian religion (1587): "A man's
. . . eyes faile because the Spirites of them fayle"; in his notes on 129.1–2, Rollins (*Variorum* I, 331) cites Thomas Tyler's 1890 edition, which "compares
Sylva Sylvarum, 1627, section 693 (Spedding's Bacon [Boston, 1862], IV, 468):
'It hath been observed by the ancients, that much use of Venus doth dim the
sight. . . . The cause of dimness of sight . . . is the expence of spirits.' " See
sonnet 56.

Ellis suspects puns on *spirit* meaning *penis erectus* in *LLL* I.ii.1–2, 116–17, in
George Herbert's "My God, where is that ancient heat towards thee," and here.
He says that "spirit"

> in phrases like 'raise a spirit,' seems to have had considerable currency as a
> humorous euphemism for the male member. Partridge, s.v. *circle* . . .
> quotes the following passage, but omits *spirit* from his Glossary:

>> *Mercutio.* This cannot anger him. 'Twould anger him
>> To raise a *spirit* in his mistress' circle
>> Of some strange nature, letting it there stand
>> Till she had laid it and conjur'd it down.
>>   (*RJ* 2.1.23–6)

> . . . .

A somewhat more circumstantial treatment of the same metaphor in rhyme
is found in "The Maids Conjuring Book" (c. 1720):

> A young Man lately in our Town,
> He went to Bed one Night;
> He had no sooner lay'd him down,
> But was troubled with a *Sprite:*
> So vigorously the *Spirit* stood,
> Let him do what he can,
> Sure then he said it must be lay'd,
> By Woman, not by Man.

> A Handsome Maid did undertake,
> And into Bed she leap'd;
> And to allay the *Spirit's* Power,
> Full close to him she crep'd:
> She having such a Guardian Care,
> Her office to discharge;
> She opened wide her Conjuring Book,
> And lay'd the Leaves at large.

> . . . .

The phallic connotations of *spirit* and *sprite* may have been due in part
to the influence of *sprit* 'a small pole or spar,' a word often homophonous
with *spirit* (Kökeritz, p. 213), though unrelated to it etymologically. [pp.
95–97]

in a waste of shame (1) in a shameful waste, in a waste that is shameful (suggesting both that to waste spirit is a shame on general principles and that this
particular action is shameful; the phrase charges both lack of economy and positive misbehavior); (2) in an action that isn't worth the shame it entails (note "the
act of shame" in *Oth* V.ii.214). Ingram and Redpath hesitantly suggest "the possibility of an image of vital energy squandered in a desert of shame"; they cite
Ham I.ii.198, "In the dead waste and middle of the night," as a possible Shakespearian use of "waste" to mean "wasteland." Kökeritz (p. 152) found a pun
here on "in a waist," which may be less farfetched than one's knowledge of anatomy would suggest; he cites Marston, *The Malcontent* II.v.89: " 'Tis now about
the immodest waist of night"; "waist" suggests the region of the hips and crotch
to Shakespeare in *Ham* II.ii.231–35: —"Then you live about her [Fortune's]
waist, or in the middle of her favours?" —"Faith, her privates we." —"In the
secret parts of Fortune? O, most true; she is a strumpet."

shame (1) ignominy, disgrace; (2) sense of guilt, self-contempt; (3) modesty,
restraining fear of offense against propriety (as in *MND* III.ii.285–86: "Have
you no modesty, no maiden shame, / No touch of bashfulness?"). Note that
"shame" was used to mean both "sexual violation" and "loss of chastity" (as
in *FQ* V.iii.13: "he fiercely rid, / To bene avenged of the shame, he did / To that
faire Damzell" and *Measure* III.i.140–41: "Is't not a kind of incest to take life /
From thine own sister's shame?").

2. *action* Like "act" and "activity," *action* was often used without modification to indicate "sexual action," "sexual intercourse"; Partridge cites *Per* IV.
ii.8–9: "they [the whores] with continual action are even as good as rotten."

1–2. The structure of these lines is emblematic of the perverse and self-defeating energy the poem describes: the first clause inverts the normal word order,
"lust in action is the expense of spirit . . ."; in the second half of line 2 *action
lust* is a chiasmus-like inversion of the first (*lust . . . action*). See *well knows/
knows well* in line 13 and *All this/this hell* (13–14); and compare the similar effect
ideationally achieved by *Past reason hunted/Past reason hated* (6–7), *proof, and
proved* (11), *Before/behind* (12), and *heav'n/hell* (14). (In *Classical Rhetoric in
English Poetry* [London, 1970], Brian Vickers labels the various rhetorical figures
in this sonnet [pp. 160–63].)

3. *bloody* = murd'rous (but *full of blame* can retroactively give the word
suggestions of "full of blood," "overfull of spirits"; Ellis [p. 96] quotes Thomas
Vicary's *The Anatomy of the Bodie of Man* [ed. F. J. and P. Furnival, 1888, p.
76]; Vicary says that blood "is made sparme . . . in men"). *full of blame*
Ingram and Redpath say " 'packed with guilt' or, just possibly, 'full of harm'.
'Blame', in either of these archaic senses, is a strong word here, and gathers
further sense from its alliteration with 'bloody'."

4. *cruel* = dissyllabic, but the time span of the two syllables is very short.
In sonnets 1 and 131, *cruel* appears at the end of lines in which it is difficult to

say whether it is the tenth syllable or the tenth and eleventh. In any case, words like *crule, jewel,* and *fuel* appear to have been pronounced much as they are now, as slurred dissyllables or very long monosyllables. Unless they appear in meter, one is hard put to label them long monosyllables or short dissyllables, and even in a case like line 4 it would be wrong to think that a seventeenth-century reader would take as long to say *cruel* as he would to say *Savage* or *extreme.* Much the same could be said about the syllabification of "heaven": Q gives "heaven" in line 14; I give *heav'n*; see 15.6, note. Shakespeare's reader would probably have pronounced the word about the same way in line 14 whatever the spelling.   *not to trust*   not to be trusted.

2–3. *lust / Is . . .*   Lust, the passion, is personified; the lines effectively refer both to its qualities and to those of any person who is under the influence of lust, any person who is "lust personified."

5–12.   From *Enjoyed* onward the references of this continuation of the string of adjectives begun in line 3 change both abruptly and smoothly with each change of logical circumstance:

"To enjoy lust" is to exercise it, to take sexual possession of the object lusted for. Here one's understanding of *Enjoyed* is necessarily colored by the fact that "to enjoy" was commonly used specifically to mean "to use sexually," "to take sexual possession of." The word thus says "made happy," "satisfied," and, by synesis, introduces the person "enjoyed" as an extra inferential object of both *Enjoyed* and *despisèd* (once lust is satisfied, the person driven by it despises himself, the passion, and the person desired and seized). In line 6, *hunted* cannot readily be understood as another predicate noun in the "*lust/Is*" series: "lust is hunted" does not make immediate sense; a reader simply continues from the implication introduced by *Enjoyed* and reads *lust/Is . . . hunted* as if it were "the person lusted for is hunted"; despite the obvious syntactic continuity of *perjured, murd'rous, . . . Enjoyed, despisèd, hunted,* the reader has experienced an unexpected, uncontrollable, instantaneous, miraculous transformation in his own merely syntactical experience that is analogous to the transformation that occurs in the exercise of sexual lust.

By the time the reader comes to *had* at the end of line 6 he is prepared to hear a play on its simple sense ("possessed") and its special sexual sense ("possessed sexually"—see 52.14, 87.13, note, and 110.9–12, note). In line 7, *hated* has the same multiple references as *despisèd,* because, unlike *had, hated* makes sense with both *lust/Is* and with "the object of lust is." In line 8, where the logic of the syntax favors *lust,* the passion, as primary reference for *laid,* and the logic of the metaphor of putting out a poisoned bait implies reference to a person who inspires lust, an extra reference to the person lusted after is evoked in a punning, bawdy suggestion of "being with a woman" and "laying a woman down" (as in *HVIII* I.iii.40); that punning reference in *laid* is of scarcely more weight than concurrent suggestions of *laid* meaning "abased" ("laid low"), of "laying a spirit" (= "causing male orgasm and loss of tumescence" as in the lines from *R&J* quoted in the note on *spirit* in line 1), and, perhaps, of "allayed" (see *OED*, s.v. "lay," v¹, I.3), "assuaged."

At the beginning of quatrain 3, *Mad* refers to *lust,* but, under the influence of *make the taker mad* at the end of quatrain 2, it also again refers pointedly to the person mad with lust. In line 10, *Had* again refers to the person lusted for and possessed; *having* and *in quest to have* refer primarily to the person who lusts, and only secondarily to *lust*, the rhetorically personified passion. *A bliss in proof* refers to the passion and to its object but not to the person who lusts; *proved* and *very woe* fit all three. *A joy* and *a dream* are presumably read as if the subject of the sentence were *lust in action*.

5. *Enjoyed* Note that the first syllable (spelled "In-" in Q) participates to an extent that varies from dialect to dialect in the pattern in *in*'s in lines 1, 2, 9, 10, and 11; in Elizabethan pronunciations the second syllable of *having* in line 10 would probably also have resembled "in" (see 83.13–14, note), and *expense* in line 1 would probably have sounded more as it does in Southwestern American dialect than as it does in Modern British English (see 37.7, note). The ideational pertinence of *in* to the topic of this sonnet goes without saying.

6,7. *reason* Shakespeare's numerous puns (see Kökeritz, pp. 138–39) suggest that *reason* was indistinguishable from "raising" (i.e. "raisin' ")—which is pertinent here, and "raisin"—which is not; compare *AYLI* I.iii.6–9, *AW* I.iii. 27–32, and *Shrew* Induction.ii.116–25, where the page masquerading as Sly's lady tells him that his "physicians have expressly charg'd" that "she" should absent "herself" from his bed:

> *Page.* I hope this reason stands for my excuse.
> *Sly.* Ay, it stands so that I may hardly tarry so long.

(There may also be some incidental phallic byplay between *straight* in line 5 and *reason* ["raisin' "].)

8. *the taker* the swallower, him who takes the bait (with overtones of "the rapist," "him who 'takes' the object of his lust"). *mad* (1) insane; (2) wild, frenzied, beyond rational self-control (note the idioms "mad on" and "mad for" meaning "wild with desire to have").

9. *Mad* = a generally accepted emendation for Q's "Made." An argument can be made for retaining the Q text and understanding the line as "Made so in pursuit and in possession." But the potential presence of that syntax is not visible until one reaches *so*, the last word in the line; by that time a reader is likely to have followed the suggestion inherent in the proximity of *mad* in line 8 and to have accepted the straightforward syntax that appears if one reads "Made" as "Mad" (and *so* as "the same way"). *OED* gives "made" as a fifteenth-century spelling of "mad"; "madde" was a common sixteenth- and seventeenth-century spelling of "mad." However he read the line, Shakespeare's reader may have heard a play on "made" in *Mad* (or on "mad" in "Made"): note *make* in line 8. Although the evidence of rhymes does not suggest that Elizabethans pronounced "made" and "mad" alike, they do seem to have resembled each other enough for punning; Kökeritz (pp. 126–27) gives several examples, including *TN* III.iv. 50–53:

> *Malvolio.* 'Go to, thou art made, if thou desir'st to be so;'—
> *Olivia.* Am I made?

> *Malvolio.* 'If not, let me see thee a servant still.'
> *Olivia.* Why, this is very midsummer madness.

Compare 147.10 and note.

11. *A bliss in proof* (1) delightful during action, delightful *in action*, delightful while being exercised; (2) delightful when tested (with a play on "which proves to be a bliss," the idea immediately contradicted in the second half of the line). *proved* (1) having been tried out; (2) having been tested; note that the ellipsis lets *proved* come near to acting twice: "once proved (once tested), proves to be (turns out to be)." *a very woe* a veritable sorrow, a perfect calamity, an absolute calamity (for similar uses of *very* and *woe* see *Much Ado* IV.i. 186 and *V&A* 455 respectively; for a justification of emending Q's "and very wo," see the note on spelling, punctuation, and emendation below). *woe* Heavyhanded puns on "woman," "woe," and "man" were commonplace; Tilley (W656) gives many examples including this from 1591: "Woman was sometimes called woe-man."

12. *Before . . . behind* in prospect . . . in retrospect, before [action]. . . after [action]. Since Q prints this line without internal punctuation, several commentators have experimented with reading it literally, as a statement about space rather than a metaphoric statement about time: e.g. Martin: "(lust is) facing a joy which lies behind a dream" (p. 61); Graves and Riding (see the note on punctuation, etc. below): "Even when consummated, lust still stands before an unconsummated joy, a proposed joy, and proposed not as a joy possible of consummation but as one only to be known through the dream by which lust leads itself on, the dream behind which this proposed joy, this love, seems to lie" (p. 90). Both these readings require considerable forcing, and neither is immediately meaningful either in itself or in context of the poem. The ostentatious parallelism of *Before* and *behind* and the non-idiomatic temporal use of *behind* can tend to revive both the long-forgotten spatial metaphor inherent in uses of "before" with reference to time and the Latin root of *proposed* (*proponere*, "to place in front of"); line 12 thus prepares the way for the spatially conceived assertion in the couplet. However, the model of line 11, which contrasts two stages in the life cycle of lust in two balanced half-lines, presumably always caused readers to read line 12 in the way confirmed by modern editorial punctuation.

proposed (1) anticipated, looked forward to; (2) promised as a reward or goal (as in *Lucrece* 132: "treasure is the meed proposed"); (3) imagined (as in *2HIV* V.ii.91–92: "Question your royal thoughts, make the case yours; / Be now the father, and propose a son"). *a dream* The various connotations of *dream* cause the line to say that, as recalled by an exhausted male, the joy of *lust in action* (a) is only dimly remembered, seems to have been an illusion; (b) seems to be a deceptive myth, a fairy-tale notion, an unrealizable ideal, seems to be a mere idea, purely imaginary; and (c) is (for him, temporarily), a physically impossible ambition. Tucker compares *Lucrece* 211–12: "What win I if I gain the thing I seek? / A dream, a breath, a froth of fleeting joy."

13–14. See Proverbs 2:12–19 (quoted in 153.8, note).

13. *the world* everybody. *well knows* is cognizant of, is aware of (with a potential play on "has experienced"; "to know," meaning "to use sexually" [as in *V&A* 525] is also generally pertinent here and could give the line additional bawdy overtones—particularly if Shakespeare's reader were accustomed to hearing the male sex organ called an *all* [see 26.1–14, note] and the female sex organ called a *well* [see 154.9, note]; the probability of punning intent is heightened by the self-conscious chiasmic repetition of *well knows* in *knows well*). *knows well knows* well enough, is wise enough.

14. *the heav'n* (1) the *bliss*, the "heavenly" pleasure; (2) the heaven-like place (with plays on "haven" [as in *Cymb* III.ii.60 and *RII* I.iii.275–76—see Kökeritz, p. 113] and *having* [i.e. "havin' " or "hav'n"] in line 10). *men* (1) human beings; (2) males. *hell* (1) agony; (2) hellish place (for the use of "hell" to refer to the female sex organ, see 144.12 and note).

1–14. *A Note on Spelling, Punctuation, and Emendation:*

Sonnet 129 was the object of "A Study in Original Punctuation and Spelling," an exercise in irresponsible editorial restraint written by Robert Graves and Laura Riding (originally called "William Shakespeare and E. E. Cummings" in *A Survey of Modernist Poetry* [London, 1927], revised and retitled for inclusion in Graves's *The Common Asphodel* [London, 1949], from which I quote it, and reprinted in Willen and Reed). The essay contains some palpable gaffes (e.g. "the Elizabethans had no typographical *v*"—which appears less than two inches from "very wo" in their transcription of the Q text of 129.11 [the Elizabethans did not use *medial v*]). However, the textual sanctimony of Graves and Riding has proved infectious. The essay starts out by describing Cummings's use of typographical idiosyncrasies for communicating nuances ("Cummings protests against the upper case being allotted to 'I': he affects a humility, a denial of the idea of personal immortality responsible for 'I'. Moreover, 'i' is more casual and detached: it dissociates the author from the speaker of the poem . . ." [p. 85]); they then introduce sonnet 129 and their intent in the essay: "By showing what a great difference to the sense juggling of punctuation marks has made in the original sonnet, we shall perhaps be able to persuade the plain reader to sympathize with what seems typographical perversity in Mr. Cummings. The modernizing of the spelling is not quite so serious a matter, though we shall see that to change a word like *blouddy* to *bloody* makes a difference not only in the atmosphere of the word but in its sound as well" (p. 86). They quote both the Q text of sonnet 129 and the modernized text in *The Oxford Book of English Verse* and then proceed to compare them. Since the Graves-Riding essay is still often treated with respect I will excerpt it at length and comment on it parenthetically in support of the proposition that an editor distorts the sonnet more for a modern reader by maintaining the 1609 text than he would if he modernized its spelling and punctuation:

"First to compare the spelling. As a matter of course the *u* in *proud* and *heauen* changes to *v*; the Elizabethans had no typographical *v*" (p. 87). (I agree that the *u*'s in Q's "proud" and "heauen" are to be read as *v*'s, but I see no benefit in making a reader interrupt his reading to translate them; moreover, leaving "proud" in Renaissance orthography is to maintain an attractive nuisance: a modern reader does well to recognize that an ocular pun on "proud" [= modern "proved"] and "proud" [= modern "proud"] may have momentarily crossed a Renaissance reader's mind and that the context of this poem is one that makes the sexual senses of "pride" and "proud" pertinent [see 151.10]; that, however, can all be managed in a note. To offer Q's "proud" to a modern reader is to invite ingenious speculations on the possibility that Shakespeare meant us to understand "proud" as "in a state of pride" *rather than* as "proved.")

"There are other words in which the change of spelling does not seem to matter. *Expence, cruell, bayt, layd, pursut, blisse, proofe, wo*—these words taken by themselves are not necessarily affected by modernization, though much of the original atmosphere of the poem is lost by changing them in the gloss. Sheer facility in reading a poem is no gain when one tries to discover what the poem looked like to the poet who wrote it" (p. 87). (I am uncertain what the authors mean by "the original atmosphere"; if this is an argument for preserving quaintness, then what is preserved is obviously not original. I do not understand the logic of "when" in "when one tries to discover," but surely to see the text Shakespeare and his contemporaries saw is not to see it as they saw it. It would not look quaint or cute to them; they would have no trouble reading it. Is it not an editor's aim to make a modern reader's experience of the text as like as possible to that of the audience for which it was written? Whenever an editor modernizes a text, he risks distorting it; whenever "the plain reader" looks at an unmodernized Renaissance text, he risks distorting it; since one of them must stick his neck out, it should be the one who is trained and paid to do it. No editor is likely to succeed perfectly in accommodating a modern reader and a Renaissance text to one another, but that is no reason to do nothing.)

"But other changes designed to increase reading facility involve more than changes in spelling. *Periurd* to *perjured*, and *murdrous* to *murderous*, would have meant, to Shakespeare, the addition of another syllable" (pp. 87–88). (Yes, but to a modern reader the change from "periurd" to "perjured" does *not* mean the addition of an extra syllable. "Murderous" is another matter; in modern English it is pronounced with two syllables or, more often, with three; "murd'rous" will indicate the dissyllabic pronunciation demanded by the rhythm.)

"*Inioyd*, with the same number of syllables as *periurd*, is however printed *Enjoy'd*; while *swollowed*, which must have been meant as a three-syllable word (Shakespeare used *-ed* as a separate syllable very strictly and frequently allowed himself an extra syllable in his iambic foot) is printed *swallow'd*. When we come to *despised*, we find in the modern version an accent over the last syllable. These liberties do not make the poem any easier; they only make it less accurate" (p. 88). (The objection to "Enjoy'd" is valid; since a modern reader customarily reads "enjoyed" as a dissyllable and since the rhythm of line 5 encourages that reading, the spelling "Enjoy'd" is a pointless gesture of editorial vigilance; however, Graves and Riding ask us to take a case against thoughtless editing as a case against all editing. The case for Q's "swollowed" is badly founded: I know of no point in any Shakespearian text where one can reliably say from the spelling of any word what pronunciation "must have been meant." The statement beginning "Shakespeare used" should begin "Thomas Thorpe's employees used" or "Shakespeare's printers used"; even so the statement is inaccurate: Shakespeare's printers did not use -*ed* so very strictly: see 26.11, 85.6, 97.8,10, 120.4, etc. Moreover, allowing for the extra final syllables of feminine rhymes, I do not see that—in the sonnets—"Shakespeare allowed himself an extra syllable in his iambic foot"—although, since spelling does not always indicate syncopation or show things like the fact that, as in modern British English, "flowers" is pronounced both dissyllabically and monosyllabically in Shakespeare, there are a good many apparent instances to the contrary, instances that prove to be ocular when one listens to the rhythm of the lines where they appear. One cannot be certain, but the case for dissyllabic pronunciation of "swollowed" ["swol-owed" or "swol-wed"], seems at least as strong as the case against. The sentence on "despised" apparently intends to register disapproval of the editorial spelling "despisèd," which seems to me only a useful signal to the modern reader that his usual pronunciation of the word is inappropriate to the rhythm of line 5 and that the usual Elizabethan pronunciation is called for instead. The assertion that editorial "liberties" make the poem less accurate is true only if one seeks an accuracy calculated to maximize the disorientation of the modern "plain reader," to make his experience of the poem less rather than more like an Elizabethan's.)

"The sound of the poem suffers through re-spelling as well as through alterations in the rhythm made by this use of apostrophes and accents. *Blouddy* was pronounced more like *blue-dy* than *bluddy*; the *ea* of *extreame* and *dreame* sounded like the *ea* in great; and *periurd* was probably pronounced more like *peryurd* than *pergeurd*" (p. 88). (Graves and Riding may well be right about the Elizabethan pronunciations of "bloody"; they could be right about "extreme" and "dream"; their speculations on "perjured" are not provoked by any evidence I know of. In any event, their real problem lies in their assumptions about the usefulness of Renaissance spellings as indicators of Renaissance pronunciations. Such assumptions are foolish in considering English spelling in any period; see Holofernes on "doubt," "debt," "calf," "half," etc. in *LLL* V.i.12ff. They are particularly foolish for Elizabethan texts in which a word may be spelled in several different ways on a single page; see 118.5, note. No Elizabethan writer or printer could have expected his reader to recognize variations in spelling as signs of variations in pronunciation. Surely we cannot assume that Shakespeare's reader heard Q's "bloody" in 50.9 differently than "blouddy" in 129.3. Graves and Riding seem to recommend the retention of "extreame" and "dreame" as guides to the Renaissance pronunciation of those words, but, even if we knew how Shakespeare heard them, Q's "ea" would not indicate the vowel sound of "great" to a modern reader. One might re-spell all of Shakespeare to conform to educated guesses about Shakespeare's dialect; a reading that pronounces "blouddy" as "blue-dy" and "dream" as "drame" and does not also readjust all the other words in the poem will turn out only an affected hybrid. Having chosen a dialect—say that of a Warwickshire boy who has spent some years in London—and having guessed at its sounds, one might then reproduce it casually, i.e. follow the method indicated by Graves and Riding in "blue-dy," which would signal one pair of vowel sounds in London, another in Chicago, and several others in the several parts of South Carolina; one might instead transcribe one's guesses into phonetic symbols, thus making Shakespeare legible only to a few specialists who could make their own transcriptions and who would probably reject one's guesswork in favor of their own. All in all, a modernized text—one that indicates rhythmic necessities with apostrophes and accent marks and uses occasional speculative notes where rhyme, rhythm, or wordplay call a change urgently to our notice—is probably the least unsatisfactory of the unsatisfactory possibilities open to us.)

Graves and Riding give the bulk of their essay to comparing and interpreting the punctuations of the Q text of 129 and the modernized text in *The Oxford Book*. They make two general points, one negative and valid, the other positive and invalid. Their whole discussion is an implicit argument against inflicting logically directive modern punctuation on lines in which a word or phrase participates in more than one syntactical structure, and in which the experience of a modern reader leads him to take punctuation marks as signals of logical limitation—as indicating which of the several relationships in which a word or phrase participates is the "right" one. Any student of the sonnets has probably at some time been dismayed by one or another instance of wanton clarification and wishes that editors would not feel obliged—and that the usual implications of punctuation did not oblige them—to authenticate one syntax in a passage and muffle the others. That discomfort with edited texts probably prompted the Graves-Riding essay and probably also accounts for the respect the essay has commanded. There are a good many points in the collection where two syntactical structures overlap (or, in the phrase of Graves and Riding, interpenetrate one another), and where a modern reader may feel the need of some clarifying and diminishing punctuation, and where most modern editors have provided it (see, for example, 89.7 and note). Unfortunately for the practical value of the Graves-Riding essay, sonnet 129 is neither diminished nor altered by modern punctuation. The text I give here is therefore not materially different from the one Graves and Riding found in *The Oxford Book* and attacked. In 129 modern punctuation gains "sheer facility in reading" and denies a modern reader nothing that Shakespeare's contemporaries would have perceived. The modern punctuation does lessen the probability that a modern reader will attempt to read the Q punctuation as a Cummings-like clue to meaning. In fact, as their justifications for retaining the Q text of 129 develop, Graves and Riding illustrate the dangers inherent in their misplaced textual fidelity by themselves demonstrating the wanton ingenuity that can result when a modern reader brings twentieth-century expectations about spelling and punctuation to an early-seventeenth-century text.

In the midst of their increasingly tortured revelations about sonnet 129, Graves and Riding offer the following persuasive platitude: "Shakespeare did not write in the syntax of prose but in a sensitive poetic flow" (p. 88). Be that as it may, readers read in the syntax of prose. If they did not, some of Shakespeare's and all of E. E. Cummings's poetic devices would fail. Graves and Riding come to grief because they ignore the power of syntactic genre to direct a reader's expectations. For example, they argue that the comma usually inserted after

"bloody" in line 3 distorts the Q text, "Is periurd, murdrous, blouddy full of
blame,": "A comma after *blouddy* makes this a separate characterization and
thus reduces the weight of the whole phrase as rhythmic relief to the string of
adjectives; it probably had the adverbial form of *blouddily*" (p. 88). I am not
sure what the authors mean by "had the adverbial form *blouddily*," but, if they
mean to suggest that Shakespeare could have expected his contemporaries to
understand "bloodily" when they read "blouddy," they are wrong. Even if
there were any evidence of "bloody" ever being used adverbially in the Renaissance, the family likeness between the ordinary adjectival sense of "bloody"
and that of "murd'rous" and "full of blame" will lead—and always would have
led—any reader to take line 3 as "Is" plus a sequence of four separate but equal
adjectival units. A Renaissance reader, brought up on haphazard printing and
casually rhetorical punctuation, must necessarily have been particularly sensitive to syntactic signals and more likely to understand "bloody" as a third entity
in the sequence "perjured, murd'rous, bloody" than modern editors or readers
are. All the retention of Q's "blouddy full of blame" achieves is the need for a
cautionary note reminding the reader that "bloody" does not occur as a British
slang substitute for "very" until the eighteenth century.

   Much the same sort of counterargument may be made to the defense of Q's
"and very wo" in line 11. One could, and Graves and Riding do, squeeze a
meaning out of the phrase; it is not impossible that Shakespeare actually wrote
"and" and not "a"; but it is highly improbable that a seventeenth-century reader
would have done other than modern editors do: "a very woe" makes ready
sense in context; "and very woe" does not. Shakespeare would have been
uncharacteristically foolish to have used the Q phrase, which (unlike the non-
communicative elements in 112.7–8,14 and 113.14), has no apparent witty
allure, and which he would surely have expected his reader to emend in passing.
E. E. Cummings could assume an audience prematurely and permanently
scarred by spelling bees and lessons in punctuation; he could communicate by
deviating from the norms. An Elizabethan reader knew no such norms. Moreover, he was used to correcting printer's errors as he read—much as we do now
when we read the haphazardly proofread "early bird" editions of daily news-
papers; even we do not infer editorial comment when we see a story datelined
"Loss, Angeles."

   Graves and Riding also overestimate the power punctuation has on modern
readers. In line 2 *The Oxford Book* text substitutes a semicolon for Q's comma
after "lust in action"; Graves and Riding complain that the change results in "a
longer rest than Shakespeare [or the printer] gave; it also cuts the idea short of
action instead of keeping *in action* and *till action* together as well as the two
lust's" (p. 88). That makes good sense in terms of handbooks on punctuation,
but I do not think one reads the line differently with a semicolon in it than with
a comma. Graves and Riding also object because "a comma is omitted where
Shakespeare [*sic*] was careful [*sic*] to put one, after *bayt*. With the comma, *On
purpose layd*—though it refers to *bayt*—also looks back to the original idea of
lust; without the comma it merely continues the figure of *bayt*" (p. 88). "On
purpose laid" has double reference whether there is or is not a comma after

"bait"; the line-end pause insures that. Even for modern readers, punctuation does not govern the logic of a sentence except in rare cases where syntax and general context do not dictate the logic. Mistakes in punctuation are usually obvious; if punctuation had the powers Graves and Riding assume for it, would we not misread all the sentences in which we note mispunctuation or in which we simply overlook misplaced commas and missing question marks.

Graves and Riding conclude their essay by citing Quince's prologue to "Piramus and Thisby" (*MND* V.i.108ff.: "If we offend, it is with our good will. / That you should think, we come not to offend, / But with good will. . . . "). The speech prompts Quince's audience of courtiers to make jokes about his bad punctuation. Graves and Riding take the passage as evidence for their thesis. Note, however, that the opening lines of Quince's prologue would have the same immediate effect if the period after "our good will" and the commas after "think" and "offend" were removed:

> If we offend, it is with our good will
> That you should think we come not to offend
> But with good will.

The line-end pause after "our good will," the effect that the resultant reading of the first line has on "That you should think," and the ellipsis between "think" and "we," all operate to an effect that the punctuation merely confirms. If Quince, a writer with a poor ear for syntactic signals, had had another and more talented actor to speak his prologue, the actor would have seen the misdirections in which the syntax leads and compensated with careful phrasing (e.g. by hurrying across the stop at the end of the first line and stressing "But" in the third). If Quince's prologue were not obviously an intentional burlesque, an editor might repunctuate the lines in an inevitably unsuccessful attempt to make them say what Quince ought to be saying in a gracious prologue. Editors do in fact do that with many passages in the sonnets that use gentler versions of the techniques Shakespeare used in making Quince ridiculous; the editors usually fail and have to write notes claiming success. Such editors are the targets for Graves and Riding, but Graves and Riding disable themselves by joining their adversaries in overestimating the power of punctuation and the efficacy of logic over syntactic habit, and in underestimating the power of idiom to lead a reader where he expects it to lead him. Shakespeare's sonnets are full of sentences in which the speaker is like Quince in that the signals inherent in his situation and the signals inherent in his syntax, diction, and idiom are at cross purposes. Editors and critics should avoid trying to strengthen some signals and diminish others, but they do no one a service if they augment Shakespeare's plentiful supply of linguistic crises by fabricating them in poems like 129.

SONNET 130

Compare sonnet 21.

This poem, a winsome trifle, is easily distorted into a solemn critical statement about sonnet conventions. The poem does gently mock the thoughtless,

A literal portrait of a beauty, from *The Extravagant Shepherd* (1654), re-produced by permission of The Huntington Library, San Marino, California. (Reduced from 6⅜ x 8¾ inches.)

mechanical application of the standard Petrarchan metaphors, but the speaker's clown act in taking hyperbolic metaphors literally appears to have no target and no aim but to be funny. (See the accompanying illustration from John Davies's *The Extravagant Shepherd* [1654].) The poem is both a wry reminder that all beloved ladies are something other and something less than they are said to be and, by virtue of the information given in sonnet 127, a comic acknowledgment that *this* beloved lady is to the ladies praised by other poets as those ladies are to heavenly bodies, roses, and goddesses. (Compare lines 1–4 of the Rowlands poem quoted in 144.12, note.)

    1. Compare *2Gent* III.i.88: "her sun-bright eye," and note the proverb "No more like than black is to white" (Tilley, B438). *nothing* in no way, not at all (compare 123.3). *the sun* Compare 49.6, and see 132.5 and note.

    3. *dun* dull grayish-tan. (Note that the line says only that *her breasts are dun* as compared with the flat white of snow; the thrust of the line is at least as much toward mocking inexact hyperbolic metaphor and illustrating the foolishness of taking hyperbole literally as toward depreciating the lady's complexion.)

    4. *wires* = monosyllabic. Comparisons of golden hair to golden wires were traditional and commonplace (see *Variorum* I, 334–35). To modern readers, at home in a world of industrial wiring and wire fences, the simile seems grotesque. To Renaissance writers and readers, the comparison of hair to wires apparently suggested a likeness to threads of beaten gold used in jewelry (compare Bartholomew Griffin, *Fidessa* [1596], 39.1: "My lady's hair is threads of beaten gold," and Thomas Watson, *Hecatompathia* [1582], 7.2: "Her yellowe lockes exceede the beaten goulde"; both poems are good examples of the tradition this sonnet plays on).

    5. *damasked* dappled. (Willen and Reed say: " 'To damask' meant to ornament with a variegated pattern; a damask rose was 'of a color betwixt red and white.' Shakespeare seems to exploit both meanings." Ingram and Redpath point out that a subsidiary train of associations might be of the soft texture of silk damask and of rose petals. *red and white* See 98.9–10, note.

    7. *some* The speaker's careful qualification, his unwillingness to say that all perfumes are sweeter than his mistress' breath, gives the line a tone of wry irony.

    8. *reeks* breathes forth, emanates. (A modern reader must be cautioned against hearing this word as the simple insult it would be if a modern writer had written the line; the primary energy of "to reek" and "a reek" was still in communicating the ideas of emitting vapor and of vapor emitted; the narrow modern senses, "to stink" and "a stench," which focus attention on the *quality* of vapor emitted, do not emerge until the late seventeenth century. However, commentators often over-caution modern readers: both the verb and the noun were already well on their way toward their modern meanings in Shakespeare's time; although "to reek" and "a reek" could be used neutrally [e.g. *Lucrece* 1377: "The red blood reek'd to show the painter's strife," and this *OED* example from 1542: "perfume being poured . . . reeketh into the air"], both words were so consistently used with reference to specifically bad-smelling vapors or in situations that are otherwise repulsive that *reeks* here would have carried suggestions of evil-smelling breath. Compare *Cymb* I.ii.1–3—"Sir, I would advise you to shift a shirt; the violence of action hath made you reek as a sacrifice"—or any

other of the twelve uses of "reek" and related words in the plays; also note the contexts of *OED*'s examples before 1700.)

9. *yet well I know*   Note the substantively irrelevant echo of 129.13; see also *well thou know'st* in 131.3.

11. *go*   walk (as in 51.14 and *Lear* I.iv.120: "Ride more than thou goest"). Tucker notes that "to 'walk like a goddess' is at least as old as Virgil's *vera incessu patuit dea* [in her gait she was revealed as a true goddess]," the conclusion of one of the most echoed passages in Renaissance literature of compliment, *Aeneid* I.326–405.

13. *by heav'n*   = a casual intensifying oath. Note, however, that it is a blunt country cousin to the rhetorical gestures of elegant courtly poets who use *heav'n itself for ornament* (21.3); it undercuts the speaker's rhetorical self-righteousness and prepares for the compliment it introduces. (Shakespeare may have expected particularly keen readers to hear an ironic, logically inconsistent pun on "put alongside heaven," "compared with heaven.") *rare*   splendid, marvelous (with a play on "unusual").

14. *she*   woman (as in *TN* I.v.225: "Lady, you are the cruell'st she alive"). *false*   (1) inappropriate, erroneously chosen, misused; (2) artificial; (3) lying; (4) insincere. *compare*   comparison (with a possible play on "a compare" meaning "a compeer," "an equal"; see 21.5, note).

SONNET 131

1. *so as*   just as. (Note the complicatedly chiasmic echo of *Thou art as* and the last syllable of *tyrannous* in *so as thou art*.)

2. *proudly*   Syntactically, *proudly* modifies, and thus to a degree personifies, *beauties*; the traditional behavior pattern—the exhibition of "daunger" by the beloved lady—draws *proudly* to modifying *cruel* by synesis. *cruel*   = dissyllabic; see 129.4, note.

3. *well thou know'st*   See 130.9, note. *dear*   (1) tender, loving (see 31.6, note), tenderly, lovingly, fondly (for *dear* used adverbially, see 115.2); (2) earnest (31.6, note), earnestly, eagerly; (3) painful (compare *RII* I.iii.151: "thy dear exile"), painfully, sorely. Ingram and Redpath point out that the adverbial action of *dear* carries suggestions of "at a high price"; it thus suggests that the speaker's *doting* costs him dearly in material or spiritual expense or in both (compare *MofV* III.ii.315: "Since you are dear bought, I will love you dear"). *doting*   (1) infatuated; (2) foolish, addled.

4. *most precious*   = an echo of *dear* in line 3, but of a sense that *dear* does not quite carry there.

5. *in good faith*   (1) indeed, verily (a mere interjection indicating the speaker's intensity); (2) speaking in good faith (an adverbial phrase modifying *say* and indicating that the sayers speak the truth). (Many editors set the phrase off in commas, but its double action occurs in any case; compare 141.1. Moreover, since this phrase leads into *some say, in good faith* can momentarily register as a direct quotation of a gossiping remark about the beloved: " 'In good faith,' some say . . . . ")

5–6. *some say that thee behold* / *Thy face hath* . . .   some who behold you say [that] your face has . . . . (The gloss reflects the logic of the completed clause. However, the standard phrase *some say that* momentarily signals an indirect quotation to follow; what does follow, *thee behold*, makes it impossible to read *that* as a conjunction and requires a reader to understand *that* as a pronoun meaning "who"; then line 6 further complicates the reader's act of preception by in fact presenting indirect discourse—discourse to which the conjunction *that* is necessary but in which it is only elliptically present. Compare 15.1–3.)

8. *to myself alone* (1) to myself in private; (2) only to myself.

9. *to be sure* (1) in order to make certain [that], in order to verify [that]; (2) to prove [that], to testify [that]; and, although *OED*'s earliest example of the phrase as an interjection is from 1657, perhaps, (3) indeed, of course, certainly (compare *in good faith* in line 5). *that is not false I swear* (1) that which I swear is true; (2) I swear that [i.e. *thy face*] is not: (a) a cosmetic illusion, (b) insincere in its expressions, a mask to hide your actual thoughts, feelings, and intents. In addition to the various permutations possible from combining the readings already cited for the two half-lines, line 9 can relate to the lines that follow as "And, to be sure that is not false, I swear [that] / A thousand groans . . . do witness bear [that] . . . ."

10. *but* merely, as a result of merely. *but thinking* The syntax makes the *groans* the thinkers (and thus personifies them); the logic of the situation dictates that the speaker be thinker (by synesis): "I have only to think on thy face, and a thousand groans . . . do witness bear."

11. *One on another's neck* one after another in quick succession (but colored by an image of vaguely personified groans weeping on one another's shoulders); Tilley (M1013) heard an echo of the proverb "One misfortune comes on the neck of another."

12. *Thy black* (1) your blackness (i.e. your dark complexion), your ugliness (see 127.1, note), and your moral foulness; and perhaps (2) your dark-complexioned face, your ugly face (taking *black* as a parodic nonce use made on the model of "fair" meaning "fair face"—as it apparently does in *AYLI* III.ii. 84–85: "Let no face be kept in mind / But the fair of Rosalinde"). *is fairest* (1) is thought to be most beautiful (compare the similar play on "fair" meaning beautiful and "fair" meaning "light-complexioned" in 127.1; (2) is thought to be purest, most spotless. *in my judgement's place* (1) in my mind, in the place where my judgment resides; (2) in my personal court of justice (Willen and Reed call attention to the courtroom metaphor generated by the context of *swear* and *witness* in lines 9 and 11; they cite *R&J* I.i.100: "old Free-town, our common judgment-place"). (The phrase also carries a self-mocking echo of "in place of my judgment" and suggests "which has displaced my judgment and now acts in its stead.")

13. *In nothing* in no respect, in no way (see 130.1; the conjunction of *In* and *nothing* could momentarily have bawdy overtones; see 20.12, note).

14. *this slander* i.e. that she is not fair, the slander reported in line 6—not the moral corruption that line 13 grants as an obvious but minor detail. *as I think* I believe, I venture to say (the tone of modest, responsible, respectful

diffidence that the speaker affects by this phrase is so at odds with the substance of the charge casually levelled in line 13 that it transforms the whole couplet into a single graceful razor stroke—one that is especially damaging because the speaker's tone assumes that his victim's values are the ones on which his supposedly comforting explanation rests and that she hasn't the moral sensitivity to notice that she has been cut apart).

SONNET 132

Note the expression "to say black is [someone's] eye," meaning "to find fault with." *OED* gives this from 1528: "They eate their belies full . . . And none sayth blacke is his eye."
Compare *LLL* IV.iii.217–77.
1. *as* as if. *pitying* = dissyllabic, by syncopation.
1,2. *eyes, heart* See 141.1–14, note.
2. The entire line is parenthetical; it modifies either *Thine eyes* or *I* ("even though I know . . .") or both. *heart* (1) inclination, attitude, feelings [toward me] (compare *V&A* 378: "Adonis' heart hath made mine hard"); (2) heart (i.e. that bodily organ as opposed to the eyes; see lines 10–12). *torment* to torment (= an elliptical form of the infinitive). From 1860 until recently, most editors assumed a misprint and substituted "torments"; although there is no evidence of a misprint, they may have been right.
4. *Looking with pretty ruth* This phrase capsules the quatrain's underlying common denominator in ideas of "looking"—the lady's eyes look (appear) as they do because of what they see when they look upon (observe) the speaker's pain. *ruth* pity. (Note the complex phonetic interrelation of the second syllable of *pretty*, *ruth*, and "truth" with *truly* in line 5; compare the effects discussed in 141.13–14, note.)
5,7. *heav'n, ev'n* See 15.6, note; *in the ev'n* ("in the evening"), may have sounded something like "in the in."
5. *morning* morning (with a play on "mourning"; the pun is enhanced by the word's phonetic echo of the present participles in each of the four preceding lines). *sun of heav'n* sun in the sky, heavenly sun (but compare 33.14 and note). Here, as in 130.1, the sun is presented as an emblem of perfect beauty—perfect golden beauty, fairness, lightness, blondness; see the following note.
6. *Better becomes* is more becoming to. *the gray cheeks* The line describes the first light of dawn in a metaphysical metaphor: the sun gives color to the gray clouds as it gives color to the cheeks of a pallid person; the wit of the conceit is increased by the fact that, although the metaphor clearly presents the sun as a cosmetically desirable means of returning "the roses" to pallid cheeks, it also necessarily contains a reminder of the other and opposite attitude toward the effects of sunlight on skin: Renaissance ladies greatly feared both being sunburned and being suntanned (probably because a suntan could cause them to be mistaken for field workers rather than ladies of leisure); a suntan diminished the fairness (lightness) of their skins and therefore their fairness (beauty) as well; the dark lady's brunette complexion is by nature what fair ladies feared theirs

would become from exposure to the sun. See *Much Ado* II.i.287, *HV* V.ii.150, *T&C* I.iii.282–83 ("The Grecian dames are sunburnt and not worth / The splinter of a lance"), and Morocco's speech, *MofV* II.i.1–3 ("Mislike me not for my complexion, / The shadowed livery of the burnish'd sun, / To whom I am a neighbour, and near bred"). A double view of the sun—as an emblem of beauty and as the destroyer of beauty—goes back at least to Song of Songs (the greatest single source of the furniture of courtly love conventions): 6:9 (6:10 in AV) says "Who is she that loketh forthe as the morning, faire as the moone, pure as the sunne . . ."; 1:4–5 say "I am blacke . . . but comelie. . . . / Regarde ye me not because I am blacke: for the sunne hathe loked upon me. The sonnes of my mother were angrie against me: thei made me the keper of the vines. . . ." *the east* Q's "th' East" testifies to the casualness of Renaissance printing and punctuation; dissyllabic pronunciation is necessary and inevitable here; see 129.1–14, note.

7. *full* bright? intensely brilliant? (*OED* gives examples like this one from 1509: "It never loketh on a man with eyes full [i.e. at full force], But ever his heart by furious wrath is dull"—but no example of *full* specifically indicating intenseness of light or color before the mid–seventeenth century. Shakespeare may have chosen to use the word because it sounds like—though it is unrelated to—two contrasting Latin words: *fulgens*, "shining" [see the English "effulgent"] and *fuligineus*, "like soot," "sooty" [see the English "fuliginous" and "fuliginousness"]; see the following note.) *that full star* Hesperus, the evening star (i.e. the planet Venus visible in the western sky just after sunset. Shakespeare may be playing with the fact that Venus is also the morning star. Quatrain 2 presents one half of each of two parallel pairs of opposites: sun-moon and morning star–evening star; lines 5 and 6 say of the morning sun what might also be said of the morning star; *full* would make immediate sense with "moon," but the moon rises in the east).

8. *sober* somber in hue, dull-colored (as in *Shrew* I.ii.129: "disguis'd in sober robes." Note *put on black* in line 3, *gray* in line 6, and *suit* in line 12).

7–8. Milton may have had these lines in his mind when he wrote *PL* IV.355 and 598–99.

9–12. Although the urgent parallelism between lines 5 and 6 (two lines on morning light in the east) and lines 7 and 8 (two lines on evening light in the west) underscores the identity of quatrain 2 as a unit, its syntax runs right across the stop phonetically implied by the completion in *west* of the quatrain rhyme pattern. The syntactic unit begun in line 5 does not conclude until the end of line 9, and the gesture of new beginning that often marks the opening of third quatrains occurs instead at the beginning of line 10: *O let it then*. A reader's effective sense of quatrain 3 as a unit is thus reduced; the formal pattern of three quatrains and a couplet (4, 4, 4, 2) is nearly overwhelmed by the pattern of logical-syntactical units (4, 5, 3, 2). However, the formal identity of quatrain 3 is quietly strengthened in a line-by-line echo of elements in quatrain 1: the word that indicates the ostensible topic of the poem, *eyes*, occurs twice, first in line 1, then in line 9; *heart* occurs in lines 2 and 10; line 3 introduces the idea of mourning, and line 11 uses it twice; line 4, on *ruth*, alliterates in *p* in its fourth, eighth, and tenth syllables; line 12, on *pity*, alliterates in *p* in its fourth and tenth syllables.

9. *mourning*   (1) black-hued; (2) grieving (with a play on *morning*).

10. *as well*   (1) just as properly, just as suitably; (2) also, in addition.   *beseem*   become (lines 6 and 9), grace, be a grace to (line 11), fit, suit (line 12).

11. *To mourn for*   (1) to grieve for, to pity; (2) to wear mourning for.   *mourning doth thee grace*   (1) wearing black gives you grace (taking *grace* as a noun and understanding the *doth* construction as it is understood in *Doth . . . glory to* in line 8; the echo of line 8 continues and further complicates the two artful equations in quatrain 2 [that between "mourning" and "morning" and that between "morning" and "evening"], by suggesting a play on "mourning" and "evening"). (2) wearing black does grace you, graces you, becomes you, beseems you (taking *grace* as a verb; the phrase thus echoes *morning sun . . . becomes* in the first half of quatrain 2).

12. *suit . . . like*   (1) dress likewise, clothe the same way; (2) likewise dress, also clothe; (3) match, make alike, make consistent.

10–12. At the end of line 10 *heart* seems to be metaphoric: "inclination" (particularly "inclination to feel love and/or pity"). As the lines progress, the literal meaning *heart* had in line 2 reemerges. The lines ask that the lady take pity on the lovelorn speaker; the vehicle for his appeal is an archly ingenious bit of courtly fancywork—an argument that the lady's heart should wear mourning as her dark eyes have been said to do. This typically contrived sonneteer's conceit is undercut by its typically Shakespearian contrary implications: the lines subsume a statement that it is consistent with the lady's "parts" (see 69.1), her qualities, her nature—i.e. her temperament (*complexion*), appearance (*complexion*), coloring (*complexion*)—that she have a black heart (see 131.13), that she be wicked to the core. (For *heart* meaning "the core," "the essence," see *MWW* II.ii.202 and *Tim* I.i.276–77: "He outgoes / The very heart of kindness." For *black* meaning "wicked," see *HVIII* I.iii.57–58: "No doubt he's noble / He had a black mouth that said other of him.")

13. See 127.1, note.   *Then*   in that case—i.e. both "therefore" and "when that happens."   *herself*   This word personifies *beauty* as "the goddess beauty," "beauty personified"; many editors anticipate the action of *herself* by capitalizing *beauty*.

14. *And all they foul that*   and [that] all those are foul who.   *foul*   ugly (playing on the fact that *foul* and *black* were both synonyms for "ugly"; since both words are also synonyms for "wicked," their conjunction continues the insulting undercurrent in lines 10–12).   *complexion*   (1) coloring (the modern sense); (2) appearance (general appearance and, specifically, appearance as it expresses a person's mood, attitude, or temperament; compare *V&A* 215: "Thou art no man, though of a man's complexion," *Measure* II.iv.129: "We [women] are soft as our complexions are," and *WT* I.ii.381: "Your chang'd complexions are to me a mirror"); (3) disposition, humor (see 45.8, note), temperament, nature (compare *Much Ado* II.i.264: "and something of that jealous complexion" [punning on "yellow-skinned"]; *OED* gives this from 1535: "Here mayst thou se of what nature and complexion [he] is").

SONNET 133

Compare the apparent situation in 133 and 134 with those in 40–42 and 144.

This sonnet continues the theme of hearts and eyes from 132; see 133.1–2,5, 9–11. Other themes and the topic of this sonnet continue in 134. See 141.1–14, note.

Some of the wit of this poem consists in the use of traditional courtly love metaphors phrased so as to evoke the connotations and implications they have outside the convention—e.g. the notion of the lover as the beloved's "servant" is traditional (see 57.8); so is the idea of being one's lady's slave; but no special context can neutralize the ugly connotations of *slavery* (line 4); the tribulations of an infatuated lover can be casually compared to torture, the beloved to a torturer or jailer; the lover can be a "prisoner of love"; but here the metaphor is so complete, so urgent, so detailed, and so flatly matter-of-fact (*jail*, line 12), that the lovers, their situation, and their behavior become grotesque. (Compare Sidney's comparable experiment in literalness in *A&S* 2—where "love's wound" seems to become gangrenous and "love's slave" has the contemptible qualities of slaves generally—and the change in connotations that occurs in the course of the sequence *serving thee, heart's slave,* and *vassal wretch* in 141.10–12.)

1. *Beshrew* fie upon, curse. *that heart* See 132.2 and 131. *Heart* and "art" may have been indistinguishable in pronunciation (see 24.13–14, note); for a Renaissance reader this line may have included by-references to the lady's artfulness and the speaker's art, his poems (also see *my poor heart* and *my heart* in lines 10 and 11).

1–2. *groan / For* groan because of. (The gloss is that demanded by *that deep wound*; momentarily, however, the "groan for" construction implies the equally pertinent meaning "groan to have," "sigh after," and seems to be moving toward something on the order of "groan for her," "groan to have that heart," "groan to have her"; compare *R&J* II.Prologue.3: "That fair for which love groan'd for" and the similar use of *for* in *JC* III.i.276: "groaning for burial.") The idea of the lover wounded by Cupid's arrow groaning in pain was a stock courtly love conceit (see Hamlet's comment, II.ii.119–21: "O dear Ophelia, I am ill at these numbers. / I have not art to reckon my groans; but that I love thee best, . . . believe it"). Here there is some wit in the fact that a heart is both weapon and target.

2. *that deep wound it gives* the serious injury it inflicts (with a play on *wound* used to describe the female sexual organ [as in *PP* 9.12–14: " 'See in my thigh,' quoth she 'here was the sore.' / She showed hers; he saw more wounds than one, / And blushing fled, and left her all alone"], and therefore with corresponding play on the literal sense of *deep* and on *gives* meaning "offers," "surrenders," "makes available"). *my friend* Most readers have quite reasonably assumed that this sonnet and 134 refer to the same friend, lady, and events alluded to in 40–42. (See also 144.) Seymour-Smith suggests "that Shakespeare wrote these at roughly the same time as 40–42, but, because they were addressed to his Mistress and not to the Friend, as 40–42 are, he included them with the other sonnets of

the series 127–152. This may not make chronological sense, but it makes good poetic sense. (There is no reason to suppose that *all* the sonnets to his Mistress were not written contemporaneously with the ones to the Friend; when Shakespeare had finished writing sonnets, he divided those that dealt primarily with the Friend from those that dealt primarily with the Mistress.)" There is, however, no solid evidence for supposing that all these sonnets *were* written at the same time; we can guess, but we cannot know.

3. *alone*   only (with a latterly emerging suggestion of "by yourself," "without help").

4. *But . . . my . . . friend must be*   without my friend becoming, without my friend being forced to be (see *OED*, s.v. *but*, 14).   *slave to slavery*   (1) enslaved (taking the phrase as a tautology for emphasis); (2) addicted to a degrading condition; (3) the slave of a slave, subservient to a "slave," a base and contemptible person (i.e. the speaker, the lady, or both; for *slave* meaning "worthless person," see *Ham* II.ii.543: "O, what a rogue and peasant slave am I"; Tucker justified understanding *slavery* as "one who is a slave" by analogy to "antiquity" used to mean "an aged person," "retention" used to mean "prison," and "nativity" used to mean "one who is born"); (4) bound to drudgery, compelled to hard labor (perhaps sexual slaving at the call of the lady's lust). The phrase plays on the traditional hyperbole by which lovers swore themselves their ladies' willing slaves.

5–6. These lines contain a muted echo and continuation of the idea of slavery in line 4; "taken from" suggests being carried off into slavery, and *engrossed*—a metaphoric extension of a business term meaning "monopolized" or "bought up wholesale"—colors the lines with suggestions of human beings degraded to the status of commodities.

2,5. Note the wit in the conjunction of *gives* and *hath taken*; "give" and "take," exact antonyms in their simple senses, are here used to virtually synonymous effect.

5. *myself*   (1) possession of myself, being my own man (compare the stock lover's expression "I am yours"); (2) my true nature, my normal state of sanity (see 13.1, note); (3) my beloved friend, *my next self* (for the idea of a friend as another self, see sonnet 39 and 36, headnote).   *thy cruel eye*   The context of *Me* and *myself* can activate a syntactically irrelevant pun on "I" (compare 136.2, note).   *cruel*   = dissyllabic; see 129.4, note.

6. *harder*   more strictly, more severely.   *engrossed*   (1) taken exclusive possession of; and, perhaps, (2) made brutish, debased (in *A Treatie of Humane Learning* [probably written about 1605, perhaps revised later, and published posthumously in 1633], Fulke Greville wrote of notions that "embody and engrosse the minde, / To make the nobler serve the baser kind"; Greville's sense of "engross" developed from its use meaning "to increase the size of," "to make fat or thick"; there may be some phallic joking in *harder hast engrossed*. Q gives "ingrossed"; note *in* in lines 9, 12, 13, and 14; for a justification of the modern spelling, see 37.7, note).

7. *myself*   me (with complicating echoes of the senses *myself* and *my next self* have at the same metrical point in the two preceding lines).

8. *A torment* = an ellipsis for "It is a torment." *crossed* thwarted (as in 90.2). The line has casual overtones of the hyperbolic proposition that the speaker's torment is more terrible than the crucifixion of Christ.

9. *Prison* imprison (an imperative). *steel* (1) steel-like, hard, unfeeling; (2) made of steel (in a sense that supplements the prison metaphor with an image of steel bars). *ward* (1) prison cell; (2) guard, custody; (3) guard, protection.

10. (1) "But in that case permit my heart to bail my friend's heart" (the sense to which the line is subsequently restricted by *Whoe'er keeps me* in line 11); (2) "But at that time [i.e. after you have imprisoned my heart] permit my friend's heart to bail mine" (a sense only temporarily present but an appropriate extension of the implied logic of lines 3 and 4: if she has the friend, she should release the speaker; many editors vouch for the presence of this temporary sense by urgently denying it in notes instructing readers to stress *my*; compare 134.13–14). *poor* (1) insignificant, unworthy, paltry; (2) unfortunate, pathetic, injured (lines 2,3,8), and therefore worthy of pity (with a play on "impecunious"). *bail* (1) bail out, redeem (the most usual sense of the word— a sense consistent with the speaker's outrage at his friend's involvement with the lady and his sense of guilt at being the cause of the friend's enthrallment, and a sense enhanced by a witty echo of the legal expression "to let to bail" meaning "to admit to bail" [*OED*, s.v. "let," 10b, gives this from 1581: "Justices of the Peace might . . . have letten to baile such persons as were indited of Felonie"]); (2) confine, imprison, guard (the sense suggested by the apparent logic of the following line; *OED* exemplifies the usage with the present line; see also "to bail" meaning "to hoop with metal bands," exemplified in this from 1594: "Close soldered, and bailde about with yron"; Willen and Reed cite the noun in *FQ* VII.vi.49: "entrapped him . . . within their baile").

11. *Whoe'er* no matter who, whosoever. *keeps* (1) keeps possession of (i.e. retains the affection of); (2) imprisons, holds captive (as in Acts 28:16: "Paul was suffred to dwel by him self with a souldier that kept him"; compare 126.7). *let my heart be* (1) permit my heart to be, please allow my heart to act as (the same kind of "let" construction as *let . . . bail* in line 10); (2) I hope that my heart may be, may my heart be (expressing vague aspiration); (3) if my heart is, given that my heart is (for similar "let" constructions, see 84.9–12, *Measure* III.ii.134: "Let him be but testimonied . . . and he shall appear . . . a scholar," and *RII* I.i.58–60: "Setting aside his . . . royalty, / And let him be no kinsman to my liege, / I do defy him"). The third reading is preserved for a modern reader only by retaining the comma with which Q closes line 11. Most editors substitute a full stop. Both punctuations can inhibit the syntactical flux of lines 11 and 12 as read by a punctuation-sensitive modern reader; since the line-end pause does some of the work of a full stop, I feel that one loses least by retaining Q's comma. *my heart* Although the metrical stresses of *my poor heart* in line 10 are doubtful, the rhythm of this line puts definite stress on *my*, thus indicating "*my heart* as opposed to *my friend's heart* and/or *that heart* [in line 1]." See 24.13–14, note (on the possible implications inherent in the pronunciation of *heart*). *guard* (1) jail cell, place of imprisonment, ward (*OED*, 17a, gives a 1613 example of *guard* meaning "guard-house," but a reader's

sense that the word refers to place derives largely from context); (2) jailer, custodian, warder; (3) protector, defender.

10–11. In addition to the relatively straightforward plays on *let* and *bail* in these lines, *let*, which was used to mean "forsake," presents a logically and syntactically incidental echo of line 7; "bale" (orthographically undistinguished from *bail*—see the Q spelling), meaning "pain," "grief," "torment," presents a logically and syntactically incidental echo of lines 1–2 and 8; and, in this context of forcible restraint, "to let" meaning "to obstruct," "to hinder" (as in *Ham* I.iv.85: "I'll make a ghost of him that lets me"), can also spill into a reader's mind and add one more element to the verbal complexities and confusions by which the complex and confused three-way love affair is both reported and imitated.

12. *then* in that case (for fear of hurting the friend, who is enclosed within the speaker and over whom the lady has no jurisdiction). *use rigor* employ harshness, be severe. (*Rigor*, a legal term, was common in phrases like "rigor of the law" meaning strict enforcement of a law; *OED* gives this from 1552: "to use agains thame the rigour of jugement." In the present context of bawdy allusions to the interaction of male and female sex organs, *rigor* can bring to mind "rig"—a "slut," a "whore" [*OED*, 4—compare "riggish" in *A&C* II.ii.244], "to rig"—"to have sexually," "to use sexually" [*OED* gives this from 1619: [he] shall reap that Maiden-head . . . he shall rig and top her"], and, perhaps, the literal sense of *rigor*, "stiffness," "rigidity.") *in* with respect to (with a play on *in* indicating place). *in my jail* in my imprisonment, in your treatment of me while I am your prisoner (with plays on "in the place where I am confined" and "within the place where I confine my friend").

13. *pent in thee* imprisoned in you (i.e. my heart is yours, my heart lives in your body—see 22.5–7; but with a play on the literal meaning). *being* = monosyllabic (as in 50.8).

14. *Perforce* of necessity. *and* and so is. *all that is in me* everything that belongs to me (i.e. the friend's affection [heart], which belongs to the speaker [is lodged in the speaker's bosom]; but with a joking allusion to the total commitment and surrender of spiritual power and physical resources in sexual emission [see 26.1–14, note]).

SONNET 134

This sonnet continues from 133.

1–2. Ingram and Redpath point out that these lines are a logically complete unit, a self-sufficient assertion that can be read as a modern reader would read it if it ended in a period or colon; Q's comma after *will* invites us to understand *now* as "now that" and the whole clause as subordinate.

2. *mortgaged* Compare *bail* (sense (1)) in 133.10. *thy will* (1) your wishes, your control; (2) your lust, your carnal appetite (compare *Oth* III.iii.34–36: "His soul is so enfetter'd to her love / That she may . . . do what she list, / Even as her appetite shall play the god"). *If* the speaker's friend is not a literary fabrication, and *if* his first name was William, *then* an informed reader would

have heard "your William," "the William who is thine," in *thy will*. See 135, headnote.

3. *so*   (1) so long as, provided that (as in 70.5); (2) in order that (note *So* in a third sense in line 1).   *that other mine*   that other self of mine, that other myself (see 133.5 and note).

4. *restore to be*   restore for the purpose of functioning as (momentarily, however, the idiom "restore to," verb-plus-preposition, may impinge on a reader's consciousness and implant a half-formed idea of "returning *that other mine* to me" in his experience of the line; one early editor was so impressed by the syntactic signal of *restore to* that he changed *be* to "me" [*Variorum* I, 342]). *still*   See 55.10, note.

5. *nor he will not be free*   (1) nor does he wish to—is he willing to—have his liberty; (2) nor shall he have his liberty (with substantively irrelevant echoes of the other senses of *will* and with plays on other senses of *be free*, i.e. "be generous," "be noble," and "be licentious"—senses retroactively generated and also contradicted by *he is kind* in line 6; see 4.4 and note, the various uses of *free* in *Oth* II.iii.326–31, and *Oth* II.iii.308: "She is of so free, so kind, so apt, so blessed a disposition, she holds it a vice in her goodness not to do more than she is requested"). The double negative is for emphasis; see 86.11, note.

6. *covetous*   grasping, greedy, and (as a result of its alliteratively underscored contrast with *kind*) selfish.   *kind*   (1) benevolent, considerate, kindly; (2) generous (as in the passage from *Othello* in the preceding note); (3) noble, of good family (*OED*, 4); (4) as his nature makes him (i.e. a healthy male—see 41.7–8; *OED* exemplifies *kind* meaning "natural," "keeping to nature" with this from 1579: "It is but kinde for a Cockes head to breede a Combe"; compare *Much Ado* I.i.22: "A kind overflow of kindness"). See 105.5.

7–8. These lines may be read as a new and independent assertion and as specific evidence that the friend is as generous as line 6 says he is.

7. *surety-like*   (1) like a guarantor, like someone who goes bail; (2) as bail, as a hostage (compare *Temp* I.ii.475: "I'll be his surety" and *2HVI* V.i.115–16: "The . . . boys . . . / Shall be the surety for their . . . father").   *write for me* (1) pledge himself on my behalf (i.e. sign his name to a pledge to make good if I defaulted—the sense indicated by the metaphor of bail); (2) act on my behalf (i.e. act as my agent in wooing; compare Don Pedro in *Much Ado* I.i.285–89:

> . . . in her bosom I'll unclasp my heart,
> And take her hearing prisoner with the force
> And strong encounter of my amorous tale.
> Then, after, to her father will I break;
> And the conclusion is she shall be thine.);

(3) use his pen in place of me, take my place in making physical love to my lady (see Hulme, pp. 135–37 [on "pen"] and 78.3,7,11, note).

8. *Under*   (1) under the terms of; (2) at the bottom of, at the place where one puts one's signature to a document (with general sexual implications).   *that bond*   (1) the bond between you and me; (2) the bond between him and me (with

a play on "the bonds that bind me, make me your prisoner"—in all relevant senses; see 133.13–14). *as fast* as tightly.

9. "You will demand everything to which your beauty entitles you." "You will exact the full penalty of the bond by which your beauty holds everything I have as surety." As used here, *statute* is a technical term indicating a bond by which a creditor was empowered to seize the property of a defaulting debtor (*OED*, 4a); "to take the statute" is an ellipsis for "to take all that is permitted by a statute"; compare Shylock's "I'll have my bond" (*MofV* III.iii.3,12,17), and Portia's injunction "Take then thy bond, take thou thy pound of flesh" (IV.i. 303). (Note the related legal metaphor in 133.12.) *statute of thy beauty* This phrase conflates two complexly derived ideas: (1) the statute—the bond—which your beauty is (the courtly compliment depends on a wittily illegitimate equation of *statute* and *bond* [which, as terms meaning "a formal legal agreement," are interchangeable—although the other meanings of the words are *not* interchangeable; compare the example from *TN* discussed in 109.6–7, note]; a *statute* is a *bond*, and *bond* describes anything that "binds"; the lady's beauty binds men to her service, is a *bond* upon them; therefore, in misplaced logic, her beauty is a *statute* [compare *that weight* in 50.6]); (2) the legal limit your beauty allows you to take (this sense, largely sustained by the logical necessities of its context [i.e. largely sustained by synesis], derives from understanding *statute*—the agreement which sets the limits of liability—as if it meant only "the full amount owed" [compare Shylock's use of "my bond" to mean "what is allowed me under the terms of my bond"], and understanding *of thy beauty* as if it were "under the terms of your beauty"—"under the terms of the bond that your beauty is").

Line 9 also anticipates the line that follows: the "take . . . of" construction and the idea of maximization give "take the statute of thy beauty" suggestions of "use your beauty to the utmost"—"take full advantage of it," "make full use of it." The words *usurer* and *use* in line 10 thus function rather like ideational puns on "take the statute of." (An ideational pun is an interplay between an idea and a word that could—but does not—express or relate to that idea. See 43, headnote and 101.10, note. Compare *shall* and *well* in 14.7; *in* in 15 and *out* in 15.8; *Sets* in 15.10 and the sunset in 15.5–9, 12; *before* and its context in 15.10; *see* and the sea in 56.7, 9–12; *arrest* and *stay* in 74.1,4; *wilfully* and *shallowest* in 80.8,9; *earth* and *world* in 81.2,6,7; *him* and *rhyme* in 107.11; *wills count* in 121.8; and *Shall will* in 135.7 [the notes on 90.6 and 141.13–14 describe related effects].)

10. *usurer* moneylender (with a play on "whore"; see 2.9, note). *all* See 26.1–14, note. *to use* (1) to be made use of; (2) to be made sexual use of; (3) for profit.

11. *sue* (1) bring a lawsuit against; (2) pursue, chase (as in *FQ* VI.ix.2: "Sewing the Blatant beast"); (3) be a suitor to, woo (as in *LLL* III.i.179: "I love, I sue, I seek a wife"); compare the pun in *LLL* V.ii.426–27: "how can this be true, / That you stand forfeit, being those that sue?" *came debtor* who became a debtor, who came to be a debtor.

12. *I lose* (1) I am bereft of; (2) I let loose, I free (see line 5 and notes; on Q's spelling, see 18.10 and 88.8, notes. *my . . . abuse* (1) the injury done to me—

by the lady and also by the friend; (2) the injury I have done, my misuse of a
friend—by having him woo for me and thus become ensnared (also see 121.10,
note—on "to abuse" meaning "to seduce" or "to ravish"). *unkind* See *kind*
in line 6 and notes.

14. *He pays the whole* (1) he pays the entire debt; (2) he is of such value that
he is worth as much as (or more than) is owed by both of us together. Following
upon the barrage of bawdy jokes in this poem, a reader may well hear a play on
"hole." As a secondary sense of the phrase, Ingram and Redpath give "He is
giving you what ought to be full carnal satisfaction." *yet* (1) even so, nonetheless; (2) even now, as yet, now as before. *free* See *free* in line 5 and note.

SONNET 135

Sonnets 135 and 136 are festivals of verbal ingenuity in which much of the fun
derives from the grotesque lengths the speaker goes to for a maximum number
and concentration of puns on *will*. (Q emphasizes the word by capitalizing and
italicizing it in ten of its twenty occurrences in the two sonnets; I have not
followed suit because a modern reader's susceptibility to orthographical signals
is so acute that Q's capitals and italics can make the poems sound even more
archly precious than they were for Shakespeare's reader; a modern reader may
also incline toward the folly of trying to dredge meaning from Q's selectivity in
singling out some *will*'s typographically and printing others in ordinary roman.
See the final note to sonnet 129.)

All the following uses of *will* come into play during the two poems: (a) "one's
will," what one wishes to have or do (see the play on *wish* and *will* in 135.1—
where *thy will* implies wilfulness: "your own way"); (b) the auxiliary verb
indicating futurity and/or purpose (see 134.5 and Abbott, par. 316); (c) lust,
carnal desire (as in 57.13, 134.2. 143.13. and *Lucrece* 243, 247, etc.); (d) the male
sex organ (e.g. *hide my will* in 135.6; Hulme [p. 96] cites the Q and F version of
T&C I.ii.82, where Pandarus is saying that Troilus is a better man than Hector:
"Hector shall not have his will this year"; see also *AW* IV.iii.14: "this night he
fleshes his will in the spoil of her honour"); (e) the female sex organ (e.g. *whose
will is large and spacious* in 135.5, *thine* in 135.6, and *it* in 136.6; compare the pun
on sense (c) in *Lear* IV.vi.271: "O indistinguish'd [i.e. limitless] space of woman's
will"; Ingram and Redpath note "the common cant sense of the *membrum
pudendum*, male or female" and that "commentators seem to have been innocent
or reticent in respect of this meaning,for which Wright's *Dictionary of Obsolete
and Provincial English*, and Partridge's *Dictionary of Slang . . .* offer any
authority necessary"; also note the first pun in the antifeminist proverb "Women
are born in Wiltshire, brought up in Cumberland, lead their lives in Bedford-
shire, bring their husbands to Buckingham, and die in Shrewsbury" [Tilley,
W699]; Tilley did not quite understand the "Wiltshire" pun, which is represen-
tative of a once flourishing minor genre; compare the "Kent" / "cunt" pun in
The Roaring Girl, II.i.336, and "She lost her maidenhead in Brecknockshire
[i.e. Break-cunt-shire]" in *A Chaste Maid in Cheapside*, I.i.117 [for "noc"—

"con" spelled backwards—meaning "cunt," see Cotgrave]); (f) William (i.e. an abbreviation of the poet's first name—as in 57.13, 80.8, and 143.13). Many commentators have speculated that William was also the name of the speaker's friend and/or of the dark lady's husband. Those speculations (and some that are farther fetched) grow not from the implications of the lines but from a fortunate correspondence between a *potential* reference in the lines and an independently concocted "key" to the identities of the friend or the lady (see Appendix 1). For example, those of the speculative biographers whose hearts are set on having William Herbert or Willie Hughes or William Hall be the friend hear themselves echoed in *thy will* in 134.2 and 136.2; those who postulate a husband for the dark lady can take the same pair of *thy will*'s as evidence that the husband existed *and* that his name was William; if read as an inventory of "Williams," the three *will*'s in 135.1–2 are useful to theorizers of both kinds.

There is very probably also a bawdy pun on *will* and "well" in 135.8–10 (see 112.3 and 154.9, notes).

Note the proverb "Will will have will though will woe win" (Tilley, W397).

1. *thou hast thy will* Compare the proverbial phrase "to be wedded to one's will" (Tilley, W392 and *LLL* II.i.210–11).

2. *to boot* too, besides, in addition. Q's "too" might strike a modern reader as an appropriate extra-syntactical auxiliary to the common substance of the phrases, the line, the quatrain, and the whole sonnet. This is the only place where the Q printer(s) spell(s) the preposition with a double *o*, but "to" and "too" were still so commonly interchanged that Shakespeare's reader is most unlikely to have noticed the variant.

3. *than* See 16.4,8,note. *enough am I* See 121.8, note (on *wills* and *I am*). *vex* The word suggests a reference both to the speaker's present railing and the lady's irritable reception of the speaker's suit as an annoyance. *still* (1) always; (2) nonetheless; (3) now as formerly, no less than before.

4. *To* The syntax immediately reveals that this word indicates attachment: "making addition to," but it can momentarily seem to introduce an infinitive completing the potential construction "more than enough to [do something]." *thy sweet will* (1) what is sweet to you, who are sweet (taking the phrase as a synesis in which *sweet* effectively acts twice); (2) your lust; (3) your sweet cunt; and possibly (4) that (other) William who is yours. (Since there is so much punning on *will* in this poem, *sweet will* also—gratuitously and presumably accidentally—suggests the flower, sweet-william; *OED* gives this from 1578: "The third [sort of gillofer] is that which we cal in Englishe Sweete Williams . . . "). *thus* by adding myself (one more William), my lust, and my penis?

5,7. *spacious, gracious* The meter could seem to suggest that both these words are trisyllabic. Both are ordinarily dissyllabic in Shakespeare, and dissyllabic pronunciations sound fine here (compare *Titus* II.i.114: "The forest walks are wide and spacious"). In the improbable event that Shakespeare expected his reader to count the syllables on his fingers and thus to read *spacious* trisyllabically (as we read "furious"), then an extra joke inheres in the conjunction of a *stretchèd meter* (17.12) and the anatomical topic of line 5.

5,12. *large*   (1) great in size, ample, capacious; (2) unconfined, unrestricted; (3) licentious (see 95.13, note); (4) liberal, generous, lavish in giving (the sense from which "largess" derives).

7. *Shall will* = an ideational pun: *Shall* and the verb "will" are effectively synonymous (see the explanation of such puns in 134.9, note, and compare *wilfully* and *shallowest* in 80.8,9).

8. *in*   with respect to? on?   *my will*   my lust? your "well," which is my own? me (the William who is mine)? Shakespeare may have sacrificed the clarity of this line to his ongoing exercise in the different uses of *in* (see lines 7,8,10, and 11; the display culminates in line 14 where one at least of *in*'s senses is overtly sexual, indicating place). *acceptance*   favorable reception (with a play on physical sexual reception of a male by a female). *shine*   (1) be visible (as in *Macb* III.i.127 and *Lucrece* 101–02: "read the subtle-shining secrecies / Writ in the glassy margents of . . . books"); (2) look favorably, beam, smile (compare *1HVI* I.ii.74–75: "Heaven and our Lady gracious hath it pleas'd / To shine on my contemptible estate").

9. Compare the proverbs "The sea complains it wants water," "The sea refuses no river," and "The sea is never full" (Tilley, S179, S181).

10. *in abundance*   (1) being in a state of abundance, being abundantly provided already (modifying the *sea*); (2) abundantly, in large quantities (modifying *addeth*).   *his*   its (but see 73.10, note).   *store*   (1) abundance; (2) stock; and perhaps (3) stud (see 84.3, 11.9, notes [on "store beasts"] and 141.10, note).

11. *So . . . add*   in the same way [you too should] add (the gloss reflects the logic necessary to the situation; the actual syntax takes its purpose as already achieved—it says that she already does as the sea does; the slipperiness of the rhetorically calculated ellipsis results in a parody of the deviousness of an unscrupulous, unskillful, and unsuccessful would-be seducer).   *being* = monosyllabic (as in 50.8).

13. The primary sense of the line is reasonably apparent from its rhythm, which a modern punctuation would mark thus: "Let 'no' unkind no fair beseechers kill;" (Tucker)—or thus: "Let 'No', unkind, no fair beseechers kill;" (Ingram and Redpath). Q's comma between *unkind* and the second *no* simply indicates a pause; compare the Q punctuation of the noun-adjective relationship between *The sea* and *all water* in line 9; here retention of the logically ineffectual Q punctuation allows the play on "a'no' " ("a spoken denial which is unkind"— the grammatical subject of the clause), and the second "no" (the negative actually operating in the clause), to evolve as and when the rhythm and diction demand; the conveniences of modernized punctuation anticipate the grammatical joke and thus deaden it by advertising its coyness; putting the first *no* in quotes also restricts its meaning to "the word 'no' " and thus undercuts the play on "a no" as "a nought," "a nothing," "a female 'will' " (on the sexual meaning of "nothing," see 20.12, 57.12, notes).   *unkind* = the negative of all the senses of "kind" in 134.6.   *fair beseechers*   (1) honorable suitors; (2) beautiful suitors; (3) suitors who "speak you fair" (i.e. are *kind* and mannerly; compare *FQ* III.viii.35: "with many gentle terms her faire besought"); (4) suitors who

woo by swearing that you are fair, who apply the epithet *fair* to you; (5) suitors
to the beautiful, beseechers of those who are fair (for the various pertinent
senses of *fair*, see 105.9; also see 127, headnote, and 127.1, note).

14. *all* (1) all the beseechers; (2) all the "will's" (of every sort); see 26.1–14,
note. *but* only (although it can momentarily seem to mean "except": "think
that all except one [are or do something]"). *Think all but one* (1) consider
them a conglomerate; (2) let it be all the same to you, consider it a matter of
indifference (for the idiom "all one" meaning "the same," "a matter of indifference," "not worth worrying over," see *TN* V.i.393: "But that's all one,
our play is done"). *one will* In effect, the phrase acts twice: "[think of me as]
one will in that conglomerate will." All the noun senses of *will* listed in the
headnote are operative here.

13,14. *beseechers, all but one* Shakespeare and/or his readers might have
heard logically incidental resonances of "besiegers" and "all but won." (See the
Irish dialect of Captain Macmorris in *HV* III.ii.102: "The town is beseech'd";
Shakespeare rhymes "liege" and "beseech" in *RII* V.iii.91–92, and probably
puns on "besiege" and "beseech" in *LC* 176–78: "And long upon these terms
I held my city, / Till thus he gain besiege me: 'Gentle maid, / Have of my suffering youth some feeling pity . . . . ' " As to "all but won," *OED* gives this 1598
example of the idiom "all but" meaning "very nearly," "almost": "Man . . .
All but resembleth God.")

13–14. In combination with the speaker's argument that one man would be
statistically negligible in the lady's hoard of paramours, the paired *no*'s in line
13 and paired *one*'s in line 14 give the couplet an aura of mathematical paradox
and suggest a proverb that Tilley cites variously as "One and none is all one,"
"One is as good as none," and "One is none" (O52). Compare the play on the
related proverb "One is no number" in 136.8 and 8.14.

SONNET 136

On the uses of *will* in this poem, see 135, headnote.

1. *soul* The reference is to "the seat of intuition," "the seat of one's
'sense' of things"; see the examples from *Hamlet* and *Much Ado* in 107.1–2,
note. The immediate context does nothing to activate the philosophical and
religious connotations of *soul*. *check* reprove (the construction is subjunctive), reproves (as in 15.6 and *AW* I.i.60–61: "be check'd for silence, / But
never tax'd for speech." This sense is dictated by the word *that*; however,
I come so near immediately reasserts the general but syntactically unharnessed relevance of "to check" meaning "to restrain," "to stop," "to repress"
[as in 15.6], because what comes too near should be stopped). *I come
so near* (1) I am so forthright [in reproving you and/or describing our
relationship], I am so candid—Willen and Reed give two related glosses: "speak
the hidden truth, come so close to the heart of the matter (Cf. Lyly, *Gallathea*
3.1: 'I think we came near you when we said you loved')" and "affect you so
deeply (Cf. *Two Gentlemen of Verona* 4.3.19: 'No grief did ever come so near
thy heart')"; (2) I approach so close to you physically, I make such bold sexual

advances [in suing for your love]. (The general context developed by sonnet 135 may evoke a play on the sexual sense of *come*—"reach climax"—but that sense is unproductive and at most a freefloating possibility to be considered and abandoned as the syntax progresses.)

1,3. *near, there*   See 140.5,7, note.

2. *thy blind soul*   The precise sense of the phrase is unclear; it demands to be figured out and probably did in Shakespeare's time as well as our own. Tucker suggested that *blind* might be "proleptic = let it shut its eyes, and then swear to it"; several commentators explain that the soul is called blind because it is shut up within the body and so cannot verify what is reported to it. The reference might be simpler: "your sensibilities, which are blinded by love" (see 137.1 and note). The reference might be more complex. Shakespeare may have chosen the locution for the sake of its sexual suggestiveness; see 137.7, 148.7–9, 153.9, and notes; compare Partridge, s.v. "eye," which he glosses as "pudend" "because of the shape, the garniture of hair and the tendency of both organs to become suffused with moisture"; Partridge cites *LLL* III.i.186–89:

> A whitely wanton with a velvet brow,
> With two pitch balls stuck in her face for eyes;
> Ay, and, by heaven, one [eye?] that will do the deed,
> Though Argus were her eunuch and her guard.

The sexual meaning of *thy blind soul* is principally evoked by the syntax, which implies a distinction between *thy soul* in lines 1 and 3 and *thy blind soul*; moreover, although *near* is the most appropriate referent for *there* in line 3, the syntax invites a reader to take *there* as a reference to *thy blind soul* or to *soul*; note also that the phrase is bracketed by two phonetic echoes of the sound of "eye": *that I* in the sixth and seventh syllables of both line 1 and line 2.

3. *admitted*   (1) acknowledged (with an abstruse play on *knows* in its here inoperative sexual sense; see 129.13, note, and the explanation of ideational puns in 134.9, note); (2) permitted to exist; (3) allowed to enter, let in.   *there* (1) near [you]; (2) into the soul (Willen and Reed note that "in the medieval psychology generally followed by the Elizabethans, intellect and will were the two rational faculties of the soul"); (3) into *thy blind soul*.

4. *for love*   out of charity.   *my love-suit sweet fulfill*   (1) my love-suit, sweet, fulfill (taking *sweet* an as epithet in direct address; editors therefore customarily isolate *sweet* in commas, thus restricting the action of the word); (2) fulfill my sweet love-suit.

4,5,6. *fulfill, fulfill, fill . . . full*   Note the gradual revelation, increasing overtness, and mounting crudity of the pun on *fulfill*, which is a synonym for "comply with"—"grant"—in line 4 (compare *Per* II, Prologue, 21: "to fulfill his prince' desire"); *fulfill* repeats that sense and also means "fill full" in line 5, and is finally restructured as *fill . . . full* in line 6; the progress of the pun is a stylistic echo of the transmutation from courtly suitor to importunate lover that line 1 appears to allude to.

5. *treasure of*   (1) precious possession which is; (2) treasure chest for,

treasury for the containing of (*OED* gives examples of *treasure* meaning "treasury" from 1550 and 1596; compare *Ham* I.iii.31–32: "or your chaste treasure open / To his unmast'red importunity"; see 20.14, note). *thy love* (1) your affection, your regard; (2) your lust; (3) your beloved; (4) what you love.

6. *Ay fill* (1) yes, fill; (2) I fill (note the Q spelling, "I"). For the same pun, see *R&J* III.ii.45–50; compare 148.9 and 152.11–14. Also note *blind* in line 2, and see 141.13–14, note (on words that, like "eye" in this poem, are absent from contexts that urgently and/or variously evoke them).

7. *In* with reference to (with a play on "within," "inside"). *things* (1) matters; (2) female sex organs (see 20.12, note). *things of great receipt* (1) treasuries, treasure chests, containers for things of great value; (2) capacious and much-used containers (note that *OED* records "receipt" meaning "the ordinary or habitual reception of strangers or travelers . . . esp. in *place of receipt*"— exemplified with this from 1608: "at the Ale-house, ther's the most receit"); (3) "in important matters," "with reference to things of value" (a sense potential to the "in things" construction and confirmed by *we prove*—compare 137.13).

8. See 8.14, note (on the proverb "One is no number"), and 135.13–14, note.

9. *in the number* among the multitude, in the throng (with a possible play on "within the number," "inside the arithmetical symbol" [which would be a zero—see 20.12, note]). *untold* (1) uncounted (compare *tells* in 12.1), ignored (because, being nothing, it is not worth taking into account [the word *untold* and the sound of its synonym "uncounted" interact in a farfetched and logically perverse pun; see 141.13–14, note—on plays on the sounds of words that do not occur in a poem but are synonyms for words that do; 58.3, note—on the bawdy potential of *account*; 63.5, note—on Shakespeare's pleasure in words and statements that say something and its opposite at once; and line 10 below]); (2) in secret, without anyone being told about it (for *untold* meaning "not recounted," "not reported," *OED* gives examples from the fourteenth century on, including this from 1623: "The cause . . . shall be to all the world untold"). There is also a syntactically irrelevant play on *untold* meaning "So numerous as to be uncountable" and "so immense as to be immeasurable"; compare the expressions "treasure untold," "untold gold" (*OED*, 2), and the modern "an untold number of."

10. *store's* Q's "stores" may be an adjectival use of the noun (i.e. "stores account" = "stores-account"), or a genitive, as most modern editors guess. The distinction is not urgent; I adopt the genitive because the collective plural "stores" is not recorded before 1636 and because *store's* makes the second of the senses given below more readily apparent to a modern reader. *thy store's account* (1) your inventory of possessions, the list of your goods on hand; (2) reports of your abundance, gossip about the great size of your hoard (see 84.3, note, on *store* meaning "abundance"; note that "a store" meaning a place where things are sold, a merchant's shop, is modern and American; *OED*'s earliest example of *store* meaning "storehouse" is half a century later than Q). There are obvious sexual overtones to *thy store's account*; see 135.10, 11.9, notes (on "store beasts"), and 58.3, note (on *account* as a synonym for the bawdy senses of "a

treasure," "a 'thing' of great receipt," "a nothing," and one sense of "will").
The topic of valuation and the surrounding diction (*untold* in line 9, *hold* in line
11, *Make* in line 13), give the phrase pertinent but non-signifying echoes of a
variety of idiomatic phrases meaning "to value, esteem, prize, make account of";
OED (6b) gives examples of "to tell store of," "to hold store of," and "to make
store of." (Note particularly the context and speaker of this example from *The
Canterbury Tales*: "And . . . I tolde of it no stoor. / They had me yeven hir lond
and hir tresoor" ["Wife of Bath's Prologue," 203–04].)

    11. *For nothing hold*   consider me nothing, hold me to be nothing. *nothing*
(1) worthless, a zero; (2) nonexistent, a "non-thing." There is also a play on "no
thing," i.e. "not a penis"; see 20.12, note; compare this song from the 1584
version of *A handful of Pleasant Delights* (ed. H. E. Rollins, 1924):

> *Fain would I haue a pretie thing,*
>   *to giue unto my Ladie:*
> *I name no thing, nor I meane no thing,*
>   *But as pretie a thing as may bee.*
> . . . .
>
> Some do long for pretie knackes,
>   and some for straunge deuices:
> God send me that my Ladie lackes,
>   I care not what the price is, thus faine, &c.
> . . . .
>
> The Mercers pull me going by,
>   the Silkie wiues say, what lacke ye?
> The thing you haue not, then say I.
>   ye foolish fooles, go packe ye. But fain &c.
> . . . .
>
> But were it in the wit of man,
>   by any meanes to make it,
> I could for Money buy it than,
>   and say, faire Lady, take it. Thus, fain, &c.
> O Lady, what a lucke is this:
>   that my good willing misseth:
> To finde what pretie thing it is,
>   that my good Lady wisheth.
> Thus fain wold I haue had this preti thing . . . .

    In context of a hectic display of bawdy puns on words like *will* and *thing*—
words that offer opportunities for further complication because they rely on
context to indicate whether they refer to male or female organs—the sexual
sense of *nothing* (see 20.12, note) is urgently pertinent and lets *For nothing* include
a sense directly opposed to "consider me worthless": "consider me as suited for
your nothing." *so*   so long as, providing that (as in 134.3).

11–12. *hold | That nothing me*   consider the nothing that I am; evaluate me, who am nothing, as (with a play on "hold . . . me" meaning "embrace me").

12. *something*   Q's "some-thing" can seem intended to acknowledge the non-idiomatic potential senses buried in the idiomatic uses of words like *nothing* and *something*; however, the extra meaning and change of ideational stress here occurs in *nothing* not *something*; moreover, the metric distortion to which a modern reader would be tempted by the orthographic signal is to be avoided. *a something sweet to thee*   (1) an object which you consider sweet (as opposed to valueless); (2) an object pleasurable to you; (3) an object of value to you, my sweet—an object which in your estimation, my sweet, is a "something" rather than a "nothing." (Compare the similarly ambiguous syntactic function of *sweet* in line 4.)

13. *Make but*   (1) make only, make no more than; (2) only make (sense (2) is confirmed by *then* in line 14 and results in the standard idiom of informal logic, "only do *X*, and then *Y* will be true").   *still*   (1) always; (2) no less than before.

14. *for*   because (introducing both justification for the speaker's assertion [since you love will, and since Will is my name, it follows that you must love me], and the reason for the lady's regard [you will find me loveable because of my name]).   *my name is Will*   (1) my name is William; (2) I am composed of will, I am will personified (compare *Ham* I.ii.146: "Frailty, thy name is woman"). I retain Q's capital in *Will* here because *name* makes the proper noun primary regardless of spelling.

SONNET 137

See the final note to 141.

1. *blind*   See 136.2 and note.   *fool*   (1) simpleton, idiot; (2) childish innocent (as in *R&J* I.iii.32, 49; see 115.13 and 151.1). Like "fool's bauble" (i.e. jester's scepter) the word *fool* may have had the specifically bawdy sense "penis." See *AW* IV.v.20–30:

> *Lafeu.* Whether does thou profess thyself—a knave or a fool?
> *Clown.* A fool, sir, at a woman's service, and a knave at a man's.
> *Lafeu.* Your distinction?
> *Clown.* I would cozen the man of his wife, and do his service.
> *Lafeu.* So you were a knave at his service, indeed.
> *Clown.* And I would give his wife my bauble, sir, to do her service.
> *Lafeu.* I will subscribe for thee; thou art both knave and fool.
> *Clown.* At your service.

Also see III.i.113–15 of Marston's *Malcontent* (ed. M. L. Wine [Lincoln, Nebraska, 1964]), where a fool is told he must "stand for [i.e. stand in for, take the place of] the fair lady" and replies: "Your fool will stand for your lady most willingly and most uprightly"; and compare *Lear* I.iv.150–54:

> *Kent.* This is not altogether fool, my lord.
>
> *Fool.* No, faith, lords and great men will not let me; if I had a monopoly out, they would have part on't. And ladies too—they will not let me have all the fool to myself; they'll be snatching.

Also see *A&C* I.i.12 where Antony is called "The triple pillar of the world transform'd / Into a strumpet's fool." *love* (1) Cupid (most editors capitalize *love*); (2) infatuation. (The proverbial idea that "love is blind" conflates "lovers are blinded by their love" [i.e. they see beauty and virtue in their beloveds that others do not see], and an allusion to the mythic embodiment of that truth, Cupid's blindness.)

2. The line echoes Psalms 115:5: "thei have eyes and se not." The Psalm pertains here in several ways: its topic is the distinction between the true god and heathen idols, which are condemned not only as false gods but as artificial ("idoles are silver and golde, even the worke of mens hands"); those who have eyes and see not include not only the idols (mere statues), but their worshippers: "Thei that make them are like unto them: so are all that trust in them" (Psalms 115:4,8; the whole passage is repeated in Psalm 135).

3. *lies* (1) is, is located, is to be found, exists; (2) deceives; (3) is artificial, is false.

5–6 *eyes corrupt by over-partial looks | Be anchored* (1) eyes corrupted by . . . looks be anchored (Shakespeare and his contemporaries commonly omitted final "-ed" in forming past participles of root words that end in the sound of *d* or *t*; see Abbott, par. 342). (2) corrupt eyes be anchored by . . . looks (taking *corrupt* as the simple adjective and *looks* as that which holds the eyes at anchor).

5–8. Compare *A&C* III.xi.55–57: "Egypt, thou knew'st too well / My heart was to thy rudder tied by th'strings, / And thou shouldst tow me after."

6. See Donne's use of "embay'd" in *Elegies* XVIII (*Loves Progress*), line 68, and compare the metaphoric overtones of sexual union as a ship come to harbor in *Oth* II.i.77–80:

> Great Jove, Othello guard,
> And swell his sail with thine own powerful breath,
> That he may bless this bay with his tall ship,
> Make love's quick pants in Desdemona's arms . . . .

In the sonnet the sexual metaphor is so triumphantly precise in its mechanics that the speaker's reliance on the wounding power of his wit makes him seem pathetic, exemplifies his degradation and frustration rather than the justice of his outrage. The intent is savage, the effect pathetic. Compare Othello's similarly pathetic wit in IV.ii.89–95 (in answer to Desdemona's protestations of innocence):

> I cry you mercy, then.
> I took you for that cunning whore of Venice
> That married with Othello.—You, mistress,

That have the office opposite to Saint Peter
And keeps the gate of hell!

Re-enter Emilia.
                                                          You, you, ay you!
We ha done our course; there's money for your pains.
I pray you turn the key, and keep our counsel.

The fact that we know Othello's charges to be unfounded and have no reason to doubt those against the dark lady does not alter the likeness between the bitter, defeated cleverness of this line and some of Othello's. *all* See 26.1–4, note.

7. Compare 129.7–8. *eyes' falsehood* (1) the misinformation delivered by the [speaker's] eyes; (2) [the lady's] deceiving oeillades, the amorous glances with which she captures hearts she never means to satisfy. (There may be a play on "to forge" meaning "to counterfeit," "to make a false imitation of" [as in *V&A* 804: "Lust full of forged lies"]; see "forgeries" in the *PP* version of sonnet 138 [quoted in 138, headnote].)

8. *tied* bound, attached (the aquatic context can color the line with incidental suggestions of tidal flux).

9. *several* = (dissyllabic) separated, fenced off, private. (The metaphor in lines 9 and 10 is from agriculture; the distinction is between enclosed private fields and common grazing land open to all. *OED* gives this from 1583: "The commons . . . are enclosed, made several"; compare the metaphor in *LLL* II.i.222 [which also follows hard upon a copulation-navigation metaphor]: "My lips are no common, though several they be.")

10. *wide* The word obviously modifies *world's*; "wide world" is a standard expression (see 19.7 and 107.2); but it can also color our understanding of the *common place*—which is also *wide* (see 135.5,12 and 136.7). *common* public. (Note "common road" in *2HIV* II.ii.160–61, "commoner," and "common customer" in *AW* V.iii.192, 280 [all meaning "common whore"]; "common house" meaning "brothel" in *Measure* II.i.43; and the name "Dol Common" in *The Alchemist*; see 69.14, note.) *common place* There may be an intentional play on "a commonplace," "something everyone knows"—in this case "something everyone knows carnally" (see 141.13–14, note).

11. *Or mine eyes, seeing this, say . . .* (1) or [why] should my eyes, beholding this, say . . . ; (2) or, if my eyes understand this, [why] should they say . . . (note the overt play on the two senses of *see*; compare the paradox in line 2). *this* the truth about the lady. *this is not* (1) "This is not" (i.e. direct address, meaning "this is not so," "the truth is not the truth," "I deny that the obvious truth is true"); (2) that this is not. *not* See 148.7–9 and note.

11–12. *say this is not / To put* (1) say, "This is not," in order to put (i.e. *To put* explains the motive for saying); (2) say, "This is not an instance of putting . . . "—say, "To do this is not to put . . . ."

12. *put . . . upon* attribute . . . to (with overtones of the idea of applying cosmetics). *fair truth* (1) lovely chastity; (2) pure honor, fair fidelity; (3) genuine beauty (as opposed to the beauty infatuation bestows); (4) natural

beauty (as opposed to cosmetically achieved beauty). (For the various senses of *fair* and *truth*, see 105.9, note; on the effective inversion of adjective and noun reflected in senses (3) and (4), see *false plague* in line 14, 13.12, 51.1, 127.4 and notes). *fair . . . foul* See 127.1,6 and 132.13–14. (The line is a wittily perverse echo of the proverbial phrase "put a good face on"—i.e. "make the best of." Tilley [F17] cites John Bale's *King Johan*: "Though it be a foul bye, set upon it a good face.")

13. *In things* See 136.7 and note.

14. *this false plague* (1) this affliction of distorted perceptions; (2) the affliction of being false, telling falsehoods; (3) this woman (the dark lady, who is untruthful and unfaithful, whose beauty is unreal [being either an illusion of infatuation or a cosmetic facade], and who is therefore an affliction to the speaker). *to . . . transferred* (1) changed into, transformed to (the sense is dictated by the context, but *OED* gives this figurative use from 1586: "*Metaphora*, which is, when a word from the proper or right signification is transferred to another neere unto the meaning"); (2) removed to, shifted to, relocated upon. (A Renaissance reader might have heard a pun on "trans-faired." The Renaissance pronunciations of vowel-plus-*r* are doubtful. We cannot be sure how *erred* and *transferred* were pronounced; surely they did not have the same vowel sound as *fair*, but the likeness of vowel sound in *err, dare, swear, fair*, and *-ferred* was probably greater in Shakespeare's pronunciation than in modern English; see 140.5, 7, note and the conjunction of *err, dare*, and *swear* in 131.7–8.)

SONNET 138

A version of this sonnet and a version of sonnet 144 were printed ten years before Q in *The Passionate Pilgrim*, a collection of twenty poems put out in 1599 by the publisher William Jaggard and advertised as "By W. Shakespeare." Five poems in *PP* are otherwise known to be Shakespeare's (the two sonnets and three lyrics from *LLL*); several others are known to be by other poets; the rest are of unknown authorship. *PP* went through two separate printings during 1599. Sonnet 138 is the first poem in *PP* (sonnet 144 is the second). This is Hyder Rollins's transcription of 138 as it appeared in the first edition of *PP* (*Variorum* I, 353–54):

> When my Loue sweares that she is made of truth,
> I do beleeue her (though I know she lies)
> That she might thinke me some vntutor'd youth,
> Vnskilful in the worlds false forgeries.
> Thus vainly thinking that she thinkes me young,
> Although I know my yeares be past the best:
> I smiling, credite her false speaking toung,
> Outfacing faults in loue, with loues ill rest.
> But wherefore sayes my loue that she is young?
> And wherefore say not I, that I am old:
> O, Loues best habit's in a soothing toung,

>   And Age in loue, loues not to haue yeares told.
>   Therefore I'le lye with Loue, and loue with me,
>   Since that our faultes in loue thus smother'd be.

Scholars have argued over whether the *PP* text represents an early version of sonnet 138 or an imperfectly remembered transcript of it; apparent evidence on both sides is abundant and inconclusive; see below.

Sonnet 138 is an exercise in logically improbable, unnatural, and uncomfortable unions that are also indivisible; the poem repeatedly points out the logical necessity of making distinctions, and it makes those distinctions impossible. The fact of impossible but undeniable fusion manifests itself in puns (e.g. the various and variously contradictory significances fused together in the word *lie*), in syntaxes that simultaneously indicate two distinct logical relationships among parts of sentences (e.g. lines 3 and 4 modify both *I do believe* and *she lies*), in the fact that every assertion in the poem is demonstrably true and also a lie (e.g. *I do believe her*, which is a statement of a fact that is and cannot be true), and in the fact that every assertion in the poem proudly reports a satisfactory relationship (the tone is downright smug), and a desperate one. A reader's *understanding* of the poem depends upon his ability to recognize simple truth; a reader exercises that ability with ease and success; but a reader's *experience* of the poem— his experience of words and sentences—is one in which he cannot recognize simple—pure, unalloyed—truth or simple falsehood. The poem as poem is like the relationship it describes; every quality or identity the poem has or presents is fused with its opposite.

(By a pure but interesting accident, thinking about the relationship of sonnet 138 and the *PP* version of sonnet 138 extends our experience of simultaneously exclusive and fused identities into another dimension.)

1. *my love* my beloved. (The sense of *love* is obvious here because of *swears* and the pronoun *she*; however, lines 11–12 [and the *PP* versions of line 8 and the couplet] play with and blur the sense of the word later in the poem by using it to suggest "the emotion called love," "the state of being a lover," and "a love relationship.") *made of truth* entirely composed of fidelity, faithfulness, honor (compare *AYLI* V.ii.77–91: "[to love] is to be all made of sighs and tears. . . . It is to be all made of faith and service . . .")—with a suggestion of "not artificial," "not cosmetically restored or improved" (see 54.2, note). (Shakespeare might also intend a syntactically unassisted play on "*a* maid of truth," "truly a virgin." "Of truth" and "of a truth," like the still current expression "in truth," were used to mean "verily," "in fact," "really"; *OED* gives this from the mid–sixteenth century: "The grit Debait and Tournament Off trewth no toung can tell." A pun on "made" and "maid" occurs in *R&J* III.ii.134–35: "He made you [the rope ladder] for a highway to my bed, / But I, a maid, die maiden-widowed." The probability of the pun increases as the poem progresses: passing off commercially experienced women as virgins to untutored youths is a traditional practice of bawds.)

2. *lies* (1) is telling a lie; (2) lies with men (see lines 13, 14 and notes).

1–2. The substantive pattern of these three clauses is synthesis, antithesis,

thesis; the unlikeliness of the sequence of propositions makes for a curious and appropriate mental experience in the reader. Line 1 subsumes the familiar paradox by which an infatuated lover is genuinely blind to what he undeniably sees: *my love* registers one element of the paradox, and, since the mere fact of swearing admits that there is some reason, valid or invalid, to disbelieve what is sworn to, *swears* registers the other (line 1 brings its situation with it—whenever one of a pair of lovers swears that he or she has been faithful, the occasion is an accusation to the contrary). Line 1 neutralizes the paradox of the totally loved and possibly unloveable beloved syntactically; the line synthesizes the coexistent contraries its elements imply into a coherent, comprehensible, and, thus, intellectually comfortable unit. As the sentence continues in *I do believe her*, the reader's comfort continues too; we understand the speaker to be saying that he is conscious of the self-delusion that results from the necessity to believe two incompatible truths. However, the actual syntax of line 2 presents its two propositions as simple truths to be understood literally; *I do believe her* and *I know she lies* cannot be effectively mediated by *though*. We understand the two lines to be telling us about the sort of synthetic compromise implied by the situation and terms of line 1, but line 2 demands that we also recognize and feel the logical impossibility of literally believing a lie. Our experience in understanding the two lines is like the speaker's experience of believing a lie: we understand the lines and understand that they cannot logically be understood.

3. *That*   so that.

4. *Unlearnèd . . . subtleties*   *PP* has "Unskilful . . . forgeries." (*Unlearnèd* relates more obviously, immediately, and self-consciously to *untutored* than *PP*'s "Unskilful" does; since arguments for the Q text of 138 as Shakespeare's revision of an earlier version printed in *PP* depend on the greater artfulness of the Q version, the less insistently artful use of "Unskilful" might argue for the *PP* version being someone's transcription from memory; on that principle *PP*'s "forgeries" for Q's "subtilties" would argue exactly the opposite. All grounds for deciding dissolve if one remembers that memorial renderings of poems usually magnify the ostentatiousness of rhetorical effects (for instance, one's memory of a heavily alliterative poem is likely to increase the alliteration); that consideration would suggest that *PP*'s "Unskilful" is unlikely to result from a memorial error in reproducing the Q text and that the phonetic and ideational crudeness of "false forgeries" relative to Q's "false subtilties" makes *PP* sound like the product of an over-eager memory. If one were foolish enough to pursue the topic, one might posit an early version of the Q poem and guess that the *PP* text is a garbled version of that.)

world's   Note that "world" and "word" were apparently hard to distinguish in Elizabethan pronunciations; both spellings were used for both words (see Hulme, pp. 207–08, 81.12, *Tim* II.ii.153: "the world is but a word," and the title John Florio gave his dictionary: *A World of Words*).

4,11,12,14.   *in*   The word functions differently each time it appears.

5. *Thus*   (1) in that way (modifying *thinking*); (2) therefore (introducing *I credit* in line 7).   *vainly*   (1) in vain, ineffectually; (2) self-conceitedly, for the

sake of personal vanity; (3) stupidly, foolishly, simply (compare *CofE* III.ii.178–79: "no man is so vain / That would refuse so fair an offer'd chain").

6. *she knows my days are*   *PP* has "I know my yeares be" (both readings suit the context, which provides no good reason for an editor to choose one over the other).

7. *Simply*   (1) naïvely, in the manner of an innocent, like *some untutored youth*; (2) foolishly (compare *simplicity* in 66.11); (3) unconditionally, absolutely (as in *MND* IV.ii.10: "he hath simply the best wit of any handicraft man in Athens").   *Simply I*   *PP* has "I smiling."

8. *simple truth*   (1) the plain facts; (2) pure honesty, plain straightforwardness (see 66.11, note); (3) non-complex truth, truth unlike the kind asserted in lines 1–2. (See 125.7, 76.4, and notes.)

3–8.   Line 8 asserts that the partnership between the two deluding and deluded lovers is equal. The justice of that assertion is witnessed not only by the substance of the five preceding lines but by their syntax. Lines 3 and 4 give a reason why the speaker believes (he wishes to seem young) and a reason why his beloved lies (she wishes to believe she has a fresh young lover). In lines 5 and 6 *Thus vainly thinking . . .* modifies *I* because the substance, construction, and diction (*thinking . . . Although . . . knows*) echo line 2 (*believe . . . though . . . know*). *Thus vainly thinking . . .* also modifies *she* because her delusion (*That she might think*) is the immediately antecedent topic of our concern (she vainly believes that she really believes the palpable untruth that she pretends to believe); lines 5 and 6 thus announce paradoxical perceptions by the lady that correspond to the speaker's own as described in line 2. The parallelism of *Simply* in *Simply I credit* at the beginning of line 7 and *vainly* in *vainly thinking* at the beginning of line 5 implies a larger parallelism by which *Thus vainly thinking . . .* is understood to have been an ellipsis for "Thus, I vainly thinking . . . ." Line 7 belatedly but effectively limits lines 5 and 6 to modifying *I*, but the limitation does not occur until after the lines have been read with their full double potential undiminished. Line 7 assures the reader that he is and has been hearing only about the speaker's mental state; line 7 thus presents line 8 as a relatively simple truth: "Thus, we are both liars, she in pretending faithfulness and I in pretending youth." However, the emphasis of line 8 is on mutuality, and it thus reasserts the suggestions of the lady's complex self-delusion that inhered in lines 3–6 and have just been suppressed by the simplified reference decreed by line 7; line 8 readmits the complex truth that both deceive, both are deceived, both recognize all the lies as lies, and both believe all the lies they hear and all they tell.

8,9,11.   The *PP* lines are quite different from Q's. In *PP*'s line 8, "Outfacing faults in love" suggests an earlier version rather than the Q line misremembered; on the other hand, "with loves ill rest" sounds like filler provided by someone who has forgotten everything about the line except that its final syllable rhymed with *best*. (If one seeks a gloss for "loves ill rest," it would have to be "love's [equally] evil remainder" and/or "love's restlessness," "love's unrestful repose." The phrase *ill-wresting world* in 140.11 invites inevitably fruitless specula-

tion on some connection between it and this phrase: 140.11 could suggest that
the *PP* version is Shakepeare's, an echo of a phrase in 138 that was later replaced; 140.11 could be pointed out as the original from which a faulty memory
generated "loves ill rest"; the likeness between the two phrases might be simple
coincidence.) *PP*'s line 9 ("But wherefore sayes my love that she is young?"),
implies either that the lady flaunts her youth (in violation of the general policy
expounded in the poem), or that she is old and pretends to youth as the speaker
does; it sounds like a mistake rather than an earlier version by Shakespeare.
PP's "habit's in a soothing toung" in line 11 sounds like a patch-up job on a
half-remembered line. The chiasmic repetition in lines 9 and 11 of the rhyme
words of lines 5 and 7 may well have been Shakespeare's own earlier tactic, but
the repetition of a rhyme or rhyme sound is a typical product of a memory
straining to recover a poem.

   9. *unjust*   (1) unfaithful in love, not *made of truth*; (2) a liar.

   11. *love's*   a love relationship's (the reference is to the whole practice of
loving and being beloved—but with lingering suggestions of *my love*, "my beloved," suggestions heightened by the succeeding clothing metaphor because a
beloved, a person, actually wears clothes).   *best*   (1) ideal; (2) most practical,
most serviceable (as opposed to ideal).   *love's best habit is in*   (1) love is best
clothed in; love's best costume is to dress in; (2) love's best mode of behavior
(customary practice, behavior pattern), consists in (consists of, has as its nature).
love's best habit is in seeming   Note that this phrase is momentarily complete in
itself and says "love's best habit is in pretense."   *seeming trust*   (1) pretense of
mutual faith, pretending to believe; (2) feigned honesty; pretense of fidelity.
(Shakespeare customarily associates clothing with deceit, concealment, and
pretense—with trying to seem other than one actually is); (3) seemly trustfulness;
(4) appropriate fidelity (*OED* gives this example of *seeming* meaning "suitable,"
"beseeming," "fitting": "The name of father . . . is semynge unto hym [God]
for dyvers causes and reasons").

   12. *age in love loves not*   (1) age when infatuated—an aged person who is in
love—dislikes; (2) in matters of love, an aged person dislikes (for *age* meaning
"aged person" as *youth* means "young person," see *WT* IV.iv.750: "Age, thou
hast lost thy labour").   *to have*   Q has "t'have," which apparently represents
an elision of "to" and " 'ave" (on the Renaissance tendency toward dropping
initial *h*, see Kökeritz, pp. 307ff.); "t'have" is metrically uncomfortable here;
PP has "to have."   *told*   (1) counted, reckoned up; (2) divulged (see 12.1).

   13. *Therefore*   (1) for the reasons given (in lines 11 and 12); (2) to achieve
that (i.e. to avert the topic of my age).   *I lie with her*   (1) I make love to her (the
usual idiomatic sense of "to lie with a woman"); (2) I lie to her, I tell lies in my
dealings with her (a non-idiomatic sense dictated by the logic of the discussion
of falsehood to which this line is logically linked by *Therefore*; note that, in doing
the work ordinarily done by "to," *with* adds its own pertinent auxiliary suggestion of cooperative mutual enterprise).

   14. *in*   (1) engaged in; (2) with respect to.   *faults*   (1) vices; (2) defects,
physical imperfections (*OED* gives this from 1599: "The women generally . . .
have three faults . . . little eyes, great mouthes, and not very smooth skin").

Faults and *false* are ideationally akin and derive from the same Latin root (*fallere*, "to deceive"), but we cannot guess with any certainty how *faults* would have been pronounced. A modern reader hears an echo of the topic of falsehood in *faults* that may have been inaudible to any but the Holofernes-like pedants among Shakespeare's readers: "fault" and "halt" rhyme in 89.1,3; "talk" and "halt" rhyme in *PP* 18.8,10; Shakespeare rhymes "caught her," "daughter," "slaughter," "halter," and "after" in *Lear* I.iv.318–22 (see 35.5, note, the Old French *faute*, and Kökeritz, pp. 310–12). On the other hand, note the phonetic implications of "if she did play false, the fault was hers; / Which fault lies on the hazards of all husbands" and "your fault was not your folly" (*John* I.i.118–19, 262), and "I do think it is their husbands' faults / If wives do fall" (*Oth* IV.iii. 84–85); note *falsely, fair, false*, and *foul faults* in 148.4,5, and 14, and see *fault* and *faults* in 96.1,3,4 set against the idea of falseness in 96.5–12.

by lies by means of falsehoods (with a play on the idea of "lying with," "lying beside," "lying by"; *by lies* presents a mirror image of the pun in *lie with*, where the sexual meaning is primary and the idea of falsehood secondary; note that *by* and *with* are potential synonyms [as prepositions indicating means]).
flattered (perhaps pronounced "flat-tred" as in *Lucrece* 296) (1) deluded; (2) gratified (with a strong suggestion of "to flatter" meaning "to caress"; see 33.2, note).

13–14. The complementary actions announced in line 13, their presentation in urgently parallel constructions (*I lie with her* and *she with me*), and the fact that each of the two clauses asserts the same necessarily cooperative action, all prepare the way for line 14, a line that sums up the speaker's grounds for cynicism, bitterness, and despair, and also one in which the unity of the two lying lovers, whose syntactic independence wanes as the poem progresses, reaches a compensating completion in the triumphantly mutual pronouns, *our* and *we*.

(The *PP* couplet is markedly different—ideationally and syntactically more awkward and ultimately less rich. It may be Shakespeare's earlier version; it may be a misremembered reconstruction of the Q version. In line 13, "I'le lye with Love, and love with me" would retroactively strengthen the potential extra sense *love's* has in line 11, "my beloved's"; "with Love" says not only "with my beloved" but "lovingly." In line 14 "faultes in love thus . . . be" says, (a) "faults by [means of] love thus . . . are"; (b) "faults as lovers thus . . . are"; and (c) "faults are thus . . . for the sake of love"—"faults are thus . . . on account of love"[compare *MND* III.ii.309–10: "in love unto Demetrius, / I told him of your stealth"]. *PP*'s "smother'd" furnishes a clumsy but apt emblematic conclusion for the bittersweet whole: the word connotes violent, hostile destruction; and in this context it denotes neutralization of vices by mutual suppression of threatening truth.)

SONNET 139

This sonnet has two topics: a sonneteer's traditional obligation to justify his beloved's cruelty to him (lines 1–2, 9–12—compare 35 and 41.1–8); and the cruelty itself (lines 3–8, 13–14—compare 41.9–14). The topics are obviously interrelated, but artistically they are joined only superficially—by the continuing pattern of imperative constructions and the octave's ideationally incidental common denominator in "speech." What little life the poem has derives from the illustration the octave's unsystematic structure provides for the speaker's unruly mood and unwillingness to suppress his anger and go through the social motions expected of him. (Shakespeare may have written the poem for the sake of playing with words and constructions that pertain to place and can be used for other purposes: in line 1 *to* introduces an infinitive, but, following *call me*, it has momentary potential for pointing toward a place to which the speaker might be summoned; in line 2 *lays upon* is almost purely metaphoric; in line 5 the effective meaning of *elsewhére* is "someone else"; also note *aside* [6], *from* [11], *elsewhére* [12], *near* [13], and *out-* [14]; the idiom *in my sight* [5] exemplifies the phenomenon in reverse.)

2,4,6. *heart, art, heart*   See 24.13–14, note.

3. *Wound me . . . with thy tongue*   This injunction is not directly related to the one in lines 1 and 2, which it both ignores and casually echoes; the action demanded here relates generally to the action that is forbidden in lines 1 and 2 (*call*), the action that is refused there (*justify*), and the occasion of those lines (*the wrong*).

4. *Use pow'r with pow'r*   (1) use your power powerfully—directly and authoritatively; and, perhaps, (2) let the powers you use against your adversary be of a kind he too possesses, fight fair, fight me on common ground and with weapons I can match.   *by art*   (1) by indirection, subtly, by cunning stratagems; and, perhaps, (2) by magic (compare Drayton, *Idea* 52.3: "have thine Eyes such Magike, or that Art"; for *art* meaning "magic," see *Temp* I.ii.24, 373 and *1HVI* II.i.15).

5–6. If a reader notices that *elsewhére* and *in my sight* are potential antonyms, the resultant incidental complexity probably seems clumsy rather than enriching. The substantively incidental relationship between *sight* and *glance thine eye* does, I think, enrich the weave of the lines, even though—perhaps because—it makes no demand for conscious notice.

6. *Dear heart*   my love, my dear (direct address); contrast the ironically different sense of the differently figurative *my heart* in line 2.   *to glance thine eye aside*   The phrase conflates two synonymous locutions: "to glance aside" and "to turn one's eyes aside"; the double construction makes the action sound purposeful and positive—a glance meaningful *toward* someone else rather than a mere turning aside *from* the speaker.

7. *What*   why.   *when thy might*   since your power (the line gets some extra energy from the occurrence of this phrase in a syntactical structure to which "when thou might'st" pertains; note the verb in line 12.

8. *o'erpressed*   too hard-pressed (but note the context [concern with speaking and not speaking], and see 140.1–2, note).   *bide*   endure, withstand (Willen and Reed compare *R&J* I.i.211: "Nor bide th'encounter of assailing eyes").

7–9. *wound, cunning, excuse, well, knows*   Concentrated as they are, these words *could* have given a logically casual bawdy cast to the lines. See the notes to 133.2 (on *wound*); 148.13 (on *cunning*); 2.9, 121.10, and 42.5,7 (on *use* [see line 4] and *excuse*); 154.9 (on *well*); and 129.13 (on *know*).

    9. *ah* The one strength of this poem is its tone; *ah* both suggests a mechanically elegant poetizer dutifully seeking, and inevitably finding, a serviceable logical trinket and gives the line the "poetic" sound of the sort of gauzy poem such a lover would turn out.

    10. *looks* (1) appearance; (2) glances.

    10,12. *enemies, injuries* In this context Shakespeare's reader may have heard these words as punning (and preciously clever) conflations of "enemy eyes" and "injur[ing] eyes." Shakespeare's other rhymes for *enemies* are "cowardize," "eyes," "flies," "guise," "lies," "tyrannize," "cries," and "voice"; his other rhymes for injuries are "exercise" and "miseries"; he rhymes "eyes" and "miseries" in *1HVI* I.i.87–88 (see Kökeritz, pp. 219–20, 434, and 453). (Also note that *injuries* [from Latin *injuria*, "contrary to justice, law, and equity"] is an incidental echo of the idea of justification in the preceding lines.)

    11,12. *turns, dart* The words are appropriate to the situation described (line 5 concerned turning eyes away, and "to dart glances" was already a stock phrase); they also participate in the metaphor of armed combat (compare *John* II.i.54: "turn your forces from this paltry siege," *LLL* V.ii.396, *AYLI* III.v.25, and "darting Parthia" in *A&C* III.i.1). Here *turns my foes* [*from*] evokes an image of the lady as knight errant turning back an attacking army that threatens her beloved.

    13. *near* nearly (with a possible play on "from being close to you").

    14. *rid* do away with, get rid of (as in *RII* V.iv.11: "I am the King's friend, and will rid his foe").

SONNET 140

    This poem continues the topic (see line 14) and imperative mood of sonnet 139. Its chief interest is phonetic; note, for example, the interplay of *w* sounds and *p* sounds in lines 1–4, and the phonetic and ideational interplay among the sixth syllables of lines 2,3,5, and 11 (alliteration in *w*), lines 2,4, and 5 (*with, pit-, wit*), and lines 3 and 11 (*words, world* [pronounced "word"—see 138.4, note]).

    1. *Be wise as thou art cruel* (1) be as wise as you are cruel, let your wisdom be as great as your cruelty; (2) inasmuch as you are cruel, be wise; be wise since you are cruel. *cruel* = dissyllabic; see 129.4, note. *press* (1) forcefully assail, beset, harass; *press* continues the military metaphor established in 139.8 (*OED* gives this from 1560: "The horsemen pressed him before, and the foteman gave the onset at his back"); metaphorically it expresses (2) distress, depress, oppress the spirits of (as in *Oth* III.iv.178: "I have . . . with leaden thoughts been press'd").

    1–2. *press* | *My tongue-tied patience* The word *tongue-tied* invokes a new and specific metaphor of torture; a person accused of a felony who "stood mute," refused to plead, underwent *peine forte et dure*, a process whereby the prisoner's body was pressed with heavy weights until he pleaded or died (see *OED*, s.v.

"peine"). Shakespeare alludes to the practice in *Measure* V.i.521 (during a discussion of slander) and in *Much Ado* III.i.76 (in a discussion of the advisability of keeping silent); see *RII* III.iv.72: "O, I am press'd to death through want of speaking" and the illogical reference in *T&C* III.ii.205–07: "because it [the bed] shall not speak of your pretty encounters, press it to death . . . Cupid grant all tongue-tied maidens here, / Bed, chamber, pander, to provide this gear!" (Note the incidental wit inherent in the juxtaposition of this metaphor with *lays upon my heart* and *o'erpressed* in 139.2 and 8.) The word *patience* (from Latin *pati*, "to suffer") has special pertinence to the metaphor of torture.

3–4. Such chain reactions of causes and effects were common in the logic of sonneteers; see *A&S* 1.1–4, 2.5–6; the rhetorical term for the device is "climax" ("the ladder"); compare lines 9 and 10 below.

4. *pity-wanting*   (1) unpitied; (2) pity-craving; (3) deserving of pity, pitiable (see 142.11, note).

5. *wit*   wisdom, good sense (as in *2Gent* II.vi.12: "he wants wit").

6. *yet, love*   (1) even so, my love; (2) no less than formerly, my love.

5,7. *were, near*   There are no grounds for guessing what pronunciation or pronunciations Shakespeare gave *were* (spelled "weare" by Q—as in 98.11), and *near*; his practice elsewhere suggests that both words could rhyme with the words we now spell "appear," "bear" (13.6,8 and 77.1,3), "err," "fair," "fear," "her," "here," "there" (136.1,3), and "wear." See Kökeritz, pp. 399ff.

10,11. *ill, ill-wresting*   The words play on one another and on *bad*; both play on *testy sick men* in line 7 (men who are "ill" ["in bad health"] and do not rest easy).

10. *speak ill of*   (1) tell bad things about, speak the ugly truth about; (2) speak wickedly about, slander.

11. *this ill-wresting world*   our present-day society in which every statement and action is maliciously construed, twisted awry so as to seem evil (with a syntactically freefloating but ideationally relevant play on "ill-wresting word" [see line 3 and 138.4, note] as well as the play on "ill-resting" (see 138.8,9,11, note]). (Willen and Reed compare *Much Ado* III.iv.30: "an bad thinking do not wrest true speaking I'll offend nobody." Note that that line occurs amid elaborate wordplay on heaviness ["my heart is exceeding heavy. . . . heavier for [the weight of] a husband"] and sickness ["I am exceeding ill"].)

12. *ears*   listeners (by synecdoche).

13. *so*   (1) mad; (2) believed. *belied*   be belied, be slandered. (The play on *be so*—which is visible in the Q text, "be lyde"—caps the pattern *Be wise, be near, believèd be* in lines 1,7, and 12. Some readers may hear—and Shakespeare may intend—a nebulous sexual play on the idea of "lying with.")

14. *straight*   (1) undeviating, directed in a single course, steady (see 139.6,11–12, and note *outright* in 139.14; compare Proverbs 4:25 [Bishops' version, 1568]: "let thyne eye liddes loke straight before thee," and note the general relevance of Proverbs 4:20–27 to this line [see 141.1–14, note]); (2) honest (*OED* gives this from 1542: "The good order strayte and true dealing of the inhabitauntes of the said towne"); (3) strait, with strict correctness (*OED*, s.v. *strait* C.6b, gives this from 1590: "they shall be judged hereafter, and give account of their steward-

ship . . . as straite as their subjects . . ."; see 121.11, note, and compare
Proverbs 4:11–12: "I have shewed thee the ways of Wysdome, & led thee into
the right pathes. / So that if thou goest in them, there no straitness hinder
thee . . ."). *heart* inclination, desire, thoughts (by traditional metonymy).
proud See 151.10, note. *go wide* (1) go astray (a metaphor from archery;
compare the idea of darting eyes, darting glances, and see 139.6–12); (2) go
wrong, stray from "the strait and narrow," wander; (3) travel widely. *wide*
See 28.14, note.

SONNET 141

1. *In faith* truly, indeed, verily (but—when read in context of the preceding
poems on constancy and faithlessness—with substantively irrelevant overtones
of "faithfully"; many editors add a comma after *faith*, but its effect is probably
greater in theory than in the fact of a reader's experience of the line; compare
131.5).

2. *errors* defects of beauty (see 127 and 132); the gloss is dictated by the
logic of the immediate context; the general context of the lady's wandering eyes
and affections (see 139, 140), combines with the root meaning of "error" (from
Latin *errare*, "to wander"), and the usual meanings of "error" (as in 117.9
and 119.5), to give the line inherent reference to faithlessness and to "moral
offenses," "misdeeds" (compare 96.7: *those errors that in thee are seen*).

3,4. *despise, despite* Both words have their usual modern English senses,
but their conjunction in a discussion of seeing activates substantively incidental
play on their common Latin root, *despicere*, which in turn derives from *de*,
"down," and *specere*, "to look," "to look at." Compare the juxtaposition of
respect and *despise* in 149.9,10; and see 83.14, 149.13–14, notes.

4. *Who* which (the heart, personified; see Abbott, par. 264; the reference of
Who is not clear from context until one reaches *is*). *in despite of view* in
spite of what is seen, regardless of appearance (Willen and Reed compare *R&J*
I.i.167–68: "Alas that love, so gentle in his view / Should be so tyrannous").
(The phrase plays casually on "in despite of you"; compare the play on "Troy-
ans' trumpet" and "Troyan strumpet" in *T&C* IV.v.64 and Barnabe Barnes's
Parthenophil and Parthenophe, sonnet 89 [an echo poem], line 8:

> What saints are like her? speak, if you be!
> *Echo.* Few be!)

is pleased to deigns to, is gracious enough to (but, since what is and is not
pleasing is a topic of these lines, and since *is pleased* momentarily registers as an
entity independent of the verb it introduces, the whole phrase is strongly
colored by overtones of "finds it pleasurable to," "delights to"; compare the
similar extra action of *desire* in line 7 where it means simply "wishes" but gives
its phrase the pertinent but not specifically harnessed energy of "lusts," "feels
physical desire"; the action of *leaves* in line 11 is also comparable. *dote* (1)
madly adore, love to distraction; (2) behave like an idiot (as in *CofE* V.i.328:
"thy age and dangers make thee dote").

5. *tune*   sound.

6. *Nor*   nor is my (for a similar ellipsis, see 65.1 and note).   *tender feeling* keen sense of touch. (The gloss is dictated by the context of *eyes* and *ears*, but the context also activates the idea of "a sense of tenderness" and gives the phrase overtones of the meaning now carried by the modern idiom "tender feeling" meaning "affection," "fond regard," "love." The second half of the line adds less highminded suggestions of "amorous caresses" and "the feel of soft, smooth skin.")   *base*   ignoble (with a possible play on "dark"—see 100.4, note—and a probable play on the simplest physical sense of *base*, "low"— indicating the location of the places touched).   *touches*   caresses, acts of touching (often used with specific reference to sexual contact, as in *Measure* III.ii.21 and *PP* 4.7–8: "To win his heart she touch'd him here and there: / Touches so soft still conquer chastity"). In the present context the word "touch" carries extra resonances: (a) from its use to refer to the operation of the hand on a musical instrument—as in *Ham* III.ii.347 and *RII* I.iii.161–65:

> And now my tongue's use is to me no more
> Than an unstringed viol or a harp;
> Or like a cunning instrument cas'd up
> Or, being open, put into his hands
> That knows no touch to tune the harmony.

(note line 5 and the incidental likeness of *base* and "bass"); (b) from its use as a synonym for *feeling*—as in *2Gent* II.vii.18: "Didst thou but know the inly touch of love"; and (c) from its use to mean "blemish," "stain," "taint" (*OED* gives this from about 1580: "They did not see how their Monsieurs honour . . . could be salved, without great touch to both").   *prone*   inclined (with a possible bawdy play on the then rare sense "lying face downward"; note in any case that the idea of decline, of descent from a higher to a baser position, is inherent in *prone*).

7. *Nor taste, nor smell*   nor does my sense of taste, nor my sense of smell.

8. *sensual*   (= syncopated, dissyllabic as in 35.9) (1) of the five senses; (2) carnal, voluptuous, of lust.   *thee alone*   you and only you (compare the last line of Donne's *Elegies* XVII: "Wee'l love her ever, and love her alone"). (The speaker specifically refuses to make the poetic lover's usual assertion that his lady is the nonpareil of women; compare *AYLI* III.v.42ff.: "I see no more in you than in the ordinary / Of nature's sale-work. . . ." Here *with thee alone* plays on the contextually pertinent sense "alone with you," "in private.")

9. *But . . . nor*   however, neither . . . nor (compare 86.9). (*But my five wits* can momentarily register as "only my five wits," "my five wits alone"; *But* thus participates in the substantively irrelevant verbal complex initiated in *alone* in line 8, complicated by *five . . . five* in this line, and completed by *one, Only,* and *count* in lines 10 and 13 [see 94.10, note—on Q's "onely"]. Since *But my five wits* looks like a positive statement ["unless my five wits" or "however, . . ." or "only . . ."] until *nor* reveals the ellipsis in the phrase that precedes it, *But my five wits* also anticipates the paradoxical reading experience evoked by the *five wits—five senses* confusion discussed below.)   *five wits*   Following

immediately upon the catalogue of the five wits in lines 1, 5, 6, and 7, *five wits* may at first seem to refer to them; in fact that was the commonest meaning of *five wits* (*OED* gives many examples including this from 1532: "There is no breade in the sacrament, nor wine, though the five wittes say all ye [i.e. all say yea]"). However, the line proceeds to assume a distinction between the *five wits* and the *five senses*, and thus demands that *five wits* be understood as most editors since Malone have indicated; Malone cited Stephen Hawes, *The Pastime of Pleasure*, 1509, chapter 24: "These are the .v. wyttes remeving inwardly: Fyrst, commyn witte [a synonym for 'common sense'], and than ymaginacyon, / Fantasy, and estymacyon truely, / And memory." "Wit" and "sense" were used interchangeably and could refer to intellectual and/or to bodily faculties of perception (see "commyn witte" above; *OED* cites this phrase from 1570: "The v. wittes bodely and ghostlye [i.e. intellectual]" and this [s.v. "sense," 7] from 1566: "his fancie and other interior senses"). In this line, then, *five wits* and *five senses* indicate intellectual and physical faculties respectively, but their juxtaposition is carefully calculated to confuse in the very act of distinguishing. The two thus participate in the ongoing disquisition on what makes sense, what the senses report, and what the speaker feels; the reader's experience of coping with synonyms used as antonyms is a miniature literary model of the speaker's incompatible feelings about the lady and his incapacity to understand why he loves what he cannot find loveable.

   10. *serving thee*   (1) being your devoted admirer (as a courtly lover was his lady's "servant," her "slave"); (2) serving you sexually, standing at stud for you (for this stockbreeder's sense of "to serve" [*OED*, 52], see *Lear* III.iv.84–87, and "service" in 149.10, *AW* IV.v.24–27, and the last lines of Donne's Elegy XX [*Loves Warre*]:

> . . . Thousands wee see which travaile not
> To warrs; But stay swords, armes, and shott
> To make at home; And shall not I do then
> More glorious service, staying to make men?

   11. *Who*   which (the heart, personified; the reference of *Who* is not clear from context until the beginning of line 12; until then, *Who* could refer to *thee*; compare *Who* in line 4).   *leaves unswayed*   lets be ungoverned, allows to be rulerless (compare *left* in 48.8 and *sway'st* in 128.3).

   11–12. Although the syntactic unit *leaves unswayed* specifies an auxiliary function for *leaves*, the sense it has standing alone is active and pertinent here (compare the potential independence of *is pleased* and *desire* in lines 4 and 7); *leaves*—"departs"—is also relevant to the sense of the next line and a half: the speaker's body is left unswayed—he is left a shell of a man—because his heart has left—has departed, has gone away—to live in his lady's bosom as a slave. (Note the new life and unexpected nature that the clichéd phrase *Thy proud heart's slave* acquires as a result of the logic its particular situation demands.)

   12. *slave*   Compare 57.1.   *vassal wretch*   See 133, headnote. Note the complex wordplay that *vassal* (someone subservient to a master) can generate among *unswayed* (i.e. ungoverned), "to vacillate," "to sway" meaning "to

swing unsteadily," and, perhaps, the swaying *leaves* of a tree (see 5.7, note).

    13. *Only . . . thus far* (1) however, to this extent; (2) thus far and no far-ther, only to this extent; (3) until now . . . only (reading (3), which is instantly cancelled by the syntactical dictates of *That she . . .* in line 14, yeilds this sense for the line: "Up until now the only thing I consider a gain is my affliction"—a sense that anticipates the piacular turn of line 14; for *thus far* used to refer to time, see *3HVI* V.iii.1–4: "Thus far our fortune keeps an upward course, . . . But . . . I spy a . . . threat'ning cloud.") (Note that the contorted syntax invites a reader to perceive the syntactically available but logically uncalled-for reading "I consider my gain—what does me good—to be a plague." Here again the reader's experience of the poem acts as a metaphor for the experience it describes.) *plague* (1) the disease of infatuation, the affliction of being a lover; (2) the lady (compare 137.14). *count* take to be, consider (the context can evoke vague bawdy suggestions of the sort *account* has in 136.10).

    14. *sin* Note the potential theological reference inherent but dormant in the stock expletive *In faith* in line 1. *pain* (1) unpleasant physical sensations, bodily suffering (a witty extension from the foregoing assertions that the lady is not pleasing to the senses—with a possible additional suggestion of the pain of venereal disease—see *plague* in line 13); (2) punishment (*OED* gives this from 1577: "Condemnation unto death set as a peine upon our heads, because of the transgression"). (Note that one of the legal senses of "to award" was "to sen-tence"; *OED* gives this from 1548: "That last judgment, which shall awarde some to eternal felicitie, and other some to everlastyng payne." Note also that *pain* was used specifically to mean punishment in hell or purgatory and to mean hell itself; *OED* gives this from 1598: "Ar now cast downe into paines lowest abysse"; see 144.12 and note.)

    13–14. The basis of the conceit here is the idea of a soul's term of imprison-ment in purgatory. Ingram and Redpath suggest "that these lines are not usually well understood. It might appear, on the surface, that there could be little advan-tage in the seductress making the poet suffer for his 'sin' with her. But Samuel Butler, alone among commentators, reveals real point in the lines. He para-phrases: 'I shall suffer less for my sin hereafter, for I get some of the punishment coincidently with the offence.' "

    Be that as it may, the couplet is not logically related to the body of the poem in any obvious or ordinary way. The couplet does pertain to a phonetic logic that underlies the whole poem—a unifying logic that is abstruse to the point of inefficiency: although the actual play on words never occurs, the first twelve lines develop a contrast between "sense" meaning "reason," "wisdom," and "the power to reason," on the one hand, and the various meanings of "sense" that pertain to sensation, on the other. The couplet jumps to the phonetically similar word *sin* (and to *pain*, which pertains to the rewards of sinfulness in one of its meanings and to sensation in another). Compare the interrelation of *I, blind, ay,* and "eye" in 136.1,2,6; that of *untold* and "uncounted" in 136.9; that of *common place*, "commonplace," and " 'thing' known to everyone" in 137.10; that among *truly write*, "rightly," and "right" in 21.9; that among *conscience* and *contented* in 151.1,2,11 and the idea of conjuring in 151.9; and that among "mansion," its Latin root *manere* ("to dwell"), "hand," and *manus* (the Latin for "hand") in Tyndale's version of 2Cor. 51:12 (quoted in 146.6, note). Also compare sonnets 13 and 79 (each is a sustained play on the word "own," which appears in neither poem); 68.1–8 (the particulars of the lines are summed up in a potential pun on "heir" and "hair"—words that do not appear in the poem); sonnet 105 (the poem is a sustained play on sexual and religious "infidelity," being an "infidel"); sonnet 7 ("sun," the key word of the sonnet, does not appear); and George Herbert's "Love bade me welcome" (the word "host" never appears in the poem and is the common denominator on which its uneasy analogies turn). Also consider the unexpressed common denominator among the ideas of houses, rule, possession, religion, and the Last Judgment that "domicile," "dominion," "dominical," their cognates, and "doomsday" could provide for sonnet 146. See also 134.9, note (on ideational puns), 90.6, note (on *conquered woe* and "conquered foe," *walks* and "talks," and *pleasure, rest, measure, best*, and "treasure chest"), and 109.13, note (on *thou, universe*, and "you").

Shakespeare was interested in progressions that do not make sense (are unreasonable) except to the senses; compare *LLL* I.i.94–99:

> *King.* How well he's read, to reason against reading!
> *Dumain.* Proceeded well, to stop all good proceeding!
> *Longaville.* He weeds the corn, and still lets grow
>   the weeding.
> *Berowne.* The spring is near, when green geese are
>   a-breeding.
> *Dumain.* How follows that?
> *Berowne.* Fit in his place and time.
> *Dumain.* In reason nothing.
> *Berowne.* Something then in rhyme.

For another play on the phonetic likeness between *sense* and *sins*, see 35.8–9, note. See also *Per* I.i.78–85 (a passage in which both topics and diction are reminiscent of this sonnet):

> But I must tell you now my thoughts revolt;
> For he's no man on whom perfections wait
> That, knowing sin within, will touch the gate.
> You are a fair viol, and your sense the strings;
> Who, finger'd to make man his lawful music,
> Would draw heaven down, and all the gods, to hearken;
> But, being play'd upon before your time,
> Hell only danceth at so harsh a chime.

1–14. *A Note on "eye and heart" poems and the problems of relationship among the sonnets in the 1609 sequence*:

The various sonnets that Shakespeare bases in self-consciously arch "eye and heart" conceits provide a good object lesson in the temptations and frustrations evoked by even the most obvious likenesses among poems and groups of poems in the 1609 sequence. Sonnet 24 is an "eye-heart" poem, and stands alone; two pairs of "eye-heart" poems, 46–47 and 132–133, relate to 24 and to each other; 93 opposes eyes and heart, but is unlike the others in manner. Each of those six poems can remind a reader of any of the other five that he has read.

Difficulty occurs only when one tries to pin down the nature and extent of their relationship. One can be drawn to speculate on some "original order" accidentally disarranged in the printer's shop. The troubles are that linking factors among the sonnets are multiple and reach in contrary directions; that, when one has noted and espoused a factor like "opposition of eye and heart," one is liable to assume that it always has the same weight (e.g. sonnet 93 is and is not like the other "eye-heart" poems); and that one can be led astray— away from the poems and the perceptions that made one suspect the presence of reassemblable groups—toward substituting the problems generated by a peremptory hypothesis for the problems that evoked the investigation in the first place (e.g. one can find oneself wanting to argue some poem out of one evident "group" and into another). Patterning factors like "eye-heart" are intriguing in themselves, useful in accounting for a strong but imperfectly maintained sense that several sonnets are a distinct group, but not necessarily at all efficient in a reader's experience of the poems.

For example, sonnet 141 seems to participate in the group of "eye-heart" sonnets begun with 137; sonnet 138 drops the topic of eye and heart, but introduces *tongue*; 139 and 140 treat of eyes, heart, and tongue; the series reaches a kind of climax in 141, which is overtly concerned with the organs of transmitting and perceiving sensation; the apparent series dwindles to an apparent close in 142.5, 10–11. One may then observe that 137–142 all have vague and various likenesses to Proverbs 4: 20–27 (Bishops' Version, 1568):

> My sonne marke my wordes and encline thine eare unto my sayings:
> Let them not depart from thine eyes, but kepe them even in the middest of thyne heart:
> For they are life unto those that finde them, and health unto all their bodyes.
> Keepe thyne heart with all diligence, for out of it issueth lyfe.
> Put away from thee a frowarde mouth, and let the lippes of slaunder be farre from thee.
> Let thyne eyes beholde that thyng that is right, and let thyne eye liddes loke straight before thee.
> Ponder the path of thy feete, and let all thy wayes be ordered aright.
> Turne not aside, neither to thy right hande nor to the left: but withholde thy foote from evyll.

That is the conclusion of Proverbs 4. In anticipation of the two contrasting loves in sonnet 144, it is worth noting that Proverbs 5 begins in a vein similar to that of the end of Proverbs 4, but that its topic is "whoredom forbidden." In conjunction, Proverbs 4 and 5 contrast the fruits of loving wisdom ("Make much of her, and she shall promote thee, yea if thou embrace her, she shall bring thee unto honour"—4:8) and loving a whore ("at the laste she is as bitter as wormewood, and as sharpe as a two edged sworde. / Her feete go downe unto death, and her steppes pearce thorowe unto hell"—5: 4,5 [Bishops']).

Altogether, one is left with a mass of valid information that *might* provide a possible clue to what was running in Shakespeare's mind when he wrote 137–142 and (perhaps) 144, a clue that can provide grounds for arguing against removing any of sonnets 137–142 from the immediate company of the others, but which demands wanton distortion if it is to support any satisfying generalization about the poems themselves, about their relationship with their neighbors (see 136.1, note and the headnotes to 134, 143, 144, and 145), or about their relationships with the earlier "eye-heart" poems and groups.

SONNET 142

1. *sin* This sonnet sounds as if it is continuing from 141.14. *dear* (1) cherished, endearing, precious; (2) loving, affectionate; (3) costly; (4) sharp, severe; (5) earnest (for examples of these five meanings of *dear*, see 31.6, 48.14, and 131.3). *virtue* (1) primary quality, chief characteristic (see 93.14, note); (2) essence (as in *Temp* I.ii.26–27: "which touch'd / The very virtue of compassion in thee"); (3) moral goodness (the opposite of *sin*); (4) chastity, sexual purity (see *Oth* IV.i.8 and "maiden virtue" in *John* II.i.98; the word can refer both to genuine chastity and to a manner that suggests or pretends to maidenly scrupulousness). *hate* is hate, is malevolence.

1–2. The two lines combine in a typically contrary Shakespearian action. They progress from self-pitying self-abuse (*Love is my sin*) to an insult to the beloved—an insult overt, unmistakable, but largely composed of potentially complimentary words (*and thy dear virtue hate*). The insult suddenly becomes genuinely complimentary in *Hate of my sin*. Thereupon *grounded on sinful loving* modifies both *sin* and *hate*, thus justifying and explaining the compliment (in a reassertion of the idea that the speaker's love is sinful), and simultaneously developing the briefly abandoned insult (by suggesting that the lady's hate—her "daunger," her primly outraged disdain, her virgin-like standoffishness—actually stems from—and is only a cover for—her illicit sexual activity. (The lines combine the use of two appropriately perverse rhetorical figures: chiasmus [inversion of the order of words, phrases, or ideas when repeated—literally "a placing crosswise"], in the interrelation of paired half-lines and in the relationship between the two lines as wholes; and anadiplosis [repetition of the last word of one unit as the first word of the next—literally "a doubling back on"].)

3. *but* only; do no more than. *compare* Note that comparison has been stylistically inherent in the first two lines.

5,10,11. *lips, eyes, heart* See 141.1–14, note.

6. *their scarlet ornaments* their redness (the phrase fits natural as well as cosmetically achieved color). The presence of *profaned* makes the whole phrase a religious metaphor: "defiled their scarlet vestments" (the conceit is awkward and may have been contrived for the sake of a play on "cardinal virtues"—

essential, primary, virtues—and "cardinal sins"; members of the College of
Cardinals are noted for their "scarlet robes" [*1HVI* I.iii.42]; Shakespeare plays
on "Cardinal" and "cardinal" in *HVIII* III.i.102–04; the context and diction
also suggest the Scarlet Whore of Babylon in Rev. 17–19; Protestants identified
her variously as Rome, Roman Catholicism, and the Pope [see the marginal
commentary in the Geneva Bible]). The metaphor in line 7 gives *scarlet ornaments* retroactive identity as red sealing wax used on bonds and deeds; see
Variorum I, 364 (note, however, that seals are one of the most prominent features
of the book of Revelation [chapters 5–10, 20, and 22]).

    7. *sealed . . . bonds of love* (1) sworn vows of indissoluble union (taking
lips as speakers, vowers; *bonds* as what is vowed; and the metaphoric force of
bonds as indicating power to bind, tie together); (2) sealed to love compacts
(taking *lips* as kissers and the metaphoric force of *bonds* as indicating legal documents; the likeness of lips to seals and of kissing to sealing [imprinting with a
stamp] is obvious, and the idea of "sealing [ratifying, confirming] a bargain with
a kiss" was already commonplace; see *2Gent* II.ii.7, *V&A* 511–12, etc.). *false*
(1) illegal, illicit; (2) insincere, fraudulent, sham; (3) faithless (to me). *as oft as
mine* (1) as often as my lips have; (2) as often as they have [kissed] my lips
(which are true).

    7–8. *as oft as mine, / Robbed . . .* as often as mine, [and] robbed . . .
(taking line 8 as an elliptical third charge against the lips, which have *profaned*,
And sealed, [*and*] *Robbed*). The comma after *mine* invites the reading given in
the gloss; if the comma were deleted, the lines would say "as often as mine have
robbed . . . "; since Q's line-end commas often turn out to be merely formal
(e.g. the Q punctuations of 31.7 and 33.5), and, since the relation of *Robbed* to
the preceding syntax is doubtful in any case, Shakespeare's reader's experience
of the line may have included both the further charge against the beloved and a
further acknowledgment of the speaker's corresponding guilt.

    8,10. *revénues, impórtune* Shakespeare used "revénue" (the etymologically
indicated accentuation), and "révenue" interchangeably (see 50.7, note); *impórtune*, which is not stressed as its Latin root is, represents Shakespeare's usual
pronunciation.

    8. *revénues* sources of income, income-yielding possessions (*OED* gives this
from 1546: "The yearely revenewse & possessions of this your Highnes realme").
"Revenue" and "rent" are potential synonyms, and the gloss given here is
retroactively dictated by *rents* and the desire to remove a tautology. The tautology must always have been perceptible, and line 8 must always have been
awkward. The general sexual reference and import of the line is obvious, but
Shakespeare may have achieved its awkwardness in the course of trying to give
an extra fillip of wit to his metaphor. Perhaps this is another example of wordplay too subtle to succeed (see 112.1–14, 113.14, and 128, notes). Shakespeare
might have hoped to evoke some sort of bawdy play on "come": the root sense
of "revenue" is "return"; the word derives ultimately from Latin *venire*, "to
come," and immediately from the French noun *revenu*, which Cotgrave glosses
as "revenew; yearelie rents, profits, or incomings." The related French adjective,

revenu ("reverted, returned, come-backe or againe; also revived . . . ; also swollen, or puft up againe") figures in the expression *revenu de queue* (literally, "revived of tail"); among his glosses for *queue* Cotgrave gives "the label [i.e. the strip of cloth to which the seal was affixed] of a Deed" and "the bable [i.e. bauble, penis] of a man"; his gloss for *revenu de queue* is "Whose taile is new growne (applicable to an old cokes or callet [i.e. old fool], growne wanton on a sudden; or to anyone which after a great weaknesse hath picked up his crummes, or is become lustie againe"). (I do not mean to suggest that Shakespeare needed French examples before he could see the punning potential of "revenue"— although he apparently thought long and playfully upon French idioms; see *anguille d'haye* ["hedge adder"] and *escorcher les anguilles par la queue* ["to go about something the wrong way"] and *Lear* II.iv.119–24, the fool's speech on the cockney, the eels, and buttered hay.)

9. *Be it* = syncopated: "beet." *Be it lawful* if it is permissible (the phrase was used as a formula like "an't please you" and "so please you" [see *RIII* I.ii.8 and *Lear* I.i.253]; here, however the phrase also carries more literal meaning: "as long as it is permissible for you to behave so"). *as thou lov'st those* (1) with the same urgency and passion you feel for those with whom you are infatuated; (2) with the same casual and unscrupulous lust with which you use your paramours.

9–10. See 139.6, 11–12 and 140.14.

11. *Root* establish, implant (an atrophied botanical metaphor revivified by *grows* in the next clause). *pity* compassion, sympathetic fellow feeling (with specific resonances from the courtly love tradition by which a spurned lover importuned his lady to pity him, to take pity on him—referring to everything from giving him a smile to giving him her body; see *pity-wanting* in 140.4, "show pity or I die" in *Shrew* III.i.76, and the parody of a courtly lover's plea in *MWW* II.i.3–15). *that* so that (the gloss is dictated by the syntax of the following line; until the end of line 12 *that* can seem to be the relative pronoun: "which, when it grows . . .").

12. *Thy pity may deserve* The phrase conflates (1) "the pity that you have shown may make you deserving" and (2) "your [own] pitiful state may be worthy." (Sense (1) is indicated by the reference line 11 establishes for *Thy pity*; the non-idiomatic reading of *deserve* is evoked by context; although "to deserve" was used to mean "to earn" [*OED* cites Marlowe's *Edward II* IV.ii: "But by the sword, my lord, 't must be deserv'd"], that sense of "to deserve" is no more idiomatic in this line than "earn to be pitied" would be. Sense (2) is also pertinent to the preceding lines; but, although *OED* [4a] gives fifteenth- and seventeenth-century examples of *pity* meaning "pitiful condition," "pitiable state," sense (2) is not evoked until demanded by the standard idiom *deserve to . . . be* ["have the right to be"].)

13. *what thou dost hide* what you withhold (i.e. pity). The logic behind using *hide* to mean "withhold" or "deny" is this: "to show" is synonymous with "to reveal," "to allow to be seen," and with "to bestow" (in such idioms as "show favor" and "show pity"); therefore "to hide" and "to withhold" are synonyms.

Note that logic has been a topic of this poem since *grounded* in line 2. The faultiness of the syllogism is both pointed up and smoothed over by the presence of the word *seek*: "try to get" relates to "withhold"; "try to discover" relates to "conceal." The presence of *seek* suggests that the use of *hide* is intended as a playful exhibition of logical-linguistic sleight of hand, but there is evidence that Shakespeare's mind just worked that way—and that the minds of his listeners effortlessly join his; consider *TN* II.v.140 and the other locutions discussed in the notes on 109.6–7, 50.6, and 149.2.

14. *By self-example* by your own example. *mayst thou* (1) it will be just if, you will justly; (2) it could happen that you will; and—reading the line like a curse—(3) I pray that you (compare 143.13), may you be, I hope you will (sense (3) completes the process by which the speaker and the lady exchange characteristics in the course of the poem and by which the distinction in line 1 becomes as genuinely meaningless as its paradoxical form initially suggests; see lines 6–10).

SONNET 143

Although the manner and spirit of this sonnet make it very different from those that precede and follow, it resembles 142.9–12 in presenting a situation in which "A" vigorously seeks "B" while "C" seeks "A" with equal vigor.

1–8. This is an epic simile (i.e. an extended simile of the sort found in Homer and imitated in later heroic poems); epic similes are characterized by their length and fullness and by the fact that at least as much effort, detail, and space is devoted to describing the action or situation to which the poet's topic is likened as is devoted to describing the primary action. This one is, in effect, mock-heroic, not because the analogous situation is domestic and non-heroic—Homer's own similes are often so—but because the scene it conjures up is ridiculous. Shakespeare may have recalled either or both of two great earlier examples of chicken-related mock-heroic verse, *Canterbury Tales* VII.3355–3401 (the lament for Chaunticleer and the description of the widow's household and barnyard in pursuit of the fox at the end of the *Nun's Priest's Tale*) and *FQ* II.iii.36 (the likening of Braggadochio to a hen: "As fearefull fowle, that long in secret cave . . .").

1. *careful* (1) attentive; (2) distressed, full of care. *housewife* = pronounced "hussif"; compare "hussy."

2. *feathered* = perhaps pronounced "feth-red." *creatures* animals. (Although *feathered creatures* obviously refers to barnyard fowl, the general context of the lady's sexual activities and of 141.12 in particular can color the simile with advance suggestions of the situation to which it will be applied. "Creature," used to mean "servant," "retainer," "minion" [as in *Tim* I.i.119], was, like its synonyms, adopted into the hyperbole of courtly love as a term for a devoted lover [as in *TNK* II.v.39–41: "When your servant / (Your most unworthy creature) but offends you, / Command him die, he shall"]; see 57, the headnote to 133, and 141.10. Here *feathered creatures* can suggest the sort of dandified rivals—the "popinjays"—of which men in the speaker's situation are

traditionally both jealous and scornful.) *broke away* which has broken away, is loose.

4. *púrsuit* Compare the accentuation of "pursue" in *MofV* IV.i.293: "We trifle time; I pray thee pursue sentence." Shakespeare uses both the Latin accentuation and the English ("pursúit," as in 129.9).

5. *holds . . . in chase* = a standard periphrastic construction meaning "chases," "gives chase" (here *holds* has special, though substantively unharnessed, pertinence in a context that concerns holding or not holding a baby in one's arms and keeping or not keeping something from getting loose).

6. *Cries* (1) clamors, urgently demands; (2) weeps. *busy care* earnest concern (with an inherent reminder of the care not given the child—who is her "care" [see 48.7 and note]). *is bent* is singlemindedly directed, is intent (as in 90.2—but with a play on "turned awry" [see 116.4 and the general final note on that sonnet]).

7. *flies* flees (as in 145.12—with an inherent, but substantively incidental, reminder that, in this particular instance, *that which flies* from a pursuer has feathers, can fly). *flies before her face* flees as she advances. The phrase is not quite idiomatic; it echoes several idioms and conflates the substance of them all. Compare these examples from the Bible: "I flee from the face of my mistresse Sarai" (Genesis 16:18—Bishops'); "I wil flee from the face of Israel: for the Lord fighteth for them . . ." (Exodus 14:25—Geneva); "The Lord shal cause thine enemies that rise against thee, to fall before thy face: they shal come out against thee one way, & shal flee before thee seven wayes" (Deuteronomy 28:7—Geneva); ". . . the Gentiles, whom God drave out before the face of our fathers" (Acts 17:45—Bishops'). The phrase calls to mind an heroic military action and also contains a down-to-earth suggestion of cornered chickens or turkeys flying in the face of a pursuer.

8. *prizing* caring about, taking account of (with a play on "to prize" meaning "to capture"; *OED* gives sixteenth-century examples and this from Chapman's Homer: "To kill the five Hippasides and prise their arms").

10. *behind* This word makes a quiet play on *before* in line 7; it is antonymous with a sense *before* does not have in line 7, "ahead."

11. *catch* (1) attain, achieve; (2) overtake and capture; (3) ensnare the affection of, captivate (as in *HVIII* II.iii.76–77; "Beauty and honour in her are so mingled / That they have caught the King"). *thy hope* (1) what you seek to have, *thy will*; (2) the person you want (with a play on the fact that children were sometimes referred to as their parents' or their nation's "hopes" [see *3HVI* IV.vi.68]).

12. *be kind* be generous and gentle, pity me (see 142.11, note); the simile in 1–8 gives the line suggestions of "act as nature intends a mother to act," "do not neglect your child"; for *kind* meaning "natural," see 105.5, note).

13. *So* in that case (with a play on *So* in line 9). *thy will* what you want (but colored by *will* meaning "lust," by a quiet play on the auxiliary verb earlier in the line, and by a blatant play on "William." Note the Q text: "*Will*"; most editors follow Q, at least to the extent of capitalizing the second *will*. See 135, headnote).

SONNET 144

Compare the apparent situation here with those in 40–42, 133, and 134; see
141.1–14, note.

A version of this sonnet was printed in 1599 in *The Passionate Pilgrim*; see
138, headnote. Rollins (*Variorum* I, 368–69) gives this transcription from the
first edition of *PP*:

> Two loues I haue, of Comfort and Despaire,
> That like two Spirits, do suggest me still:
> My better Angell, is a Man (right faire)
> My worser spirite a Woman (colour'd ill.)
> To win me soone to hell, my Female euill
> Tempteth my better Angell from my side:
> And would corrupt my Saint to be a Diuell,
> Wooing his puritie with her faire pride.
> And whether that my Angell be turnde feend,
> Suspect I may (yet not directly tell:)
> For being both to me: both, to each friend,
> I ghesse one Angell in anothers hell:
> > The truth I shall not know, but liue in dout,
> > Till my bad Angell fire my good one out.

Trying to decide the relationship between the *PP* and Q versions is as difficult as
it is in the case of 138, and for similar reasons. In line 2 *PP*'s "That" and Q's
Which tell us nothing. The *PP* version of line 13 is more straightforward than
Q's, which, though not really preferable, signals a new formal and logical departure with *Yet*, and thus sounds more like Shakespeare's usual couplet practice; on the whole, the *PP* version sounds more like the work of someone trying
to remember the Q line than like an early draft. On the other hand, the *PP*
version of line 11 seems more like an early draft by the author than the product
of someone else's lapsed memory; *PP*'s "to" makes line 11 easier to understand,
but Q's *from* accentuates the fact that the speaker's *two loves*, who are his by
virtue of love for them, are not his in any practical sense because both are absent
from him; the Q line is a bit more elliptical, but it gives up none of the sense of
the *PP* version and adds a considerable amount.

The rhyme between "sight" and *pride* in lines 6 and 8 of the Q version sounds
wrong to modern readers, and very probably is so. *PP*'s "side" probably warrants emendation of Q. However, Renaissance poets did occasionally rhyme
words in which the final consonants differ (the practice may have been more
acceptable when the discrepancy resulted from grammatical inflection—compare
fleet'st/*sweets* in 19.5,7 and "enur'd"/"procure" in the Q text of *LC* 251–52).
Moreover, even if we were to assume that the "sight"/*pride* rhyme would have
been unacceptable to Shakespeare, we could still not be altogether certain that
the Q printer misread his copy text when he printed "sight" in line 6: Q might
reproduce the *PP* text in a partially revised text that Shakespeare was still tinker-
ing with when the sonnets came into Thorpe's possession. Two of the five sub-

stantive differences between the two versions relate to the *side/pride* rhyme in quatrain 2. If, as is probable, *worser spirit* in line 4 is to be pronounced "worser sprite," then it forms a complex ideational and phonetic chiasmus with *right fair* in line 3. *PP*'s "faire pride" in line 8 does too: "faire pride" comes close to saying "fair wrong" and to sounding like "fair right"; perhaps the Q text derives from a MS in which Shakespeare was trying to achieve an even more complicated inversion of *right fair* and to crowd just a little more wit into his creation (compare 112 and 142 and notes); Q's "sight" in line 6 is closer to *right* in *right fair* than *side* is; moreover, "sight" pertains to two of the sonnet's topics: perceiving fairness (of all kinds), and being able to know rather than guess (lines 10–14); on the other hand, the context of *hell*, the *female evil*, and temptation gives *from my side* logically unavailable potential for suggesting "out of my side" and the creation of Eve out of a rib taken from Adam's side (Gen. 2:21–23; the expression "from the side" does not figure in the Biblical account, but it was standard in references to the creation of Eve; see *PL* VIII.536, IX.965, Milton's play on "out of my side" and "by my side" in *PL* IV.484–85, and—for pre-Shakespearian evidence—*OED*'s examples s.v. "side" and "rib"). *PP*'s "faire pride" in line 8 has much more ideational resonance than Q's *foul pride* (Ingram and Redpath say that "faire pride" lacks "the strong oxymoron" that *foul* affords to the Q version; but the bad connotations of *pride* are at least as strong as the good ones, and so "faire pride" is a strong oxymoron too). It seems unlikely, but is not impossible, that a mistaken memory would be subtler than a Shakespearian original, and so the evidence of "faire"/*foul* in line 8 would seem to weigh in favor of the theory that the Q text of 144 derives from a Shakespearian revision of the version printed in *PP*—perhaps a revision in which he was still experimenting, giving up "faire" in favor of *foul*, a phonetically and ideationally complex link between line 8 and *right fair* in line 3, and trying to find a rhyme for "sight" that is ideationally as well as phonetically suited for being set against *right* in line 3. On the other hand, the argument that *PP*'s flat-footed line 13 is the creation of someone's struggling memory remains intact—as does the undeniable probability that Q's "sight" is the printer's error it has always seemed to be. . . . All in all, this small problem, one for which we have more evidence than is usually available to solvers of the problems of Shakespeare's sonnets, provides an excellent object lesson in the frustration that goes with scholarly and non-scholarly theorizing about the 1609 quarto.

1. "I have two beloveds; one gives me comfort, and the other drives me to despair." (Until the qualities are distributed in lines 3 and 4, *of comfort and despair* can refer equally to both *loves*; *PP* and some modern editions set the phrase off in commas, but that has no effect on the logic of the line. Note also that, although both *comfort* and *despair* are used generally here, they are both terms in theology, an area which the poem immediately invades.)

2,4. *spirits, spirit* The word is apparently dissyllabic in line 2 and monosyllabic in line 4; see 86.5, note.

2. *suggest me* prompt me, urge me on (compare *RII* I.i.100–01: "he did . . . / Suggest his soon-believing adversaries" and *HVIII* I.i.163–65: "Only to show his pomp . . . [he] suggests the King . . . this last costly treaty"; Shake-

speare's similar uses of "'to suggest'" usually occur where the suggester is a tempter urging evil action by making it seem desirable [e.g. *RII* III.iv.75–76: "What Eve, what serpent, hath suggested thee / To make a second fall of cursed man?"]). *still* continually.

3. *right fair* beautiful indeed (but *coloured ill* retroactively adds "fair complexioned," "blond," to the sense of *fair*; see 127.1, 131.12, 132.13, and notes).

5,7; 9,11. The rhymes *evil*/*devil* and *fiend*/*friend* sound odd to a modern ear and, appearing in context of speculations on degenerative transformations, might invite interpretation as illustrative phonetic effects. However, the *fiend*/*friend* rhyme occurs again in *V&A* 638, 640; and *fiend* rhymes with *end* in 145.9, 11 and *Phoenix* 6,7. The *evil*/*devil* rhyme is very common in verse before and after Shakespeare and in Shakespeare's plays. See Kökeritz, pp. 188–89 and 192–93.

6. *side* = the *PP* reading; see headnote.

7. *my saint* my virtuous beloved (like such still-current phrases as "my angel," this epithet is in the courtly love tradition, in which poets customarily spoke to and about their beloveds in the manner and language of vassals to, or about, lords or worshipers to, or about, saints; compare *A&S* 61 and *Amoretti* 22 and 61, and see sonnet 130.

8. *foul* (1) ugly, not fair; (2) morally evil (see 132.14 and 137.12). *pride* (1) splendor, show of finery, gorgeousness (compare 99.3); (2) lust (compare *Oth* III.iii.408, quoted in 76.1, note)—with a play on the fact that pride is preeminently the Devil's sin.

9. *whether that* as to whether it is true that. (The gloss of *whether that* as an ellipsis is dictated by *Suspect I may* in line 10; "to suspect whether" is not idiomatic.)

10. *directly* Ingram and Redpath say, "Some or all of the following senses seem to be present: (1) 'by direct evidence', (2) 'completely' (see *OED.* 4), and (3) 'as yet' (literally, 'immediately', in time); though (1) is probably primary."

11. "But since both are absent from me, and since each is a friend of the other." (The gloss on the last part of the line is dictated by its likeness to the first and reflects an elliptical form of "both being friend to each"; the awkwardness of *both to each friend* presumably derives from Shakespeare's desire to assert the alliance between the two loves grammatically in the word *both* and to balance *both from* with *both to*; *both from* and "both friend" would have made a good phonetic pair, and "both friend to each" would have maintained the "from"/"to" contrast without being any more awkward than the phrase Shakespeare chose. However, *both from me both to each friend*, which has the practical advantage of providing a rhyme for *fiend* in line 9, has the greater virtue of presenting the idea that each becomes the other's "friend" instead of the speaker's in a near-image of the two loves, made one by the pronoun, acting in consort to leave the speaker—go *from* him, and moving toward each other— going *to each* other. Most editors put a clarifying comma between *both from me* and *both to each* [compare the punctuation of the *PP* version]. I retain the Q punctuation because it includes the idea that the alliance of the two beloveds occurred only because they were introduced by the mutual friend they have

betrayed: they came together *from* being—as a result of being—friends of the speaker [compare the *PP* version: "For being both to me"].)

12. *one angel in another's hell*   (1) each is a punishment to the other; they are one another's punishment; (2) one angel (the man) is in the other's (the woman's) hell. Seymour-Smith provides this note on the metaphors of line 12:

> A. Forbes Sieveking quotes this description of the game of Barley-break, or Last-in-hell, in *Shakespeare's England* (1916): 'It was played by six persons, three of each sex, coupled by lot. A piece of ground is divided into three compartments, the middle one being called "hell". The couple condemned to hell try to catch the others advancing from the extremities; if they succeed, the hell-pair change places with the couple taken. In the catching, the middle pair were not to be separate before they succeeded, while the others might loose hands at any time if pressed. When all had been taken the last couple was said to be "in hell", and the game ended.' Hussey's assertion (ed. 1888) that this line contains a reference to Barley-break has been challenged; but lines 5–7 seem to bear him out. 'Hell' also has here an obvious physical connotation.

And Ingram and Redpath say this:

> Several meanings appear to be present: (1) they are both in the 'Hell' or middle-den of a game of barley-break; (2) as contemporaries averred, such a position was often used as a pretext for a sexual tumble; (3) 'Hell' is probably also, as in Boccaccio's story of Rustico and Alibech (*Decameron*, III, 10), the female sexual organ. In the case . . . of sense (3) 'one angel' is the man, and 'another' is the woman.

See *hell* in 119.2 and 129.14; compare *Lear* IV.vi.127–28 and hhe following exercise in obscenity (Epigram 15 in Samuel Rowlands's *The Letting of Humours Blood* [1600], which J. Q. Adams justly suggested was written in imitation of 144; see *Variorum* I, 370):

> Amorous *Austin* spendes much Balleting,
> In rimeing Letters, and loue Sonnetting.
> She that loues him, his Ynckehorne shall be paint her,
> And with all *Venus* tytles hee'le acquaint her:
> Vowing she is a perfect Angell right,
> When she by waight is many graines too light:
> Nay all that do but touch her with the stone,
> Will be depos'd that Angell she is none,
> How can he proue her for an Angell then?
> That proues her selfe a Diuell, tempting men,
> And draweth many to the fierie pit,
> Where they are burned for their ent'ring it.
> I know no cause wherefore he tearmes her so,
> Vnlesse he meanes shee's one of them below,
> Where *Lucifer*, chiefe Prince doth domineere:

If she be such, then good my hartes stand cleere,
Come not within the compasse of her flight,
For such as do, are haunted with a spright.
This Angell is not noted by her winges,
But by her tayle, all full of prickes and stinges.
And know this lustblind Louer's vaine is led,
To prayse his Diuell, in an Angels sted.

Also see the bawdy-pretty, Ophelia-like ravings of the Jailer's Daughter in *TNK* IV.iii.29–40 where she describes her future in Elysium and contrasts it with the punishment of the damned: "Faith, . . . sometime we go to barley-break, we of the blessed. Alas, 'tis a sore life they have i' th' tother place, such burning, frying, boiling, hissing . . . ." (The speech occurs in a context of incidental references to coins and coining; see the note on Gresham below.)

14. The line is incredibly full. It says "Until she gets tired of him and kicks him out" and "Until he shows symptoms of venereal disease" (see Rollins's comment in *Variorum* I, 371). Both senses are enhanced by incidentally bawdy suggestions of "smoking a fox" from its hole (compare *Lear* V.iii.22–23: "He that parts us shall bring a brand from heaven / And fire us hence like foxes"); moreover, *fire* sustains the metaphor of hell and also embodies the idea of punishment for sin (compare 141.13–14 and the traditional popular interpretation of the statement in the second commandment that the sins of the fathers are visited upon the children unto the third and fourth generation). The line also makes a comically apt allusion to—and conflation of—four substantively interchangeable proverbs: "One fire [or heat] drives out another." "One love drives out another." "One nail drives out another." "One wedge drives out another" (Tilley, F277, L538, N17, and W234—part of the wit here derives from the fact that the context of this sonnet gives the proverbs a bawdy relationship in their particulars [fire, love, nail, wedge] as well as in their tenor). Last but not least, the line activates one of the favorite Renaissance puns, that on *angel* meaning a spiritual being and the coin called "an angel" (see 119.9, note, *MWW* I.iii.50–54, etc.). The pun is activated by the splendidly comic echo of "Gresham's Law," an economic axiom propounded by Sir Thomas Gresham in a letter to Queen Elizabeth in 1558: "Bad money drives out good."

SONNET 145

This, the slightest of the sonnets, is the only one in tetrameters. Many commentators have hoped that it is not by Shakespeare (see *Variorum* I, 372–73). One cannot be certain that the sonnet is Shakespeare's, but the effect it describes —that of being surprised by a sentence that signals one direction and then takes another—is an effect that Shakespeare is very fond of actually achieving in his reader; what the speaker tells us happened to him as he listened to his lady is what actually happens to a reader time after time as he reads these sonnets (see, for example, 15.1–2, 35, 75.3, 79.5, and the four successive syntactic identities that emerge in the course of the first two lines of sonnet 13). Other commentators have felt that 145 might be Shakespeare's but does not belong in this sequence. It does, however, take up the topic of damnation and salvation that is the common denominator of 144 and 146. If we are to believe that 145 is spurious, we must assume that it was chosen and placed by a literary pirate who was either improbably careful or improbably serendipitous.

1. *love's* Cupid's. (The personification is immediately made apparent by *own hand*; Q capitalizes the word.)

2,9,13; 14. *I hate*; *not you* Modern editors often put these phrases in quotation marks, thus giving the poem greater clarity than it had for Shakespeare's reader.

5. *Straight* immediately, straightaway.

7. *Was used in* used to be used in, was customarily employed for (a conflation of two senses of *used*). *doom* sentence, judgment (see 107.4).

8. *greet* address me (compare *HV* II.iv.76–78: "thus he greets your Majesty : / He wills you . . . / That you . . .").

10–11. *day* / *Doth follow night* The idea was proverbial (Tilley, N164) as an emblem of inevitability (as in *Ham* I.iii.79) and of hope (as in *Macb* IV.iii.240).

12. *is flown* has fled (with a suggestion of "has flown through the air," evoked by the fact that fiends—fallen angels—are traditionally winged; compare *flies* in 143.9).

13. *hate away* Andrew Gurr persuasively suggests a pun on "Hathaway" ("Shakespeare's First Poem: Sonnet 145" in *Essays in Criticism*, XXI [July 1971], 221–26). (Since *And* was regularly pronounced "an" [see Kökeritz, p. 271], there may be a pun on Shakespeare's wife's first name as well; line 14 may have sounded like "Anne saved my life . . . .")

SONNET 146

The following notes draw heavily on a sequence of three articles which are discussed in detail in a long final note on this sonnet: Donald A. Stauffer, "Critical Principles and a Sonnet," *The American Scholar*, XII (Winter 1942–43), pp. 52–62; B.C. Southam, "Shakespeare's Christian Sonnet. No. 146," *SQ*, XI (Winter 1960), 67–71; and Charles A. Huttar, "The Christian Basis of Shakespeare's Sonnet 146," *SQ*, XIX (Autumn 1968), 355–65.

Michael West has recently documented the kinship of this poem with medieval verse debates between body and soul—a genre revived in the seventeenth century ("The Internal Dialogue of Shakespeare's Sonnet 146," *SQ*, XXV [Winter 1974], 109–22); in particular, West cites this anonymous "Dialogue betweene the Soule and the Body" from Francis Davison's *Poetical Rhapsody* (1602):

> *Soule* Ay me, poore Soule, whom bound in sinful chains
> This wretched body keepes against my will!
> *Body* Aye mee poore Body, whom for all my paines,
> This froward soule causlesse condemneth stil.
> *Soule* Causles? whenas thou striv'st to sin each day?

> *Body* Causles: when I strive thee to obay
> *Soule* Thou art the meanes, by which I fall to sin
> *Body* Thou art the cause that set'st this means awork
> *Soule* No part of thee that hath not faultie bin
> *Body* I shew the poyson that in thee doth lurke.
> *Soule* I shall be pure when so I part from thee:
> *Body* So were I now, but that thou stainest mee.

West also offers examples of other analogous turns of thought and phrase among Shakespeare's contemporaries.

This sonnet and *Ham* V.i.1–236 are variously related in themes, diction, and thought processes.

1. *Poor soul* Although the succeeding lines indicate that *Poor* indicates pity and *soul* refers to the immortal spirit of the speaker, *Poor soul* momentarily stands alone and can give the lines that follow overtones of the well-established idiom meaning "poor creature" (compare *Shrew* IV.i.168–69: "she, poor soul, / Knows not which way to stand, to look, to speak"); the phrase already implied a position of detached superiority from which the user benevolently but casually condescends. (Moreover, in context of a collection of love poems, the whole of line 1 can seem to be an apostrophe to the speaker's beloved, the center of his world; the reference of *soul* does not solidify until line 2 [note that one of the traditional locations of hell is the center of the earth—see 144.12].) *center* The reference of the epithet is the center of a circle, the point by which the circle is defined and around which it revolves. Here *center* must be understood figuratively as an indication of relative value; see the Neo-Platonic use of the circle-center metaphor in the passage quoted from *Courtier* in the final note to sonnet 93. Ingram and Redpath say, "Most editors cite *R&J.* II.i.2: 'turn back, dull earth, and find thy centre out'; but do not offer to elucidate the meaning of 'centre' there either. Both here and there it refers to what is, or ought to be, the center of attraction, the being which should be served, in the one case by Romeo, in the other by the body." The word also suggests the location of the soul as imagined in concrete terms; the soul is loosely but traditionally imagined as the inmost element in the body (compare *John* III.ii.20–21: "Within this wall of flesh / There is a soul counts thee her creditor"). In context of this line, *earth* also invokes overtones of "the center" used as an ellipsis for "the center of the earth" (*OED* gives an example from the fourteenth century, one from *The Atheist's Tragedy*, and *Ham* II.ii.156–58: "I will find / Where truth is hid, though it were hid indeed / Within the centre"). The line has logically gratuitous but philosophically suggestive complication from the fact that "the earth," as the center of the Ptolemaic universe, and "the center" were potential synonyms (as in *T&C* I.iii.85–86: "The heavens themselves, the planets, and this centre, / Observe degree, priority, and place"). *my . . . earth* (1) the substance of which my body is composed (the reference is to earth as the grossest of the four elements [see 44.1 and 44.11, note]; see also Genesis 2: 7: "The Lord God also made the man of the dust of the grounde, and breathed in his face breath of life, and the man was a living soule" and 1Cor. 15: 45–50, which, along with "earth

to earth, ashes to ashes, dust to dust," is included in the burial service); (2) the world, my world (with overtones of the commonplace notion of the body as a microcosm, a little world; compare *JC* II.i.67–69 and Donne, *Holy Sonnets* V: "I am a little world made cunningly / Of elements, and an Angelike spright, / But black sinne hath betraid to endless night / My worlds both parts, and (oh) both parts must die . . .").

The elements of line 1 can lead the mind toward the Eden myth. Immediately following the account of man's creation from dust comes this: "And the Lord God planted a garden Eastwarde in Eden, and there he put the man whome he had made" (Gen. 2:7,8). More particularly the conjunction of *earth* and *center* in a spatial conception of hierarchical value can suggest the various formal and informal traditions whereby Eden was at the geographical center of the earth (e.g. the idea that it was at the equator [alluded to in *PL* IV.282] and the spatial implications of Gen. 2:10) and the related idea of man created to "rule over the fish of the sea, and over the foule of the heaven . . . & over all the earth" (Genesis 1:26).

Line 1 prepares the way for all the ideas from which and toward which the poem develops; it reaches toward the intermeshed paradoxes by which man is made of earth and has dominion over earth ("made . . . to have dominion in the workes of [God's] hands . . . [and has] all things under his fete"— Psalms 8:6), and by which man has the earth for domicile, has the body for "his earthly house," and has another "buylding given of God, that is an house not made with hands, but eternal in the heavens," a house for which

> we sigh, desiring to be clothed with our house, which is from heaven. / . . . / For in dede we that are in this tabernacle, sigh and are burdened, because we wolde not be unclothed, but wolde be clothed upon, that mortalitie might be swalowed up of life. / And he that hathe created us for this thing, is God, who also hathe given unto us the earnest [i.e. down payment] of the Spirit. / Therefore we are alway bolde, thogh we knowe that whiles we are at home in the bodie, we are absent from the Lord. / . . . / . . . we are bolde & love rather to remove out of the bodie, and to dwell with the Lord. / Wherefore also we covet, that bothe dwelling at home ["In this bodie"—marginal note, Geneva], and removing from home, we may be acceptable to him. / For we must all appeare before the judgement seat of Christ . . . . [2Cor. 5:1–10]

This opening line suggests the beginning of human history, implies its course, and implies its end, which is also the focus of the poem's end, the Last Judgment, doomsday—when the bodies and souls of the righteous shall be reunited in eternal life and death shall have "no more dominion" over them (Romans 6:9).

2. Q reads "My sinfull earth these rebbell powres that thee array." Sisson, who called this "the prize crux of the Sonnets," sums up the problem and its solutions: "It is apparent that the compositor has repeated *my sinful earth* as a sort of catchword, and left out two syllables which would have completed the sense of 1.2. Conjecture is free, subject to a decision upon the trend of thought of the missing words, which could be 'against,' 'the aim or butt of,' 'a prey to,' or as C.

Leech suggested privately, 'feigning to deceive by brave shows,' etc. An infinity of suggestions is possible. . . . Recent editors, perhaps wisely, eschew conjecture" (I, 214). Sisson himself decided that, "taking all into account," "Fenced by" was the most satisfactory guess; perhaps wisely, he did not say what the "all" he considered was. Ingram and Redpath, who choose "Foil'd by," explain how they came to do so. Nonetheless, their arbitrary choice is just as good as Sisson's or any of several others that Rollins lists (*Variorum* I, 374). If I had to offer my own no less arbitrary preference, I would choose "pressed with," which participates in the phonetic pattern set in motion by the consonants in *Poor soul* and which pertains variously to the ideas of weight, siege, and penalties that run through the whole sonnet (see *o'erpressed defence* in 139.8, *press* in 140.1, and 140.1–2, note).

these rebel pow'rs   the body and the passions (see the final note on this sonnet).   *array*   "In Shakespearian usage the word has a wide range of meaning. In a semi-technical sense, given the military context of line two, it would mean 'marshal for battle': thus the physical being ('these rebbell powres') mobilizes and exploits the soul, who should rule, to its own ends. As we come on to line three this meaning would give way to the second sense—'to ill-treat, to bring to a lowly condition'. While, with the house-decoration of line four, 'array' could be understood as meaning 'to dress, to decorate'. Not one of these meanings is exclusive and they all operate to amplify the situation in obedience to the varying associations which the neighboring lines suggest" (Southam, p. 69). Of these meanings, "to dress," "to clothe," was the commonest in Shakespeare's time; in context of a developing contrast between the soul and its mortal trappings, *array* might have carried a pertinent reminder of its use in the Sermon on the Mount (Matt. 6:28–29, quoted in 94.12, note). Shakespeare uses the noun "array" in the military sense in *3HVI* V.i.62–63: "Stand we in good array, for they . . . / Will issue out again and bid us battle." *OED* exemplifies "to array" meaning "to afflict" with this from around 1600: "Vyce . . . which hathe hym so Encombered and arayed."

3. *pine*   (1) suffer, undergo pain; (2) long eagerly, hunger; (3) starve, waste away for want of food (as in 75.13).   *pine within*   (1) pine inwardly, pine but make no outward show of grief or need (compare the expression "to eat one's heart out" and the behavior described in *TN* II.iv.109–11: "She never told her love, / But let concealment, like a worm i' th' bud, / Feed on her damask cheek. She pin'd in thought"); (2) stay inside and pine (i.e. behave like the occupant of a besieged city).   *suffer*   (1) undergo the anguish of; (2) bear patiently; (3) acquiesce in (compare 58.5).   *dearth*   want, famine, deprivation (with a strong suggestion of "death"—a word *dearth* suggests phonetically, a word suggested by *suffer*—which was used intransitively to mean "suffer death," "pay the penalty of death," "be executed" [*OED* gives this from 1570: "al Gods Sainctes that suffered in Q. Maries time"; compare *Macb* III.ii.16: "let the frame of things disjoint, both the worlds suffer"], and a word so pertinent to a discussion of the soul's peril that one early editor—or, more probably, one early printer—changed *dearth* to "death" in his text of the sonnet [*Variorum* I, 375]).

1–3. Compare the diction of Proverbs 19:15–16 "slouthfulnesse bryngeth

sleepe, and a soule accustomed with craft, shall suffer hunger. / Who so kepeth
the commandement kepeth his owne soule: but he that regardeth not his wayes,
shall dye" (Bishops' Version).

1–4. Note that the *rebel pow'rs* are both the besiegers and the besieged; they
imprison and they protect. The paradox inherent in the perfectly fluid fusion of
metaphors is emblematic of the whole poem.

3–14. See 1Tim. 6:12–19: "Fight the good fight of faith: laye holde of eternal
life, whereunto thou art also called . . . / I charge thee . . . / That thou kepe
this commandement without spot, and unrebukeable, until the appearing of our
Lord Jesus Christ . . . / . . . / Who onely hathe immortalitie, & dwelleth
in the light that none can atteine unto, whome never man sawe, nether can se
. . . / Charge them that are riche in this worlde, that they be not high minded,
and that they trust not in uncerteine riches, but in the living God . . ./ That
they do good, & be riche in good workes . . . / Laying up in store for them
selves a good fundation against the time to come, that they may obteine eternal
life." See also Matt. 13: 44–49:

> Againe the kingdome of heaven is like unto a treasure hid in the field,
> which when a man hathe founde, he hideth it, & for joye thereof departeth
> and selleth all he hathe, and byeth that field.
>
> Againe the kingdome of heaven is like to a marchant man, that seketh
> good perles,
>
> Who having founde a perle of great price, went and solde all that he had,
> and boght it.
>
> Againe the kingdome of heaven is like unto a drawe net cast into the
> sea, that gathereth of all kindes of things.
>
> Which, when it is ful, men drawe to land, and sit and gather the good into
> vessels, and cast the bad away.
>
> So shal it be at the end of the worlde. The Angels shal go forthe, and
> sever the bad from among the just . . . .

4. (1) "paying attention to mere outward show"; (2) "paying attention to
what is on the outside and therefore of no benefit to what is inside." *Painting*
For the cosmetic overtones in *Painting*, see 21.2 and 82.13; compare *Ham*
V.i.189. *costly* (1) gorgeously; (2) extravagantly, expensively (with strong
overtones of "at such a sacrifice," "at such dire cost to yourself," "which is so
harmful"). *gay* (1) showy, brightly colored (*OED*, 3); (2) excellent, estimable
(*OED* gives this from 1563: "This maie seme to some, a gaie saiyng where as in
deede, it is bothe foolishe, and wicked"); (3) specious, flimsy, unreliable (*OED*
gives this from 1548: "Thei with money, and gay promises, first corrupted a
Miller").

5. *cost* expenditure (compare 64.2). *having* since you have. *lease* See
107.3, note.

6. *fading* (1) losing its brightness and color; (2) decaying, declining (like a
withering flower), dying. *mansion* dwelling place, house. (The word did not
yet carry implications of grandeur; compare the French *maison*.) *Mansion* was a
stock metaphor for the human body as residence of the soul—perhaps because

it accidentally contains the sound "man," and "house" and "dwelling" do not. This is Tyndale's version of 2Cor. 5:1–2: "We know surely yf oure erthly mancion wherin we now dwell were destroyed, that we have a bilding ordeyned of God, an habitacion not made with hondes, but eternall in heaven. / And herefore sigh we, desiringe to be clothed with oure mansion which is from heaven." See 95.9, note.

7. *inheritors* See 94.5, note (on *inherit*). *of this excess* (1) of this unnecessary superfluity; (2) of this extravagant expense (with a play on "as a result of this departure, this going out"; the literal sense of *excess* is "departure"; see *OED*, 1, and compare the use of Latin *excessus* to mean "a departure from life").

8. *thy charge* (1) what you have spent, the *large cost, this excess*; (2) what is entrusted to you, that over which you are guardian, i.e. the body (compare *T&C* V.ii.6–7: *Diomedes*: "How now, my charge!" / *Cressida*: "Now, my sweet guardian"); (3) your burden, that which weighs you down. The coexistence of senses (2) and (3) in the word *charge* makes it an emblematic summary of the problematic relationship between body and soul: the body, which protects, houses, shelters, the soul, also holds the soul prisoner within it—has charge of the body, holds it in charge; the soul, God's viceroy in the body, is charged with responsibility for it. *end* (1) fate (colored by the pertinence of *end* meaning "death," "destruction"); (2) purpose.

9. *live . . . upon* (1) live off, sustain yourself by means of (see *feed on* in line 13); (2) attain eternal life by means of, avoid spiritual death by means of. ("To live" has extra-logical pertinence because its here inactive sense "to dwell" echoes the topics of residence and real estate in lines 4–7.)

10. *that* thy servant, the body. *pine to* suffer in order to (intensified by the momentary resemblance between this construction and "pine-plus-infinitive" meaning "yearn to do or have something"). *aggravate* increase. (*OED* gives three examples of similarly neutral uses of the word, one from a 1549 English version of a Latin original, the second a self-consciously pedantic display from 1635, and the third a doubtful example from 1698. The gloss on *aggravate* in this line is dictated by the logic of the context: the sentence does not make sense unless the word is understood in its most literal Latin sense rather than the various English senses that derived from figurative Latin uses of *aggravare*, "to make heavier." All *OED*'s examples of idiomatic uses of *aggravate* involve the infliction of hardship or injury, but several Renaissance senses actively retain the idea of placing or adding weight. Thus, although the sense of *aggravate* in this line would have felt strange and strained to Shakespeare's reader, *aggravate* would have had a general pertinence to this context of burdens and penalties that a modern reader may not hear; note particularly that the word had legal associations; *OED* gives this 1583 example of *aggravate* meaning "to load something heavy upon": "If the punishment . . . were aggravated and executed upon the offenders," and this 1626 example of *aggravate* meaning "bring as a charge against": "Aggravating it as an act of Rebellion." However, despite contextual reinforcement of *aggravate* as a simple synonym for "increase," the word inevitably infuses the line with overtones of the senses "to aggravate" still has—"to make worse," "to annoy," "to inflame." Those senses do not modify the dis-

cursive sense, but they can aggravate a reader's sense of uneasiness about a re-
commendation of spiritual values couched in terms appropriate to a petty,
mundane, vindictive vow to revenge in kind.) *thy store* your resources, your
stock of treasure.

11. Stauffer quotes Elizabeth Drew to the effect that line 11 "simultaneously
carries on three threads of thought: concerning marketing, time and value. It
also sets up oppositions for each. And all three threads of thought merge to
suggest the superiority of the spirit to matter, of immortality to evanescence
. . ." (p. 57). *Buy* purchase (although, when heard, *Buy* can be momentarily
mistaken for "by" and seem to indicate the means of increasing, the substance to
be added, and/or the size of the addition). *terms* set period of time (like the
span of a *lease* or the periods during the year during which law courts or schools
are in session); *terms divine*, therefore, refers to "eternity" and is in effect an
oxymoron: *terms*—from Latin *terminus*, "boundary," "limit," "end"—are by
definition finite; what is divine is infinite; note the ideational interplay among
lease in line 5, *end* in line 8, *terms divine*, and the idea of the Last Judgment—an
idea that hovers behind this poem throughout and is expressly evoked in line 14.
(The mercantile metaphor can also evoke echoes of *terms* meaning "stipula-
tions" and give the line a suggestion of making a deal with God.)

12. *without be* (1) externally be; (2) let the outside, the *outward walls*, be
(colored by the general pertinence of the syntactically irrelevant prepositional
sense of *without* meaning "lacking").

13. Compare 1Cor. 15:54 (which is included in the burial service): "Death is
swallowed up in victory."

14. See 1Cor. 15:26 (which is also included in the burial service): "The last
enemy that shall be destroyed, is death"; Isaiah 25:8: "He wil destroye death for
ever"; and Rev. 21:4: "and there shal be no more death."

1–14. *A note on the functions of criticism:*

I have elsewhere examined several critical accounts of sonnet 94 in an effort to
demonstrate the illogic and folly of habitually thinking about a Shakespeare
sonnet in terms of "either . . . or" and "is . . . but" and to recommend thinking in terms of "both . . . and" and "is . . . and is also" (*An Essay on Shakespeare's Sonnets*, New Haven, 1969, pp. 152–68). Sonnet 146 is a subtler poem
than 94 and the experience of reading it is less jarring intellectually, but both
place their readers' minds so as to look at facts from a single point of view (thus
inviting critics to demonstrate the exclusive pertinence of that point of view),
and also lead them inevitably to look at the same facts from other and incompatible points of view (thus inviting critics to deny that their minds wander
from the frame of reference the poet demands or to deny that the overt intent and
effect of the sonnet are what they seem to be). Sonnet 146 has recently prompted
two valuable essays (cited in the preceding notes)—B.C. Southam's, which takes
issue with the critical consensus on the sonnet, and Charles Huttar's, which takes
issue with Southam. The essays are valuable in themselves and valuable as demonstrations that this sonnet (like most of Shakespeare's sonnets) is satisfying
to read, unsatisfying to think about, and likely to evoke critical analyses that
satisfy only by *making* the poem satisfying to think about. These two essays are

more open-minded, more responsible, and more sensible than essays in the controversy over sonnet 94 have been, but in a sophisticated form they too exhibit
the debilitating effects of insisting that anything that is true must be exclusively
true and that the presence of one implication necessarily diminishes the force
of counter implications that are also present.

One of my purposes in writing the present commentary on the sonnets is to
advertise a criticism that does not try to say how a work should be read or
should have been read in the past but instead concerns itself with how the work
is read, how it probably *was* read, and why. The following cavilling comments
on the Southam and Huttar essays are intended as witness to the wisdom and
practical necessity of a criticism that admits that every impression that a poem
evokes in the majority of its modern readers and can be demonstrated as a probable response in the majority of the poet's contemporaries is and was a part of
that poem and cannot be argued away. I hope that the following discussion will
also explain how the glosses I provide throughout this commentary are to be
used and why I gloss in the pluralistically-committed way I do.

I will start with Huttar's efforts to gloss a single phrase, *these rebel pow'rs* in
line 2. He successfully argues that the phrase refers to non-physical faculties, to
the passions, the affections, the emotions, the lower powers of the soul. He
quotes John Wylkinson's 1547 translation of Aristotle's *Ethics* in probably unnecessary support of his point:

> The Solle of Man hath thre powers, one is called the lyfe vegitable: in the
> whiche man is partener with trees & with plantes: The second power, is
> the life sensible in the whiche a man is partener with beastes, for why al
> beastes haue lifes sensible. The third, is called solle reasonable, by the
> whiche a man differeth from all other thinges, for there is none reasonable
> but man. And this power reasonable is sometyme in acte, and sometime
> in power, from whence the Beatitude is whan it is in acte and not when it is
> in power. [p. 358]

However, Huttar does not succeed in his argument that Southam and the world
at large are "wrong to take 'these rebbell powres' as referring to 'the physical
being.' "

Huttar stresses the distinction between the flesh and desires of the flesh.
Huttar assumes not only that making the distinction is valid, which it is, but that
the distinction bears on this poem, which it does not. He offers Donne's Holy
Sonnet XIV ("Batter my heart"), *FQ* II.xi.1–2, and other examples of the
Renaissance commonplace by which "the relation of reason to the other powers"
of the soul is presented in images of war—particularly civil war—between reason
and the passions and in images of reason besieged by the affections; he harnesses
them thus:

> The affections are part of the soul; yet they besiege "the fort of reason" in
> order "to bring the soule into captiuitie". Here is precedent for Shake-
> speare's addressing himself to the whole soul in line one, then referring to
> only a part, reason, by the "thee" of line two. The role of the body is to

augment the onslaught of affections through the infirmity of the flesh; but if the servant is obedient to the master . . . *both body and soul are saved together.*

The insistence of the Christian creeds on the resurrection of the body clearly shows that the concept of the body as a prison, which the soul is better off rid of, is rejected. . . . In Christian thought the body is not to be done away with but to be redeemed (Rom.viii:23) by being changed (Phil. iii:21; I Cor.xv:20,35–54) . . . . The body is not inherently evil but potentially good or evil, as Romans vi:12–19 makes clear.

I think that a major source of the misunderstanding is the ambiguity of the terms "flesh" and "body" in the New Testament. The Epistle prescribed by the *Book of Common Prayer* for the third Sunday after Easter admonished Christians to "abstain from fleshly lusts, which war against the soul." St. Paul testifies, "I know that in me (that is, in my flesh,) dwelleth no good thing" (Rom.vii:18), and "I keep under my body, and bring it into subjection" (I Cor.ix:27). Flesh and spirit are clearly opposites (Rom.viii:5–13; Gal. v:16ff.). Christians are to "mortify the deeds of the body" (Rom. viii:13, part of the Epistle for the eighth Sunday after Trinity). It is easy to see how such passages could be read Platonically. [p. 360]

In fact it is hard to see how they could be read otherwise; Pauline and Platonic thinking were intertwined from the beginning and became more so with the passage of time. The best evidence of their fusion is the long history of efforts by philosophers and theologians to disentangle them; no one works at disentangling what is not entangled. Huttar cites, quotes, and joins the disentanglers: "The Reformers resisted" the idea that the body is necessarily evil:

Calvin commented on Romans vii:18: "Both these names therefore, as wel of the flesh as the spirit agree vnto that which reteyneth stil his naturall affection." "Flesh" then in Scripture was taken as symbolic of the "rebbell powres" of the soul, the affections. This metaphorical sense is obvious in Galatians v:24, "They that are Christ's have crucified the flesh with the affections and lusts." To read "have crucified the flesh" literally is absurd. But unless we are on guard we shall read "flesh" and "body" literally and thereby risk the error of calling biblical that which is really neo-Platonic. We shall be in danger of forgetting that extreme asceticism actually is frowned upon in the Bible (e.g. Col. ii:23; I Tim.iv:4). [p. 360]

The danger Huttar fears is surely genuine; the reformers' urge to avert it, the traditional readings of the sonnet, Huttar's urge to deny them, and the sonnet itself all testify to that. However, it is doubtful that the word "danger"— meaning something that *can* be averted, something that is not inevitable, and something that *should* be averted—is appropriate to discussing this sonnet; the elements that evoke the responses Huttar finds theologically inappropriate are ingrained in the sonnet, and a discussion that excludes them as "mistaken" can have validity only in an essentially biographical argument that Shakespeare wanted to write a poem other than the one we have and failed to see that he had

not written it. Such an argument would be hard to sustain but would be a legitimate enterprise; such an argument would not, however, be about this poem but
about something else. Huttar's logic finally carries him so far from the poem itself that he can say that "there is no notion of revenge" in the last six lines (p.
362)—an assertion demonstrably undermined by the fact that the poem occasions it. In short, his "reading" of the poem does not arise from the poem but
from his research into its topic.

Huttar would never have set off on his reasonable but irrelevant and disorient-
ing side trip if he had not assumed that, if *rebel pow'rs* refers to the body, it
cannot refer to the affections. He therefore sets out to "prove" that it does not
refer to the body. His failure to do so and his folly in trying are demonstrated
by the last phrase in his article: "the obvious, but erroneous, assumption that
'rebbell powres' means the 'body.' " One cannot reasonably deny that a word or
phrase has a reference that generations of careful and informed readers have
assumed it to have—unless one does so on historical grounds, on the basis of a
demonstration that in the given context the audience for whom the work was
written would not have taken the meaning later readers take from the word or
phrase in question. One can reasonably argue that a writer's own audience would
have taken more (or more complex) meaning than we do, but to do that is not to
demonstrate that a meaning obvious to us was not always obvious. Huttar introduces his quotation from Aristotle with this: "It is wrong to take 'these rebbell powres' as referring to 'the physical being' (Southam, p. 69). A contemporary reader would have seen without hesitation that this spoke of the powers of
the soul." I am not at all certain about the validity of the second of those sentences; I surely do not see the probability that Shakespeare's reader would have
been more aware of or more on the lookout for the Aristotelian theory of the
three souls than the modern scholars who have commented on the poem; I am
certain that the implied logical connection between these two sentences is
illegitimate.

(The particular case of *rebel pow'rs* in sonnet 146 both strengthens and weakens my general thesis that neither a disquisition on what a word or phrase or
poem should have meant to its readers nor a demonstration that previous readings have been incomplete should be mistaken for proof that previous readings
have been erroneous: *these rebel pow'rs* are said to *array* the soul, and one sense
of *array* demands that the *pow'rs* be understood as the body because the body is
to the soul as clothing is to the body. However, even if the reference of *pow'rs*
did not demonstrably include the body, I would be loathe to assume that the
scholarly consensus on *these rebel pow'rs* can be dismissed [compare 94.9, note—
on the universal equation of the *summer's flow'r* with "them" *that have pow'r*.])

The kind of thinking behind Huttar's discussion of *rebel pow'rs* is not unusual
in criticism, but it is surprising to find it in this critic in this article. Huttar's
general assertion of poetic value is a model of sense, sensitivity, and precision:
"I take it that the power to sustain a single image through a passage of several
lines is of a higher order than the power to create (or borrow) a series of images,
each one apt but unrelated to the others. Better yet is the poet who can sustain
an image, and in the same words flash before the reader's attention the enriching

association of disparate images" (pp. 360–61). In the main, Huttar's practical criticism of sonnet 146 admirably reflects those generalizations. Moreover, the stated purpose of his essay is to answer Southam's article and take him to task for making just the sort of unreasoningly reductive agrument about the poem as a whole that Huttar then makes about *rebel pow'rs*.

Southam's argument progresses in the traditional manner of demonstrations that the critical history of a work is the product of an informal conspiracy to misread:

> This sonnet is generally accepted as a statement of Shakespeare's sympathetic attitude towards a commonplace of Christian doctrine. The theme is understood to be a combination of "I keep under my body, and bring it into subjection" (I Cor.9.27.) and "O death, where is thy sting? O grave, where is thy victory?" (I Cor.15.55.), and the commentary and criticism on the poem reveal an impressive unanimity: Shakespeare's Christian sentiments are applauded; the clarity of expression and the absence of ambiguity are noted; and it is allowed a place among the greatest of the sequence. . . . [Southam then quotes a number of comments to demonstrate that] both scholar and ordinary reader concur. They find that Shakespeare endorses bodily subjugation as a means to spiritual health, and thereby, to a conquest of death. The sonnet is hailed as an unqualified statement of orthodox Christian belief and, as such, a unique document in the Shakespeare canon. Only once have I seen it suggested that this reading may not necessarily be definitive. In *The American Scholar*, Vol. XII, under the title "Critical Principles and a Sonnet," D. A. Stauffer records a discussion between five critics which centered upon Sonnet 146. During the course of the discussion John Crowe Ransom remarked: "I am struck by the fact that the divine terms which the soul buys are not particularly Christian: there are few words in the poem that would directly indicate conventional religious dogma. Rather, in the notion that the soul is a mere tenant of the body, a prince who has fallen to the condition of a sentinel in the world's garrison, a stranger coming from another realm, the sonnet seems in spirit to be Platonic." This comment was not amplified by Ransom, nor did his companions take it up, and although I am not able to agree with him in particulars of his criticism his overall impression that the sonnet is not merely an endorsement of Christian asceticism hints that a more penetrating reading is possible. [pp. 67–68]

The crucial word in the passage is "merely" in the last sentence. Had Southam stayed with it, his essay would have had greater validity. As the comments quoted in the foregoing notes illustrate, Southam demonstrates that quatrain 1 requires a reader to see the soul personified in several different roles and that it evokes both pity and blame for the soul. He is less detailed in describing the next two quatrains, but his focus is upon the elements in them that make a reader morally uneasy about the selfishness of the soul. In his eagerness to correct his predecessors' urgent insistence that 146 is an *uncomplicated* Christian exposition of *contemptus mundi*, he allows an argument that starts off in a demonstration

that the "feeling, thought, and expression" of this poem are not in perfect harmony throughout to drift into argument that 146 is not a Christian exposition of
contemptus mundi at all. Finally, he abandons the admirable effort at correcting
an oversimplification; he replaces the oversimplification with its much less
justifiable and equally reductive opposite; he finally disappears down an all-
purpose critical rabbit hole by declaring an irony:

> Luce calls the sonnet "an exact epitome of the Biblical yet lofty morality
> of Shakespeare's time." There are, true enough, a number of Biblical echoes
> which superficially run the poem along a conventional course, and the
> values of the poem seem to be those of the prosperous Elizabethan world.
> But it is Shakespeare the humanist speaking, pleading for the life of the
> body as against the rigorous asceticism which glorifies the life of the spirit
> at the expense of the vitality and richness of sensuous experience. Neither
> spiritual nor bodily life can be fulfilled at the other's cost, for the whole
> man, body and spirit indivisible, will suffer thereby. We can see how very
> much higher is the charity which motivates this sonnet than the type of
> Christianity which moves on the surface of the poem, and at which the
> irony is directed. [p. 71]

One alternative to analyses that are emotionally and intellectually satisfying
in their own terms but are otherwise unsatisfactory is an analysis that avoids
conceding to the intellectual convenience of the critic and his readers, and
therefore does not provide the satisfaction we are accustomed to getting by
writing and reading criticism. Both Southam and Huttar learned from—and
failed to learn the lesson of—Donald Stauffer's insufferable and invaluable
memorial reconstruction of a conversation about sonnet 146 held in the early
1940's by Reuben Brower, John Crowe Ransom, Daniel Aaron, Elizabeth Drew,
and Stauffer himself. Stauffer's article (cited in the preceding notes) admits more
of the truth about sonnet 146 than anything before or since and also comes
closer than anything I know to capturing the experience of reading any great
poem. It is as wholesome an example as one could set for a serious student of
literature. And yet, although the distinction of the participants in the discussion
should have been enough to insure a general audience for Stauffer's essay, it is
omitted from most bibliographies and ignored in the anthologies of sonnet
criticism by Willen and Reed and by Barbara Herrnstein—both of which contain
an otherwise excellent sampling of the best criticisms available in the early 1960's
and also show considerable barrel-scraping. Edward Hubler did acknowledge
Stauffer's account of the conversation (*The Sense of Shakespeare's Sonnets*
[N.Y., 1952], pp. 60–63), but did so only to make fun of the participants as
having ignored "Shakespeare's warning that 'they that dally nicely with words
may quickly make them wanton' " (p. 61); in the sanctimony of his clearheaded-
ness Hubler forgot that, as Viola's line shows, Shakespeare was the Don Juan of
verbal dalliance.

The reasons Stauffer's report has been rejected or ignored are, I think, two.
The first is trivial. The essay is embarrassing to read; its style is that of a love

child of James Fenimore Cooper and Geoffrey Chaucer; its format is both coyly and pedantically imitative of Classical and Renaissance pastoral dialogues and also sports some trimmings from the *Symposium* of Plato. The second reason goes deeper. Reading the essay is like thinking about the sonnet, not like reading critical analyses of it. The essay tells the truth without focusing on *one* truth about the poem and subordinating the others to it.

Most critical articles leave a reader knowing more facts than he did before, but their chief achievement, function, and value is actually to allow a reader to know *less* about a work than he knew before, to excuse him from the inconvenience of admitting all of his experience of a work into his memory of it. As one reads through Stauffer's dialogue, the five critics keep questioning, modifying, negating, and dismissing each others' statements, but, except for a few rare and mentally refreshing moments of transparent nonsense, one is likely to find oneself feeling that each speaker is making, or pointing the way to, the definitive statement about the poem; each seems to be saying *the* thing one thought as one read the poem, and one forgets that one has accepted the preceding speakers' comments as equally summary. Each of the five voices tries to establish one angle of vision on the poem; each succeeds, and none can maintain its absolute truth as exclusive. The five critics keep agreeing with each other and registering surprise at the extent of their agreement; it does not seem possible to them that so many conclusive statements are not mutually exclusive. The five critics talking to each other are like a single mind at the point when it perceives the need to pick out one thread in the poem and subordinate everything else to it. Since they are five individual minds, they cannot do that. They just go home.

Stauffer packages the hodge-podge of unaccommodated truths in a narrative framework that makes the whole essay a mere literary curiosity, but had he not done so, had he not acted as an artist, packaging truth rather than trying to flatten it out and line it up on an expository grid, he would not have been able to retain all of the discussion or as much of the poem as he did. The preceding notes on sonnet 146 are a different sort of attempt to admit that all that occurs in this poem exists. The notes are not unsatisfying in the particular way that Stauffer's appear to have been, but they are surely unsatisfying. If Hubler had lived to see them, he would probably have scorned them as he scorned Stauffer's ideologically unmediated reproduction of a conversation; any critic determined to demonstrate the reasonable but mistaken assumption that a simple straightforward poem like sonnet 146 must derive its clarity from some one expository assertion (which is embodied in it and for which the particulars of the poem are only a many-colored coat) would have to do the same. Such a critic assumes that, when someone else focuses on any incidental ideational element in a poem, he offers it as the real "point" of the poem, a substitute for the clear and clearly intended substance of the poet's sentences. As I have previously said, that is often true: critics often—critics usually—make such reductions. But that is not necessarily true, and it is particularly untrue about the five critics in Stauffer's dialogue. Whatever fears of false conclusions individual statements in that conversation may have inspired in Hubler, I suspect that his main dissatisfaction arose not from individual instances of misguided absolutism but from the in-conclusiveness of the whole. The five critics never made up their minds about sonnet 146.

The value of making up one's mind about a poem is not the same as the value of making up one's mind about real-life events that one's decision can influence. Nothing one says or thinks about a poem can change it. What one says about a poem can sometimes change the angle of a reader's perception of it, but one cannot stop the poem from doing all that it does or argue it into doing what it does not do. No interpretive description of a poem can nullify any of the actions the poem performs upon a reader's understanding. A piece of information unknown to the reader can put additional actions into the poem; so can chang-ing its context; an historically irrelevant response (e.g. the special wit that "A True Maid" by Matthew Prior [1664–1721] can have for a reader familiar with "The Sick Rose" by William Blake [1757–1827] and the misunderstandings that flow from ignorance of the history of the word "interest" [see 74.3, note]) can be corrected and, perhaps, in time forgotten (although I personally find that I still must actively reject a reference to a horse when I read 127.3 and that Dickens's Mr. Guppy makes me think of an eager little fish—even though *Bleak House* was published during 1852–53, and the Reverend R. J. L. Guppy of Trinidad did not send the first recorded specimen of *lebistes reticulatus* to the British Museum until the following decade). An interpretive description can even convince a reader that some of his experience of a poem does not or should not occur, but that is not at all the same thing as actually doing away with those responses. Moreover, critics regularly admit the existence of responses they deny by the very act of arguing against them. To argue against a reading that results from an historical accident (Prior and Blake are both in our past, and we are accustomed to the idea that "to be interested in" is "to have one's attention engaged by"), or for a reading lost by a similar accident of the progress of time may not lead to perfect practical success, but such activity is surely benign in both intention and effect. Arguments against a reading that the poem evokes and that it can be legitimately argued to have evoked for its first audience are usually benign in intent (we like to know exactly what something is and what it is not), but they are not benign in effect: such criticisms leave a reader with a clearer sense of what the poem means than the poem itself ever gave; such criticisms are intellectually comforting—but only so long as the reader does not go back and reread the poem on which he now has so firm a grasp.

It is as unreasonable and unprofitable to argue that sonnet 146 does not espouse an orthodox Christian position on the relative value of mortal and immortal considerations as it is to deny that the poem generates the ideational static Ransom and Southam point out.

That brings us to another familiar and inviting way of packaging disparate truths: I would not want to recommend any account of this poem that called it a Christian exhortation tempered by, or modified by, other considerations; to do so would be to recommend homogenizing the experience of the poem. It would be intellectually convenient to say that the standard descriptions of this poem as a straightforward exercise in Christian resolve are products of wishful thinking, but the fact that such critical descriptions protest too much attests not only to the presence of other and complicating elements in the poem but *also* to the fact that the poem itself evokes those descriptions; that is to say that sonnet 146 *is* the simple unalloyed exhortation it is said to be and that those of its details which make such descriptions difficult (make it necessary to sprinkle one's descriptions with words like "surely," "obviously," "unqualified," and "unambiguous," and to insist on the poem's undeniable likeness to Sidney's "Leave me o Love"), coexist with the obvious statement of religious resolve but do not diminish its force, simplicity, or singlemindedness. It does not seem reasonable that such a coexistence should be possible, that the elements would not immediately resolve themselves in a mixture comparable to the one that results from mixing black paint and white paint, or that the critic's job would be other than determining the proportions of black to white and thus the particular shade of gray. However, the incompatible elements, points of view, and responses do retain their independence, do not undergo synthesis. Such improbable coexistence occurs regularly in human experience: take, for example, the idea of "love-hate" relationships so popular with amateur psychologists. The sonnets regularly take such paradoxical situations for topics and reproduce them in the reader rather than resolving them. If the 1609 sequence has a common denominator it is the unity of divisible things and the divisibility of units; the speaker repeatedly presents his reader with things that at once have an absolute identity and just as absolutely do not.

I have attached this editorial plea to my annotation of sonnet 146 because its topic—the total unification of separable spiritual elements (reason, passions) as one element in a unified pair of separable elements (soul, body), which are distinguishable as immortal and mortal and are each also both immortal and mortal—is one of the few topics where the human mind has traditionally been most urgently unsuccessful in pacifying itself by the rational exercise of categories and subordination. One of my purposes in annotating the sonnets is to recommend an unmediated analysis of works of art (or an analysis that at least tries to resist mediation), an analysis that is not satisfying in anything like the way its subject is satisfying, an analysis that does not try to decide which of a poem's actions should be acknowledged but instead tries to explain the means by which all a poem's improbably sorted actions coexist and cohere within the poem and, for the duration of the poem, within the mind of its reader. If I am to have any success, sonnet 146 is the proper place to make my plea. The idea of the soul as a politic, parasitic exploiter of the body should seem ridiculous; all the traditions of western culture make us reject the implications that the metaphors of master and servant, landlord and tenant bring with them. As presented in sonnet 146, the relationships of master and servant, and of landlord and tenant are simply not analogous to the relationship of soul to body. Yet we are used to these metaphors as vehicles for discussing the relationship of the mortal and immortal parts of human beings; these metaphors are the Bible's own, and they do not ordinarily give us trouble. Moreover, the speaker gives us no hint that we are to view the argument here as any less noble than we are used to finding it. The last line, in fact, is moving in its serenity. Sonnet

146 is, as readers have traditionally thought, a Christian exhortation to reject transient pleasures and gain eternal life. As we read the poem we know we are reading a traditional statement of *contemptus mundi*. As we read the poem we see the relation of body and soul as our impressions of Christian doctrine (rather than a course of study in St. Paul) make us expect to see it. The speaker uses the traditional metaphors for vivifying the relationship and enabling us to see things in a single frame of reference; he achieves *exactly* the effect we would expect such a poem to have; *and* (not *but*) he lets the metaphors of servant and master, tenant and landlord run free to evoke the responses that those relationships evoke when they are not limited by an illustrative purpose but are real business relationships between human beings who try to exploit and avoid being exploited. That is to say that 146 enables us singlemindedly to espouse spiritual values *and* to do so in a genuinely narrow vision that genuinely includes pertinent reminders of the considerations and attitudes it successfully excludes; 146 achieves a genuinely restricted frame of reference that *feels* as all-inclusive as the logic of Christianity asks us to believe it is.

The great virtue of poetic embodiments of human experiences is that they house undeniable contrarieties of response instead of translating experience into thesis, antithesis, and synthesis. There should therefore be reason to value a criticism that offers complex descriptions of complex objects. Why should we take it as the critic's job to deny the poem's achievement? Why should we argue that the elements that cohere in a poem are by nature any more or less compatible with one another than they ordinarily are when the poem is read by an informed reader (i.e. a reader in command of as much of the mental furniture of the poet's contemporaries as we can discover and recondition)? A criticism that denies its audience the comfort Joseph offered Pharoah and his servants when he interpreted their dreams as coded messages offers the comfort of admitting that great poems, not being god-made, do not dissolve under the ministrations of prophets. A criticism that can admit the justice of John Benson's confidence that readers of Shakespeare's poems will "finde them, seren, cleere and eligantly plaine, such gentle straines as shall recreate and not perplexe your braine, no intricate or cloudy stuffe to puzzell intellect, but perfect eloquence . . . " (from the preface to *Poems: Written by Wil. Shakespeare*, 1640), and can *also* admit that the complexities modern critics see in the sonnets are there and that their discoverers cannot justly be dismissed as ingenious unless they try to convert the sonnets into mere vehicles for elements they are themselves surprised to discover—a criticism that admits that arguments for dating the sonnets by reference to English history or to the themes and styles of the various plays, the belief in a lost original order of the sonnets, the quasi-alchemical efforts to restore it, the expeditions to find "Mr. W. H." and "The Rival Poet," and the games of pin the tail on "The Dark Lady" have all been failures, and that admits that the sonnets and their interrelations in the 1609 sequence constantly tempt the mind toward similar follies—such a criticism may ask more tolerance and greater patience than is convenient, but, since the usual alternatives offer their comforting illumination by temporarily darkening all but a selected few of the lights in a sonnet or in the sequence, the unsatisfying criticism

I propose may be worth trying. We have tried to come to terms with the sonnets
by seeing them in light of this or in light of that. I suggest that we try coming to
terms with them in all the terms they bring with them, that we attempt and attempt to tolerate a criticism that is genuinely, literally, conservative.

SONNET 147

See 118.14, note.
1. *My love* my infatuation, the passion I feel. (The gloss reflects only the
limited sense invited by the words that follow. Momentarily, however, *My love*
is open to being understood as "my beloved"; that sense, which never takes
firm hold, does however ease the logically straightforward but rhetorically
sudden transition from the topic of the speaker's longings in lines 1–12 to their
object in the couplet. [Note that *fair*, the sixth syllable of line 13, is a contracted
mutation of the sixth and seventh syllables of line 1, *fever*.]). *as* like. *longing* The word modifies both *love* and *fever*. *still* (1) always (as in 9.5); (2)
yet, no less than before.
2. *longer* for an additional period of time (with a play on *longing*; note the
extra-logical interrelations among the sounds and meanings of *longing*, *still*,
and *longer*: *For* limits the meaning of *longing still* to "still desiring," but the
ideational kinship between *long-* and the notion of continuation in *still* gives
line 1 a suggestion of "still lengthening," a suggestion that *longer* reasserts within
an instant of the limitation dictated by *For* ["to long" neaning "to lengthen"
was apparently obsolete by Shakespeare's time; the by-meaning *longing*
has here is contextual not semantic]). *For that* In view of the preceding notes,
it might be argued that *For that* could carry suggestions of "because of that"
(thus giving ". . . still prolonged because of that which nurseth . . . " as a
secondary reading for lines 1 and 2), but the standard sense of "to long" and the
standard idiom "to long for" presumably always overwhelmed that possibility.
nurseth (1) fosters, ministers to, takes care of; (2) promotes the well-being of,
strengthens (playing on the inherent echo of the idea of nursing a patient in an
effort to overcome the disease); (3) feeds (the basic literal sense of *nurseth*).
3. *ill* (1) illness; (2) evil.
1–3. Note that, since any regimen based on the theory of the four humors
(see 45.8, note) would presumably forbid a feverish patient food, the metaphors
by which the speaker presents his unwholesome mental state are especially
pertinent and efficient; compare the modern proverb "feed a cold and starve
a fever."
3–4. The parallelism of *longing* . . . / *For that which* in lines 1 and 2 and
Feeding on that which in line 3 indicates *love* and/or *fever* as antecedent for both
phrases; physical proximity suggests *disease* as antecedent for *Feeding*. Since
the sense of lines 1–4 is the same in any reading, the indifferent syntax is a
stylistic metaphor for—and vouches for the validity of—the simile it amplifies.
Much the same is true of the insignificant "uncertainties" in line 4—where
Th' . . . *appetite* refers to *love* and/or *fever* and/or *disease*, and where [*in
order*] *to please* modifies *longing* and/or *nurseth* and/or *preserve* and/or

Feeding. (Compare the interplay of *longing, louger,* and *still*; of *still* and *preserve*; of *nurseth* and *Feeding*; of *ill* and *sickly*; and of *longing* and *appetite.*)

3–4,8. Compare the topics and diction of 146.11–14.

4. *Th'uncertain* (1) the capricious, the changeable, the variable; (2) the unreliable (see the use of *uncertain* in 1Tim.6:17 [quoted in 146.1–14, note]). *appetite* (1) desire, lust (as in *Lucrece* 8–9: "that name of 'chaste' unhap'ly set / This bateless edge on his keen appetite"); (2) desire for food and/or desire for particular dishes; (3) caprice, whim (*OED* gives this from 1580: "I have an appetite it were best for me to take a nap").

5. *my love* my infatuation.

6. *prescriptions* (1) directions, orders (involving positive action—as do recipes for medicines to be taken); (2) proscriptions (*OED* gives this from 1560: "The same outlawing or prescription is against the laws"); (3) specified restrictions, limitations, exceptions (compare the legal concept of "negative prescription"). *kept* observed, followed. (This context sets off vague, complex reverberations of logically unharnessed senses of "to keep": (a) "to preserve" [as in *HV* V.i.62: "God bye you, and keep you, and heal your pate"]; (b) "to provide the food for," "to support" [*OED* gives this from 1616: "What shall become of my poor family? They . . . must keep themselves"]; (c) "to stay within" [as in *T&C* I.iii.190: "keeps his tent"]; (d) "to stay the same," "to continue in one course or condition" [as in *RII* V.ii.7–10: "the Duke . . . kept on his course"]. The word *kept* carries incidental echoes of the ideas of preservation and maintenance in quatrain 1; moreover, since the extra energies of *kept* are already activated, the potential but syntactically irrelevant opposition of *kept* and *left* [line 7] can also contribute to the poem's aura of gratuitous perversity.)

7. *Hath left me* (1) has departed from me (leaving me insane); (2) has abandoned me; (3) has abandoned hope of curing me (compare *Tim* III.iii.11–12): "His friends, like physicians, / Thrice give him over"; *OED* gives "to leave off" as a late seventeenth-century idiom meaning "to give up [a patient] as incurable"). *I desp'rate* I, who am desperate. *desp'rate* (1) in despair; (2) despaired of, given up as incurable (*OED* gives this from 1581: "The Physician delivereth the desperate sicke bodie to the Divines care"); (3) wild and reckless (made mad by despair, *frantic mad*). *approve* (1) demonstrate, am proof that; (2) find by experience that (*OED* gives this from 1591: "Unto them a spectacle, and a resolution sildom approved, to see one ship turne toward so many enemies"); note that "to approve" meaning "to commend," "to pronounce to be good"—a sense logically inappropriate to lines 7 and 8—pertains to, and thus, in a way, is echoed in, lines 13 and 14.

8. *Desire is death* The phrase has a Biblical ring; compare Romans 6:19–23, 8:6, and Eph. 2:1–3. *which* The antecedent can be either *Desire* or *death*. *which physic did except* (1) medicine proscribed desire; (2) medicine kept out death; (3) desire rejected medicine. (*OED* gives "to object to," "to take exception to" as one meaning of "to except," but finds only two examples: *RII* I.i.72—in which the *OED* reading is obviously erroneous [see Peter Ure's note in his 1955

Arden edition of *RII*], and this line—in which the special modulations of "to except" ["to leave out," "to exclude"], are dictated by context.)

9. "Past cure past care" was proverbial (Tilley C921); Ingram and Redpath point out that "Shakespeare is here not merely reproducing the proverb (as he does in *LLL*.V.ii.28], but playing with it, for . . . he has here inverted it. The case is past cure, because the physician has ceased to care." *now* now that, since. *is past care* has ceased to be concerned (with plays on "is no longer giving me medical care" and "is so far deteriorated that medicine is powerless to help"; the line thus leaves doubt whether *reason* is the patient [cared for] or the physician [as line 5 says it is]).

9–11. Line 10 is both a continuation of the clause begun in line 9 ("I am past cure and frantic mad"), and the first element of the clause that emerges in line 11 ("And, frantic mad . . . , my thoughts are as . . ."—i.e. "my thoughts, which are frantic mad . . . , are as . . . ").

10. "Desire has no rest" was proverbial (Tilley D211). *frantic mad with* (1) frantic-mad as a result of, frantically mad as a result of; (2) made wild by (Q reads "madde"; for the potential confusion between the words we spell "mad" and "made," see 129.9 and note); (3) frantic-mad, and exhibiting (*with* indicating an adjunct quality; compare the uses of *with* in 128.11, 132.4, and *AYLI* II.vii.155: "[the justice] With eyes severe"). *evermore* constant, incessant (for the adjectival use of adverbs, see 7.2, note).

11. *my discourse* my speech, what I say.

12. *At random* in a headlong course, haphazardly. (The English word *random* is adapted from the French *randon*, "a violent rush." The Q spelling, "randon," is at least as common in sixteenth-century texts as *random*. Since the change is phonetically negligible in the harmony of the poem, and since retaining the old spelling [as some editors have justly done] can distract a modern reader and appear either quaint or like a printer's error, emendation probably comes closer to duplicating the reading experience of Shakespeare's contemporaries than "randon" does. Note that *random* and the French *randon* derive from French *randonner*, "to run swiftly," and can revivify the idea of running in *discourse* and evoke a play on the simplest meaning of its source, the Latin *discurrere*, "to run different ways, to run about in various directions.") *vainly* (1) futilely, ineffectually; (2) senselessly, foolishly (*OED* gives this from 1588: "She spoke somwhat idlie and vainlie, by reason of . . . her sickness").

14. *as black as hell* = proverbial (Tilley, H397).

13–14. Compare 150.4. *fair, bright, black, dark* · All four words refer simultaneously to the lady's complexion and her morality (see 127.1,6; 132.10–14; 137.12; and 152.13–14).

SONNET 148

1–2. Q puts an exclamation point after *O me* and commas at the ends of lines 1 and 2; Q's first full stop comes with the question mark at the end of line 4. It is never easy to differentiate between interrogatively phrased exclamations and genuine questions (see 97.2–4, note). Here the opening exclamation invites an exclamatory reading of lines 1 and 2; the structure and substance of the rest of line 1 signals a question, but the hyperbolic sound of line 2 makes the whole sound exclamatory. I put an exclamation point at the end of line 2 in order to acknowledge that, although lines 1–6 are composed of three two-line questions, the first is a mixture of exclamation and question, in which the exclamatory dominates. (The second is half question, half exclamation; and the third is a mixture in which puzzlement, simple questioning, is stronger than surprise and outrage.)

1. *love* (1) infatuation, the emotion called love; (2) the god of love, Cupid. (Line 1 conflates a statement that passion transforms and its mythological equivalent in which Cupid, as a god, has power to create and transform. See 137.1, note: the answer to the momentarily independent question *what eyes hath love*, "what kind of eyes does Cupid have?" would also answer an interrogative reading of the whole of lines 1 and 2.)

2. (1) "Which have no likeness to eyes that see accurately," "Which contradict the reports of normally efficient eyesight"; (2) "Which never make contact with what is actually visible," "Which are blind to reality."

4. *censures* judges (the modern narrow elliptical sense, in which "to censure" = "to censure unfavorably," was only just emerging in Shakespeare's time; the nature of the judgment was still specified by an adverb; see "censure well the deed," meaning "judge the deed favorably" in *2HVI* III.i.275). (Note the accidental presence in *censures* of the sounds of two words generally pertinent to the sonnet's topic: "sense" and "sure.") *falsely* (1) erroneously; (2) dishonestly.

4,5,14. *falsely; fair, false; foul faults* See 138.14, note.

5. *false* (1) unreliable, deceiving as a result of error; (2) lying, deceptive by design (*false eyes* also revives the image in line 1: love providing the speaker with artificial eyes, glass eyes). *dote* See 141.4, note.

6. *What means* (1) what reason has, what prompts; (2) how dare.

7–9. The speaker's puzzled progression through a series of explanations for the discrepancy between what he esteems beautiful and what the world esteems so is mirrored in a reader's experience of these lines. Line 7 is potentially self-contained, and the line-end pause gives temporary identity to the statement, "If what I take to be beautiful is not beautiful, *then* [introducing a logical necessity following from the situation stipulated in the *if* clause] love reports things as they really are" (for *denote* meaning "make known" see *Ham* I.ii.82–83: "all forms, moods, shapes of grief, / That can denote me truly"). But that reading of line 7 is self-contradictory. Therefore (whether the text retains Q's comma after *denote* or not), the reader moves on to take *denote* transitively and look for a reasonable sense for line 7 as an adjunct of line 8: "love doth well demonstrate that [or doth well demonstrate the following:] love's eye is not so true as all men's [eye is]." However, although *all men's* concludes one logically acceptable potential identity for lines 7 and 8, there is still one more word in line 8: *no*. The Q punctuation of lines 8 and 9 (see below), cannot satisfy a modern reader accustomed to logically directive punctuation. A Renaissance reader, accustomed to loosely used punctuation and printer's variations on it (see the notes to sonnet 129), would probably have been ready to perceive all these successive sentences: (1) "Love's eye is not so true as all men's." (2) "Love's eye is not so true as all men's 'no' " (i.e. "Love's 'ay' ['yes,' affirmation] is not so true as the world's 'no' " [compare the puns in 136.6 and 152.13, the repetition of the *eye* / "ay" pun in line 9, and the *I* / "eye" pun in line 11]); (3) ". . . as all men's. No. How can it? . . . ," and, perhaps, (4) ". . . as all men's. How can it know? . . ."

These three lines have a vaguely bawdy cast, derived from (a) the concentration of the phonetically related words *not*, *-note*, *no*, and *O*; (b) the word *well*; and (c) the fact that each of those five words is, or is related to, a slang term for vulva (see 20.12, 108.5, 129.13, 154.9, and notes; Partridge, s.v. "O"; and "virgin knot" in *Temp* IV.i.15 and *Per* IV.ii.148); such a context can give logically free-floating special significance to *Love's eye is not so true*, and "all men's no": "Love's eye, the vulva [see 136.2, 153.9, notes], is not so faithful, so chaste" [compare *eyes' falsehood* in 137.7 and *O cunning love* in line 13], and "a public 'nothing' " (compare *the bay where all men ride* and *wide world's common place* in 137.6 and 10). If indeed *all* had sexual senses, then it too presumably colored this line (see 26.1–14, note).

8–9. *all men's: no.* / *How can*   The Q punctuation is

> . . . all mens: no,
> How can . . . .

No modern repunctuation can satisfactorily register the multiple relationships of *no* to the syntaxes that precede and follow it. The unsatisfactory punctuation given here is designed *only* to insist on the simultaneous necessity and illegitimacy of making a choice between "all men's 'no'. / How can . . . " and "all men's. No; / How can . . . ". Like Ingram and Redpath, I am inclined to "believe that Shakespeare may have intended two readings of the line to be possible, and that the strange punctuation of Q was designed to permit a syntactical play in addition to the pun on 'eye'."

10. *with watching*   by wakefulness, by being constantly open.

11. *No marvel then though*   therefore it is not surprising if.   *I*   I, the personal pronoun (with a pun on "eye").   *mistake my view*   (1) mis-perceive what I look upon; (2) misjudge, misunderstand, what I see. (The phrase includes both the alternatives in quatrain 1.)

13. *cunning*   crafty, artful (with a sexual pun—as in *Cymb* I.iv.87 [quoted in 154.9, note; see Ellis, pp. 216–18]. *Cunning* meaning "cute," "little, pretty, and loveable," is a nineteenth-century American innovation).   *love*   Ingram and Redpath say this: "In line 1 'love' could only mean either (1) the act of loving or (2) the god of love. In lines 7, 8, and 9 sense (1) prevails. In line 13, however, as a stroke of wit, a new reference of the word—to the mistress—is introduced; for in line 14 'thy foul faults' clearly refers primarily to the mistress. Concurrently, however, the whole couplet probably alludes to the way in which Love (the god) deludes men."

14. *foul faults*   (1) defects of physical appearance; (2) immoralities (compare 147.13–14).   *faults*   See 35.5, note.

SONNET 149

1. *cruel* = dissyllabic; see 129.4, note.

2. *When* since (although the succeeding suggestions of reference to occasions when speaker and beloved made love [when the speaker "took her part"?] can activate overtones of "whenever"; note *spend* in line 7, and see 151.6, note [on the sexual sense of *part*]). *against myself* Compare 35.11, 49.11, 88.3, and 89.13; here *against myself* suggests "against my better judgment" as well as "in opposition to my own interests." *with thee partake* take your part, side with you. (On this unique use of "to partake," Willen and Reed say, "We know of no other identical usage, but cf. Holinshed's *Chronicles* 3.495: 'some fray or tumult might rise amongst his nobles, by quarreling or partaking,' and also 'partaker' in *OED* quotation: 'And all his partackers I shall slea'." Although this usage is etymologically warranted and sustained by idiomatic uses of the cognates Willen and Reed cite, this use of *partake* is itself grossly unidiomatic and thus has the effect of a witty malapropism based on the logical assumption that, since "to take someone's part" means "to join forces with him," "to partake with someone" means the same thing [compare the examples cited in 50.6, 109.6–7, 142.13, and 152.11, notes].) *partake* = a simple modernization of Q's "pertake." (Renaissance writers and printers used "-er" and "-ar" interchangeably to represent the sounds now ordinarily represented by "-ar." They sometimes used "-ar" to represent sounds ordinarily represented by "-er." *OED* gives "partain" as a variant spelling of "pertain" and gives "pert," "pertake," and "pertener" as variants of "part," "partake," and "partner." Compare the histories of the now independent words "parson" and "person," and note the modern British pronunciations of "clerk," "Derby," and "Berkeley.")

3. *think on thee* (1) think about you (i.e. remember you—note *forgot* in the next clause); (2) consider your welfare, show consideration for you. *when* (1) at such time as, whenever; (2) since.

3–4. *when I forgot | Am of myself all tyrant for thy sake* No modern, logically directive punctuation can maintain all the syntaxes crushed together in these lines: (1) "when I, forgot, am . . . " = (a) "when, forgetting myself (i.e. forgetting my own best interests), I am . . ." and/or (b) "when, forgotten by you (i.e. overlooked, ignored), I am . . ." (reading (1) is encouraged by the line-end break between *forgot* and *Am*); (2) "when I forgot am of myself—all, tyrant, for thy sake" = "when, tyrant, I forget about myself only for your sake" (with the implication in *all* that the speaker has no purpose or identity in life except to serve the beloved—that the beloved is his all and his all is the beloved's; reading (2) is encouraged by the model of the vocative in line 1 and the ideational associations between cruelty and tyranny); (3) "when I forgot am all of myself, tyrant, for thy sake" = "when, tyrant, for your sake I forget myself entirely" (reading (3) is encouraged by such locutions as "to be quite forgot," "to be all forlorn," and, perhaps, "to be all forgotten" [meaning "to be unable to remember anything," as in *A&C* I.iii.91]); (4) "when I, forgot, am of myself all tyrant for thy sake" = (a) "when for your sake I, forgotten, am all tyrant (i.e. a perfect tyrant) over myself" and (b) "when, in your behalf, I, forgotten, am tyrannous voluntarily (i.e. all on my own, by my own natural inclination, without being urged or forced at all"; compare the *of* construction in *MWW* IV.i.61: "which they'll do fast enough of themselves"; reading (4) is encouraged by the word order and echoes of the voluntary self-abuse proclaimed in line 2).

4,11. *all*   See 26.1–14, note.

5. In his edition of 1780, George Steevens compared Psalm 139:21: "Do not I hate them, o Lord, that hate thee?" (*Variorum* I, 304).

5,6. *that, that*   whom, whom (the context makes it obvious that the antecedents are *Who* in line 5 and *whom* in line 6, but note that syntactically the readiest antecedents are *thee* and *thou*; the speaker would call his beloved [whether female or male] *friend* and does indeed fawn upon her [or him—see 126, headnote]).

7. *lour'st*   = monosyllabic.   *lour'st on*   frown upon, scowl at.   *spend*   take, mete out (Ingram and Redpath). (The sense is clear from context but "to spend revenge" is most unidiomatic. This line is strange and strained generally; *lour'st* is an ostentatiously flat repetition of the idea in *frown'st* in the preceding line. Since "to lower," meaning "to let descend," and "to lower," Q's standard variant on "to lour," are homonymic, lines 7 and 8 might be the product of an unsuccessful effort at a clever reference to a method of sexual intercourse in which the woman lowers herself upon the man. If lines 7 and 8 registered a successful double entendre, then the poem, which seems gratuitously preoccupied with the words *on* and *upon*, and which uses language rich in potential sexual connotation [e.g. *with thee partake, proud, service, motion,* and perhaps, *all* and *Commanded*], would sustain several covert references to the temporary sexual suicide of male orgasm. See 129.1, note—on the sexual sense of *spend*.)

8. *present*   immediate (as in *Lucrece* 1262–63: "with circumstances strong / Of present death").   *moan*   (1) lamentation, show of grief; (2) grief, suffering (compare 30.11).

9. *respect*   (1) regard with reverence, consider worthy; (2) pay attention to, take into consideration (as in 85.13).

10. "That is so proud as to despise being your servant."   *proud*   (1) splendid, exalted, worthy of respect and admiration; (2) pride-generating, inspiring of self-satisfaction and haughtiness (but see 151.10, note).   *thy service*   The reference is to the courtly love convention by which the lover spoke of his relationship to his lady as that of vassal to lord. (The other of the two basic analogies of courtly compliments, that of worshiper and deity, is reflected in line 11.) For the sexual suggestions in *service,* see 141.10, note.

11. Compare the groom's statement in the marriage service: "with my body I thee *worship*: and with *all my* worldly *goods* I thee endow" (the italics are mine). *When*   (1) since; (2) at such time as, whenever.   *thy defect*   (1) your imperfection, your lack of worthy qualities (see 150.2); and perhaps (2) that particular anatomical deficiency that makes you attractive (compare 20.9–12). See *worst* and *best* in 150.8.

12. *motion*   (1) movement, glances (compare 140.14); (2) commandment, instruction (Willen and Reed cite AV, Translator's Preface 5: "with this motion: 'Read this, I pray you' "). For "motions" meaning the "hot impulses and

the actual physiological stirrings and bodily movements of physical desire," see
Partridge and *Measure* I.iv.57–61.

13. *love, hate on* my beloved (a vocative), go on hating (an imperative);
this complex variation on oxymoron is also a variation on the confusion between
love referring to affection and *love* used as an epithet for the speaker's beloved
(compare 40 and 51.1, note).

13–14. The couplet seems inappropriate—uncalled for by what precedes it,
a sudden and arbitrary recurrence to the topic of sonnet 148 and an implied
and not at all witty contradiction of 148.13–14. Until line 12, eyesight figures
in this poem only incidentally in *frown'st* and *lour'st* and as a substantively
inactive common denominator between *respect* and *despise* (see 141.3, 4, note).

SONNET 150

1. *from what pow'r* (1) by means of what faculty, what ability; (2) by means
of what strength; (3) from what supernatural being (compare *Temp* III.iii.
72–74: "for which foul deed / The pow'rs . . . have / Incens'd the seas and
shores"); (4) by what authority, by what right of sway (compare *Measure*
I.i.80–81: "A pow'r I have, but of what strength and nature / I am not yet in-
structed").

2. *insufficiency* (1) unfitness, incapacity, deficiency, inadequacy (see *defect*
in 149.11); (2) weakness, lack of power (Willen and Reed cite Spenser, *State
of Ireland*: "reject them as incapable and insufficient"). *sway* rule, govern,
control (as in 128.3, but strongly colored by "to sway" meaning "to turn aside"
or "to cause to waver" [*OED* gives this from 1586: "He was swayed with all
. . . as everie winde of passions puffed him"; compare *MofV* IV.i.50–52:
"affection, / Mistress of passion, sways it to the mood / Of what it likes or
loathes" and *1HIV* III.ii.130–31: "God forgive them that so much have sway'd /
Your Majesty's good thoughts away from me"]).

2,6,8. *in-, in, in* Note that the same sound occurs in three different senses
as the second syllable of three different lines (*in* occurs again at the end of line
13 amidst heavy but random bawdy play).

3. *give the lie to* accuse of lying, call a liar (the phrase, a hyperbolic way of
saying "behave as if I did not trust the evidence of," may have included a play
on "overthrow," "throw down"; see *Macb* II.iii.22 and 35: "Was it so late,
friend, ere you went to bed that you do lie so late?" "I believe drink gave thee
the lie last night").

4. This line combines two different kinds of hyperbole: it attests to the degree
of the speaker's infatuation by presenting a ridiculously exaggerated example
of the nonsense he is willing to speak ("And even swear that it is dark in the
daytime," ". . . that the sun is not there when it is"—compare 147.13–14 and
Shrew IV.v.1–22), and by saying that the speaker not only takes ugliness for
beauty but takes beauty for ugliness ("And even swear that sunshine does not
make the day beautiful"—compare 132.13–14; for "to grace" meaning "to
adorn," see 67.2). Note that, like 33, 130, and 132, this line equates the sun with

beauty; as usual, the speaker tends to equate beauty with lightness of complexion and both with lights.

5. *becoming of things ill* (1) the power to make bad seem good, ugliness seem beautiful, defect seem perfection, and insufficiency seem sufficient (the noun use of *becoming* to mean "power to beautify," "ability to make comely," derives from "to become" meaning "to set off to advantage," "to grace"; compare 132.6). The presence of the word *this* makes sense (1) primary, but the conjunction of *becoming* and *ill*, the particular context of line 4, and the general context of the speaker's conviction that the lady destroys, corrupts, and perverts the nature of things, all combine to make the phrase include the opposite of its overt substance: (2) the power to ill-become things, the power to set things off to disadvantage. *things* See 136.7 and 11, notes.

6. *the very refuse of thy deeds* (1) those of your deeds that are least worthy, the absolute worst of your deeds, those of your deeds that should be most repellent; (2) the plain rubbish that your deeds are; (3) the least of your deeds (e.g. your incidental by-actions, casual gestures, mundane, everyday activity).

7. *warrantise* evidence, assurance of the presence of, warranty. *skill* capability, know-how, expertness, cunning.

8. See 149.11 and, for a possible meaning of *thy worst all*, 26.1–14, note.

11,12. The meaning of *abhor* is the same in both lines: "loathe," "shrink from in disgust"; but the context and the model of words like "abuse" in which the prefix "ab-" indicates "wrongly" here activate a play on "whore" in both lines. *Abhor* carries extra-logical suggestions of "use as a whore," "shun because of whorishness," and, in *abhor my state*, "make me cuckold-like" (compare the name "Abhorson" in *Measure* and *Oth* IV.ii.162–65: "I cannot say 'whore'; / It does abhor me now I speak the word; / To do the act might the addition earn, / Not the world's mass of vanity could make me").

12. *With others* along with other people [who scorn me] (with a play on "by lying with other men").

13. *raised* evoked (but see 151.9, 12–14).

14. *Worthy* See 72.4, note.

13–14. The couplet conflates two logics: (1) since I had so little to tempt me to love you and so little to gain from loving you, my unselfish generosity has earned your love in return; (2) since you are unworthy and I find unworthiness loveable, I am a fitting person for you to love (with the implication that love of unworthiness makes the lover as unworthy as the object of his love—the idea that the lover takes on the virtues of the thing loved is a Platonic commonplace).

SONNET 151

1. *Love* (1) Cupid (the reference immediately specified by *is too young*; Cupid is traditionally thought of as a baby—see 115.13); (2) the passion (love) of which Cupid is the emblem and, by extension, those that feel that passion, people who are infatuated. "It is impossible to love and be wise" and "Love is without reason" were proverbial (Tilley, L558 and L517). *too young to know*

what conscience is too young to have a sense of right and wrong, too young
to be held responsible for moral choices. (The logic behind the line appears to
derive from two related and often confused legal concepts: in canon law, a
person under the age of reason [i.e. under the age of seven years] is not considered morally capable or responsible; in both civil and canon law a person is
not held capable of making vital decisions for himself until he reaches the age
of discretion, which traditionally occurs at or about the age of puberty, the age
of *physical* adulthood. This line plays elaborately on the capacity to know mentally and the capacity to know carnally (see 129.13, note).

Compare line 1 with *Penis erectus non habet conscientiam*, which Archer
Taylor cited as proverbial (*The Proverbs* [Cambridge, Mass. 1931], p. 171).

1,2,13. *conscience* (1) ability to recognize right and wrong; (2) sensitivity
and obedience to an inner moral sense. The poem also plays on the etymology
and sound of the word: literally *conscience* means "knowledge with" and derives,
through Latin *conscientia* ("privity to shared knowledge") from Latin *con*
("together") and *scire* ("to know"); any word with *con* in it appears to have
invited Shakespeare and his contemporaries (see Cotgrave, s.v. *con* and *noc*)
to play on the commonest name for the female sex organ. Here Shakespeare
seems to derive a reading of *conscience* that is roughly paraphrasable as "cunt
knowledge." (Compare *contented* in line 11 and "conceit" in the second poem
quoted in the note on line 6 below.) For similarly baroque bawdy punning see
HV V.ii.285–321.

2. Aside from its vague bawdy suggestiveness, this line seems to refer to the
traditional idea that love ennobles the lover, makes him eager to be worthy of
his mistress' love. There is incidental wit in the fact that Venus (*love*) is literally
the mother of Cupid (*Love*) and that bearing and babies are variously pertinent
to these lines.

3. *gentle cheater* = an oxymoron; compare *tender churl* in 1.12. *urge
not* Willen and Reed give two readings: (1) "do not charge [me] with" (which
they exemplify with *RIII* III.v.80–81: "urge his hateful luxury / And bestial
appetite"), and (2) "do not provoke," "do not incite" (for which they give this
OED example from 1594: "forbeare ambitious Prelate to urge my griefe").
amiss misdeed, offense (as in 35.7).

3–5. Line 4 operates in two distinct logics. As one reads line 4 it relates only
to sense (1) of *urge* in line 3: as a justification of the injunction against accusing,
it warns the lady of the tactical folly of calling the kettle black—warns her
against making an issue of vices of which she herself may also be justly
accused. However, line 5 begins *For*, "because," and thus seems to present an
explanation of line 3 or line 4 or both. The first phrase of line 5, *For thou
betraying me*, does indeed point out a fault of which the lady is guilty, and
betraying suggests that the fault is the one we would expect to hear of in this
context—sexual infidelity; but *betraying* turns out to operate in an altogether
different logic ("Because, since you betray me, I do betray . . ."), a logic
which retroactively narrows the sense of *urge* in line 3 to "incite," "provoke,"
and dictates that lines 3–5 be understood to say ". . . do not provoke me
sexually lest you be justly charged with being responsible for my (involuntary)

sexual response and thus for my sin, because your betrayal of me into sin, your seduction of me, causes me to sin."

5–6. See 146.1–2.

6. *nobler part* soul (see line 7) or mind; the phrase plays on *part* meaning "bodily part" (see 17.4, note) and specifically the male member—the heroic "part" which is betrayed into involuntary servitude. For *part* meaning "penis" and/or "vagina," see Ellis, pp. 71–72; among his examples Ellis cites *AW* II.iii.243–44, *LLL* V.ii.498–506, and this old rhyme:

> Now if any of my Parts, or all,
> You will then to Tryal call,
> You shall both see, and feel, and taste,
> Lest you repent your bargain past:
> Then Part and Part let us Compare,
> There's no deceit in open Ware.
>
> . . . .
> But yet that part that all must bind,
> O shew not, lest you strike me Blind.

See also "part and whole [hole]" in this stanza from a bawdy parody of lovers' blazons that begins "Give me leave to love thee lasse" (the twenty-sixth poem in [Nicholas Breton's?] *The Arbor of amorous Devises* [1597]):

> Thy hidden parts I recommend,
> To his conceit who is thy friend,
> Whose labour sure doth onely tend,
> in part and whole to love thee.

6–7. Compare sonnet 146.

7. *My soul* my spirit, the morally responsible agent within me (with a play on "my beloved," "my lady," "my love" [see *call* / *Her love* in lines 13–14 below], she who licenses the speaker's sexual activity; for *my soul* as a term of endearment, see *MND* III.ii.246: "My love, my life, my soul, fair Helena").

8. *Triumph* = sometimes accented on the first syllable in Shakespeare, sometimes on the second (Kökeritz, p. 397); here a modern reader has no way of knowing whether Shakespeare expected the word to be read as an iamb (like *in love*) or a trochee (like *Love is*). *stays* waits for (as in *2Gent* II.ii.13: "My father stays my coming"). *farther* (1) longer; (2) further (with a possible play on "father"). *reason* (1) intellect, the guiding and governing faculty of the mind; (2) justification, excuse, ground for action (with a logically casual play on "raising" [pronounced "raisin' "], which is evoked by the phonetically and ideationally related word *rising* in line 9—see Kökeritz, pp. 138–39 and *Shrew* Induction. ii. 119–25:

> *Page [as lady].* . . . For your physicians have expressly charg'd,
> In peril to incur your former malady,
> That I should yet absent me from your bed.
> I hope this reason stands for my excuse.

Sly. Ay, it stands so that I may hardly tarry so long. But I would be loath to fall into my dreams again. I will therefore tarry in despite of the flesh and the blood).

stays no farther reason (1) no longer waits for reason; (2) waits for no additional reason. (The diction gives the phrase extra-syntactical but pertinent overtones of "is no longer stayed by—is no longer restrained by—intellect.")

9. *rising at thy name* The overt reference is to sexual erection, but the phrase is a metaphor of conjuring—in which names were used to conjure *up* spirits. See Cassius on the powers of the names "Brutus" and "Caesar": "Conjure with 'em: / 'Brutus' will start a spirit as soon as 'Caesar' " (*JC* I.ii.146–47); see the bawdy passage from *HV* cited above and the one from *R&J* quoted in 129.1, note. See 141.13–14, note.

9–11. *point, prize, proud, pride, poor* These words, variously interrelated by sound (e.g. the vowel sounds of *prize* and *pride*, the dental endings of *point*, *proud*, and *pride*, etc.) and by sense (e.g. *proud* and *pride* are cognates; the actions of pointing and becoming *proud* are interrelated), are most obviously related by alliteration in *p* and, for the last four, *p*-plus-*r*. Ellis (Appendix II, pp. 220–23) convincingly documents his guess that both *p* and *r* were generally used as popular non-polite euphemisms for "penis." (Compare the word game played, I am told, by Sicilians on the eve of a wedding; the guests sit around and drink and take turns naming things they would like to give the bride; the object of the game is to avoid naming any object with an *r* in it.)

10. *triumphant prize* prize of victory, prize to exult over, swagger about, and celebrate, prize that it is glorious to have achieved (see 51.1, 13.12, and notes); but see the irony in 41.8—the prize is as much the triumphant taker as the triumphantly taken. *proud* (1) vainglorious (swollen with pride); (2) made splendid (compare *proud* in 64.2 and *pride* in 25.7, 52.12, and 103.2); (3) lustful (compare *Lucrece* 705–06: "While Lust is in his pride, no exclamation / Can curb his heat or rein his rash desire" and "salt as wolves in pride" in *Oth* III.iii.408 where "in pride" has the meaning "in heat" has now); (4) swollen, tumescent (as in *Lucrece* 712: "The flesh being proud, Desire doth fight with Grace"; this sense relates to *proud* meaning "swollen," "high," "in flood," to describe rivers and to *proud* meaning "tumid" to describe plants; see 104.4, note). *of* (1) with respect to (designating *this pride* as that in which *flesh* takes pride—see the standard idiom "to be proud of" some possession, talent, person, etc.); (2) by (designating *this pride* as that which makes *flesh* splendid —as fine clothes make their wearers fine); (3) with (as in "swell with pride"). *pride* (1) vaingloriousness, haughtiness; (2) splendor; (3) lust; (4) tumescence.

11. *contented* See 1, 2, 13, note above; here the joke seems to involve understanding the word as if its first syllable occurred twice. Compare 1.11, 119.13, and *V&A* 213 and 513–14: "To sell myself I can be well contented, / So thou wilt buy, and pay, and use good dealing."

1,2,10,11. *conscience, proud, pride, contented* Compare the bawdy play of "contagious," "proud," and "continents" in the description of the swollen rivers in *MND* II.i.90–92: "Contagious fogs . . . falling in the land, / Hath every pelting river made so proud / That they have overborne their continents."

12. As in line 9, the overt reference is sexual; here the metaphor is of a soldier's loyalty to his commander or comrades or of a knight's loyalty to his king. *stand in thy affairs* be steadfast in the services it does for you, act in your behalf and never retreat. (In context of *stand* and *in*, *affairs* takes on the anatomical sense its synonym, "matters," has in "country matters" and "women's matters" [see 87.14, note], and that Enobarbus gives its synonym, "business," in *A&C* I.ii.165–69:

> *Antony.* The business she hath broached in the state
> Cannot endure my absence.
> *Enobarbus.* And the business you have broach'd here cannot be without
> you; especially that of Cleopatra's, which wholly depends on your abode.

Also see 52.1–2, note [on *stand in*] and 57.10, note [on *affair*].) *by thy side* (1) along with you, or fighting shoulder to shoulder beside you; (2) while we are lying side by side.

13. *want* lack. *conscience* (1) consciousness, awareness, judgment (as in *Tim* II.ii.176–77: "Canst thou the conscience lack / To think I shall lack friends?"); (2) ability ro recognize right and wrong; (3) sensitivity to an inner moral sense. See 1,2,13, note above. *hold it* consider it (an imperative). Since *of conscience* was a stock expression, used almost as an interjection, this line can carry an appropriate extra sense: "Do not, by all that is fair and reasonable, consider it a lack that . . ." (*OED* gives this 1568 example of *of conscience* meaning "in conscience": "I cannot of conscience favour them therein"; see the 1609 quarto of *Per* IV.ii.20: "there's two [whores] unwholesome, a' conscience").

13–14. *call* / *Her love* call her "my love."

14. *for* (1) for the sake of; (2) as the result of; (3) to get. *dear* See 87.1, 102.12, 37.3, and notes. *I rise and fall* ". . . the 'rising and falling' is singularly appropriate to [the poem's] theme of involuntary lust; the point is that it is *not* a metaphor" (Seymour-Smith).

SONNET 152

1. *I am forsworn* I break faith with another lover. (Whether or not the statement has specific reference(s) depends upon a reader's knowledge about the author [Shakespeare was a married man], and his knowledge of the 1609 collection [the speaker has sworn to be true to the beloved friend addressed earlier in the Q sequence—e.g. 123.14]; for a reader who knows both, line 2 can be ironic because, like the lady, the author/speaker is *twice forsworn*—he "urges" an "amiss" of which he himself is guilty [see 151.3–4]. Note that lines 5–14 respond to a more general meaning of *I am forsworn*: "I have told a lie.")

2. Paired with the model provided by the syntax of line 1, the body of line 2 invites a reader to understand it as "in swearing to me that you love me you are twice forsworn." However, the word *But* signals a contrast between the forsworn speaker and the lady; *twice forsworn* confirms the signal. In order to make sense, the contrast must be understood not as a contrast between the speaker's physical

infidelity and the lady's oath (swearing love). Aversion to solemn promises is one of the strongest threads running through Shakespeare's work (e.g. *R&J* II.ii. 107–20, *JC* II.i.112–40, *Ham* I.v.143–81, *AW* IV.ii, entire and V.iii.284–85, *LLL* I.i, entire, *WT* V.ii, entire); and the distinction between doing what one has sworn not to do and making a new vow that contradicts a previous one is explicitly developed in lines 3 and 4 (*act, vowing*). However, the body of commentary on this sonnet does not lead one to suppose that readers make that distinction as they read lines 1 and 2; and—since the rhetorical implication that *loving thee* in line 1 and *to me love swearing* are to be read as synonyms is so strong, and since line 3 provides a clear and satisfactory gloss on line 2—there is no reason to expect that any reader pauses to puzzle over the logic of lines 1 and 2. Moreover, a reader's probable knowledge of the lady's conduct as reported earlier in the 1609 sequence can lead him to anticipate the gloss provided in line 3 and read *thou art twice forsworn* as "you have broken your faith with another (previous) lover, and you have broken your faith with me as well (by going to bed with a third person or by going to bed again with the lover you betrayed by loving me)." *thou art . . . forsworn to me love swearing* (1) you are perjured (break an earlier vow) as a result of swearing to me that (a) you love me and (b) will continue to love me, will be faithful; (2) you are perjured when you swear to me that you love me (i.e. the new promise is a lie); (3) you are forsworn to me (i.e. you break your oath to me) in swearing love (to me? to your former love? to a third lover?); (4) you are forsworn to love-swearing me (i.e. to me who swear to love you).

3. *In act* (1) in action, physically; (2) in doing "the act," performing the sexual act, having sexual relations (for the specifically sexual sense of *act*, see *Oth* IV.ii.164 [quoted in 150.11,12, note] and *MofV* I.iii.78: "woolly breeders in the act"). *bed-vow* marriage vow (whether formal or informal; compare the note on the specific reference of *I am forsworn* in line 1). *broke* broken (see 47.1, note and Abbott, par. 343). *faith* vow (compare *LLL* V.ii.283: "Berowne hath plighted faith to me"). *torn* broken, breached (compare *LLL* IV.iii.280–81: "Berowne, now prove / Our loving lawful, and our faith not torn"; Tucker observed that *torn* here suggests nullifying a written contract by tearing it up).

4. *hate* (1) hatred for me (whom you lately swore to love and for whom you broke your bed-vow); (2) hatred for your former lover; (3) hatred for your newest lover (i.e. a third lover who has superseded the speaker). *new love bearing* (1) feeling love for someone new (i.e. for me); (2) feeling love for someone new (i.e. for someone who has replaced me); (3) bearing the physical weight of a new lover, allowing a new lover to lie with you.

3–4. Line 3 explains *twice forsworn*: "[thou art forsworn] in breaking your bed-vow and in breaking your new bed-vow (i.e. the new and adulterous oath to be faithful to me) by going to bed with a third man or by resuming obedience to your marriage vows." Line 4 adds a new oath—a third oath, a solemn renunciation of the speaker—to the physical infidelity implied by the parallel actions in line 3 (*In act thy bed-vow broke* and [*in act thy*] *new faith torn*).

1–4. The overlapping syntaxes and logics of the quatrain successively present: (a) physical violation of the terms of an earlier vow (*In loving thee I am forsworn* and, by implication, "in [you] loving me"); (b) a new oath that falsifies and is falsified by the earlier vow (*to me love swearing*); (c) physical violation of the terms of the new vow (*new faith torn, new love bearing*); and (d) a still newer vow that falsifies and is falsified by the vow it supersedes (*In vowing new hate*). The quatrain is generally imitative of its substance: its syntax is promiscuous, and it is calculatedly confusing in demonstrating change in the apparent constancy of the anaphora of three *In* phrases, the four participles (*loving, swearing, vowing, bearing*), and the densely interrelated phrases *new faith, new hate,* and *new love*. (The next line continues the careful confusion by complexly echoing the sound and sense of line 2:

> But . . . twice forsworn to me . . . .
> But . . . two oaths' breach do I . . . .

Also compare the interplay of constant and constantly changing sound, form, sense, and logic in the complex anaphora of *For all | And all* [lines 7,8], *For I have sworn deep oaths | And to* [9,11], and *For I have sworn thee fair | To swear* [13,14].)

5. *breach*   breaking, violation (with a logically freefloating pun on the anatomical senses of *breach* and "breech" (as in *2HIV* II.iv.49, *Lucrece* 469, and *AW* I.i.119).

7. *but to*   (1) to do nothing except; (2) merely to; (3) only intended to; (4) which only.   *misuse thee*   (1) debauch, illicitly use you sexually (*OED* gives this from about 1540: "Bicause I have myseused here [i.e. her] I intende to make [her] a goode woman"); (2) deceive you, delude you (as in *Much Ado* II.ii.25: "Proof enough to misuse the Prince, to vex Claudio, to undo Hero, and kill Leonato"); (3) revile you, speak evil of you (as in *Shrew* II.i.156–58: "she did call me rascal fiddler / And twangling Jack . . . / As had she studied to misuse me so"); (4) lie about you, misrepresent you (i.e. say you are fair and virtuous). Sense (4), of which *OED* finds no other examples, does not emerge until lines 9 and 10 demand it.

8. (1) "And all my confident trust of you is gone," "I no longer trust you"; (2) "And because of you all my honorable trustworthiness is lost," "I am no longer trustworthy" (with a suggestion of *honest* meaning "chaste" [as it does throughout *Oth*] and a bawdy play on *in thee* indicating the site of the loss). Sense (1) is evoked by the presence of the idiomatic construction "to have faith in" (e.g. Mark 11:22: "Have faith in God"), but does not immediately relate to the logic of lines 7 and 9; sense (2) is not idiomatic, but is dictated by context. Compare *2Gent* V.iv.46–52:

> Read over Julia's heart, thy first best love,
> For whose dear sake thou didst then rend thy faith
> Into a thousand oaths; and all those oaths
> Descended into perjury, to love me.

> Thou hast no faith left now, unless thou'dst two,
> And that's far worse than none; better have none
> Than plural faith, which is too much by one.

9. *deep oaths* (1) solemn oaths, heartfelt oaths (Tucker cites George Turberville's *Tragical Tales*, 1587: "they all . . . gan to sweare by deepe And very
solemne othes"); (2) mouth-filling, resounding, oaths; (3) extreme oaths, excessively extravagant oaths (*OED* gives this from 1577: "Deep swearings, not only
needlesse, but also hurtfull"). *thy deep* your vast, your great (*OED* gives this
from 1616: "This consideration . . . hath in deep measure seized upon mee");
presumably Shakespeare intends some sort of play here on *deep* indicating great
downward or inward extension (also note *all* in lines 7 and 8 and the initial vowel
sound of *oaths*; see 26.1–14, note [on *all*], Partridge, s.v. "O" and 20.12, note
[on zero]. *kindness* generosity. Presumably Shakespeare intends some genital
reference here—suggested by the consonants of *kind-*, and/or by the surface
relationship between *kindness* and "deed of kind" (*MofV* I.iii.80), and/or by the
ideationally related anatomical sense of "favors"—as in *Ham* II.ii.231–34:

> *Hamlet.* Then you live about her waist, or in the middle of her favours?
> *Guildenstern.* Faith, her privates we.
> *Hamlet.* In the secret parts of Fortune? O, most true; she is a strumpet.

Partridge compares Shakespeare's bawdy uses of *kind* with "the obsolete French
literalism, *la nature*, the pudend, the female genitalia." Farmer and Henley give
these Scots lines from the early eighteenth century: "The fair one frightened for
her fame / Shall for her kindness bear nae blame. . . . "
  11. *to enlighten thee* (1) to give you wisdom (the obvious sense, one that gives
the line a biblical cast [see Hebrews 6:4, Isaiah 35:5, 42:7, John 9, Ephesians
1:18, etc.], and one that seems irrelevant to its context); (2) to make you fair (a
witty malapropism based on a logic that says: fair coloring = light coloring; to
be fair = to be beautiful; thus, "to enlighten" = "to make beautiful"; see 149.2,
note). *gave eyes to blindness* (1) saw beauty I could not see; (2) gave my eyes
over to blindness, became voluntarily blind (but continuing the irrelevant topic
of intellectual or spiritual enlightenment).
  12. (1) "Or made my eyes report the opposite of what they see"; (2) "Or
suborned the eyes to deny the truth, contradict the evidence before them"
(*swear against* suggests two witnesses giving contradictory testimony in a law
case). *the thing* Compare 136.7 and 11.
  13. *eye* Many editors read "I." Q's *eye* is richer, embodying "I" and "ay"
as well as "eye"; compare the puns on "I" and "ay" in 136.6 and "I," "ay," and
"eye" in 148.8, 9, and 11. *more perjured eye* the eye is (and/or I am, and/or
my "ay"—my affirmation—is), therefore, even more guilty of perjury (in that the
lie sworn is such a foul one). Ingram and Redpath say that "the force of the pun
on 'eye' would seem to depend on the word 'truth' in line 14. The poet is a more
perjured kind of 'eye' than his falsely swearing eyes were. They swore the opposite of what they saw. He has sworn the opposite of what he knows to be the
truth. The poet is, however, also asserting that he is a 'more perjured *I*'—more

perjured in this particularly foul lie than in any he has admitted to in the rest of the sonnet."

13,14. *fair, foul*   Foul both evaluates the speaker's lie (it is extreme—all the antonyms of all the pertinent senses of *fair* describe the lady), and refers to its substance (calling foul fair); *fair* and *foul* pertain to the lady's complexion and to her morality (see 127.1, 6; 132.10–14; 137.12; and 147.13–14).

SONNET 153

Both this sonnet and 154 are variations on a conceit of which the earliest known use occurs in a six-line epigram by Marianus Scholasticus in the Greek Anthology. A version of the epigram was printed in Florence in 1594, but it is most unlikely that Shakespeare knew the Greek text. There are various Renaissance myth-making exercises on the topic of cold springs turned hot by Cupid's torch of love, but there is no saying what Shakespeare's immediate source was. The question was treated definitively by James Hutton in "Analogues of Shakespeare's Sonnets 153–54: Contributions to the History of a Theme" (*Modern Philology*, XXXVIII [May 1941], 385–403). Hutton gives this translation of Marianus's epigram: "Beneath these plane trees, detained by gentle slumber, Love slept, having put his torch in the care of the Nymphs; but the Nymphs said one to another: 'Why wait? Would that together with this we could quench the fire in the hearts of men.' But the torch set fire even to the water, and with hot water thenceforth the Love-Nymphs fill the bath." The Greek epigram and those of its descendants found by Hutton all have vague but considerable potential for bawdy anatomical reference. Shakespeare heightens that potential; his two sonnets on Cupid's torch and heated baths play on the common denominator among (1) the female sex-organ—a *valley-fountain*, a *cool well*—which grows hot with use (and, with misuse may come to burn and to burn subsequent users with the perpetual fire of venereal disease); (2) public baths; (3) natural hot springs (generally thought to have curative powers), and (4) sweating tubs (the tubs of hot water in which victims of venereal disease were steeped as part of their cure—see *Tim* IV.iii.82–87 and Francis Beaumont, *The Knight of the Burning Pestle* III.iii.110–38). See the notes on *well* in 154.9, and note the conjunction of senses in the following related words: "bagnio" = "brothel" (derived from Italian *bagno*, "a public bath"); "stew" = (1) fish pond; (2) public bath (like a Turkish bath); (3) brothel (akin to French *estuver* = "to soak in warm water," *s'estuver* = "to sweat in a hot-house," "to wash oneself in hot waters," *estuves* = "brothels," "hot-houses," and *estuy* [modern *étui*] = "a sheath," "a case" for instruments such as pens, needles, pen-knives, "an etwee"); "hot-house" = (1) a bathing house with hot baths (often considered curative—as in this *OED* example from 1544: "The pacient must . . . sweate in baths or whote houses"); (2) brothel (as in *Measure* II.i.64). Note also that spas, watering places, and hot baths have from Roman times been noted for lasciviousness (see Martial XI.lxxx) and as paradoxical places (James Revel Smith puts the paradox elegantly in *Springs and Wells in Greek and Roman Literature* [N.Y., 1922]: "Life about the Springs of Baiae moved in that eccentric round of opposite purposes that seems to become its natural orbit in most of the world's gay watering places, where a part of the visitors are feverishly seeking a respite from sickness in draughts and baths, while others, without maladies, are plunging into every variety of dissipation and depravity that conduce to the destruction of health and sow the seeds of disease" [p. 62]). The poems play with and intertwine a number of related paradoxes: the cure for love is loving (to cool the heat of desire a man puts himself into a warm place); that cure is not permanent; the cooling of male desire inflames the female sex organ; the female sex organ may set the male aflame with disease; the cure for the disease (tubbing), resembles the action by which the disease was contracted.

Shakespeare's authorship of 153 and 154 has been regularly but unconvincingly challenged; see *Variorum* I, 391 and II, 42–53, but note the couplet rhymes of 152 and 153.

1. *laid by*   put aside, put down (with a possible play on "lay down beside"; compare the juxtaposition of *lying* and *Laid by* in 154.1–2).   *brand*   torch. (Compare Martial III.xciii.27: *intrare in istum sola fax potest cunnum*; aside from the simple obscenity of *fax in cunnum*, Martial's joke hinges on *fax*, "a torch"—specifically a nuptial torch [a torch carried in bridal processions], or one used to light funeral pyres, and metaphorically anything that inflames; used of that which kindles desire, *fax* carries extra and specific energy from "nuptial torch" [see Horace, *Odes III*.ix.13].)

2. *A maid of Dian's*   (1) one of the virgin huntresses who serve Diana, virgin goddess of the hunt; (2) a virgin.   *advantage*   favorable opportunity, chance (as in *V&A* 129: "Make use of time, let not advantage slip").   *found*   The word acts two ways to the same effect: syntax (*advantage found*), indicates that the maid discovered an opportunity; context (*this . . . found*), and idiom ("to find someone or some material thing"), indicate that she discovered Cupid.

3. *quickly*   (1) immediately; (2) hastily (although it is unlikely that any reader ever heard a play on "quick" meaning "alive" here, the word has an extra and extra-logical "feel" of pertinence in context of *love-kindling fire* and of *dateless lively heat* in line 6).

4. *of that ground*   nearby, which was in the place where the maid found Cupid sleeping.

5. *this*   The word has no clear antecedent; the antecedent—Cupid's brand— is dictated by synesis (i.e. the logic of the situation substitutes for syntactic precision). One early editor changed *this* to "his" (*Variorum* I, 391).   *holy* divine, sacred (because Cupid is a god)—with a play on "holey" (as in *AW* I.iii.32: "I have other holy reasons [for marriage]"; see 127.7, note, "Committed holy rapes upon the will" in Thomas Carew's "An elegy upon the death of Doctor Donne" [line 17], "thrice holy hill" in the Barnes poem quoted in 154.9, note, and *A&C* I.ii.169, quoted in 151.12, note).   *of*   (1) belonging to, pertaining to; (2) which is; (3) caused by, from.   *love*   (usually capitalized by editors) (1) Love, Cupid; (2) affection, the emotion or passion called "love."

6. *dateless*   (1) eternal (as in 30.6); (2) eternally (some editors hyphenate *dateless lively* to indicate the adverbial reading).   *lively*   (1) living (as in 67.10); (2) vigorous.   *still*   (1) always, forever; (2) constantly (with suggestions of

"even after that has happened," "nevertheless"—suggestions pertinent to the underthemes of satisfying desire and curing disease). *endure*   Q has "indure" (see 37.7, note).

7. *grew*   became.   *yet*   (1) *still* (in all the senses given above); (2) to this day. *prove*   find, discover to be (as in 72.4; note the ideational pun on *found* in line 2). (The gloss given here reflects the sense to which line 8 subsequently narrows *prove*; line 7 is momentarily a complete, self-contained clause, and *prove* can momentarily register as "put to the test," "try out," "use," and, perhaps, "become," "are transformed to" [as in 48.14].)

8. *strange*   Q gives "strang"; *OED* gives "strang" as a variant spelling of *strange* from the fourteenth to the seventeenth century and as a variant spelling of "strong" from the thirteenth to the sixteenth. Tucker adopted "strong" in his text because he did not find *strange* appropriate to the context, but, as Ingram and Redpath point out, "the word was often used to mean 'exceptionally great, extreme' (*OED*, sense 9), and in that sense does not differ greatly from 'strong.' " Moreover, *strange* meaning "unusual," "exotic," "surprising," is perfectly appropriate to the context and is also capable of carrying pertinent suggestions of the standard expression "strange woman" meaning "harlot" (as in Proverbs 2:12–19: "[Wisdom shall] deliver thee from the evil way . . . / And from them that leave the waies of righteousnes to walke in the waies of darknes: / Which rejoyce in doing evil, & delite in the frowardnes of the wicked, / Whose wais are croked and they are lewde in their paths. / And it shal deliver thee from the strange woman, even from the stranger, which flattereth with her wordes. / Which forsaketh the guide of her youth [*That is, her housband* . . . —Geneva, marginal gloss], and forgetteth the covenant of her God. / Surely her house tendeth to death, & her paths unto the dead [*To them that are dead in bodie and soule*—Geneva, marginal gloss]. / All thei that go unto her, returne not againe, nether take they holde of the waies of life").

9. *eye*   For the traditional idea that the eyes of a beloved inspire the lover, see 78.5–8. Here (and, if Q is correct, in line 14) Shakespeare probably intends a play on the genital sense of "eye" (see 136.2, 148.7–9, notes, "naked seeing self" in *HV* V.ii.293, and "hir nether ye" in the last lines of Chaucer's "Miller's Tale"). *new-fired*   newly ignited.

10. *for trial*   to test it (note the ideational pun on *prove* in line 7).   *trial* = dissyllabic (like *dial* in 77.2,7).

11. *withal*   therefrom (but with a possible play on "from 'all' "; for speculation on a sexual sense for "all," see 26.1–14, note).   *bath*   (1) a medicinal bath; (2) a watering place; (3) Bath, the city named for its hot springs. (Whether or not Shakespeare's reader would have heard a specific reference to Bath is much debated. Ingram and Redpath say, "Bath was certainly visited for its curative waters in Elizabethan times, and 'thither hied' might allude to such a visit. On the other hand, Bath had no pre-eminence among spas such as it was to attain in the eighteenth century, and the line might refer to any curative spa in use at the time." However, in favor of the specific reference, one may note that the expression "Go to Bath!" meaning "You are insane" *may* already have been current; Farmer and Henley cite this from 1588: "Such two Justices may . . .

License diseased persons (living of almes) to travel to *Bathe* or to *Buckstone*, for remedie of their griefe." Moreover. one element in some of the poems derived from the Marianus epigram was special reference to some particular watering place (e.g. Baiae or Baden—see Hutton).

12. *hied* hastened. *distempered* (1) diseased (in body and/or in mind—Willen and Reed cite *2HIV* III.i.41–42: "a body yet distempered; / Which to his former strength may be restored . . . " and *R&J* II.iii.33–34: "it argues a distempered head / So soon to bid good morrow to thy bed"); (2) out of sorts, ill tempered. (Note that steel is tempered by plunging it into water.)

14. *eye* See the note on line 9 above. Rhymes like *lies/eye* are unusual in Renaissance poetry, but not unheard of. Most editors perfect the rhyme by giving "eyes." (The emendation is recommended by its possible pun on "ice." Wyatt rhymed "eyes" and "ice" in "Avysing the bright bemes"; for the "eyes"/ "ice" pun, see Herrick's "To Mistress Amie Potter," and, perhaps, "two stemyng Ise" in Wyatt's "My mothers maydes" [line 53]. Note that sonnets 153 and 154 are in a poetic tradition in which love's paradoxes are expressed as miraculous perversions of the natural order of the four elements and the four humors [see 45 and notes, and compare such exercises in oxymoron as Drayton's "When I first ended, then I first began" and "Those teares, which quench my hope" and sonnet 30 of Spenser's *Amoretti*].)

SONNET 154

See 153, headnote.

1–2. Hutton noted that "the first two lines are deficient in sense; they make the love-god in his sleep perform the act of laying aside his brand" (p. 401). The deficiency is less apparent if *brand* is understood in an obscene sense (see 153.1, note and 87.13, note—on the Renaissance literature on sexual dreams).

2. *Laid by* Note the play on *laid by* in 153.1.

5,7. *votary, general* The rhythm suggests that both are trisyllabic.

6. *legions* multitudes (in the following line *the general* activates a retroactive—and incidental—pun on *legions* meaning "armies").

7. *of* (1) *of* indicating that which the general commands; (2) *of* indicating that of which he was disarmed, what was taken from him.

8. *Was sleeping by a virgin hand disarmed* "While asleep was disarmed by . . ." (*by* indicates agency, but the line includes a momentary play on "was sleeping beside—next to—a virgin"). Note also the incidental play of *hand* and "arm" in *disarmed*.

9. *well* Like *valley-fountain* in 153.4, *well* is probably intended both literally and as a bawdy metaphor for the female sex organ. I find no indisputable use of *well* in that sense before *Cooper's Well*, an obscene eighteenth-century comic parody, a topographical description of a whore named Cooper. However, see the intricate interplay of "will" and *well* in this conversation between Parolles and Helena about virginity:

> *Parolles.* . . . . Will you anything with it [your virginity]?

> *Helena.* Not my virginity yet.
> There shall your master have a thousand loves,
> A mother, and a mistress, and a friend,
> A phoenix, captain, and an enemy,
> A guide, a goddess, and a sovereign,
> A counsellor, a traitress, and a dear;
> His humble ambition, proud humility,
> His jarring concord, and his discord dulcet,
> His faith, his sweet disaster; with a world
> Of pretty, fond, adoptious christendoms
> That blinking Cupid gossips. Now shall he—
> I know not what he shall. God send him well!
> The court's a learning-place, and he is one—
> *Parolles.* What one, i' faith?
> *Helena.* That I wish well. 'Tis pity—
> *Parolles.* What's pity?
> *Helena.* That wishing well had not a body in't
> Which might be felt . . . .   [*AW* I.i.152–70]

(For the sexual senses of "will," see 135, headnote; for the phonetic likeness of *well* and "will," see 112.3, note.) Also see *MWW* I.iii.46 (quoted in 112.3, note); and Proverbs 5 (forbidding whoredom and prodigality)—this is the Bishops' Bible version of verses 15 and 18: "Drinke of the water of thyne owne well, and of the rivers that run out of thyne owne spring [Marginal gloss: *Content thyselfe with thyne owne wyfe, and desire not other*]." "Let thy well be blessed, and be glad with the wyfe of thy youth." The Geneva version of Proverbs 5:15 is "Drinke the water of thy cisterne, and of the rivers out of the middes of thine owne well"; compare *Oth* IV.ii.60–63 (the comparison of Desdemona to a fountain [i.e. a spring], and a cistern):

> The fountain from the which my current runs,
> Or else dries up—to be discarded thence!
> Or keep it as a cistern for foul toads
> To knot and gender in!

For other related ideas, compare the Spanish *pozo nupcial*; *WT* I.ii.192–95: "And many a man there is . . . / . . . holds his wife by th'arm / That little thinks she has been sluic'd in's absence, / And his pond fish'd by his next neighbour"; and *Cymb* I.iv.983–89:

> You may wear her in title yours; but you know strange fowl light upon neighbouring ponds. Your ring may be stol'n too. So your brace of unprizable estimations, the one is but frail and the other casual; a cunning thief, or a that-way-accomplish'd courtier, would hazard the winning both of first and last.

See also Barnabe Barnes, *Parthenophil and Parthenophe*, Madrigal 26 (in *Elizabethan Sonnets*, ed. Sidney Lee [New York & Edinburgh, 1904], I, 235–36):

> I dare not speak of that thrice holy hill,
>   Which, spread with silver lilies, lies;
> Nor of those violets which void veins full fill,
>   Nor of that maze on love's hill-top:
> These secrets must not be surveyed with eyes!
>   No creature may those flowers crop!
>   Nor bathe in that clear fountain,
> Where none but Phoebe with chaste virgins wash!
>   In bottom of that sacred mountain—
> But, whither, now? Thy verses overlash!

Donne plays with the idea in lines 3–7 of *Upon Mr. Thomas Coryats Crudities*: "Venice [i.e. Venice's—with a play on Venus'] vast lake thou hadst seen, and would seek than / Some vaster thing [see 135.7, 11], and found'st a Curtizan. / That inland sea having discovered well, / A Cellar gulfe, where one might saile to hell / From Heydelberg, thou longdst to see. . . ." And in *Elegies*, XVII.21–22 Donne uses *well* in the suggestive company of "die" (see *Much Ado* V.ii.87: "die in thy lap"), "do" (see 110.9–12, note), and "service" (see 141.10, note): "I love her well, and would, if need were, dye / To doe her service."

by   nearby. (This is the fourth of five *by*'s in the poem: lines 2, 4, 8, 9, and 13; no two of them are used in quite the same way.)

10. *fire, perpetual*   The rhythm is doubtful: *fire* is ordinarily monosyllabic (as in line 5); if *fire* is pronounced as one syllable, *perpetual* has four and provides a limp rhyme for *thrall* in line 12; the rhythmically improbable alternative, giving *fire* two syllables and *perpetual* three (as in 56.8), is even less satisfactory. *heat*   (1) warmth; (2) lust.

11. *Growing*   becoming.   *bath*   medicinal hot natural spring.

13. *Came*   In this context a reader may hear a play on the sexual sense of "to come" (as in *Much Ado* V.ii.20–22: *Margaret*. "Well, I will call Beatrice to you, who, I think, hath legs." *Benedick*. "And therefore will come"; and *TN* III.iv.29–30: *Olivia*. "Wilt thou go to bed, Malvolio?" *Malvolio*. To bed? Ay, sweetheart, and I'll come to thee").   *prove*   (1) demonstrate to be true; (2) discover to be true, find (as in 153.7).   *this*   the following truth.   *that*   (1) the fact that I am my mistress' slave; (2) the fact that I *Came there for cure*; (3) the events described in lines 1–12.

14. *water cools not love*   Mr. Ronald Jaeger kindly let me see an advance copy of a note in which he points out that this phrase echoes Song of Songs 8:7: "Muche water can not quenche love, nether can the floods drowne it . . ." (*Notes and Queries*, XIX, 125). See 153.14, note.

Abbreviations Used in the Commentary

Abbott	E. A. Abbott, *A Shakespearian Grammar*, 3rd ed. London, 1870.
A&C	*Antony and Cleopatra.*
A&S	Philip Sidney, *Astrophel and Stella.*
AV	The Authorized Version of the Bible (also called the King James Bible), 1611.
AW	*All's Well That Ends Well.*
AYLI	*As You Like It.*
Baldwin	T. W. Baldwin, *On the Literary Genetics of Shakespeare's Poems and Sonnets.* Urbana, 1950.
BCP	*The Book of Common Prayer* (here cited in the 1559 version as given in *Liturgies and Occasional Forms of Prayer Set Forth in the Reign of Queen Elizabeth*, ed. for The Parker Society by W. K. Clay. Cambridge, Eng., 1847).
Beeching	*The Sonnets of Shakespeare*, ed. H. C. Beeching. Boston, 1904.
Bible	Unless otherwise specified, references are to the Geneva Bible of 1560.
Brooke	*Shakespeare's Sonnets*, ed. Tucker Brooke. New Haven, 1936.
CofE	*The Comedy of Errors.*
Cor	*Coriolanus.*
Cotgrave	Randle Cotgrave, *A Dictionarie of the French and English Tongues.* London, 1611.
Cruttwell	Patrick Cruttwell, *The Shakespearean Moment.* London, 1954.
Cymb	*Cymbeline.*
Dowden	*The Sonnets of William Shakespeare*, ed. Edward Dowden. London, 1881.
Ellis	Herbert Alexander Ellis, *Shakespeare's Lusty Punning in "Love's Labour's Lost."* The Hague, 1973.
Empson, *Seven Types*	William Empson, *Seven Types of Ambiguity.* Rev. ed. New York, 1947.
Empson, *Some Versions*	William Empson, *Some Versions of Pastoral.* London, 1935.
Farmer and Henley	J. S. Farmer and W. E. Henley, *Slang and Its Analogues.* 7 vols. London, 1890–1904.
Florio	John Florio, *Queen Anna's New World of Words.* London, 1611 (a revision of *A Worlde of Wordes*, London, 1598).

FQ   Edmund Spenser, *The Faerie Queene.*

Golding   *The. xv. Bookes of P. Ovidius Naso, entytuled Metamorphosis, translated . . . by Arthur Golding.* London, 1567.

1HIV, 2HIV   *The First Part of King Henry the Fourth, The Second Part of King Henry the Fourth.*

HV   *King Henry the Fifth.*

1HVI, 2HVI, 3HVI   *The First Part of King Henry the Sixth, The Second Part of King Henry the Sixth, The Third Part of King Henry the Sixth.*

HVIII   *King Henry the Eighth.*

Ham   *Hamlet.*

Harbage   *Shakespeare's Sonnets,* The Pelican Edition, ed. Douglas Bush and Alfred Harbage. Baltimore, 1961.

Hubler   Edward Hubler, *The Sense of Shakespeare's Sonnets.* Princeton, 1952.

Hulme   Hilda M. Hulme, *Explorations in Shakespeare's Language.* London, 1962.

Ingram and Redpath   *Shakespeare's Sonnets,* ed. W. G. Ingram and Theodore Redpath. London, 1964.

JC   *Julius Caesar.*

John   *King John.*

Kökeritz   Helge Kökeritz, *Shakespeare's Pronunciation.* New Haven, 1953.

LC   *A Lover's Complaint.*

Lear   *King Lear.*

Leishman   J. B. Leishman, *Themes and Variations in Shakespeare's Sonnets.* London, 1961.

LLL   *Love's Labour's Lost.*

Lucrece   *The Rape of Lucrece.*

Macb   *Macbeth.*

Malone   Edmund Malone, *Supplement to the Edition of Shakespeare's Plays published in 1778 by Dr. Samuel Johnson and George Steevens.* 2 vols. London, 1780.

Martin   Philip Martin, *Shakespeare's Sonnets: Self, Love, and Art.* Cambridge, Eng., 1972.

Measure   *Measure for Measure.*

Met.   Ovid, *Metamorphoses.*

MofV   *The Merchant of Venice.*

MWW   *The Merry Wives of Windsor.*

MND   *A Midsummer Night's Dream.*

Much Ado   *Much Ado About Nothing.*

Noble   Richmond Noble, *Shakespeare's Biblical Knowledge.* London, 1935.

OED   *The Oxford English Dictionary* (also called *A New*

English Dictionary or *Murray's Dictionary*), ed. J. A. Murray et al. 13 vols. Oxford, 1884–1928.

Onions C. T. Onions, *A Shakespeare Glossary*. Oxford, 1911.

Orgel Ben Jonson, *The Complete Masques*, ed. Stephen Orgel. New Haven, 1969.

Oth *Othello.*

Partridge Eric Partridge, *Shakespeare's Bawdy*. London, 1947.

Per *Pericles, Prince of Tyre.*

Phoenix *The Phoenix and the Turtle.*

PL John Milton, *Paradise Lost.*

Pooler *The Works of Shakespeare: Sonnets,* The Arden Edition, ed. C. K. Pooler. London, 1918.

PP *The Passionate Pilgrim.*

Prayer Book See *BCP.*

Q *Shakespeares Sonnets*, The First Quarto. London, 1609.

RII *King Richard the Second.*

RIII *King Richard the Third.*

R&J *Romeo and Juliet.*

Ringler *The Poems of Sir Philip Sidney*, ed. William A. Ringler, Jr. Oxford, 1962.

Rollins See *Variorum.*

SC Edmund Spenser, *The Shepheardes Calender.*

Schaar Claes Schaar, *An Elizabethan Sonnet Problem*, Lund Studies in English, 28. Lund, 1960.

Schmidt Alexander Schmidt, *Shakespeare-Lexicon*, 2 vols. Berlin, 1874–75.

Seymour-Smith *Shakespeare's Sonnets*, ed. Martin Seymour-Smith. London, 1963.

Shakespeare Unless otherwise specified, references to Shakespeare's plays and poems are keyed to *The Tudor Shakespeare*, ed. Peter Alexander. London, 1951 and New York, 1952.

Shrew *The Taming of the Shrew.*

Shumaker Wayne Shumaker, *The Occult Sciences in the Renaissance*. Berkeley, 1972.

Sisson C. J. Sisson, *New Readings in Shakespeare*. 2 vols. London, 1956.

Smith William Shakespeare, *Sonnets*, ed. Barbara Herrnstein Smith. New York, 1969.

SQ *Shakespeare Quarterly.*

T&C *Troilus and Cressida.*

Temp *The Tempest.*

Tilley Morris Palmer Tilley, *A Dictionary of The Proverbs in England in the Sixteenth and Seventeenth Centuries*. Ann Arbor, 1950.

Tim   *Timon of Athens.*

Titus   *Titus Andronicus.*

TN   *Twelfth Night.*

TNK   The Two Noble Kinsmen (references are keyed to the text given in *The Riverside Shakespeare*, ed. G. Blakemore Evans et al. Boston, 1974).

Tucker   *The Sonnets of Shakespeare*, ed. T. G. Tucker. London, 1924.

2Gent   *The Two Gentlemen of Verona.*

V&A   *Venus and Adonis.*

Variorum   *A New Variorum Edition of Shakespeare: The Sonnets,* ed. Hyder Edward Rollins. 2 vols. Philadelphia, 1944.

WT   *The Winter's Tale.*

Whitney   Geoffrey Whitney, *A Choice of Emblemes.* Leiden, 1586.

Willen and Reed   *A Casebook on Shakespeare's Sonnets*, ed. Gerald Willen and Victor B. Reed. New York, 1964.

Wilson   *The Sonnets*, The New Cambridge Shakespeare, ed. John Dover Wilson. Cambridge, Eng., 1966.

Wright and LaMar   *Shakespeare's Sonnets*, ed. Louis B. Wright and Virginia LaMar, The Folger Library General Reader's Shakespeare. New York, 1967.

Appendix 1

The following survey is brief because the facts are so few and because the theories are so many, so foolish, and so well described in Hyder Rollins's *A New Variorum Edition of Shakespeare: The Sonnets* (2 vols., Philadelphia, 1944). There have been isolated outbreaks of definitive rearrangement and inferential biography since the *Variorum*, but Rollins's examples still adequately represent the state of the art. My sketch of the fuss about Mr. W. H. illustrates the quality of speculation.

TEXT: Aside from 138 and 144, the two sonnets that appear in *PP*, the 1609 Quarto is the only text. A notice of intention to publish the sonnets occurs in the Stationers' Register for 1609: "20 Maij Thomas Thorpe Entred for his copie vnder thandes of master Wilson and master Lownes Warden a Booke called Shakespeares sonnettes." In talking about the Renaissance book trade, "bookseller" and "publisher" are generally interchangeable terms, but Thomas Thorpe, the "T.T." of the Quarto title page and dedication, did not have a shop of his own; although a member of the Stationers' Company, Thorpe was a small-time entrepreneur who speculated in such manuscripts as he could come by; he arranged to have them printed and sold. How and where Thorpe got the text of the 1609 Quarto (which included *A Lover's Complaint* as well as the 154 sonnets), is unknown. George Eld, in whose shop Q was printed, was also the printer for *Troilus and Cressida*. The Q title page exists in two forms: seven of the thirteen surviving copies have "to be solde by *John Wright*, dwelling at Christ Church gate," and four have "to be solde by William Apsley" (two copies lack title pages). Eld and the booksellers Wright and Apsley were all better established than Thorpe, and each published books. Wright, for example, was one of the syndicate that printed the First Folio in 1623. Rollins, *Variorum* II, 1–5, gives the whereabouts of and variations among the thirteen known copies of Q; also see my note on 89.11. The copy reproduced here is the Huntington–Bridgewater copy. The reproduction of the variant title page is from the Elizabethan Club copy.

The sonnets were not published again until 1640 when John Benson, another bookseller, used all but eight as the basis for a hybrid called *Poems: Written by Wil. Shakespeare. Gent.* Benson's book, a carelessly executed attempt to make money on forgotten poems to which he did not hold publishing rights, included most of *PP* and had *LC*, *Phoenix*, and poems by Thomas Carew, Thomas Carey, Ben Jonson, Herrick, Milton, and several other poets tacked on at the end. Benson rearranged the sonnets, interspersed poems from *PP* among them, grouped the resulting hodge-podge into 72 "poems," gave fatuous titles to his new units, and changed words here and there so as to make poems to a man into poems to a woman. Benson's text was the basis of many eighteenth-century editions and competed with editions based on Q, but, except as a fact of editorial history, the Benson version may be dismissed as irrelevant to the study of the sonnets. Rollins gives a more than adequate account of the 1640 text and its subsequent influence (II, 18–36).

The Q text was reprinted in a responsibly edited version in 1709. Other and more scholarly editions followed, but not for half a century: George Steevens's in 1766, Edward Capell's in the same year, and the still essential annotated edition by Edmond Malone in 1780.

SHAKE-SPEARES

SONNETS.

Neuer before Imprinted.

AT LONDON
By *G. Eld* for *T. T.* and are
to be folde by *iohn wright,*dwelling
at Chriſt Church gate.
1609.

An example of the Wright imprint of the Quarto title page, reproduced
by permission of the Elizabethan Club of Yale University.

AUTHENTICITY: There is no reason to doubt that the 154 poems Thorpe published as Shakespeare's are by Shakespeare. There is, of course, no certainty that they are. For various reasons (sometimes specified, always arbitrary, never persuasive) most of the sonnets in Q have at one time or another been questioned. The most frequently banished have been 145 (presumably because its form is deviant and because it is not a good poem) and 153–154 (the last two sonnets, both variations on a classical original, and neither related to the situations implied in the first 152); but 145 describes a rhetorical effect that is a Shakespearian favorite, and the couplet rhymes of 153 echo those of 152.

DATES OF COMPOSITION: Versions of two Q sonnets appeared in 1599 as part of *PP* (see 138 and 144, headnotes). Otherwise the only certainty about the date of the 154 sonnets in Q is the publication date, 1609. In *Palladis Tamia*, registered on September 7, 1598, Francis Meres praised Shakespeare's *V&A* and *Lucrece* and "his sugred Sonnets among his private friends, &c." That testifies to nothing except that Meres knew of some Shakespeare sonnets by 1598; whether he referred to all or any of the sonnets in Q is a matter of pure guesswork. The same is true of all efforts to date some or all of the sonnets by internal details (see 104 and 107, headnotes), by their style, by their subject matter, or by biographical speculation.

FORM: All but three of the 154 poems in Q consist of fourteen pentameter lines— three quatrains and a couplet—and rhymed *abab, cdcd, efef, gg* (a form introduced by Henry Howard, Earl of Surrey, and anticipated by Thomas Wyatt's "The flamyng sighes that boile within my brest," a twenty-eight-line poem in fourteen-line, seven-rhyme stanzas rhymed *abba, cddc, effe, gg*). The three exceptions in Q are 99 (fifteen lines long), 126 (six couplets), and 145 (tetrameters).

SOURCES: The last two sonnets in Q ultimately derive from a specific source, an epigram in the Greek Anthology (see 153, headnote). Otherwise, "source" is an inappropriate and misleading term in discussing the literary antecedents of the sonnets. It is more to the point to talk about literary traditions and conventions (notably those of courtly love literature as specialized by Petrarch, the continental sonneteers who followed him, and Sidney and Daniel in England). Shakespeare also echoes, alludes to, and plays on classical works, traditional philosophic commonplaces, passages from the Bible and the Christian liturgy, proverbial expressions, and—and above all—the standard English idioms of stock situations. With one exception, such matters are treated in the notes to the specific sonnets. The exception is Book XV of Ovid's *Metamorphoses*, which is excerpted at length in Appendix 2. *Metamorphoses* XV is the particular literary text most echoed in the sonnets, but it is principally a local source for local effects; Shakespeare uses Book XV the way he uses proverbs and liturgical echoes: as an extension of the language, a source of well-made, well-known building blocks; I single it out for special treatment for economy of presentation and (secondarily) to illustrate the extent to which Shakespeare had assimilated the particular passages he echoes.

In general I have neither noted analogues to Shakespearian conceits and ideas in the work of his predecessors and contemporaries nor speculated on indebtedness or its direction; such matters are ably treated by Baldwin, Leishman, Schaar, and Rollins.

ARRANGEMENT: Since most people guess the 1609 Quarto to be unauthorized, we have no strong reason to assume the 1609 order to be either the order of their writing or the order in which Shakespeare would have wanted them read had he published them himself. Benson reordered the poems in his 1640 edition, but he presumably did so for the simple commercial purpose of disguising a pirated reprint as something new. Benson's precedent was, moreover, unnecessary. As one reads the sonnets in their 1609 sequence, one feels their continuity as both urgent and wanting; the 1609 sequence regularly feels purposeful and as regularly seems to have just barely failed of its purpose. Efforts to put the order "right" were almost inevitable. None of the proposed rearrangements has been more satisfactory than Q's.

Many of the nineteenth- and twentieth-century reorganizations were determined by supposititious biographies which they were thereupon said to support. They warrant only sociological attention, and Rollins has provided it. Others, however, derive from efforts to ratify perceptions evoked by any reading of the 1609 sequence; such reorganizations do not command respect, but the instinct that prompts them demands sympathy of any reader who has ever found himself lost in the maze of road signs posted in the 1609 sequence.

The continuity of the 1609 sequence is obvious and insistent, but sporadic and inconsistent in the factors by which relationship is perceived. In a sequence of, say, six sonnets that feel continuous, the first and second may be syntactically linked (like 5–6, 27–28, 44–45, 89–90, and the three pairs linked by *But*); the second and third may be linked by logic (like 88–89 and 92–93); the first four and the sixth by topic (like 1–17, 40–42, 46–47, 50–51, 71–72, 132–133, 133–134, 134–136, and 153–154); and the fourth, fifth, and sixth by a common denominator of tone, incidental diction, metaphor, or secondary topic (see 18.12, note). As the preceding examples indicate, a single poem can be an obvious participant in several obvious groups determined by different obvious connecting factors. To point out or construct a group usually requires that a grouper arbitrarily dictate his chosen focus as paramount and determinate. For instance, within the 1609 order, the decision that a group begins or ends at a given point is almost always arbitrary. If one perceives a "rival poet" group in 78–80, 82–86, then sonnet 81 interrupts it; but sonnet 81 picks up the idea of decay at the end of 80 and, like 80 and 82, is about verse writing; 77 is also about writing; and 87 sounds like a logical next step from the surrender of 86. Moreover, 87 leads into and can be considered a part of a "self-defeating" group that begins with 88 and could be said to end with 89, if 90 did not begin with a syntactic gesture of logical continuation: *Then hate me when thou wilt.* Sonnet 91, *Some glory in their birth, some in their skill*, seems to depart radically from sonnet 90, but both conclude by making the same point. Sonnet 92 begins *But* and continues consideration of the beloved's abandonment of the speaker; 92 ends with *Thou mayst be false, and yet I know it not*, and 93 begins with the speaker's comparison of himself to a deluded cuckold. Sonnet 94 can look and feel like an isolated pronouncement, but its last six lines have a botanical common denominator with the last lines of 93 and the first of 95. . . .

A rearranger can also come to grief if he sees a strong connection between two sonnets isolated from one another in the 1609 order. Sonnets 34 and 120 seem to pertain to one another, but they also pertain to their neighbors in Q. The same is true of 77 and 122. One could feel that 40–42 and 133–134 belong together, but if one moved them one would disrupt the union of 132–133 ("eye–heart" poems) and 134–136 ("will" poems).

My point in the foregoing examples is that, although the sonnets invite scholarly rearrangements that fulfill the various kinds of continuity they signal, it is folly to accept the invitation. For further object lessons in the folly of grouping, see the final note on 141 and my discussion of 33–37 in *An Essay on Shakespeare's Sonnets* (New Haven, 1969), pp. 1–12. On the apparent break between 1–126 and 127–152, 153, 154, see 126, 127, headnotes.

BIOGRAPHICAL IMPLICATIONS, THE "STORY" BEHIND THE SONNETS: Some biographical prospectors in the sonnets have been content with mining them for illegitimately derived details (e.g. that Shakespeare was physically lame [37 and 89] and ashamed of being an actor [110 and 111]), but the desire to know more and the nature of the collection itself has evoked some notoriously creative scholarship. Like most love poetry, the sonnets presume a reader who is aware of their situation; they put a reader in a position comparable to those into which audiences are thrust (and from which they are quickly rescued) during the opening lines of some plays—for example, *King Lear*, in which the opening lines remark on a surprising change in a situation we know nothing about. The sonnets keep us in that position. We constantly overhear comments on situations which we know only from inferences inherent in the comments on them. We have no difficulty understanding the comments, and, since in doing so we make effortless and efficient use of background information we do not have, the sonnets convince us that we have such information and can tempt us to reproduce it for our fellows. Of those who have succumbed to the temptation, most have fallen under the following headings.

THE YOUNG MAN AS/AND MR. W. H.: Speculation on the identity of the young man rests on one or more from a series of assumptions that are reasonable but nonetheless pure: (a) the assumption that there is a biographical basis for the events apparently referred to in the sonnets (i.e. that there is a young man to identify); (b) the assumption that all references to a male beloved are to the same person; (c) the assumption that the Mr. (i.e. Master) W. H. of Thorpe's dedication is the young man addressed in the sonnets.

The two most popular candidates for Mr. W. H. have been Henry Wriothesley, third Earl of Southampton (1573–1624) and William Herbert, third Earl of Pembroke (1580–1630). Southampton and Pembroke, both noblemen and literary patrons, are recommended by the widespread implication that the speaker is addressing a man of high rank (an implication that could just as well derive from the courtly love tradition of addressing beloved ladies as if they were feudal lords) and the recurrent references to the relations of poet and patron (see sonnets 26, 38, and 78–86). The "evidence" for Southampton includes his initials (W. H. reversed), Shakespeare's dedication of *V&A* and *Lucrece* to him, and his marital activities (in 1590 he refused to cooperate in a projected match between himself and Lord Burghley's granddaughter, Lady Elizabeth Vere; in 1598 he contracted a hasty and secret marriage with one of the Queen's ladies-in-waiting, Elizabeth Vernon, who was pregnant at the time of her marriage but—to the sorrow of those who would have her the dark lady—relentlessly chaste thereafter). The "evidence" for Pembroke includes his initials (W. H.), the fact that Shakespeare's colleagues Heminges and Condell dedicated the First Folio to him and his brother Philip, and an unsuccessfully negotiated marriage between him and the Lord Chamberlain's granddaughter, Elizabeth Carey, in 1595. Southampton was first nominated in 1817, Pembroke in 1832. Campaigns on their behalf have filled so many pages for so many years that their rivalry has itself become part of literary history, and arguments against one have been unreasonably assumed to be arguments for the other.

Other speculators who take Thorpe's reference to Mr. W. H. as a reference to the man addressed in the sonnets have put forth other of Shakespeare's real or imaginary contemporaries as the male beloved: William Hart (Shakespeare's brother-in-law); William Hart (Shakespeare's nephew, baptized on August 28, 1600); William Hughes (a figment born of a supposed pun on *hues* in 20.7); several William Hathaways (e.g. a dramatist [inconveniently named Richard], Shakespeare's brother-in-law, and Shakespeare's father-in-law [also named Richard]); William Hervey (Southampton's mother's third husband, a candidate pushed forward regularly since 1867); William Hatcliffe (Lord of Misrule at Gray's Inn during Christmas celebrations in 1587/8); William Hammond (a manuscript of Middleton's *Game at Chess* was dedicated to a William Hammond, and someone of that [not improbable] name lived in Kent), William Haughton (a minor dramatist), William Holgate (an innkeeper's son who might have written verse); another William Herbert (Pembroke's cousin), William Harrison (topographer, clergyman, and speculative biologist—the author of *The Description of Eng-*

land in Holinshed's *Chronicles*, who was long and well married by 1577 and dead of old age by 1593); Kaiser Wilhelm Hohenzollern (1859–1941) . . . .

Nominators friendly to chiasmic disguise have put forth some H. W.'s to join Southampton: e.g. "Henry" Walker (Shakespeare's godson, baptized William on October 16, 1608), and Henry Willobie (author of—and, as "H. W.," a principal character in— *Willobie His Avisa* [1594], in which a character called "W.S." also figures [see *Variorum* II, 295–313]).

Other proposed identities for Mr. W. H. include William Shakespeare. One theory makes W. H. stand for "William Himself." Another, more obviously lunatic, notion says that W. H. refers to the man addressed in the poems and Shakespeare is that man: he is addressed by the author of the sonnets, one Anne Whateley (a nun fabricated from an error by the clerk who recorded Shakespeare's marriage license); she called Shakespeare Mr. W. H., using the second letter of his last name in order to confuse people.

Theorists who do not assume that the young man addressed is to be identified with Mr. W. H. have sharked up other candidates for the male beloved (the principal qualification for candidacy being that the nominator have heard of the nominee): Robert Devereux, second Earl of Essex; Hamnet Shakespeare (the poet's son, who died at age 11 in 1596); an illegitimate son of William Shakespeare (whose existence is not otherwise suspected); Edmund Shakespeare (the poet's younger brother); Robert Southwell, S.J.; Henry V (1387–1422); Elizabeth I (whose unmarried condition is well known to have been chronic, and whose sex Shakespeare disguised either from tact, as a tribute to her "masculine" mind, or for the sake of literary variety in the sonnet convention); Prince Henry (1594–1612, eldest son of James I, to whom George Chapman [a candidate for rival poet] dedicated an early installment of his "Homer"); and many more. (I ignore candidates proposed by Baconians, Oxfordians, and such.)

Some people, putting Thorpe's use of "begetter" under pressure, think that "Mr. W. H." does not refer to the man addressed in the sonnets but the man who obtained the manuscript for Thorpe. William Hervey, who survived Southampton's mother and executed her will, gets most of his support from this group; the younger Hart and the hypothetical Hughes have also seen service as procurers rather than inspirers of the manuscript. Various thin lines of argument lead to a Mr. W. H. named William Hall. An early suggestion was that Thorpe's "M^r. W. H. ALL. HAPPINESSE." is a misprint for "M^r. W. HALL. HAPPINESSE." William Hall is a common name; there was a stationer's assistant named William Hall in the 1590's and early 1600's; a William Hall, perhaps the same man, set up as a printer in 1608; he (or one of them) would have known Thorpe and *could* have been his accomplice in procuring the manuscript. The same is true of a bookseller named William Holme.

Another convenient and supposititious misprint would make Mr. W. H. an error for Mr. W. S., William Shakespeare.

HOMOSEXUALITY: William Shakespeare was almost certainly homosexual, bisexual, or heterosexual. The sonnets provide no evidence on the matter. See 126.4, note.

(The first 126 sonnets are full of incidental and incidentally bawdy sexual innuendo; some references make literal sense in reference to either male or female organs; some are specifically male, some specifically female [e.g. the *con-, cun-* jokes]. Hermaphroditic wordplay is not likely to confuse any readers but those who treat the poems as biographical spoor: sexual wordplay has always been anatomically eclectic—as any reader of walls knows. Moreover, Shakespeare makes overt rhetorical capital from the fact that the conventions he works in and the purpose for which he uses them do not mesh and from the fact that his beloveds are not what the sonnet conventions presume them to be [e.g. sonnet 20 and sonnets 1–17—wooing sonnets that woo not a female beloved but a male one and beg sexual favor not for the sonneteer but for someone else, anyone else, who is female—and sonnets 127–152—where the beloved is of the sex appropriate to the convention but is otherwise unworthy]. The sonnets, even those that most playfully engage themselves in incidental sexual-verbal trivia, often ring with passion and sincerity, but to assume therefore that they reflect particulars of Shakespeare's sex life is to be as unreasonable as Hamlet would be if he assumed that the first player was a chum of Hecuba's. The sexual undercurrents of the sonnets are of the sonnets; they probably reflect a lot that is true about their author, but I do not know what that is; they reveal nothing and suggest nothing about Shakespeare's love life.)

THE DARK LADY: Sonnets 127–152 include several that refer to or address a woman (or, improbably, some women) of dark complexion and whore-like habits. She, like the male friend, may be a literary creation; if Shakespeare was talking about real people and events, we have no clue whatsoever as to the woman's identity. Speculation on her identity has ranged from wanton to ludicrous and need not be illustrated.

THE RIVAL POET (OR POETS): Several of the sonnets (i.e. 78–80 and 82–86) mention a poet (or some poets) with whom the speaker seems to be in competition for the love and/or patronage of the beloved. Most Elizabethan poets whose names and work have survived have been suggested as *the* rival poet of the sonnets. George Chapman is the leading candidate (presumably because he wrote both pompously and well); Christopher Marlowe is in second place. There are no valid grounds for favoring any one poet or any coalition. There are no grounds for certainty that Shakespeare had any real particular poet(s) in mind.

Appendix 2

EXCERPTS FROM BOOK XV OF *The. xv. Bookes of P. Ovidius Naso, entytuled Metamorphosis, translated . . . by Arthur Golding* (1567)

The following passages are those echoed in the sonnets and referred to in the commentary. The copy text for Golding's version is that of W. H. D. Rouse in *Shakespeare's Ovid, being Arthur Golding's Translation of the Metamorphoses* (London, 1904).

The bulk of the fifteenth and last book of *Metamorphoses* is a long speech by Pythagoras; it begins with a passage on the barbarity of eating animal flesh; the final argument against butchering livestock is this (lines 96–110 in Ovid's Latin):

>   . . . But that same auncient age
> Which wee have naamd the golden world, cleene voyd of all such rage,
> Livd blessedly by frute of trees and herbes that grow on ground,
> And stayned not their mouthes with blood. Then birds might safe and sound
> Fly where they listed in the ayre. The hare unscaard of hound
> Went pricking over all the feeldes. No angling hooke with bayt
> Did hang the seely fish that bote mistrusting no deceyt.
> All things were voyd of guylefulnesse: no treason was in trust: 110
> But all was freendshippe, love, and peace. But after that the lust
> Of one (what God so ere he was) disdeyning former fare,
> Too cram that cruell croppe of his with fleshmeate did not spare,
> He made a way for wickednesse. And first of all the knyfe
> Was staynd with blood of savage beastes in ridding them of lyfe.
> And that had nothing beene amisse, if there had beene the stay.
> For why wee graunt, without the breach of godlynesse wee may
> By death confound the things that seeke too take our lyves away.
> But as too kill them reason was: even so agein theyr was
> No reason why too eate theyr flesh. . . .   120

Pythagoras goes on to expound the theory of metempsychosis in a passage that possessed the imaginations of Marlowe, Shakespeare, and Ben Jonson. This is Golding's version of *Met.* XV.165–269. (Lines 165–76 [Golding's 183–92] are incidentally illuminating; their assertion of the paradox of constancy and constant change presents a good description of a prime stylistic characteristic of the first fourteen books of *Metamorphoses* [in which Ovid straightforwardly announces changes in topic, and in which the details of a new topic are regularly those of the preceding old one, and in which each topic anticipates, suggests, and seems already to have begun on the topic that succeeds it], and of Shakespeare in the individual sonnets, in their interrelation, and in the structure of his plays.)

> All things doo chaunge. But nothing sure dooth perrish. This same spright
> Dooth fleete, and fisking heere and there dooth swiftly take his flyght
> From one place too another place, and entreth every wyght,
> Removing out of man too beast, and out of beast too man.
> But yit it never perrisheth nor never perrish can.
> And even as supple wax with ease receyveth fygures straunge,

And keepes not ay one shape, ne bydes assured ay from chaunge,
And yit continueth alwayes wax in substaunce: So I say   190
The soule is ay the selfsame thing it was, and yit astray
It fleeteth intoo sundry shapes. Therfore least Godlynesse
Bee vanquisht by outragious lust of belly beastlynesse,
Forbeare (I speake by prophesie) your kinsfolkes ghostes too chace   ⎫
By slaughter: neyther nourish blood with blood in any cace.   ⎬
And sith on open sea the wynds doo blow my sayles apace,   ⎭
In all the world there is not that that standeth at a stay.
Things eb and flow, and every shape is made too passe away.
The tyme itself continually is fleeting like a brooke.
For neyther brooke nor lyghtsomme tyme can tarrye still. But looke   200
As every wave dryves other foorth, and that that commes behynd
Bothe thrusteth and is thrust itself: Even so the tymes by kynd
Doo fly and follow bothe at once, and evermore renew.
For that that was before is left, and streyght there dooth ensew
Anoother that was never erst. Eche twincling of an eye
Dooth chaunge. Wee see that after day commes nyght and darks the sky,
And after nyght the lyghtsum Sunne succeedeth orderly.
Like colour is not in the heaven when all things weery lye
At midnyght sound a sleepe, as when the daystarre cleere and bryght   ⎫
Commes foorth uppon his milkwhyght steede. Ageine in other plyght   ⎬210
The morning *Pallants* daughter fayre the messenger of lyght   ⎭
Delivereth intoo *Phebus* handes the world of cleerer hew.
The circle also of the sonne what tyme it ryseth new
And when it setteth, looketh red, but when it mounts most hye,   ⎫
Then lookes it whyght, bycause that there the nature of the skye   ⎬
Is better, and from filthye drosse of earth dooth further flye.   ⎭
The image also of the Moone, that shyneth ay by nyght,
Is never of one quantitie. For that that giveth lyght
Too day, is better than the next that followeth, till the full.
And then contrarywyse eche day her lyght away dooth pull.   220
What? seest thou not how that the yeere as representing playne
The age of man, departes itself in quarters fowre? first bayne
And tender in the spring it is, even like a sucking babe.
Then greene, and voyd of strength, and lush, and foggye is the blade,
And cheeres the husbandman with hope. Then all things florish gay.
The earth with flowres of sundry hew then seemeth for too play,
And vertue small or none too herbes there dooth as yit belong.
The yeere from springtyde passing foorth too sommer, wexeth strong,
Becommeth lyke a lusty youth. For in our lyfe through out
There is no tyme more plentifull, more lusty whote and stout.   230
Then followeth Harvest when the heate of youth growes sumwhat cold,
Rype, meeld, disposed meane betwixt a yoongman and an old,
And sumwhat sprent with grayish heare. Then ugly winter last
Like age steales on with trembling steppes, all bald, or overcast
With shirle thinne heare as whyght as snowe. Our bodies also ay   ⎫
Doo alter still from tyme too tyme, and never stand at stay.   ⎬
Wee shall not bee the same wee were too day or yisterday.   ⎭
The day hath beene, wee were but seede and only hope of men,
And in our moothers woomb wee had our dwelling place as then,

Dame Nature put too conning hand and suffred not that wee   ⎫ 240
Within our moothers streyned womb should ay distressed bee,   ⎬
But brought us out too aire, and from our prison set us free.   ⎭
The chyld newborne lyes voyd of strength. Within a season tho
He wexing fowerfooted lernes like savage beastes too go.
Then sumwhat foltring, and as yit not firme of foote, he standes
By getting sumwhat for too helpe his sinewes in his handes.
From that tyme growing strong and swift, he passeth foorth the space ⎫
Of youth, and also wearing out his middle age a pace,   ⎬
Through drooping ages steepye path he ronneth out his race.   ⎭
This age dooth undermyne the strength of former yeeres, and throwes   250
It downe: which thing old *Milo* by example playnely showes.
For when he sawe those armes of his (which heeretoofore had beene
As strong as ever *Hercules* in woorking deadly teene
Of biggest beastes) hang flapping downe, and nought but empty skin,
He wept. And *Helen* when shee saw her aged wrincles in
A glasse, wept also: musing in herself what men had seene,   ⎫
That by twoo noble princes sonnes shee twyce had ravisht beene. ⎬
Thou tyme, the eater up of things, and age of spyghtfull teene, ⎭
Destroy all things. And when that long continuance hath them bit,
You leysurely by lingring death consume them every whit.   260
And theis that wee call Elements doo never stand at stay.   ⎫
The enterchaunging course of them I will before yee lay.   ⎬
Give heede thertoo. This endlesse world conteynes therin I say ⎭
Fowre substances of which all things are gendred. Of theis fower
The Earth and Water for theyr masse and weyght are sunken lower.
The other cowple Aire and Fyre the purer of the twayne
Mount up, and nought can keepe them downe. And though there doo remayne
A space betweene eche one of them: yit every thing is made
Of themsame fowre, and intoo them at length ageine doo fade.
The earth resolving leysurely dooth melt too water sheere,   270
The water fyned turnes too aire. The aire eeke purged cleere
From grossenesse, spyreth up aloft, and there becommeth fyre.
From thence in order contrary they backe ageine retyre.
Fyre thickening passeth intoo Aire, and Ayër wexing grosse
Returnes to water: Water eeke congealing intoo drosse,
Becommeth earth. No kind of thing keepes ay his shape and hew.
For nature loving ever chaunge repayres one shape a new
Uppon another, neyther dooth there perrish aught (trust mee)   ⎫
In all the world, but altring takes new shape. For that which wee ⎬
Doo terme by name of being borne, is for too gin too bee   ⎭ 280
Another thing than that it was: And likewise for too dye,
Too cease too bee the thing it was. And though that varyably
Things passe perchaunce from place too place: yit all from whence they came
Returning, doo unperrisshed continew still the same.
But as for in one shape, bee sure that nothing long can last.
Even so the ages of the world from gold too Iron past;
Even so have places oftentymes exchaunged theyr estate.
For I have seene it sea which was substanciall ground alate,
Ageine where sea was, I have seene the same become dry lond,
And shelles and scales of Seafish farre have lyen from any strond,   290

And in the toppes of mountaynes hygh old Anchors have beene found.
Deepe valleyes have by watershotte beene made of levell ground,
And hilles by force of gulling oft have intoo sea beene worne.
Hard gravell ground is sumtyme seene where marris was beforne,
And that that erst did suffer drowght, becommeth standing lakes.

Pythagoras goes on to list "alterations" by which "see we all things are chaungeable."
The list includes the phoenix (XV.392–407 in the Latin):

One bird there is that dooth renew itself and as it were
Beget itself continually. The Syrians name it there
A *Phœnix*. Neyther corne nor herbes this *Phœnix* liveth by,
But by the jewce of frankincence and gum of *Amomye*.
And when that of his lyfe well full fyvehundred yeeres are past,
Uppon a Holmetree or uppon a Date tree at the last
He makes him with his talants and his hardened bill a nest:
Which when that he with Casia sweete and Nardus soft hathe drest, }
And strowed it with Cynnamom and Myrrha of the best,   } 440
He rucketh downe uppon the same, and in the spyces dyes.
Soone after, of the fathers corce men say there dooth aryse
Another little *Phœnix* which as many yeeres must live
As did his father. He (assoone as age dooth strength him give
Too beare the burthen) from the tree the weyghty nest dooth lift,
And godlyly his cradle thence and fathers herce dooth shift.
And flying through the suttle aire he gettes too *Phebus* towne,
And there before the temple doore dooth lay his burthen downe.

Ovid concludes his poem in his own voice (XV. 871–79 in the Latin):

Now have I brought a woork too end which neither *Joves* feerce wrath,
    Nor swoord, nor fyre, nor freating age with all the force it hath
Are able too abolish quyght. Let comme that fatall howre
Which (saving of this brittle flesh) hath over mee no powre,
And at his pleasure make an end of myne uncerteyne tyme.
Yit shall the better part of mee assured bee too clyme
Aloft above the starry skye. And all the world shall never   990
Be able for too quench my name. For looke how farre so ever
The Romane Empyre by the ryght of conquest shall extend,
So farre shall all folke reade this woork. And tyme without all end
(If Poets as by prophesie about the truth may ame)
My lyfe shall everlastingly bee lengthened still by fame.

Index to the Commentary

This index is not to be confused with, and cannot serve as a substitute for, a concordance. Its references are to the notes in which various words and topics are discussed; this list is thus not a reliable index to the lines where those words and topics appear in the sonnets themselves (e.g. *wane*, which appears in 11.1, is listed here as appearing in 11.2 because the word is discussed during the note on the second line of sonnet 11).

Key

"15.1,3" would refer to a note numbered "1,3" in the commentary on sonnet 15.

"15.1–3" would refer to a note numbered "1–3" in the commentary on sonnet 15.

"15.2; 15.5–11; 15.1–14" would refer to three separate notes in the commentary on sonnet 15.

"15" would indicate that notes on the word or topic in question occur throughout the commentary on sonnet 15.

"15,h" would refer to a headnote to the commentary on sonnet 15.

Notes numbered 1–14 (e.g. 112.1–14) are usually long, general notes, placed at the end of the commentary on a particular sonnet.

If entries can be profitably ranked in order of importance, I do so; otherwise references are listed in order of their appearance in the commentary.

Where confusion is unlikely to result, I simplify the form listed in the index and lump obviously related words like *make* and *made* under one heading. I do not separate homonyms in the index because the substance of the notes referred to is so often an assertion that the distinction has been blurred (thus all uses of *use* appear under one heading; the same is true of the adjective *long* and the verb *to long*). I also lump a gloss on the word *meter* and comments on metrics under one heading.

Not every word and topic of the sonnets in listed here; nor does the list include every word glossed in the commentary or every topic mentioned. I have included and excluded entries on the basis of what I hope is common sense. Generally, simple glosses (e.g. *carcanet* = "necklace") are omitted; although *carcanet* is glossed in a note on 52.8, I left it out of the index because anyone wanting to know which sonnet has *carcanet* in it will presumably go to a concordance; anyone wanting to know what it means and not remembering where it is in the sonnets will presumably go to the *OED*. However, any word that does any double semantic duty is listed.

The commentary on the sonnets may be useful to students of Shakespeare's plays and other poems, to students of Shakespeare's language, and to students of the works and language of Shakespeare's contemporaries. The index is designed to help such students as much as possible in the smallest possible space.

The lists are illustrative rather than exhaustive (e.g. headings like "style as metaphor" present only a sampling of instances), although the listings for little words (like *in*, *to*, and *by*) that are casually treated in most literary reference books are fuller than might seem reasonable.

Passages cited from Shakespeare's other works or from other Renaissance writers are not indexed except in cases where my note can be considered informative about the illustrative example.

Index of First Lines

Additional Notes (1978)

(Five of these seven new notes derive from responses to this edition by W. L. Godshalk. The note on 1.4 summarizes a portion of Godshalk's "Puns in Shakespeare's Sonnet 1, Line 4," which is scheduled to appear in *ELN* during 1979. The notes on 16.9, 73.3–4, 94.4, and 149.13–14 draw on Godshalk's review of this edition; by the time these notes are printed a version of that review will have appeared in an issue of *JEGP*. I quote Godshalk from drafts that he kindly forwarded in time for me to pirate them. The long, repentant note on my now-rejected emendation in 111.1 was prompted by broadly significant research by Randall McLeod. I thank Professor Godshalk and Professor McLeod for their work and for their generosity in letting me use it here.)

1.4 (p. 136). *tender heir*   In a note explaining and sustaining an assertion in M. M. Mahood's *Shakespeare's Wordplay* (London, 1957, p. 92), Godshalk convincingly argues that *tender heir*—pronounced "tender air"—is a complex bilingual pun on Latin *mulier* ("woman") via Latin *mollis aer* ("tender air") by which line 4 conveys a witty extra meaning: " 'His *woman* might bear [i.e., give birth to], his memory, i.e., his child.' " The pun is nothing like so improbable as it may seem: wittily erroneous derivation of *mulier* from *mollis aer* was traditional, and so was its easy extension into macaronic punning (see the Soothsayer's extravagant parlay on "tender air," "virtuous daughter," *"mollis aer,"* *"mulier,"* and "wife" in *Cymb* V.v.444–50). Godshalk's note gives an account of the Latin tradition—"Tertullian attributes the derivation [of the false etymology of *mulier*] to Cicero's friend, Varro"—and of the Latin-English tradition—"Caxton in *The Game of the Chesse* (1474–75) apparently brought the pun into England: 'For the Women ben lykened unto softe waxe or softe ayer, and therfore she is callyd Mullier whiche is as moche to saye latyn as mollis aer and in englissh softe ayer.' [William Caxton, *The Game of the Chesse,* ed. Vincent Figgins (London, 1855), sig. G8ʳ]." Godshalk also refers his reader to the Variorum *Cymbeline* (Philadelphia, 1913) for a note (p. 435), in which H. H. Furness discusses the bilingual pun and its development.

16.9 (p. xiii). *lines of life*   Godshalk suggests "a pun on 'loins of life,' with suggestions of copulation, pregnancy, and birth. . . . I heard the same pun in 74.3: 'My life hath in this line some interest,' and I was shocked by the bawdy potential of 86.13 ['But when your countenance filled up his line']." Kökeritz (pp. 125, 217) argues that the two words were homonyms; *OED* gives "to loin" as a variant of "to line" ("to cover on the inside"; "to stuff"; "to copulate with"), and gives this example from 1587: "The Indians, who tie their sault bitches often in woods, that they might be loined by tigers." For "loins" as the seat of generative power and "loin" meaning "offspring" "descendants," see *OED,* s.v. "loin," *sb.,* 2.b. Godshalk notes that Ellis (pp. 156–57) finds the "lines/loins" pun in *LLL* IV.iii.55 and *R&J* I.Prologue.5. The phonetic likeness of *line* and "loin" may also have enhanced the play on two senses of "to line" in *AYLI* III.ii.95–96: "Winter garments must be lin'd, / So must slender Rosalinde."

73.3–4 (p. 259). Godshalk suggests "that one reading of these lines (not apparently observed by former commentators) is this: the 'boughs . . . shake against the cold, bare, ruined choirs, where late the sweet birds sang.' What we have in this reading is one image, not two: the autumnal trees rub against the ruins of an old church; the 'sweet birds' of summer 'sang' in both trees and ruins."

94.4 (p. 306). *cold* The Q spelling is "could," which *OED* lists among sixteenth- and seventeenth-century spellings of *cold*. Commenting on the emendation, Godshalk says that *cold* in the modernized text "looks like a simple emendation of an obvious mistake or, to those familiar with the vagaries of Renaissance spelling, a simple modernization. But look at the line in the context of the first quatrain: "They that haue powre to hurt, and will doe none, / . . . . / Vnmooued, could, and to temptation slow.' And we sense what is really lost by simple modernization, for in Q's line 'could' stands for something like 'cold potential'—'cold could.' " Since the word's syntactical position demands that it be read as an adjective, Godshalk overstates his case in saying that "could" "stands for" the noun phrases he suggests; however, in this context of curbed potential, he is right to recognize the incidental reverberation inherent in the mere presence of a spelling that in a suitable syntax would register a form of the verb "can." (The same sort of point might be made about "proud"—the Q spelling of *proved* in 129.11—and about "ore"—in Q's spelling of *o'ersways* in 65.2—and their contexts.)

111.1 (p. 359). *wish* In the first printing of this edition the modernized text of sonnet 111.1 reads "with"; my note on the emendation cavalierly dismisses *wish* as "an obvious misprint." Both the emendation and the casual confidence behind it are traditional. Charles Gildon—who emended whimsically and at will—started the tradition in his edition of 1709, and—although Gildon's other unfounded innovations have long since been dismissed—only one significant subsequent edition (Seymour-Smith's, 1963) has questioned and rejected Gildon's renovation of 111.1. A case can be made that the emendation improves—or, at least, simplifies—the sonnet, but that is the only kind of case that can be made.

The presumption and folly of substituting "with" for Q's *wish* is definitively demonstrated by Randall McLeod in a not-yet-published essay presented at the 1978 meeting of the Shakespeare Association of America and titled "Unemending Shakespeare's Sonnet 111." McLeod notes the vital but customarily ignored fact that the "sh" in Q's *wish* is a ligature—letters combined into a single composite character and cast on a single type-body (e.g., long "s" and "t," long "s" and "h," "c" and "t," "f" and "l" [all exemplified in sonnet 1], "f" and "i" [as in 2.2], and double long "s" [2.8,12]). Since the "sh" the Q compositor set to make *wish* was a single type, and since setting "th" would have required him to use a "t" and an "h"—two separate pieces of type, one cannot reasonably suppose that the compositor set *wish* because he picked up a long "s" when he wanted a "t." He must have meant to set the word he did set (or, improbably, some other three-type word). Thus—whatever it may be—Q's *wish* is not a simple mechanical error.

McLeod goes on to consider and deny the probability that the compositor's longhand copy text read "with" and was misread as *wish*. McLeod argues that final "th" in a secretary hand is unlikely to have been mistaken for final long "s" and "h." On the basis of McLeod's illustration of "th" and "sh" in a secretary hand, the mistake seems more probable to me than it does to him—not as probable as misreading printed *w–i–t–h* for printed *w–i–long-s–h,* but not improbable either. After demolishing the notion that Q's *wish* resulted from a slip of the compositor's hand, and after rejecting the idea that *wish* resulted from a misreading of the copy text, McLeod considers and allows the possibility that the copy text "read 'with' but the compositor misremembered it as 'wish.' " I have neither the space, the skill, nor the graphic resources to do justice to the bibliographic evidence. I trust that by the time this is printed McLeod's essay will itself be in print. Here I need only say that, if in fact—in altogether unascertainable fact—Q's *wish* is not the work Shakespeare wrote, it is surely not "an obvious misprint."

McLeod goes on to argue that emendation of 111.1 is unnecessary. Like Seymour-Smith, he demonstrates that the unemended line makes sense read as the imperative it appears to be; he paraphrases it as "Wish for my sake that Fortune chide" and notes that its apparent masochism is consistent with the similarly perverse instructions that the speaker issues in 90.1–3 (*Then hate me . . .*). McLeod points out also that the Q line makes sense read indicatively ("You wish Fortune to chide me for my own good") or interrogatively (McLeod suggests reading quatrain one "with a tone of incredulity: 'Surely you don't for my sake wish Fortune to chide; don't you know what she has done for me thus far . . .'").

The most readily available reading is the imperative one, and McLeod gives it most of his attention in describing the relationship of the unemended line to those that follow. He notes that line 8—the imperative line that openly contrasts with line 1 whether line 1 is or is not emended—also instructs the beloved to wish: *Pity me then, and wish I were renewed.* He also calls attention to the general aura of contradiction and paradox that derives from casual word play like *whilst . . . willing . . . will* in line 9 (where, as McLeod observes, the context of the reference to *my name* in line 5 makes 111 one with the other poems that play on the poet's Christian name), from oxymoronic effects, from the full scale paradox of line 11, and from the speaker's vow in quatrain three to seek out curative pain. McLeod sums up:

> Will . . . is a "willing patient," who "will" drink potions, who will think no bitterness bitter, and who will think double penance not too correct correction. The wishes of the Friend are seen to express a contradiction through time, as first he is to have one wish, and then its opposite. The activity of the Friend leads to a similarly contradictory activity (staged as a re-activity) in the persona; but now the contradiction is embodied simultaneously, as in the attitude that bitter is not bitter, and in such an oxymoron as "willing patience," the paradox of which we perceive when we remember the etymon of "patience" (*pati,* to suffer). The idea of "desiring to suffer," which is essential in "penance" and in submitting to a "cure," takes us back to the question of the masochistic persona suing for rejection in line 1, and we can see that "masochism" by itself is too simple a term to apply to the persona here. The neurotic masochism is part of a larger dialectical design symbolized more positively by the concepts of cure (l. 14) and penance (12), which dialectical whole transvalues initial and partial assumptions.

Granting, then, that there is no need to search for a substitute for Q's "wish" in 111.1, one interesting question remains: why have generations of editors blandly assumed that the line needs reparation? The readiest answer—that we simply followed tradition—is demonstrably insufficient to explain why otherwise rigorous modern editors casually reject *wish;* they are the same editors who elsewhere question traditional emendations and justify retaining as many Q readings as possible. A better answer, I think, lies (a) in the fact that the syntactically acceptable but elliptical and verb-cluttered construction *do you wish fortune chide* is not syntactically ordinary, (b) in the fact that "chide with" is (and was—see Genesis 31:36, Numbers 20:3, and Judges 8:1) a stock idiom, and (c) in the fact that the

three following lines—usually read as appositive to fortune—and the three-line
conclusion based on those lines (*Thence comes it . . .*) do themselves chide the
goddess Fortune—accuse her with the vehemence and in the detail that the verb
"to chide" suggests. If one grants that Shakespeare intended to open sonnet 111
with an improbable and apparently perverse request of the sort that opens sonnet
90, one must—on the evidence of the many editors who confidently and carelessly
accepted *wish fortune chide* as an error for "with fortune chide"—also grant that
by using an elliptical construction (one that depends on an understood "that"), by
including the verb "chide," and by following it up with six lines that *do* chide
with fortune, Shakespeare blurred the rhetorical power of his bizarre request.

Sonnet 111 thus becomes a candidate for the sort of theorizing in which I engage during my discussions of sonnet 112 (which picks up topics and diction from
111) and sonnet 113. In my commentaries on the cruxes in sonnets 112 and 113
(112.7–8, 14; 113.14), I suggest that those two poems *might* be unfinished sonnets
or sonnets abandoned in frustration by a poet who customarily contrived to fold
potentially disruptive, often counter-suggestive, extra-logical, extra-syntactical
ideational complications into his sentences without disturbing the smooth fabric of
their exposition, a poet who worked more subordinate effects into sonnets 112 and
113 than he could accommodate in straightforward logic and syntax—upon which
the efficacy of such complications necessarily depends. Speculation about the cause
of the long-assumed crux in 111.1 is as pure as that about 112 and 113, but I suspect that in 111.1—a line in which "for my sake" does double duty, specifying a
motive for both the beloved's wish and fortune's chiding—Shakespeare was also
trying for another and more spectacular doubleness, trying to achieve a locution
that would say " . . . wish fortune to chide" *and* anticipate the contrary spirit of
the imperative in line 8 by suggesting the stock construction "chide with." That
explanation is pretty farfetched, but in view of the similarly complicated cruxes in
the two sonnets that immediately follow 111 in the Quarto, in view of the readiness
of two centuries of editors to "correct" 111.1, and in view of those editors' una-
nimity in assuming "with fortune chide" to be the "true" reading, my speculations
become somewhat less wanton than they might otherwise seem.

125.11 (p. 428). *seconds* Although "second" as a measure of time was evidently rare in Shakespeare's lifetime (*OED*'s only instance before 1695 is from a
1588 translation of a Latin text), I recently stumbled on this example in I.iv. 77–84
of Ben Jonson's *The Divell is an Asse* (acted 1616, printed 1631, published 1640;
I quote the Herford and Simpson text, Volume VI [1938] of the Oxford Ben Jonson):

> *Fit[zdottrel]*.   For the short space
> You doe demand, the fourth part of an houre,
> I think I shall, with some convenient study,
> And this good helpe to boot, bring my self to't.
> *Wit[ty-pol]*. I aske no more.
> *Fit*.   Please you, walk to'ard my house,
> Speake what you list; that time is yours: My right
> I have departed with. But, not beyond,
> A minute, or a second, looke for. . . .

The casualness with which Jonson has Fitzdottrel say "not beyond, / A minute or
a second" implies an audience reasonably familiar with *seconds* as units of time.
I am therefore more inclined than I previously was to believe that Shakespeare's

contemporaries might have heard suggestions of "which has nothing to do with time" in *Which is not mixed with seconds.*

149.13–14 (p.524). Godshalk points out an arcanely witty propriety in this seemingly inappropriate couplet. He observes that my commentary on sonnet 149 "misses completely the puns on 'I/eye' in lines 1, 2, 3, 5, 6, 7, 9, 12, which are activated by the final couplet." The wit of the couplet thus derives from the simultaneity of its obvious impertinence to the expository surface of lines 1–12 and the pun-based relevance of blindness to the series of variously lost *I*'s that leads up to the word *blind;* the relationship of the couplet to the rest of the poem thus echoes the physics of *love, hate on*—the complex oxymoron at the beginning of line 13. For another super-subtle exercise on *I* and *eye,* see 113 and notes.